A COMPANION TO LATE ANTIQUE LITERATURE

BLACKWELL COMPANIONS TO THE ANCIENT WORLD

This series provides sophisticated and authoritative overviews of periods of ancient history, genres of classical literature, and the most important themes in ancient culture. Each volume comprises approximately 25 and 40 concise essays written by individual scholars within their area of specialization. The essays are written in a clear, provocative, and lively manner, designed for an international audience of scholars, students, and general readers.

ANCIENT HISTORY

Published

A Companion to the Roman Army
Edited by Paul Erdkamp

A Companion to the Roman Republic
Edited by Nathan Rosenstein and Robert Morstein-Marx

A Companion to the Roman Empire
Edited by David S. Potter

A Companion to the Classical Greek World
Edited by Konrad H. Kinzl

A Companion to the Ancient Near East
Edited by Daniel C. Snell

A Companion to the Hellenistic World
Edited by Andrew Erskine

A Companion to Late Antiquity
Edited by Philip Rousseau

A Companion to Ancient History
Edited by Andrew Erskine

A Companion to Archaic Greece
Edited by Kurt A. Raaflaub and Hans van Wees

A Companion to Julius Caesar
Edited by Miriam Griffin

A Companion to Byzantium
Edited by Liz James

A Companion to Ancient Egypt
Edited by Alan B. Lloyd

A Companion to Ancient Macedonia
Edited by Joseph Roisman and Ian Worthington

A Companion to the Punic Wars
Edited by Dexter Hoyos

A Companion to Augustine
Edited by Mark Vessey

A Companion to Marcus Aurelius
Edited by Marcel van Ackeren

A Companion to Ancient Greek Government
Edited by Hans Beck

A Companion to the Neronian Age
Edited by Emma Buckley and Martin T. Dinter

A Companion to Greek Democracy and the Roman Republic
Edited by Dean Hammer

A Companion to Livy
Edited by Bernard Mineo

A Companion to Ancient Thrace
Edited by Julia Valeva, Emil Nankov, and Denver Graninger

A Companion to Roman Italy
Edited by Alison E. Cooley

A Companion to the Etruscans
Edited by Sinclair Bell and Alexandra A. Carpino

A Companion to the Flavian Age of Imperial Rome
Edited by Andrew Zissos

A Companion to Science, Technology, and Medicine in Ancient Greece and Rome
Edited by Georgia L. Irby

A Companion to the City of Rome
Edited by Claire Holleran and Amanda Claridge

A Companion to Greeks Across the Ancient World
Edited by Franco De Angelis

A Companion to Late Antique Literature
Edited by Scott McGill and Edward J. Watts

A COMPANION TO LATE ANTIQUE LITERATURE

Edited by

Scott McGill and Edward J. Watts

WILEY Blackwell

This edition first published 2018
© 2018 John Wiley & Sons, Inc.

All rights reserved. No part of this publication may be reproduced, stored in a retrieval system, or transmitted, in any form or by any means, electronic, mechanical, photocopying, recording or otherwise, except as permitted by law. Advice on how to obtain permission to reuse material from this title is available at http://www.wiley.com/go/permissions.

The right of Scott McGill and Edward J. Watts to be identified as the author(s) of the editorial material in this work has been asserted in accordance with law.

Registered Office(s)
John Wiley & Sons, Inc., 111 River Street, Hoboken, NJ 07030, USA

Editorial Office
101 Station Landing, Medford, MA 02155, USA

For details of our global editorial offices, customer services, and more information about Wiley products visit us at www.wiley.com.

Wiley also publishes its books in a variety of electronic formats and by print-on-demand. Some content that appears in standard print versions of this book may not be available in other formats.

Limit of Liability/Disclaimer of Warranty
While the publisher and authors have used their best efforts in preparing this work, they make no representations or warranties with respect to the accuracy or completeness of the contents of this work and specifically disclaim all warranties, including without limitation any implied warranties of merchantability or fitness for a particular purpose. No warranty may be created or extended by sales representatives, written sales materials or promotional statements for this work. The fact that an organization, website, or product is referred to in this work as a citation and/or potential source of further information does not mean that the publisher and authors endorse the information or services the organization, website, or product may provide or recommendations it may make. This work is sold with the understanding that the publisher is not engaged in rendering professional services. The advice and strategies contained herein may not be suitable for your situation. You should consult with a specialist where appropriate. Further, readers should be aware that websites listed in this work may have changed or disappeared between when this work was written and when it is read. Neither the publisher nor authors shall be liable for any loss of profit or any other commercial damages, including but not limited to special, incidental, consequential, or other damages.

Library of Congress Cataloging-in-Publication Data

Names: McGill, Scott, 1968– editor. | Watts, Edward Jay, 1975– editor.
Title: A companion to late antique literature / edited by Scott McGill, Edward J. Watts.
Description: New York : Wiley, 2018. | Series: Blackwell companions to the ancient world |
Identifiers: LCCN 2018004193 (print) | LCCN 2018005932 (ebook) | ISBN 9781118830369 (pdf) | ISBN 9781118830352 (epub) | ISBN 9781118830345 (cloth)
Subjects: LCSH: Latin literature–History and criticism. | Greek literature–History and criticism. | Christian literature, Early–History and criticism. | Literature, Medieval–History and criticism. | Middle Eastern literature–History and criticism.
Classification: LCC PN641 (ebook) | LCC PN641 .C657 2018 (print) | DDC 809/.021–dc23
LC record available at https://lccn.loc.gov/2018004193

Cover image: School scene, circa 190, courtesy of GDKE-Rheinisches Landesmuseum Trier.
Photograph © INTERFOTO/Alamy Stock Photo
Cover design: Wiley

Set in 11/13.5pt Galliard by SPi Global, Pondicherry, India
Printed in Singapore by C.O.S. Printers Pte Ltd

10 9 8 7 6 5 4 3 2 1

Contents

Notes on Contributors ... ix

PART ONE   Late Antique Literature by Language and Tradition   1

Introduction ... 3
Scott McGill and Edward J. Watts

1 Greek ... 9
   Scott Fitzgerald Johnson

2 Latin ... 27
   Ian Wood

3 Syriac ... 47
   John W. Watt

4 Coptic ... 61
   David Brakke

5 Armenian ... 75
   Robin Darling Young

6 Georgian ... 87
   Stephen H. Rapp, Jr.

7 Middle Persian (Pahlavi) ... 103
   Touraj Daryaee

8 Languages of Arabia ... 123
   Kevin T. van Bladel

PART TWO Literary Forms — 141

9 Classicizing History and Historical Epitomes — 143
   Michael Kulikowski

10 Ecclesiastical History — 161
   Peter Van Nuffelen

11 Chronicles — 177
   R.W. Burgess

12 Epideictic Oratory — 193
   Alex Petkas

13 Panegyric — 209
   Roger Rees

14 Epic Poetry — 221
   Mary Whitby and Michael Roberts

15 Epigrams, Occasional Poetry, and Poetic Games — 241
   Bret Mulligan

16 Christian Poetry — 259
   Laura Miguélez-Cavero and Scott McGill

17 Prosimetra — 281
   Joel C. Relihan

18 Philosophical Commentary — 297
   Han Baltussen

19 Biblical Commentary — 313
   Marie-Pierre Bussières

20 Christian Theological Literature — 327
   Josef Lössl

21 Sermons — 343
   Jaclyn Maxwell

22 Travel and Pilgrimage Literature — 359
   Jan Willem Drijvers

23 Biography, Autobiography, and Hagiography — 373
   Sarah Insley and Jeanne-Nicole Mellon Saint-Laurent

24 Epistolography — 389
   Cristiana Sogno and Edward J. Watts

| 25 | Pseudepigraphy
Javier Martínez | 401 |
| 26 | Legal Texts
Charles N. Aull | 417 |
| 27 | Handbooks, Epitomes, and *Florilegia*
Marietta Horster and Christiane Reitz | 431 |
| 28 | Grammar
Alessandro Garcea | 451 |
| 29 | School Texts
Lillian I. Larsen | 471 |
| 30 | Literature of Knowledge
Marco Formisano | 491 |
| 31 | Inscriptions
Raymond Van Dam | 505 |
| 32 | Translation
Daniel King | 523 |
| 33 | Antiquarian Literature
Christopher Kelly | 539 |

PART THREE Reception — 555

| 34 | Late Antique Literature in Byzantium
Anthony Kaldellis | 557 |
| 35 | The Arabic Reception of Late Antique Literature
Kevin T. van Bladel | 569 |
| 36 | Late Antique Literature in the Western Middle Ages
Joseph Pucci | 583 |
| 37 | Early Modern Receptions of Late Ancient Literature
Diane Shane Fruchtman | 597 |
| 38 | Edward Gibbon and Late Antique Literature
Gavin Kelly | 611 |
| 39 | Nineteenth- and Twentieth-Century Visions of Late Antique Literature
James Uden | 627 |

Index — 643

Notes on Contributors

Charles N. Aull holds a PhD in History from Indiana University. His research focuses on political and legal history.

Han Baltussen is the Walter W. Hughes Professor of Classics at the University of Adelaide and a Fellow of the Australian Academy of Humanities. He has held fellowships at the Center for Hellenic Studies, Washington DC and the Institute for Advanced Study, Princeton. He has published books on Theophrastus (2000), Simplicius (2008), the Peripatetics (2016), and co-edited volumes on ancient commentaries (2004), consolations (2012), and self-censorship (2013). He is currently preparing a study of consolation strategies in antiquity and a new translation of Eunapius's *Lives of Philosophers and Sophists*.

David Brakke is Joe R. Engle Chair in the History of Christianity and Professor of History at the Ohio State University. He has published books and essays on early Egyptian Christianity, monasticism, and Gnosticism, including *Demons and the Making of the Monk: Spiritual Combat in Early Christianity* (2006). He and Andrew Crislip translated a selection of Shenoute's works in *Selected Discourses of Shenoute the Great: Community, Theology, and Social Conflict in Late Antique Egypt* (2015).

R.W. Burgess has been a professor of Classics at the University of Ottawa since 1989 and is a fellow of the Royal Society of Canada. He has written five books, almost 50 articles and chapters, and almost 70 encyclopedia entries on chronicles, numismatics, consuls, late Roman and Byzantine historiography, and late Roman history.

Marie-Pierre Bussières, Associate Professor in Classics at the University of Ottawa (Canada), specializes in late antique Latin literature. She has published an edition and translation of two fourth-century Latin polemics against the pagans and astrology by the anonymous author known as Ambrosiaster and is currently working on an edition and translation of the *Questions and Answers on the Old and New Testament* by the same author.

Touraj Daryaee is the Maseeh Chair in Persian Studies and the Director of the Dr. Samuel M. Jordan Center for Persian Studies and Culture at the University of California, Irvine. He is a historian of ancient Iran and works on Pahlavi texts and the history of Zoroastrianism.

Jan Willem Drijvers is Senior Lecturer in Ancient History at the University of Groningen. He has published widely on a variety of topics concerning late antiquity. He is author of *Helena Augusta* (1992) and *Cyril of Jerusalem: Bishop and City* (2004), and co-author of the *Philological and Historical Commentary on the Res Gestae of Ammianus Marcellinus XXII–XXXI* (1995–2017). See also http://www.rug.nl/staff/j.w.drijvers

Marco Formisano is Professor of Latin Literature at Ghent University, Belgium. He has published extensively on ancient technical and scientific writing: *Tecnica e scrittura* (Rome 2001); *Vegezio, Arte della guerra romana* (Milan 2003); *War in Words: Transformations of War from Antiquity to Clausewitz*, co-edited with H. Böhme (Berlin 2012); *Vitruvius. Text, Architecture, Reception*, co-edited with S. Cuomo (*Arethusa*, 49.2, 2016); and *Knowledge, Text and Practice in Ancient Technical Writing*, co-edited with P. Van der Eijk (Cambridge 2017). He is the editor of a series devoted to late antique literature entitled *The Library of the Other Antiquity* (Winter).

Diane Shane Fruchtman is Assistant Professor of Religion at Rutgers University and specializes in Western Christian Thought from Augustine to the Reformation. She is currently working on a monograph, *Surviving Martyrdom: Martyrdom without Death in the Late Ancient West and Beyond*, which uncovers the historical diversity of understandings of martyrdom by focusing on the phenomenon of "living martyrs" in Christian history. She received her PhD in History of Christianity from the Department of Religious Studies at Indiana University in 2014.

Alessandro Garcea is Full Professor of Latin Language and Literature at the University of Paris-Sorbonne and member of the Institut Universitaire de France. His main works include *Gellio et la dialettica* (Turin 2000), *Cicerone in esilio: L'epistolario e le passioni* (Hildesheim 2005); *Caesar's De analogia* (Oxford 2012). He coordinates the *CGL – Corpus Grammaticorum Latinorum* and *FLG – Fragmentary Latin Grammarians* web projects.

Marietta Horster is Chair in Ancient History, University of Mainz. She shares an interest with Christiane Reitz (see below) in technical writing and the processes of the transformation of knowledge and condensation of texts. Her main working fields are Greek cult, the Roman imperial family, and Roman imperial and late antique administrative and organizational developments.

Sarah Insley is the Dean of Branford College at Yale University. A specialist in postclassical Greek philology and literature, her research focuses on monastic literature, hagiography, and liturgical texts in late antiquity and Byzantium. She is currently completing a translation of the *Letters* of Gregory of Nazianzus for the Dumbarton Oaks Medieval Library.

Scott Fitzgerald Johnson is Associate Professor of Classics and Letters at the University of Oklahoma. He has published widely on late antique literature and culture, including the recent monograph *Literary Territories: Cartographical Thinking in Late Antiquity* (Oxford, 2016).

Anthony Kaldellis is Professor of Classics at the Ohio State University. He has published widely on many aspects of Byzantine history, culture, and literature and has also translated many Byzantine authors, especially the historians. For more, see http://kaldellispublications.weebly.com.

Christopher Kelly is Professor of Classics and Ancient History in the University of Cambridge and a Fellow of Corpus Christi College. His books include *Ruling the Later Roman Empire* (2004), *The End of Empire: Attila the Hun and the Fall of Rome* (2009), and *Theodosius II: Rethinking the Roman Empire in Late Antiquity* (2013). He is editor of the *Journal of Roman Studies*.

Gavin Kelly studied Classics at Gonville and Caius College, Cambridge, and at Gibbon's old Oxford College, Magdalen, before holding Research Fellowships at Peterhouse, Cambridge, and the University of Manchester. He has taught since 2005 in the department of Classics at the University of Edinburgh, where he is Professor of Latin Literature and Roman History. He is the author of *Ammianus Marcellinus: The Allusive Historian*, two edited books, and articles on authors including Ammianus, Claudian, Sidonius, and Symmachus.

Daniel King is Associate Research Fellow (formerly Lecturer) at Cardiff University, specializing in Syriac Studies. Major publications include *The Syriac Versions of the Writings of Cyril of Alexandria* (Peeters, 2008) and an edition of *The Earliest Syriac version of Aristotle's Categories* (Brill, 2010); he also regularly translates works out of Syriac, Greek, and Latin. In addition, he is an advisor and consultant for the translation of the Bible into modern Bantu languages in East Africa for the Summer Institute of Linguistics.

Michael Kulikowski is Professor of History and Classics at Penn State and Head of the Department of History. He is the author of several monographs, most recently *The Triumph of Empire: The Roman World from Hadrian to Constantine* (2016), and editor-in-chief of the Landmark Ammianus Marcellinus project.

Lillian I. Larsen holds a PhD in Religious Studies from Columbia University in New York City. She currently serves as Associate Professor and Chair of Religious Studies at the University of Redlands, in Southern California. Her research – long focused on rewriting the history of monastic education – is represented in a series of articles addressing monastic pedagogy. These publications likewise represent a conceptual core of the recently concluded "Monastic and Classical Paideia Project" at Lund University in Sweden. She is currently completing work on a forthcoming compendium, *Monastic Education in Late Antiquity: The Transformation of Classical Paideia*, co-edited with Samuel Rubenson and published by Cambridge. Her revisionary monograph, which rereads narrative, regulatory, and material refractions of monastic pedagogy "against the grain," is under contract and near completion. Work on a complementary catalog of monastic school texts is likewise underway.

Josef Lössl is Professor of Religious Studies and Theology at Cardiff University. He is Director of the *Cardiff Centre for Late Antique Religion and Culture* and Editor-in-Chief of the *Journal for Late Antique Religion and Culture* and *Vigiliae Christianae: A Review of Early Christian Life and Language*. His *Companion to Religion in Late Antiquity*, co-edited with Nicholas Baker-Brian, is in press.

Javier Martínez is Professor of Greek Philology at the University of Oviedo. He has translated works of Plato and Aristophanes into Spanish, with commentary, and published articles on Greek literary tradition and philosophy. He has edited several volumes on the subject of fakes, forgers, and forgeries in classical literature: *Falsificaciones y falsarios de la Literatura Clásica* (2011), *Mundus vult decipi* (2012), *Fakes and Forgers of Classical Literature – Ergo decipiatur!* (2014), and *Splendide Mendax: Rethinking Fakes and Forgeries in Classical, Late Antique, and Early Christian Literature* (2016).

Jaclyn Maxwell is Associate Professor in the departments of History and Classics/World Religions at Ohio University. Her publications include *Christianization and Communication in Late Antiquity: John Chrysostom and his congregation in Antioch* (Cambridge: Cambridge University Press, 2006), "Social Interactions in a Rural Monastery: Scholars, Peasants, Monks and More in the *Life of Hypatius*," in

Motions of Late Antiquity: Essays on Religion, Politics, and Society in Honour of Peter Brown, edited by Jamie Kreiner and Helmut Reimitz (Turnhout: Brepols, 2016), and "Popular Theology in Late Antiquity," in *Popular Culture in the Ancient World*, edited by Lucy Grig (Cambridge: Cambridge University Press, 2017).

Scott McGill is Professor of Classical Studies at Rice University in Houston, Texas. He is the author of *Virgil Recomposed: The Mythological and Secular Virgilian Centos in Antiquity* (New York: Oxford University Press, 2005), *Plagiarism in Latin Literature* (Cambridge: Cambridge University Press, 2012), and *Juvencus' Four Books of the Gospels: Evangeliorum libri quattuor* (London: Routledge, 2016).

Laura Miguélez-Cavero (Junior Research Fellow, Balliol College, University of Oxford; Co-Investigator of the Project "Greek Epic of the Roman Empire: A Cultural History," Faculty of Classics, University of Cambridge) specializes in late antique Greek poetry and has worked mainly on Egyptian authors. She is the author of *Poems in Context: Greek Poetry in the Egyptian Thebaid, 200–600 AD* (Berlin: De Gruyter, 2008) and *Triphiodorus: The Sack of Troy* (Berlin: De Gruyter 2013).

Bret Mulligan, Associate Professor and Chair of Classics at Haverford College, has published on Martial, Statius, Claudian, epigram, and, most recently, Nepos's *Life of Hannibal*. He is currently working on a translation of Ennodius's poetry, a commentary on Martial, book 10, and the image of disease in Latin poetry.

Alex Petkas is a lecturer at the University of California, San Diego. He is completing his PhD dissertation in Classics at Princeton University, writing on the philosophical letter collection of Synesius of Cyrene. His research interests include the history of Greek rhetoric and criticism, epistolography, and the cultural reception of philosophy in antiquity. He is co-editor of a forthcoming volume on Hypatia of Alexandria and has also presented papers on imperial panegyric, animals in Greek literature, and late antique invective.

Joseph Pucci is Professor of Classics, of Medieval Studies, and of Comparative Literature, Brown University. He is the author of *Medieval Latin*, 2nd ed. (1997); *The Full-Knowing Reader* (1998); *Venantius Fortunatus: Poems to Friends* (2010); *Augustine's Virgilian Retreat: Reading the Auctores at Cassiciacum* (2014); *Classics Renewed: Reception and Innovation in the Latin Poetry of Late Antiquity* (ed. with Scott McGill, 2016); General Editor of the Routledge Series in Late Latin Poetry; and co-editor of Brill's Late Antique Literature series.

Stephen H. Rapp, Jr. received his PhD at the University of Michigan in 1997 and has taught at Georgia State University, the Russian State

Humanities University (RGGU), and Sam Houston State University. His research explores the overlap and negotiation of the Iranian and Romano-Byzantine worlds through the prism of late antique Caucasia, one of Eurasia's most vibrant cultural crossroads. His latest monograph, *The Sasanian World through Georgian Eyes: Caucasia and the Iranian Commonwealth in Late Antique Georgian Literature*, was published by Ashgate in 2014.

Roger Rees is Reader in Latin at St. Andrews University, UK. His research focuses on panegyric. He is part of a collaborative team working on the *Panegyrici Latini* collection (see, for example, *Arethusa* 46.2, 2013, co-edited with Bruce Gibson). His commentary on the speech to Theodosius by Pacatus Drepanius is in press with Cambridge University Press.

Christiane Reitz is Chair in Classical Philology (Latin), University of Rostock. She shares an interest with Marietta Horster (see above) in technical writing and the processes of the transformation of knowledge and condensation of texts. Her main working fields are ancient epic and classical reception.

Joel C. Relihan is in his 25th year at Wheaton College in Norton, Massachusetts, where he is Professor of Classics. He is currently preparing an annotated translation of Pseudo-Lucian, *The Ass*, and laying the groundwork for a wide-ranging literary study, *Panopticon: A History of Menippean Satire*.

Michael Roberts is the Robert Rich Professor of Latin at Wesleyan University. He has published a number of books and articles on the literature, especially the poetry, of late antiquity, including *The Jeweled Style: Poetry and Poetics in Late Antiquity* (Ithaca, NY, 1989) and *The Humblest Sparrow: The Poetry of Venantius Fortunatus* (Ann Arbor, 2009).

Jeanne-Nicole Mellon Saint-Laurent is Assistant Professor of Theology at Marquette University. She is the author of *Missionary Narratives and the Formation of the Syriac Churches*, published by University of California Press. She is also the editor of a two-volume digital catalog of Syriac saints and their lives, *The Gateway to the Syriac Saints*, produced by Syriaca.org.

Cristiana Sogno is Associate Professor of Classics at Fordham University. She has worked on the correspondence of Symmachus and has recently co-edited a volume on late antique letter collections together with Bradley Storin and Edward Watts.

James Uden is an Associate Professor of Classical Studies at Boston University. He is the author of *The Invisible Satirist: Juvenal and Second-Century Rome* (Oxford, 2015), and numerous articles and book chapters on late antique literature.

Kevin T. van Bladel is Professor of Near Eastern Languages and Civilizations at

Yale University. He has published books and articles on the Classical Near East including *The Arabic Hermes* (2009) and *From Sasanian Mandaeans to Ṣābians of the Marshes* (2017).

Raymond Van Dam is Professor emeritus of History and Near Eastern Studies at the University of Michigan. His books include *Rome and Constantinople: Rewriting Roman History during Late Antiquity* (2010) and *Remembering Constantine at the Milvian Bridge* (2011).

Peter Van Nuffelen is Professor of Ancient History at Ghent University. He publishes on Roman religion and philosophy, early Christianity, and late antiquity. Recent publications include *Orosius and the Rhetoric of History* (Oxford University Press, 2012) and *Penser la tolérance durant l'Antiquité tardive* (Editions du Cerf, 2018).

Edward J. Watts is Alkiviadis Vassiliadis Chair in Byzantine Greek History and Professor and the University of California, San Diego. In addition to a co-edited volume on letter collections, he has recently published two monographs that make extensive use of letter collections: *The Final Pagan Generation* (UC Press, 2015) and *Hypatia: The Life and Legacy of an Ancient Philosopher*, (Oxford, 2017).

John W. Watt is Honorary Research Fellow in the School of History, Archaeology and Religion at Cardiff University. His research has focused on Syriac rhetoric and philosophy, and in these areas he has edited major treatises of Antony of Tagrit (Louvain: Peeters, 1986) and Bar Hebraeus (Leiden: Brill, 2005). Several of his articles are collected in his *Rhetoric and Philosophy from Greek into Syriac* (Farnham: Ashgate, 2010).

Mary Whitby is Faculty Lector in Greek and Latin language and a lecturer at Merton College, Oxford. Her research interests focus on the poetry of late antiquity, which she has explored in a number of articles.

Ian Wood is Professor emeritus at University of Leeds. He taught at Leeds from 1976 to 2015. His D.Phil. was on Avitus of Vienne (Oxford, 1980). His books include *The Merovingian Kingdoms* (1994), *The Missionary Life* (2001), *The Modern Origins of the Early Middle Ages* (2013), and, with Fred Orton and Clare Lees, *Fragments of History: Rethinking the Ruthwell and Bewcastle Monuments* (2007). Editions and translations are: with Danuta Shanzer, *Avitus of Vienne* (2002); and with Chris Grocock, *Abbots of Wearmouth and Jarrow* (2013) and *Jonas of Bobbio, Life of Columbanus, Life of John of Réomé, and Life of Vedast* (2017).

Robin Darling Young has translated and studied works in classical Armenian, including Armenian translations of late ancient Greek works. She is Associate Professor of Church History at the Catholic University of America.

PART ONE

LATE ANTIQUE LITERATURE BY LANGUAGE AND TRADITION

Introduction

Scott McGill and Edward J. Watts

This volume presents a set of essays highlighting the richness and creativity of late antique literature. Our description of that literature will surprise far fewer readers today than it would have throughout most of the twentieth century. A consensus existed then, especially in the Anglophone world, that late antique texts were generally derivative, uninteresting, and reflective of decline across the Mediterranean. Indeed, with a few exceptions (notably Augustine), late antique literature was largely dismissed if acknowledged at all.

The declinist approach that reigned in the twentieth century and relegated late antiquity to the dusk before the Dark Ages has not yet disappeared. But it has widely given way to responses that shed the old prejudices – however inscribed they remain in school curricula – and recognize the quality, interest, and value of late antique literature.

Late antiquity was an extremely productive time in literary history. A great amount of Greek and Latin texts in prose and verse survives from the mid-third to the early seventh century, the period upon which this book centers. Alongside that work, moreover, stand large corpora written in Coptic, Syriac, Armenian, Georgian, Pahlavi, Arabic, and a host of other regional languages. Taken together, the surviving literature from these centuries exceeds the sum total of surviving texts from the Mediterranean during the preceding millennium.

Late antique literature was also profoundly innovative. It was marked by modes of productive reception in which authors updated and transformed what came before them and by the emergence of new subject matter, new genres, new settings for literary production, new textual functions, and new

---

A Companion to Late Antique Literature, First Edition.
Edited by Scott McGill and Edward J. Watts.
© 2018 John Wiley & Sons, Inc. Published 2018 by John Wiley & Sons, Inc.

reading practices (see Herzog 1989, p. 33). As a result, late antiquity has much to tell us about the dynamics of literary history: how the cultural past creates, and is created by, what succeeds it, and how traditions are endlessly in movement as they flow through the manifold channels of reception. What is more, late antique literature is an indispensable witness to a period of seismic cultural changes. The corpus of texts, with its huge size and variety, sheds much light on the late antique world across vast swaths of territory and across linguistic, religious, and class lines.

The chapters comprising this volume give an overview of the literature of late antiquity, while also providing a selective account of its reception history. The book centers on Greek and Latin texts; these were, of course, predominant in the literary culture of the late Roman Empire, which is the primary focus of this *Companion*. But the volume also expands to include literature in other languages. This reflects the multicultural and polyglot world of late antiquity, in which the literature of Greek- and Latin-speaking Romans was situated among and interacted with the texts of different kingdoms and peoples. The period was a time when a broad range of Greek and Latin texts crossed political, linguistic, and cultural borderlands into the emerging and vibrant vernacular literatures of the Mediterranean, the Caucasus Mountains, the Iranian Plateau, and the Arabian Peninsula. To get a more developed sense of the literature of the period, it is therefore crucial to break free of the Greek/Latin binary and to encompass a broader range of languages and traditions (Humphries 2017).[1] The creative energy of late antiquity can only be appreciated when the extent of its reverberations are recognized.

Late antique literature demands, too, that we be flexible with the binary classical/Christian. Late antiquity represented one of the great transitional eras in literary history. Its authors, especially but not exclusively those working in Greek and Latin, were trained to appreciate classical forms and rhetoric, and many developed great familiarity with the works of classical authors. This training deeply influenced both their conception of literature and the sorts of projects they undertook. While established classical genres and literary models often framed the work that late antique authors undertook, these men and women were not at all stuck in or constricted by the past. Instead, late antique authors recast the classical inheritance to create texts that reflected contemporary tastes and needs and that fit with new cultural and historical developments. Foremost among those developments was the rise of Christianity into a culturally and politically dominant force. The literature that accompanies the emergence of Christianity as a privileged religion in the Roman world represents a significant late antique innovation. Christian authors remade established genres and specific textual models from the classical past, but they also departed from that past by responding to a separate authoritative tradition comprising the Scriptures and other Christian writings while producing texts in styles and for settings and uses with no precedent in classical culture. Christian literature thus lies both within and outside of the classical tradition; organizations of knowledge and of cultural history in which the classics stand on one side and Christianity on the other are entirely inadequate to deal with that body of material (Elsner and Hernández Lobato 2017, pp. 3–6).

The chronological limits of the late antique world cannot be precisely defined. We have chosen to center the volume on the period between the middle of the third century and the roughly first third of the seventh century. The boundaries we have set require both some explanation and some flexibility. The mid-third century represents a significant point of demarcation between the literature of the high Roman Empire and the literature that begins to emerge in the fourth century. While it is true that some authors like Plotinus, Cyprian, and Bardaisan stand astride this divide, most of the major developments we want to consider in Greek and Latin as well as in the various vernacular literatures take distinctive turns in the later third and early fourth centuries. To give just three examples, these years saw the flowering of Syriac poetry, the emergence of several new forms of Christian literature, and an expansion in the texts treated and approaches utilized by exegetical commentators.

It is also clear that many of these literary developments reach a natural end point in the first decades of the seventh century. This is the case with Greek poetry, for instance, whose last late antique representative is George of Pisidia, and is essentially true of Latin poetry, despite the history of Visigothic verse. There are also distinct and dramatic breaks in the Greek medical, philosophical, and astrological commentary traditions. Likewise, after Theophylact Simocatta and Isidore of Seville in the first third of the seventh century, there will be no major authors of Greek or Latin historiography active for more than a century. Admittedly, the date has less meaning in some areas, including Syriac and Coptic literature, and little significance at all in Persia. Still, the dramatic decrease in surviving Greek and Latin literature written after ca. 630 means that most of the essays in this volume do not understand late antiquity to extend beyond the first half of the seventh century.

While our chronological boundaries are relatively well demarcated, our definition of literature is a capacious one. The modern restriction of the word to creative works, particularly poetry, drama, and prose fiction, is alien to antiquity (Goldhill 1999; Vessey 2012, 2015), and we follow convention in the field of classical studies in applying the term to an array of texts that today would be classified differently. "Literature" is in our formulation a broad rubric, and it covers a wide range of textual means, both written and oral, through which individuals in late antiquity represented, organized, and understood the world around them. We recognize that the line between the literary and the nonliterary/subliterary is sometimes uncertain. We acknowledge, too, some restrictions in our approach: For the most part in this book, the category "literature" comprises only texts to which authors and textual communities assign value that separates them from the purely functional and the disposable. This includes school exercises, which, even when they were throwaway student efforts, belonged to literate culture and were designed to train the young to attain some level of rhetorical skill. Those exercises can also be placed within the bounds of literature for the same reason that texts like technical treatises and laws can be: They defy attempts to classify them as nonliterary because they possess features, notably linguistic self-consciousness, representational strategies, rhetorical characteristics, and intertextual ties to authoritative textual models, associated with the literary. Intertextuality is, in general, another important marker of literature in our formulation. Literary works operate within or against (at times multiple) discursive systems with different histories; they belong to and participate in diachronic fields of marked textuality, including when they update and remake that inheritance. Paraliterary and metaliterary compositions – e.g. commentaries, epitomes, and handbooks, all of which are characteristic of late antiquity – are not separate from the literary, moreover, but are extensions of it.

A broad examination of the textual resources that were transmitted and transmissible in late antiquity provides an expansive view of literary production in the period. The essays gathered in the volume examine the forms, histories, characteristics, audiences, and functions of many different kinds of late antique literature. In the process, contributors demonstrate how modern analytic techniques developed primarily for a narrower band of literary forms can be applied productively to a wider group of texts.

The volume is organized into three sections. In Part One, the chapters consider the processes through which the literary outline of the ancient world was expanded as more authors began working in a broader group of languages. The chapters in this section present the diverse linguistic literary histories of the period, and they connect literature to currents in political, religious, and cultural history throughout the later Roman, Sasanian, and Arab worlds. Collectively, the bodies of literature reveal varied and sustained sets of literary projects through which authors over vast territories used literature to deal with topics and to articulate worldviews within and, at times, across the cultures of the late antique world.

The second and longest section of the volume considers a wide range of late antique literature. It is organized around the concept of a literary form. The concept includes genres, which are fluid and dynamic in late antiquity:

An important characteristic of late antique literature is the way in which authors pushed against and beyond inherited generic conventions and develop new variations on traditional genres (including by combining them) or new genres altogether. But "form," as we are using it, is a more elastic term than "genre." By "form" we mean a body of texts linked, sometimes in a broad sense, by formal properties, subject matter, method, tone, or function (or some combination of these). The texts might lie within or across genres, or they might lie outside of the traditional, recognized generic matrix. The category "form" provides a balance of coherence and flexibility, and it enables the section to cover a very wide amount of material. A clear sense of the variety and vitality of late antique literature emerges from the chapters. Contributors analyze the sets of characteristics that define the different literary forms and the ways that the forms reveal a distinctive late antique culture of literary experimentation and growth.

The final section of the volume considers the reception of late antique literature. It is, of course, impossible to deal exhaustively with the subject. The chapters instead examine particular epochs, as well as major individuals, in the reception history of late antiquity. Contributors consider the transmission of late antique texts, the interpretation of them in the respective ages, and the resonance they enjoyed. The chapters show how the literature of the period now known as late antiquity was made and remade over the course of its long and varied history. There are many late antiquities that emerge during its reception; with the past as our guide, we can expect that there will be many more in generations to come.

We are now at a time of reengagement, which has brought much late antique literature back from the brink of scholarly extinction and has led to considerable reevaluation of late antique texts and literary culture. This volume is an attempt to further those developments. Our strong wish is that the book will help scholars and students to understand late antique literature on its own terms. This, in turn, will enable them not only to know better the world of late antiquity but also to appreciate more deeply ways in which literary creativity can be expressed.

NOTE

1. Circumstances beyond the editors' control made a chapter on Jewish literature impossible. On that literature, see Fergus Millar, Eyal Ben-Eliyahu, and Yehuda Cohn, eds. (2013), *Handbook of Jewish Literature from Late Antiquity, 135–700 CE* (Oxford: Oxford University Press).

REFERENCES

Elsner, Jaś, and Hernández Lobato, Jesús. (2017). Introduction: Notes towards a poetics of late antique literature. In: *The Poetics of Late Latin Literature* (ed. Jaś Elsner and Jesús Hernández Lobato), 1–22. Oxford: Oxford University Press.

Goldhill, Simon. (1999). Literary history without literature: Reading practices in the ancient world. *SubStance* 88: 57–89.

Herzog, Reinhart. (1989). Einführung in die Lateinische literatur der spätantike. In: *Restauration und Erneuerung: Die lateinische Literatur von 284 bis 374 n. Chr.* (ed. Reinhart Herzog), 1–44. Handbuch der lateinischen Literatur der Antike, vol. 5. Munich: C.H. Beck.

Humphries, Mark. (2017). Late antiquity and world history. *Studies in Late Antiquity* 1 (1): 8–37.

Vessey, Mark. (2012). Literature, patristics, early Christian writing. In: *The Oxford Handbook of Early Christian Studies* (ed. Susan Ashbrook Harvey and David G. Hunter), 42–65. Oxford: Oxford University Press.

Vessey, Mark. 2015. Literature, literary histories, Latin late antiquity: The state of the question. In: *Spätantike Konzeptionen von Literatur* (ed. Jan R. Stenger), 27–39. Heidelberg: Universitätsverlag Winter.

CHAPTER ONE

Greek

Scott Fitzgerald Johnson

Greek in late antiquity is not easily categorized. It was a language of empire, a language of philosophy and theology, a marker of identity, a language of routine daily life and commerce, and, above all, a language with symbolic power for both the literate and illiterate in the language. Greek in late antiquity was a heritage language due the literary legacy which characterized it in the period, but it was also, in linguistics terms, a "prestige" language, a status signaled by the innumerable translations made out of Greek into all the early Christian languages, such as Latin, Syriac, Coptic, Ethiopic, Armenian, Georgian, Arabic, and Old Church Slavonic. As such, Greek held an innate value for speakers of other languages, who, over the course of late antiquity, developed their own claim on the language and, in certain cases, their own distinctive brands of Greek literacy and pedagogy. Thus, Greek in late antiquity took on a sociocultural role distinct from the literature written in it. This chapter investigates that sociocultural role and draws attention to the symbolic value of the language as a marker of identity in the period.

This sociocultural role was never divorced from the literature written in Greek both before and during late antiquity. The relationship between the two categories was perpetuated by the premium placed on Greek in the Roman educational system, especially in the eastern Mediterranean (Marrou 1956; Cribiore 1999, 2001; Too 2001; Van Hoof and Van Nuffelen 2015; Kaster 1983, 1988; Watts 2006). In other words, Greek was valued for the intellectual and literary riches to which it offered its readers access, in a similar manner to how it is still taught in university Classics departments today. Education allowed for advancement in society and participation in a much

---

A Companion to Late Antique Literature, First Edition.
Edited by Scott McGill and Edward J. Watts.
© 2018 John Wiley & Sons, Inc. Published 2018 by John Wiley & Sons, Inc.

larger intellectual and social world than merely the local, where the quotidian language was often not Greek. The rhetorical training embedded in late Roman education was especially valuable, as in earlier centuries, for gaining public office and engaging literate society (Brown 1992; Quiroga Puertas 2013; Webb 2009).

The many Greek letter collections from the period, moreover, attest to Greek – paralleled, of course, by Latin – as a medium of intellectual communication across the late Roman Mediterranean (Neil and Allen 2015; Gillett 2012). Late antiquity is justly famous as a period of self-reflective correspondence, and many letter collections seem to have been drawn up by the authors themselves or at least by their immediate circles. This was the case for the Christian monastic founder Pachomius (Choat 2015) and the bishop Isidore of Pelusium (Evieux 1997), for example, as much as it was for the pagan orator Libanius (Bradbury 2004). Libanius's collection reveals not just a skilled letter writer but also how his voluminous correspondence coincided with the real-world movement of Greek students and teachers throughout the eastern Mediterranean. Libanius's letters thus reflect the evolution of Roman patronage networks within the late antique school system. One letter (*Ep.* 1098), to the Jewish patriarch Gamaliel in Jerusalem, concerns Gamaliel's son, who studied Greek rhetoric with Libanius at Antioch after having studied with Libanius's former pupil Argeios at Caesarea or Berytus (Beirut) (Stemberger 2014, p. 32).

At the same time, levels of Greek literacy varied considerably, and the language was often used as a blunt instrument at the barest functional level (Bagnall 2011). The key difference between the late antique role of Greek and our modern pedagogy of "classical Greek" is that these low-level exchanges in late antiquity were very much still Greek-in-use, even if they are formulaic and unsophisticated by comparison to the literary Greek we teach and prize today. This has certainly always been the case in the history of Greek – it was and remains a living language, after all – but for late antiquity we are privileged to have a marvelous record of these low-level exchanges, a record that does not survive for, say, classical Athens in the fifth century BCE (Horrocks 2010). Mountains of papyri from late Roman and early Byzantine Egypt attest voluminously to quotidian Greek.

The Egyptian papyri similarly attest to the near constant interaction between Greek and Coptic (Bagnall 2011, pp. 75–111). As its own medium of literature and exchange, Coptic developed alongside and in relation to Greek. Sociolinguistics of late antique Egypt is a vibrant field, and none of its researchers today would allow for one of the languages, on a cultural level, to be divorced from the other (Cribiore 2007; Papaconstantinou 2007, 2008, 2010; Bagnall 2009; MacCoull 1988, 2013). To put it differently, "the Greek of Egypt" is not a real category for cultural study; instead, we should think about Greek in terms of what roles it was used for in tandem with the roles Coptic played at the same time (and these roles shifted over the course of late antiquity). This axiom is true for all of the many varied linguistic contexts in which Greek was taught and used (Johnson 2015a), yet it does not preclude the delineation of characteristic features of Greek in a given locale, such as Egypt (Gignac 1976; Fournet 1999).

Because Greek was the medium of theological exchange, it held a special value for the highest-stakes debates in late antiquity. There was a venerable legacy of Greek among Christians since, as everyone knew in the period, the New Testament was written in Greek and the first churches were all Greek-speaking (Porter and Pitts 2013a, 2013b; Karrer and Vries 2013). The same was largely true for the Old Testament, since the Septuagint, the Greek translation of the Hebrew Bible made by Jews in the Hellenistic period, was the dominant version of the Old Testament in earliest Christianity (Aitken and Paget 2014; Rajak 2009). All the indigenous early Christian communities translated the Bible into their own languages early in their history; such translations were, indeed, markers of their own Christian identity. But it was never forgotten that these were translations, and knowledge of the original Greek of the Bible, where available, was prized.

There has been a vibrant discussion in recent scholarship over why exactly Greek became the language of theological debate. Was it because Greek was venerated as the language of the Bible? Or was it a practical question, because Greek was the medium of power and law (the *Rechtssprache*) in the eastern Mediterranean under Rome (Millar 2006b; cf. Johnson 2015a, esp. pp. 8–17)? The technical terminology of Christian doctrine that developed over the course of the seven ecumenical councils, from Nicaea I (325) to Nicaea II (787), and in the numerous theological treatises emerging around and fueling these councils was hard won and could not be relinquished easily. But was institutional inertia the main driving force? I return to this question below, though suffice it to say that the relationship between this Greek technical terminology and Greek as the language of empire is complex.

Of course, theologians were not the first to coin technical terms and formulae in Greek. Philosophy had a long history of working out its logical and argumentative apparatus in Greek. Systematization of philosophy – Neoplatonism, in particular, but also Aristotelianism – was a trend characteristic of late antiquity across many genres and in several centers of intellectual endeavor. (See the "Ancient Commentators on Aristotle" series, ed. Richard Sorabji [http://www.ancientcommentators.org.uk]; Sorabji 2004; Gerson 2010; Falcon 2016.) The overlap of philosophical, legal, and rhetorical schools in the East – in Alexandria (Watts 2006), Gaza (Johnson 2015a, pp. 31–35; Downey 1958; Bitton-Ashkelony and Kofsky 2004, 2006), Berytus (Hall 2004), Athens (Cameron 1969; Watts 2006), and Constantinople (Wilson 1996, pp. 28–60) – reinforced the above-mentioned value of Greek for social advancement through education while at the same time encouraging the attachment of value to the charisma of specific philosophical teachers and schools at these centers. Porphyry's important output, not least the editing and publication of Plotinus's *Enneads*, provided an indispensable educational tool in Greek, which was subsequently translated into Latin, Syriac, Arabic, and other languages (Johnson 2013; Magny 2014; Brock 1988, 1989b). Greek became, over the course of late antiquity, a type of holy language for Greek philosophy because of the canonical works expressed in it, such as Plotinus, Aristotle, and, of course, Plato himself, especially his later "cosmological" dialogues (the *Timaeus* above all) (Baltussen 2008; Tarrant 2007–2013). Translations by scholars like Calcidius (fourth century) into Latin and Jacob of Edessa (seventh century) into Syriac became standard in their own milieux but never existed wholly without reference to Greek (Magee 2016; Romeny 2008). Indeed, the eagerness with which Syriac Christian scholars repeatedly went back to the Greek originals for their Syriac and Arabic translations of philosophical and medical treatises shows the continued notional value of the language, even after the texts were readily available in other (albeit less accurate) translations (Brock 1983, 1991, esp. 2004). In the Latin West this direct access to Greek for philosophical work seems to have been lost after John Scotus Eriugena and even well before him in some quarters (Jeauneau 1987, pp. 85–132; Herren and Brown 1988).

Bringing these two strands together, I would emphasize that Greek was also the medium of disputation between Christians and Neoplatonic philosophers. This was already in evidence at the time of Origen's *Contra Celsum* (248 CE), but in the sixth century, in the context of the vibrant commentary movement on Plato and Aristotle, many different thinkers engaged one another at a highly technical level in the medium of Greek. The literary debates between Simplicius, John Philoponos, and Cosmas Indicopleustes in Justinianic Alexandria are perhaps a high water mark of this type of engagement (Baltussen 2008; Anastos 1946, 1953; Pearson 1999; MacCoull 2006). It is clear that formal public debates also occurred regularly, sometimes modeled on the literary debates but also providing inspiration for literature that created imagined disputations from whole cloth (Cameron 2014). Connected to this technical literature are the many magical/theurgic (Burnett 1996; Noegel, Walker, and Wheeler 2003; Lewy 1978), numerological (Kalvesmaki 2013), and astrological (Hegedus 2007; Magdalino 2006) treatises produced by both Christians and Neoplatonists (and others) in the period and shared across religious affiliation. These are evidenced by surviving treatises on such subjects but also in many papyri and casual inscriptions in Greek, often on moveable objects like incantation bowls, from throughout the eastern Mediterranean. Many of the Greek incantations are paired with other languages. A trilingual anti-demonic amulet in the Ashmolean Museum (Oxford, UK) dating to the fifth century contains inscriptions in Greek (the nonsensical "magic words"), Aramaic (anti-demonic incantation), and Hebrew (prophylactic psalm attributed to David), all apparently written by the same scribe (Bohak 2014, pp. 249–50). Thus, like other languages, Greek sometimes possessed magical properties, even if it never rose to the level of being a mystical divine tongue bearing a metaphysical code in its very structure, as did Hebrew, Arabic, and in some cases Latin.

Certain genres thrived in Greek during late antiquity, while others fell into disuse (Cameron 1992, 2006). Poetry became an area of vibrant experimentation (Agosti 2012). Nonnos of Panopolis (fl. ca. 430) was the author of the longest epic poem to survive from antiquity, the *Dionysiaca*, and he also wrote a fascinating paraphrase of the Gospel of John in epic verse (Accorinti 2016). Nonnos's style was very influential and was imitated by a number of poets, some of whom wrote on classical themes and others on Christian (Whitby 1994; Agosti 2001). Poets such as Synesius of Cyrene wrote in a more hymnic or lyrical mode, mixing classical and religious material (Bregman 1982), while George of Pisidia in the seventh century employed verse for varied genres, including panegyric and biblical commentary (Whitby 1995, 2014). Eventually, classicizing, quantitative verse fell out of fashion, and in its place came liturgical poetry. Romanos the Melode, originally from Emesa in Syria, produced dozens of *kontakia* in Constantinople during the reign of Justinian (Maas 1906; Grosdidier de Matons 1977). These poems served as verse homilies, mostly on biblical subjects, and are written in complicated syllabic meters. Romanos's style was itself developed from Syriac verse models, and Romanos shares many interpretative strategies with Ephrem the Syrian (Maas 1910; Brock 1989a).

Like poetry, historiography was an area of innovation and expansion. Histories in the classical mode continued to be written in Greek throughout the fourth to sixth centuries and into the seventh, though several texts survive only in fragments (Blockley 1981). The sixth century, with major histories by Procopius and Agathias, was the apex of this tradition (Cameron 1970, 1985). Contemporary with late classicizing history came a new genre of ecclesiastical history, inaugurated by Eusebius of Caesarea (Johnson and Schott 2013). Eusebius had many continuators: Socrates, Sozomen, and Theodoret in the fifth century and Evagrius Scholasticus in the sixth (Allen

1981; Whitby 2000). While these were narrative church histories, they followed chronology very closely. Building on the work of Julius Africanus, Eusebius also demonstrated an interest in the chronicle, another popular historical genre in late antiquity (Mosshammer 1979). Later texts such as John Malalas's *Chronicle* (Jeffreys, Jeffreys, and Scott 1986), the *Chronicon Paschale* (Whitby and Whitby 1989) and the *Chronicle* of Pseudo-Zachariah Rhetor (surviving in Syriac; Greatrex, Phenix, and Horn 2011) demonstrate the continued interest in literary models established in the fourth century. In the course of the seventh century Greek historiography slowed to a trickle, even as Syriac historiography, based partly on Greek models, thrived outside of the empire (Debié 2015).

Biography was another rich area of Greek literature in late antiquity (Hägg and Rousseau 2000; Williams 2008). Biographical texts were written about holy men and women, bishops, emperors, and other worthy subjects (Efthymiadis 2011–2014). Perhaps more than any other literary mode, biography in late antiquity intersects with fictional writing (or the modes of "fictionality" and "fictiveness," in the terms of De Temmerman 2016). Much work has been done to show how the influence of the Greek novel and the early Christian Apocryphal Acts stimulated the writing of biography in a hagiographical mode (Johnson 2006), and it has been argued that the longest and most complex Greek novel, Heliodorus's *Aithiopika*, is indeed from the fourth century (Bowersock 1994). The lines between narrative fiction, biography, hagiography, and panegyric were frequently blurred in experimental literary texts throughout late antiquity (Cameron 2000). Formal, public panegyric has survived less in Greek than in Latin, but evidence exists that it was vibrant (Whitby 1998), and the corpus of Procopius offers competing examples of both panegyric and invective in connection with the life and deeds of Justinian (Cameron 1985). Certain related genres, such as miracle collections and apocalypses, took on a major role in shaping the Greek imagination around the supernatural and the end of the world (Talbot and Johnson 2012; Garstad 2012).

The recognized late antique modes and genres, such as poetry, historiography, and biography, are familiar from literary histories of the period. Less well known are the instances of Greek language and literary culture outside of the Roman sphere. Beginning before and continuing into late antiquity, Greek inscriptions in Bactria and Central Asia show the continued influence of Alexander's conquests in those regions (Millar 2006a). The "Throne of Adulis" in the Axumite Kingdom of Ethiopia, meanwhile, described by Cosmas Indicopleustes in the sixth century, retained a lengthy Greek inscription; it is one of numerous multilingual inscriptions on Ethiopian *stelai* from late antiquity (Bowersock 2013). At the end of our period, Theodore of

Tarsus (ca. 602–690), a native Greek speaker, became Archbishop of Canterbury and established the study of Greek among English clergy (Lapidge 1995). Despite the clear value of Greek for multilingual exchange throughout the Roman Empire and, indeed, far beyond it, no comprehensive study of Greek in multilingual environments has been produced that would complement the important work done on Latin for the whole of the classical and medieval worlds (Adams 2003, 2007, 2013; Adams, Janse, and Swain 2002; Mullen and James 2012; Mullen 2013).

Indeed, it is through the interactions between languages that one can glimpse the social role of Greek, a role which shifted over time in different communities. This role was often linked to translation, as noted above. Greek into Syriac is one well-studied vector that provides ample evidence over many centuries for gauging the place of Greek (Brock 1982, 1983). In general, the trend in Syriac in late antiquity was toward greater Hellenization in translation. This is notable because Syriac continued to thrive as a literary language throughout the medieval period and was never in danger of losing its role in the liturgies and thought of the Syriac churches. The movement toward Hellenization provides an indication that Greek theological terms held their own value after the fifth century and that the post-Chalcedonian theological arguments were often taking place with Greek as the lingua franca (Brock 1989a).

To take the example of the Bible, the Old Testament Peshitta had been translated very early (second century) into Syriac directly from Hebrew, perhaps with the Jews of Edessa doing some or most of the translating (Weitzmann 1999). In very few places does it show any interference from the Septuagint (Brock 1995, pp. 34–36). However, from the late fifth century on, the trend among Syriac (especially Syrian Orthodox) translators was to ape the Greek version: thus, the so-called Philoxenian (ca. 507/508) and Harklean/Syro-Hexaplan translations (ca. 616), made by Syrian Orthodox scholars, follow the Greek very closely, even to the point of imitating its word order and producing awkward Syriac in the process. This was a revisionist project, which feared that the standard, idiomatic translation of the Peshitta was being misused or misunderstood (by dyophysites, either "Nestorian" or Chalcedonian). This occurred even though, for the Old Testament, the Peshitta translation was very early and had been made from the original Hebrew. The desire to return *ad fontes* to the Septuagint, itself a translation, demonstrates the value of Greek for theological argument among non-Greek communities well into the seventh century.

Many ante-Nicene and Nicene-era Greek church fathers were translated into Syriac, and the availability of Greek theological and monastic texts in Syriac compares closely with what was available in Latin in late antiquity

(Brock 1995, p. 37). The habit of revising earlier translations for the sake of accuracy to the Greek occurred also for theological texts: the corpus of Pseudo-Dionysius was translated first by Sergius of Reshaina (d. 536), within a few decades of its composition in Greek, and this translation was revised by Phokas of Edessa at the end of the seventh century (Brock 1995, pp. 39–40). Philosophical and medical literature in Greek was highly prized by Syriac translators, and the "translation-movement" project at the court of Abbasid Baghdad was almost completely the work of Church of the East (aka "Nestorian") translators (Troupeau 1991). Thus, translations of Aristotle, Porphyry, and Galen were translated from Greek into Syriac before being translated from Syriac into Arabic (Brock 1989b; Brock 2004). The *Categories*, for example, were translated multiple times into Syriac: the earliest in the sixth century, then revised in the early eighth century by Jacob of Edessa, and then again in the ninth century by Hunayn ibn Ishaq, one of the premier translators under the Abbasids. Therefore, in a period when the philosophical commentary tradition had ceased in Constantinople – the seventh and eighth centuries – the Greek tradition was being actively cultivated by Syrian Orthodox and Church of the East translators outside the Byzantine Empire.

This brings us back to the question of what forces promoted the value of Greek in late antiquity. By 700 the Byzantine Empire had seemingly given up its hopes of returning the eastern provinces to its fold (Haldon 2016). Yet the interest in Greek remained strong, and even intensified, in areas under Islamic dominion, where Arabic was increasingly the language of commerce and administration (Hoyland 2004). Indeed, some of the most prominent Greek writers of early Byzantium, such as John of Damascus and Cosmas the Melode, came from outside of the Byzantine Empire, but are today firmly considered Byzantine writers who contributed substantially to the development of late antique Greek literature. Was the motivating factor imperial, i.e. that these writers wanted their works read by Greek readers within the empire?

The answer depends on a combination of factors. Throughout late antiquity, both before and after Chalcedon, and before and after the Arab Conquests, Greek remained a prestige language for theological, philosophical, and literary (e.g. verse) writing. There was never a time, however, when it was not surrounded by writing in other languages. The church of Jerusalem in John of Damascus's day, for example, was producing texts in Christian Palestinian Aramaic, Arabic, and Georgian at the same time John was writing his massive corpus in Greek (Johnson 2015a, pp. 58–88). Most scholars think John himself was fluent in Arabic and may have known a dialect of Aramaic as well, which only further emphasizes that John's choice of Greek was intentional (Griffith 2011). I would suggest the affiliation of the Palestinian monasteries with the Chalcedonian faith was one primary factor. For comparison, St. Catherine's Monastery in the Sinai, also Chalcedonian and thus under the Patriarch of Constantinople, retains one of the finest libraries of early Byzantine Greek manuscripts in the world (Mango 2011). At the same time, all the other early Christian languages are present there too, in great numbers, and the colophons of these manuscripts make it clear than several of them originated in Mar Sabas monastery near Jerusalem (according to tradition, the home of John of Damascus). Greek thus retained a prestige for certain writers even when other languages were flourishing in the same locations at the same times and, importantly, when Greek was not the language of daily life. Coptic largely replaced Greek in Egypt in the immediate aftermath of the Arab Conquests, a transition that occurred earlier and more completely than it would in Aramaic and Arabic contexts (Papaconstantinou 2012, Johnson 2015a, pp. 36–58).

I return, therefore, to the pedigree of Greek as a language for the communication of ideas. That is not to say that Syriac or Armenian, for instance, were not also vehicles for conceptual writing: they certainly were, and their literary histories are remarkable on their own terms, quite apart from Greek. However, the affiliation of Byzantium with Greek, from the time of Justinian on, provided a touchstone for Christian writers of all stripes, both within and outside the empire itself, and often under a different (Arabic-speaking) imperial power. This was the imperial influence, even if clearly not related to the borders of the Byzantine Empire. Entangled with the imperial influence is the fact that a rich Christian literary corpus, since the beginning, had been produced in Greek and had, importantly, provided the toolkit of concepts and terminology that allowed the writers of late antiquity the ability to interact with a heritage that went back to the New Testament. The association of the church with the Roman Empire from the time of Constantine further solidified the authority of this corpus. Additionally, the apparatus of argument in late antiquity, for the Christians as much as for the Platonists, was founded on received and accepted philosophical and logical writings in Greek from pre-Christian times. And likewise, on top of all this, the characteristic conservatism of liturgy and the increasing value of biblical translations from the Greek, especially in monastic and school contexts, reinforced the primacy of the language. Thus, the circles that perpetuated the use of Greek in late antiquity were in many ways strikingly different from those of the earlier Roman world yet nevertheless remained just as pivotal for the emergence of new forms of thought and new vectors of exchange in late antiquity.

REFERENCES

Accorinti, Domenico. ed. (2016). *Brill's Companion to Nonnus of Panopolis*. Brill's Companions in Classical Studies. Leiden: Brill.

Adams, J.N. (2003). *Bilingualism and the Latin Language*. Cambridge: Cambridge University Press.

Adams, J.N. (2007). *The Regional Diversification of Latin, 200 BC–AD 600*. Cambridge: Cambridge University Press.

Adams, J.N. (2013). *Social Variation and the Latin Language*. Cambridge: Cambridge University Press.

Adams, J.N., Janse, Mark, and Swain, Simon. ed. (2002). *Bilingualism in Ancient Society: Language Contact and the Written Text*. Oxford: Oxford University Press.

Agosti, Gianfranco. (2001). L'epica biblica nella tarda antichità greca: Autori e lettori nel IV e V secolo. In: *La scrittura infinita. Bibbia e poesia in età medievale e umanistica* (ed. Francesco Stella), 67–104. Florence: Sismel.

Agosti, Gianfranco. (2012). Greek poetry. In *The Oxford Handbook of Late Antiquity* (ed. S.F. Johnson), 361–404. Oxford: Oxford University Press.

Aitken, James K. and Paget, James Carleton. ed. (2014). *The Jewish-Greek Tradition in Antiquity and the Byzantine Empire*. Cambridge: Cambridge University Press.

Allen, Pauline. (1981). *Evagrius Scholasticus, the Church Historian*. Spicilegium Sacrum Lovaniense 41. Leuven: Spicilegium sacrum Lovaniense.

Anastos, Milton V. (1946). The Alexandrian origin of the "Christian topography" of Cosmas Indicopleustes. *Dumbarton Oaks Papers* 3: 73–80.

Anastos, Milton V. (1953). *Aristotle and Cosmas Indicopleustes on the Void: A Note on Theology and Science in the Sixth Century*. Thessaloniki: Hetaireia Makedonikōn Spoudōn.

Bagnall, Roger S. (2009). *Early Christian Books in Egypt*. Princeton, NJ: Princeton University Press.

Bagnall, Roger S. (2011). *Everyday Writing in the Graeco-Roman East*. Sather Classical Lectures. Berkeley: University of California Press.

Baltussen, H. (2008). *Philosophy and Exegesis in Simplicius: The Methodology of a Commentator*. London: Duckworth.

Bitton-Ashkelony, Brouria and Kofsky, Arieh. ed. (2004). *Christian Gaza in Late Antiquity*. Jerusalem Studies in Religion and Culture 3. Leiden: Brill.

Bitton-Ashkelony, Brouria and Kofsky, Arieh. ed. (2006). *The Monastic School of Gaza*. Supplements to *Vigiliae Christianae* 78. Leiden: Brill.

Blockley, R.C. (1981). *The Fragmentary Classicising Historians of the Later Roman Empire: Eunapius, Olympiodorus, Priscus, and Malchus*. 2 vols. ARCA, Classical and Medieval Texts, Papers, and Monographs 6, 10. Liverpool: F. Cairns.

Bohak, Gideon. (2014). Greek-Hebrew linguistic contacts in late antique and medieval magical texts. In: *The Jewish-Greek Tradition in Antiquity and the Byzantine Empire* (ed. J.K. Aitken and J.C. Paget), 247–260. Cambridge: Cambridge University Press.

Bowersock, G.W. (1994). *Fiction as History: Nero to Julian*. Sather Classical Lectures 58. Berkeley: University of California Press.

Bowersock, G. W. (2013). *The Throne of Adulis: Red Sea Wars on the Eve of Islam*. Oxford: Oxford University Press.

Bradbury, Scott. (2004). *Selected Letters of Libanius: From the Age of Constantius and Julian*. Translated Texts for Historians 41. Liverpool: Liverpool University Press.

Bregman, Jay. (1982). *Synesius of Cyrene, Philosopher-Bishop*. The Transformation of the Classical Heritage 2. Berkeley: University of California Press.

Brock, Sebastian P. (1982). From antagonism to assimilation: Syriac attitudes to Greek learning. In: *East of Byzantium: Syria and Armenia in the Formative Period* (ed. Nina G. Garsoïan, Thomas F. Mathews, and Robert W. Thomson), 17–34. Washington, DC: Dumbarton Oaks.

Brock, Sebastian P. (1983). Towards a history of Syriac translation technique. In: *III Symposium Syriacum, 1980: Les Contacts Du Monde Syriaque Avec Les Autres Cultures (Goslar 7–11 Septembre 1980)* (ed. R. Lavenant), 1–14. Orientala Christiana Analecta 221. Rome: Pontifical Oriental Institute.

Brock, Sebastian P. (1988). The earliest Syriac translation of Porphyry's *Eisagoge*: 1st edition. *Journal of the Iraqi Academy, Syriac Corporation* 12: 316–366.

Brock, Sebastian P. (1989a). From Ephrem to Romanos. *Studia Patristica* 20: 139–151.

Brock, Sebastian P. (1989b). Some notes on the Syriac translations of Porphyry's *Eisagoge*. In: *Mélanges en hommage au professeur et au penseur libanais Farid Jabre*, 41–50. Publications de l'université libanaise, section d'études philosophiques et sociales 20. Beirut: Université Libanaise.

Brock, Sebastian P. (1991). The Syriac background to Hunayn's translation techniques. *ARAM* 3: 139–162.

Brock, Sebastian P. (1995). The Syriac background to the world of Theodore of Tarsus. In: *From Ephrem to Romanos: Interactions between Syriac and Greek in Late Antiquity*, 30–53. Variorum Collected Studies Series CS664. London: Ashgate Variorum.

Brock, Sebastian P. (2004). Changing fashions in Syriac translation technique: The background to Syriac translations under the Abbasids. *Journal of the Canadian Society for Syriac Studies* 4: 3–14.

Brown, Peter. (1992). *Power and Persuasion in Late Antiquity: Towards a Christian Empire*. The Curti Lectures, 1988. Madison, WI: University of Wisconsin Press.

Burnett, Charles. (1996). *Magic and Divination in the Middle Ages: Texts and Techniques in the Islamic and Christian Worlds*. Aldershot: Variorum.

Cameron, Alan. (1969). The last days of the academy at Athens. *Proceedings of the Cambridge Philological Society* 195: 7–29.

Cameron, Averil M. (1970). *Agathias*. Oxford: Clarendon.

Cameron, Averil M. (1985). *Procopius and the Sixth Century*. London: Duckworth.

Cameron, Averil M (1992). New themes and styles in Greek literature: Seventh–eighth centuries. In: *The Byzantine and Early Islamic Near East: Papers of the First Workshop on Late Antiquity and Early Islam* (ed. Averil M. Cameron and Lawrence I. Conrad), 81–105. Studies in Late Antiquity and Early Islam 1. Princeton, NJ: Darwin Press.

Cameron, Averil M. (2000). Form and meaning: The *Vita Constantini* and the *Vita Antonii*. In: *Greek Biography and Panegyric in Late Antiquity*. The Transformation of the Classical Heritage 31 (ed. T. Hägg and P. Rousseau), 72–88. Berkeley: University of California Press.

Cameron, Averil M. (2006). New themes and styles in Greek literature. A title revisited. In: *Greek Literature in Late Antiquity: Dynamism, Didacticism, Classicism* (ed. S F. Johnson), 11–28. Aldershot: Ashgate.

Cameron, Averil M. (2014). *Dialoguing in Late Antiquity*. Hellenic Studies Series. Washington, DC and Cambridge, MA: Center for Hellenic Studies and Harvard University Press.

Choat, Malcolm. (2015). From letter to letter-collection: Monastic epistolography in late-antique Egypt. In: *Collecting Early Christian Letters: From the Apostle Paul to Late Antiquity* (ed. B. Neil and P. Allen) 80–93. Cambridge: Cambridge University Press.

Cribiore, Raffaella. (1999). Greek and Coptic education in late antique Egypt. In: *Ägypten und Nubien in spätantiker und christlicher Zeit* (ed. Stephen Emmel et al.), 2: 279–286. Wiesbaden: Harrassowitz.

Cribiore, Raffaella. (2001). *Gymnastics of the Mind: Greek Education in Hellenistic and Roman Egypt*. Princeton NJ: Princeton University Press.

Cribiore, Raffaella. (2007). Higher education in early Byzantine Egypt: Rhetoric, Latin, and the Law. In: *Egypt in the Byzantine World, 300–700* (ed. R.S. Bagnall 2007), 47–66. Cambridge: Cambridge University Press.

Debié, Muriel. (2015). *L'Écriture de l'histoire en Syriaque: Transmissions interculturelles et constructions identitaires entre hellénisme et islam: avec des répertoires des textes historiographiques en annexe*. Late Antique History and Religion, vol. 12. Leuven: Peeters.

De Temmerman, Koen. (2016). Ancient biography and formalities of fiction. In: *Writing Biography in Greece and Rome: Narrative Technique and Fictionalization* (ed. Koen De Temmerman and Kristoffel Demoen), 3–25. Cambridge: Cambridge University Press.

Downey, Glanville. (1958). The Christian schools of Palestine: A chapter in literary history. *Harvard Library Bulletin*, 12: 297–319. [Reprinted in Johnson 2015b, 281–303.]

Efthymiadis, Stephanos. ed. (2011–2014). *Ashgate Research Companion to Byzantine Hagiography*. 2 vols. Farnham: Ashgate.

Evieux, Pierre. (ed. (1997). *Isidore de Péluse: Lettres*. 2 vols. Sources chrétiennes 422, 454. Paris: Éditions du Cerf.

Falcon, Andrea. ed. (2016). *Brill's Companion to the Reception of Aristotle in Antiquity*. Brill's Companions to Classical Reception 7. Leiden: Brill.

Fournet, Jean-Luc. (1999). *Hellénisme dans l'Égypte du VIe siècle: La bibliothèque et l'oeuvre de Dioscore d'Aphrodité*. 2 vols. MIFAO 115. Le Caire: Institut Français d'Archéologie Orientale.

Garstad, Benjamin. (2012). *Apocalypse Pseudo-Methodius: An Alexandrian World Chronicle*. Dumbarton Oaks Medieval Library 14. Cambridge, MA: Harvard University Press.

Gerson, Lloyd P. ed. (2010). *The Cambridge History of Philosophy in Late Antiquity.* 2 vols. Cambridge: Cambridge University Press.

Gignac, Francis T. (1976). *A Grammar of the Greek Papyri of the Roman and Byzantine Periods.* 2 vols. Testi e documenti per lo studio dell'antichità 55. Milan: Istituto editoriale cisalpino-La goliardica.

Gillett, Andrew. (2012). Communication in late antiquity: Use and reuse. In: *The Oxford Handbook of Late Antiquity* (ed. S.F. Johnson) 815–846. Oxford: Oxford University Press.

Greatrex, Geoffrey, Phenix, Robert R., and Horn, Cornelia B. (2011). *The Chronicle of Pseudo-Zachariah Rhetor: Church and War in Late Antiquity.* Translated Texts for Historians 55. Liverpool: Liverpool University Press.

Griffith, Sidney H. (2011). John of Damascus and the Church in Syria in the Umayyad era: The intellectual and cultural milieu of orthodox Christians in the world of Islam. *Hugoye* 11(2): 207–237.

Grosdidier de Matons, José. (1977). *Romanos le Mélode et les origines de la poésie religieuse à Byzance.* Beauchesne Religions 1. Paris: Beauchesne.

Hägg, Tomas, and Rousseau, Philip. ed. (2000). *Greek Biography and Panegyric in Late Antiquity.* The Transformation of the Classical Heritage 31. Berkeley: University of California Press.

Haldon, John F. (2016). *The Empire That Would Not Die: The Paradox of Eastern Roman Survival, 640–740.* Cambridge, MA: Harvard University Press.

Hall, Linda Jones. (2004). *Roman Berytus: Beirut in Late Antiquity.* London: Routledge.

Hegedus, Tim. (2007). *Early Christianity and Ancient Astrology.* New York: Peter Lang.

Herren, Michael W. and Brown, Shirley Ann. ed. (1988). *The Sacred Nectar of the Greeks: The Study of Greek in the West in the Early Middle Ages.* King's College London Medieval Studies 2. London: King's College London.

Horrocks, Geoffrey C. (2010). *Greek: A History of the Language and Its Speakers.* 2nd ed. Chichester: Wiley Blackwell.

Hoyland, Robert G. (2004). Language and identity: The twin histories of Arabic and Aramaic (and: Why did Aramaic succeed where Greek failed?). *Scripta Classica Israelica* 23: 183–199.

Jeauneau, Édouard. (1987). *Études érigéniennes.* Paris: Études Augustiniennes.

Jeffreys, Elizabeth, Jeffreys, Michael, and Scott, Roger. (1986). *The Chronicle of John Malalas.* Byzantina Australiensia 4. Melbourne: Australian Association for Byzantine Studies.

Johnson, Aaron P. (2013). *Religion and Identity in Porphyry of Tyre: The Limits of Hellenism in Late Antiquity.* Greek Culture in the Roman World. Cambridge: Cambridge University Press.

Johnson, Aaron P. and Schott, Jeremy M. ed. (2013). *Eusebius of Caesarea: Tradition and Innovations.* Hellenic Studies 60. Washington, DC and Cambridge, MA: Center for Hellenic Studies and Harvard University Press.

Johnson, Scott Fitzgerald. (2006). Late antique narrative fiction: Apocryphal Acta and the Greek novel in the fifth-century life and miracles of Thekla. In: *Greek literature in late antiquity: Dynamism, didacticism, classicism* (ed. S.F. Johnson), 190–207. Aldershot: Ashgate.

Johnson, Scott Fitzgerald. (2015a). Introduction: The social presence of Greek in eastern Christianity, 200–1200 CE. In: *Languages and Cultures of Eastern Christianity: Greek* (ed. S.F. Johnson) 1–122. Farnham: Ashgate.

Johnson, Scott Fitzgerald. ed. (2015b). *Languages and Cultures of Eastern Christianity: Greek.* The Worlds of Eastern Christianity, 300–1500, 6. Farnham: Ashgate.

Kalvesmaki, Joel. (2013). *The Theology of Arithmetic: Number Symbolism in Platonism and Early Christianity.* Hellenic Studies Series 59. Washington, DC and Cambridge, MA: Center for Hellenic Studies and Harvard University Press.

Karrer, Martin and de Vries, Johannes. ed. (2013). *Textual History and the Reception of Scripture in Early Christianity – Textgeschichte und Schriftrezeption im frühen Christentum.* Septuagint and Cognate Studies 60. Atlanta: Society of Biblical Literature.

Kaster, Robert A. (1983). Notes on "primary" and "secondary" schools in late antiquity. *TAPA* 113: 323–46.

Kaster, Robert A. (1988). *Guardians of Language: The Grammarian and Society in Late Antiquity.* The Transformation of the Classical Heritage 11. Berkeley: University of California Press.

Lapidge, Michael. ed. (1995). *Archbishop Theodore: Commemorative Studies on His Life and Influence.* Cambridge Studies in Anglo-Saxon England 11. Cambridge: Cambridge University Press.

Lewy, Yochanan. (1978). *Chaldaean Oracles and Theurgy: Mysticism, Magic and Platonism in the Later Roman Empire* (ed. Michel Tardieu). Rev. ed. Paris: Études Augustiniennes.

Maas, P. (1906). Die Chronologie der Hymnen des Romanos. *Byzantinische Zeitschrift* 15: 1–43.

Maas, P. (1910). Das Kontakion. *Byzantinische Zeitschrift* 19: 285–306.

MacCoull, Leslie S.B. (1988) *Dioscorus of Aphrodito: His Work and His World.* The Transformation of the Classical Heritage 16. Berkeley: University of California Press.

MacCoull, Leslie S.B. (2006). The historical context of John Philoponus' *De Opificio Mundi* in the Culture of Byzantine-Coptic Egypt. *Zeitschrift für Antikes Christentum* 9: 397–423.

MacCoull, Leslie S.B. (2013). Niches in an ecosystem: The choice of Coptic for legal instruments in late antique Egypt. *Analecta Papyrologica* 25: 257–276.

Magdalino, Paul. (2006). *L'orthodoxie des astrologues: La science entre le dogme et la divination à Byzance, VIIe-XIVe siècle.* Réalités byzantines 12. Paris: Lethielleux.

Magee, John. (2016). *Calcidius: On Plato's Timaeus.* Dumbarton Oaks Medieval Library. Cambridge, MA: Harvard University Press.

Magny, Ariane. 2014. *Porphyry in Fragments: Reception of an Anti-Christian Text in Late Antiquity.* Ashgate Studies in Philosophy and Theology in Late Antiquity. Farnham: Ashgate.

Mango, Cyril A. ed. (2011). *St Catherine's Monastery at Mount Sinai, Its Manuscripts and Their Conservation: Papers Given in Memory of Professor Ihor Ševčenko, 27 November 2010, Stelios Ioannou Centre for Classical and Byzantine Studies, University of Oxford*. London: Saint Catherine Foundation.

Marrou, Henri Irénée. (1956). *A History of Education in Antiquity* (trans. George Lamb). New York: Sheed and Ward.

Millar, Fergus. (2006a). Alexander's legacy: The imprint of the Greek language east of the Euphrates. Review of F. Canali De Rossi, *Iscrizioni dello estremo oriente Greco* (Bonn, 2004). *Ancient East and West* 5: 287–296.

Millar, Fergus. (2006b). *A Greek Roman Empire: Power and Belief Under Theodosius II (408–450)*. Sather Classical Lectures 64. Berkeley: University of California Press.

Mosshammer, Alden A. (1979). *The Chronicle of Eusebius and Greek Chronographic Tradition*. Lewisburg, PA: Bucknell University Press.

Mullen, Alex. (2013). *Southern Gaul and the Mediterranean: Multilingualism and Multiple Identities in the Iron Age and Roman Periods*. Cambridge: Cambridge University Press.

Mullen, Alex and James, Patrick. ed. 2012. *Multilingualism in the Graeco-Roman Worlds*. Cambridge: Cambridge University Press.

Neil, Bronwen and Allen, Pauline. ed. (2015). *Collecting Early Christian Letters: From the Apostle Paul to Late Antiquity*. Cambridge: Cambridge University Press.

Noegel, Scott B., Walker, Joel Thomas, and Wheeler, Brannon M. ed. 2003. *Prayer, Magic, and the Stars in the Ancient and Late Antique World*. University Park, PA: Pennsylvania State University Press.

Papaconstantinou, Arietta. (2007). "They shall speak the Arabic language and take pride in it": Reconsidering the fate of Coptic after the Arab Conquest. *Le Muséon* 120: 273–299.

Papaconstantinou, Arietta. (2008). Dioscore et la question du bilinguisme dans l'Égypte du VIe siècle. In: *Les archives de Dioscore d'Aphrodité cent ans après leur découverte: Histoire et culture dans l'Égypte byzantine*. (ed. Jean-Luc Fournet) 77–88. Études d'archéologie et d'histoire ancienne. Paris: De Boccard. [Reprinted and translated in Johnson 2015b, 249–260.]

Papaconstantinou, Arietta. ed. (2010). *The Multilingual Experience in Egypt, from the Ptolemies to the Abbasids*. Farnham: Ashgate.

Papaconstantinou, Arietta. (2012). Why did Coptic fail where Aramaic succeeded? Linguistic developments in Egypt and the Near East after the Arab Conquest. In: *Multilingualism in the Graeco-Roman Worlds* (ed. Alex Mullen and Patrick James), 58–76. Cambridge: Cambridge University Press.

Pearson, Carl. (1999). Scripture as cosmology: Natural philosophical debate in John Philoponus' Alexandria. PhD diss. Harvard University.

Porter, Stanley E. and Pitts, Andrew W. ed. (2013a). *Christian Origins and Greco-Roman Culture: Social and Literary Contexts for the New Testament*. Text and Editions for New Testament Study 9. Leiden: Brill.

Porter, Stanley E. and Pitts, Andrew W. ed. (2013b). *The Language of the New Testament: Context, History, and Development.* Linguistic Biblical Studies 6. Leiden: Brill.

Quiroga Puertas, Alberto J. ed. (2013). *The Purpose of Rhetoric in Late Antiquity: From Performance to Exegesis.* Studien und Texte zu Antike und Christentum 72. Tübingen: Mohr Siebeck.

Rajak, Tessa. 2009. *Translation and Survival: The Greek Bible of the Ancient Jewish Diaspora.* Oxford: Oxford University Press.

Romeny, Bas ter Haar. ed. (2008). *Jacob of Edessa and the Syriac Culture of His Day.* Leiden: Brill.

Sorabji, Richard. ed. (2004). *The Philosophy of the Commentators, 200–600 AD: A Sourcebook.* 3 vols. London: Duckworth.

Stemberger, Günter. (2014). Jews and Greco-Roman culture: From Alexander to Theodosius II. In: *The Jewish-Greek Tradition in Antiquity and the Byzantine Empire* (ed. J.K. Aitken and J.C. Paget), 15–36. Cambridge: Cambridge University Press.

Talbot, Alice-Mary Maffry and Johnson, Scott Fitzgerald. (2012). *Miracle Tales from Byzantium.* Dumbarton Oaks Medieval Library 12. Cambridge, MA: Harvard University Press.

Tarrant, Harold. ed. (2007–2013). *Proclus: Commentary on Plato's Timaeus.* 5 vols. Cambridge: Cambridge University Press.

Too, Yun Lee. ed. (2001). *Education in Greek and Roman Antiquity.* Leiden: Brill.

Troupeau, Gérard. (1991). Le rôle des syriaques dans la transmission et l'exploitation du patrimoine philosophique et scientifique grec. *Arabica* 38: 1–10.

Van Hoof, Lieve and Van Nuffelen, Peter. ed. (2015). *Literature and Society in the Fourth Century AD: Performing Paideia, Constructing the Present, Presenting the Self.* Mnemosyne Supplements: Monographs on Greek and Latin Language and Literature 373. Leiden: Brill.

Watts, Edward J. (2006). *City and School in Late Antique Athens and Alexandria.* Berkeley: University of California Press.

Webb, Ruth. (2009). *Ekphrasis, Imagination and Persuasion in Ancient Rhetorical Theory and Practice.* Farnham: Ashgate.

Weitzman, Michael. (1999). *The Syriac Version of the Old Testament: An Introduction.* Cambridge: Cambridge University Press.

Whitby, Mary. (1994). From Moschus to Nonnus: The evolution of the Nonnian style. In: *Studies in the Dionysiaca of Nonnus* (ed. Neil Hopkinson), 99–155. Cambridge: Cambridge Philological Society.

Whitby, Mary. (1995). The devil in disguise: The end of George of Pisidia's Hexaemeron reconsidered. *Journal of Hellenic Studies* 115: 116–131.

Whitby, Mary. ed. (1998). *The Propaganda of Power: The Role of Panegyric in Late Antiquity.* Mnemosyne, Bibliotheca Classica Batava 183. Leiden: Brill.

Whitby, Mary. (2014). A learned spiritual ladder: Towards an interpretation of George of Pisidia's hexameter poem "On Human Life." In: *Nonnus of Panopolis in Context* (ed. K. Spanoudakis), 435–457. Berlin: De Gruyter.

Whitby, Michael. (2000). *The Ecclesiastical History of Evagrius Scholasticus.* Translated Texts for Historians 33. Liverpool: Liverpool University Press.

Whitby, Michael and Whitby, Mary. (1989). *Chronicon Paschale 284–628 AD.* Translated Texts for Historians 7. Liverpool: Liverpool University Press.

Williams, Michael Stuart. (2008). *Authorised Lives in Early Christian Biography: Between Eusebius and Augustine.* Cambridge Classical Studies. Cambridge: University of Cambridge.

Wilson, Nigel Guy. (1996). *Scholars of Byzantium.* 2nd ed. London: Duckworth.

CHAPTER TWO

Latin

Ian Wood

Over the course of the fourth to sixth centuries Latin literature changed fundamentally, if not absolutely. The shift can be related to the broader shifts in religion, politics, and society, including Christianization; the failure of the Western Roman Empire; the development of the so-called successor states, with their different patronage systems; and a change in schooling. In the fifth century the core curriculum was based on what is now referred to as the *trivium* (grammar, logic, and rhetoric) and the *quadrivium* (arithmetic, geometry, astronomy, and music) (Marrou 1969). This division of education into the so-called seven liberal arts can be found in the *De nuptiis Philologiae et Mercurii* of the fifth-century African jurist Martianus Capella (Shanzer 1986), although the actual term *quadrivium* seems to have been coined in the sixth century by either Boethius (d. 524) or Cassiodorus (d. ca. 585), while *trivium* first appears in the Carolingian period. Both Augustine (d. 430) and Paulinus of Pella (d. post 461) refer to this traditional education. Already by the early sixth century, however, such an educational system was in decline, even though one can find some evidence for rhetorical schools in a number of cities, including Milan (for which we have the evidence of Ennodius of Pavia [d. 521]; Kennell 2000), in the post-Roman period. What evidence we have for schooling in the seventh century suggests that it was largely in the hands of the clergy: There was certainly some religious education at a parish level (we hear of children learning the psalms), and there are indications that episcopal households could act as educational centers. (Riché 1976.) So, too, could the courts of kings, although exactly what was taught,

---

A Companion to Late Antique Literature, First Edition.
Edited by Scott McGill and Edward J. Watts.
© 2018 John Wiley & Sons, Inc. Published 2018 by John Wiley & Sons, Inc.

and how it was taught, is unclear. Essentially, the urban education system of antiquity ended in the fifth and sixth centuries.

Equally important for the changes in Latin literature was the removal of the imperial court, which had served as a focus for certain types of public oratory, notably panegyric, while the collapse of the senatorial aristocracy removed an additional source of patronage and, indeed, of audiences and circles of literary production. Certainly the courts of the kings of the early medieval West could still function as foci for literary production, and literature could still be produced in aristocratic households (Hen 2007). But while some of this literature looked back to the traditions of oratory and letter writing that had been central to the imperial aristocracy of the fifth and sixth centuries, of much greater significance was the production of religious texts, and not least of works of hagiography. An ideal guide to the learning of educated Christians at the end of the sixth century may be found in Cassiodorus's *Institutions of Divine and Secular Learning* (Halporn and Vessey 2004).

A further complication was linguistic change. Although late antiquity saw the production of a number of grammar books, notably those of the fourth-century Donatus and the sixth-century Priscian, the Latin language – like any language – changed. There were sound changes and shifts in orthography, as well as changes in prosody and meter, with accentual meter replacing the stress patterns of classical poetry, and with rhyme coming to be increasingly prominent. As a result, the language of a seventh-century text seems radically different from that of a cultivated author of the fourth century, but what we might regard as proto-Romance was, in fact, the Latin of the day (Grandgent 1907; Wright 1982; Banniard 1992).

When considering the changes in literary production over the late antique period, it is useful to examine individual genres, although as we will see, there is considerable overlap between some forms of literary production. We will begin with the most official forms (panegyric and oratory in general). After a brief glance at philosophical writing, we will turn to poetry (which overlaps with panegyric) and epistolography (which overlaps with poetry, and occasionally with panegyric). Thereafter, we will look at history writing and at its relationship with what is sometimes called pseudo-history and with hagiography.

2.1 Panegyric and Secular Oratory

In many ways the fourth century was the golden age of panegyric (Whitby 1998; Rees 2012). Although the genre was not new, developments in imperial and senatorial public display from the reign of Diocletian (284–305) onwards provided a context for the delivery of extremely elaborate praise speeches, initially in prose, although, by the beginning of the fifth century, also in verse. Thus, assumption of major office, including the imperial title, as well as the consulship, together with important anniversaries, provided an excuse for the public delivery of a panegyric. These were more than simple laudatory exercises, in that they also functioned as works of justification, explaining public policy or the political position of the individual being lauded. The most significant collection of prose panegyrics is that known under the title *Panegyrici Latini*, made in the reign of Theodosius I (379–395) by Pacatus, which gathers together a sequence of 12 panegyrics, covering the century from 289 to 389, from the days of the Tetrarchy down to the compiler's own offering (Nixon and Rodgers 1994). The collection was prefaced by Pliny's panegyric to Trajan, which served as a model.

Among other panegyrics of the late fourth century there are the orations of Symmachus, the first of which is addressed to Valentinian I (364–375), and Ausonius's *Gratiarum Actio* offered to Gratian (375–383) in 379 for granting him the consulship (Lolli 2006). Symmachus's flowery style, the so-called *stylum pingue atque floridum*, was thought particularly apposite for such formal addresses. The tradition of prose panegyrics continued into the fifth century, as can be seen in the fragments of that of Merobaudes for the *magister militum* Aetius (d. 454) (Clover 1971), and it even lasted into the sixth. Another fragmentary panegyric is that addressed by Cassiodorus to the Ostrogothic king Theodoric (493–526), who is also the subject of an extensive work by Ennodius of Pavia (Rohr 1995), although there is some doubt as to whether this was delivered as a spoken oration.

Equally characteristic of the public literary scene was the verse panegyric, which in the opening years of the fifth century became the dominant form of public address as a result of the works of Claudian, acting as the mouthpiece for the *magister militum* Stilicho (d. 408) (Cameron 1970; Schindler 2009, pp. 227–309). Claudian's verse panegyrics were highly elaborate allegorical exercises, which could even include discussion between the Olympian gods. Indeed, there is no hint of Christianity in his work, despite the fact that the audience by this time was almost entirely Christian; he himself, however, is described as a pagan by both Orosius (d. post 418) and Augustine. Claudian's verse panegyrics provided the model for Sidonius Apollinaris (d. ca.489), in the sequence of public poems addressed to the emperors Avitus (455–456), Majorian (457–461), and Anthemius (467–472), which he composed in the middle of the fifth century (Harries 1994; Watson 1998). Sidonius seems to have had no immediate successor in the West – a lacuna which can no doubt be explained by the collapse of the imperial court, although Sidonius himself did write a poem in praise of the Visigothic king Euric (466–484).

In Constantinople, however, the Latin verse panegyric was clearly still in vogue in the second half of the sixth century, as can be seen from the *In Laudem Iustini*, written in praise of Justin II (565–574) by the African poet Corippus (Cameron 1976, Schindler 2009). But even in the West, verse that was inspired by the tradition of panegyric did continue in the immediately post-Roman kingdoms. At the very end of the fifth century Dracontius (d. 505) wrote his *Satisfactio ad Gunthamundum*, as a plea for pardon for some unspecified political crime (Conant 2012, pp. 141–148). In the second half of the sixth century the Italian Venantius Fortunatus (d. ca. 600) wrote a considerable amount of verse for formal occasions at the Frankish courts of Merovingian kings, including praise poems and an epithalamium (George 1992, 1995; Roberts 2009). Fortunatus wrote in a style that has been described as "jeweled" (Roberts 1989, esp. pp. 138–142, 151), a variant of the earlier *stylum atque floridum*. He would seem to have learned his skills in Justinianic Ravenna.

Panegyric was, of course, only one genre of public oratory: In addition to his oration for Valentinian, Symmachus wrote a number of speeches, most famously the third *Relatio* (384), which argued for the restoration of the Altar of Victory to the Senate House (Barrow 1976). Also close in kind to panegyric and to epithalamia, marking imperial or aristocratic marriages, were funerary orations. Among the most significant of these were those delivered by Ambrose, bishop of Milan (374–397), for Valentinian II (375–392) and for Theodosius I (Liebeschuetz 2005). These, of course, were both laudatory and, at the same time, religious. As such, they point to the strong connection between secular and religious oratory.

2.2 Sermons

The fourth and fifth centuries were as much a golden age for the composition of sermons as they were for the composition of panegyric. Some of the finest preachers had been trained as rhetors, among them both Ambrose and Augustine (395–430), as well as the late fifth-century religious teacher Julianus Pomerius. Although we tend to understand sermons as essentially spiritual, there is no doubt that congregations in the fifth and sixth centuries appreciated them as rhetorical exercises (Maxwell 2006, pp. 1–64) and were stirred to strong emotion by them (Brown 2000, p. 248, on Augustine). The sermons of Caesarius of Arles (502–542) in the early sixth century were highly regarded and survive in large numbers, although many of those that are now attributed to him were either attributed to Augustine or are anonymous in the manuscripts (Klingshirn 1994, pp. 9–10). Other Gallic sermons of the late fifth century are preserved in a collection known now as that of Eusebius Gallicanus, which seems to include works by a number of ecclesiastics, including Faustus of Riez (Bailey 2010). We know that Avitus of Vienne (d. 518) compiled a volume of sermons for the ecclesiastical year, some of which have come down to us, while others of his sermons, intended for specific occasions, notably the dedication of churches, were preserved among his letters (Wood 1986, 2014). That his sermons were assessed as oratorical displays is clear from the fact that in one of his letters he has to defend himself from the charge leveled by a fellow bishop of having wrongly stressed a syllable in the course of his preaching.

Of course, the theological content of a sermon was ultimately more important than its oratorical qualities. Sermons, indeed, overlap with full-blown works of theology. A number of the most important theological works of Gregory the Great (590–604), including the commentaries on Ezekiel and those on Job, were delivered as homilies. Drawing a line between literature and theology is thus extremely difficult – and not just with regard to homiletic writing. Augustine's works are particularly challenging in this respect. It is useful, here, to remember Sidonius's description of the library of his friend Ferreolus. The section closest to the seats intended for men included works that were distinguished by their eloquence, despite the difference of their subject matter and opinions: The authors shelved together are named by Sidonius as Augustine, Varro, Horace, and Prudentius, as well as Origen, in Rufinus's translation – although he does note their varying doctrinal positions. The section closest to the seats intended for the women, by contrast, is described as holding the religious works. Apparently Origen and Augustine were valued by Ferreolus for their style more than their content.

2.3 Philosophy

Even nowadays it is possible to make a connection between Augustine and Varro, given the attention paid to the philosopher by the bishop of Hippo in the *City of God*. Just as one needs to note the overlap between panegyrics and sermons, so, too, one needs to remember that theology and philosophy were overlapping categories. Augustine's *Cassiciacum Dialogues* belong firmly to the work of late antique philosophical thought.

Philosophy was to be found not only in the theological works of the fifth century. In addition to Martianus Capella, whose *De nuptiis Philologiae et Mercurii* constitutes an allegorical guide to the liberal arts, there is Macrobius's commentary on the *Dream of Scipio*, which offers a philosophical and especially Neoplatonist reading of the cosmos (Cameron 2011, pp. 269–270).

A century later Boethius wrote the last of the great philosophical works of antiquity, the *Consolation of Philosophy*, while imprisoned in Ravenna in 524, awaiting execution on the orders of the Ostrogothic ruler Theodoric the Great. Although this is the most famous of Boethius's works, his output reflected the full range of learning noted by Martianus Capella, with volumes on music, arithmetic, and commentaries on Aristotle. In addition, he was the author of a number of short theological treatises dealing with Trinitarian questions (Chadwick 1981; Marenbon 2003, 2009).

2.4 Secular Verse

Although the late antique period can be seen as a golden age of panegyric and, indeed, of homiletic writing, its poetry tends to be less highly regarded, being unfavorably compared with both the Augustan Age of Virgil and Ovid and the Silver Age of Statius. Yet the verse of the period is not insignificant. We have already noted the verse panegyrics of Claudian and Sidonius. Claudian also left an incomplete poem on the *Rape of Proserpine*. Another substantial mythological work, the *Orestes*, was composed in the Vandal kingdom around the year 500 by Dracontius (Díaz de Bustamente 1978; Bureau 2003). Post-Roman North Africa, indeed, seems to have been a center of poetic production, much of it – including some of Dracontius's work – slight in scale (Kay 2006). A significant number of the poems collected in the *Latin Anthology* appear to have been written in late fifth-century Africa, among them the often risqué poems of Luxorius. Africa after the fall of the Vandals provided the setting for the last substantial secular, albeit not mythological, epic, Corippus's account of the campaigns of John Troglita against the Moors (Gärtner 2008).

The best-known secular poems of the period, however, are not substantial epics but rather works, often smaller in scale, that treat rather more mundane themes. Toward the end of the fourth century Ausonius, for instance, wrote works on his family, in the *Parentalia*, and on the professors of Bordeaux, where his own rhetorical career had begun, as well as his most famous poem, the *Mosella*, describing and musing on the landscape of the river valley (Green 1991, Sivan 1993). The contemporary landscape is also central to one of the most significant large-scale secular poems of the early fifth century, Rutilius Namatianus's now-fragmentary account of his journey from Rome, where he had been city prefect, to his homeland in Gaul, in 416 – the *De Reditu Suo* (Wolff 2007; Malamud 2016). Although the world that Rutilius describes is one that had recently suffered from the passage of the Visigoths, the gloss that he puts on the situation is one of imminent renewal, *ordo renascendi* (Matthews 1975, pp. 329–376). It is unfortunate that the concluding books of the poem are lost, since they would have shed more light on the literary circles of Gaul, which at this time provided an audience for the one surviving late antique theatrical work, the *Querolus*, which deals comically with the problems facing a minor aristocrat of the period (Lassandro and Romano 1991).

2.5 Religious Verse

A contemporary of Rutilius, also belonging to the senatorial aristocracy – indeed even more socially distinguished – was Paulinus of Pella, the grandson of Ausonius. His great poem, however, while concerned with recent events, is religious in orientation. The *Eucharisticos* is Paulinus's thanksgiving to God for his survival, despite the disasters of the early fifth century that had led to his losing almost all his inheritance – which he narrates in some detail (McLynn 1995). Other poets of the period, writing perhaps slightly before Paulinus, also took as their subject matter the state of Gaul following the invasions of the Vandals, Alans, and Sueves, followed by the arrival of the Visigoths. Among the poems is the *Commonitorium*, ascribed to bishop Orientius of Auch, which, like the *Carmen de providentia Dei*, is sometimes attributed to Prosper of Aquitaine, turns the crisis into a springboard for spiritual exhortation (Marcovich 1989; Gillett 2003, pp. 138–143; Fielding 2014).

Perhaps the most influential of the Christian poets was the Spaniard Prudentius, who died ca. 413. Already in the early 380s he had written an attack on Symmachus's appeal for the return of the Altar of Victory to the Senate House (Tränkle 2008). In the long term the work that would have most impact was the *Psychomachia*, an allegorical text describing the conflict between vice and virtue. For historians of late antique spirituality, however, his *Peristephanon*, a collection of verses on Christian martyrs, and most especially Spanish martyrs, has provided more insights, illustrating the application of poems and hymns to the growing cult of the saints (Roberts 1993) – something that can also be seen in the poetry of Paulinus of Nola (d. 431). The tradition would continue throughout the fifth and sixth centuries and finds one of its most extended illustrations in the poetic *Life of Martin* by Venantius Fortunatus (Roberts 2002).

The main body of large-scale Christian poetic works from the period, however, is made up of versifications of the Bible, which both paraphrase and comment on the text (Herzog 1975; Nodes 1993; Green 2006). The earliest of these, Juvencus's versification of the Gospels, dates to the Age of

Constantine (McGill 2016). A second poetic version of the Gospels, the *Carmen Paschale*, was composed, probably in Italy, by the rhetor Sedulius in the first half of the fifth century (Springer 1988, 2013). A century later Arator, a north Italian protegé of Ennodius of Pavia, penned his versification of the Acts of the Apostles.

The New Testament seems to have attracted poets rather more often than did the Old Testament. The first major versification of the Heptateuch is ascribed to a fifth-century Gallo-Roman known to us as Cyprian (though some prefer simply to talk of the Heptateuch Poet). At the end of the fifth century Dracontius, alongside his other poems, wrote an account of the Creation in his *De Laudibus Dei* (Tizzoni 2012). At almost exactly the same time, and perhaps influenced by Dracontius's example, Avitus of Vienne set about versifying Genesis and Exodus, or rather, in the case of Genesis he versified one of Augustine's commentaries on the biblical book (Wood 2001). In addition to five substantial poems on the Old Testament, Avitus wrote a lengthy verse work in praise of chastity, which largely revolves around the piety of women of his own family.

Chastity, or rather virginity, was also the subject of one of Venantius Fortunatus's major, and most extended, religious poems, the *De Virginitate*, written for his patroness and friend, Radegund, the ascetic founder of the monastery of the Holy Cross at Poitiers. Like other of Fortunatus's poems, this proved a model to later generations, providing inspiration in particular for the late seventh-century Anglo-Saxon poet Aldhelm.

2.6 Letter Writing

Avitus and Venantius Fortunatus bring us to another of the major genres of late antique literature: letter writing (Sogno, Storin, and Watts 2017; Müller, forthcoming). Of course, the writing and preservation of letters was well established in the classical period, and, indeed, Pliny's letters were often regarded as a model, both as individual pieces and as a collection. The fourth, fifth, and sixth centuries can be seen as a major period of letter writing, and, as in the case of panegyric, the flowery style could be appropriate. There are the obvious collections, especially those of Symmachus and Sidonius Apollinaris, the latter of whom looks back specifically to both Symmachus and Pliny.

The early sixth century boasts a remarkable number of collections of letters. The best known is the large collection of Cassiodorus's official correspondence, the *Variae*, compiled during the author's enforced sojourn in Constantinople in the middle of the sixth century (Bjornlie 2013). Closer in kind to the collection of Sidonius are those of Ruricius of Limoges (d. ca. 510) (Mathisen 1999),

Avitus of Vienne (Wood 1993; Shanzer and Wood 2002), and Ennodius of Pavia (Kennell 2000). Equally, from the end of the sixth century, there is the collection of occasional verses made by Venantius Fortunatus, the majority of which are, in fact, verse letters (Williard 2014). Covering the whole of the period from the late fifth to the late sixth century there is the multi-authored collection known as the *Epistolae Austrasicae* (Barrett and Woudhuysen 2016). This tradition of letter writing lasted into the seventh century, with the letters of Desiderius of Cahors (d. ca. 655) (Mathisen 2013). Many of these letters contain little information of significance: Their main purpose seems often to have been the cultivation and maintenance of networks of friendship, and, indeed, they are frequently described as letters of *amicitia*. As such, they have been central to the reconstruction of fourth-, fifth-, and sixth-century groups of families and friends.

All these letters have been interpreted in the light of the Sidonius collection, although in fact some of them differ significantly. Unlike the collections of Symmachus, Sidonius, Cassiodorus, or Fortunatus, those of Avitus, Ruricius, and Ennodius are not authorial. They were put together from archive collections, some perhaps as early as the sixth century, but others, including those of Ennodius, Desiderius, and the *Epistolae Austrasicae*, in the eighth and ninth centuries, which is when the letters of Pope Gregory the Great (590–604) were organized into a *Register*. Some groups of letters that have been presented as collections (most notably the *Epistolae Arelatenses Genuinae*) were, in fact, only put together in the nineteenth century (Wood, forthcoming).

The question of when and how these letters were gathered together is an important one, because it suggests that the interpretation of them as exercises in friendship radically underestimates their range of functions. Some letters undoubtedly were regarded as models for the exercise of friendship and also as models for epistolary style. One small group of seventh-century letters, of Frodebert of Paris and Importunus of Tours, is even preserved alongside the Formulary of Sens in a Paris manuscript (Walstra 1962; Shanzer 2010; Hen 2012). Other letters, however, have very different functions and were preserved in collections of theology and canon law. They thus have much in common with early collections of papal letters, like the *Collectio Avellana*, which was apparently put together in the late sixth century (Viezure 2015). The prose works of Avitus present a good example of the range of genres to which letters can be assigned. They seem to have survived in the archives of the Church of Vienne, where they were consulted to create several different collections; and they include a sizeable number of letters that can readily be compared with the epistolary output of Sidonius (who may indeed have been his uncle) and that appear alongside political pieces, which can be best described as mini-panegyrics, as well as short theological treatises. In addition, the archive, and the earliest known collection made from it, included sermons for special occasions, which would not have been appropriate for the author's *Homiliary*, a collection of sermons for the standard feasts of the year. Thus, in talking of the significance of letters among the output of late antiquity, we should be aware that the genre is concerned with far more than the topic of *amicitia*, which has most attracted historians.

2.7 History Writing

Sidonius wrote letters, panegyrics, and also masses for the church, although these have not survived. He refused, however, to write an account of the war in Gaul with the Huns in the time of Attila (*Ep.* 8.15.1–2). That he should have been invited to write such a work is a reminder that the senatorial aristocracy had been involved in the production and edition of historical works. Symmachus is known to have undertaken the preparation of a new text of Livy (*Ep.* 9.13). Ammianus Marcellinus's great history would seem to have had an aristocratic, probably even a court, audience, to judge from the fact that the Greek rhetor Libanius had heard of the success of his public readings (Fromara 1992). His judgment on the strengths and weaknesses of individual emperors and generals was thus addressed to the most influential levels of society.

The same can be said of some of the other historical works of the period, including the two historical epitomes, the *De Caesaribus* of Aurelius Victor, who was even appointed governor of Pannonia Secunda by the emperor Julian in 361 (Bird 1994), and the *Breviary* of Eutropius, who, while not personally so distinguished, was nevertheless appointed *magister epistolarum* by Constantius before 361 and *magister memoriae* by Valens in 369 (Bird 1993). The *Historia Augusta*, a collection of imperial biographies purporting to have been written by several authors in the third century, but, in fact, the product of a single forger in the second half of the fourth century, would seem to belong to this same world (Thomson 2012). Historians and their audiences, thus, were drawn from the world of imperial bureaucrats and from the aristocracy – although Ammianus Marcellinus's earlier career had been as a soldier. Not surprisingly, like panegyric, history was intended to carry a political message.

It is worth noting that the *Historia Augusta* is not the only forged history to have been in circulation in the fourth century, although other examples are not usually categorized as histories. Thus, the story of Troy, which was thought of as historical, saw a remarkable revival in late antiquity. It seems to have been in the fourth century that an abridged version of Homer in Latin, known as the *Ilias Latina*, composed probably in the first century, attracted attention (Scaffai 1982). In addition, another version of the fall of Troy, the *Ephereridos* of Dictys of Crete, was translated into Latin, apparently in the fourth century (Yavuz 2015). Among the works that would prove most popular in later generations is the *De Excidio Troiae* ascribed to Dares of Frigia, but which was apparently a late antique forgery (Yavuz 2015; Clark, forthcoming). Exactly when Dares's text was written is unclear, nor is it known whether it was based on a Greek original. The Latin text opens with a letter supposedly from Cornelius Nepos to Sallust, announcing the discovery of the work. As a forgery it bears some comparison with the *Historia Augusta*.

Another figure who would seem to have been associated with the senatorial classes was Filocalus, the calligrapher who created the so-called *Calendar of 354*, a compilation that brought together information on the Caesars, the consuls, and the urban prefects of Rome, alongside the bishops and martyrs of Rome, and attached that information to what is now called a World Chronicle, and a Chronicle of the City of Rome (Salzman 1991). Whereas the epitomes of Aurelius Victor and Eutropius, as well as of the *Historia Augusta* and the *Res Gestae* of Ammianus, look back to classical history writing, part of the Filocalus compilation belongs to the traditions that were gaining popularity in Christian circles. Filocalus himself was closely connected to Pope Damasus and, it would seem, to the pious senatorial matron Melania the Elder.

2.8 Christian History and Hagiography

Christian historical writing, of course, goes back to the Bible, but what was perhaps the historical work to have most influence was the *Chronicle* compiled by Eusebius of Caesarea in the reign of Constantine (306–337), which was subsequently translated and extended by Jerome (d. 420) (Burgess 1999; Burgess and Kulikowski 2013). Unlike the prose narrative of Ammianus (which drew its literary inspiration most obviously from Tacitus), Eusebius's *Chronicle* was rather a vast annalistic compilation, providing a remarkable synchronization of events in the various empires past and present, each set out in its own column. Although annalistic (in other words, comprising short entries detailing the major event or events in each year) and thus extremely terse in nature, it provided an interpretation of world history through its choice of information and by gradually whittling down the number of empires in existence, until only the Roman Empire remained, thus highlighting its position in Providential History. Most chronicle writing in the early Middle

Ages followed the model of Eusebius, often transcribing the Eusebian text as translated by Jerome, with minor alteration, and then continuing the annalistic scheme. Thus, the Eusebian scheme was continued by Prosper of Aquitaine (d. ca. 455) and Hydatius of Tuy (d. 469) in the fifth century, by Marcellinus Comes (d. 534), Cassiodorus, and Marius of Avenches (d. 596) in the sixth, and by Isidore of Seville (600–636) in the seventh (Muhlberger 1990; Croke 2001; Burgess and Kulikowski 2013; Wood 2010, 2015).

This, however, was not the only pattern followed by historians and, especially, by historians writing in the post-Roman kingdoms. Thus, Victor of Vita in late fifth-century North Africa wrote a *History of the Vandal Persecutions* (Moorhead 1992; Merrills 2011) and Cassiodorus a (now lost) *History of the Goths*, which served as a point of departure for Jordanes in Constantinople in the middle years of the sixth century, as he interrupted his *Historia Romana* to write his *Getica* (the *Gothic History*) (Christensen 2002). In subsequent decades Gregory of Tours (573–594) set about writing his *Ten Books of Histories* (Heinzelmann 2001; Reimitz 2015). These used to be classified as "Barbarian histories" because at first sight each one focused on a particular barbarian group (Goffart 1988). In recent years it has rightly been observed that they do not have a great deal in common, and that each of the so-called Barbarian histories follows a different pattern, although most of them have a strong religious bent. For Victor of Vita the main focus is obviously the Catholic Church and the persecution that it faced in Vandal Africa. For Gregory of Tours the church is also the center of attention, much more so than the Franks.

The historical writings of Victor and Gregory are closely allied to the biographies of saints, and, indeed, Gregory wrote almost as much hagiography as history. Already in the third century accounts of martyrdom were set down, among the earliest being the passion of the African virgin Perpetua (Berschin 1986; Bremmer and Formisano 2012; Cooper 2013, 105–130). Such accounts, revolving around the arrest, interrogation, and execution of the martyr, became increasingly popular and continued to be written long after the period of persecutions; many of the later acts concerned fictitious saints, who were invented to justify, promote, or explain a saint cult. They were often composed in the context of ecclesiastical conflict, as in the case of a substantial number of *acta* produced in Rome in the early sixth century. They were frequently short and, on occasion, were composed to be read on the feast day of the martyr. Usually they are anonymous, although some, for instance that of St. Maurice and the Theban Legion, written by Eucherius of Lyons (d. ca. 449), were written by ecclesiastics with a fine sense of rhetorical style.

With the end of the persecution hagiographers also began to write about saints who had not died as martyrs. Whereas the martyr acts were concerned largely with the assertion of Christianity, the lives of confessors had a rather broader range of concerns, promoting particular styles of asceticism, episcopal practice, or attachment to specific theological positions. The first life of a confessor to have a major impact was that of Antony, written by Athanasius of Alexandria in ca. 360, but already translated into Latin by Evagrius of Antioch before 374. This initiated a vogue for the writing about the desert fathers, both in the lives of individual saints, and also in collections of anecdotes about the holy men of Egypt (Harmless 2004). Among Latin writers Jerome contributed to the hagiographical literature of the desert with his, at least partially fictional, lives of Hilarian, Malchus, and Paul the First Hermit (Bastiaensen 1994), while John Cassian (d. 435) set out his knowledge of the desert fathers as a model for the ascetic life in his *Conferences* and *Institutes* (Stewart 1998).

Hagiography of the desert fathers, together with an interest in the Holy Land, which emerged as a focus for pilgrimage after the days of Constantine and, more particularly, after the journey to Jerusalem undertaken by his mother Helena (d. 330), led to the development of a further literary genre: the travelogue concerned with visits to the holy places. The earliest of these was that of the Bordeaux pilgrim, composed in 333. This was followed in the 380s by an account written by a woman known to us as Egeria. Among several later accounts is that of the so-called Piacenza pilgrim, dated to the 570s. Descriptive writing about the Holy Land, admittedly largely secondhand, would continue through into the eighth century (Hunt 1982; Wilkinson 2002).

The West could scarcely boast a desert setting as could Egypt, Syria, and Palestine. It could, however, boast ascetics, most notably Martin of Tours (d. 397), who, although he ended his life as bishop of Tours, was initially an ascetic and a monastic founder. His life by Sulpicius Severus became one of the cornerstones of Western hagiography (Stancliffe 1983). It was followed by Sulpicius's *Dialogues*, written in large measure to show that Martin was the equal of the desert fathers. The *Life of Martin* was followed by a number of other hagiographical works devoted to Western ascetics and monastic founders, notably a cluster of lives concerned with the island monastery of Lérins and, from the early sixth century, a substantial tripartite life, the anonymous *Life of the Fathers of Jura* (Martine 1968).

Monks and abbots, however, did not provide the dominant material for hagiography in the fifth- and sixth-century West, although there was something of a resurgence of monastic hagiography in the seventh century. Rather, the major texts tended to be devoted to the lives of bishops. Among the earliest, and the most influential, were Paulinus's *Life of Ambrose*, written in 422, and Possidius's *Life of Augustine* (written before 439). Both of these are regularly cited as models by later hagiographers. Also of considerable importance is the *Life of Germanus of Auxerre*, written ca. 480 by Constantius, a priest of

Lyons, at the request of his bishop, Patiens, but addressed additionally to Sidonius Apollinaris (Thompson 1984). Among significant episcopal lives from the first half of the sixth century there are that of Fulgentius of Ruspe by Facundus and that of Caesarius of Arles, written by Cyprian of Toulon together with a number of friends. From the second half of the century there is a sizeable collection of lives penned by Venantius Fortunatus (Collins 1981).

Although not exactly hagiography, there is also the collection of papal lives known as the *Liber Pontificalis*. The first group of these apparently belongs to the very late fifth century. Subsequently lives were added, albeit somewhat spasmodically. Rather than presenting the popes as saints, the collection was rather more concerned with their rulership of the Roman Church, with the result that in certain respects the lives are closer to imperial biographies than the hagiography of saints (Davis 2000).

By the sixth century literature was unquestionably associated primarily with the church and with Christian religion. So, too, learning was increasingly dominated by the church, with the result that it ceased to be associated with centers of court or aristocratic influence – it is notable that the fifth and sixth centuries saw the first surviving literary works to be composed by Britons in the British Isles, the *Confessio* of Patrick (Howlett 1994) and the *De Excidio Britonum* of Gildas (George 2009) while Spanish authors like Hydatius of Tuy made their careers in the land of their birth rather than gravitating toward the Mediterranean (Burgess 1993). The collapse of the urban school did not mean that the skills of the grammarian or the rhetor were entirely lost, although written Latin came more and more to reflect everyday usage, rather than the artificial language of the rhetorical schools. The classics were not entirely forgotten; indeed the earliest manuscripts of most classical texts come from the Merovingian and, more particularly, the Carolingian world. Classical narratives survived, although not always in ways that Virgil would have recognized, as one can see from the forgery ascribed to Dares of Phrygia. Above all, the requirements of the new Christian and sub-Roman world were different from those of the Empire, and even of the late Empire, and this is reflected in the literature.

REFERENCES

Bailey, Lisa Kaaren. (2010). *Christianity's Quiet Success: The Eusebius Gallicanus Sermon Collection and the Power of the Church in Late Antique Gaul*. South Bend, IN: University of Notre Dame Press.

Banniard, Michel. (1992). *Viva voce: Communication écrite et communication orale du IVe an IXe siècle en Occident latin*. Paris: Brepols.

Barrett, Graham and Woudhuysen, George. (2016). Assembling the *Austrasian Letters* at Trier and Lorsch. *Early Medieval Europe* 24: 3–57.

Barrow, Reginald Haynes. ed. (1976). *Prefect and Emperor: The Relationes of Symmachus, AD 384*. Oxford: Oxford University Press.

Bastiaensen, A.A.R. (1994). Jérôme hagiographe. In: *Hagiographies*. Vol. 1 (ed. Guy Phippart), 110–119. Turnhout: Brepols.

Berschin, Walter. (1986). *Biographie und Epochenstil im lateinischen Mittelalter. Vol. 1, Von der Passio Perpetuae zu den Dialogi Gregors des Großen*. Stuttgart: Anton Hiersemann.

Bird, Harold W. (1993). *Eutropius: Breviarium*. Translated Texts for Historians 14. Liverpool: Liverpool University Press.

Bird, Harold W. (1994. *Aurelius Victor: De Caesaribus*. Translated Texts for Historians 17. Liverpool: Liverpool University Press.

Bjornlie, Shane. (2013). *Politics and Tradition between Rome, Ravenna and Constantinople: A Study of Cassiodorus and the Variae, 527–554*. Cambridge: Cambridge University Press.

Bremmer, Jan N. and Formisano, Marco. ed. (2012). *Perpetua's Passions: Multidisciplinary Approaches to the Passio Perpetuae et Felicitatis*. Oxford: Oxford University Press.

Brown, Peter. (2000). *Augustine of Hippo: A Biography*. New ed. Berkeley: University of California Press.

Bureau, Bruno. (2003). Épique et romanesque: l'exemple de deux épopées tardives, L'Enlèvement de Proserpine de Claudien et la Tragédie d'Oreste de Dracontius. *Interférences Ars Scribendi* 1.

Burgess, R.W. (1993). *The Chronicle of Hydatius and the Consularia Constantinopolitana: Two Contemporary Accounts of the Final Years of the Roman Empire*. Oxford: Clarendon.

Burgess, R.W. and Kulikowski, Michael. (2013). *Mosaics of Time: The Latin Chronicle Traditions from the First Century BC to the Sixth Century AD. Vol 1: A Historical Introduction to the Chronicle Genre from Its Origins to the High Middle Ages*. Turnhout: Brepols.

Burgess, R.W. with Witakowski, Witold. (1999). *Studies in Eusebian and Post-Eusebian Chronography*. Stuttgart: Steiner.

Cameron, Alan. (1970). *Claudian: Poetry and Propaganda at the Court of Honorius*. Oxford: Clarendon.

Cameron, Alan. (2011). *The Last Pagans of Rome*. Oxford: Oxford University Press.

Cameron, Averil. (1976). *In Laudem Iustini Augusti Minoris: Flavius Cresconius Corippus*. London: Athlone, University of London.

Chadwick, Henry. (1981). *Boethius: The Consolations of Music, Logic, Theology and Philosophy*. Oxford: Oxford University Press.

Christensen, Arne Søby. (2002). *Cassiodorus, Jordanes and the History of the Goths: Studies in a Migration Myth*. Copenhagen, Museum Tusculanum.

Clark, Frederic. (Forthcoming). *The First Pagan Historian: The Fortunes of a Fraud from Antiquity to the Present*. Oxford: Oxford University Press.

Clover, F.M. (1971). Flavius Merobaudes: A translation and historical commentary. *Transactions of the American Philosophical Society* n. s. 61: 1–78.

Collins, Richard. (1981). Observations on the form, language and public of the prose biographies of Venantius Fortunatus in the hagiography of Merovingian Gaul. In: *Columbanus and Merovingian Monasticism* (ed. Howard B. Clarke and Mary Brennan), 105–131. British Archaeological Reports 113. Oxford: British Archaeological Reports.

Conant, Jonathan. (2012). *Staying Roman: Conquest and Identity in Africa and the Mediterranean, 439–700*. Cambridge: Cambridge University Press.

Cooper, Kate. (2013). *Band of Angels: The Forgotten World of Early Christian Women*. London: Atlantic Books.

Croke, Brian. (2001). *Count Marcellinus and His Chronicle*. Oxford: Oxford University Press.

Davis, Raymond. (2000). *The Book of Pontiffs (Liber Pontificalis)*. 2nd ed. Translated Texts for Historians 6. Liverpool, Liverpool University Press.

Díaz de Bustamente, J.M. (1978). *Draconcio y sus carmina profana: Estudio biográfico, introducción y edición crítica*. Santiago: Universidad de Santiago, Secretariado de Publicaciones.

Fielding, Ian. (2014). Physical ruin and spiritual perfection in fifth-century Gaul: Orientius and his contemporaries on the "landscape of the soul." *Journal of Early Christian Studies* 22: 569–585.

Fromara, Charles W. (1992). Studies in Ammianus Marcellinus: I: The letter of Libanius and Ammianus' connection with Antioch. *Historia* 41: 328–344.

Gärtner, Thomas. (2008). *Untersuchungen zur Gestaltung und zum historischen Stoff der Johannis Coripps*. Berlin: De Gruyter.

George, Judith. (1992). *A Latin Poet in Merovingian Gaul*. Oxford: Clarendon.

George, Judith. (1995). *Venantius Fortunatus: Personal and Political Poems*. Liverpool: Liverpool University Press.

George, Karen. (2009). *Gildas's De Excidio Britonum and the Early British Church*. Woodbridge: Boydell.

Gillett, Andrew. (2003). *Envoys and Political Communication in the Late Antique West, 411–533*. Cambridge: Cambridge University Press.

Goffart, Walter A. (1988). *The Narrators of Barbarian History (A.D. 550–800): Jordanes, Gregory of Tours, Bede, Paul the Deacon*. Princeton, NJ: Princeton University Press.

Grandgent, C.H. (1907). *An Introduction to Vulgar Latin*. London: D.C. Heath.

Green, R.P.H. (1991). *The Works of Ausonius*. Oxford: Clarendon.

Green, R.P.H. (2006). *Latin Epics of the New Testament: Juvencus, Sedulius, Arator*. Oxford: Oxford University Press.

Halporn, James W. and Vessey, Mark. (2004). *Cassiodorus: Institutions of Divine and Secular Learning*. Liverpool: Liverpool University Press.

Harmless, William S.J. (2004). *Desert Christians: An Introduction to the Literature of Early Monasticism*. Oxford: Oxford University Press.

Harries, Jill. (1994). *Sidonius Apollinaris and the Fall of Rome, AD 407–485*. Oxford: Oxford University Press.

Heinzelmann, Martin. (2001). *Gregory of Tours: History and Society in the Sixth Century.* Cambridge: Cambridge University Press.

Hen, Yitzhak. (2007). *Roman Barbarians: The Royal Court and Culture in the Early Medieval West.* Basingstoke: Palgrave Macmillan.

Hen, Yitzhak. (2012). Chrodobert, Boba, and the wife of Grimoald. *Revue Belge de Philologie et d'Histoire* 90: 225–44.

Herzog, Reinhart. (1975). *Die Bibelepik der lateinischen Spätantike 1: Formgeschichte einer erbaulichen Gattungen.* Munich: Wilhelm Fink.

Howlett, David. (1994). *The Book of Letters of Saint Patrick the Bishop.* Dublin: Four Courts.

Hunt, E.D. (1982). *Holy Land Pilgrimage in the Later Roman Empire.* Oxford: Oxford University Press.

Kay, N.M. (2006). *Epigrams from the Anthologia Latina: Text, Translation and Commentary.* London: Bloomsbury.

Kennell, S. A. H. (2000). *Magnus Felix Ennodius: A Gentleman of the Church.* Ann Arbor, MI: University of Michigan Press.

Klingshirn, William E. (1994). *Caesarius of Arles: The Making of a Christian Community in Late Antique Gaul.* Cambridge: Cambridge University Press.

Lassandro, D. and Romano, E. (1991). Rassegna bibliografica degli studi sul *Querolus*. *Bolletino di Studi Latini* 21: 26–51.

Liebeschuetz, J.H.W.G. with Carole Hill. trans. (2005). *Ambrose: Political Letters and Speeches.* Liverpool: Liverpool University Press.

Lolli, Massino. (2006). Ausonius: Die "Gratiarum actio ad Gratianum imperatorem" und die "Maiestatis laudibus": Lobrede auf den Herrscher oder auf den Lehrer? *Latomus* 65: 707–726.

Malamud, Martha. (2016). *Rutilius Namatianus' Going Home: De reditu suo.* London: Routledge.

Marcovich, Miroslav. (1989). *Prosper of Aquitaine: Text, Translation and Commentary.* Leiden: Brill.

Marenbon, John. (2003). *Boethius.* Oxford: Oxford University Press.

Marenbon, John. ed. (2009). *The Cambridge Companion to Boethius.* Cambridge: Cambridge University Press.

Marrou, Henri Irénée. (1969). Les arts libéraux dans l'Antiquite classique. In: *Arts libéraux et philosophie au Moyen Âge* (ed. Henri Irénée Marrou), 6–27. Paris: Vrin; Montreal: Institut d'études médiévales.

Martine, Francois. (1968). *Vie des Pères du Jura.* Sources Chrétiennes 142. Paris: Éditions du Cerf.

Mathisen, Ralph W. (1999). *Ruricius of Limoges and Friends: A Collection of Letters from Visigothic Gaul.* Translated Texts for Historians 30. Liverpool: Liverpool University Press.

Mathisen, Ralph W. (2013). Desiderius of Cahors: Last of the Romans. In: *Gallien in Spätantike und Frühmittelalter: Kulturgeschichte einer Region* (ed. Steffen Diefenbach and Gernot Michael Müller), 455–469. Berlin: De Gruyter.

Matthews, John. (1975). *Western Aristocracies and Imperial Court, A.D. 364–425.* Oxford: Clarendon.

Maxwell, Jaclyn. (2006). *Christianization and Communication in Late Antiquity.* Cambridge: Cambridge University Press.

McGill, Scott. (2016). *Juvencus' Four Books of the Gospels: Evangeliorum libri quattuor.* London: Routledge.

McLynn, Neil. (1995). Paulinus the Impenitent: A study of the *Eucharisticos. Journal of Early Christian Studies* 3: 461–486.

Merrills, Andrew H. (2011). *Totum subuertere uoluerunt*: "Social Martyrdom" in the *Historia persecutionis* of Victor of Vita. In: *Unclassical Traditions. Vol. 2: Perspectives from East and West in Late Antiquity* (ed. Christopher Kelly, Richard Flower, and Michael Stuart Williams), 102–115. Cambridge Classical Journal Suppl. 35. Cambridge: Cambridge University Press.

Moorhead, John. (1992). *Victor of Vita: History of the Vandal Persecutions.* Translated Texts for Historians 10. Liverpool: Liverpool University Press.

Muhlberger, Steven. (1990). *The Fifth-Century Chroniclers: Prosper, Hydatius, and the Gallic Chronicler of 452.* Leeds: Francis Cairns.

Müller, Gernot H. ed. (Forthcoming). *Zwischen Alltagskommunikation und literarischer Identitätsbildung: Kulturgeschichtliche Aspekte lateinischer Epistolographie in Spätantike und Frühmittelalter.* Stuttgart, Steiner.

Nixon, C.E.V. and Rodgers, Barbara Saylor. (1994). *In Praise of Later Roman Emperors: The Panegyrici Latini.* Berkeley: University of California Press.

Nodes, Daniel J. (1993). *Doctrine and Exegesis in Biblical Latin Poetry.* ARCA Classical and Medieval Texts, Papers and Monographs, vol. 31. Leeds: Francis Cairns.

Reimitz, Helmut. (2015). *History, Frankish Identity and the Framing of Western Ethnicity, 550-850.* Cambridge: Cambridge University Press.

Riché, Pierre. (1976). *Education and Culture in the Barbarian West, Sixth through Eighth Centuries* (trans. John J. Contreni). Columbia, SC: University of South Carolina Press.

Roberts, Michael. (1989). *The Jeweled Style: Poetry and Poetics in Late Antiquity.* Ithaca, NY: Cornell University Press.

Roberts, Michael. (1993). *Poetry and the Cult of the Martyrs: The Liber Peristephanon of Prudentius.* Ann Arbor, MI: University of Michigan Press.

Roberts, Michael. (2002). Venantius Fortunatus's Life of Saint Martin. *Traditio* 57: 129–187.

Roberts, Michael. (2009). *The Humblest Sparrow: The Poetry of Venantius Fortunatus.* Ann Arbor, MI: University of Michigan Press.

Rohr, Christian. ed. and trans. (1995). *Der Theoderich-Panegyricus des Ennodius.* MGH Studien und Texte 12. Hannover: Hahnische Buchhandlung.

Salzman, Michele Renee. (1991). *On Roman Time: The Codex Calendar of 354 and the Rhythms of Urban Life in Late Antiquity.* Berkeley: University of California Press.

Scaffai, Marco. ed. (1982). *Baebii Italici Ilias Latina.* Bologna: Pàtron.

Schindler, Claudia. (2009). *Per carmina laudes: Untersuchungen zur spätantike Verspanegyrik von Claudian bis Coripp.* Beiträge zur Altertumskunde 253. Berlin: De Gruyter.

Shanzer, Danuta. (1986). *A Philosophical and Literary Commentary on Martianus Capella's De nuptiis Philologiae et Mercurii Book 1*. Berkeley: University of California Press.

Shanzer, Danuta. (2010). The tale of Frodebert's tail. In: *Colloquial and Literary Latin* (ed. Eleanor Dickey and Anna Chahoud), 376–405. Cambridge: Cambridge University Press.

Shanzer, Danuta and Wood, Ian. (2002). *Avitus of Vienne: Letters and Selected Prose*. Translated Texts for Historians 38. Liverpool: Liverpool University Press.

Sivan, Hagith. (1993). *Ausonius of Bordeaux: Genesis of a Gallic Aristocracy*. London: Routledge.

Sogno, Cristiana, Storin, Bradley K., and Watts, Edward J. ed. (2017). *Late Antique Letter Collections: A Critical Introduction and Reference Guide*. Berkeley: University of California Press.

Springer, C.P.E. (1988). *The Gospel as Epic in Late Antiquity: The Paschale carmen of Sedulius*. Leiden: Brill.

Springer, C.P.E. (2013). *Sedulius: The Paschal Song and Hymns*. Atlanta, GA: Society of Biblical Literature.

Stancliffe, Clare. (1983). *Saint Martin and His Hagiographer: History and Miracle in Sulpicius Severus*. Oxford: Clarendon.

Stewart, Columba. (1998). *Cassian the Monk*. New York: Oxford University Press.

Thompson, E.A. (1984). *Saint Germanus of Auxerre and the End of Roman Britain*. Woodbridge: Boydell.

Tizzoni, Mark. (2012). *The Poems of Dracontius in Their Vandalic and Visigothic Contexts*. PhD diss., University of Leeds.

Thomson, Mark. (2012). *Studies in the Historia Augusta*. Collection Latomus 337. Brussels: Latomus.

Tränkle, Hermann. (2008). *Prudentius: Contra Symmachum, Übersetzt und eingeleitet*. Turnhout: Brepols.

Viezure, Dana Iuliana. (2015). *Collectio Avellana* and the Unspoken Ostrogoths: Historical reconstruction in the sixth century. In: *Shifting Genres in Late Antiquity* (ed. Hugh Elton and Geoffrey Greatrex), 93–103. Farnham: Ashgate.

Walstra, Gerardus Joannes Josephus. (1962). *Les cinq épitres rimées dans l'appendice des formules de Sens*. Leiden: Brill.

Watson, Lynette. (1998). Representing the past, redefining the future: Sidonius Apollinaris' panegyrics of Avitus and Anthemius. In: *The Propaganda of Power: The Role of Panegyric in Late Antiquity* (ed. Mary Whitby), 177–198. Leiden: Brill.

Whitby, Mary. ed. (1998). *The Propaganda of Power: The Role of Panegyric in Late Antiquity*. Leiden: Brill.

Wilkinson, John. (2002). *Jerusalem Pilgrims before the Crusades*. Warminster: Aris & Phillips.

Williard, Hope D. (2014). Letter-writing and literary culture in Merovingian Gaul. *European Review of History* 21: 691–710.

Wolff, Étienne ed. (2007). *Rutilius Namatianus: Sur son retour*. Paris: Belles Lettres.

Wood, Ian. (1986). The audience of architecture in post-Roman Gaul. In: *The Anglo-Saxon Church* (ed. L.A.S. Butler and R.K. Morris), 74–79. London: Council for British Archaeology.

Wood, Ian. (1993). Letters and letter-collections from antiquity to the early Middle Ages: The prose works of Avitus of Vienne. In: *The Culture of Christendom: Essays in Medieval History in Commemoration of Denis L. T. Bethell* (ed. Marc Meyer), 29–43. London: Hambledon.

Wood, Ian. (2001). Avitus of Vienne, the Augustinian Poet. In: *Society and Culture in Late Antique Gaul: Revisiting the Sources* (ed. Ralph W. Mathisen and Danuta Shanzer), 263–277. Aldershot: Ashgate.

Wood, Ian. (2010). Chains of chronicles: The example of London, British Library ms. Add. 16974. In: *Zwischen Niederschrift und Wiederschrift. Frühmittelalterliche Hagiographie und Historiographie im Spannungsfeld von Kompendienüberlieferung und Editionstechnik* (ed. Richard Corradini, Max Diesenberger, and Meta Niederkorn-Bruck), 67–77. Forschungen zur Geschichte des Mittelalters 18. Vienna: ÖAW.

Wood, Ian. (2014). The homilies of Avitus. In: *Sermo doctorum: Compilers, Preachers and Their Audiences in the Early Medieval West* (ed. M. Diesenberger, Y. Hen, and M. Pollheimer), 81–97. Turnhout: Brepols.

Wood, Ian. (2015). Universal chronicles in the early Medieval West. *Approaches to Comparison in Medieval Studies* 1: 47–60.

Wood, Ian. (Forthcoming). Why collect letters? In: *Zwischen Alltagskommunikation und literarischer Identitätsbildung: Kulturgeschichtliche Aspekte lateinischer Epistolographie in Spätantike und Frühmittelalter* (ed. Gernot H., Müller). Stuttgart, Steiner.

Wright, Roger. (1982). *Late Latin and Early Romance in Spain and Carolingian France*. Liverpool: Francis Cairns.

Yavuz, Nurgül Kivilcim. (2015). *Transmission and Adaptation of the Trojan Narrative in Frankish History between the Sixth and Tenth Centuries*. PhD diss., University of Leeds.

CHAPTER THREE

Syriac

John W. Watt

Syriac literature flourished throughout late antiquity, especially in its homelands east of the Euphrates. The extant literature is almost entirely Christian, and the adoption of Syriac as the preferred literary medium by Christians in that region no doubt contributed to its widespread use, although it is likely that it, or one or more closely related Aramaic dialects, was also employed by other religious groups. It is only in the fourth century, particularly in the writings of Ephrem Syrus, that we can see a form of Christianity clearly differentiated from movements such as Marcionism and Manichaeism, and even in the early fifth century, in the text known as the *Doctrine of Addai*, a "proto-orthodox" group still appears to be battling for supremacy against competing movements and claiming apostolic foundation for itself in Edessa. Whether or not some Syriac texts prior to the fourth century should be categorized as Christian often depends, therefore, on how tightly one draws the boundary in relation to these groups that were later rejected, as well as on difficulties of interpretation inherent in the texts themselves. In the subsequent period, the rejection of the Council of Chalcedon in favor of a miaphysite Christology by the majority of Roman Syrians, and the independent development in the Persian Empire of a dyophysite Christology that did not recognize Chalcedon, led to a theological, in addition to an institutional, division between the West Syriac and East Syriac Churches (and the Greek Orthodox) and their writers. Although in Christology the thought of the two Syriac churches clearly diverged, admiration not only of Ephrem but also of some major Greek theologians, particularly Gregory of Nazianzus, was nevertheless common to both.

A Companion to Late Antique Literature, First Edition.
Edited by Scott McGill and Edward J. Watts.
© 2018 John Wiley & Sons, Inc. Published 2018 by John Wiley & Sons, Inc.

3.1 Biblical Commentary

Biblical interpretation was an important part of Syriac literature throughout late antiquity. While not exactly a commentary, the *Diatessaron* of Tatian, the harmonized narrative created from the four Gospels, is nevertheless a striking literary creation derived from the Bible. Whether it was first created in Greek or Syriac, and whether in Rome or the East, is still open to dispute, but its influence in the Syriac-speaking area is unquestioned, even though the complete Syriac text is not extant (Petersen 1994). The earliest Syriac version of the individual Gospels is that known as the Old Syriac, extant in two fifth-century manuscripts. While translated from a Greek text, the version also made use of the *Diatessaron*. The Old Syriac Gospel text probably originated in the third or early fourth century, and the translators knew (at least parts of) the Syriac version of the Old Testament later known as the Peshitta (the "Simple" version), which may be as early as the second century. It was translated from the Hebrew by many translators, among whom were probably both Jews and Jewish converts to Christianity.

Biblical commentary in the stricter sense begins with the exegetical writings of Ephrem (d. 373). His fame rests primarily on his poetic works, but he also wrote extensively in prose. Commentaries are attributed to him on Genesis, Exodus, the Diatessaron, Acts, and the Pauline epistles, but the latter two are extant only in Armenian. The contents and literary character of the three extant Syriac works are varied, but in the main they may be said to offer notes on the text or to offer explanations of a fairly simple theological nature of the passages which most interested him. For example, in Genesis he is particularly interested in the primal history. In the story of Adam and Eve, he explains at some length the command not to eat of the tree of the knowledge of good and evil as a test of the use of their free will, but much of the later narrative of the book he passes over with little or no comment. Many comments in the two Old Testament commentaries appear to be taken, probably indirectly and orally, from Jewish sources. In the commentary on the *Diatessaron*, however, there are some longer lyrical passages in which his more sophisticated symbolical theology, well known from his hymns (considered below), is given full rein (Griffith 2003).

After Ephrem, extended biblical commentary in Syriac is known in two works of Philoxenus of Mabbug: one on Matthew and Luke, the other on the prologue to John. Since neither of the two is preserved intact, some caution is advisable in their overall characterization, but the contrast with Ephrem is nevertheless quite striking. They are sophisticated theological treatises expounding a miaphysite Christology, intended to win readers to the miaphysite cause and to counteract the exegetical writings of the dyophysites Diodore and Theodore. While that on Matthew and Luke, preserved only in fragments, appears to oscillate between extended theological expositions of the author's key Christological passages (e.g. Luke 2:52) and only brief comments on the others, the enormous commentary on the prologue of John is devoted exclusively to that alone. Philoxenus considered Ephrem's Christological terminology too inexact, and also found fault with the existing translations of the New Testament and the Creed, as a result of which he commissioned fresh ones. The expression "put on a body," for example, found in the current Syriac version (the Peshitta) of Hebrews 5:7 and 10:5 and of the Creed, and used frequently by Ephrem, was considered by Philoxenus to open the door to "Nestorianism" and replaced in later versions by more exact terms ("embodied," "enfleshed") (de Halleux 1963). Ephrem and Philoxenus are the two most notable Syriac biblical commentators of late antiquity, but from the fifth century we also have a commentary on Ecclesiastes by John of Apamea and an elaboration on the Joseph story in the form of an epic poem by Balai. Biblical interpretation, if not commentary as understood in the schools, is found in much Syriac poetry, not only in Balai and anonymous works, but most notably in the works of Ephrem and Jacob of Serugh.

3.2 Poetry

Unlike Philoxenus's concern with exact Syriac terminology and its correspondence with that of the Greek, Ephrem's linguistic usage is allusive, his thinking metaphorical and symbolic, and his most favored literary form the poetic. Theology expressed and advocated through poetry is the most striking aspect of Syriac within late antique literature, and its two greatest poets, Ephrem and Jacob of Serugh, are generally thought to have been only lightly if at all affected by Greek philosophy or rhetoric, though recently some studies have argued for a stronger Greek influence on the former than has generally been supposed (Possekel 1999). Although the corpus of Ephrem's poetry is the most impressive known in Syriac, it was not the earliest. The *Odes of Solomon*, a group of 42 short poems preserved virtually complete in Syriac, have been variously ascribed to the first, second, or third century, and their original language is thought to be either Syriac or Greek. While some passages are suggestive of a Christian origin, much of their material remains difficult to interpret (Lattke 1999–2005). Bardaisan of Edessa (154–222) is known to have written poetry in Syriac, though he also understood Greek, but none of his poetry has survived. Some of Ephrem's theological poems were composed for the express purpose of combating Bardaisan's teaching, so it is possible that Ephrem was to some extent inspired to write theological poetry by the example of Bardaisan.

Syriac poetry from Ephrem onwards (but not the Syriac form of the *Odes of Solomon*) is distinguished by a regulated syllable count. Ephrem employed two forms: the *madrasha* (*hymnus*), composed of stanzas in which the lines may or may not have the same syllable count, but in which the pattern remains constant throughout the entire piece; and the *memra* (*sermo*), not structured in stanzas but composed of couplets with the same syllable count throughout, which in Ephrem's case is always 7 + 7. Ephrem spent most of his life in Nisibis, but when it was ceded to the Persians, he moved to Edessa. He was a vigorous advocate of Nicene Christianity and opponent of those who adhered to the doctrines of Bardaisan, Marcion, or Mani. His poetry was very influential in later Syriac Christianity and even inspired imitations in Greek. Today he is admired principally for the richness of his poetic imagery and the imaginative use he made of it in his theological and spiritual teaching (Brock 1992; Murray 2006). A good example of his method is his *madrasha De fide* 82, where contemporary ideas about the pearl are presented as a symbol of the nativity and life of Christ (Brock 2013).

Two smaller poetic corpora are attributed to writers from the early fifth century, Cyrillona and Balai, although it is not certain that all the individual pieces stem from them. Their content and their form are quite varied. The six in the former group are mostly theological or biblical, but one concerns an incursion of the Huns (ca. 396). The latter comprises a number of short poems on ecclesiastical or liturgical matters and also an epic poem, in 12 *memre*, on the biblical Joseph. Their true author is disputed; Ephrem has been proposed, which is consistent with their 7 + 7 meter, but the attribution to Balai has also been defended. They present a striking meditation on the Joseph story, not without some similarities with Jewish interpretations and elaborations of the biblical narrative, and have also been thought to exhibit acquaintance with Greek rhetorical practice (Phenix 2008). A larger body of material is attributed to Narsai (d. ca. 502), consisting of several *memre* each on the Creation, Old Testament topics, Gospel parables, church sacraments, and feasts, and the three principal theologians particular to the East Syriac Church, namely, Diodore, Theodore, and Nestorius (Brock 2009). Narsai also has been thought to be familiar with some Greek rhetorical practice (McVey 1983). A considerable amount of anonymous poetry (*memre*) on biblical themes also probably belongs to the fifth or sixth century.

The outstanding Syriac poet after Ephrem is Jacob of Serugh (d. 521). He produced a vast number of *memre*, in the 12-syllable meter, as well as a small number of *madrashe*. Unlike Ephrem, he was little concerned with combating "heresy" or establishing a particular "orthodoxy." While opposed to the

Chalcedonian Christological formula, he did not make his opposition a theme of his poems, and in some of them he even appears to have been influenced by the works of Theodore, which will probably have been a result of his education at the strongly dyophysite School of the Persians in Edessa. His poems are mostly on biblical and ecclesiastical themes, including liturgical feasts and portraits of various saints (Kiraz 2010).

3.3 Theology

From the foregoing it will be evident that much theological, spiritual, and paraenetic literature in Syriac exists in poetic forms. Even the great poets, however, also composed such literature in prose. Six prose homilies survive from Jacob's hand, and theology in prose comes, too, from that of Ephrem. From him two discourses (*memre*) and a letter are extant in artistic prose, while in normal prose we have, in addition to his biblical commentaries (above), works against Bardaisan, Marcion, and Mani. Two other significant series of such works come from the fourth century. One is a set of 23 *Demonstrations* attributed to Aphrahat (or in some manuscripts to a Jacob), whose identity is unknown but who must have been a significant figure in the church in the Persian Empire. The *Demonstrations* fall broadly into two groups. The first deals with various aspects of Christian life (e.g. "Faith," "Love," "Prayer," "Humility"), and one, on "The Children of the Covenant," has received particular attention on account of its significance for the study of early Syriac asceticism. The second appears to be directed to Christians who were attracted by Judaism or by some Jewish practices and is devoted to subjects such as "Circumcision," "The Sabbath," "The Distinction between Foods," and "The Peoples Who Have Replaced the People." This second group may have arisen at a time of persecution (the subject of *Demonstration* 21) of Christians in the Persian Empire, and it has been thought to reflect the differing positions of Christians (pro-Roman) and Jews during Persian–Roman hostilities. An interesting feature of the collection is that the first 22 *Demonstrations* form an alphabetic acrostic of the letters of the Syriac alphabet. Roughly contemporary with Aphrahat, and also from an unidentified author within the Persian Empire, is another paraenetic work entitled (by its modern editor) *Liber graduum* (Book of Steps). The "steps" refer to the ascetical ascent to the heavenly city, marked by two broad stages. The "Upright" observe the "lesser commandments" marked by charity; the "Mature" or "Perfect" the "greater commandments" characterized by the imitation of Christ (Juhl 1996; Heal and Kitchen 2014).

The outstanding theologian of the following century was Philoxenus of Mabbug (d. 523). His miaphysite Christology found expression in his biblical commentaries, in numerous letters, in a number of short discourses, and in two substantial works: Ten *memre* "On one of the Holy Trinity was embodied and suffered," and Three *memre* "On the Trinity and the Incarnation." His concern for precise Syriac terminology modeled on the Greek has already been noted, together with his belief that disdain or indifference to this in Syriac opened the door to false doctrine. An extensive set of discourses on the ascetic life picks up the binary division known from the *Liber graduum* and was widely read in monastic circles. Like Jacob of Serugh, Philoxenus had been educated at the School of the Persians in Edessa, and although (like Jacob, but more forcefully) he rebelled against the Christological doctrine advanced there, it may be that it was there that he came across the writings of Evagrius of Pontus and perhaps also learned something of the rudiments of Greek (Aristotelian) philosophy. His works display knowledge not only of Evagrius's ascetical teaching but also of his cosmological system in the form of the common Syriac version of the *Kephalaia gnostica* (de Halleux 1963, Michelson 2014). He was, however, opposed to the more radical form of Evagrianism expounded by Stephen bar Sudhaili, against which he warned in a letter to two priests, Abraham and Orestes, who had been in contact with Stephen. Stephen was the author of *The Book of the Hierotheos*, or at least of what has been considered by some scholars to be its first layer, clearly indebted to Evagrius's writings. The attribution to Hierotheos, the alleged teacher of "Dionysius the Areopagite," connects it with the Pseudo-Dionysian corpus and may be part of a second layer, perhaps stemming from Stephen's disciples. The doctrine concerns the ascent of the mind to the divinity and the eschatological unification of all (Pinggéra 2002).

3.4 Biography and Hagiography

Our information about the lives of significant authors is limited by a lack of genuine biographies, but some of them are the subjects of hagiographical accounts. As is well known, hagiography is not the same as critical biography but is nevertheless related to it and also to panegyric. It does not necessarily provide reliable historical information about a figure but may illuminate instead the cultural and ideological concerns of the hagiographer who praises his subject's saintliness. In the case of Ephrem, there is a biographical tradition stemming probably from the sixth century, which is now extant in late manuscripts exhibiting three recensions. It is not a reliable source for his life, but it seemingly reflects the ideal picture of a monk held by later Greek Orthodox tradition. While, for example, the *memra* on Ephrem by Jacob of Serugh (correctly) connects him with the Syriac ascetic tradition of the "Children of the Covenant" (cf. above), the Syriac *vita* (biography) associates him with Basil and Egyptian monasticism (Amar 2011). *Vitae* of Philoxenus and Jacob of Serugh are known only from a much later date.

There is a substantial amount of Syriac hagiography from the fifth or sixth century, though dating is sometimes problematic. Many of the works can be classified as *vitae* in the restricted sense described above, such as the *Life of Simeon Stylites*. Others are martyr acts, such as those dealing with martyrdoms under various Persian shahs (Shapur II, Yezdgerd I, Bahram V, Yezdgerd II). Some are collections of short pieces or anecdotes on holy men and women known to the author, notably the *Lives of the Eastern Saints* by John of Ephesus (Harvey 1990). Some *vitae* merge into panegyric, such as the *Life of Rabbula* and the *Life of John bar Aphthonia*.

The *Acts of Thomas*, extant in both Syriac and Greek versions, were probably written in the third century and present a legendary account of the apostle Thomas's mission to India, culminating in his martyrdom under king Mazdai. Embedded in this romance is material of diverse origin, including two notable poems: the "Hymn of the Bride," and the "Hymn of the Pearl" (Klijn 2003). Another legendary account of supposedly apostolic times is the *Doctrine of Addai*, containing the famous alleged correspondence between Jesus and King Abgar of Edessa, and the apostle Addai's mission to the city and its conversion (Desreumaux 1993). The origin of this Syriac text (as distinct from the shorter version, claimed by Eusebius to have existed in the archives of Edessa, which he presented in his *Ecclesiastical History*) is probably to be located in fifth-century Edessa, from which also came a group of Edessene martyr *Acts*, including the *Acts of Sharbel* and the *Acts of Barsamya*. They purport to tell of their heroes' martyrdom under Trajan and have features in common with the *Doctrine of Addai*. These fifth-century Edessene texts aim to exalt the Christian status of the city. Probably also of Edessene origin is the *Julian Romance*, though the date and unitary origin of the work are disputed. It is a polemical work against the emperor Julian, with legendary accounts of his accession and death but with praise for his successor Jovian.

3.5 Rhetoric and Epistolography

In Greek, similarities have been observed between some hagiographic *vitae* and the prescriptions for an encomiastic speech presented in rhetoric handbooks, such as the *progymnasmata* and the treatises of Menander Rhetor.

No treatise on rhetoric of a similar age is known in Syriac, but some, at least, of the prescriptions could have been known to Syriac writers, either because they themselves knew Greek, or because they had learned of them through others who did. Furthermore, there is a lengthy treatise on rhetoric from a Syriac author probably of the ninth century, Anton of Tagrit, which, although differing in several ways from known Greek treatises, nevertheless shows knowledge of many of the prescriptions. It is hard to see why such knowledge would have come into Syriac at that late date, and it is most natural to suppose that the treatise embodies a tradition of rhetoric instruction in Syriac which goes back to an earlier time (Watt 2010).

Arguments have, therefore, been advanced that in a number of the works mentioned above the influence of classical rhetorical teaching can be detected. Deliberative rhetoric has been seen in the *Liber graduum*, with its exhortations to a life of perfection, and in forensic rhetoric in the *memra* of Narsai in defense of the three doctors of the East Syriac Church, Diodore, Theodore, and Nestorius. In Balai's poem on Joseph, an influence from classical rhetoric has been suggested in the arrangement of the speeches and the author's use of rhetorical figures and techniques of persuasion (Phenix 2008).

What appear to be the clearest examples of such influence, however, fall within the sphere of epideictic: the oration (*memra*) on John bar Aphthonia by an anonymous monk of the monastery of Qenneshre, and that on Severus of Antioch by George, bishop of the Arab tribes (d. 724). The monastery of Qenneshre was originally located near Antioch and migrated to Qenneshre on the banks of the Euphrates around 530, under the leadership of John, who himself, as far as we know, wrote exclusively in Greek. In subsequent years the monastery was celebrated as a center for the study of Greek, and its alumni included most of the notable Syriac Aristotelian scholars of the seventh century, including George. It is reasonable, therefore, to assume that classical rhetorical theory was taught there both before and after the migration from the Orontes to the Euphrates (Watt 2010, chapter 5). Syriac writers who studied Greek philosophy may be assumed, like their Greek counterparts, to have previously studied rhetoric. Thus it is not surprising to find evidence of rhetorical knowledge in the prologue to Sergius of Reshaina's *Commentary on Aristotle's Categories* (Hugonnard-Roche 2004, chapter 8). About the same time, the early sixth century, a highly rhetorical prologue was prefaced by Joshua the Stylite to his historical work (on both these writers, see below).

The oldest example of Syriac epistolography is the *Letter of Mara bar Serapion to His Son Serapion*, which has been variously dated from the first to the fourth century. The letter is in the style of advice from a pagan philosopher to his son and may be one of the few remaining pieces of pagan Syriac literature. However, its allusions to Jesus as a "wise king" and its references to his death at the hands of the Jews and the fall of Jerusalem make a Christian origin perhaps more likely (Merz and Tieleman 2012). Indubitably from the fourth century, we have a *Letter of Ephrem to Publius* in artistic prose on eschatological matters, and from the fifth, the legendary correspondence between Jesus and Abgar of Edessa already noted above in the *Doctrine of Addai*. Among numerous letters from writers of the fifth and sixth centuries, particularly worthy of note are a considerable number by Philoxenus, frequently comprising lengthy theological arguments, and two historically important letters of (the miaphysite) Simeon of Beth Ashram (possibly revised in transmission), dealing respectively with the martyrs of Najran and the influence of Barsauma of Nisibis on the spread of dyophysite Christology.

3.6 Historiography

Most Syriac historiography is in the form of chronicles (Debié 2009; Witakowski 1987). The earliest local chronicle is the sixth-century *Chronicle of Edessa*, which covers events in Edessa from 133 BCE to 540 CE, although the first and longest entry is an account of a flood in 201 CE that mentions damage done to "the sanctuary of the church of the Christians." It knows nothing of the story of the beginning of Christianity in Edessa told by Eusebius and the *Doctrine of Addai*. The *Chronicle of Arbela* has an account of the beginning of Christianity there, but it is uncertain whether it is a sixth-century work, as claimed by its editor, or a forgery. An important work of a later date, the *Khuzistan Chronicle* from the seventh century, is a valuable source for the period of Heraclius, the end of the Sasanian Empire and the Arab conquests. Other local chronicles from the late antique period have not survived as independent works but have sometimes been incorporated, in whole or in fragments, in chronicles assembled in a later period. The genre of the world chronicle became known in Syriac through Syriac versions of those of Hippolytus and Eusebius, but original Syriac examples of the genre, or chronicles utilizing either of these sources, are known only from the seventh century and later.

Earlier than the sixth century translation of Eusebius's *Chronicle* was the fifth-century version of his *Ecclesiastical History*, which, unlike the *Chronicle*, has mostly survived. It served as the model for this genre in Syriac, for which there are two important works from the sixth century. From John of Ephesus's three-volume work, only the third is complete, ending in 588 CE, but book 2, covering the period 449–571, was used and adapted in the late eighth-century *Chronicle of Zuqnin* (Harvey 1990; van Ginkel 1995). The

Ecclesiastical History of Pseudo-Zacharias is a complex work. Books 1–2 consist of diverse historical or legendary pieces, while books 3–6 are an adapted translation of part of the *Ecclesiastical History* of Zacharias Rhetor. Later books, some of them preserved only fragmentarily or in some cases completely lost, cover the reigns of the emperors Anastasius, Justin I, Justinian, and Justin II (Greatrex 2011). Slightly later, on the East Syrian side there is an *Ecclesiastical History* by Barhadbeshabba Arbaya, and by Barhadbeshabba of Halwan (possibly, but probably not, the same person) a history entitled *Cause of the Foundation of Schools*, going back to biblical and classical times but with a focus upon the Persian School of Edessa and the School of Nisibis.

Even earlier than the *Chronicle of Edessa* is an anonymous work generally known as *The Chronicle of Joshua* [or Pseudo-Joshua] *the Stylite*, also preserved not independently, but incorporated in the *Chronicle of Zuqnin*. It is, however, in its form not purely a chronicle or in its content purely local. The first of the two main sections is, indeed, a local Edessene chronicle, providing an annalistic account of plague, famine, and epidemic in the city in 494–502. The second, however, is a continuous narrative of the Roman–Persian war of 502–506, in which Edessa is merely one of the locations. The work begins with a rhetorical prologue addressed to a (real or fictitious) abbot named Sergius, continues with an account of events in the Roman and Persian Empires leading up to the war, and ends, following the two main sections, with a rhetorical epilogue. While the Edessene section covering 494–502 can therefore be characterized as a chronicle, the work as a whole is more akin to the genre of a political history, albeit with some elements of Christian divine intervention (Luther 1997; Trombley and Watt 2000).

3.7 Philosophy and Translation

The earliest known Syriac writer on philosophy is Bardaisan, but nothing of his work has survived except for brief citations or allusions found in later writers mostly opposed to him, such as Ephrem. A philosophical dialogue, probably by his pupil Philip, has however survived, in which he appears as a speaker. Known as the *Book of the Laws of the Countries* from an ethnographic section, it is a treatise on fate and freewill and was much influenced by Alexander of Aphrodisias (Drijvers 1965; Dihle 1979; Teixidor 1992; Ramelli 2009). Nothing more of serious philosophical interest is known from the earlier part of the period, but the situation changes radically for the late fifth or early sixth century, when Syriac interest in Aristotelian philosophy, in its late antique Neoplatonic form, suddenly comes into view. Its beginnings are associated with Sergius of Reshaina (d. 536), who studied in

Alexandria, translated many works of Galen, and became an *archiatros* in Reshaina. Sergius may have been drawn to Alexandria to study medicine there, but it is clear that he also studied philosophy. As previously noted, he wrote a commentary on Aristotle's *Categories* and intended (as he made clear in it) to do the same for the entire Alexandrian Aristotelian curriculum, but for whatever reason we know only of that on the *Categories*. He did, however, also write a shorter introduction to philosophy addressed to a Philotheos (Aydin 2016), and he translated two philosophical treatises supposedly by Aristotle but outside the Alexandrian school corpus: *De mundo* and *On the Causes of the Universe* (the latter known from an Arabic version to be by Alexander of Aphrodisias). In addition to Alexander, Sergius may have been sympathetic to some aspects of the thought of Bardaisan, and later Bardesanites may in turn have been appreciative of the cosmological writings of Sergius (King 2011).

In the prologue to the *Commentary on the Categories*, Sergius credits Aristotle with being the principal source and beginning of knowledge not only for Galen and physicians like him but also for all subsequent philosophers. Unlike his Alexandrian teachers, he gives no indication that the study of Aristotle should be followed by that of Plato. Sergius was a Christian (who perhaps knew Philoponus in Alexandria) and presumably, on this account, did not follow Proclus's reading of Plato, which he could have heard in Alexandria from Ammonius, which in effect offered a philosophical rationale for pagan religion. However, a further translation made by him was that of the Pseudo-Dionysian corpus, and from his work known as *A Treatise on the Spiritual Life*, which he (subsequently) prefaced to this translation, it appears that he envisioned Pseudo-Dionysius's Neoplatonizing interpretation of the Bible, rather than Proclus's of Plato, as the culmination for Christians of the Aristotelian curriculum. He may well have recognized Pseudo-Dionysius's dependence on Proclus and might even have known the true identity of the "Areopagite." Later sixth-century Syriac writings on Aristotle are commentaries on the *Isagoge*, *De interpretatione*, and *Analytica priora* I.1–7 by Proba and two works by Paul the Persian: a *Treatise on Logic* and an *Elucidation of the De interpretatione* (Hugonnard-Roche 2004, chapters 5–12).

While Sergius wrote in Syriac, if he expected his readers to read Aristotle himself, he must have assumed they would do so in Greek. Nevertheless, anonymous translations of *Categories*, *De interpretatione*, and *Analytica priora* I. 1–7 did appear in the course of the sixth century (Hugonnard-Roche 2004, chapters 1–4; King 2010). Sergius certainly did not assume that his readers would or could access the first of these (which might be later than his lifetime); it is possible, but not at all certain, that Proba was responsible for the other two. With philosophy it is therefore particularly clear what is, however, also the case in many of the other literary areas and authors surveyed here, namely, that much late antique Syriac literature, while distinctive in several ways, has nevertheless to be seen in close association with the Greek. Greek influence came about in two ways: through the fact that many Syriac speakers (including of course the translators) were bilingual, or at any rate were proficient readers of Greek; and through the translations themselves. From the biblical translations of the second to third and subsequent centuries through the numerous translations of Christian theological works (among which the *Homilies* of Gregory of Nazianzus are worthy of particular mention both for their extent and their influence) to the secular philosophical and medical versions from the fifth and sixth centuries, translations from Greek form an important part of Syriac literature (Brock 1999; Schmidt and Gonnet 2007). This activity continued without interruption into the Islamic period, during the first few centuries of which Syrians and Syriac literature played an important part in the intellectual life of the new civilization and contributed to the impact of late antique culture on the Islamic world. Late antique Syriac literature is thus an important element both of pre-Islamic late antique culture and of the continuing vitality of that culture in the years following the Arab conquest of the region (Lössl and Watt 2011, pp. 165–257). Many texts extant in Syriac manuscripts have still to be published, and future research on this literature may be expected to add not only to our knowledge of individual authors within it but also to our appreciation both of its links with, and distinctiveness from, late antique Greek literature and of its importance to the intellectual and cultural history of the Middle East.

REFERENCES

Amar, Joseph. (2011). *The Syriac Vita Tradition of Ephrem the Syrian*. Louvain: Peeters.

Aydin, Sami. (2016). *Sergius of Reshaina: Introduction to Aristotle and his Categories. Syriac text, with introduction, translation, and commentary*. Leiden: Brill.

Brock, Sebastian. (1992). *The Luminous Eye: The Spiritual World Vision of St. Ephrem*. Kalamazoo, MI: Cistercian Publications.

Brock, Sebastian. (1999). *From Ephrem to Romanos: Interactions between Syriac and Greek in Late Antiquity*. Aldershot: Ashgate.

Brock, Sebastian. (2009). A guide to Narsai's homilies. *Hugoye* 12 (1): 21–40.

Brock, Sebastian. (2013). *The Harp of the Spirit: Poems of Saint Ephrem the Syrian*. Cambridge: Aquila Books.

Debié, Muriel. ed. (2009). *L'historiographie syriaque*. Paris: Geuthner.

de Halleux, André. (1963). *Philoxène de Mabbog: Sa vie, ses écrits, sa théologie*. Louvain: Université catholique de Louvain.

Desreumaux, Alain. (1993). *Histoire du roi Abgar et de Jésus.* Turnhout: Brepols.
Dihle, Albrecht. (1979). Zur Schicksalslehre des Bardesanes. In: *Kerygma und Logos: Beiträge zu den geistesgeschichtlichen Beziehungen zwischen Antike und Christentum. Festschrift für Carl Andresen zum 70. Geburtstag* (ed. Adolf Martin Ritter), 123–135. Göttingen: Vandenhoek & Ruprecht.
Drijvers, Han. (1965). *Bardaisan of Edessa.* Assen: Van Gorcum.
Greatrex, Geoffrey. ed. (2011). *The Chronicle of Pseudo-Zachariah Rhetor: Church and War in Late Antiquity.* Liverpool: Liverpool University Press.
Griffith, Sidney. (2003). Ephrem the Exegete. In: *Handbook of Patristic Exegesis: The Bible in Ancient Christianity* (ed. Charles Kannengiesser), 2: 1395–1448. Leiden: Brill.
Harvey, Susan. (1990). *Asceticism and Society in Crisis: John of Ephesus and the Lives of the Eastern Saints.* Berkeley: University of California Press.
Heal, Kristian and Kitchen, Robert. ed. (2014). *Breaking the Mind: New Studies in the Syriac "Book of Steps".* Washington DC: Catholic University of America Press.
Hugonnard-Roche, Henri. (2004). *La logique d'Aristote du grec au syriaque: Études sur la transmission des textes de l'Organon et leur interprétation philosophique.* Paris: Vrin.
Juhl, Diana. (1996). *Die Askese im Liber graduum und bei Afrahat: Eine vergleichende Studie zur frühsyrischen Frömmigkeit.* Wiesbaden: Harrassowitz.
King, Daniel. (2010). *The Earliest Syriac Translation of Aristotle's Categories: Text, Translation and Commentary.* Leiden: Brill.
King, Daniel. (2011). Origenism in sixth century Syria: The case of a Syriac manuscript of pagan philosophy. In: *Origenes und sein Erbe in Orient und Okzident* (ed. Alfons Fürst), 179–212. Münster: Aschendorff.
Kiraz, George. ed. (2010). *Jacob of Serugh and His Times: Studies in Sixth-Century Syriac Christianity.* Piscataway, NJ: Gorgias Press.
Klijn, Albertus. (2003). *The Acts of Thomas: Introduction, Text, and Commentary.* Leiden: Brill.
Lattke, Michael. (1999–2005). *Oden Salomos: Text, Übersetzung, Kommentar.* Freiburg: Universitätsverlag Freiburg Schweiz.
Lössl, Josef and Watt, John. ed. (2011). *Interpreting the Bible and Aristotle in Late Antiquity: The Alexandrian Commentary Tradition between Rome and Baghdad.* Farnham: Ashgate.
Luther, Andreas. (1997). *Die syrische Chronik des Josua Stylites.* Berlin: de Gruyter.
McVey, Kathleen. (1983). The memra of Narsai on the three Nestorian doctors as an example of forensic rhetoric. In: *III Symposium Syriacum* (ed. René Lavenant), 87–96. Rome: Pontificio Istituto Orientale.
Merz, Annette and Tieleman, Teun. eds. (2012). *The Letter of Mara bar Sarapion in Context: Proceedings of the Symposium Held at Utrecht University, 10–12 December 2009.* Leiden: Brill.
Michelson, David. (2014). *The Practical Christology of Philoxenos of Mabbug.* Oxford: Oxford University Press.
Murray, Robert. (2006). *Symbols of Church and Kingdom: A Study in Early Syriac Tradition.* London: T & T Clark.

Petersen, William. (1994). *Tatian's Diatessaron: Its Creation, Dissemination, Significance, and History in Scholarship*. Leiden: Brill.

Phenix, Robert. (2008). *The Sermons on Joseph of Balai of Qenneshrin*. Tübingen: Mohr Siebeck.

Pinggéra, Karl. (2002). *All-Erlösung und All-Einheit: Studien zum "Buch des heiligen Hierotheos" und seiner Rezeption in der syrisch-orthodoxen Theologie*. Wiesbaden: Reichert.

Possekel, Ute. (1999). *Evidence of Greek Philosophical Concepts in the Writings of Ephrem the Syrian*. Louvain: Peeters.

Ramelli, Ilaria. (2009). *Bardaisan of Edessa: A reassessment of the evidence and a new interpretation*. Piscataway: Gorgias.

Schmidt, Andrea and Gonnet, Dominique. eds. (2007). *Les pères grecs dans la tradition syriaque*. Paris: Geuthner.

Teixidor, Javier. (1992). *Bardésane d'Edesse: La première philosophie syriaque*. Paris: Éditions du Cerf.

Trombley, Frank and Watt, John. (2000). *The Chronicle of Pseudo-Joshua the Stylite: Translated with Notes and Introduction*. Liverpool: Liverpool University Press.

van Ginkel, Joop. (1995). *John of Ephesus: A Monophysite Historian in Sixth-Century Byzantium*. Groningen: Rijksuniversiteit Groningen.

Watt, John. (2010). *Rhetoric and Philosophy from Greek into Syriac*. Farnham: Ashgate.

Witakowski, Witold. (1987). *The Syriac Chronicle of Pseudo-Dionysius of Tel-Maḥrē: A Study in the History of Historiography*. Uppsala: Uppsala University.

CHAPTER FOUR

Coptic

David Brakke

Coptic literature originated and reached its highest level of achievement in late antiquity, and its study engages some of the central themes of late ancient history, among them the relationships between a wider Mediterranean tradition ("Greece" or "Rome") and a regional/national tradition ("Egypt") and between religious life and literary culture. The question of bilingualism and thus of biculturalism is apparent in the Coptic language itself, for it is the last stage of the Egyptian language written in the Greek alphabet (plus between six and eight Egyptian characters), and even works that native Coptic speakers composed feature numerous Greek loan words (Greco-Coptic). Nearly all works of Coptic literature are religious in nature, and its only truly great author, Shenoute (347–465), was a monastic author who addressed issues of Christian theology, ethics, and ascetic practice with a rhetorical brilliance that would have dazzled any ancient orator. The struggle over imperial attempts to impose the Council of Chalcedon colored and inspired much of what Copts wrote after 451. Translation, Christianization, and empire gave birth to Coptic literature, determined its forms and genres, and motivated its most outstanding works.

4.1 The Problems of "Coptic Literature" and its History

Although scholars have written several excellent overviews (in English Orlandi 1986, 2006; Wilfong 2001; Emmel 2007), a full history of Coptic literature lies in the future, thanks primarily to the fragmentary state of its preservation (Emmel 2006). Literary historians have as their top priority the publication and identification of the countless fragments of frequently dismembered Coptic manuscripts that libraries and museums in Egypt, Europe, and North America possess. Especially after the Arab conquest, the production and reproduction of literary manuscripts in Egypt became concentrated in a few large monastic communities, especially the White Monastery near Panopolis (Orlandi 2002) and the Monastery of the Archangel Michael in the Fayum (Depuydt 1993; Emmel 2005). Copying may have reached a peak in the ninth and tenth centuries, but the gradual replacement of Coptic with Arabic as the living language of Coptic Christians caused manuscript production to decline and eventually to cease, except for liturgical aids. Existing Coptic manuscripts fell into neglect and suffered damage. Finally, when European collectors began to acquire the manuscripts, they seldom did so in large complete groups. Instead, codices from the same Egyptian hoard usually ended up in different locations, with portions of already dismembered individual codices dispersed (Louis 2008). Reconstructing the manuscript tradition of Coptic literature remains the field's most urgent task.

Even if and when scholars complete that task, writing a history of Coptic literature will still face the difficulty of contextualizing numerous works that are pseudonymous and even whose original language is uncertain (Orlandi 1986, pp. 70–73). Many martyrdoms, encomia, homilies, apocrypha, and other works that survive in Coptic are anonymous or bear authorial attributions that scholars doubt, usually to prominent church fathers who wrote in Greek, such as Athanasius of Alexandria, John Chrysostom, or Basil of Caesarea. Was, for example, a homily on Michael the Archangel attributed to Basil in a ninth-century manuscript originally composed in Greek or Coptic (Depuydt 1991, 1:10–16, 2:10–17)? When was it composed, and was the original context Egyptian? At what point did the attribution to Basil enter the history of transmission? Although many sermons can be assigned to "cycles" that date to the seventh or eighth centuries (Orlandi 1991), an individual sermon that shows affinities with traditions found in late ancient Greek and Coptic sources may in truth come from any number of settings in the late ancient and early

Byzantine East from the fourth through the ninth centuries. At some point it found a receptive audience in the monastically dominated environment of Coptic Christianity.

If pseudonymous homilies provide a challenge to contextualization, so too do some works that bear attribution to a known Coptic Christian. For example, four fragmentary White Monastery manuscripts from the ninth to eleventh centuries (now dispersed among eight different libraries) attribute two sets of homilies, one on Matthew and another on Luke, to Rufus, who is known to have been bishop of Shotep in the final decades of the sixth century. If the attribution is correct, then the homilies illustrate a literary revival among Coptic Christians during the patriarchate of Damian (578–607), when the anti-Chalcedonian church achieved a new level of unity and strength after a period of disarray. Moreover, the works are indebted to Alexandrian traditions of exegesis associated with Origen and Didymus the Blind and show knowledge of these authors and of others such as Irenaeus and Evagrius of Pontus, and so they would testify to the persistence of this theological current well into the post-Chalcedon era and to a lively intellectual culture in Upper Egypt (Sheridan 1998). On the other hand, some scholars have argued that these Alexandrian, even "Origenist," elements indicate that the homilies are Coptic translations of Greek works from the late fourth or early fifth century (Luisier 1998; Lucchesi 2000). In that case, as one scholar puts it, we would gain "some works of considerable interest for the history of the Origenist controversy" but "lose one of our native Coptic authors" (Emmel 2006, p. 180).

The controversy surrounding the homilies of Rufus raises the question of what we mean by "Coptic literature" in general. If we restrict the term only to literary works that were composed in Coptic, we could not be certain whether the homilies of Rufus and countless other works belong to that category at all. In fact, Lucchesi (2000, p. 87) has argued that we should assume the existence of a Greek original behind every Coptic text until we can prove the contrary. In that case Coptic literature dwindles to very little, and its contents become deeply uncertain. For these reasons, most scholars maintain a capacious sense of Coptic literature as embracing nearly all the literary works that survive in the language. The bilingualism that appears on every page in the form of Greco-Coptic words represents Coptic literature's distinctive character as a literature on the border between Greek and Egyptian, between traditional Egyptian religion and Christianity, and between absolute literary authorities (like the Bible) and creative innovation.

4.2 Translation and the Origins of Coptic Literature

Christianity is a religion of translation: In late antiquity as today, Christians were eager to translate their scriptures, rituals, and practices from their original languages and idioms into those of the cultures they sought to missionize. The use of Greek characters to write vernacular Egyptian dates to the second and possibly even first century CE: The earliest examples are horoscopes, spells, and invocations that reflect traditional Egyptian religion (Old Coptic). Christians took up the practice to translate and teach the Bible and so "brought Coptic out of the cloistered environments in which it had been used by non-Christians," elevated its literary quality, and made it available to Egyptians to write personal documents and literary works (Choat 2012, p. 589). The earliest Coptic (as opposed to Old Coptic) manuscripts date to the third and early fourth centuries and contain glosses on Old Testament texts, select biblical works, and hymns. To represent a language that was primarily oral in the third century, Coptic uses the 24 letters of Greek, along with a small set of Egyptian characters drawn from the Demotic script to express sounds lacking in Greek. Dialectical variation characterized Egyptian as it was spoken up and down the Nile, and thus Coptic, too, features a variety of regional dialects (Funk 1991). Nonetheless, in late antiquity Sahidic emerged as the prestige dialect, probably thanks to its central location in Middle Egypt, to its relative similarity to the other dialects, and to Christianity's drive toward standardization (Layton 2011). After the Muslim conquest, Bohairic, based in northern Egypt, became dominant and remains (along with Arabic) the liturgical language of Coptic Christians. A critical edition of the Sahidic Bible, whether Old or New Testament, is a major desideratum in Coptic studies, which projects at Münster and Göttingen hope to fill. The significance of the Bible for Coptic language and literature exceeds that of the King James Version for modern English: Its grammar, syntax, and vocabulary profoundly shaped all the literary works that followed. The New Testament (especially the Gospels), Psalms, and Proverbs are the most frequently found biblical works in early manuscripts, which provide important evidence also for the Greek text of the Bible before it was standardized in the Byzantine period (Wilfong 2001).

A vast portion of the earliest attested Coptic texts (from the fourth and fifth centuries) consists of additional works translated from Greek and perhaps Syriac/Aramaic. Christianity was not the only missionary religion active in Egypt: So, too, Manichaeans sought converts, formed communities, and translated their sacred literature. For example, the apparently seven codices that make up the so-called Medinet Madi Library probably date to the first decades of the fifth century (Robinson 2013; Gardner, BeDuhn, and Dilley 2015). The poor state of their preservation has made conserving and editing the codices a major challenge; a team of scholars is currently making progress on one of the most damaged but perhaps most historically fascinating codices, which contains a work entitled *The Chapters of the Wisdom of My Lord Manichaios* and which is now in the Chester Beatty Library in Dublin. Written in the Subachmimic or Lycopolitan dialect, the Medinet Madi texts have traditionally been considered translations from Syriac/Armenian, but the possibility of Greek originals for at least some cannot be ruled out. Whatever their original social location, the works suggest a thriving Manichaean literary culture in Coptic during the early fifth century, for they include teachings of Mani and episodes from his life, psalms, homilies, letters, and even a church history.

More famous by far are the 13 codices discovered at Nag Hammadi in 1945 (Brakke 2005), which contain an astonishing variety of early Christian works, most of which ancient church leaders would have considered heretical. Although the hoard of manuscripts is often referred to as a "library," scholars have no definitive evidence for the context of the manuscripts' creation and collection. While many if not most have argued for a monastic setting (Lundhaug and Jenott 2015), monks were not the only ascetically and intellectually inclined Christians in late ancient Egypt. The scripts, writing materials, and dialects of the manuscripts are diverse. It has been estimated that the handwriting of as many as 14 different scribes can be detected in the codices. Although all the texts are in Coptic, some are in the Sahidic dialect and others in Subachmimic, with great variation even within these two broad categories. It seems likely, therefore, that the manuscripts were copied at different locations and subsequently collected by a person or group. Several of the leather covers contain cartonnage, scraps of discarded papyrus glued together to make the cover firm: The latest of the scraps can be dated to 348 CE, and thus the codices must have been constructed later than 350, and an increasing number of scholars argue for some time during the early fifth century.

The 46 different tractates contained in the Nag Hammadi codices vary widely in their genres and theologies. Although most can be considered Jewish or Christian in the sense that they draw on the Hebrew Bible, the New Testament, and other Jewish and Christian literature, others, such as a fragment of Plato's *Republic*, certainly did not derive from a Jewish or Christian milieu. All of the texts were originally composed in Greek and subsequently translated into Coptic; thus, they could have originated in locations throughout the eastern Mediterranean or among Greek-speaking communities in the

West. Many of the tractates are apocalypses or revelations, in which a divine figure (e.g. Jesus) or authoritative human being (e.g. Adam) reveals future events, cosmological secrets, or theological doctrines to an elect person or group. Other works are or include theological treatises, sermons, prayers, hymns, and wisdom books. Several tractates are called "gospels," but none resemble the Gospels of the New Testament, which present a narrative of Jesus's ministry emphasizing his passion and death. Rather, the *Gospel according to Thomas*, for example, presents a collection of Jesus's sayings, in the manner of the biblical book of Proverbs, without any narrative.

Literary historians must ask what motivated the translation of these works from Greek into Coptic. Advocates of the monastic hypothesis for the codices' origin suggest that the translations were intended for Egyptian monks with poor knowledge of Greek (Lundhaug and Jenott 2015). Others argue that, because many of the works present complex mythologies and theological arguments and are studded with Greek loan words, it seems likely that most readers interested in such literature would have known Greek as well as Coptic. Moreover, much of the Coptic is poor (especially if the translations date to the fifth century), and many of the translations muddled. Some have suggested that the translators were neophytes in Coptic (at least in writing it) and were practicing. Or perhaps the works reflect a fascination with Egyptian as an ancient language of mystic lore, the best medium for works that often transmit esoteric knowledge (*gnōsis*) (Emmel 2008). In some monastic settings Coptic, the language of Antony, Pachomius, and other admired pioneers, may have had greater prestige than Greek. Whatever the motivation, the translation of these works brought them into the world of Coptic literature, where they encountered resistance and influenced religious thought in ways that scholars are only beginning to explore.

4.3 Original Coptic Literature: From Pachomius and Shenoute to the Muslim Conquest

Literature composed in Coptic originated in Christian monasticism, that is, organized ascetic life apart from the traditional household. Epiphanius reports that Hieracas, the leader of an ascetic community in Lycopolis in the early fourth century, wrote psalms in Coptic, but if he did, they have been lost (Goehring 1999, pp. 110–133). A set of letters attributed to Antony, the famous hermit who died around 356, survives in several languages, and he may have written them in Coptic (Rubenson 1995). Several works on the monastic life bear the name of Paul of Tamma, who appears to have lived in the late fourth century (Orlandi 1988). We are on more secure ground with the writings of Pachomius and his colleagues in the Koinonia, the federation of monasteries that he founded and led until his death in 346. The Koinonia was a bilingual community that generated rules, biographies, letters, and homilies in both Greek and Coptic (Veilleux 1980–1982). Pachomius himself may have written some of the early rules in Coptic, and he certainly composed most if not all of his letters in Coptic. Some of the letters are obscure, written in a code that modern historians labor to decipher (Joest 2014). Letters and rules are the earliest and among the most basic genres of monastic literature – and thus of Coptic literature as well.

The Pachomian *Rules* form the first point on a trajectory that leads to the *Rule of St. Benedict* (Veilleux, 1980–1982, vol. 2; Rousseau 1985, pp. 48–53). They come down to us as a whole only in Jerome's Latin translation of 404, in which they divide into four sections, or books. Although it is reasonable to assume that some of this material in written form dates back to the lifetime of Pachomius, the *Rules* doubtless are the product of several decades of development and ad hoc legislation. For the most part individual rules take the form of legislative commands: The monk or the housemaster or the superior or whoever "shall" or "shall not" do something. Frequently a particular situation is presupposed with a conditional clause: "If anyone does" this, "he shall" do that. Literary influences include legal texts and wisdom literature, both biblical and Egyptian. Although there appears to be some rationale behind the creation of one or more of the sections – for example, "Precepts and Institutes" may address specific officials, not monks in general – the rules often follow no clear organizational scheme and so reflect their origins in ad hoc legislating over a long period of time rather than in a single author's vision. Still, one can see here the beginnings of the classic *regula* of the Benedictine type.

Apart from rules and letters, then, there were few precedents in native Coptic when Shenoute made his literary debut in the 380s. Shenoute was a monk in a monastery founded by his uncle Pcol near Atripe, across the Nile from Panopolis and not far from the leading Pachomian monastery at Pbow. As the (deceased) founder's nephew and a young man of obvious education and rhetorical talent, Shenoute must not have been just any monk, but he held no known official position when he produced his first major work – a long open letter to his monastic community that accuses its leadership of covering up major instances of sin and announces the author's decision to withdraw to a hermitage in the nearby desert (Emmel 2004a, 2004b, pp. 558–565). Now the opening work in the first volume of Shenoute's *Canons*, this piece resembles other early Coptic works in its genre (letter), its extensive quotations from the community's rules, and its reliance on the Bible for its vocabulary and imagery. And yet it is startlingly new: The style mixes polished rhetoric, biblical diction, and colloquial informality; the voice is both completely assured of its moral rectitude and deeply anguished in its emotional pitch; and the author tells a series of mysterious parables that sound vaguely scriptural but are, rather, allegories for communal events.

Shenoute's innovation consists, on the one hand, in the brilliance of his variations on existing Coptic literary forms (letter, rules, homilies) and works (the Bible) and, on the other, in his use of Greek rhetorical techniques to extend the complexity of Coptic syntax and to develop a distinctive literary voice. In a sermon from late in his career (440s), Shenoute acknowledges that "there are many people who speak the word because they want the people who hear them to praise them as orators," rather than "so that souls might be saved," and that some hearers are more interested in critiquing the preacher's rhetorical skills than in benefiting spiritually. Shenoute insists that he speaks as he does only "because I want our labor to profit us, both speaker and listener" (Brakke and Crislip 2015, p. 278), but one can imagine that it was not only the content of Shenoute's teachings that drew crowds to hear his occasional public sermons or that caused prominent politicians and military leaders to visit him and request a private oration. It is difficult to know, however, how in the 380s Shenoute's first letter would have been published or to imagine how its addressees would have received it. In any event, it opened a remarkable literary career that spanned some seven decades and that achieved a level of excellence that no other native writer of Coptic would ever approach.

The reconstruction of Shenoute's literary corpus by Stephen Emmel (2004b) is one of the great achievements of Coptic literary history. The codices that contained Shenoute's writings, nearly all of which were produced and transmitted in the White Monastery, suffered dismemberment and damage during the late Middle Ages, and in the early modern period the fragments were dispersed among libraries in Europe, North America, and Egypt. Emmel's reconstruction of those codices revealed that most of Shenoute's works were organized into two major collections. Shenoute himself created nine volumes of *Canons*, which contain works having to do with the monastery's internal life. Because he continued to live as a hermit until nearly the end of his life and because he oversaw three federated monasteries (two for men and one for women), Shenoute exercised much of his leadership by letters, which he expected to be read aloud to gathered monks. These works have been described as "sermonizing diatribe and excited self-presentation" that sometimes addressed specific problems or crises and that drew on the Bible and collections of rules (Layton 2014, p. 35). Most likely after his death, an editor or editors created eight volumes of *Discourses*, which contain works addressed to wider audiences, including sermons that Shenoute delivered to congregations of monks and lay people in the primary monastery's church (Brakke and Crislip 2015). Additional works survive outside these two primary collections, including letters addressed to persons outside the monastery, such as bishops of Alexandria.

Thanks to Shenoute's dominant authorial voice, monastic legislation in the White Monastery took a literary path different from that of the Pachomian works. Layton (2009, 2014) has determined that Shenoute made use of one or more lists of already written rules that he inherited from the Pachomian federation, his predecessors as leaders of the White Monastery, and possibly other authoritative monks (all of whom he often referred to collectively as "our fathers"); he doubtless augmented and revised the rules that he had received. No such lists survive from the White Monastery, however; rather, Shenoute quotes and cites over 500 such rules in the *Canons*. Most of Shenoute's rules follow the legislative form of Pachomius's ("shall"/"shall not"), but a substantial group consists of curse formulas: "Cursed be anyone who…" or "Anyone who…shall be under a curse." It seems likely that Shenoute or one of his predecessors derived this form from the legislation found in Deuteronomy 27:15–26. Although surely the lists of rules that Shenoute used and revised must have survived him to be used in later generations, it is his *Canons* that Shenoute ordered to be read to assemblies of monks and that were transmitted in the monastery into the medieval period.

The brilliance of Shenoute's style and rhetoric leaves other Coptic writers of the fourth and fifth centuries looking rather dull in comparison. For example, while Shenoute demonstrated a seemingly effortless ability to improvise on biblical vocabulary and diction, Besa, Shenoute's successor as head of the White Monastery federation, relies more heavily on simple quotations from the Scriptures (as well as from monastic literature like Antony's letters) (Kuhn 1956). In this respect, he resembles the Pachomian leader and author Horsiesius, whose letters and instructions quote extensively from the Bible (Veilleux 1980–1982, vol. 3). The author known as "Pseudo-Shenoute" seems to have been content to replicate the work of the master to the best of his ability (Kuhn 1960). Although the sheer excellence of Shenoute's intellect and literary talent cannot be discounted, scholars have yet to consider thoroughly the reasons for this decline in literary quality. A single answer is likely impossible, but it may lie in changing modes of education in monastic communities; the extent to which later authors sought the same public role that Shenoute played (even if he denied seeking it); and a conservative attitude that such great fathers as Athanasius, Cyril, and Shenoute had already said what Christians needed to know and believe.

If one looks in vain for outstanding individual authors other than Shenoute, the vitality of Coptic literature can be found in the hagiography that flourished from the fourth through eighth centuries, whether translated from Greek or composed in Coptic (Papaconstantinou 2011). These works include lives of saints, acts of martyrs, collections of miracle stories, homilies, and encomia. Like letters and rules, lives of saints originated with monastic communities. The various *Lives of Pachomius*, which date to the decades before and after the turn of the fifth century, continued the didactic agenda of Athanasius of Alexandria's Greek *Life of Antony*, while drawing upon it for literary motifs (Veilleux 1980–1982, vol.1; Rousseau 1985, pp. 38–48). Pachomius's life provided a template for monks seeking to live out the values of the Pachomian federation. Recounting the story of Pachomius, however, also fostered a specific communal identity for the monks of the Koinonia. By extending their narratives to include the lives of Horsiesius and Theodore, Pachomius's successors, the authors created a communal history for the federation with which the monks could identify, enhancing group solidarity (Watts 2010, pp. 99–107).

Because these works belonged to the living literature of monastic life and liturgical celebration, they could be revised and circulate under different versions, as in fact the lives of Pachomius did. Similarly, the *Life of Shenoute* may survive as a complete work in Bohairic attributed to Besa, but it is unlikely to be the unified composition of a single author. Instead, various hagiographic vignettes about the archimandrite, some of which may date back to the decades after his death, appear in different such "lives" in Arabic as well as Coptic (Lubomierski 2007). Likewise, the well-known *Panegyric on Macarius of Tkôw*, attributed to Dioscorus of Alexandria, survives in different recensions in Bohairic and Sahidic (Johnson 1980). The popularity of this literature motivated continual revision to speak to contemporary audiences.

The *Panegyric on Macarius* reveals also one important source of the energy that motivated the production of hagiographical texts in the fifth and later centuries: the opposition to the Council of Chalcedon (451) and its "two-nature" Christology. Its hero, Macarius, dies when he refuses to subscribe to the *Tome* of Leo and an imperial officer kills him. In other works martyrs may suffer for their Christian beliefs under pagan emperors, but their heroism served to encourage Egyptian Christians resisting Chalcedonian Christian emperors. The famously repetitive and grisly nature of Coptic martyr accounts fostered a martyrological self-understanding among anti-Chalcedonians and reflected this literature's liturgical context, in which formulaic yet vivid narratives supplemented biblical readings.

In the late fifth and sixth centuries, Coptic authors engaged the Egyptian church's struggle to define its relationship with the Chalcedonian imperial Church. The Coptic *History of the Church*, probably first composed in the 470s, survives only fragmentarily, much of it incorporated into the medieval Arabic *History of the Patriarchs (of Alexandria)* (Orlandi 2007). The *History of the Church* presented much of Eusebius of Caesarea's *Ecclesiastical History* in Coptic and then continued the narrative by emphasizing heroes of Egyptian Christianity like Athanasius, Cyril, Shenoute and Dioscorus; the Egyptian church played a central role in defining orthodoxy for the imperial church, which had gone astray as the Copts remained faithful. Derived from this work is the Coptic *Life of Athanasius*, which became the central piece of a dossier of Coptic texts celebrating Athanasius or presenting homilies that he purportedly delivered (Orlandi 1968). By representing their past and especially their greatest theologians and leaders, Coptic authors began to create an identity for the Egyptian church that was related to but separate from that of imperial Chalcedonian Christianity. Already in Shenoute's works the term *hellēnes* functioned negatively and flexibly to mean "pagan," "obscenely rich," "cultured in the wrong way," and so on. It is unlikely, however, that anti-Chalcedonianism motivated the use of Coptic rather than of Greek; the use of Greek declined as knowledge of it among the non-elite Christians that writers hoped to reach declined and as, after the Arab conquest, elites turned to Arabic (Mikhail 2014, pp. 9–105).

That project of literary self-definition reached a new peak during the patriarchate of Damian (578–607). Damian led a revival of the Egyptian church after a difficult period in which the anti-Chalcedonians had to fend off the emperor Justinian's more aggressive attempts to impose Chalcedonian doctrine, even as they struggled with their own theological and political divisions. For the first time since the days of Pachomius, Shenoute, Besa, and company, we have works from several named authors: Constantine of Siout (ca. 550–640), Pisentius of Koptos (569–632), John of Shmun (ca. 600), John of Parallos (ca. 600), and possibly (as we saw above) Rufus of Shotep (Orlandi 2006, 567–70). These authors wrote mostly homilies and encomia and demonstrated a level of rhetorical flair and an ability to exploit Coptic grammar and syntax that had not been seen since Shenoute, even if none can be placed on a par with him. Despite their literary quality and apparent engagement with Greek and Coptic literary traditions, however, these works rehearse traditional themes, and none of their authors developed a distinct literary voice as Shenoute did (Emmel 2007, p. 97).

With only one outstanding native writer, Coptic literature may suffer in comparison with other "regional" literatures of late antiquity, especially Syriac. One looks in vain for a line of outstanding and innovative theologians like Aphrahat, Ephrem, and Philoxenus among the Syrians. Instead, most Coptic literature represents the collective voice of a religious community, one profoundly shaped, first, by monasticism and, then, by struggle with a "heretical" imperial church. Coptic served as a vehicle of translation and Christianization and later of Egyptian self-definition vis-à-vis a Greek-speaking Roman Empire. As such the literary heritage of the early Copts epitomizes many of the most important themes of late antiquity and its study, above all, what "Hellenism" meant in a bilingual society.

REFERENCES

Brakke, David. (2005). Nag Hammadi. In: *Encyclopedia of Religion* (ed. Lindsay Jones), 6395–6399. 2nd ed. Detroit, MI: Thomson Gale.

Brakke, David, and Crislip, Andrew. ed. (2015). *Selected Discourses of Shenoute the Great: Community, Theology, and Social Conflict in Late Antique Egypt.* Cambridge: Cambridge University Press.

Choat, Malcolm. (2012). Coptic. In: *The Oxford Handbook of Roman Egypt* (ed. Christina Riggs), 581–593. Oxford: Oxford University Press.

Depuydt, Leo, ed. (1991). *Homiletics from the Pierpont Morgan Library: Seven Coptic Homilies Attributed to Basil the Great, John Chrysostom, and Euodius of Rome.* 2 vols. Louvain: Peeters.

Depuydt, Leo. (1993). *Catalogue of Coptic Manuscripts in the Pierpont Morgan Library.* Louvain: Peeters.

Emmel, Stephen. (2004a). Shenoute the Monk: The early monastic career of Shenoute the Archimandrite. In: *Il monachesimo tra eredità aperture: Atti del simposio "Testi e temi nella tradizione del monachesimo cristiano" per il 50e anniversario dell'istituto monastico di Sant'Anselmo, Roma, 28 maggio-1e guigno 2002* (ed. M. Bielawski and D. Hombergen), 151–174. Rome: Pontificio ateneo S. Anselmo.

Emmel, Stephen. (2004b). *Shenoute's Literary Corpus.* 2 vols. Louvain: Peeters.

Emmel, Stephen. (2005). The library of the Monastery of the Archangel Michael at Phantoou (al-Hamuli). In: *Christianity and Monasticism in the Fayoum Oasis: Essays from the 2004 International Symposium of the Saint Mark Foundation and the Saint Shenouda the Archimandrite Coptic Society in Honor of Martin Krause* (ed.Gawdat Gabra), 63–70. Cairo: American University in Cairo Press.

Emmel, Stephen. (2006). A report on progress in the study of Coptic literature, 1996–2004. In: *Huitième congrès international d'études coptes (Paris 2004): I. Bilans et perspectives 2000-2004* (ed. Anne Boud'hors and Denyse Vaillancourt), 173–204. Paris: De Boccard.

Emmel, Stephen. (2007). Coptic literature in the Byzantine and early Islamic world. In: *Egypt in the Byzantine World, 300–700* (ed. Roger S. Bagnall), 83–102. Cambridge: Cambridge University Press.

Emmel, Stephen. (2008). The Coptic Gnostic texts as witnesses to the production and transmission of Gnostic (and other) traditions. In: *Das Thomasevangelium. Entstehung, Rezeption, Theologie* (ed. Jörg Frey, Enno Edzard Popkes, and Jens Schröter), 33–49. Berlin: Walter de Gruyter.

Funk, Wolf-Peter. (1991). Dialects, morphology of Coptic. In: *The Coptic Encyclopedia.* 8 vols. (ed. Aziz S Atiya), 8:101–108. New York: Macmillan.

Gardner, Iain, BeDuhn, Jason, and Dilley, Paul. (2015). *Mani at the Court of the Persian Kings: Studies on the Chester Beatty "Kephalaia" Codex.* Leiden: Brill.

Goehring, James E. (1999). *Ascetics, Society, and the Desert: Studies in Early Egyptian Monasticism.* Harrisburg, PA: Trinity Press International.

Joest, Christoph. (2014). *Die Pachom-Briefe: Übersetzung und Deutung.* Louvain: Peeters.

Johnson, D. W. (1980). *A Panegyric on Macarius Bishop of Tkôw Attributed to Disocorus of Alexandria*. Louvain: Secrétariat du CorpusSCO.

Kuhn, K. H. (1956). *Letters and Sermons of Besa*. 2 vols. Louvain: Peeters.

Kuhn, K. H. (1960). *Pseudo-Shenoute: Om Christian Behaviour*. 2 vols. Louvain: Secrétariat du CorpusSCO.

Layton, Bentley. (2009). The monastic rules of Shenoute. In: *Monastic Estates in Late Antique and Early Islamic Egypt: Ostraca, Papyri, and Essays in Memory of Sarah Clackson* (ed. Anne Boud'hors, James Clackson, Catherine Louis, and Petra Sijpesteijn), 170–177. Cincinnati: American Society of Papyrologists.

Layton, Bentley. (2011). *A Coptic Grammar*. 3rd ed. Wiesbaden: Harrassowitz.

Layton, Bentley. (2014). *The Canons of Our Fathers: Monastic Rules of Shenoute*. Oxford: Oxford University Press.

Louis, Catherine. (2008). The fate of the White Monastery library. In: *Christianity and Monasticism in Upper Egypt* (ed. Gawdat Gabra and Hany N. Takla), 83–90. Cairo: American University in Cairo Press.

Lubomierski, Nina. (2007). *Die Vita Sinuthii: Form- und Überlieferungsgeschichte der hagiographischen Texte über Schenute den Archimandriten*. Tübingen: Mohr Siebeck.

Lucchesi, Enzo. (2000). La langue originale des commentaires sur les Évangiles de Rufus de Shotep. *Orientalia* 69: 86–87.

Luisier, Philippe. (1998). Review of Sheridan 1998. *Orientalia Christiana Periodica* 64: 471–473.

Lundhaug, Hugo, and Jenott, Lance. (2015). *The Monastic Origins of the Nag Hammadi Codices*. Tübingen: Mohr Siebeck.

Mikhail, Maged S.A. (2014). *From Byzantine to Islamic Egypt: Religion, Identity and Politics after the Arab Conquest*. London and New York: I.B. Tauris.

Orlandi, Tito. (1968). *Testi Copti: 1. Encomio di Atanasio; 2. Vita di Atanasio*. Milan: Cisalpino.

Orlandi, Tito. (1986). Coptic literature. In: *The Roots of Egyptian Christianity* (ed. Birger A. Pearson and James E. Goehring), 51–81. Philadelphia: Fortress.

Orlandi, Tito. (1988). *Paolo di Tamma: Opere*. Rome: CIM.

Orlandi, Tito. (1991). Cycles. In: *The Coptic Encyclopedia*. 8 vols (ed. Aziz S. Atiya), 3:666–668. New York: Macmillan.

Orlandi, Tito. (2002). The library of the Monastery of Saint Shenute at Atripe. In: *Perspectives on Panopolis: An Egyptian Town from Alexander the Great to the Arab Conquest. Acts from an International Symposium held in Leiden on 16, 17, and 18 December 1998* (ed. A. Egberts, B. Muhs, and J. van der Vliet), 211–231. Leiden: Brill.

Orlandi, Tito. (2006). Patristic texts in Coptic. In: *Patrology: The Eastern Fathers from the Council of Chalcedon (451) to John of Damascus (†750)* (ed. Angelo Di Berardino), 491–570. Cambridge: James Clarke.

Orlandi, Tito. (2007). The Coptic ecclesiastical history: A survey. In: *The World of Early Egyptian Christianity: Language, Literature, and Social Contex* (ed.James E. Goehring and Janet A. Timbie), 3–24. Washington DC: Catholic University of America Press.

Papaconstantinou, Arietta. (2011). Hagiography in Coptic. In: *The Ashgate Research Companion to Byzantine Hagiography* (ed. Stephanos Efthymiadis), 1:323–344. Farnham: Ashgate.

Robinson, James M. (2013). *The Manichaean Codices of Medinet Madi.* Eugene, OR: Cascade Books.

Rousseau, Philip. (1985). *Pachomius: The Making of a Community in Fourth-Century Egypt.* Berkeley: University of California Press.

Rubenson, Samuel. (1995). *The Letters of St. Antony: Monasticism and the Making of a Saint.* Minneapolis: Fortress.

Sheridan, Mark. (1998). *Rufus of Shotep: Homilies on the Gospels of Matthew and Luke.* Rome: CIM.

Veilleux, Armand. (1980–1982). *Pachomian Koinonia.* 3 vols. Kalamazoo, MI.: Cistercian.

Watts, Edward. (2010). *Riot in Alexandria: Tradition and Group Dynamics in Late Antique Pagan and Christian Communities.* Berkeley: University of California Press.

Wilfong, Terry G. (2001). Coptic literature. In: *The Oxford Encyclopedia of Ancient Egypt* (ed. Donald B. Redford), 1:295–302. Oxford: Oxford University Press.

CHAPTER FIVE

Armenian

Robin Darling Young

The Armenian language – Hayeren in the language itself – may date from about 1500 BCE, having been brought to the area of the southern Caucasus and eastern Anatolia by a group emigrating from the northeast and eventually replacing its predecessor Urartian culture. From north of the Black Sea, or possibly from northwestern Thrace, this group came to the mountainous region including the southern Caucasus, western Anatolia, and the headwaters of the Tigris and Euphrates rivers. Thus the center of Armenian's geographical spread was, in antiquity, the lands from Lake Van in the west to Urmia in the east; its modern varieties continue to be spoken in the modern Republic of Armenia and in the large international diaspora.

Armenians are first described as Armin/Arminiya in an old Iranian Behistun inscription of about 520 BCE that commemorates Darius the Great. With the rise of the first (Achaemenid) Persian Empire under Cyrus the Great in the mid-sixth century BCE, the region became a satrapy under the administration of a native governor and, apart from the brief interruption of Seleucid kings following the conquests of Alexander the Great, continued to exist as a distinctive region and culture under the cultural domination and political domination of the Arsacids (ca. 250 BCE–244 CE), a subgroup of which remained the dominant Arshakuni clan in Armenia even after the rise of the Sasanians (244-651 CE). Yet Armenians also had contacts to the west (in Greek-speaking Asia Minor and Greece) and south (Syriac-speaking Mesopotamia and Syria), and these would become more important in late antiquity.

A Companion to Late Antique Literature, First Edition.
Edited by Scott McGill and Edward J. Watts.
© 2018 John Wiley & Sons, Inc. Published 2018 by John Wiley & Sons, Inc.

Armenian occupies a distinct branch of the Indo-European language spectrum, a satem (Indo-Iranian) variant whose nearest neighbors are now-dead languages of Anatolia (for example, Phrygian). Its connection with Iranian culture is more than linguistic: Iranian culture of the Arsacid and Sasanian empires formed the texture and much of the content of Armenian thought and literature through late antiquity. The dynamic and often warring relationship between Byzantium and Iran also permeates the "classical" Armenian literature of late antiquity and reflects an "Iranian substrate" (Garsoian 1982) that persisted alongside its adoption of Greek and Syriac Christian topics and terminology. (Jensen, 1939; Meillet, 1936; Schmitt, 1981).

Thus the Armenian language and its oral culture is much older than Armenian literature, which is almost entirely Christian in late antiquity and, indeed, developed as a vehicle for Christian culture. Until the early fourth century CE, the religions of Armenia were pagan (native, Semitic, and Persian in origin), with much smaller Jewish and, later, Christian communities. Written languages, where they were used, were Aramaic and sometimes Greek – for instance, in the ca. 200 BCE inscriptions at Armavir. Syriac appeared later as a spoken language in the south, and texts in Greek and Syriac likely circulated from the second century CE forward, brought by traders and missionaries. Like the dominant Persian culture around them, Armenians before the arrival of Christianity preferred oral recitations and spoken communication; the *gusans*, or "bards," traveled through the region to perform epic poetry, but only scattered verses and folk traditions recorded by later Christian opponents have survived as the remains of this once-large and flourishing tradition (Bournoutian, 1993).

Internally, late ancient Armenians largely lacked an urban network and preferred the social organization of tribal chieftains (*naxarars*) with a hereditary king (*tagawor*); clans occupied their own regions, building fortress-castles to guard crops and the cultivation of horses. Many laborers were the equivalent of serfs (*anazat*, "unfree"). The few cities in the region served as trading posts for merchants traveling east or west between the Mediterranean and East Asia. Nonetheless, Armenian speakers traveled to the major cities of the eastern Roman Empire. Their Christian communities were recorded by Eusebius, and they had traveled to Jerusalem by the fourth century, sending emissaries from Armenia but also leaving behind fifth-century graffiti that are the earliest examples of Armenian script (Stone 1982, 1992, 1993). Between 314 and 336, Macarius, bishop of Jerusalem, wrote a letter of instruction responding to the second Armenian catholicos, Vrtanes, concerning baptism and the Eucharist – witnessing to both the rise of Armenian Christian groups and their reliance on Greek for written communication.

The spread of Christianity in Armenia, strengthening with the conversion of King Trdat and his family (traditional date 301; revised date 317), did not result immediately in a written language. Rather, churches' religious rituals, including the liturgy, and public readings of sacred texts, including the Bible, resulted in the practice of simultaneous oral translations from Greek in the west and Syriac in the south. Such a practice presupposes a cadre of learned bilingual clergy, trained in spoken and written Greek or Syriac, who also carried out the missionary efforts dramatically portrayed in the histories of the next century. Meanwhile, the leader of Armenian Christian communities – the catholicosate – during the fourth century was a hereditary office, with father (beginning with Gregory the Illuminator) passing his office to eldest son, mirroring the Persian preference for succession among the clans and the royal dynasty; although the efforts of singular ascetics and their disciples feature strongly in the later histories, there seem to have been no large monasteries for either men or women in late antiquity. The lack of large-scale asceticism at the time when it was spreading to the south and west suggests an Armenian culture in agreement with Persian insistence on the importance of marriage and family obligations. Such small kinship groups may have obviated the need for a library of works in the native language until Christianity became more populous in the fifth century (Garsoian, 1985).

Written literature was nonetheless occasionally prized in Armenia from earlier antiquity. King Tigran, who ruled a large area of northern Syria and southern Armenia during the period of Roman expansion eastward, was celebrated by Greek authors for his appreciation of Greek culture, including plays; he caused the construction of a city modeled on Greek cities further to the west, and included a temple in classical form. His son, Artwawzd, was recorded by Plutarch to have written tragedies, orations, and histories. Furthermore, Armenians steadily went west to participate in Hellenistic and then Greco-Roman civic life and culture. Prohaeresius, rhetorician in Athens and teacher of Basil of Caesarea and Gregory of Nazianzus, is a parade example but not the only one; he was an Armenian (and a Christian); before he became Basil's dear friend, Gregory initially took the side of a group of Armenian students ("not a simple people, but very crafty and cunning") hazing the great future bishop (*Funeral Oration* 17). Many students of the well-known rhetorical instructor Libanius were Armenians too. Presumably they pursued careers in the west, that is, in Greek-speaking cities of the Empire, at a time when many provincials migrated toward the metropolises of the east.

Thus Armenian literature began much later than Armenian-speaking culture, because, although the language was spoken in a wide range of countryside, it did not gain an alphabet and the means to compose works in the

Armenian for native speakers until after the beginning of the fifth century. Thanks to the catholicos Sahak and the learned ascetic (Mesrop) Mashtots, and with the support of the Armenian royal house (*tun*), a group of men called the "Holy Translators" began to create an Armenian Christian library for the country. Trained in Greek and Syriac, they traveled to cities outside the territories of Armenia, where they used the new alphabet to create a group of translated works. Mashtots himself had been educated in Greek literature as a young man, and his service to the Arsacid court indicates the value of his talent. An associate, Rufinus, had a similar education. Thus it is not surprising that the translators were commissioned to journey to Antioch, Edessa/Urhai, Emesa, Jerusalem, Constantinople and Alexandria (major centers of Christian scholarship) in order to collect texts and to translate the first group of works from Greek and Syriac that would form the basis for Armenian literature. Since none of the theological disputes that resulted in the creation of separate churches, such as the Church of the East or the miaphysite churches, had yet broken out, Armenians translated the Scriptures, beginning with the Book of Proverbs, as well as liturgical books, biblical commentaries, patristic treatises, biographies and hagiographies, and histories – including the *Church History* and later the *Chronicle* of Eusebius of Caesarea. This period (405–460) has been called the "Golden Age" of Armenian literature, not only because of its translations, but also because of the creation of a native literature originating in Armenian (Inglisian, 1963).

Probably under the direction of their sponsors, the first scholars equipped with the Armenian language turned to the translation of the Bible and liturgical books. The first biblical version translated was from Syriac, which had probably arrived in the country with missionaries coming from Mesopotamia to the south. But the increasing involvement of some Armenian bishops with Constantinopolitan clerical authorities led to the retranslation of the Scriptures from Greek, which Armenian was able to reproduce thanks to its complex features – strongly inflected, with grammatical and syntactical similarities to Greek. As with scriptural texts, liturgical texts – lectionaries (such as the fourth-century Jerusalem Lectionary) and books of rites for ceremonies such as baptism and the Eucharist – also were created for Armenian churches through translation from Greek and Syriac. Current liturgical scholarship continues to identify various layers of transmission and tradition. The *Sharakan*, the Armenian hymnal, contains some liturgical poetry from the late ancient period. Hagiographies were also composed in the early period; one such is *The Martyrdom of Shushanik*, about an Armenian Christian woman imprisoned and tormented for her beliefs by her pagan, Zoroastrian husband. Other hagiographies were inserted in the histories of the fifth and sixth centuries. These include the torments of Gregory the Illuminator and the female martyrs Gayane, Hripsime, and their companions (in Agat'angelos's history) as well as an account of the monk Daniel (in the *Buzandaran*).

In addition to books specifically for reading aloud in church in the native language, early Armenian scribes made the effort to translate the works of Christian writers who, in the fourth and fifth centuries, were already being labeled "fathers of the church" and whose work had been gathered into florilegia in support of varying theological positions. These included Ignatius, Aristides, Irenaeus, Hippolytus, Dionysius of Alexandria, Gregory Thaumaturgus, Athanasius, Gregory Nazianzus, Gregory of Nyssa, Basil, Macarius of Jerusalem, Cyril of Jerusalem, John Chrysostom, Epiphanius, Evagrius of Pontus, Cyril of Alexandria, and Syriac authors including Aphrahat (identified in the Armenian translation as the notable bishop Jacob of Nisibis) and Ephrem the Syrian. They also translated the works of Origen, Apollinarius, Diodore of Tarsus, and Theodore of Mopsuestia – but these authors' works were later destroyed, after the controversies of the fifth and sixth centuries led to their condemnation in the church of the Empire. After the final split of the eastern Armenian church from the Byzantine church, however, certain works remained available in Armenian that were destroyed in Greek. This included some of the works of Evagrius of Pontus, for instance (suppressed after 553 in the west), and the works of Philo and Pseudo-Philo, Aristides, Eusebius, and Irenaeus (the *Demonstration of the Apostolic Preaching*) (Thomson, 1997).

5.1 Ecclesiastical and Theological Works in Prose

With the exception of hymns and prayers, all of early Armenian theological literature consists of prose writings like letters, treatises, and canon laws. Poetry would not develop in Armenia until after late antiquity, apart from early hymns preserved in the hymnal the *Sharakan* (van Lint, 2014).

The first theological work to be written in Armenian is the *On God/Against the Sects*, by Eznik Kolbac'i (390–455), or Eznik of Kolb. Eznik, one of the translators under Mashtots, drew on sources from the Greek and Syriac traditions, as well as on his own knowledge based on orally communicated teachings, to expose the errors of paganism, Zoroastrianism, Greek philosophical views, and the Christian sect of Marcionism, the other religions present in Armenia. In the first part, Eznik attempts to rebut pagan beliefs in the existence of many gods; the belief in metaphysical dualism, with its insistence upon the substantial existence of evil; and a belief in fate, resulting in moral determinism. In the second part, Eznik attacks the Zurvanite form of Zoroastrianism, and in particular its triune set of deities: Zurvan, the original divine being and his sons Ormizd and Ahriman. In the third section, Eznik rebuts Greek philosophers, including Plato and Aristotle, for their understanding of the cosmos and of God. Finally, Eznik assembles a critique of Marcionism, with its particular style of ascetic practice, as well as its rejection of the Old Testament (allegedly authored by an evil deity) and its promotion of a limited version of the New Testament (Luke, Paul, and the Acts of the Apostles) ascribed to the intervention of a good God of love. Eznik's work attests to the presence in Armenia of a large library of early Christian controversialists because he quotes from no less than 12 previous Greek and Syriac sources, among whom were apologists, heresiologists, biblical interpreters, and doctrinal writers: the second-century apologist Aristides, Hippolytus, Irenaeus, Methodius of Olympus, Origen, Basil of Caesarea, Epiphanius, Cyril of Alexandria, Theodore of Mopsuestia, and Ephrem the Syrian. The latter name demonstrates the still-important connection between Syriac sources and Armenian writers of the fifth century.

Eznik's work is particularly interesting for its intricate composition in a classical Armenian free of rhetorical embellishments and reflecting the complex grammatical structure of the language. Its influence on later Armenian works was slight, however; his style gave way to a more expansive and repetitive prose, and the controversial positions he analyzed and debunked were of little interest to later authors. *On God* reflected the apologetic stances of the earlier Christian authors from whom Eznik quoted; later Armenian authors did not have to combat the opinions of philosophers or Marcionites. Struggles continuing against Zoroastrian Persians until the rise of Islam tended to be reflected in historical, rather than theological, works (Blanchard and Darling Young, 1998).

Two other early works are letters of Sahak and Mashtots. The first is the response of the two to Proclus, bishop of Constantinople, and the second is Sahak's response to Acacius of Melitene. Both are found in the later-assembled *Book of Letters* (thirteenth century), and they contain correspondence of Armenians with Constantinople concerning the doctrine of the natures of Christ. At some time in the fifth century, Koriwn (390–447), one of the original group of translators commissioned by Sahak, wrote a hagiographical biography of Mashtots, describing the miraculous appearance of the Armenian alphabet, his organization of the first translation efforts, and his missionary travels to Georgia and Albania (present Azerbaijan), where he invented alphabets for their peoples as well.

After Koriwn, six authors of theological prose represent the total of Armenian theological works, properly speaking, that comprise what remains of pre-Islamic Armenian literature. Many of these works are theological exegeses of biblical books, often with hortatory or disputative purposes. Two works were ascribed to Gregory the Illuminator – the *Teaching of St. Gregory* and the *Collected Discourses*. The first is a long sermon allegedly preached to the court of Trdat in the early fourth century; it is included in the *History* of Agat'angelos. It seems to have been composed in the late fifth century. The second work, a collection of twenty-three homilies, also was traditionally attributed to Gregory the Illuminator (or sometimes Mashtots) but is not given a historical context. This so-called *Hadjakhapatoum Djark'* contains discussions of the Trinity and Christ, with a last homily – possibly adapted from a work of Basil – containing a monastic rule. Vrt'anes K'ertol (550–620), catholicos of the Armenian church from 604 to 607, wrote *Concerning Iconoclasm*, a treatise that defends and explains icon veneration in the Armenian church of late antiquity, touches on the relationship between Armenians and Greeks with respect to icons, and discusses the materials used in the practice of writing icons (Maranci, forthcoming).

Following K'ertol, the catholicos Komitas (610–628), has been credited as the author of numerous works reassigned to Yovhannes Mayravanec' (575–667) and has also been alleged to be the author of hymns about the martyr Hrip'sime (Néve 1886).

The final three theological authors of late antiquity are (Pseudo-) Yovhannes Mandakuni (575–668), Yovhannes Ojnec'i (650–729), and Grigor Arsharui (650–729). The first author composed a collection of 25 sermons attributed to the genuine Yovhannes Mandakuni (420–490), intended to criticize lingering pagan practice and institute Christianizing reforms.

Yovhannes Ojnec'i, became Catholicos in 718 and was granted the title *imastaser* (philosopher). A reformer of the church and of the liturgy, he presided at the councils of Div in 719 and Manazkert in 726. He wrote shorter treatises, including the *Synodal Discourse*, *Against the Fantasiasts*, and *Against the Paulicians*, as well as numerous sermons on the topic of the church for the dedication of churches and for liturgical offices. He also compiled canonical legislation. Finally, Arsharui wrote a commentary on the liturgical lectionary. None of these authors has been extensively studied in Western scholarship. A number of works are ascribed to "David the Invincible Philosopher," a sixth-century syncretistic Neoplatonist and Armenian native trained in Alexandria, to whom is credited an original work, the *Definitions and Divisions of Philosophy*, and commentaries on Porphyry's *Isagoge* and on the Aristotelian texts, the *Categories* and the *Prior Analytics*.

5.2 Historians

Of all the works of late ancient Armenian literature, the histories have received by far the most modern scholarly attention. Whereas extensive poetry and works of theological sophistication developed only later, after the end of late antiquity, with its post-Islamic Conquest reorganization of Armenian politics and society, Armenian authors wrote histories of their own countries that are valuable not only because they provide the context for the spread, and for the difficulties among Armenians, of Christianity in the country but also because they describe the interaction of Sasanian Persian and missionary Christian culture in a region set between the two great empires of the period. They also provide a strongly differing perspective on the period from other early Christian works. Although they include hagiographical sections, catechetical orations, moralizing sermons, and accounts of miracles, as well as sometimes long sections tinged with apocalyptic discourse, and although they were written by men of the church, they nevertheless reflect the concerns of their patrons in a social world that had far more similarities to Persia than it did to its late Roman or Byzantine contemporaries.

Although bishops (such as Sahak) were patrons or sometimes authors of theological works, the patrons of historical works were not bishops but members of noble families who wished to have their exploits recorded and celebrated in the written language in addition to (or instead of in) oral accounts. For this reason the histories recount crucial events in the history of the country from the perspective of one family or clan. They sometimes show a particular family in alliance with other families in war and trade, but they also are often in conflict with other clans, particularly as Christianity spread in Armenia with its Sassanian overlords. It was in just that situation of conflict and warfare that Armenian literature as a whole seemed to flourish. Indeed, the sections of Armenia that became part of the Roman Empire with the treaties of the fourth or sixth century did not produce a distinctively Armenian theological or historiographical tradition.

Six historians have left accounts of the events of Armenian society in late antiquity: Agat'angelos, the author of the *Buzandaran* (Pseudo-Faustus of Byzantium), Elishe, Lazar of Parp', and Sebeos all date from the period of the fourth through the seventh centuries, while Movses Khorenat'si pretends to be an eyewitness to events of the fifth century but in actuality dates from the eighth century. Two historians – Agat'angelos and the author of the *Buzandaran* – wrote in the late fifth century but claimed to write in the fourth. Elishe and Lazar wrote in the late fifth century about the struggle between Armenians loyal to Persia and Zoroastrianism and those who had become Christianized; Sebeos wrote in the seventh century and is an important source for the final period of Sassanid reign.

Agat'angelos claimed to be a scribe in the court of Trdat', the Armenian king who converted to Christianity as the result of the mission of Gregory the Illuminator in the early fourth century. Agat'angelos's *History of Trdat and Saint Gregory* survives in numerous languages and in varying editions: It tells the dramatic story of Gregory's conversion to Christianity; his alliance with the See of Caesarea and his long imprisonment by the pagan Trdat'; the arrival of Christian virgins fleeing from the emperor Diocletian's sexual predations; their martyrdom under Trdat'; Trdat's transformation into a boar; his subsequent repentance and acceptance of Christianity; and his alliance with Constantine and Christianity. Known as the "received history," it has had a long and continuing influence in Armenian Christianity, similar to that of Eusebius in the Greek and Latin west and the Syriac-speaking south. Yet it was composed to celebrate the Arshakuni dynasty of Armenian kings and reflects just one perspective on the coming of Christianity to the region.

Garsoian's recently translated, richly annotated publication of the *Buzandaran* (also known, inaccurately, as "Faustus of Byzantium") has allowed for a differing, complementary account of the arrival of Christianity that highlights the strong resistance to it among the Armenian clans, with their ongoing cultural and religious connections to Sassanid-ruled Persia. Reflecting the history of the southern district of Taron, the *Buzandaran* also recounts the missionary efforts of Syrian monks from the south among the successors of the house of Gregory the Illuminator. Instead of a clear transition from paganism to Christianity, the *Buzandaran* shows the persistence of Zoroastrian and native religious traditions among Armenian ruling families and the celebration of warfare and epic tradition.

The two historians of the fifth century, writing in the sixth, tell the story of the war between the Armenian Christian lords and Persians and Armenians loyal to them as a history of a "nation" struggling against a powerful overlord. Both celebrate the deeds of the Mamikonian clan and, in particular, of Vardan Mamikonian, the hero of the war. Yeghishe's *History of Vardan and the Armenian War* is devoted to the period of 449–451, concluding with the defeat of Vardan and the Christian Armenians at the battle of Avarayr. It is a combination of battle accounts and martyrology centering on the "deeds of heavenly valor" of Vardan and his companions. These figures accommodated the pagan Persian's insistence on Zoroastrian observance only to repent and die defending Christianity, thus leading ultimately to the Persians granting Armenians the freedom to practice Christianity.

Lazar of Parp', educated in the fifth century in Armenia and Constantinople, wrote his *History of Armenia* at the behest of Vardan's heir, Vahan Mamikonian. He gives a much longer account of Armenian history, beginning in the fourth century and culminating in the war of 449–451. An example of a wider set of contacts among Armenians, he returned to Siunik', where he worked for the Kamsarakan clan, until Vahan Mamikonian noticed his talents and brought him to Vagharshapat. Finally, suffering from opposition from the anti-Byzantine side of Armenian church life, he moved to the city of Amida (current Diyarbakr, Turkey) and completed his history.

A historian writing in the seventh century has been traditionally named Sebeos; he chronicles the sixth and seventh centuries – the period of the emperor Heraclius and his war against the Persians up to the first Islamic civil war. His title, "Bishop of the Bagratunis," also points to the remarkable Armenian practice in which bishops and priests were attached to ruling families instead of presiding over urban Sees. One of few sources for the campaigns of Heraclius, he was also one of the earliest Western writers on early Islam, and he signals the end of Armenian connection with both Byzantium – from whose form of Christianity Armenians had already broken – and Sasanian Persia, the culture and religion of which would be replaced by Islam. The new Islamic reign would lead to further Armenian independence, with the diminution of the two great empires of late antiquity. Armenian literature continued, its histories sponsored by aristocratic families and its religious literature by large monastic establishments that appeared in the post-ancient period.

In sum, Armenian literature before the Arab conquest was largely the creation of the Armenian clergy, and through the ancient and medieval periods, it remained largely the province of that class. Whether they were historians in the service of one or another ruling house or were clerics or monks, they represented and served the church and its projects, refracted through the dominant themes of Armenian religious culture. In this way, Armenian literature was like that of the Syriac-speaking populations to the south and east: it was a creation of Christian institutions established in the fourth century, in the wake of Constantine and Theodosius's gradual establishment of Christianity. Nonclerical Armenian stories were not literature, because they were not recorded until the nineteenth century, at which point their form and contents had developed, but they also reflected ancient compositions. When the epic stories (Sasnadzrer) of the heroes of Sasun (Sanasar, Balthasar, Mher the Great, and David of Sasun) were recorded in the nineteenth century, they provided a distant reflection of the Armenian oral culture that had been sidelined since the fifth century.

REFERENCES

Blanchard, Monica and Darling Young, Robin. (trans.) (1998). *A Treatise on God Written by Eznik of Kolb (fl. c. 430–c. 450)*. Leuven: Peeters.

Bournoutian, George A. (1993). *A History of the Armenian People*. Costa Mesa, CA: Mazda Publishers.

Garsoian, Nina. (1985). *Armenia between Byzantium and the Sasanians*. London: Variorum.

Garsoian, Nina. (1989). *The Epic Histories Attributed to P'awstos Buzand* (Buzandaran Patmut'iwnk'). Cambridge, MA: Harvard University Press

Inglisian, Vahan. (1963). Die armenische Literatur. In: *Armenisch und kaukasische Sprachen* (ed. Gerhard Deeters). Handbuch der Orientalistik, 1.7. Leiden: Brill.

Jensen, Hans, 1939. *Altarmenische Grammatik*. Heidelberg: C. Winter Universitätsverlag.

Maranci, Christina. (Forthcoming). *The Art of Armenia: A Critical Art History of Ancient and Medieval Armenia, With a Concluding Chapter on Cultural Heritage*. New York and London: Oxford University Press.

Meillet, Antoine. (1936). *Esquisse d'une grammaire comparée de l'armenien classique*. 2nd ed. Vienna: Imprimerie des pp. Mékhitharistes.

Néve, Félix. (1886). *L'Arménie chrétienne et sa littérature*. Louvain.

Schmitt, Rüdiger. (1981). *Grammatik des Klassisch-Armenischen*. Innsbruck: Innsbrucker Beitrage zur Sprachwissenschaft.

Stone, Michael. (1982). *The Armenian Inscriptions from the Sinai with Appendixes on the Georgian and Latin Inscriptions by Michel van Esbroeck and W. Adler*. Harvard Armenian Texts and Studies, 6 (ed. R.W. Thomson). Cambridge: Harvard University.

Stone, Michael. (1992). *The Rock Inscriptions and Graffiti Project, Catalogue of Inscriptions. Vols. 1–2: Inscriptions 1–6000*. Society of Biblical Literature Resources for Biblical Study, 28–29, Atlanta: Scholars Press.

Stone, Michael. 1993. *The Rock Inscriptions and Graffiti Project, Catalogue of Inscriptions. Vol. 3: Inscriptions 6000–8500*. Society of Biblical Literature Resources for Biblical Study. Atlanta: Scholars Press.

Thomson, Robert W. (1981). Armenian literary culture through the eleventh century. In: *The Armenian People from Ancient to Modern Times, v.1, The Dynastic Periods: From Antiquity to the Fourteenth Century* (ed. Richard G. Hovannisian), 199–240. New York: St. Martin's Press.

Van Lint, Theo. (2014). Medieval poetic texts. In: *Armenian Philology in the Modern Era. From Manuscript to Digital Text* (ed. Valentina Calzolari with the collaboration of Michael E. Stone), 377–413. Leiden-Boston: Brill.

CHAPTER SIX

Georgian

Stephen H. Rapp, Jr.

Since the pioneering work of Peter Brown of the 1970s, the Christianizing Roman Empire has been touted as the bedrock of late antiquity. Nevertheless, ensuing scholarship has enlarged the social, cultural, and imperial horizons of that cross-cultural enterprise. Thus a growing cadre of specialists reject the persistent image of Iran and the expansive Iranic (Persianate) world as hostile interlopers and instead envision them as fundamental and contributory components of late antiquity from its beginning (Canepa 2009; cf. Bowersock, Brown, and Grabar 1999). The push beyond the Graeco-Roman Mediterranean has sparked interest in zones of sustained cross-cultural encounter: the Horn of Africa, Central Eurasia, and, the subject of this essay, Caucasia (on these Eurasian perspectives, see Johnson 2012). In late antiquity, Christian and Iranian/Iranic threads were entwined in a cohesive "Christian Caucasian civilization" stretching from the Black to the Caspian Seas (Toumanoff 1963). Bolstered by three of the world's earliest royal conversions, the Christian faith achieved dominance across the isthmus named for the Caucasus Mountains in the fourth and fifth centuries. Significantly, all three royal houses – and some of their leading aristocrats – were descended from prominent Parthian families, including the Arsacids. And although Christianity successfully dislodged several polytheisms, vestiges of these earlier religions persisted for centuries to come. Substantial remnants of the hybrid Zoroastrianisms that had prevailed since the Iron and Hellenistic Ages continued deep into the medieval period (Russell 1987).

Caucasia's Christianization owed little to the direct intervention of the Roman imperial core. Rather, it was chiefly the result of holy women and

---

A Companion to Late Antique Literature, First Edition.
Edited by Scott McGill and Edward J. Watts.
© 2018 John Wiley & Sons, Inc. Published 2018 by John Wiley & Sons, Inc.

men associated with Syria, Cappadocia, and Pontus. Late antique Caucasia has no equivalent of the imperially sanctioned mission of Cyril and Methodius to the Slavs in the ninth century. Yet we observe a fascinating parallel: The triumph of Christianity among the Slavs and the peoples of southern Caucasia was enhanced by the formulation of alphabetic scripts. In the latter case, scripts for the Armenian, Georgian, and Albanian languages were created toward the end of the fourth century (Gamqreliże 1989). The Armenian monk Maštoc' (Mesrop) played a pivotal role in this cross-cultural endeavor, though his received memory is conditioned by subsequent ecclesiastical and political rivalries. The internal, pan-Caucasian project to promote Christianity through local tongues equipped with their own scripts triggered the formation of new literary societies that, despite their sharp individuality and clashing agendas in later epochs, were tightly interlocked in their infancy.

6.1 Earliest Original Georgian Literature: Hagiography

The genesis of Georgian literature is typically connected to the inland hub of K'art'li, which commanded the central basin of the Kura/Mtkuari River; this realm, which was established at the collapse of the Achaemenid Empire, roughly corresponds to Greco-Latin Iberia (for an accessible overview of Georgian literature, see Rayfield 1994). From their beginning the dynastic monarchs of K'art'li were based at Mc'xet'a/Mtskheta and its citadel, Armazis-c'ixe, both located at the strategic confluence of the Mtkuari and Aragwi Rivers. Not only did Mc'xet'a occupy the political, religious, economic, and agricultural epicenter of the Georgian lands, but it was also the gateway to one of the principal passes through the Caucasus Mountains, the Darial Gate. In the sixth century the royal seat was transferred just downriver on the Kura to Tp'ilisi, "T'bilisi" according to modern orthography.

Under the impulse of Christianity, literary centers arose throughout eastern Georgia and in adjacent areas to the south cohabited by K'art'velians and Armenians. Outstanding among the latter is Somxit'i/Gugark', the Armeno-K'art'velian marchlands governed by dynastic border lords brandishing the Middle Persian title *bidaxš*, rendered *pitiaxši* in Georgian and *bdeašx* in Armenian (Rapp 2014a, pp. 62–75). Major scriptoria later operated to K'art'li's southwest in the Armeno-K'art'velian lands of Tao/Tayk' and Klarjet'i/Kłarjk' (Childers 2013, p. 296). Christian activity here reached its apex in the early medieval period. The locus of the initial phases of Georgian literary production was by no means restricted to Caucasia. In late antiquity, Jerusalem and Palestine were anchors of Georgian and Armenian literature.

Already by the fifth century, eastern Georgian ascetics were established at monasteries in the Holy Land, including Mar Saba. Procopius mentions a monastery of the Iberians in Jerusalem and another of the western Georgian Laz in the desert nearby (*Buildings* 5.9.6–7). It is conceivable, though not definitively proven, that the Georgian script was invented in the Levant. In subsequent centuries, Georgian scriptoria operated elsewhere in the Byzantine and Islamic spheres, including the Black Mountain in Syria, Mount Sinai, and Mount Athos (Menabde 1961 and 1980).

The Gospels and other primary religious texts were the first works set into Georgian. Original Georgian compositions followed soon thereafter, but the identity and date of the first homegrown source remains uncertain because of the relatively late and incomplete nature of surviving manuscripts. Among known narratives, the place of honor is usually afforded to *The Passion of Šušanik*, a concise hagiography ascribed to the priest Iakob C'urtaveli/Jacob of Tsurtavi. According to this text, the pious Armenian noblewoman Šušanik, daughter of the famous Vardan Mamikonean, was martyred by her Zoroastrianizing husband, Va[r]sk'en, the *bidaxš* of Somxit'i-Gugark'. Varsk'en had renounced his familial Christianity as he aligned himself with the Sasanian *šāhan šāh* in a bid to minimize the interference of the kings of K'art'li and Armenia Major. Šušanik's steadfast refusal to apostatize brought incarceration and brutal torture. Šušanik's *vita* appears to have been composed shortly after her death in the late fifth century. Although the narrative shows signs of later adjustment, its basic structure belongs to the decades immediately after Šušanik's martyrdom.

In the same period a short Georgian *vita* was composed that commemorates the martyrdom of nine newly converted children from Kolay/Kola. The anonymous author recounts the children's clandestine baptism and subsequent murder by their enraged "pagan" parents. This hagiography is devoid of explicit chronological and geographical markers: Other than a bald reference to Kolay in eastern Anatolia, the generic story might have been set anywhere Christians commingled with polytheists. Its apparent sixth-century date has been determined by language and syntax.

The Martyrdom of Evstat'i Mc'xet'eli is the latest surviving Georgian *vita* from late antiquity. Its Iranian hero, born Gwrobandak, spent his early years in Ganzak, a city in northwestern Iran near a prominent Zoroastrian shrine. In Ganzak the young Gwrobandak abandoned his ancestral training as a Zoroastrian *mowbed* and seems to have joined a Manichaean congregation (Mgaloblishvili and Rapp 2011). Only after migrating to the K'art'velian capital, the reason for which is not revealed, Gwrobandak received Christian baptism and took a Christian name and wife. Complaints lodged by Mc'xet'a's community of Iranian émigrés compelled the local Sasanian official to interrogate the renamed

Evstatʻi (< Gk. Eustathius) about his renunciation of Zoroastrianism. Evstatʻi refused to return to the Zoroastrian fold and was executed at the *marzbān*'s order, thus securing his place among Iranian martyrs. The date of Evstatʻi's death is contested: While most scholars advocate the mid-sixth century under the Sasanian *Šāhan šāh* Xusrō I, the correct date is probably ca. 600 under Xusrō II (Rapp 2014a, pp. 80–87). Assuming a composition shortly after his martyrdom, Evstatʻi's *vita* derives from the early seventh century.

A small number of Georgian hagiographies were consigned to writing as late antiquity dissolved into the medieval age, most notably Iovane Sabanis-że's *Passion of Habo* and Giorgi Merčʻule's lengthy *Deeds of Grigol Xanżtʻeli*. Habo was an Arab perfumer who migrated to eastern Georgia, where he was martyred by the Arab administrator of eastern Georgia in 786. By contrast, Grigol Xanżtʻeli/Gregory of Khandzta was not a martyr. He founded several monastic complexes in Tao-Klarjetʻi in the eighth and ninth centuries. The contents of a few other surviving Georgian *vitae* are chronologically situated in late antiquity, but these were comprehensively reworked by medieval scribes and are therefore more valuable for later periods. For example, the Georgian *Life of Peter the Iberian* diverges substantially from the Syriac *vita* by John Rufus and exhibits signs of thorough rewriting (for a recent study of Peter, see Horn 2006). The extant Georgian recension conveys nothing about Peter's challenge to dyophyistism. Likewise, hagiographies celebrating the martyr Ražden, a fifth-century Iranian convert from Zoroastrianism, as well as the pious Thirteen Syrian Fathers were comprehensively rewritten in later times. The substantially revised *vita* of Davitʻ and Kostantine has been connected to a hypothesized Georgian-language chronicle of the sixth century, though this is far from certain (Sanaże and Araxamia 2013).

Thus, the earliest works of original Georgian literature were compact hagiographies whose basic purpose was the expansion and solidification of Christianity in Caucasia's cosmopolitan and cross-cultural atmosphere (translations in Lang 1976). The oldest were devoted to martyrs. In the medieval period, the focus shifted to prominent monks and other holy men. The religious nature of these initial specimens of Georgian literature is to be expected given the fourth-/fifth-century Christian provenance of *asomtʻavruli*, the first dedicated Georgian script. The hagiographies celebrating Šušanik, Evstatʻi, and the children of Kolay display no textual interdependence and concentrate narrowly upon their devout subjects. Collectively, they project a basic image of early Christian Kʻartʻli and its neighbors. These sources embody a nonethnocentric Christianity untouched by later obsessions with orthodoxy, heresy, and institutional autonomy. Hardened ethnolinguistic and confessional positions – which reinforced one another – are evident only from the seventh century, when autocephalous "national" churches began to crystallize among the Armenians, eastern Georgians, and Caucasian Albanians (for the period, see the *magnum opus* of Garsoïan 1999). As is exemplified in Gwrobandak's trek from Zoroastrian priest-in-waiting to Manichaean convert and then to expatriate Christian, the religious milieu of late antique Caucasia was plural, heterodox, and syncretic.

6.2 Christian K'art'li and the Iranian Commonwealth

Early Georgian hagiographies communicate no systematic persecutions of Christians by Sasanian officials and Zoroastrian *mowbed*s. While Gwrobandak-Evstat'i's death was ordered by the Sasanian *marzbān* headquartered in Tp'ilisi, this episode unfolded in the wake of lurid complaints registered by the local Iranian community. Despite the strong influence of Iran, escalating religious antagonism, and fierce imperial competition in strategic "borderlands" such as Caucasia, early Georgian hagiographies are remarkably ambivalent toward Iran and Zoroastrianism. Christian K'art'velians do not seem to have produced dedicated polemic against Zoroastrianism, as was the case in Armenia, e.g. Eznik Kołbac'i's *On God*.

Critical readings of the three earliest Georgian hagiographies expose the tight interconnection of Iran and Caucasia, a situation extending in some respects back to Achaemenid rule. As it had in earlier centuries, the social structure of late antique Caucasia resembled that of Iran, with great aristocratic houses and their hereditary prerogatives dominating the social landscape. Élites favored Iranian and Iranic names, which often had Zoroastrian backgrounds. Among K'art'velian royalty we encounter, for example, Mirian (Mihrān), Bak'ar (Bahkar/Pakur), Trdat (Tīrdād), P'arsman (Farsamana), Mirdat (Miϑradāta), and Vaxtang (cf. Vahrām/Bahrām and Vərəϑraɣna). More broadly, the Georgian language along with Armenian and probably Caucasian Albanian were studded with Iranian and Iranic terminology (Gippert 1993). Some Georgian words commonly used in Christian ecclesiastical settings – including *netari* (blessed < MPers. *nēttar*), *šaravandi* (consecration < MPers. **šahrawand*, cf. Arm. *ašxarawand*), and *tažari* (palace, temple < Parth. *tažar*) – were derived from Middle Iranian languages, sometimes *via armeniaca*, or developed in tandem with these tongues. Other manifestations of Caucasia's profound association with Iran include synchronisms in the *vitae* of Šušanik and Evstat'i pointing to the reigning *šāhan šāh* and not the Roman emperor. This convention is deployed in Georgian inscriptions – e.g. in the late fifth-century foundational inscription of Bolnisi

Sioni (Silogava 1994). It is also encountered in contemporaneous Armenian and Albanian sources as well.

On the whole, the earliest Georgian hagiographies are silent on the Roman Empire, the Roman emperor, and other Roman luminaries, institutions, and events. Indeed, across late antiquity, Romano-Byzantine influence and interventions in the inland Georgian districts were relatively minimal when compared to those emanating from Iran (cf. Furtwängler et al. 2008; Braund 1994). This is especially true before the reign of Heraclius and his march through Caucasia during his campaign against the Sasanians. At one point Heraclius stood before the citadel of Tpʻilisi. When the most ancient Georgian *vitae* evoke an imperial or large-scale cultural ("civilizational") context, they prioritized the familiar sociocultural world of Ērānšahr – what might be called the Iranian Commonwealth – to which peoples across the Caucasian isthmus had belonged since the Iron Age, including nomads such as the Alans/Ovsis in Northern Caucasia. The Irano-Caucasian nexus did not vanish as a result of public, royally sanctioned Christianization. Except for the Roman annexation of Armenian territories in eastern Anatolia, which were restructured socially and administratively along Roman lines (Adontz 1970), other Caucasian lands, including eastern Georgia and Persarmenia, preserved their traditional Iranian and especially Iranic institutions throughout the premodern epoch. In many cases Christianity was tailored to the existing Iranian/Iranic sociocultural pattern more than the other way around.

6.3 Conversion Stories and Acculturating Parthians

Beyond the hagiographical texts already surveyed, the first phase of original Georgian literature comprehends the earliest known Georgian-language account of the Christianization of Kʻartʻli: the seventh-century *Conversion of Kʻartʻli*. Although a manuscript of the thirteenth/fourteenth century associates a deacon named Grigol with the text's transmission (chapter 13, Abulaże, 86_{29-32}), the identity of the original author remains a mystery. The brevity of *The Conversion* is disproportionate to its significance. While the story it relates is valuable for reconstructing the Christianization of the Kʻartʻvelian monarchy, especially the baptism of King Mirian in 326 (for the date, see Patariże 2000), of equal importance is the deliberate repackaging of these events in the seventh century. The underlying narrative of the received tale is quite old; its contours are delimited by Rufinus, who wrote his *Ecclesiastical History* in Latin back around the year 400. Rufinus – in this case probably via the lost church history of Gelasius of Caesarea – repeats the testimony of the well-placed nobleman Bakur/Bacurius, heir to the independence-minded *bidaxšate* of the Armeno-Kʻartʻvelian marchlands. We possess no definitive evidence of the Kʻartʻvelian author of *The Conversion* having possessed direct knowledge of Rufinus and/or Gelasius. However, the same core story is found in both sources.

None of the earliest traditions of Kʻartʻli's conversion expressly mention Christianity's competition with specific faiths. The details of the story featuring a menacing and well-organized idolatry, first encountered in the longer *Life of Nino* of the ninth/tenth century, belong to a medieval effort to demonstrate the inherent autocephaly of the Kʻartʻvelian Church and the viability of a distinctive eastern Georgian society and monarchy. Accordingly, an autonomous Kʻartʻvelian Christianity had supplanted an autonomous Kʻartʻvelian polytheism.

Although it employs Iranic vocabulary and imagery akin to earlier Georgian hagiographies, *The Conversion of Kʻartʻli* represents a marked literary evolution. This is exemplified by the synchronism in its initial passage referring not only to "the days of King Constantine" but also to the Ascension of Christ (*Conversion of Kʻartʻli*, chapter 1). Iran and Iranians are afforded no role in this later textual monument to eastern Georgia's Christianization. *The Conversion*'s narrative purpose is to celebrate the good deeds of the holy woman Nino. Having migrated to Caucasia from Roman domains (Cappadocia in medieval traditions) with a group of female ascetics, Nino secured the conversion of Queen Nana and eventually of her reluctant husband, Mirian. (Foreigners are conspicuous in the history of early Christian Caucasia; King Mirian, Šušanik, Gwrobandak-Evstatʻi, and the later Thirteen Syrian Fathers and Habo were non-Georgians.) The chief function of the text is to establish the *autonomous* Christianization of the Kʻartʻvelians back in the early fourth century by creatively exploiting the cross-cultural traditions circulating in seventh-century Caucasia. As it happens, Nino's supposed companions, the holy women Hṙipʻsimē and Gaianē, are central characters in the conversion story of the Armenian King Trdat as conveyed by a cycle of texts associated with a fifth-century Armenian author called Agatʻangełos (< Gk. Agathangelos). While the historical Nino's attachment to this company of women cannot be authenticated, *The Conversion*'s author – or authors – certainly capitalized upon the regional popularity of Agatʻangełos. Simultaneously, the later Kʻartʻvelian writer was cautious to avoid any impression of the subordination of his church to its neighbors, especially the Armenians.

The timing of *The Conversion of Kʻartʻli* was not fortuitous. At the dawn of the seventh century, Heraclius's passage through eastern Georgia, the destabilization of the Sasanian Empire, and the Kʻartʻvelian Church's repudiation of the regional protectorate asserted by its Armenian counterpart contributed to a formal schism between the two ecclesiastical organizations. Following the condemnation of the K'art'velian Katholikos Kwrion at the Armenians' Third Council of Duin in 607, eastern Georgian prelates aligned themselves with the imperial Roman church to an unprecedented degree as they declared autocephaly. This entailed inter alia the silencing of lingering objections to the diophysite christology adopted at the Fourth Ecumenical Council of Chalcedon back in 451; the yet unrivaled, selective influx of Romano-Byzantine art and architecture; and the eventual replacement of the liturgy of Jerusalem with that of Constantinople. As the sun set on late antiquity, eastern Georgian Christianity's customary orientation toward Syria and the Holy Land, as well as toward Armenia and eastern Anatolia, was yielding to one looking toward Constantinople to an unprecedented degree.

The Conversion of K'art'li is the first Georgian religious text to feature a dynastic monarch. It is true that Varsk'en the *bidaxš* of Somxit'i/Gugark' is a central character in *The Passion of Šušanik* and that he imagined himself to wield royal authority (Rapp 2014a). But Varsk'en's literary role is to refute Christ and to inflict the brutalities leading to the martyrdom of his pious wife. Mirian (r. 284–361) at first resisted Nino's God; however, the king eventually entered the Christian fold after a miracle that transpired during an ill-fated royal hunt. Following Mirian's baptism and the alleged dispatch of "Greek" priests by none other than Constantine the Great, the swift conversion of his realm to Christianity is reported. By the end of the fourth century, Christianity was unquestionably achieving dominance with royal and aristocratic support throughout southern Caucasia. However, several written sources, including the *vita* of Abibos Nekreseli (one of the Thirteen Syrian Fathers credited with establishing monasticism in eastern Georgia in the sixth century), attest the tenacity of Caucasia's indigenous Zoroastrianisms and newly imported Sasanian variants. Material evidence includes the foundations of an impressive Zoroastrian temple at Nekresi below the monastic complex founded by Abibos. This site was still active in the fourth century. Accordingly, Christianization was a long-term, cross-cultural process. Moreover, local and newly reinvigorated Sasanian strains of Zoroastrianism did not suddenly vanish. Some Zoroastrian elements were Christianized, including sacral models of royal authority.

It soon became evident that the succinct *Conversion* could not compete with more sophisticated traditions, foreign and perhaps domestic. Some noble houses, including the *bidaxš*es of the Armeno-K'art'velian marchlands, may once have brandished their own oral and written conversion tales. Under two Byzantinizing forces, the Georgian Church and the royal Bagratid dynasty, *The Conversion* was superseded in the ninth/tenth century by the expanded *Life of Nino*. This latter work has remained the standard account of eastern Georgia's conversion to the present day.

The Conversion of Kʻartʻli might seem an important literary step toward the articulation of Georgian historiography. However, a new interpretation of early Georgian literature repositions the primary links of this literary chain to a lost historiographical tradition that was put into writing in the sixth century (Rapp 2014a). At the heart of this development are expatriate Parthian families who assimilated into the Caucasian aristocracy. The process commenced during Arsacid rule over the Parthian Empire and continued into the fourth century when Mirian, a young Parthian aristocrat, migrated to Kʻartʻli. There Mirian assumed royal authority and inaugurated the Xosroiani/Chosroid dynasty. Parthian migrants wove themselves inextricably into the social fabric of Caucasia. Several Parthian aristocratic branches acculturated, including Arsacids who sat on the thrones of Caucasia's three kingdoms. Significantly, the first monarchs of Armenia Major, Kʻartʻli, and Albania to embrace Christianity were acculturated or acculturating Parthians at the time the Sasanians governed Iran. Some Christian holy men and women also had Parthian backgrounds, including Gregory the Illuminator whose activities won the conversion of King Trdat, an Armenian Arsacid. The Parthian contribution to Caucasian history (and Caucasia's contribution to Parthian history!) was considerable and helps to account for the timing of Caucasia's royal conversions. With regards to the highest social stratae, women and men with Parthian backgrounds frequently stood at the vanguard of public conversion to Christianity in late antiquity.

6.4 The Dawn of Georgian Historiography: *Hambavi mepʻetʻa*

The Parthian presence throughout Caucasia had many long-term consequences. In early phases of late antiquity, prior to royal Christianization, Caucasia's Zoroastrianisms underwent momentous change. Acculturated Parthians were an energetic conduit for renewed linguistic dialogue between Caucasia and Iran. The period is characterized by an upsurge of Middle Iranian terminology. The invention of the three Caucasian scripts may have been inspired by scripts created for local languages in Iran toward the end of the Parthian Arsacid regime (Häberl 2006 for Mandaic). In addition, there was a literary dimension. Later Sasanians and their allies sponsored a self-promoting historiography. Eventually acquiring written form, the lost *Xwadāy-nāmag* is known principally through Islamic-era narratives such as Ferdowsī's eleventh-century *Šāhnāma*. *Xwadāy-nāmag* blended epic and history into a single story that presented the Sasanian dynasty as uniquely legitimate through its possession of royal *xwarrah*, its unparalleled magnanimity, and its station as the exclusive source of hero-kings. Originally intended to glorify the Sasanian family, the *Xwadāy-nāmag* was a living tradition to which others contributed, including the Parthian aristocracy clustered in Iran's northern districts.

Caucasia's Parthians contributed to the *Xwadāy-nāmag*, though in an unconventional way. Acculturated Parthians in eastern Georgia, along with other noble elements likewise embedded in Iranian culture, created their own epic-history paralleling the *Xwadāy-nāmag*. Although its oldest form is lost, the sixth-century *Hambavi mepʻetʻa* profoundly influenced Georgian historical literature between the eighth and tenth centuries (Rapp 2014a). At the beginning of this period, whole passages from *Hambavi mepʻetʻa* were absorbed into historiographical texts. It should be stressed that *Hambavi mepʻetʻa* is not a Georgian translation or close adaptation of the Iranian *Xwadāy-nāmag*. Although it incorporates personalities and events of the *Xwadāy-nāmag* (especially for remote eras, such as Farīdūn, Īrāj, Key Kāvus, Farīburz, Siyāwaxš, and Key Xusrō), *Hambavi mepʻetʻa* is an original Georgian composition paralleling the structure and purpose of its Iranian analogue. For instance, the first monarch of the Kʻartʻvelians, Pʻarnavaz (r. 299–234 BCE), is presented as a foundational king akin to the primordial Iranian monarchs acclaimed in the *Šāhnāma* and its antecedents. As the royal architect of his society, Pʻarnavaz is imputed with the establishment of the dynastic monarchy, an administrative apparatus based on officials called *eristʻavi*s, and the invention of the Georgian script (or at least the introduction of literacy). The Greco-Roman Mediterranean plays a far less important political and cultural role than the Iranian Commonwealth in late antique historiography, in terms of both narrative content and historiographical structure. This is but one index of Georgia's intimate membership in the Iranian cultural world.

Though lost, extensive remnants of *Hambavi mepʻetʻa* lie at the heart of two Georgian histories composed between ca. 790 and 813. *The Life of the Kʻartʻvelian Kings*, the longest premodern narrative devoted to eastern Georgia's "pagan" history, is customarily but erroneously ascribed to the eleventh-century archbishop Leonti Mroveli (Rapp 2003, 157–163). Mroveli was not the original author but a creative medieval editor who also inserted several notices from Judaeo-Christian antiquity. The bulk of *The Life of the Kings* derives from *Hambavi mepʻetʻa*. It celebrates the pre-Christian kings of Kʻartʻli and the foundations of their power: dynastic right, possession of *xwarrah*, special attachment to the realm's polytheism (whose core was, in fact, a hybrid Zoroastrianism), and aptitude in combat as hero-kings who were buttressed by titanic champions called *bumberazi*s. The particular manner in which *The Life of the Kings* conveys these attributes was directly inspired by the late antique *Hambavi mepʻetʻa*; this, in turn, parallels the Iranian epic tradition.

6.5 Christian History in Iranic Colors

Similar Iranic imagery is applied to *Christian* K'art'velian kings in the ca. 800 *Life of Vaxtang Gorgasali*. Following brief treatments of his Chosroid grandfather and father, Arč'il (r. 411–435) and Mirdat V (r. 435–447), the narrative concentrates on the long reign of Vaxtang Gorgasali (Vakhtang I, r. 447–522). Vaxtang's royal biography is the first extant Georgian historiographical source to focus on a solitary ruler; it also contains the richest Georgian-language accounts of the single combat characterizing the epic-histories of the Iranian Commonwealth. The model of Iranic kingship articulated in *The Life of the Kings* is repeated in *The Life of Vaxtang* with a noteworthy exception: After Mirian's fourth-century conversion, certain Christian images were inserted into the existing Iranic conception of royal authority. The Christian Vaxtang is presented as one of the *bumberazi*s of old, joyfully entering into single combat against a variety of gigantic adversaries, including, we are told, a (Christian) Roman *logothetēs* named Polycarpus. But the religious context has changed: Vaxtang credits his victories to the Christian God. At the same time, as a king ruling in the Iranian cultural world, Vaxtang never engages Iranian champions in single contests and even has Zoroastrian Iranian *bumberazi*s under his command.

The early Christian kings of K'art'li did not embrace the central tenets of eastern Roman imperial ideology. Crucial among these were Roman republicanism and Eusebius's theory of Christian kingship, the basic premise of which prevailed in the Romano-Byzantine Empire for a thousand years (for the former, see Kaldellis 2015). Instead, K'art'velian monarchs developed their own paradigm, which synthesized traditional Iranic elements with (Judaeo-) Christian ones. The creative fusion of traditions is illustrated by the claimed descent of the Christian Chosroids from Nimrod. As was the case elsewhere in the Near East, the biblical hunter was reimagined as the initiator of potent kingship upon the Earth and as the first monarch of Iran (Rapp 2014b). Although the tenor of Vaxtang's interaction with the Sasanian Empire was highly variable (in moments of tension with the Christian Romans, the Iranians sometimes attempted to shatter the K'art'velian kings' attachment to Christianity), words are put into Vaxtang's mouth applauding Zoroastrianism as an honorable faith. The Christian hero-king even comes to the defense of Zoroastrianism: "Although the Iranians are not in the true religion yet they know God the Creator and believe in the spiritual life" (Qauxč'išvili 1955, p. 193 = Thomson 1996, p. 209).

A third Georgian-language historiographical narrative was produced around the year 800. The untitled continuation of *The Life of Vaxtang* is usually credited to a certain Juanšer Juanšeriani, although there are sound reasons to reject this attribution. Pseudo-Juanšer treats the period from the reign of Vaxtang's son and successor Dačʻi (r. 522–534) through that of St. Arčʻil (r. 736–786), the Chosroid prince of Kaxetʻi/Kakheti. Often lacking the Iranic disposition of *The Life of the Kings* and *The Life of Vaxtang*, this text engages the transition from late antiquity to the medieval age, including the final war waged by the Sasanians and Romans, Muḥammad and the ascendancy of Islam, and the ruin of the Sasanian Empire. The royalist writer reports the suppression of the Kʻartʻvelian monarchy by the Sasanians around 580 and covers the initial phase of the interregnum, which stretched to the late ninth century.

Like the *vitae* produced in late antique Georgia, historiographical works celebrating the monarchy situate the Kʻartʻvelian and larger Caucasian experience principally within an Iranian – and not Romano-Byzantine – matrix. This said, Pseudo-Juanšer displays a relatively greater knowledge of Byzantium. When previous Georgian historiography evokes the Roman Empire, references tend to be short, vague, and devoid of historical veracity. Sometimes they have been manipulated so as to nudge the Kʻartʻvelians onto the center stage of Afro-Eurasian history. Accordingly, *The Life of the Kings* casts Constantine's conversion as a desperate reaction to an Irano-Kʻartʻvelian invasion, and *The Life of Vaxtang* reports Vaxtang's successful assault on Roman Anatolia (Qauxčʻišvili 1955, pp. 69–70). Once again, the political and cultural framework deployed by early Kʻartʻvelian historians was the Iranian and not the Romano-Byzantine world.

Hambavi mepʻetʻa's influence extends to the succinct historiographical components of another literary corpus called *Mokʻcʻevay kʻartʻlisay*, literally "The Conversion of Kʻartʻli." This compendium features its namesake seventh-century text and the longer *Life of Nino*, composed in the ninth/tenth century. Four short historiographical accounts, often no more than king lists, supply rudimentary background. *The Primary History of Kʻartʻli* and the three *Royal Lists* show signs of having drawn upon the late antique *Hambavi mepʻetʻa*. But in these cases, *Hambavi mepʻetʻa* was handled not as a model to be emulated but as a storehouse of information. Thus, *Mokʻcʻevay kʻartʻlisay*'s four brief narratives mostly lack Iranic trappings and explicit acknowledgments of Caucasia's Iranian orientation. However, not all such imagery was curbed. Sometimes the Iranian and Iranic names of the early kings of Kʻartʻli are more accurately preserved in the historiographical components of *Mokʻcʻevay kʻartʻlisay* than they are in the densely Iranic *Life of the Kings* and *Life of Vaxtang*. Common indebtedness to the *Hambavi mepʻetʻa* tradition accounts for the similarities of *The Life of the Kings* and *The Life of Vaxtang*, on the one hand, and *The Primary History* and three *Royal Lists*, on the other. But differences, including divergent traditions about the first king of K'art'li in the early Hellenistic period, also imply *Hambavi mep'et'a*'s existence in more than one recension and simultaneous rendition in oral and written forms.

In their received states, vestiges of the lost *Hambavi mep'et'a* are thus transmitted through several filters. As a cohesive text, *Hambavi mep'et'a* fell from favor in the eighth and ninth centuries and vanished in the twilight of late antiquity. Notwithstanding its removal from the literary canon, *Hambavi mep'et'a*'s historiographical approach, vocabulary, imagery, and, in some cases, whole passages were absorbed into the ca. 800 *The Life of the Kings* and *The Life of Vaxtang*. Then, in the eleventh century, during the heyday of the medieval Bagratids, Archbishop Leonti Mroveli gathered existing Georgian historiographies and assembled what may have been the first iteration of *K'art'lis c'xovreba* (*Kartlis Tskhovreba*), the compendium commonly but inaccurately termed "the Georgian Chronicles." Mroveli re-edited existing accounts, homogenizing their narratives and stripping them of overt Iranian, Iranic, and Zoroastrian elements. It was probably Mroveli who discarded the original treatment of Mirian's reign – which must have been distinguished by a strong Iranic flavor – with one downplaying Mirian's cultural association with Iran. Further, Mroveli injected several Judaeo-Christian notices into the pre-Christian section of *The Life of the Kings*. Unfortunately, all of the manuscripts from this time are lost. What have reached us are Georgian manuscripts copied at the end of the fifteenth century and thereafter. However, a late thirteenth-century redaction of an Armenian-language adaptation of *K'art'lis c'xovreba*, called *Patmut'iwn Vrac'* or *History of the Georgians*, demonstrates the stability of the corpus's constituent texts throughout the medieval era.

Early Georgian literature exhibits continuities with the past and innovations pointing to the future. Particularly important was the acceptance and promotion of Christianity by the crown, which enabled the unprecedented growth of the religion throughout eastern Georgia and contributed to the displacement of polytheistic faiths, especially local Zoroastrianisms. Clearly, Christianization did not result in the obliteration of Caucasia's entrenched Iranic culture and opulent Iranian heritage. In many respects, Christianity was grafted onto existing cultural and social structures that belonged foremost to the Iranian world. In instances of blatant incompatibility, including but by no means limited to the religious bases of K'art'velian royal authority, Christianity trumped Zoroastrianism. But symbols and conventions with stout Zoroastrian backgrounds could be perpetuated. One such example is the "spread wings" motif regularly adorning late antique and early medieval Caucasian crosses (Compareti 2010). All the while, early Georgian hagiographical and historiographical literature communicates a muted knowledge of the Roman Empire and its institutions and luminaries. K'art'li's traditional orientation toward the Iranian Commonwealth thus remained fundamentally intact through Christianization, beyond the collapse of Sasanian power, and even well into the early medieval epoch, at which time *The Life of the Kings* and *The Life of Vaxtang* attained their familiar forms.

Finally, it must be emphasized that the value of early Georgian historiographical literature rests not in its "hard facts" – its literal recollection of what "actually happened" – but in the contemporaneous values, attitudes, and orientations saturating its narratives. Accordingly, texts like *The Life of the Kings* and *The Life of Vaxtang* open unique windows into late antiquity and are poignant reminders that a Christian society need not be a fundamentally Romano-Byzantine one, despite the rhetoric emanating from Constantinople and modern Mediterranean-privileging scholarship (for the former, see Haldon 2016). Indeed, the experience of Caucasia demonstrates that late antiquity was a cross-cultural enterprise stretching across not only the Mediterranean but the Black, Caspian, and Red Seas as well.

REFERENCES

Adontz, Nicholas with Nina G. Garsoïan. (1970). *Armenia in the Period of Justinian: The Political Conditions of the Naxarar System*. Lisbon: Calouste Gulbenkian Foundation.

Bowersock, G.W., Brown, Peter, and Grabar, Oleg. ed. (1999). *Late Antiquity: A Guide to the Postclassical World*. Cambridge, MA: Belknap Press of Harvard University Press.

Braund, David. (1994). *Georgia in Antiquity: A History of Colchis and Transcaucasian Iberia, 550 BC–AD 562*. Oxford: Clarendon Press.

Canepa, Matthew P. (2009). *The Two Eyes of the Earth: Art and Ritual of Kingship between Rome and Sasanian Iran*. Berkeley: University of California Press.

Childers, Jeff W. (2013). The Georgian version of the New Testament. In: *The Text of the New Testament in Contemporary Research: Essays on the* Status Quaestionis (ed. Bart D. Ehrman and Michael W. Holmes). 2nd ed., 293–327. Leiden–Boston: Brill.

Compareti, Matteo. (2010). The spread wings motif on Armenian steles: Its meaning and parallels in Sasanian art. *Iran and the Caucasus* 14: 201–232.

Conversion of K'art'li. (1963). In: *Mok'c'evay k'art'lisay*, in Żveli k'art'uli agiograp'iuli literaturis żeglebi (ed. Ilia Abulaże), vol. 2, 83–91. T'bilisi: Sak'art'velos ssr mec'nierebat'a akademiis gamomc'emloba.

Furtwängler, A., Gagoshidze, I., Löhr, H. et al. ed. (2008). *Iberia and Rome: The Excavations of the Palace at Dedoplis Gora and the Roman Influence in the Caucasian Kingdom of Iberia*. Langenweißbach: Beier & Beran.

Gamqreliże, Tʻamaz. (1989). *Ceris anbanuri sistema da żveli kʻartʻuli damcerloba.* Tʻbilisi: Tʻbilisis universitetis gamomcʻemloba. Translation: Thomas V. Gamkrelidze (1994). *Alphabetic Writing and the Old Georgian Script: A Typology and Provenience of Alphabetic Writing Systems.* Delmar, NY: Caravan Books.

Garsoïan, Nina. (1999). *L'eglise arménienne et le grand schisme d'Orient.* Corpus Scriptorum Christianorum Orientalium, vol. 574, sub., vol. 100. Louvain: In Aedibus Peeters.

Gippert, Jost. (1993). *Iranica Armeno-Iberica: Studien zu den iranischen Lehnwörtern im Armenischen und Georgischen.* Österreichische Akademie der Wissenschaften philosophisch-historische Klasse, Sitzungberichte, vol. 606. Vienna: Österreichische Akademie der Wissenschaften.

Häberl, Charles G. (2006). Iranian scripts for Aramaic languages: The origin of the Mandaic script. *Bulletin of the American Schools of Oriental Research* 341: 53–62.

Haldon, John. (2016). *The Empire That Would Not Die: The Paradox of Eastern Roman Survival, 640–740.* Cambridge, MA: Harvard University Press.

Horn, Cornelia B. (2006). *Asceticism and Christological Controversy in Fifth-Century Palestine: The Career of Peter the Iberian.* Oxford: Oxford University Press.

Johnson, Scott Fitzgerald. ed. (2012). *The Oxford Handbook of Late Antiquity.* Oxford: Oxford University Press.

Kaldellis, Anthony. (2015). *The Byzantine Republic: People and Power in New Rome.* Cambridge, MA: Harvard University Press.

Lang, David Marshall. (1976). *Lives and Legends of the Georgian Saints.* rev. ed. Crestwood, NY: St. Vladimir's Seminary Press.

Life of the Kings. (1955). In: *Kʻartʻlis cʻxovreba* (ed. S. Qauxčʻišvili), 3–71. Tʻbilisi: Saxelgami.

Life of Vaxtang. (1955). In: *Kʻartʻlis cʻxovreba* (ed. S. Qauxčʻišvili), 139–204. Tʻbilisi: Saxelgami.

Menabde, Levan. (1961 and 1980). *Żveli kʻartʻuli mcerlobis kerebi.* 2 vols. Tʻbilisi: Tʻbilisis universitetis gamomcʻemloba.

Mgaloblishvili, Tamila and Rapp Jr., Stephen H. (2011). Manichaeism in late antique Georgia? In: *"In Search of Truth": Augustine, Manichaeism and Other Gnosticism: Studies for Johannes van Oort at Sixty* (ed. Jacob Albert van den Berg, Annemaré Kotzé, Tobias Nicklas et al.), 263–90. Leiden and Boston: Brill.

Patariże, Lela. (2000). Kʻartʻveltʻa gakʻristianeba 'kʻartʻlis cʻxovrebis' mixedvitʻ. In: *Kʻristianoba sakʻartʻveloši (istoriul-etʻnologiuri gamokvleveni)*, 8–16. Tʻbilisi: n.p.

Rapp Jr., Stephen H. (2003). *Studies in Medieval Georgian Historiography: Early Texts and Eurasian Contexts*, Corpus Scriptorum Christianorum Orientalium, vol. 601, sub., vol. 113. Louvain: In Aedibus Peeters.

Rapp Jr., Stephen H. (2014a). *The Sasanian World through Georgian Eyes: Caucasia and the Iranian Commonwealth in Late Antique Georgian Literature.* Aldershot: Ashgate.

Rapp Jr., Stephen H. (2014b). The Georgian Nimrod. In: *The Armenian Apocalyptic Tradition: A Comparative Perspective: Essays Presented in Honor of Professor Robert*

W. *Thomson on the Occasion of His Eightieth Birthday* (ed. Kevork Bardakjian and Sergio La Porta), 188–216. Leiden and Boston: Brill.

Rayfield, Donald. (1994). *The Literature of Georgia: A History.* Oxford: Clarendon Press.

Russell, James R. (1987). *Zoroastrianism in Armenia.* Cambridge, MA: Harvard University Department of Near Eastern Languages and Civilizations.

Sanaże, Manana and Araxamia, Goneli. (2013). *VI s. istoriuli k'ronika „davit' da kostantines camebaši".* T'bilisi: Sak'art'velos universitetis gamomc'emloba.

Silogava, Valeri. (1994). *Bolnisis užvelesi k' art' uli carcerebi* (The Oldest Georgian Inscriptions of Bolnisi). T'bilisi: Mec'niereba.

Thomson, Robert W. (1996). *Rewriting Caucasian History: The Medieval Armenian Adaptation of the Georgian Chronicles.* Oxford: Clarendon Press.

Toumanoff, Cyril. (1963). *Studies in Christian Caucasian History.* Washington, DC: Georgetown University Press.

CHAPTER SEVEN

Middle Persian (Pahlavi)

Touraj Daryaee

Sometime in the ninth century, several important Zoroastrian priests, Adūrbād ī Ēmēdān, Adūrbād ī Farroxzādān, and Zādspram ī Gošanjām, wrote down the teachings of the Mazdean (Zoroastrian) religion for posterity (Boyce 1968, p. 44). Why did they decide to put to pen the tradition of the preceding sages at this time in the history of the Near East? There are a few possible reasons for such a monumental writing and rewriting of the Zoroastrian tradition in Middle Persian in the ninth and the tenth centuries CE. First, there was the loss of adherents of the Good Religion in the face of Islamic expansion. With the Abbasid Caliphate, the idea of what may be called "Persianate Islam" had taken hold and become a vehicle for the spread of the new religion throughout the Iranian Plateau and Central Asia (Eastern Iranian World) and beyond. It can be argued that by the year 1000 CE, approximately the same time that Christianity became the dominant religion in Europe, Islam had become dominant on the Iranian Plateau and the Iranian World (Daryaee 2015, pp. 111–112). Second, a number of religious movements, a mélange of Iranian and Semitic, had begun, as well as other nativist movements that brought new ideas at odds with the established Zoroastrianism of the Sasanian period (224–651 CE) (Crone 2012). These Zoroastrian priests were living at a turning point in the history of the region and of the Iranian people, and it seems that there was a need to put on paper what had come to pass, to etch in the minds of their coreligionists what had happened in the past as well as rules and regulations, so that they would not be forgotten. There was also a need for a defense not only against the newly

---

A Companion to Late Antique Literature, First Edition.
Edited by Scott McGill and Edward J. Watts.
© 2018 John Wiley & Sons, Inc. Published 2018 by John Wiley & Sons, Inc.

dominant religion of Islam and older religions such as Christianity but also against what were deemed heretical religious movements in the eighth and the ninth century CE (Daryaee 2016, pp. 136–137).

Thus, when we refer to Pahlavi literature in late antiquity we are speaking of a body of texts written in Middle Persian from roughly the third century to the eleventh century CE. The Aramaic script in different forms was used to write the Middle Persian texts (Weber 2003a), and writings are found from Egypt to China, be it on papyri, parchment, leather, textile, ostraca, or paper (Weber 1992, 2003b). The earliest remains are Pahlavi writings on rock from the time of the founder of the Sasanian Empire, Ardaxšīr I (224–240 CE) at Naqš-e Rostam, as well as his coins and those of his father and brother. They are short but loaded in meaning and ideology. The Sasanian king claims that he is the king of kings of the Iranians and that he is born of the seed of the gods. By the time of the second ruler Šāpūr I (240–270 CE), Pahlavi inscriptions become longer and a narrative is provided that draws from both the oral and written tradition from the Achaemenid period, in contact with the religious literature of the Iranian world.

Pahlavi inscriptions are mainly from the third and the fourth centuries CE and were commissioned by the kings and by the high priest, Kerdīr. They are formulaic in structure and their compositions resemble Achaemenid inscriptions. Some have suggested that this was part of the oral literary tradition that was prevalent in ancient Persia and used by the writers of the inscriptions and texts (Shayegan 2012; Huyse 1990; Skjærvø 1985). The later Sasanian inscriptions (post fourth century) are rarely royal, are shorter, and are commissioned by individuals or local lords for remembrance, building campaigns, and funerary dedications which are much shorter. The script used for the inscriptions represents the archaic version of the Aramaic script. This may be a continuation of a tradition that was first developed by the Achaemenids for their royal chancery. The characters are written separately from right to left, while the later inscriptions are almost Arabesque-like and the letters are joined and much more cursive. This is similar to the Book Pahlavi or Middle Persian texts that were written in the late Sasanian and post-Sasanian period.

The content of the early inscriptions is boastful, and the structure is such that first the king makes sure that it is known that he is a Zoroastrian (*Māzdēsn* = worshipper of Mazda). His genealogy is given next, and then the territories under his rule. A narrative story often follows, as in the case of Šāpūr's Naqsh-e Rostam inscription (Huyse 1999; Back 1978) in which there is a story of the defeat of the Romans and what became of them as a result of their aggression. By the middle of the inscription, the boastful nature of the king and his epic actions is evident. This seeking after heroism is also apparent from a short inscription of Šāpuūr at Hājjīābād, where he tells us that he has shot an arrow that has gone very far and dares anyone else to do the same (MacKenzie 1978). This resembles the tale of the great Iranian archer, Arash, whose feats were remembered and recited in Eastern Iran. Thus we already can see traces of Persian epic on the third-century inscriptions (Daryaee 2014).

The other long inscription is that of Narsē from the fourth century CE. This begins in the same way as Šāpūr's, although Narsē's concern is to justify his taking of the throne from Wahrām, king of the Sakas. Narsē plays the dualism of Zoroastrianism very well in this period, portraying himself as just and the forces of Wahrām and his accomplice Wahnām, son of Tatrus, as purveyors of falsehood. He tells us his election was the result of the grandees' election of him over his opponent, when they met him and asked him to become the King of Kings (Shayegan 2012; Skjærvø 1985, p. 54).

After Narsē in the fourth century, the economy of the inscriptions gives us very little historical information, with the exception of the time of Šāpūr II. The subject of the two inscriptions at the time of Šāpūr II is quite valuable and interesting for several reasons. Both of these inscriptions were commissioned by local kings at Persepolis, one by the king of the Sakas, Šāpūr Sagānšāh and the other by a Seleukos the scribe. These inscriptions reveal the territorial extent of the Sasanian Empire in the fourth century, the local administrative and military apparatus of the Sasanian kings, and finally the importance of Persepolis for the Sasanians.

Mihr-Narseh, who was the grand Wazīr or minister *Wuzurg-framādār* in the fifth century (Henning 1954), has left a short inscription by a bridge that he commissioned for the sake of his and his son's souls. The inscription attests to the Zoroastrian conception of building for salvation in this period, be it a common person or a grand Wazīr (Henning 1954, p. 101). By the end of the Sasanian and the beginning of the early Islamic period several small private inscriptions exist. The most prominent include the two inscriptions at Maqsūd Abād. These deal with the owner of a piece of land, its well, and reconstruction of castles. Other inscriptions have been found in Byzantium (de Blois 1990) and east in India (West 1880) and as far as China (Harmatta 1971).

Written Pahlavi texts, meanwhile, begin to appear in the fifth century and become more common in the sixth. The first texts are the *Zabūr* or Psalms, which are translations of Biblical texts into Middle Persian (Andreas and Barr 1933; Gignoux 2002). The internal evidence demonstrates that they were translations from Syriac by authors whose primary language was Persian (Skjærvø 1983, pp. 47–62). In the second half of the fifth century CE, the Catholicos Aqāq translated a summary of the Christian religion from Syriac into Middle Persian for the Sasanian king of Kings, Kawād I (Sims-Williams 2011).

There is also evidence of translation of the *Book of Enoch* and other Christian apocryphal works, as well as other hymns that suggest the importance and number of the Christian community in Persia.

Pahlavi texts (Cereti 2001; Macuch 2009) are mainly the product of Zoroastrian priestly writing, and so they are colored by a religious outlook. Still, we do find what may be called "secular" texts that give us a view of the rich literary heritage that once existed in late antiquity (Utas 1979). We can securely believe that there was a larger amount of Middle Persian literature in various genres, but because of the hardships faced by the Zoroastrian community throughout the ages, only those books that were of utmost importance for the religion and communal solidarity were copied by the priests. Personal choice and taste were also to preserve some of the rarer texts that do survive. Different genres are represented among the surviving texts. We will divide this large corpus into the following categories: commentaries on the Avesta (*zand*); philosophical and debate texts; apocalyptic texts; didactic texts (*Rivāyat* texts or *andarz*); geographical and epic texts; legal texts (*dādīg*); cultural texts; and dictionaries (*frahang*).

7.1 Commentary on the *Avesta*

By far the largest group of texts are commentaries and elaborations on the Zoroastrian holy text, which was given final written form in the sixth century CE, probably during the reign of Khusro I and his high priest Weh-Šāpūr (Andrés-Toledo 2015). Here the chief priest or the Mowbedān Mowbed at the council of Khusro I established the 21 *nask*s (chapters/sections) of the *Avesta* (Vevaina 2015, p. 227). Of the 21 *nask*s, most are now lost, but it is the *Zand* or Middle Persian commentaries that give us information on the lost portion of the *Avesta*. However, their content and the manner in which the authors of the Pahlavi commentaries discuss them is difficult to comprehend. What seems to have taken place, according to Y. S.-D. Vevaina, is that the exegetical narrative in the Pahlavi texts is woven into a new textual narrative. The Pahlavi authors appear to have been giving new meanings to the sacred texts, and at the same time to have been using myth, epic, and legal metaphors to make them understandable (Vevaina 2010, pp. 228–229).

The major text that is important for the understanding of the Zoroastrian worldview is the *Bundahišn* (The Book of Primal Creation), first compiled in the Sasanian period and then added to it in the early Islamic period, last compiled by Farrbay, the son of Ašwahišt, (Anklesaria 1956). In the preface to the text, the scribe mentions that he is redacting these Zoroastrian teachings in a time of hardship, when the number of adherents is dwindling in the face of conversion to Islam. Hence what we can gain from this text is a sense of urgency on the part of the priest to hand down what he thought was most important for the preservation of the good religion. The text provides a catalog of learning: material on cosmology and cosmogony; a good deal of information on deities and demons; and an encyclopedia of botany, zoology, ethnography, geography, and history.

The other copious work is the *Dēnkard* (Acts of Religion). This is another encyclopedic work, at times written in a difficult and cryptic language (Sanjana 1916; West 2013a). The *Dēnkard* originally was composed in nine books, where books one and two have been lost (Gignoux 2001). Book three is concerned with a host of issues, from the composition of human body to opinions regarding church and state in the Sasanian period (de Menasce 1973). Here one finds the famous Persian dictum of the inseparability of church and state, which still rings true in the religious circles: *hād xwadāyīh dēn ud dēn xwadāyīh...pad awēšān xwadāyīh abar dēn ud dēn abar xwadāyīh winnārdagīh* "Know that kingship is religion and religion is kingship...for them kingship is arranged based on religion and religion based on kingship" (*Dēnkard*, 470). Book four has been called the Book of Manners or Customs *ēwēn-nāmag* and is perhaps the most difficult book, since it deals with not only the history of the sacred texts but also Greek and Indic science, which will be dealt with below. Book five begins with a series of questions put forth by a nonbeliever to a Zoroastrian sage, and it deals with different issues, especially the idea of *xwēdodāh* or consanguineous marriages (Amuzegār and Tafazzolī 2001; West 2013b). Book six may be called a Book of Counsel *Andarz-nāmag* (Shaked 1979), while book seven particularly deals with the story of Zoroaster, from his birth to his death (Molé 1967; Amuzegār and Tafazzolī 2001). Book eight is important because it is a description of the contents of the 21 *nask*s of the *Avesta*. Each *nask* is named and its contents are briefly mentioned, while book nine concentrates on three *nask*s (West 1897). There are other encyclopedic works such as the *Wīzīdagīhā ī Zādsparam* (The Selections of Zādsparam) (Gignoux and Tafazzolī 1993; Rashid 1366 [Rašēd Mohassel 1987]). The other important body of texts is known as the *Pahlavī Rivāyat*s, which are concerned with legal precepts as well as history, mythical creatures, and customs (Tafazzolī 1998, pp. 153–155). These legal texts give us some understanding of Zoroastrian life in late antiquity, drawn from the *Avesta*, which can in turn be compared with (contemporaneous?) Christian and Jewish legal texts such as that of the Syriac *Law Book of Yišoboxt* and the *Babylonian Talmud* (Mokhtarian 2015).

7.2 Philosophical and Debate Texts

Several texts in Middle Persian, mainly from the eighth and ninth centuries CE, represent the end stage of Middle Persian literature. The *Draxt ī Asūrīg* (The Assyrian Tree) is outstanding in its content and antiquity in its genre (Brunner 1980). The vocabulary of the text suggests its Parthian antecedents and its content Mesopotamian influence. This text presents a debate between a date tree and a goat, typical of the ancient Mesopotamian debate poetry that was read during banquets. The debate is about which of these two (date/goat) is more useful. Other texts are from the early Islamic period, such as the important *Škand ī Gūmānīg Wīzār* (Doubt Dispelling Explanation), which asserts the supremacy of Zoroastrian theology and the deficiency of such religions as those of the Fatalists (*Dahris*), Manichaeans, Christians, Jews, and Muslims (de Menasce 1945). The author systematically tackles the tenets of these religions and sometimes quotes verbatim from the holy texts of these religious traditions. The method of argumentation is also noteworthy in that it resembles the analytical method of debate known in Islamic Theology (*'Ilm al-Kalam*) and may have been influenced by that tradition of Islamic thought and literature, most probably as a result of contact with the Mu'tazila. *Gizistag Abāliš* (The Accursed Abāliš) (Chacha 1936) is a short text about the debate between Abāliš, who appears to be a heretic or atheist, the Zoroastrian high priest, and Jewish, Christian, and Muslim theologians at the court of the Caliph Ma'mūn in the ninth century CE. The last text has survived in its Pazand form (Middle Persian written in the Avestan script). The text known as *Pus ī Dāneš Kāmag* (The Youth in Desire of Knowledge) is written in the same vein as the *Škand ī Gumānīg Wīzār*, but there is little reference to the Islamic period. The work is concerned with Zoroastrian matters, such as the reason for wearing the sacred belt, the *kustīg*.

7.3 Apocalyptic and Visionary Texts

This genre of Middle Persian literature is the most interesting of the Pahlavi corpus. These texts predict the way in which the world will come to an end and the fate of the people and that of *Ērānšahr*, the empire of the Sasanians. First, however, there is an important visionary text, the *Ardā Wirāz Nāmag* (The Book of Righteous Wirāz), which is about the journey of a righteous man, Wirāz, to heaven and hell; it may be compared with Dante's famous work, the *Divina Commedia*. Not only is the journey itself interesting, but the preparation for the journey into paradise and hell by Wirāz also gives us a sense of ritual initiation in late antique Iran. Having been properly cleansed and laid on a bed, he is given a concoction of hemp called *mang ī wištāsp* "hemp of Wištāsp," which enables him to make the journey (Vahman 1986). *Ardā Wirāz Nāmag* was seemingly a didactic as well as a visionary text, as Zoroastrians read the text to understand and learn how and by which acts one ends up in heaven, hell, or what is known in Pahlavi as *hamīstagān* (limbo or purgatory). The reference to Alexander of Macedon as an Egyptian is unique in the corpus of Middle Persian literature; it suggests a late antique, perhaps a Sasanian, vision of the past.

In the apocalyptic text *Zand ī Wahman Yasn* (The Commentary of the Wahman Yasn), Zoroaster is given the *xrad ī harwisp āgāhīh* (Wisdom of complete knowledge) by means of Ohrmazd, which is poured as water into his hands for him to drink; the water induces seven days and nights of dreaming, as in the case of Wirāz. Zoroaster is able to see the future in a mysterious form (a tree with seven trunks), which is explained to him to be seven eras (in another part of the text, there are four eras that sound very much like Hesiod's division in the *Theogony*). These eras span the beginning of Zoroastrianism to the time of the Turkic conquest of Persia (Cereti 1995).

These texts predict the fate of the Zoroastrians: They will face hardships and will only achieve supremacy at the end of the world, when sinners will be punished and those Zoroastrians who have endured hardship will go to heaven, which Wirāz had seen and had described to believers. The apocalyptic nature of the text is clear, as the majority of the text discusses calamities both natural and man-made. The sun becomes motionless, while a host of evil forces attack, and it is through the intervention of the deities and Iranian heroes that the suffering stops. Interestingly, the Romans (Byzantines) appear in the apocalyptic vision as invaders, as do the Huns from the other side of the Iranian world. The fifth-century Sasanian king Wahrām Gur stands as a vanquisher of heresy, while Wahrām ī Warzāwand (The Miraculous Wahrām), who may be the son of Yazdgerd III, comes to save the day (Cereti 1996). There are few personages who are given the power to look into the future by means of hallucinogens, such as Zoroaster, King Wištāsp, his minister Jāmāsp, and Wirāz. One must also mention Kerdīr, whose inscription suggests his campaign be included into the host of righteous personages who were able to make the journey (Daryaee 2001).

The *Jāmāsp Nāmag* is another one of these texts (Agostini 2013). Again, Jāmāsp is endowed with a vision of what is to come. As in the *Zand ī Wahman Yasn*, the text describes a great deal of natural and political disasters until the saviors appear, and men and women arise from the dead to be judged. There is a strong historical dimension to the text: Iranian history according to the Zoroastrian tradition is given; the Sasanians receive a full genealogy; and an account of their rule extends to the arrival of the Arabs, who come from the lineage of the demon of Wrath (Xēšm) (Agostini 2013, pp. 108–109).

7.4 Didactic Texts

A large amount of Pahlavi texts attempts to elucidate matters relating to the Zoroastrian tradition. They either are known as *Rivāyat* texts or *andarz* (wise sayings). A noteworthy example of a *Rivayat* text is the *Dādestān ī Dēnīg* (Jaafari-Dehaghi 1998), an important encyclopedic text full of history, myth, and practical advice on how to live. The *Epistles of Manūščihr* (Dhabhar 1912), meanwhile, present a series of questions and answers on how and what priests and people should do in life. The *Rivāyats*, however, are the most enduring type of literature in the Zoroastrian tradition, written not only in Pahlavi but also later in Persian. They include the *Pahlavi Rivāyats Accompanying the Dādestān ī Dēnīg* (Williams 1990) and the *Rivāyat ī Emēd ī Ašawahištān* (Safa-Isfahani 1980), as well as the *Pahlavi Rivāyat of Adurfranbay* (Anklesaria 1969; Rezā'ī Bāgh-Bīdī 2005). *Wīzādagīhā ī Zadspram* is an interesting text in the same genre. This contains important wisdom material but also deals with medicine and the body (Gignoux and Tafazzolī 1993; Rašēd Mohassel 1987). *Mēnog ī Xrad*, is another notable text, with a series of questions and answers that provide us with much information about Zoroastrian history and tradition. It was most likely written before the Islamic period (Tafazzolī 1986).

Andarz texts or wisdom literature are abundant and are usually attributed to wise sages or people of authority in the Zoroastrian tradition. These texts give didactic ordinances about the religion, social order, good and bad conduct, and proper rules. One notable example deals with children and youth, enumerating their daily duties and discussing their education (Junker 1912). Priests, kings, important personages, and wise men all are given credit for these *andarz*.

7.5 Geographical and Epic Texts

There is good evidence to show that as early as the time of Kawād I, the Sasanian court was in possession of a geographical text (Zakeri 2011, pp. 221–222). This text would partly be in the tradition of the *Avesta*, where a chapter in the *Wīdēwdād* gives us information on the different regions and people who inhabited them. A short text known as *Abādīh ud Sāhagīhā ī Sīstān* (Utas 1980) is concerned with the Province of Sīstān, which had special importance for Zoroastrianism in the Sasanian period: It was thought to be the center of Zoroaster activity and the homeland of the Kayanid king, Wištāsp (Gnoli 1980, 2000) The text may be seen as a progenitor of the later Islamic geographical texts and local histories such as the Persian *Tārīx-e Sīstān* (History of Sīstān) as well as other local histories and geographical texts.

The longest text is known as the *Šahrestānīhā ī Ērānšahr* (The Provincial Capitals of Ērānšahr); it discusses different capital cities in different regions. All the cities are mentioned as part of the Sasanian Empire; they include Mecca, Medina, and parts of Africa. The author identifies the builder and rebuilder of a specific city and the important events that took place there. The text is not an exact geographical-administrative history, but has epic features, is imperialistic in outlook, and reflects Zoroastrian dogma (Daryaee 2002a).

A Pahlavi epic is the *Ayādgār ī Zarērān* (Memoir of Zarēr) (Monchi-Zadeh 1981; Russell 1996), which focuses on the court of King Wištāsp, the patron of Zoroaster, and the bloody war with their enemies, the Tūrānians. The epic relates that victory will come to the Zoroastrians only after many heroes and princes have fallen in battle. The epic of *Ayādgār ī Zarērān* is tragic because the minister of Wištāsp, Jāmāsp, who is endowed with the knowledge of future, is able to foretell to the king the death of many heroes in battle. The other epic deals with the career of the founder of the Sasanian dynasty, Ardaxšīr ī Pābagān. The sixth-century *Kārnāmag ī Ardaxšīr ī Pābagān* (The Book of the Deeds of Ardaxšīr, the Son of Pābag) describes Ardaxšīr's origins as a descendant of King Dārā, i.e. Achaemenid Darius. The epic treats Ardaxšīr' as a great hero who is good at all he does, from polo to board games, and who successfully challenges the last Parthian king, Ardawān (Artabanus) (Grenet 2003). This story also found its way into Medieval Persian epic.

7.6 Legal Texts

The *Wīdēwdād*, part of the *Avesta*, is mainly concerned with the laws of purity and pollution; the Pahlavi translation of this text adds commentaries as glosses in the text (Moazami 2014). There is also a more copious *Zand* of the *Wīdēwdād* that has not been translated. If we are to accept the contents of *Dēnkard* (book eight) as having been the topics of the lost portions of the *Avesta*, we realize that much of this text was concerned with legal matters as well. There is also a prodigious amount of legal commentary in Middle Persian. The most important legal text of the Sasanian period is the *Madīyān ī Hazār Dādestān* (The Exposition of One Thousand Judgments) (Macuch 1981, 1993; Perikhanian 1973, 2000). This work deals with legal cases brought to the Sasanian court. The *Šāyest nē Šāyest* (*Licit and Illicit*) (Kotwal 1969) is another significant text; it covers judgments of the Zoroastrian judges and theologians who sometimes disagree with one another over legal injunction. These texts provide insights into the legal world of the Zoroastrian tradition and the concern with purity and pollution as well as with the rights of men, women, and children.

7.7 Cultural Texts

The texts that tell us much about the cultural life and social norms of the Sasanian period are mainly short works. They include a variety of subjects, such as food, games, ideas of beauty, giving speeches, dinner manners, and how to write properly. The most interesting is the text of *Kusrō ud Rēdag* (King Khusro and the Page), which lays out the courtly ideals of "good living." The page recounts his training not only as a chef, but also as a calligrapher, his athletic prowess as a master polo player and horseman, his religious upbringing, and his morality. The suggestion is of an ideal Zoroastrian man in late antiquity (Azarnouche 2013). The text also mentions board games such as chess. This is the subject of another small work in Middle Persian known as *Wizārišn čatrang ud Nēw-ardaxšīr* (Explanation of the Game of Chess and Backgammon). The treatise explains why the two games were invented and gives their rules, which are treated from a Zoroastrian perspective and placed in a Zoroastrian cosmological setting (Daryaee 2002b; Panaino 1999).

Sūr ī Suxwan (Banquet Speech) is another text that sets out to describe the ancient Iranian banquet etiquette and the list of people who sit before the royal table, including the King of Kings (*šāhān šāh*) and the Grand Wazīr (*wuzurg-framadār*), but also those of the lower ranks (Daryaee 2007). There is also a text on how to write properly for different matters, *Abar Ēwēnag ī Nāmag Nibēsišnīh* (On the Manner of Book/Letter Writing) (Zaehner 1939). The survival of these texts points to the sophistication of Persian culture and society, where varied aspects of life were discussed and standards were established.

The nobility acquired some of its cultural knowledge and capital in the *frahangestān*, "House of Culture." Activities included memorizing sacred utterances, scribal instruction and calligraphy, horsemanship, jousting, polo, playing musical instruments, singing, poetry, dancing, studying astrology, and mastering board games (Azarnouche 2013). Naturally, warriors were trained in the art of combat, and not only in shooting but also in horse racing and jousting. In fact, it is in Persia that we find some of the earliest reliefs on jousting scenes and the art of one to one combat. These are all familiar to the Medieval European world, where their Persian equivalent, i.e. the knights (Middle Persian *āzādān*), did the same, except much earlier.

7.8 Dictionaries

Two Middle Persian dictionaries (*frahang*) have survived. The first is the *Frahang ī Pahlawīg*, which is mainly concerned with difficult words that were written with the Aramaic ideograms. The authors took pains to show the Middle Persian word in question in its usual ideographic and its simple representation. For example, the word for "night" was written with the Aramaic ideogram *LYLYA*, which was read as Middle Persian *šab*. To demonstrate that this word stood for night, the author wrote the word without the ideogram as *šb*. The glossary also reflects ancient Near Eastern tradition in the way the subject headings are organized, based on cosmology, waters, fruits, metals, etc. A more recent recension of this glossary exists that approaches the words alphabetically (Nyberg and Utas 1988). The other major dictionary or glossary is the *Frahang ī Ōīm-ēwag*, a dictionary of Avestan words. In the preface the author states that the work is intended to understand the *zand* (Middle Persian translation of the *Avesta*) (Reichelt 1900).

7.9 Christian and Manichaean Literature in Middle Persian

A relatively large number of Christians appear to have lived in the Iranian Plateau by the late Sasanian period. This was the result, first, of the influx of Christian captives and their settlement into the empire, and second, of later conversions to the Christian faith. In Mesopotamia the Persian (Syriac Persian) Christian community who received converts from the royal family became subjects of martyrologies and hagiographies of late antiquity (Brock and Harvey 1998). The Christians were also active in translating Christian texts, especially the New Testament, into Middle Persian. The *Zabūr* or Psalms are translations of these biblical texts into Middle Persian (Andreas and Barr 1933). These are the main non-Zoroastrian Middle Persian texts that survive, along with a few Christian funerary monuments. They were probably done for and by the Nestorian community, using the Syriac versions of the Bible. There is also evidence of translation of the *Book of Enoch* and other Christian apocryphal works as well as of hymns; this suggests the importance and size of the Christian community in Iran.

Another group of Middle Persian texts is the product of Manichaean religious life; Manichaeans were an important community in the Near East and the eastern Mediterranean region in the late antiquity. A large corpus survives, but most of the texts are fragmentary in nature, and are usually called Manichaean Middle Persian texts. They are quite varied in topic and parallel the Zoroastrian texts in subject matter (Klimkeit 1993). The most important Manichaean Middle Persian text is the *Šāpūragān*, which was written by Manī for his patron Šāpur I. This summarizes the teachings of Manī in the court language of the Sasanian Empire, although the text is difficult because of its esoteric and apocalyptic style (MacKenzie 1978). There are other fragments and texts in Middle Persian that may be called Manichaean hagiography and martyrology. Finally, there are sermons and addresses by Manichaean leaders (the Elect) after Manī's death to the adherents.

7.10 Pahlavi Literature in Contact with Greek and Sanskrit Literature and Islam

In Pahlavi texts, we come across word compounds that appear to define technical religious and scientific terminology and that were foreign to Persian. These terms are further evidence for the translation of foreign works into Middle Persian. Some Syriac and Greek words that were translated in Middle Persian are as follows: *dašnēzādagān* for Syriac *banyā yāminā* "righteous ones;" *gēhān ī kōdak* for Greek *mikros kosmos* "microcosm;" *xraddōšagīh* for Greek *philosophia* "philosophy;" and *zamīg-paymānīh* for *geōmetria* "geometry" (Rezā'ī Bāgh-Bīdī 2000, pp. 148–149) The evidence suggests a vibrant translation campaign by the Sasanian scholars to understand the world and their neighbors. This runs contrary to the common view of the Sasanian world as one that was static and hostile to non-Zoroastrian ideas.

In the fourth book of *Dēnkard*, we read that during the reign of Šāpūr I texts on medicine, astronomy, logic and other crafts and skill that existed in India and Rome and other lands were gathered and a copy of them were made (Choksy 2004; Shaki 1981). As to the nature of these texts, we do have some ideas. In another part of book four of *Dēnkard* the name of some of these texts are given: the Indian *Kāla Koa*, "Treasury of Astronomy," and Pahlavi *Magistīg* (Almagest) of Ptolemy (Bailey 1971, p. 86; Shaki 1981, p. 123). In the *Bundahišn* we also find several pieces of evidence that the author(s) was familiar with Greek texts and sciences, namely the use of the Hippocratic treatise *Peri hebdomádōn* (MacKenzie 1989).

A place for the dissemination of Greek knowledge among others in the Sasanian Empire was the city of *Weh-andīōg-Šāpūr* (Gundēšāpūr). This city, which was built during the reign of Šāpūr I, was comprised of Syriac-speaking Christians of the city of Antioch, who established the famous medical center there. It was in this place that Greek medical books were translated into Syriac in the sixth century CE by Sargis, while Indian medical treatise also reached this location (MacKenzie 1989, p. 81). Thus, the Sasanians made possible the meeting of Greek and Indian sciences. Also, Aristotelian texts and other Greek texts dealing with *bawišn ud vināhišn*, "on coming to be and passing away," *Jatag-wihīrīh*, "change of form," and *nibēg ī zamīg paymānīh*, "measurement of the earth," i.e. geometry, were translated into Middle Persian (Bailey 1971, pp. 81–82; Shaki 1970). So, too, books on logic by Paul the Persian and a book on Aristotelian physics, theory of the soul, meteorology, and biology by Priscianus Lydus found their way to the Persian court (Gutas 1998, 26; Walker 2002).

Persian knowledge of Indian learning is clear, mainly in the field of philosophy and astronomy. Books on logic called *tark* (Sanskrit *tarka*) were translated from Sanskrit into Middle Persian (Bailey 1971, p. 86). Indian influence on astronomy *āwyākrn* (Sanskrit *vyākarana*) is well known. One can state that Persia was a conduit for the transmission of knowledge between the Hellenic and Indic world in late antiquity; consequently, it became a meeting ground of old and new ideas. All of this would be inherited by Muslim civilization, which transmitted these ideas to the West when it had forgotten its philosophical and scientific tradition.

Astrology (MacKenzie 1964, p. 171) played a prominent part in Sasanian society which while the Avesta provided the initial inspiration, it was the Babylonian, Greek, and Indian tradition that impacted it; its importance can be seen from the number of terms used for those professions such as *star-gōwišnīh* "star-telling," *axtar-āmar* "zodiac-teller," *stār-hangār* "star-reckoner," and *hangām-šnāsag* "time-knower." The Sasanian king, we are told, consulted fortune-tellers or astrologers to find out about the future and the courses of action that should be taken. The best example is found in the Ardaxšīr Romance, *Kārnāmag ī Ardaxšīr ī Pābagān*, where Pābag has a series of dreams about the progenitor of the house, i.e. Sāsān. One night Pābag dreams that the sun shines from the head of Sāsān; the second night he sees Sāsān sitting on a white elephant and everyone in the empire paying homage to him; and the third night he dreams that the three sacred Zoroastrian fires were shining on Sāsān's house. Pābag has to ask the "dream interpreters" *xwamn-wizārān* to tell him the meaning of his dreams.

7.11 Conclusion

What remains of Pahlavi texts is only a fraction of what existed. The reason for this loss is mainly that much of it was translated into Arabic, especially the wisdom literature, and above all to instruct the Caliph on how to rule and how to deal with his subjects. The survival of some of the Pahlavi texts was because of the diligence of a number of priests who wanted to keep the tradition alive and give answers to their Zoroastrian community in the face of conversion and loss of status and wealth in the new Islamic empire that stretched from China to Spain. Thus, what was important for religion was copied by the priests from generation to generation. Still, much was lost, and among the agents of destruction were bigoted emirs who had forgotten that the Zoroastrians were also a people of the book and their ancestors.

What remains apparent, however, is that there was a vibrant literary tradition in the late the antique period. Nor did writing in Pahlavi stop with the coming of the Arabs (de Menasce 1975; Weber 2011): Rather, it continued for a group of scholars and priests who were devoted to the religion of Zoroastrianism and in daily economic (Gignoux 2010) and legal matters (Gignoux 2012). From the remains of late antique Pahlavi texts, we can observe a sea of learning that was the product of imperial and scholastic efforts to understand the world. It was first the Zoroastrian priests who were able to incorporate Greek philosophy into a unified Zoroastrian philosophical and religious outlook. The Muslims only followed this tradition, until Al-Ghazali challenged the late antique trend. The Pahlavi texts also exhibit a dialogue between Greek and Sanskrit and other literary traditions on the Iranian Plateau. The now lost Pahlavi text *Hazār Afsān* (A Thousand Tales), is a good clue for the new trend at the end of the late antique period (Beyzaie 2013), which in Arabic came to be known as the *Thousand and One Nights*. Lastly, such tales as the story of Sindbad may have been originally a Sasanian tradition that was associated with one of the great ancient heroes of Iran, namely the voyages of Garšāsp, which became popularized among the masses (Zakeri 2006).

REFERENCES

Agostini, Domenico. (2013). *Ayādgār ī Jāmāspīg: Un texte eschatologique zoroastrien*. Rome: Gregorian and Biblical Press.

Amuzegār Jaleh and Tafazzolī, Ahmad. (2001). *Dēnkard V*. Cahiers de Studia Iranica. Leuven: Peeters.

Andreas, Friedrich and Barr, Kaj. (1933). *Bruchstücke einer Pehlevi-Übersetzung der Psalmen*. Berlin: Akademie der Wissenschaften.

Andrés-Toledo, Miguel Angel. (2015). Primary sources Avestan and Pahlavi. In: *The Wiley Blackwell Companion to Zoroastrianism* (ed. Michael Stausberg and Yuhan Sohrab-Dinshaw Vevaina with Anna Tessmann), 519–528. Malden, MA: Wiley Blackwell.

Anklesaria, Behramgore. ed. and trans. (1956). *Zand Ākāsīh. Iranian or Greater Bundahišn*. Bombay: No publisher.

Anklesaria, Behramgore, ed. and trans. (1969). *The Pahlavi Rivāyat of Āturfarnbag and Farnbag-Sroš* (ed. posthumously Peshotan Anklesaria (vol. 1), and M. K. JamaspAsa (vol. 2)). Bombay: No publisher.

Azarnouche, Samra. (2013). Husraw ī Kawādān ud Rēdag-ē. Khosrow fils de Kawād et un page. Paris: Association pour l'avancement des études iraniennes.

Back, Michael. (1978). *Die sassanidischen Staatsinschriften*. Leiden :Brill.

Bailey, Harold Walter. (1971). *Zoroastrian Problems in the Ninth-Century Books*. Oxford: Oxford University Press.

Beyzaie, Bahram. (2013). *Hazār afsān kojāst?* Tehran: Roshangaran.

Boyce, Mary. (1968). Middle Persian literature. In: *Iranistik, Handbuch der Orientalistik*, 32–66. Leiden: Brill.

Brock, Sebastian and Harvey, Susan. trans. (1998). *Holy Women of the Syrian Orient*. Berkeley: University of California Press.

Brunner, Christopher. (1980). The fable of the Babylonian tree. *Journal of Near Eastern Studies* 39: 191–202.

Cereti, Carlo. (1995). *The Zand ī Wahman Yasn. A Zoroastrian Apocalypse*. Rome: Istituto italiano per il medio ed estremo Oriente.

Cereti, Carlo. (1996). Again on Wahram ī Warzāwand. In : *Atti del convegno internazionale (Roma, 9–12 novembre 1994): La Persia e l'Asia Centrale da Alessandro al X secolo*, 629–39. Rome: Accademia Nazionale dei Lincei.

Cereti, Carlo. (2001). *La letteratura pahlavi. Introduzione ai testi con riferimenti alla storia degli studi e alla tradizione manoscritta*. Milan: Mimesis.

Chacha, Homi. (1936). *Gajastak Abalish: Pahlavi Text with Transliteration, English Translation, Notes, and Glossary*. Bombay: Trustees of the Parsi Punchayat Funds and Properties.

Choksy, Jamsheed. (2004). Incorporation of medieval science into Zoroastrian scripture and exegesis: Some evidence from *Dēnkard* book 4. In: *Menog ī Xrad: The Spirit of Wisdom: Essays in Memory of Ahmad Tafazzoli* (ed. Touraj Daryaee and Mahmoud Omidsalar), 58–63. Costa Mesa: Mazda.

Crone, Patricia. (2012). *The Nativist Prophets of Early Islamic Iran: Rural Revolt and Local Zoroastrianism*. Cambridge: Cambridge University Press.

Daryaee, Touraj. (2001). Kerdīr's Naqsh-e Rajab inscription: *Nāme-ye Irān-e Bāstān. International Journal of Ancient Iranian Studies* 1: 3–10.

Daryaee, Touraj. (2002a). *Šahrestānīhā ī ērānšahr*. Costa Mesa: Mazda.

Daryaee, Touraj. (2002b). Mind, body, and the cosmos: The game of chess and backgammon in Ancient Persia. *Iranian Studies*, 35: 281–313.

Daryaee, Touraj. (2007). The Middle Persian text Sūr ī Saxwan and the late Sasanian court. In: *Des Indo-Grecs aux Sassanides: Données pour l'histoire et la géographie historique* (ed. Rika Gyselen), 65–72, Res Orientales 1. Leuven: Peeters.

Daryaee, Touraj. (2014). Araš ī šawātīr ke būd? *Bokhara* 95–96: 167–176.
Daryaee, Touraj. (2015). Zoroastrianism under Islamic rule. In: *The Wiley Blackwell Companion to Zoroastrianism* (ed. Michael Stausberg and Yuhan Sohrab-Dinshaw Vevaina with Anna Tessmann) 103–118. Malden, MA: Wiley Blackwell.
Daryaee, Touraj. (2016). Refashioning the Zoroastrian past: From Alexander to Islam. In: *The Zoroastrian Flame: Exploring Religion, History and Tradition* (ed. Alan Williams, Sarah Stewart, and Almut Hintze), 135–146. London: I.B. Tauris.
De Blois, François. (1990). The Middle Persian inscription from Constantinople: Sasanian or post-Sasanian? *Studia Iranica* 19: 209–218.
De Menasce, Jean-Pierre. trans. (1945). *Škand-Gumānīk Vičār: La solution décisive des doutes: Une apologétique Mazdéenne du IXe siècle*. Fribourg: Librairie de l'Université.
De Menasce, Jean-Pierre. trans. (1973). *Le troisième livre du Dēnkart*. Paris: Klincksieck.
De Menasce, Jean-Pierre. (1975). Zoroastrian literature after the Muslim conquest. In: *The Cambridge History of Iran*, vol. 4 (ed. Richard Frye), 543–565. Cambridge: Cambridge University Press.
Dhabhar, Bamanji Narsavanji. (1912). *Nâmakîhâ i Mânûshchîhar. The Epistles of Mânûshchîhar*. Bombay: No publisher.
Gignoux, Philippe. (2001). La composition du *Dēnkard* et le contenu du livre V. In: *Tafazzoli Memorial Volume* (ed. A. A. Sadeghi), 29–38. Tehran: Sokhan.
Gignoux, Philippe. (2002). Pahlavi psalter. *Encyclopaedia Iranica*. http://www.iranicaonline.org/articles/pahlavi-psalter (accessed 22 February 2017).
Gignoux, Philippe. (2010). La collection de textes attribuables à Dādēn-vindād dans l'Archive pehlevie de Berkeley. In: *Sources for the History of Sasanian and post-Sasanian Iran* (ed. Rika Gyselen), 11–134, Res Orientales 19. Bures-sur-Yvette: Groupe pour l'Étude de la Civilisation du Moyen-Orient.
Gignoux, Philippe. (2012). Une archive post-sassanide du Tabaristān (I). In: *Objets et documents inscrits en pārsīg* (ed. Rika Gyselen), 29–96, Res Orientales 21. Bures-sur-Yvette: Groupe pour l'Étude de la Civilisation du Moyen-Orient.
Gignoux, Philippe and Tafazzolī, Ahmad. (1993). *Anthologie de Zādspram: Édition critique du texte pehlivi traduit et commenté*. Studia Iranica, Cahier 13. Paris: Peeters.
Gnoli, Gherardo. (1980). *Zoroaster's Time and Homeland*. Naples: IsMEO.
Gnoli, Gherardo. (2000). *Zoroaster in History*. New York: Bibliotheca Persica.
Grenet, Frantz. (2003). *Le geste d'Ardashir fils de Pâbag. Kārnāmag ī Ardaxšēr ī Pābagān*. Die: Éditions A Die.
Gutas, Dimitri. (1998). *Greek Thought, Arabic Culture: The Graeco-Arabic Translation Movement in Baghdad and Early 'Abbāsid Society (2nd–4th / 8th–10th centuries)*. New York: Routledge.
Harmatta, János. (1971). The Middle Persian-Chinese bilingual inscription from Hsian and the Chinese–Sāsānian relations. In: *Atti del Convegno internazionale sul tema: La Persia nel Medioevo (Roma, 31 marzo–5 aprile 1970)*, 363–76. Rome: Accademia Nazionale dei Lincei.
Henning, Walter Bruno. (1954). The Inscription of Firuzabad. *Asia Major* 4: 98–102.

Huyse, Philip. (1990). Noch einmal zu Parallelen zwischen Achaemeniden- und Sāsānideninschriften. *Archäologische Mitteilungen aus Iran* 23: 177–183.

Huyse, Philip. (1999). Die dreisprachige Inschrift Šābuhrs I. An der Kaʿba-i Žardušt (ŠKZ). 2 vols. Corp. Iscrip. Iran. III, vol. I, Text I. London.

Jaafari-Dehaghi, Mahmoud. (1998). *Dādestān ī Dēnīg. Part I*. Paris: Association pour l'avancement des études iraniennes.

Junker, Heinrich. (1912). *Ein mittelpersisches Schulgespräch. Pāzandtext mit Übersetzung und Erläuterungen*. Heidelberg: Winter.

Klimkeit, Hans-Joachim. (1993). *Gnosis on the Silk Road: Gnostic Parables, Hymns, and Prayers from Central Asia*. San Francisco: HarperSanFrancisco.

Kotwal. Firoze M. (1969). *The Supplementary Text to the Šāyest nē-šāyest*. Det Kongelige Danske Videnskabernes Selskab. Historisk-filosofisk Meddelelser 44.2. Copenhagen: Munksgaard.

Macuch, Maria. (1981). *Das Sasanidische Rechtsbuch "Mātakdān i Hazār Dātistān" (Teil II)*. Wiesbaden: Deutsche Morgenlandische Gesellschaft.

Macuch, Maria. (1993). *Rechtskasuistik und Gerichtspraxis zu Beginn des siebenten Jahrhunderts in Iran. Die Rechtssammlung des Farroḥmard i Wahrāmān*. Wiesbaden: Deutsche Morgenlandische Gesellschaft.

Macuch, Maria. (2009). Pahlavi literature. In: *The Literature of Pre-Islamic Iran: Companion Volume I to a History of Persian Literature* (ed. Ronald Emmerick and Maria Macuch), 110–116. London: I.B. Tauris.

MacKenzie, David Neil. (1964). Zoroastrian astrology in the Bundahišn. *Bulletin of the School of Oriental and African Studies* 27: 511–329.

MacKenzie, David Neil. (1978). Shapur's shooting. *Bulletin of the School of Oriental and Africa Studies* 41: 499–511.

MacKenzie, David Neil. (1989). Bundahišn. *Encyclopaedia Iranica*. http://www.iranicaonline.org/articles/bundahisn-primal-creation (accessed 21 February 2017).

Moazami, Mahnaz. (2014). *Wrestling with the Demons of the Pahlavi Widēwdād*, Leiden: Brill.

Mokhtarian, Jason. (2015). *Rabbis, Sorcerers, Kings, and Priests: The Culture of the Talmud in Ancient Iran*. Berkeley: University of California Press.

Molé, Marijan. (1967). *La Légende de Zoroastre selon les textes pehlevis*. Paris: Klincksieck.

Monchi-Zadeh, Davoud. (1981). *Die Geschichte Zarēr's*. Uppsala: Acta Universitatis Upsaliensis.

Nyberg, Henrik Samuel and Utas, Bo. (1988). *Frahang ī Pahlavīk*. Wiesbaden: Otto Harrassowitz.

Panaino, Antonio. (1999). *La novella degli scacchi e della tavola reale*. Milan: Mimesis.

Perikhanian, Anait. (1973). *Sasanidskiĭ sudebnik*. Yerevan: Izd-vo AN Armianskoĭ SSR.

Perikhanian, Anahit. (2000). *Book of a Thousand Judgements: A Sasanian Law-Book* (trans. Nina Garsoian). Costa Mesa: Mazda.

Rašēd Mohassel, Mahmud. (1987). *Gozidahā-ye Zādesparam*. Tehran: Pajuheshkadeh Olum-e Ensani.

Reichelt, Hans. (1900). *Der Frahang I Oīm*. Vienna: WZKM.

Rezā'ī Bāgh-Bīdī, Hassan. (2000). Sassanian neologisms and their influence on Dari Persian. *Nāme-ye farhangestān* 15: 148–149.

Rezā'ī Bāgh-Bīdī, Hassan. (2005). *The Revāyat of Ādur-Farrōbay ī Farroxzādān*. Tehran: Markaz-i Dā'irat al-Ma'ārif-i buzurg-i islāmī.

Russell, James. (1996). A Parthian Bhagavad Gita and its echoes. In: *From Byzantium to Iran: Armenian Studies in Honor of Nina G. Garsoian* (ed. Jean-Pierre Mahé and Robert Thomson), 17–35. Atlanta, GA: Scholars Press.

Safa-Isfahani, Nizhat. (1980). *Rivāyat-i Hēmīt-i Ašawahistān: A Study in Zoroastrian Law*. Cambridge, MA: Harvard University Press.

Sanjana, Darab Dastur Peshotan. (1916). *The Dēnkard*. London: Kegan Paul, Trench, Trübner & Co.

Shaked, Shaul. (1979). *Wisdom of the Sasanian Sages*. Boulder, CO: Caravan.

Shaki, Mansor. (1970). Some tenets of the eclectic metaphysics of the *Dēnkard*. *Archiv Orientální* 38: 277–312.

Shaki, Mansor. (1981). The *Dēnkard* account of the history of the Zoroastrian scriptures. *Archiv Orientální* 49: 114–125.

Shayegan, M. Rahim. (2012). *Aspects of History and Epic in Ancient Iran: From Gaumāta to Wahrām*. Cambridge, MA: Harvard University Press.

Sims-Williams, Nicholas. (2011). Christianity IV. Christian literature in Middle Iranian. *Encyclopaedia Iranica*. http://www.iranicaonline.org/articles/christianity-iv (accessed 22 February 2017).

Skjærvø, Prods Oktor. (1983). Case in inscriptional Middle Persian, inscriptional Parthian and Pahlavi psalter. *Studia Iranica* 12: 47–62.

Skjærvø, Prods Oktor. (1985). Thematic and linguistic parallels in the Achaemenian and Sassanian inscriptions. In: *Papers in Honour of Professor Mary Boyce* (ed. H. W. Bailey, A.D.H. Bivar, J. Duchesne-Guillemin et al.), 593–603. Leiden: Brill.

Tafazzolī, Ahmad. (1986). *Mēnō-ye Xrad*, Tehran: Tus Publishers.

Tafazzolī, Ahmad. (1998). *Tārīḵ-e adabiyāt-e Irān-e piš az Eslām*. Tehran.

Utas, Bo. (1979). Non-religious book Pahlavi literature as a source to the history of Central Asia. In: *Studies in the Sources on the History of Pre-Islamic Central Asia* (ed. János Harmatta), 119–128. Budapest: Akadémiai Kiadó.

Utas, Bo. (1980). The Pahlavi treatise Avdēh u sahikēh ī Sakistān or "Wonders and Magnificence of Sistan." *Acta Antiqua Academiae Scientiarum Hungaricae* 28: 259–267.

Vahman, Fereydun. (1986). *Ardā Wirāz Nāmag, The Iranian "Divina Commedia."* London: Curzon.

Vevaina, Yuhan Sohrab-Dinshaw. (2010). Relentless allusion: Intertextuality and the reading of Zoroastrian interpretive literature. In: *The Talmud in Its Iranian Context* (ed. Carol Bakhos and Rahim Shayegan), 206–234. Tübingen: Mohr Siebeck.

Vevaina, Yuhan Sohrab-Dinshaw. (2015). Theologies and hermeneutics. In: *The Wiley Blackwell Companion to Zoroastrianism* (ed. Michael Stausberg and Yuhan Sohrab-Dinshaw Vevaina with Anna Tessmann), 211–234. Malden, MA: Wiley Blackwell.

Walker, Joel. (2002). The limits of late antiquity: Philosophy between Rome and Iran. *The Ancient World* 33: 45–69.
Weber, Dieter. (1992). *Pahlavi Papyri, Pergamente und Ostraca.* Corpus Inscriptionum Iranicarum. London: School of Oriental and African Studies.
Weber, Dieter. (2003a). Remarks on the development of the Pahlavi script in Sasanian times. In: *Proceedings of the Copenhagen Symposium on Religious Texts in Iranian Languages (Copenhagen, 18th–22nd May 2002)*, 185–195. Copenhagen: Historisk-filosofiske Meddelelser.
Weber, Dieter with the assistance of W. Brasheart and photographs by Margarete Büsing and Eva Maria Borgwaldt. (2003b). *Papyri, Pergamente und Leinenfragmente in mittelpersischer Sprache.* Corpus Inscriptionum Iranicarum. London: School of Oriental and African Studies.
Weber, Dieter. (2011). An Interesting Pahlavi letter from early Islamic times (Berk. 245). *Zeitschrift der Deutschen Morgenländischen Gesellschaft* 161: 91–98.
West, Edward William. (1880). The Pahlavi inscriptions at Kanheri. *Indian Antiquary*, 265–268.
West, Edward Willam. (1897). Pahlavi literature. In: *Grundriss der Iranischen Philologie* (ed. Wilhelm Geiger and Ernst Kuhn), 75–129. Strassburg: Karl J. Trübner.
West, Edward William. (2013a). *Pahlavi Texts. Vol. 4: Contents of the Nasks.* Cambridge: Cambridge University Press.
West, Edward William. (2013b). *Pahlavi Texts. Vol. 5: Marvels of Zoroastrism.* Cambridge: Cambridge University Press.
Williams, A.V. (1990). *The Pahlavi Rivāyat Accompanying the Dādestān ī Dēnīg.* Copenhagen: Munksgaard.
Zaehner, Robert Charles. (1939). Nāmak-nipēsišnih. *BSOAS* 9: 93–109.
Zakeri, Mohsen. (2006). *Persian Wisdom in Arabic Garb, 'Alī b. 'Ubayda al-Rayḥānī (D. 219219/834) and His Jawāhir al-kilam wa-farā'id al-ikam.* Leiden: Brill.
Zakeri, Mohsen. (2011). Qawādiyān (Kawādiyān) Balkhī-Istakhrī Atlas and its Middle Persian ancestry. In *Mediaeval and Modern Iranian Studies: Proceedings of the 6th European Conference of Iranian Studies* (ed. Maria Szuppe, Anna Krasnowolska, and Claus Pedersen), 213–224. Paris: Association pour l'avancement des études iraniennes.

CHAPTER EIGHT

Languages of Arabia

Kevin T. van Bladel

In typical accounts, the Arab-Islamic conquest of the seventh century marks the end of late antiquity and the beginning of a new period. In this view, Arabic is treated as a source language mainly for the subsequent period and, therefore, accounts of Arabic literature would not belong in a volume on literatures of late antiquity. Such treatment of Arabic materials as "post-late antique" overlooks the survival of numerous texts in Arabian languages from throughout the late ancient period (third to the early seventh centuries), a tradition of writing with roots as old as the eleventh century BCE. These are the extant portions of late ancient Arabian literatures, the bulk of which is presumably lost.

Many specialists in Arabic have themselves been quite skeptical about pre-Islamic Arabian literatures. They tend not to believe that there was much writing of any kind in late ancient Arabia. What we have is poetry or song lyrics written down much later. Arabists, therefore, resort to notions of an "oral society," an ill-defined term, but one that connotes the idea that literature was essentially only orally performed and that writing was scarce. Adopting this approach, scholars of Arabic have assumed that nothing substantial was written in Arabic until the Qurʾān. There are, however, numerous ancient Arabian written texts, from late antiquity and from long before, and references to more, but lost, written material, enough to make one think again about pre-Islamic literacy. In the main, three sorts of texts survive from the Arabian Peninsula originating from late antiquity. First, there are tens of thousands of known inscriptions in various ancient Arabian languages (and not just in Arabic proper), from graffiti to royal monumental inscriptions;

A Companion to Late Antique Literature, First Edition.
Edited by Scott McGill and Edward J. Watts.
© 2018 John Wiley & Sons, Inc. Published 2018 by John Wiley & Sons, Inc.

second, there are hundreds of poems preserved in early Arabic, thought to have originated from the seventh, sixth, and even the fifth century CE, as well as prose tales and moral exhortations deriving from the period, purportedly transmitted orally and recorded in early strata of the medieval Arabic manuscript tradition; third, there is the Qur'ān, Islam's foundational scripture, which would turn out to be by far the single most influential literary composition of late antiquity. Each of these three kinds of texts poses distinct problems for the student and historian of the literatures of the third to the early seventh century, problems effectively requiring anybody wishing to use these texts for other purposes to adopt a position in the midst of complicated and often unresolved debates. This chapter briefly describes the texts and literature surviving from the Arabian Peninsula and the arid plains and deserts between Iraq, Jordan, and Syria, here collectively "Arabia" for short, during the period adopted for "late antiquity" in this volume.

Maps of Arabia in this period often depict a wide, blank space easily imagined as uninterrupted desert. This is misleading. The 3.25 million square kilometers of terrain in the peninsula were and are highly varied, comprising not only wide sandy deserts of different hues and extensive fields of black volcanic rock but also mountains (some of them wooded), numerous seasonally irrigated gullies and gulches, scattered permanently watered oasis depressions, hot shores with abundant access to the resources of the seas, and a vast, arid, rocky shrubland plateau fit for the grazing of livestock. There were also cities, towns, and villages where water was available.

It should come as no surprise that such a large and diverse territory was home to many different peoples having different means of subsistence and speaking different languages. At least five different populations distinguished by language lived in the Arabian Peninsula in the period under discussion. All of their languages were historically related to one another as members of the Semitic language-family – meaning that their languages all evolved separately from a much more ancient prehistoric common ancestor – although they were for the most part mutually incomprehensible by the period under consideration here. Most of these languages do not provide us with much written material, but registering their existence helps to contextualize historically the emergence of classical Arabic, which would go on to become the vehicle of an extremely copious medieval literature and the most widespread heir of all the various literatures of late antiquity discussed in this volume. It should be remembered foremost that what we call "Arabic" evolved as one language among several languages of Arabia. By contrast, outsiders in antiquity tended to refer to all the inhabitants of the Arabian Peninsula as Arabs (or, in late antiquity, as Saracens in Greek and Latin and as Ṭayyāye in Aramaic, or by specific tribal names) without differentiating clearly between them. Modern scholars, too, have sometimes overlooked the linguistic heterogeneity of Arabia, which must correlate with ethnic heterogeneity, and have concluded that the Arabia of Muḥammad around 600 was basically ethnically homogeneous. This was surely not the case, but much research remains to be done to explain the fate of that ancient heterogeneity and the ethnic and linguistic "Arabization" of Arabia, a question scarcely addressed because it is taken for granted as a preexistent condition.

In the interior basin within the mountains of Yemen, people spoke a group of languages dubbed today Ancient South Arabian (in scholarly literature also sometimes Ṣayhadic or Old, or Epigraphic, South Arabian). This was the region called Arabia Felix in Roman sources of late antiquity. Its sedentary inhabitants prospered by means of reservoirs catching seasonal floods from the surrounding highlands, preserving waters used to cultivate cereal crops and palm orchards. Preeminent among their languages was that of the ancient kingdom of Sheba, Arabic *Saba'*, called Sabaic today. About ten thousand inscriptions survive written in Sabaic and its cousins in the region, Qatabānic, Maʿīnic, and Ḥaḍramitic. These are written in a distinctive script of 29 consonantal glyphs, one per phoneme, and are dated from the eleventh century BCE until the sixth century CE, with the latest dated inscription from the year 554 CE. They attest to the veneration of numerous local gods and, eventually, Jewish and Christian monotheism (Gajda 2009). Many of them commemorate specific events, building foundations, and military expeditions. Relatively recent discoveries have revealed thousands of polished wooden sticks etched with a handwritten form of the same script used for Ancient South Arabian inscriptions. These minuscule texts, called *zabūr*, were preserved by the dry climate. Those extant are thought to derive from one northern Yemeni find-area at which they have survived. These economic documents and private letters show what anybody might have guessed before they were discovered: that the speakers of Ancient South Arabian languages, living in towns in a prosperous region cultivated with large irrigation works, did not restrict their literacy to inscriptions on stone alone. As the extant minuscule texts show, they kept records and wrote correspondence on perishable materials. Formal poetry existed, too, as demonstrated by an earlier Sabaic inscription in what is clearly some kind of verse, still opaque, but with consonant end-rhymes like those occurring in later classical Arabic verse. For the most part, the inscriptions in Ancient South Arabian languages hint at what may well have been copious literature, written on perishable materials and therefore lost, much in the manner of literature in other ancient languages like Parthian (cf. the more hesitant Stein 2011).

In the mountain highlands above the Ṣayhad lived the people called Ḥimyar, who spoke a language known in Arabic sources as Ḥimyaritic.

The Ḥimyarites came to possess an extensive kingdom encompassing the Ancient South Arabian-speaking lowlanders. They wrote a form of locally standard Sabaic for the purposes of almost all of their known inscriptions, with three exceptions that appear to be in poetry but defy interpretation. Scholars have disagreed about whether the language of Ḥimyar was a late species of Ancient South Arabian or an entirely different Semitic language extant essentially just in these poetic inscriptions. The lack of agreement is surely due to the paucity of identifiable traces of the Ḥimyarite language that survive. For Peter Stein (2008), this just suggests that the Ḥimyarites spoke a form of Ancient South Arabian. It will be difficult to say more about their speech without further discoveries. Their inscriptions in Sabaic, as well as sources by outsiders in other languages, attest that the rulers of the Ḥimyarites adopted a form of Judaism as their religion in the fifth century and that they remained Jewish until the disintegration of their kingdom in the sixth.

Today, in the wadis, mountains, and deserts of eastern Yemen and western Oman, an isolated branch of the west Semitic language-family survives, entirely different from Ancient South Arabian, called conventionally the Modern South Arabian languages. The existence of these languages in antiquity is unattested, but their survival in the present as the languages of some two hundred thousand people demonstrates the otherwise invisible regional variety that certainly existed among the population of the peninsula in antiquity.

In northern Arabia inscriptions remain from the major oases of Tayma and Duma, as do tens of thousands of graffiti in the deserts and basalt fields spanning Saudi Arabia, Jordan, Syria, and Iraq. These are written in a variety of scripts known collectively as Ancient North Arabian, expressing different Semitic languages and dialects known also in the scholarly literature as Ancient North Arabian, attested from perhaps as early as the middle of the first millennium BCE into the third century CE. Ancient North Arabian is, therefore, a category encompassing different languages having in common local variations of the same script, which is closely related to the Ancient South Arabian script. Some Ancient North Arabian texts are written in languages closely related to Old Arabic (the ancestor of Arabic proper); others are still poorly understood and are probably not Arabic strictly speaking. Their mutual differences are still being teased apart (Al-Jallad 2015). The Ancient North Arabian inscriptions and graffiti consist almost entirely of the names of their authors along with occasional brief remarks to commemorate an event of personal significance. Inscriptions include invocations of gods, prayers, curses, laments, celebrations, notes for friends, signatures, labels for doodles scratched on stone, labels on tombs, and commemorations of events notable to the authors. Examples of three inscriptions in the copious corpus of Safaitic texts, left by pastoralists in the rocky deserts of southern Syria, are given here in Ahmad Al-Jallad's rendering. The strings of consonants here represent proper names the vocalization of which is uncertain.

> By ʿd son of Ġt son of ʿd son of ʿd son of Ġt son of Wdm son of S¹r son of Ṣbḥ: he wept and grieved for his father, who was murdered, so, O Lh, he will have vengeance; and he longed for his paternal uncle and all of his companions; and may he who would efface (this inscription) go blind. (LP 243; Al-Jallad 2015, p. 266)
>
> By ʾbs¹ʿd son of Ḥny son of ʾbd son of S¹ʿd: he found the traces of his companions, for those who remain despair, and then he was sad on account of the sheep which had gone hungry. (C2713; Al-Jallad 2015, p. 237)
>
> By Mty son of Ḥzn: he rebelled against Rome the year the Persians came to Bosrā, so, O Lt, let there be security. (SIJ 78; Al-Jallad 2015, p. 281)

The ancestor of classical Arabic, which specialists call Old Arabic, emerged in a historical context and by a historical process that, it must be said, scholars have not fully understood. Different approaches have been taken to explain the origins of classical Arabic and the people who spoke it. For much of the twentieth century and still today it has been widely held that, essentially, the Arabs have effectively always been in Arabia, speaking an undocumented, very early form of Arabic. This view appears often in works on the origins of Islam in which "the Arabs," the default agents in the narrative, are united by Islam and undertake a vast conquest. The focus of such explanation is not on Arab ethnogenesis, because a uniform Arab ethnic group is taken for granted, but on the organization of Arabs into a state or the like.

A second approach emphasizes the relative newness and changeability of Arab identity and seeks to discover the history of Arab ethnogenesis, while taking seriously the traditional literary Arabic narratives of pre-Islamic times compiled by genealogists, Arabic language scholars, and antiquarians from the eighth century onward. Selected epigraphical and archaeological materials are used in this theory to support the account in which the genesis of Arab tribes who carried out the conquests of the seventh century occurred in the wake of a long period of staggered migrations of pastoralist peoples from southern Arabia into the highland (Arabic *Najd*) interior of the Arabian Peninsula and still further toward the north into Syria and Iraq, starting in the third and fourth centuries and continuing – and, in a way, culminating – in the Arab conquests of the seventh and eighth centuries (Hoyland 2001, pp. 229–247). As Michael Zwettler (2000) and Robert Hoyland (2009) have argued, the family and tribal names attested in the thousands of Ancient North Arabian inscriptions of the period 200–400 mostly disappear from use, only to be replaced eventually by tribes first mentioned in the south in Ancient South Arabian inscriptions and whose names – such as Tanūkh – are all attested and made famous later in the period from the seventh-century conquest. They take these epigraphic data to corroborate independent literary sources of later times: the massive genealogical compendia of the Arabs after the conquest, surviving from the ninth century onward, as well as a number of detailed collections of pre-conquest Arabian lore aggregated by specialists such as Ibn al-Kalbī (d. ca. 820) and al-Aṣmaʿī (d. 828). These collections of initially orally transmitted Arabian tribal and family tradition describe just such migrations from south to north. For now, however, this account remains to be tested by archaeology and careful source analysis. A new analysis, presented by Webb (2016), argues that the Arab identity was generated in the midst of or in the wake of the Islamic conquests and that it did not exist as such before.

A third approach ignores the later Arabic traditions and emphasizes the comparative method of historical linguistics as applied to the Semitic languages; it adheres most closely to the epigraphic evidence and their precise distribution, studying also the genesis of the Arabic script. The view from this approach suggests Arabic was an ancient language that was long prevalent in and local to northwestern Arabia, including the Ḥijāz mountain region. Arabic comes into our view when speakers of Old Arabic who had access to the Nabataean script began to use it. Scholarship in this vein has largely not addressed the development of classical Arabic during and after the conquest but regards isolating and defining the earliest form of Old Arabic as a precondition to determining the later history of the language.

Still other views on the problem of Arab ethnogenesis can be found, holding various elements in common with the approaches just described. Suffice it to say here that the demographic and linguistic changes in late ancient Arabia are the subject of intensive ongoing research and have been explained in mutually incompatible ways by different scholars. It is a controversial subject and the picture may change radically or, it is hoped, come into focus sharply. Several factors have inhibited research into the topic, but a shortage of unambiguous sources and the default assumption of ethnic homogeneity across much of Arabia have been some of the chief ones. A recent collaborative volume edited by Greg Fisher (2015) usefully gathers and introduces many of the relevant materials with the help of experts in subfields.

The first signs of what would become classical Arabic occur in a small number of inscriptions over several centuries written in Old Arabic. These appear first in the vicinity of modern Jordan and Syria. There are several ancient inscriptions of the first centuries CE that may lay claim to being partly or wholly Old Arabic (MacDonald in Fisher 2015, pp. 395–417), but the Namāra inscription of 328, from southeastern Syria, presents the oldest uncontroversially entirely Old Arabic text. It is a grave inscription of a King Imru'alqays, and it commemorates his victory over Arabian peoples as far as Najrān, near the present-day Yemeni–Saudi border. From the sixth century several more Arabic inscriptions appear on a Christian martyrion, on a church doorframe, and in a graffito. These late ancient Old Arabic texts were not written in a variety of the script used across ancient Arabia but in a late cursive variety of the Aramaic script used in the Nabataean Kingdom and in the Roman province of Arabia, a territory roughly corresponding with present-day Jordan.

The earlier stages of Old Arabic are evident in ancient inscriptions on the fringes of the Nabataean Kingdom (incorporated into the Roman Empire as a province in 106), in northwestern Arabia, and in Arabic words and phrases used in Nabataean Aramaic texts. These point to the primary language of their authors. A tiny number of short inscriptions in the Nabataean script, in unspecifiable Semitic languages from the first century CE (and perhaps earlier), contain linguistic features otherwise known only from Arabic. These plausibly represent earlier relatives of Old Arabic. What is clear, however, is that Arabic as we know it comes to be employed regularly only in late antiquity, being put to writing in the Nabataean Aramaic letters, the ancestor of the cursive Arabic script. During this period, its use must have been largely on perishable materials. Otherwise, it would be very difficult to explain the continuous use of a late form of the Nabataean script to write Old Arabic, long after Nabataean Aramaic had disappeared from available records.

The history of Arabic before the seventh-century conquests is known primarily from these inscriptions. It is a matter of debate whether the language of northern and central Arabia was relatively uniform or highly variegated by dialect. Common sense, along with reports about dialectal variation among Arab tribes in the ninth and tenth centuries, supports the latter interpretation. There does survive, however, a remarkable quantity of poetry, Arabic *ši'r*, from this ancient Arab population, dating to the fifth, sixth, and seventh centuries (and beyond late antiquity, of course, in unbroken tradition until the present, constituting one of the bases of Arabic literature throughout its history). Arabic poetry from before the Arab conquest, like most extant ancient poetry, survived only because it was useful and entertaining to later readers and listeners who preserved it. The manner of its oral intonation in the time of its composition is not exactly known today, but it is clear that we are dealing with the lyrics to rhythmic songs of a kind. The verb typically used for the recitation of this poetry, *inšād*, connotes calling out in a loud voice. After the Arab conquest, *ši'r* became recognized as different from the poetry of other nations in two ways. Phonemic vowel quantity (long and short vowels) contributed to endowing heavy and light syllables in Arabic with meaningful distinctions, just as in classical ancient Greek and Latin verse but on different patterns in their own tradition. Arabic poetry cast in these meters was called *mawzūn*, or "measured," as on a scale. Its second major formal characteristic was the rhyme of final consonants, called *qāfiya*; every verse was to end in the same consonant or consonant-vowel syllable. We might add a third, important feature: The language of this poetry used a set of case- and mood-endings which in most instances constituted whole syllables (and were thus essential to the meter). Such grammatical endings eventually disappeared almost entirely in all vernacular varieties of Arabic after the conquest but remained part of the classical ideal of the medieval literary language. The grammatical noun endings were, as modern linguists have discovered, highly conservative, in that they reflect the proto-Semitic system of inflection very closely and find their closest extant match in the Akkadian of the third and second millennia BCE. Presumably such linguistic conservatism reflects the isolation of the population of its users, and specifically indicates that very few non-native speakers learned this form of Arabic before the conquests.

There were different sorts of poetry. The rhyming *rajaz* verse was used for boasts and taunts before battle, laments, and various short folk tunes. The more elaborate *qaṣīda* or "ode" came to be most prestigious and represented *šiʿr* proper. Although some short poems were regarded as "snippets," *qiṭʿa*s, the archetypical *qaṣīda* was conceived as comprising three parts in about 75–100 long lines in total. The first part, the *nasīb*, is often called in English the "amatory prelude." It sets a nostalgic tone of longing as the poet describes a place where he camped and met a beloved, or a place in which people dear to him had been but are no longer. The poet mentions or describes an abandoned site reminding the poet of a loss. (This is a frequent theme, too, in the Northern Arabian graffiti described above, suggesting perhaps that the graffiti reflected a culture of song contemporary with it.) The nostalgic prelude leads to an episode representing a journey, *riḥla*, typically through the desert and often by night, sometimes involving detailed descriptions of the poet's mount and elaborate similes. Lastly comes the boast, *fakhr*, or another topic motivating the composition such as praise of a patron. Throughout, the poet may illustrate his point with a proverb, *mathal*, or words of wisdom, *ḥikma*. The tripartite construction came to be remarkably consistent, even if quite a few *qaṣīda*s actually lacked the neat structure. The three ideal parts of the *qaṣīda* were quite susceptible to use for various purposes. In later times, for example, "amatory preludes" could refer to longing for God, or despair for a deceased patron, or any number of other sorts of longing. Poets of later ages were ingenious in adapting the ancient standards to new ends.

Hundreds of late-ancient Arabic poems survive, entire or as fragments, but the question of their authenticity has rightly been a major concern for scholars. The doubts about it have come from several sources. One is the gap of centuries between the alleged times of composition down to the time of earliest attestation in writing. Another is the large number of textual variations between different attestations of the same verses, suggesting a text so unstable as to be unverifiable. These factors even led a few twentieth-century scholars to suppose some or all of the early Arabic poetry to be a late fabrication (e.g. Margoliouth 1925). It seems safe to say that few if any now adhere to this highly skeptical view. Another approach follows the theories of "Oral Formulaic" verse fostered by Parry, Lord, and others. On this hypothesis the early Arabic poetry was composed extemporaneously and orally, and differently on each occasion, by professional versifiers who used metrical formulae to fill out lines spontaneously in the same manner as twentieth-century Serbian bards. This would mean that the early Arabic poetry of which we possess records, transmitted as written in medieval books, of course, represents only specific iterations of poems that varied on each occasion. The application of the "Oral Formulaic" hypothesis to early Arabic poetry (most concertedly made by Zwettler 1978) has, however, essentially been invalidated by the research of Gregor Schoeler (2006, pp. 87–110), who has documented reports of the great effort that early Arabic poets took to prune and edit their own poetry over long periods, months or more, until they were finished. Explicit statements by early medieval students of this poetry show that it was not spontaneous and formulaic. Arabic poetry was certainly orally performed, and there are reports of spontaneous versification over the centuries (reported because it was remarkable), but long poems represented a specially honed craft of deliberate, thoughtful, sometimes time-consuming composition.

The numerous variations in the recorded versions of individual Arabic poems have several sources. One is surely just the error and whimsy of devoted reciters (*rāwī*s) and copyists who, unfamiliar with ancient or dialectal words and expressions, replaced them mistakenly or deliberately with words that made more sense to them and their contemporary audience. Another is the sort of variation that one encounters in song lyrics today, too, whereby the words may be changed when either remembered imperfectly, so as to make sense, or deliberately, to make a point. There is no single source of variation in the lyrics, then, of these popular poems and songs but, in short, they seem to be due primarily just to the lively long-lived human appreciation and reiteration they enjoyed, as with all ancient textual traditions preserved by copying. Sometimes modern scholars romantically attribute almost supernatural memories to premodern peoples, but a moment's reflection reminds us that, even today, individuals may know the lyrics to hundreds of popular songs and musicians may be able to recall countless tunes, even if sometimes imperfectly. In view of this, the survival of many genuine ancient Arabic songs in writing, with considerable variations, is not strange.

Another matter of debate concerns the nature of the Arabic language in which the poetry is composed. A typical view is that the language of the early Arabic poetry is a "supra-tribal koine," more or less artificial, employed by nobody as an everyday language and used only for poetry and special, solemn occasions. In a strong, widely held version of this theory, the ancient Semitic nominal case endings used in the poetry were confined to it and to non-poetic solemn utterances. This view retrojects the modern Arabic diglossia (the concurrent use of colloquial varieties for ordinary communication and a universal literary standard for formal and written communication) onto antiquity without regard for the social circumstances and system of education that generate modern Arabic diglossia. Contrariwise, other scholars, seemingly currently a minority, hold that the Arabic of the poets represents a normal language of general use up to the time of the Arab conquests. Its use in poetry was certainly in a poetic register, but is not endowed with special grammatical systems of inflection used only in poetry. In this minority view, the Arabic poets intended their songs to be appreciated by a normal, untrained audience. The stance one adopts on the Arabic language of the poetry may make a difference in how one interprets it and uses it for history.

Numerous sources indicate that the Arabic language of everyday life underwent drastic changes following the Arabic conquest. The reports come from the earliest Arabic linguists, from the eighth century onward, who strove to preserve the language in a classical state from the "corruption" that they perceived it to be undergoing due to social mixing with conquered peoples. The very survival of late ancient Arabic poetry, along with the standardization of an idealized pre-Islamic Arabic language maintained among bedouin who had not mixed with colonized peoples, is therefore partly due to the attempt of those scholars to record early, "uncorrupted," aesthetically pleasing, and especially authentic-seeming samples of that language. This, they believed, was the language known to their prophet and used in their scripture. Without their effort to find, preserve, collect, and evaluate the corpus of old lyrics and verses available to them, we would have almost no literary products from late ancient Arabia besides the inscriptions.

The poetry of late ancient Arabia, representing mostly the sixth and early seventh centuries, is remarkable in its apparent isolation from other contemporary forms of literature in the languages of neighboring peoples. It is not that Arabic poetry was produced in a world sealed off from the outside. It is rather that Arabic poetry seems to have been unknown to outsiders. It had its own forms and conventions. It refers largely to a world aware of and often oriented toward the great and powerful states of the Romans, Persians, and Ḥimyarites, but on the margins of that world. The setting of ancient Arabic poetry is rather a society of mostly pastoralist tribes in competition over resources of water, pasturage, and livestock, who were not part of large, complex states. The inhabitants of this world are portrayed as having no laws but those of revered custom, the might of arms levied by kings, warlords, or bands, and the overriding connections of kinship. Small-scale violence appears to have been common. The poets impart melancholic wisdom about the inevitability of death and seek refuge in the glory of victory at arms and the good reputation of one's family and tribe, transitory though they may be. They praise unstinting generosity. They long for happy days spent with friends now gone away by distant roads. Poetry by women is preserved, mostly in the form of moving laments for brothers who died violently, of whom only the report of their distant death returns. Other poems survive in the voice of the outcast or brigand, the *ṣuʿlūk*, glorifying a harsh but independent life.

Numerous translations are available for nonspecialists who want access to this world of late ancient Arabic verse. Here I single out three translations for the English-speaking scholar venturing into ancient Arabic poetry for the first time. An accessible modern English rendering of a group of early *qaṣīdas* called *Muʿallaqāt* is that of Michael A. Sells (1989). These poems were among those which, around 800 CE, Arabic scholars in Iraq selected in groups of six or seven as canonical classics. The poems actually selected varied from collection to collection; Sells has chosen six typical and famous ones. The name *Muʿallaqāt*, which can be interpreted as "the hung (ones)," fostered a legend that they had been embroidered in cloth and hung upon the Kaʿba in Mecca because of their excellence. Much larger is Charles J. Lyall's edition of the *Mufaḍḍalīyāt*, accompanied by a useful English translation and commentary (1918–1924). Named for its compiler al-Muafaḍḍal ibn Muḥammad al-Ḍabbī of Kūfa (d. 780 or 786), it contains 128 Arabic poems, mostly ancient. The best place to begin for the aspiring researcher may be, however, Alan Jones's edition, translation, and commentary of 15 shorter laments and outcast poems with 10 longer *qaṣīda*s, entitled *Early Arabic Poetry* (2011), equipped with invaluable introductory materials and bibliography.

There is space here for the example of just one poem. ʿAbīd ibn al-Abraṣ, of the tribe of Banū Saʿd ibn Thaʿlaba, composed a number of poems that proved popular and were anthologized in later times and that were studied closely in later ages. References in ʿAbīd's lyrics to the Arab king Ḥujr ibn al-Ḥārith al-Kindī, to that king's death, and to Ḥujr's son Imruʾalqays would (if authentic) place his activities in the first half of the sixth century. ʿAbīd's poems are often strongly characterized by the melancholic nostalgia widely appreciated in early Arabic verse. The poem here, excerpted partially from Jones's thoughtful and learned translation (2011, pp. 309–335 with minimal modifications here), addresses the inevitability and cruelty of old age both directly and metaphorically. It was composed in a somewhat idiosyncratic meter, suggesting a work antedating the canonization of meters authorized by later critics. This poem begins typically with reflections on abandoned and deserted sites. In this case it seems they are lands out of which his people were driven.

> Desolate, without its people, is Malḥūb; likewise al-Quṭaybiyyāt; likewise al-Dhanūb;
> ...
> Likewise ʿArda; likewise Qafā Ḥibirr – there is not one of the [tribe] in those places.
> They have taken in wild things instead of their people; things have changed their state.
> It is a land that has been inherited by death; everyone who dwelt in it has been despoiled –
> Either slain or dead in some other way – and grey hair is a [mark of] shame for those who [survived and now] have grey hair.
> Your eyes – their tears flow copiously, as if their tear-ducts were a water-skin full of holes
> Worn out, or water flowing [down] the surface, running quickly from a hill on the front of which are run-off gullies.
> ...
> You yearn for the excitement of youth. How can you yearn so? How, when grey hair has warned you?
> If [the land] has become changed and its people removed, they are not the first [to suffer so] and they do not cause wonder.
> If the broad expanse [of these places] is now desolate of its people, and dearth and drought have beset [the area],
> Everyone with any happiness will have it snatched away, and everyone with hope will be deceived.
> Everyone with any camels will have them inherited, and everyone who gains spoils will himself be despoiled.
> Everyone absent on a journey can return, but the one absent by death will not return.
> Is a barren woman the equal of one with a fertile womb, or is the one who gains spoils the equal of one who fails?

> ...
> Many is the stretch of water covered with slime that I have come to, the road to which is fearful and barren.
> Feathers of [dead] pigeons lie in the vicinity – one's heart beats fearfully through terror of [the place].

In the next verses – the description of a journey typical in the middle of a *qaṣīda* – the poet passes forbidding, desolate places, riding a stout she-camel. The camel is likened to a strong wild ass and then an oryx, both described in specific terms. Then he imagines riding a horse, and the horse is like an eagle, which is like an old woman, its feathers white-edged like the woman's hair. But the eagle, like old age, seeks prey:

> Just then [the eagle] saw a fox in the distance, with a barren desert between him and her.
> At that she shook her feathers and stirred herself and [made] herself ready for flight.
> Then she launched herself towards him with all speed, aiming to reach him in one fell swoop.
> Hearing her flight, he raised his tail and was filled with fear; his action was that of a terrified creature.
> Seeing her coming, he moved on at a crouch, showing the whites of his eyes as he turned them to look up at her.
> Then she overtook him and flung him down, and her prey was in agony beneath her.
> She threw him up, then flung him down, and the stony ground scratched his face.
> He squeals as her talons bite into his flank. There is no escape – his breast is pierced.

The world of this poetry is to an extent idealized, and it is probably misleading about that world because it is implicit in the bulk of what was preserved. That is, there must also have been other sorts of compositions, some perhaps pertaining directly to Christianity or Judaism, or liturgies of the gods of Arabian polytheists. There must have been written correspondence and other sorts of writing in the languages of ancient Arabia, including Old Arabic. But the survival of the poetry almost alone has led both medieval and modern scholars to conceive of a world barren of literary production apart from poetry and song and, then, to regard the ancient Arabians as extolling poetry far beyond any other forms of art. That may have been, but equally it may be the illusion caused by the selective survival of texts.

Tales of Arabian life before Islam do survive, transmitted as Arabic prose in later compilations, but these have collectively received much less scholarly attention. Most hold that such texts are effectively oral folklore and unreliable as records, with a small minority of scholars considering such material to have been transmitted in written form from an early stage. There are several genres of such texts. Claiming to derive from the fifth, sixth, and early seventh century, but collected in eighth- and ninth-century (and later) compilations of antiquarian lore, there are wise sayings (*ḥikma*), advice in the form of testaments from kingly fathers to princely sons (*wasīya*), genealogies (*nasab*) with accompanying historical accounts (the plain report, *khabar*, and the biographical *sīra*), orations and sermons (*khuṭba*), transcripts of letters (*risāla*), stories of famous battles (*ayyām*), and copious recorded memories of the early Islamic community. Robert Serjeant (1983) usefully surveys early Arabic prose. Albrecht Noth (1973) and Fred Donner (1998) propose methods to address the question of historicity in Arabic narratives from late antiquity, focusing on the genesis of Islam. Recently, Arabic papyri have begun to receive closer attention, including some quite early documents and epistles, the earliest extant dated one from 22 AH (643 CE). For an overview of the still-incipient field of Arabic papyrology, see Petra Sijpesteijn (2009). Long labors are still required to exploit the Arabic prose texts claiming late antique derivation.

The most important literary work of Arabian late antiquity, and perhaps of all late antiquity, is the Qurʾān. Sometimes the Qurʾān is considered as the beginning of Arabic literature, notwithstanding the numerous references in both the poetry and the Qurʾān itself to written texts (many of these collected in Jones 2003). An ongoing debate concerns the possibility of prior translations of biblical texts into Arabic before the Qurʾān (summarized, with a negative conclusion, by Griffith 2013, pp. 7–53). In any case, barring future discoveries, the Qurʾān is effectively the oldest extant Arabic book. It is thought to be the revelation of the prophet Muḥammad ibn ʿAbdallāh of Mecca, a town nestled in the western mountain range of Arabia, about 70 kilometers from the coast of the Red Sea. Muḥammad is said to have delivered the contents of the Qurʾān piecemeal and in serial form, occasionally revising verses with the passage of time. It is conceived as God's communication to Arabic speakers through his prophet. It was subsequently arranged in 114 sections called *sūra*s, as long as 286 verses (themselves of varying length) and as short as three. Related mostly in a rhythmic, strophic style rich in assonance, called *sajʿ*, the Qurʾān bears a complex message addressing matters universal, cosmic, and eschatological, on the one hand, and specific events in Muḥammad's career, on the other. Throughout, it returns again and again to a few major points. It vehemently and constantly warns its audience of the dire, imminent judgment of humans by God. It glorifies God; proclaims his manifest, awesome, and exalted power and omniscience; and demands obedience to him and his commands. Severe punishments in the Fire await those who do not believe and obey. It promises heavenly postmortem rewards for those who believe and perform justice. Relatively few passages are legislative in character. More are paraphrases or retellings of stories that the audience was expected to know about figures such as Joseph, Jesus, and, most of all, Moses. The Qurʾān soon came to be the foundational scripture of the religion Islam. From its first appearance until today, the Qurʾān has been used to offer guidance in life for billions of people, interpreted in countless ways for the ends of different sects that themselves changed over time.

The nature of the Qurʾān and its composition and codification remain controversial problems among critical historians. Most scholars, but not all, have agreed with traditional accounts that hold that its contents were related by Muḥammad as revelations over a period of 23 years until his death around 632, and that Muḥammad's earliest followers recorded his revelations on various materials and recited them to memorize them. Its importance was guaranteed by the conquests by Muḥammad's followers of the Sasanian Persian Empire and half of the Roman Empire. The third successor of Muḥammad as head of this militant community, the caliph ʿUthmān (r. 644–656), is said to have ordered the creation of a standard version. Variant copies of the Qurʾān were reportedly replaced by copies of this "ʿUthmānic recension." Today, very early fragments of seventh- or eighth-century Qurʾān manuscripts survive in special collections. They have been treated with intensive study in recent years (summarized by Déroche 2013). Their existence more or less invalidates earlier theories of a minority of scholars that the Qurʾān may have been a later composition, but we still do not know whether the traditional accounts of its codification are true. Indeed, there is no consensus on many questions concerning this extraordinary text, even as modern scholarship on the Qurʾān flourishes. For orientation and copious bibliography, one may consult several major reference works on the Qurʾān that have been published in recent years (e.g. McAuliffe 2001–2006; Leaman 2005; Rippin 2006). In 2013, a new academic society was created for its study, the International Qurʾanic Studies Association.

Scholarship on the Qurʾān has recently engaged intensively with the historical context out of which the book appeared: late antiquity. One may gain a sense of the new directions in Qurʾānic studies from three volumes of such studies, collections of contributions of varying success: Gabriel Reynolds (2008, 2011) and Angelika Neuwirth, Nicolai Sinai, and Michael Marx (2011). In an important monograph Reynolds (2010) argues that the Qurʾān is ultimately homiletic in character, thus relating it to a late ancient genre thriving in the world of its historical genesis. He joins many other scholars in making the case, now clearly established, that the Qurʾān assumes an audience with plenty of knowledge about the Bible and related texts. It has not yet been determined when or how the community that followed Muḥammad came to abandon or to be deprived of a tradition of direct experience with the biblical texts and tales that would have rendered the Qurʾān's accounts fully comprehensible to them, but this must have happened in the first generations after Muḥammad, because within one hundred years of Muḥammad's life, various forms of exegesis and storytelling began to be composed to fill in that background knowledge for those who followed the guidance of the Qurʾān. In another recent work similarly worthy of attention, Holger Michael Zellentin (2013) has elucidated substantial features shared by both the legal culture implicit in the Qurʾān and that of the third-century *Didascalia Apostolorum*, leading him to propose a Jewish Christian background long sought also by many other researchers in different ways. These and other major problems in the study of the Qurʾān await definitive resolution. Many other important recent contributions to the study of the Qurʾān could be pointed out, but generally it is researchers with experience in the study of late antique texts that have made the most decisive gains in recent years. While specialists certainly can never exclude the Islamic reception and massive tradition of commentarial works (*tafsīr*) of the Qurʾān from their research – for it is the spectacular reception of the Qurʾān that endows it with unmatched importance – the Qurʾān itself must be understood first of all with reference to its own historical context. So long as we employ late antiquity as a period, then the Qurʾān is a product of that period – indeed, it is its single most influential work. Scholars of late antiquity wishing to approach the Qurʾān in translation have innumerable versions available to them. Not all English translations have scholarly value. Those of Tarif Khalidi (2008) and Arthur J. Droge (2013), among a few others, succeed in legibility, fidelity to the Arabic, and integrity.

Whether one is interested in ancient Arabian inscriptions, early Arabic poetry, or early Arabic accounts of the pre-Islamic times, a single new volume edited by Greg Fisher (2015) presents a thorough collection of primary sources, both literary and epigraphic, about all of these subjects. Many of the data it gathers have been scattered and relatively inaccessible even to specialists in Arabic, let alone to specialists in late antiquity. The varied contributions raise the fundamental question about the genesis of the Arab peoples but do not answer it, nor are they able to historicize adequately the category "Arab." We still do not have a consensus about exactly how "the Arabs" came to be, nor do we yet have a historically sound vocabulary for talking about the peoples of Arabia before Islam. Fisher's volume, nevertheless, can be consulted with great profit and may be regarded now as a solid starting-point for scholars interested in Arabian literatures of late antiquity and their origins.

REFERENCES

Al-Jallad, Ahmad. (2015). *An Outline of the Grammar of the Safaitic Inscriptions*. Leiden: Brill.

Déroche, François. (2013). *Qurʾāns of the Umayyads: A First Overview*. Leiden: Brill.

Donner, Fred. (1998). *Narratives of Islamic Origin: The Beginnings of Islamic Historical Writing*. Princeton, NJ: Darwin.

Droge, Arthur J. (2013). *The Qurʾān: A New Annotated Translation*. Sheffield: Equinox.

Fisher, Greg. ed. (2015). *Arabs and Empires before Islam*. Oxford: Oxford University Press.

Gajda. (2009). *Le royaume de Ḥimyar à l'époque monothéiste*. Paris: Académie des inscriptions et belles-lettres.

Griffith, Sidney. (2013). *The Bible in Arabic*. Princeton, NJ: Princeton University Press.

Hoyland, Robert. (2001). *Arabia and the Arabs*. London: Routledge.

Hoyland, Robert. (2009). Arab kings, Arab tribes and the beginning of Arab historical memory in late Roman epigraphy. In: *From Hellenism to Islam: Cultural and Linguistic Change in the Roman Near East* (ed. Hannah M. Cotton, Robert G. Hoyland, Jonathan J. Price et al.), 374–400. Cambridge: Cambridge University Press.

Jones, Alan. (2003). The word made visible: Arabic script and the committing of the Qurʾān to writing. In: *Texts, Documents, and Artefacts: Islamic Studies in Honour of D.S. Richards* (ed. Chase Robinson), 1–16. Leiden: Brill.

Jones, Alan. (2011). *Early Arabic Poetry: Select Poems*. Reading: Ithaca.

Khalidi, Tarif. (2008). *The Qurʾan*. New York: Viking.

Leaman, Oliver. (2005). *The Qurʾan: An Encyclopedia*. New York: Routledge.

Lyall, Charles J. 1918–1924. *The Mufaḍḍalīyāt: An Anthology of Ancient Arabian Odes*. 3 vols. Oxford: Clarendon.

Margoliouth, D.S. (1925). The Origins of Arabic Poetry. *Journal of the Royal Asiatic Society*, 25: 417–449.

McAuliffe, Jane Dammen. (2001–2006) *Encyclopaedia of the Qurʾān*. 6 vols. Leiden: Brill.

Neuwirth, Angelika, Sinai, Nicolai, and Marx, Michael. (2011). *The Qurʾān in Context: Historical and Literary Investigations into the Qurʾānic Milieu*. Leiden: Brill.

Noth, Albrecht. (1973). *Quellenkritische Studien zu Thema, Formen, und Tendenzen frühislamischer Geschichtsüberlieferung*. Bonn: Selbstverlag des orientalischen Seminars der Universität. 2nd ed. *The Early Arabic Historical Tradition: A Source-Critical Study*, with Lawrence Conrad (trans. Michael Bonner). Princeton, NJ: Darwin. 1994.

Reynolds, Gabriel. ed. (2008). *The Qurʾān in Its Historical Context*. New York: Routledge.

Reynolds, Gabriel. (2010). *The Qurʾān and Its Biblical Subtext*. New York: Routledge.

Reynolds, Gabriel. ed. (2011). *New Perspectives on the Qurʾān: The Qurʾān in Its Historical Context 2*. New York: Routledge.

Rippin, Andrew. (2006). *The Blackwell Companion to the Qurʾān*. Malden: Blackwell.

Schoeler, Gregor. (2006). *The Oral and the Written in Early Islam* (trans. Uwe Vagelpohl, ed. and intr. James E. Montgomery). London: Routledge.

Sells, Michael A. (1989). *Desert Tracings: Six Classic Arabian Odes by ʿAlqama, Shánfara, Labíd, ʿAntara, Al-Aʿsha, and Dhu al-Rúmma*. Middletown, CT: Wesleyan University Press.

Serjeant, R.B. (1983). Early Arabic prose. In: *The Cambridge History of Arabic Literature: Arabic Literature to the End of the Umayyad Period* (ed. A.F.L. Beeston, T.M. Johnstone, R.B. Serjeant et al.), 114–153. Cambridge: Cambridge University Press.

Sijpesteijn, Petra. (2009). Arabic papyri and Islamic Egypt. In: *The Oxford Handbook of Papyrology* (ed. Roger S. Bagnall), 452–472. Oxford: Oxford University Press.

Stein, Peter. (2008). The "Ḥimyaritic" language in pre-Islamic Yemen: A critical reevaluation. *Semitica et Classica* 1: 203–212.

Stein, Peter. (2011). Literacy in pre-Islamic Arabia: An analysis of the epigraphic evidence. In: *The Qurʾan in Context: Historical and Literary Investigations into the Qurʾānic Milieu* (ed. Angelika Neuwirth, Nicolai Sinai, and Michael Marx), 255–280. Leiden: Brill.

Webb, Peter. (2016). *Imagining the Arabs: Arab Identity and the Rise of Islam*. Edinburgh: Edinburgh University Press.

Zellentin, Holger Michael. (2013). *The Qurʾān's Legal Culture: The* Didascalia Apostolorum *as a Point of Departure*. Tübingen: Mohr Siebeck.

Zwettler, Michael. (1978). *The Oral Tradition of Classical Arabic Poetry*. Columbus, OH: Ohio State University Press.

Zwettler, Michael. (2000). Maʿadd in late-ancient Arabian epigraphy and other pre-Islamic sources. *Wiener Zeitschrift für die Kunde des Morgenlandes* 90: 223–309.

PART TWO

LITERARY FORMS

CHAPTER NINE

Classicizing History and Historical Epitomes

Michael Kulikowski

The Greeks and Romans followed strict and consistent rules of genre when writing about the past. They did not, however, have a consistent vocabulary with which to describe their genres, which poses difficulties for the modern historian trying to describe them and the lines between them (Burgess and Kulikowski 2013, pp. 1–62; 2016). Alongside historical biography, which was shaped by the contours of an individual's life even when organized thematically, there was a major division between what we may call chronicle and history. The former genre, which existed in Greek from at least the fourth century BCE, and in Latin from the first century BCE, had as its primary purpose the recording of dated events over a relatively long period of time, in a way that allowed large historical periods to be apprehended rapidly and distant events to be correlated with one another. History, by contrast, which went back to Herodotus and Thucydides in Greek and to Livy in Latin, told a story of greater or lesser chronological length, but at a considerably more leisurely pace; moral purpose and narrative thrust might vary but always went beyond the simple presentation of events in sequence. In the later first century CE, these long traditional histories began to share space with much shorter *breviaria* (epitomes or abbreviated histories), which at first took the shape of abridgments of Livy, like that of Florus and others. Sometimes as short as a chronicle, *breviaria* lacked that genre's overarching chronological focus, often organized by reign rather than annalistically.

A Companion to Late Antique Literature, First Edition.
Edited by Scott McGill and Edward J. Watts.
© 2018 John Wiley & Sons, Inc. Published 2018 by John Wiley & Sons, Inc.

We will leave chronicles aside in the following discussion and focus instead on histories and *breviaria*, both in Greek, where we can trace a continuous tradition throughout late antiquity, and in Latin, where the evidence for history on the grand scale is much poorer. Beginning in the third century, as the empire became more and more Christian, church history emerged as a genre in its own right. Greek and Latin authors who imitated older, classical traditions of history-writing strove, with partial success, to exclude neologisms associated with the religious changes of the later empire and cleave to pre-Christian models of what was and was not a suitable topic for serious history; as late as the sixth century, a Christian author like Procopius would introduce references to priests and monks as if they were slightly exotic creatures with which readers might not be familiar. At its most extreme, the Greek classicizing impulse went so far as to exclude language that was not yet in use when Herodotus, Thucydides, and Xenophon were writing (a habit of the Second Sophistic milieu from which many history writers emerged). Other authors might admit neologisms that reflected the passage of time and the realities of the Roman imperial polity, but without altering the canon of appropriate historical topics, sticking to the political and military affairs that had always been the focus of proper history and perpetuating classical nomenclature for neighboring peoples (Scythians for Huns, Massagetae for Goths, Parthians for Persians and so on).

The majority of such history is in Greek, because the great Trajanic author Cornelius Tacitus was both apex and abortive endpoint of Latin historiography on the grand scale. Although the fourth-century histories of Ammianus Marcellinus represent a nearly equal pinnacle of literary and imaginative qualities, they belong as much to the Greek as to the Latin tradition (Wilamowitz-Moellendorf 1907, p. 201; Norden 1909, pp. 646–650). Too little survives of other putative classicizing histories in Latin to say much about them, while the claims made for a lost *Annales* of Nicomachus Flavianus (Ratti 2010) are at best wildly exaggerated, at worst borderline demented (demonstrated in Cameron 2010, pp. 627–690). Late antique Latin historiography, Ammianus aside, is thus almost exclusively a matter of chronicles, *breviaria*, and church history.

The Greek tradition, by contrast, is both abundant and lively right down to the early seventh century, when Greek historiography went into hibernation for several hundred years. Much of this classicizing Greek tradition survives only in fragments, for a series of reasons. One is that the well-known transition from papyrus roll to codex culled the ranks of third- and fourth-century authors. Thereafter, the cost of writing materials ensured that authors whose appeal did not conform to later tastes tended to be palimpsested: The sixth-century *Ethnica* of Stephen of Byzantium refers to a great many historians whose work was unknown to the Greek Middle Ages. In the West, the majority of the Greek heritage had probably disappeared before the Carolingians conquered the heartlands of western classical culture, which left the survival of the rest very much dependent upon the shifting tastes of Middle Byzantine antiquarians. The *Myriobiblion* or *Bibliotheca* of the Constantinopolitan patriarch Photius, of disputed ninth-century date (Treadgold 1980; Markopoulos 2004); the collections of historical excerpta compiled on the instructions of the emperor Constantine Porphyrogenitus (Toynbee 1973, pp. 575–605); and the maddeningly eclectic encyclopedia known as the *Suda* – all are among our best testimony for, and sources of text from, the classicizing historians of late antiquity. Our dependence on middle Byzantine tastes come with certain problems. There is a preference for the exemplary and the improving, for the clever folkloric anecdote, and for whatever helps point a moral agreeable to the Christian, Constantinople-centric world in which the antiquarians worked. In evaluating the fragmentary historians, therefore, we need to account, not so much for deliberate misrepresentation on the part of the Byzantine compilers, but rather for the distortion that follows from selection criteria that we only partially understand. The selection of fragments that happens to be extant can have a serious impact on how one interprets an author's larger work and purpose, as one can see in the discussion of Olympiodorus below.

A consideration of Greek classicizing histories needs to begin with Dexippus of Athens, a third-century author whose work survives in sufficiently large fragments to allow a confident assessment (*FGrH* 100; Millar 1969; Janiszewski 2006, pp. 39–54, 109–113, 145–149; Martin 2006; Mecella 2013). Publius Herennius Dexippus came from a prominent Athenian family and had a career in local government marked out by his personal and familial prestige (he was eponymous archon in the early 250s). During the "Scythian" invasions of the third century, he was one of the locals who rallied the city to repel the marauders in a gesture of self-help. His posthumous prestige rested more on his historical writings than on his political career, and his style, much admired by the Byzantines, accounts for the survival of his work in substantial excerpts; excitingly, he is a rare ancient historian whose corpus has recently been expanded by new discoveries. He is known to have written three works, including a *Chronichè historía*, or *Súntomos historikós*, composed either in the 270s (Janiszewski 2006, p. 52) or a decade or two earlier (Millar 1969). This was universal history in multiple books, a genre popular with Greek authors since the Second Sophistic and reaching its apogee with the *Romaiká* of Cassius Dio under the last Severans. Dexippus's contribution ran from an uncertain starting date down to the reign of Claudius II (r. 268–270), probably covered a millennium of history, and was perhaps organized by the annual archonships of Athens. Dexippus also wrote a *Tà metà Aléxandron* in four books, borrowing liberally from his predecessor Arrian of Nicomedia, and a *Skuthiká*, recounting the third-century invasions by Goths, Heruls, and other generic "Scythians" in at least three books. It is not always possible to assign the extant fragments precisely to one or another of Dexippus's works, but the sieges recounted in the fragments preserved by Constantine Porphyrogenitus, and in the newly published papyrus fragments from Vienna, are all almost certainly from the *Scythica* (Martin and Grusková 2014a, 2014b; Mallan and Davenport 2015). In general, Dexippus affects a Thucydidean tone of cautious observation, suitable in a man who had personally participated in public affairs. The selection bias of our excerptors may give more of a military cast to the history than it possessed in reality, and while the *Scythica* must certainly have concentrated on the Balkan wars of the 250s–270s, there is no reason to think it was quite so heavily concerned with sieges as we once thought – there is considerable war of maneuver in the new fragments.

The achievement of Dexippus was recognized already in antiquity. Whereas writers like Asinius Quadratus, Nicostratus of Trebizond, or Onasimus are barely more than names to us – and were no more than that to their fourth-century successors – Dexippus was used by quite a number of them. Ammianus Marcellinus certainly knew Dexippus, and the author of the *Historia Augusta* drew on him for what little genuine information can be extracted from his dismal biographies of the later third-century emperors. Eunapius of Sardis, however, went much further, and took the close of Dexippus's histories as the starting point for his own fourteen-book *History*, which survived down to the time of Photius in two editions. The first edition was written in the direct aftermath of Adrianople as a sort of "instant history" of how the empire had come to so awful a pass; the latter ran into the early fifth century, with some of its anti-Christian bile perhaps expunged, whether by Eunapius himself or a later bowdlerizer (Barnes 1978; Blockley 1981, pp. 1–26; Blockley 1983, pp. 2–151; Baldini 1984). Eunapius, sadly, is not a patch on his third-centry predecessor, and that does not simply reflect our having more of Eunapius from which to recoil. Where Dexippus is precise, Eunapius is grandiloquent; where Dexippus is careful, Eunapius is slapdash. Indeed, the explicit contempt that he directs toward precision in chronology – "what do dates add to the wisdom of Socrates" (frag. 1, Blockley 1983) – is matched by his practical neglect of it in the surviving fragments.

Eunapius is, nonetheless, one of the main controlling sources we possess for events of the fourth century, both in the fragments preserved by Constantine Porphyrogenitus and in the large stretches of Zosimus's *Historia*

Nova that merely abridge Eunapius and deflate the soaring rhetoric and Atticisms of the original. (Zosimus, as Photius, *Bibl. Cod.* 98, says, essentially copied out Eunapius rather than actually writing history himself.) Because Zosimus is so literal, we can be more certain of the overall contents of Eunapius's work than of Dexippus or those other fragmentary authors who survive mainly in excerpts. This makes it possible to see the moralizing priggery and shrillness that are the hallmarks of the historian. No one – emperor, courtier, or otherwise – escapes a withering judgment. All are cowardly or envious or deceitful in various ways. Until Julian. The pagan emperor is, for Eunapius, an object of what can only be called devotion; he knew Julian's companion, the doctor Oribasius of Pergamum, and used the latter's notes on the emperor's campaigns. The emperors that succeeded the pagan martyr come in for renewed scorn: Valens for his blindness and incompetence and Theodosius for what Eunapius regards as lamentable softness on the barbarian enemy. While this perspective underpins just about everything in the text, Eunapius and Zosimus's witness to him serves to check the narrative of Ammianus where they overlap. Likewise, the survival of a text written so close to the events at Adrianople gives us a much better sense of the range of immediate reactions to that shattering Roman defeat.

Along with Eunapius, a classicizing source probably contemporary to him had an outsized impact on the historical record while leaving only indirect evidence for its existence. There has long been a recognition that very late Byzantine universal *breviaria* like those of Zonaras (Banchich and Lane 2009) and Cedrenus preserve good information on the fourth century that confirms and supplements Ammianus and Eunapius but doesn't seem to depend upon either of them, and that material on the third century in these late sources might potentially be just as valuable. The difficulty has always been threefold: The precise interconnection between the extant late Byzantine authors has never been properly worked out; there is every likelihood that, as with the Irish chronicle tradition, no clear stemma can be reconstructed because there is cross-contamination among texts in each successive generation; and a suitably critical edition of most Byzantine texts has not yet been produced (this is changing, but our texts of George the Monk, Zonaras, Cedrenus, and Glycas remain deeply inadequate). That said, a careful study of Zonaras (Bleckmann 1992) seems to have demonstrated the existence of the long-suspected common late antique source, despite lacking a fully probative display of manuscript collation and subsequent textual criticism. This source is generally called *Leoquelle* (after Leo Grammaticus, the traditional name of one of the texts that shows evidence of this source, though Leo has now been revealed as nothing more than a recension of Symeon the Logothete; Wahlgren 2006). It will have been written in good classicizing Greek, somewhere in the fourth-century East. It ran parallel to both Dexippus and Eunapius, may or may not show familiarity with the latter's history, and was certainly not identical with the work of either author. Where the narrative picked up is unclear (perhaps after Dio's *Romaiká* petered out), but it ran down to Julian or Jovian. Despite vigorous, if also ludicrous, efforts to demonstrate that the *Leoquelle* was first composed in Latin and was, therefore, actually the lost *Annales* of Nicomachus Flavianus, there can be no question that the *Leoquelle* was Greek and that the content we can ascribe to it provides a genuine alternative to information found in Dexippus, Eunapius, and Ammianus. Unique information in the late Byzantine historians, or information shared by them in versions unfamiliar to the extant earlier sources, therefore needs careful evaluation on its own merits, but it cannot be dismissed out of hand as unusable because so late. That said, any systematic assessment of the good information preserved in Pseudo-Symeon Logothetes, Zonaras, Cedrenus, and Glycas will have to await the publication of properly critical editions of those authors, only one of which (Wahlgren 2006) now exists.

Apart from Eunapius and the *Leoquelle*, other third- or fourth-century historians are revealed to us only in very exiguous fragments (Janiszewski 2006 covers most of them). To take one of the better examples, a Eusebius (*FGrH* 101) who has never been satisfactorily identified was the author of two substantial fragments preserved in a Paris codex that deal with sieges in the Balkans and Gaul, though these events cannot be dated; whether they are the work of a Eusebius said by Evagrius Scholasticus (5.24) to have written a history from Augustus to Carus or of some other unattested Eusebius is unclear, but they reveal a classicizing author at home between the later third and later fourth centuries (Janiszewski 2006, pp. 54–77, with bibliography), very much in the same manner as the more broadly visible, if unidentifiable, *Leoquelle*.

Dexippus, Eunapius, and, from what we can tell, their more shadowy analogues belong to a recognizable type of the later Second Sophistic. Though undoubtedly public figures with local careers in their contemporary world, they still moved in circles that fetishized the *polis* and its patriotism and that claimed as its heritage a pristine, if largely invented, Hellenism, prizing genres that stood in a direct and definable line with the practices of late Hellenistic predecessors. They were, in other words, the sorts of people whom Libanius laments leaving the schools of rhetoric for the schools of Roman law, their *polis* and its pride for Constantinople. The generation of Eunapius was the last in which such men would dominate the Greek literary scene, because their cultural centrality had greatly declined. In their place came new elites whose route to wealth, power, and prestige came from, and was sustained by, imperial service. While these new men could imitate and continue the stylistic mannerisms of the Hellenistic past, their outlook had changed dramatically, in keeping with their changed world. This meant that, by the fifth century, the sort of men who wrote history in Greek were little different from those who had long dominated the much poorer tradition of Latin historiography.

As already noted, Latin historical writing on the grand scale seems to have stopped entirely with Tacitus. His rough contemporary L. Annaeus Florus pointed the alternative way forward with his epitome of Livy. From Florus on, this sort of *breviarium* was the most characteristic product of Latin historiography; if there was a living third-century tradition of classicizing history, it has escaped us. (On the other hand, the consular Marius Maximus wrote biographies during the Severan period that were later sources of the *Historia Augusta*, and consularia did continue to be compiled during this period.) It is likely, if conjectural, that *breviaria* in the mode of Florus continued to be composed in the third century, but at some time in the middle of the fourth century, a *breviarium* by an unknown author emerged and had enormous significance for the future. Its existence was noticed and proven by Alexander Enmann in 1884 (whence it is known as the *Enmannsche Kaisergeschichte*, or *EKG*). The *Kaisergeschichte* itself is lost and probably did not long survive the fourth century, but its existence is proved irrefragably by a host of shared information and, crucially, shared errors among a variety of fourth- and fifth-century authors (Eutropius, Aurelius Victor, the *Historia Augusta*, the *Epitome de Caesaribus*, Orosius, and so on). The success of Eutropius in particular rendered otiose the older *Kaisergeschichte*; hence its disappearance and our lack of information about its author.

Probably, though, he was a bureaucrat or civil servant in the fourth-century administrative hierarchy, for that is the background of nearly every Latin historical writer of the period, including the breviarists Aurelius Victor and Eutropius. The former came from a *petit bourgeois* North African background and had risen through the civil bureaucracy until a timely decision to back Julian against Constantius II opened the position of *consularis Pannoniae II* to him, setting him on a career that would even win him an urban prefecture under Theodosius (Bird 1984, 1994). Eutropius was a contemporary of Victor, was from Gaul, and was perhaps of a slightly more elevated background. He served as *magister epistularum*, joined Julian's campaigns, and then pursued a career in the East where he served under Valens and governed Asia as proconsul in 370 (Bird 1993).

The two men had in common more than their career trajectories: They produced strikingly similar works, each of real though limited utility for modern historians. Victor's *Caesares* is written in a convoluted, not to say tortured, syntax designed to show off the author's intellectual attainments – a classic case of trying too hard. Running from the first emperor to the reign of Constantius II, it is particularly useful for the hints it gives of chronology in the otherwise poorly datable first half of the fourth century. Eutropius's *Breviarium*, more popular than Victor's because its Latin is astoundingly simple, became the most influential textbook of Roman history ever produced. Dedicated to the emperor Valens, it was just the sort of thing that the *Pannonius subagrestis* could have benefited from, with a lightly didactic tone that, nevertheless, whisks one from Romulus to the present in a hundred short pages. More elegant, though equally dependent on the *Kaisergeschichte*, is the so-called *Epitome de Caesaribus*, a late fourth-century production that may reveal traces of Greek influence in its Latin text. Like Victor's and Eutropius's works, it is an intermittently valuable witness to otherwise poorly attested emperors, though like them, its reliability is hard to control for. An *Annales* written by Virius Nicomachus Flavianus, Roman senator and reluctant rebel against Theodosius, is attested in two honorific inscriptions (*CIL* 6: 1782; 6: 1783 = *ILS* 2947–48) that record his career. Literally thousands of pages have been devoted to constructing out of this single inscribed line a magnificent work of genius that influenced every extant text of the fourth and fifth centuries, standing as a monument to the last pagans of Rome (e.g. Paschoud 2006; Ratti 2010; but Flavianus has since the late 1980s been a sort of patron deity of Paschoud's revived *Historia Augusta* colloquia). Every positive argument adduced for this phantom work has been comprehensively exploded (Cameron 2010, pp. 627–690), but it is likely to haunt scholars for decades to come. If the epigraphically attested *Annales* were ever more than an aristocrat's squib or feuilleton, they were most likely a breviary of the *EKG*/Victor/Eutropius variety, perhaps on Republican rather than imperial history.

Towering over all these works, real and imagined, stands the figure of Ammianus Marcellinus, with Ambrose, Jerome, and the young Augustine the finest Latin prose writer of the century, and also the most eccentric. A balanced bilingual in Greek and Latin, he was nevertheless a Greek-speaker by birth, from an Antiochene family well connected to either the civilian or military bureaucracy. *Quondam miles et Graecus* ("a Greek, once a soldier," as he famously calls himself), he began a promising career as a *protector domesticus*, as did many other privileged young men of his generation. The *scholae domesticorum* served as a de facto officer training corps for the Constantinian empire, and no doubt it was there that Ammianus began to shape his knowledge of Roman history. In the *scholae*, young men of staggeringly diverse backgrounds (provincial gentry, Frankish princelings, exiled royals from Persia and the Caucasus, sons of illiterates who had prospered in the ranks and risen in the world) were provided a common set of references and a received narrative to orient them to the history of the world they would govern – like its dedicatee Valens, they would have found Eutropius most instructive. Ammianus, however, took his historical interests much further and developed as profound a knowledge of republican and imperial history as it was possible to acquire in the fourth century. In that lies one paradox of his *Res Gestae*, for though he often thought in Greek, and one struggles with his Latinity until the Greek substructure becomes clear, his whole framework of historical reference is Roman. His *exempla*, his moralizing, his arguments from analogy are all drawn from a Roman past, not a Greek one; and though in many places he seems to be arguing against political discourses current in the Greek world (both Eunapius and the consummate courtier Themistius are obvious targets), he attacks them with Roman weapons and disregards the *polis*-land repertoire of contemporary sophists (Kelly 2008; Kulikowski 2012).

But such inherent contradiction is not all that gives Ammianus his enduring appeal – his outlook on the empire is so beguiling that to escape it, once read, requires a conscious effort. Like Tacitus (and like Gibbon, who admired both authors), Ammianus searches for the human motivations that make history, mainly the discreditable ones – the mistakes, the venalities, the self-regard that render this sublunary world so disappointing a place. As is not the case with Tacitus, it is possible to distinguish a theology of sorts in Ammianus's pages, a genuine belief in the working, if not of gods, then of inexorable forces outside human control (Camus 1967, pp. 133–238; Meslin 1974; Rike 1987). Ammianus's gods punish; they never reward. In all of this it is possible to see elements of the man's own thwarted career, but the biographical fallacy is fatally easy to indulge in the case of Ammianus and we need to guard against practicing amateur psychology upon an author whose apparent self-revelation is at times actively deceptive (cf., e.g. Matthews 1989 and Barnes 1998).

The *Res Gestae* once began where Tacitus ended, at the death of Domitian. Whether the original composition was in 31 or 36 books (Barnes 1998), the first tranche of these had already disappeared when the grammarian Priscian was writing in the sixth century, and only the final 18 were extant, numbered 14 through 31 in the received tradition. These 18 books cover the years between 353 and 375/378, which suggests that Ammianus's accounts of the second and third centuries must have been quite cursory (attempts to prove where the text assumed its present fullness are necessarily speculative and none has been successful). The extant text of book 14 picks up just as the usurper Magnentius has been defeated and the hideous *agens in rebus* Paul the Chain is charged with rooting out and chastising his supporters.

Ammianus goes on to cover the disaster of the Caesar Gallus's brief tenure of power, the supposed usurpation of Silvanus in Gaul (15.5), Constantius's triumphal entry into Rome (16.10, a famous set-piece), and the endless wars with Persia on the eastern front (18–19). In many of these events, Ammianus was a direct participant, and he inserts himself into the first-person narrative with a vividness unique to Latin historians. Ammianus's first hero is his commanding officer Ursicinus, and he goes to great lengths to whitewash his character, as in the assassination of Silvanus, and to present him as a victim of Constantius's implacable suspicion; Ammianus can even portray a promotion as a deliberate slight (Thompson 1947, pp. 42–55). In Ammianus's account of the eastern campaigns, his eyewitness perspective is peculiarly gripping, revealing both the efficiency of the Roman army and the banality of cruelty in its world. The description of the siege and fall of Amida in books 18 and 19 is perhaps the least stylized such account to survive from antiquity (Lenski 2007). But parallel to these eastern events, the main hero of the extant books is emerging in the shape of the Caesar Julian, the figure on whom Ammianus pinned his highest hopes and expectations. He sees his hero's flaws, not least his addiction to ostentatious and otiose sacrifices and an impetuosity that could be as costly as it was magnificent, but he either fails to notice or does not mind the bitter malice that renders the emperor's own writings such heavy going for a modern reader.

The rest of the *Res Gestae* follows the emperor's ill-fated Persian invasion, and the military history of the Roman Empire could not be written as it nowadays is if that account did not exist. Ammianus had at one point evidently decided to end his history there, with the emperor's heroic if pointless death, the parlous extraction of the army from Persia, and the sad anticlimax of Jovian's reign (Heather 1999), which the historian treats as a hollow sham. It was after the Persian campaign that he himself left the army. A pagan, perhaps even an apostate like his hero Julian (Barnes 1998), he may have felt his prospects limited after the accession of yet another Christian ruler, but even before that his career had not prospered as had other *protectores* of his generation: Two slightly older contemporaries, Jovian and Valentinian, had risen to the purple after all. Instead of active service, he traveled, collecting materials for his history, living for extended periods in Antioch and then in Rome. We do not know when he began writing, or where, but he altered his original plan to stop with Julian, perhaps in light of the grotesque hecatomb that was Adrianople. Books 26–30 lack the precision and control of the earlier sections, but they have the same power to shape the historical imagination and have duly done so: the thuggish but soldierly Valentinian, the thick-witted paranoiac Valens, the improbable perfection of the elder Theodosius under whose son Ammianus was writing. Then, at the end, comes the monographic book 31, a fully rounded account of the circumstances that led to Adrianople, portrayed not as divine punishment but as a tragic train of human incompetencies (see Lenski 1997; Kulikowski 2012). The empire would recover, Ammianus says: It always had before. He himself died in the 390s, possibly without putting the finishing touches on his history. Brilliant though it is, it found no audience, no continuators, no posterity. Ammianus was simply too difficult, and too subtle. With few models of his own, he served as a model for no one. Eutropius, by contrast, proliferated in a rich manuscript tradition and two separate Greek translations, all with a long future serving as a primer of Roman history that lasted right into the eighteenth century.

With Ammianus, Latin historiography on a grand scale effectively comes to an end. The fragments of Renatus Profuturus Frigeridus and Sulpicius Alexander that are preserved in Gregory of Tours's sixth-century *Historiae* have some of the grandeur that we associate with the classicizing tradition, but they are too few and lack too much context to be reliably identified as belonging to it. What little fifth-century history was produced in Latin was church history, much of it translation from the Greek or hypertrophied *breviaria* like Orosius's *Historiae*. Sidonius explicitly disclaims any willingness to write a history of his times (a good thing – a lost history by Sidonius would generate a fantasist cottage industry à la Flavianus). By the time of Gregory of Tours, writing at the end of the first Merovingian century, the world had entirely changed and the bishop's work was a strange hybrid alien to the developed late Latin genres. In the interim, Cassiodorus had produced both a consularia (which we can identify as his only because it is explicitly said to be) and a Gothic history, now lost. This latter was probably an overgrown *breviarium*, like the *Getica* that Jordanes wrote in Justinianic Constantinople after a brief consultation of Cassiodorus's text (Christensen 2002). (Readers should beware prolific references in the scholarship to an *Origo Gothica*, whether it is attributed to Cassiodorus or not – it is a figment of *germanisches Altertumskunde* aiming to salvage some sort of primeval Gothic orality from Jordanes's thoroughly Byzantine text.) Jordanes's other work, a *Romana*, is little more than a reworked Eutropius, still more evidence that the *breviarium* is as characteristic a genre of late antiquity as the chronicle.

The Constantinople in which Jordanes wrote was one of the few places in the East where writing in Latin made sense – the military of the era was still recruited in large measure from those parts of the Latin-speaking Balkans that remained under imperial control, and by the 540s there was a large cadre of Italian exiles awaiting the outcome of Justinian's peninsular war. Elsewhere, though, the empire was becoming more and more Greek, Justinian's *novellae* appearing in both languages and the law school at Berytus slipping as an unchallenged center of eastern Latinity. Jordanes was thus very much an exception, and eastern historiography, both secular and ecclesiastical, was predominantly and proudly Greek. But it was a changed historiography, the old classicizing form and manner surviving, but the matter becoming less stylized and more willing to acknowledge contemporary reality.

Perhaps the best example of these changes is Olympiodorus of Thebes in Egypt (Matthews 1970; Blockley 1981, pp. 27–47; Gillett 1993). He is preserved in fragments by Photius, but because of his slightly rough-hewn style and his willingness to use Latin loanwords, he was much less to the patriarch's taste than was the polished, if hollow, prose of Eunapius. But Olympiodorus was used by the Nicene Constantinopolitan Church historian Sozomenos and the anti-Nicene Philostorgius, and also by faithful Zosimus in his fifth and sixth books. As Zosimus did with Eunapius, he follows Olympiodorus so closely that the two years between the breaking off of the former and the start of the latter are simply missing from Zosimus's history. According to Photius (*Bibl. Cod.* 80), Olympiodorus began his 22 books in the year 407 and carried it forward to 425, when Valentinian III and Galla Placidia were placed on the western throne with the backing of an eastern army, to which expedition Olympiodorus was an eyewitness. More or less by chance, his work became the last detailed account of western imperial affairs that we know to have existed. Olympiodorus has long been a favorite of modern scholars because of his precision, his experience as an ambassador of the imperial court, and his personal involvement in many of the events he describes, not least travels in various parts of the empire where other late ancient writers tended not to venture, like the Great Oasis and the land of the Blemmyes, a five-day march into the desert from Philae (frags. 32; 35,2, Blockley 1983). The fact that he admits technical vocabulary and declines to operate in a half fictional *polis*-land is another mark in his favor, as is the charming detail of the singing, dancing, and talking parrot who was his companion for twenty years (frag. 35,1, Blockley 1983). More difficult is knowing quite what attitude he took toward the politics of his time, and this is in large part a function of his fragmentary survival. An easterner, a representative of the eastern court no less, he might have been expected to take a triumphalist approach to the successful eastern mission to prop up the west. Certainly the fragments preserved by Photius suggest that perspective, but a reading of Philostorgius introduces very real doubt: The last episode in the latter's account of the western expedition is not the triumphant ascent of the *nobilissimus* Valentinian to the rank of Augustus, but rather the arrival of the rogue general Aëtius with 60,000 barbarian mercenaries and the bloody pitched battle they fought against the eastern army – with the result that Placidia compromised with the cynical warlord and brought him into the empire's military hierarchy (frag. 43,2, Blockley 1983). Did Olympiodorus want his readers to welcome the triumphant success of the imperial restoration? Or did he want to foreshadow the decades of violence that Aëtius and his rivals inflicted on the western empire? Was he hailing an *ordo renascendi* or was he reminding us it would all be in vain? In the fragmentary state of the evidence, there is no way of telling, an illustration of the sorts of difficulties we face with such sources.

Later fifth-century historians like Priscus of Panium (Blockley 1981, pp. 48–70) continued as much in the vein of Olympiodorus as in the older sophistic tradition. Priscus, who famously served on the embassy of Maximus to Attila's court in 448, wrote a history in eight books about eastern affairs, though whether this was organized along the lines of a classicizing history or of a monographic account of the Hunnic wars is unclear. Unknown to Photius, he is instead preserved in large chunks by the Constantinian *Excerpta*, so we have to fall back on the *Suda* and the excerpts themselves for our understanding of the author. What they reveal is a figure after the Olympiodoran model, a rhetorician of skill who was nevertheless concerned to give verisimilitude rather than idealized classicism to his evidence. Certainly he is a more interesting writer than Malchus of Philadelphia (Blockley 1981, pp. 71–85), author of seven books of imperial history from Leo I's death to the deaths of Julius Nepos and Zeno, though Malchus is highly esteemed by Photius for the elegance and clarity of his style. Malchus's contemporary Candidus (Blockley 1983, pp. 464–473), an Isaurian historian under Anastasius, wrote an account of the reigns of Leo and Zeno, of which Photius gives a quite hostile account, approving only the author's piety, not his style or historical skills.

With Candidus and Malchus we move to the sixth century, where everything inevitably lies in the shadow of Procopius (Cameron 1985; Kaldellis 2004). This is not an unmixed blessing, as the vast bulk of the Justinianic writer distracts from the sometimes more interesting productions of Menander, Agathias, and Theophylact. That said, all these authors reflect, not merely the disappearance of the old sophistic model of history writing, but also an increasingly evident transition to a post-Classical, medieval worldview. This manifests itself chiefly in the way that exotic and digressive matters are introduced to the story. Whereas the classicizing traditions of Ammianus and the fragmentary Greek authors at whom we have been looking turned to formal *excursus* as a way of including learned asides or technical discussion, Procopius tends to bury the same sort of material in folkloric guise. Thus Ammianus (18.7.4–5) might have an excursus on lions triggered by the geography of the Tigris valley, but he sets it off as a digression and alters his tone into that of the learned schoolroom. Procopius, by contrast, loads his digressions with stock motifs and folkloric topoi: In narrating the death of the shah Peroz in battle against the Hephthalites (*Bella* 1.4.1429), he introduces a sort of shaggy-dog story about a great pearl beloved by, and lost with, the Persian king and then gives us the history of the pearl and an improbable tale of oysters and sharks. This reliance on folkloric motifs is something that we find also in the church histories of the period, and in the hypertrophied *breviarium* composed in Antioch by John Malalas at roughly this same time (Jeffreys, Croke, and Scott 1990; Meier, Radtki, and Schulz 2016).

A related development is the almost total ignorance of the history of the Latin West revealed by the histories of both Vandalic and Gothic wars. While Procopius is modestly reliable on western events of Justin's and Justinian's reigns, the fifth century is a virtual blank. This goes well beyond the sort of mythologizing of Constantine, for good and ill, that had already afflicted the fourth century (Lieu and Monserrat 1998a, 1998b). It is, rather, a fundamental unfamiliarity with the sequence of events or even the main players in them. Procopius, that is, reveals the disjuncture between East and West that the fifth-century crisis had produced: Even a man who had traveled in Italy and put considerable effort into understanding the course of events that led to the Gothic war simply could not muster the evidence in an accurate way. A combination of both trends – the folkloric and the ignorant – is best illustrated in Procopius's tale (*Bella* 3.7) of the fifth-century emperor Majorian's wandering incognito in the Vandal camp in order to spy on Gaiseric and learn his plans.

Procopius looms large over the last two generations of Greek classicizing history. Writing under Justin II and Tiberius, the rhetor Agathias picked up the history of Justinian's reign where Procopius broke off in 550 and continued the narrative – almost exclusively a military narrative – down to 558, though he had clearly intended to cover the whole of Justin II's reign and must have died before completing his work (Cameron 1970). This is implied by his successor Menander (a courtier under Maurice whose honorific military title of Protector is usually treated as part of his name). Menander carried Agathias's narrative down to 582 and, like him, imitated as best he could the stylistic affectations of Procopius (Blockley 1985). Finally, Theophylact Simocatta, writing under Heraclius, continued the story through to the death of Maurice in 602 (Whitby 1988).

The classicizing tradition comes to an end with Theophylact, and, indeed, the entire tradition of narrative history writing in Greek effectively ended at the start of the seventh century. By that time, classical traditions in the Latin world had completely disappeared. The Middle Ages, in both East and West, would reinvent many of antiquity's historical genres – but they would be doing so in imitation of the past, not as the direct inheritors of it.

REFERENCES

Baldini, Antonio. (1984). *Ricerche sulla storia di Eunapio di Sardi. Problemi di storiografia tardopagana.* Bologna: CLUEB.

Banchich, Thomas and Lane, Eugene. (2009). *The History of Zonaras from Alexander Severus to the Death of Theodosius the Great.* London: Routledge.

Barnes, Timothy D. (1978). *The Sources of the Historia Augusta.* Brussels: Latomus.

Barnes, Timothy D. (1998). *Ammianus Marcellinus and the Representation of Historical Reality.* Ithaca, NY: Cornell University Press.

Bird, H.W. (1984). *Sextus Aurelius Victor: A Historiographical Study.* Liverpool: Francis Cairns.

Bird, H.W. (1993). *Eutropius: Breviarium.* Liverpool: Liverpool University Press.

Bird, H.W. (1994). *Aurelius Victor: De Caesaribus.* Liverpool: Liverpool University Press.

Bleckmann, Bruno. (1992). *Die Reichskrise des III. Jahrhunderts in der spätantiken und byzantinischen Geschichtsschreibung. Untersuchungen zu den nachdionischen Quellen der Chronik des Johannes Zonaras.* Munich: Tuduv.

Blockley, Roger C. (1981). *The Fragmentary Classicising Historians of the Later Roman Empire I: Eunapius, Olympiodorus, Priscus and Malchus.* Liverpool: Francis Cairns.

Blockley, Roger C. (1983). *The Fragmentary Classicising Historians of the Later Roman Empire II: Text, Translation and Historiographical Notes.* Liverpool: Francis Cairns.

Blockley, Roger C. (1985). *The History of Menander the Guardsman: Introductory Essay, Text, Translation and Historiographical Notes.* Liverpool: Francis Cairns.

Burgess, Richard W. and Kulikowski, Michael. (2013). *Mosaics of Time. The Latin Chronicle Traditions from the First Century BC to the Sixth Century AD. Vol I: A Historical Introduction to the Chronicle Genre from its Origins to the High Middle Ages.* Turnhout: Brepols.

Burgess, Richard W. and Kulikowski, Michael. (2016). The historiographical position of John Malalas. Genre in late antiquity and the Byzantine Middle Ages. In: *Die Weltchronik des Johannes Malalas. Autor – Werk – Überlieferung* (ed. Mischa Meier, Christine Radtki, and Fabian Schulz), 93–118. Stuttgart: Franz Steiner.

Cameron, Alan. (2010). *The Last Pagans of Rome.* New York: Oxford University Press.

Cameron, Averil. (1970). *Agathias.* Oxford: Clarendon.

Cameron, Averil. (1985). *Procopius and the Sixth Century.* Berkeley: University of California Press.

Camus, P.M. (1967). *Ammien Marcellin. Témoin des courants culturels et religieux à la fin du iv-e siècle.* Paris: Les Belles Lettres.

Christensen, Arne Soby. (2002). *Cassiodorus, Jordanes and the History of the Goths. Studies in a Migration Myth.* Copenhagen: Museum Tusculanum.

Enmann, Alexander. (1884). Eine verlorene Geschichte der römischen Kaiser und das Buch De viris illustribus urbis Romae. *Philologus* supp. 9: 337–501.

Gillett, Andrew. (1993). The date and circumstances of Olympiodorus of Thebes *Traditio* 48: 1–29.

Heather, Peter. (1999). Ammianus on Jovian: History and literature. In: *The Late Roman World and Its Historian. Interpreting Ammianus Marcellinus* (ed. Jan Willem Drijvers and David Hunt), 105–116. London: Routledge.

Janiszewski, Pawel. (2006). *The Missing Link: Greek Pagan Historiography in the Second Half of the Third Century and in the Fourth Century AD*. Warsaw: Journal of Juristic Papyri.

Jeffreys, Elizabeth, Croke, Brian, and Scott, Roger. ed. (1990). *Studies in John Malalas*. Melbourne: Australian Association of Byzantine Studies.

Kaldellis, Anthony. (2004). *Procopius. Tyranny, History and Philosophy at the End of Antiquity*. Philadelphia: University of Pennsylvania Press.

Kelly, Gavin. 2008. *Ammianus Marcellinus: The Allusive Historian*. Cambridge: Cambridge University Press.

Kulikowski, Michael. (2012). Coded polemic in Ammianus book 31 and the date and place of its composition. *Journal of Roman Studies* 102: 79–102.

Lenski, Noel. (1997). *Initium mali romano imperio*: Contemporary reactions to the Battle of Adrianople. *Transactions of the American Philological Association*, 127: 129–68.

Lenski, Noel. (2007). Two sieges of Amida (AD 359 and 502–503) and the experience of combat in the late Roman Near East. In: *The Late Roman Army in the Near East from Diocletian to the Arab Conquest*: Proceedings of a colloquium held at Potenza, Acerenza and Matera, Italy (May 2005) (ed. Ariel S. Lewin and Pietrina Pellegrini), 219–236. Oxford: Archaeopress.

Lieu, Samuel N.C. and Montserrat, Dominic. ed. (1998a). *From Constantine to Julian: Pagan and Byzantine Views*. London: Routledge.

Lieu, Samuel N.C. and Montserrat, Dominic. ed. (1998b). *Constantine: History, Historiography and Legend*. London: Routledge.

Mallan, C. and Davenport, C. (2015). Dexippus and the Gothic invasions: Interpreting the new Vienna fragment (*Codex Vindobonensis Hist. gr.* 73, ff. 192v–193r). *Journal of Roman Studies* 105: 203–26.

Markopoulos, Athanasios. (2004). New evidence on the date of Photios' *Bibliotheca*. In: *History and Literature of Byzantium in the 9th–10th Centuries*, item XII. Aldershot, Hants: Variorum.

Martin, G. (2006). *Dexipp von Athen. Edition, Übersetzung und begleitende Studien*. Tübingen: Narr.

Martin, G. and Grusková, J. (2014a). Dexippus Vindobonensis? Ein neues Handschriftenfragment zum sog. Herulereinfall der Jahre 267/8. *Wiener Studien* 127: 101–120.

Martin, G. and Grusková, J. (2014b). Scythica Vindobonensia by Dexippus (?): New fragments on Decius' Gothic Wars. *Greek, Roman and Byzantine Studies* 54: 728–754.

Matthews, John F. (1970). Olympiodorus of Thebes and the history of the West (A.D. 407–425. *Journal of Roman Studies* 60: 79–97.

Matthews, John F. (1989). *The Roman Empire of Ammianus.* Baltimore: Johns Hopkins University Press.

Mecella, Laura. (2013). *Dexippo di Atene. Testimonianze e frammenti.* Rome: Tored.

Meier, Mischa, Radtki, Christine, and Schulz, Fabian. ed. (2016). *Die Weltchronik des Johannes Malalas. Autor – Werk – Überlieferung.* Stuttgart: Franz Steiner.

Meslin, Michel. 1974. Le merveilleux comme langage politique chez Ammien Marcellin. In: *Mélanges d'histoire ancienne offerts à William Seston* (ed. J. Tréheux), 253–263. Paris: Boccard.

Millar, Fergus. (1969). P. Herennius Dexippus: The Greek world and the third-century invasions. *Journal of Roman Studies*, 59: 12–29.

Norden, Eduard. (1909). *Antike Kunstprosa.* 2nd ed. Leipzig: Teubner.

Paschoud, François. (2006). *Eunape, Olympiodore, Zosime. Scripta Minora.* Bari: Edipuglia.

Ratti, Stéphane. (2010). *Antiquus error. Les ultimes feux de la résistance païenne. Scripta varia augmentés de cinq études inédites.* Turnhout: Brepols.

Rike, R.L. (1987). *Apex Omnium: Religion in the Res Gestae of Ammianus.* Berkeley: University of California Press.

Thompson, E.A. (1947). *The Historical Work of Ammianus Marcellinus.* Cambridge: Cambridge University Press.

Toynbee, Arnold. (1973). *Constantine Porphyrogenitus and His World.* London: Oxford University Press.

Treadgold, Warren T. (1980). *The Nature of the Bibliotheca of Photius.* Washington, DC: Dumbarton Oaks.

Wahlgren, Staffan. ed. (2006). *Symeonis Magistri et Logothetae Chronicon.* Berlin: De Gruyter.

Whitby, Michael. (1988). *The Emperor Maurice and His Historian: Theophylact Simocatta on Persian and Balkan Warfare.* Oxford: Clarendon.

Wilamowitz-Moellendorf, Ulrich. (1907). *Die griechische und lateinische Literatur und Sprache*, 2nd ed. Leipzig: Teubner.

CHAPTER TEN

Ecclesiastical History

Peter Van Nuffelen

The history of ecclesiastical historiography in late antiquity seems, at first sight, straightforward. It was created by Eusebius of Caesarea (d. 339) at the beginning of the fourth century, flourished in Greek, never really caught on in Latin, transferred into Syriac in the sixth century, and died out at the end of late antiquity, with Evagrius Scholasticus as the last major representative of the genre at the end of the sixth century. The genre seems to have a strong internal cohesion. Individual works carry the Greek title *ekklesiastike historia* or any of its derivatives in Latin and Syriac. They generally espouse the form chosen by Eusebius: Ecclesiastical affairs are narrated in nonclassicizing language with regular citation of documents and other texts. To some scholars, formal similarity seems backed up by a shared theological outlook: Church histories are supposed to trace the plan of God in history. On this view, ecclesiastical history might well be the late antique literary genre par excellence: the expression of the rise of the church and its self-affirmation as a historical actor in late antiquity. Logically, the demise of the genre by the seventh century is then to be explained by the dawn of a new period, in which church and state became indistinguishable (e.g. Markus 1975; Momigliano 1977; Chesnut 1986; Cameron 1998). The traditional view certainly has truth in it. Its weakness lies in the fact that it is constructed on the basis of the six preserved Greek and Latin orthodox church historians (I give their dates of publication): Eusebius of Caesarea (ca. 325), Rufinus (ca. 402–403; the only one writing in Latin), Socrates (439–440), Sozomen (ca. 445), Theodoret of Cyrrhus (ca. 448–451), and Evagrius (ca. 594–600). This chapter argues

---

A Companion to Late Antique Literature, First Edition.
Edited by Scott McGill and Edward J. Watts.
© 2018 John Wiley & Sons, Inc. Published 2018 by John Wiley & Sons, Inc.

that considerable nuance is added to the picture if we take the fragmentary material into account, look at other languages, and shed some long-held presuppositions.

10.1 Origins

If Eusebius created ecclesiastical history, it certainly was not ex nihilo. Self-conscious as any ancient author, he claims in his preface that he is "now the first to enter upon this subject, as if I am trying to walk a deserted and untrodden path" (*Church History* 1.1.3). This claim to originality has had two effects on scholarship. One is to distance Eusebius from classical historiography. Indeed, the statement strikes a chord with the modern scholar, who notices that the *Ecclesiastical History* has features absent in classical historiography, such as the quotations of other texts in extenso. This has led to the suggestion that Eusebius was more inspired by "parahistoriographical" genres, such as lives of philosophers and antiquarian historiography, than by mainstream classical historiography (Momigliano 1990, p. 138; Winkelmann 1991). The idea needs to be nuanced. Eusebius consciously seeks to insert himself into the grand tradition of classical historiography by indicating warfare, albeit against the powers of evil, as his subject (*Church History* 1.1.4, 5.pr.3–4). Documents were also cited within the classical tradition from historians such as Thucydides (5.23–24, 5.47) and Polybius (3.22–25, 3.27.2-10, with Marincola 1997, pp. 101–103), although we should avoid reducing classical historiography to these canonized luminaries; the genre was varied, including national and local histories. One can best understand Eusebius as intending to write the history of the distinct people that the Christians claimed to be (see Johnson 2014).

Eusebius's claim to originality also has the purpose of lifting him above his predecessors, who are silenced or at least downgraded. Scholarship has tended to follow Eusebius and to dismiss earlier attempts at writing history of the church as not really history. Yet, this was not the view of late ancient Christians, who could point to Clement of Alexandria, Hegesippus, and Julius Africanus as predecessors of Eusebius, as well as describe the evangelists and Moses, the author of the Pentateuch, as historians (Jerome, *De viris illustribus* 22; Macarius Magnes, *Apocriticus* 11.17; Philostorgius, *Church History* 1.1; Sozomen, *Church History* 1.1.12; Evagrius Scholasticus, *Church History* 5.24). There is undoubtedly a difference between Eusebius and his predecessors: He combines a theological conception of the church with a social one, which allows him to clearly define his subject matter with reference to its specific representatives, such as bishops, famous writers, heresies, and martyrs (*Church History* 1.1.1–2). Indeed, a more advanced institutionalization may well have been a social precondition for writing a history of the church, for which a more or less clear identification of the church within society was necessary. If, then, there is indeed a qualitative difference between Eusebius and his predecessors, his claim to be the first to write history has led to a lack of recognition of the other forms of writing about the past that preceded him. Indeed, Eusebius should also be seen as incorporating impulses toward historical writing from martyrology, heresiology, and apologetics (Morgan 2005; Morlet 2006; DeVore 2013).

It is, ultimately, more fruitful to ask in what context Eusebius situated his history, rather than what the origins of his historiography were. Indeed, there are many ways in which one can narrate the past of one's religious community. An interest in the development of the community and its doctrine can be found in other late antique faiths as well. A life of Mani has been preserved in the Mani Codex from Cologne (ca. 300), and fragments from two Coptic codices with "church historical" content await edition (Sundermann 1986). Within Christianity, a series of apocryphal gospels exists, texts that were usually shaped by theological rather than by historiographical concerns but, nevertheless, added to the traditions about the origins of the Christian faith. What sets Eusebius apart from such forms of writings is a clear choice to insert ecclesiastical history within the tradition of Greco-Roman historiography by depicting Christianity as a people with its own history. Besides illustrating the degree of cultural integration of Christianity in ancient civilization, it also hints at the fact that Eusebius was probably writing not just for a clerical or even Christian audience; he espoused the cultural forms of the ancient elite in order to address it and demonstrate to it the true nature of Christianity (Verdoner 2010; Corke-Webster 2013).

10.2 Genre

Later church historians would readjust the Eusebian program to their own needs but would never abandon the view of ecclesiastical historiography as part of general historiography. Greek church historians have a clear awareness of a division of labor: Events dealing with the empire were the preserve of what we would call classicizing history, whereas ecclesiastical history dealt with everything that related to the church. This can be observed in the case of Procopius, who, besides his history of Justinian's wars, in which the church is by and large absent, planned an ecclesiastical history (Procopius, *Wars* 8.25.13; *Anecdota* 11.33.). There was, obviously, plenty of overlap between ecclesiastical and secular events, and historians reflected about this: Socrates affirms that one cannot assign a strict priority to either sphere, whereas Sozomen sees ecclesiastical events as having causal priority: Peace in the church assures peace in the empire (Socrates, *Church History* 5.pr; Sozomen, *Church History* 6.2.13–16, 8.25.1 with Wallraff 1997, 99–109 and Van Nuffelen 2004, pp. 117–124, 156–158). There were other differences between the two genres, too. Ecclesiastical historians felt less bound by the strict imitation of classical models, and they would, therefore, have less classicizing elements, without them being entirely absent. For the same reason they were more open to the quotation of entire documents in the original, as Eusebius had already been. Yet the quotation of documents was not an automatism: Sozomen, for example, clearly had reservations because their inclusion risked distorting the narrative balance (*Church History* 1.1.14), while Rufinus has virtually no documents at all and the Eunomian historian Philostorgius (ca. 424–438) very few if the extant fragments are anything to go by (Bidez et al. 2013; Bleckmann and Stein 2015).

The paradigmatic status ascribed by scholars to Eusebius's *Ecclesiastical History* and the apparent conformation to that model by the preserved successors in Greek (Socrates, Sozomen, Theodoret, and Evagrius) has led to the perception of the genre as essentially an imitation and emulation of Eusebius. Ecclesiastical history then appears as a genre that writes about the recent and contemporary history of the church in general and that continues a preceding history, so as to insert itself into a continuous history from Christ to the end of times. This perception is the product of the choice by later generations to preserve these Greek histories because they were perceived to form an authoritative account of the past and offered together a continuous account from Christ to the sixth century. This is most clearly expressed in the fact that Socrates, Sozomen, and Theodoret, who all wrote about the church in the fourth and early fifth century, were gathered into a single tripartite history by Theodore Lector in 518, who, in turn, inspired a similar work in Latin by Cassiodorus (ca. 540–550). In that authoritative sequence, then, the needs of later readers are found, and not the intentions of the individual authors.

Moreover, the canonization of these four works led to the loss or marginalization of a series of other church histories, whose authors often made other choices for the organization of their material. A church history could take on a monographic character and focus on a single event, as do, for example, the Anonymous of Cyzicus (after 476) on the Council of Nicea (325) and Hesychius of Jerusalem (ca. 434–439) on that of Ephesus (431). Alternatively, the work could be more expansive and include the history of the church from its very origins: Sozomen says he composed an epitome of Eusebius in two books (*Church History*, Dedication) and, in Syriac, the

Miaphysite John of Ephesus started his church history with Caesar (ca. 588), whereas the Nestorian Daniel Bar-Maryam started with Christ (seventh century). Ecclesiastical historiography could also be local, as demonstrated by the Coptic church history of Alexandria. Finally, ecclesiastical histories could also take the form of compilations, as illustrated by Theodore Lector, Cassiodorus, and Pseudo-Zachariah (568). Each of these forms could express a particular historiographical strategy: "Supersessionist" accounts such as the one by John of Ephesus allowed a rewriting of the past from the perspective of current orthodoxy; compilations allowed to marshal past authorities for contemporary issues, as did Cassiodorus by selecting episodes to question Justinian's church policy; monographs could highlight the finding of truth that was challenged by contemporary heretics; local histories could express local identities.

If the genre of ecclesiastical history was internally diversified, its boundaries were fluid. I shall illustrate this by looking at four types of texts that were close enough to ecclesiastical history to be sometimes assimilated to it. First, a singular undertaking was the Christian history by Philip of Side (ca. 426–439), who wrote a narrative history from Adam to his own day. Its title clearly indicates it was consciously not an ecclesiastical history, as it started before the existence of the church. This Christian history can be understood as the combination of church history and "sacred history," the origins of which were often assigned to Moses.

Second, collections of documents were an omnipresent tool of public argument in late antiquity: Documents were gathered in a sequence, often guided by a brief narrative framework, and served to prove a particular position. The best-known examples of the genre are the so-called *Historia Arianorum* of Athanasius (ca. 295–373) and his *Apologia Secunda*. Not only were these collections important sources for church historians; they could also be labeled "ecclesiastical history," as happened with the collection of Timothy the Apollinarian and, probably, with the so-called ecclesiastical history of the Alexandrian Episcopate (Van Nuffelen 2002a; Bausi and Camplani 2013). As church historians often quoted documents, the transfer of title need not cause surprise. Yet, in these collections the balance was clearly tilted toward documents and against narrative.

Third, Eusebius described his church history as a more extensive version of his chronicle (Eusebius, *Church History* 1.1.7) and there was, indeed, overlap in content between both genres: Chronicles written by Christians always included ecclesiastical events. Moreover, contrary to what their annalistic format suggests, chronicles could be every inch as argumentative as narrative histories, as is shown at the end of the sixth century by the chronicles of Victor of Tunnuna and John of Biclar, who challenged Justinian's policy on the Three Chapters. When chronicles took on a narrative form in the sixth century, they started to incorporate material from ecclesiastical history, as John Malalas illustrates. In the Syriac tradition, as we shall see, this led to a division of chronicles into a secular and an ecclesiastical part.

Finally, biography was an important part of late ancient Christian literature production. If hagiography often assimilates itself to history, the similarities with church histories are the greatest in the case of serial biographies – for example, so-called histories of monks (e.g. *Historia monachorum in Aegypto*) and collections of martyr accounts. As the example of Eusebius, author of *On the Martyrs of Palestine*, shows, church historians could write both types of texts, as did Theodoret of Cyrrhus and John of Ephesus. The fact that part of the manuscript tradition of Eusebius's church history includes the *Martyrs of Palestine* as a book of the church history, demonstrates that both could be assimilated (Cassin, Debié, and Perrin 2012). At the same time, it is clear that such biographical narratives were seen as distinct from the broader scope of a church history and that monks and martyrs were only part of its subject matter. It is, indeed, striking that the tradition of serial biography of bishops or abbots, best attested for Rome in the *Liber pontificalis*, is never called a church history in the Greek and Latin tradition, an observation that is, with some exceptions such as the Chronicle of Arbela, also correct for the Syriac tradition.

Ecclesiastical history, thus, interacted creatively with other forms of historical writing, both within and outside the church. This is an obvious reflection of its nature: Being history, it was influenced by what late ancient authors thought was historiography, a tradition that was inherited from classical antiquity; being a history of the church, it had a potential interest in all aspects of ecclesiastical life and was open to the various genres that focused on partial aspects. Ecclesiastical history, therefore, can be defined in a tautology: It is a history of the church, that is, an account of the Christian institution and community in the mold of what was considered to be historiography.

10.3 History and Theology

Scholars have often defined the genre in theological terms, in two respects. First, as a history of the church, it presupposes a view of the Christian community – that is, the church – and it is thus conditioned on an ecclesiology. Second, as histories, church histories express the Christian view about history and about God's impact on it. Both propositions are correct, if easily overstated. Having to deal with all the components of the church, from bishop to laity, church histories project views of the church. Yet they are not to be read as developing an ecclesiology that would be theoretically coherent. Rather, an ecclesiology is presupposed and shimmers through in the narrative. In other terms, ecclesiastical histories reflect ecclesiology but do not necessarily reflect on it. The most fruitful recent suggestion in this respect is that of Philippe Blaudeau (2006), who sees church histories as reflecting "geo-ecclesiologies." In the doctrinal controversies that marked the ancient church, the various patriarchal sees understood themselves as incarnating the right theology, which was, in turn, related to presuppositions on how the relations between the various churches needed to be organized. Ecclesiology thus had a geographical focus. Indeed, church histories usually have a clear geographical focal point, which normally coincides with the see the history implicitly identifies as the norm of orthodoxy. Theodore Lector, for example, has a clearly Constantinopolitan focus, whereas Zachariah Scholasticus (492–495) focuses on Alexandria. Theodoret of Cyrrhus, in turn, has a clearly Antiochean focus.

It is often assumed that ecclesiastical historians hold strong presuppositions about the theology of history. The fundamental aim of church history is defined as tracing the plan of God in history and determining how each event contributes to the history of salvation. This has led to dismissive judgments, for church historians are supposed not to be interested in "real history," as they already know how events will develop (Timpe 2001; Meier 2004). Such a view relies on a misunderstanding of late ancient theology of history, which generally emphasizes that our human capacities are too limited to fully understand God and, hence, the world. If a church historian (as any late ancient author) believes that the hand of God ultimately lies behind everything, he also affirms his own incapacity to define the precise significance of each event. Indeed, properly theological works are the place to discuss explicitly the meaning of what happens in the world, but history is not the genre to pontificate on the meaning of history. There is more theology of history in Theodoret's *Homilies on Providence* than in his *Ecclesiastical History*. In addition, late ancient historians leave ample space for human causality and do not attribute everything that happens directly to God. Indeed, the Syriac chronicler Pseudo-Joshua the Stylite engages in extensive reflection on how one can reconcile human and divine causality (*Chronicle*, preface). As with ecclesiology, ecclesiastical histories are not texts designed to reflect on the theology of history: They start out from assumptions, they reflect on the difficulties of attributing causes to God, man and the devil, and they wonder about the meaning of things, but they never achieve a high level of coherent theoretical reflection. In this, the genre remains true to its vocation of historiography as defined in the ancient tradition – to record truthfully what had happened – but does this within a changing intellectual environment.

10.4 Development

Because of the fractious nature of the late ancient church, there were many different views on its past available. All sides in the debates about orthodoxy and heresy engaged in the writing of history, which could provide proof of the true tradition. The preservation of texts was, obviously, influenced by orthodoxy: In Greek and Latin, preserved histories are Chalcedonian; in Syriac, Miaphysite or Nestorian. Yet, many orthodox works are also lost. While chance certainly was a factor, works with a wider scope and a smaller explicitly polemical intent seem to have had greater chance of survival, as they had a greater interest in the eyes of posterity. In this section, I shall survey the various traditions of ecclesiastical historiography according to language, including the fragmentary material so as to offer as complete an image as possible.

In Greek, the tradition of writing ecclesiastical history seems robust from Eusebius until Evagrius, with the five standard Greek histories. As we have seen, the integration of fragmentary evidence considerably nuances the picture of the genre produced by these five preserved works, and the same can be said for its development. The second generation of historians, Philostorgius, Socrates, Sozomen, and Theodoret, consciously start where Eusebius left off. Yet some church histories are attested for the fourth century, such as that by Philo of Carpasia (ca. 375–400), who seemed to have focused on edifying stories about martyrs and confessors (Van Hoof, Manafis, and Van Nuffelen 2017). A late Syriac source attests to a history written for the time from Christ to Constantine by a certain Sabinus the Arian (Nau 1915–1917). He may be identical to Sabinus of Heracleia (second half of the fourth century), a homoiousian, who composed a collection of documents on fourth-century church history, but the evidence is too limited to build much of an argument from it. As we have seen, Timothy the Apollinarian composed a collection that went under the title of church history. The so-called Anonymus Arian historiographer is not a church historian but a chronicler who continued an earlier continuation of Eusebius's *Chronicle* until 363 (Burgess 1999; Van Nuffelen forthcoming). On the Nicene side evidence is not much better: Alexandria may have produced a history of its see under Theophilus (385–412), but its aspect, as we can gather from the fragments, is that of a collection of documents. Gelasius of Caesarea (d. 395) is said to have composed a church history at the end of the fourth century, but extant fragments indicate a use of Socrates, which turns this into a pseudonymous work (Winkelmann 1966; Van Nuffelen 2002b).

In the fifth century, church history was written when the history of the church seemed to take on its final shape. Philostorgius writes fully aware of the fact that his Eunomian sect is a tiny outlawed minority in the Theodosian Empire and draws on apocalyptic tropes in his last books. Socrates and Sozomen, by contrast, affirm the return of peace after a century-long struggle against Arianism and other evils. The church history of Theodoret aligns itself at first sight with these works and with the ideology of the Theodosian court. Yet his decision to end his history before the start of the Nestorian controversy, in which he himself was heavily involved on the wrong side, shows that his history reflects strongly on the permanent dangers posed to orthodoxy. Even if these general histories dominate our view of ecclesiastical historiography in the age of Theodosius II, we should not forget that other forms existed, such as the work focused on the council of Ephesus by Hesychius of Jerusalem (Van Hoof, Manafis, and Van Nuffelen 2016).

After the council of Chalcedon (451), we witness a series of ecclesiastical histories of all stripes and colors: The genre now becomes one of the literary genres in which rights and wrongs are claimed. On the Chalcedonian side, histories start with Chalcedon (Basil of Cilicia [after 512], Theodore Lector), whereas Miaphysite histories often went back to the Nestorian controversy (Timothy Aelourus [457–477], John Diacrinomenus [after 512]), thus expressing their view that Chalcedon had actually returned to Nestorius. But other options were available to them: Zachariah Scholasticus started with the run-up to Chalcedon, whereas John of Aegea (after 488) started with the council of Nicaea. All of these histories are to be dated in the last decades of the fifth and early-middle sixth century, and there does not seem to have been an immediate forerunner for Evagrius Scholasticus, writing at the very end of the sixth century. Indeed, the ecclesiastical troubles of the second half of the sixth century seem to have spurred the writing of church history in Syriac rather than in Greek, as we shall see below. Evagrius also represents a new, somewhat more settled way of approaching church history: He is willing to use the heretical history of Zachariah as a source of information, thus accepting that truthful and good information can be found there. His narrative is supersessionist, in that it goes back to Nestorianism and covers events already described by others, yet it preserves dissonant voices.

The end of church history in Greek has generated much scholarly interest. The traditional explanation is that, in a Christianized empire, it became increasingly hard to separate ecclesiastical from secular events. As evidence for this, the last book of Evagrius, which is by and large secular in nature, is usually adduced. Yet earlier historians, like Philostorgius and Sozomen, also shifted their narrative toward secular events in the last books, and, as we have seen, ecclesiastical historians pondered the difficulties of separating both realms. It has also been suggested that we witness a shift toward chronicles that started with the Creation, but chronicles and ecclesiastical histories had existed side by side for a long time. The end of the need for an apologetic genre of writing history has also been adduced, but on this account one would expect to see ecclesiastical history resurface at every conflict – for example, iconoclasm (Wallraff 2015). An alternative suggestion would be to think about church history as the social activity of a particular group. Writing a church history implied affirming the church as an autonomous sphere of society and was, therefore, also a form of social self-affirmation. We see it practiced by clerics or individuals closely aligned with a religious lifestyle. The fact that Socrates, Sozomen, and Evagrius, authors of three of the five preserved Greek histories, were lay persons seems, at first sight, to contradict this suggestion. Yet all of them were closely aligned with religious groups, Evagrius being, for example, legal aide to the patriarch of Antioch. It may be, then, that the end of ecclesiastical history in Greek is due to the fact that after the progressive Christianization in the sixth century and the transformations of the state in the "dark" seventh and eighth century, the Byzantine clerical and secular elite were more strongly integrated, thus generating less need for a self-affirmation of the church as an independent entity.

In Latin, ecclesiastical history never took off, and when it occurs, it is under the influence of the Greek-speaking East. We have seen that Rufinus translated and updated Eusebius (402–403), a work ordered by Chromatius of Aquileia to serve as a consolation to his flock in the face of recent troubles. In Constantinople, ca. 540–550, Cassiodorus had a Latin compilation made of Socrates, Sozomen, and Theodoret, inspired by a similar work in Greek by Theodore Lector and probably with the aim of finding ammunition against Justinian's condemnation of the Three Chapters. The *breviarium* of Liberatus has the same function (ca. 565) and is an ecclesiastical history in all but name. In the ninth century, Anastasius the Librarian (871–874) produced Latin translations of Greek historiographical works for John Hymonides, who intended to produce an ecclesiastical history, but the project never materialized. The only exception is Bede's *Ecclesiastical History of the English People*, a work inspired by Rufinus and Cassiodorus but original in its outcome: It picks up the Eusebian idea of ecclesiastical history as a narrative of the people of God but transfers this to a single people. By that maneuver, the English become a particular locus of God's attention and its readers are reminded of the high charge placed on them.

The question why ecclesiastical histories were rarely composed in the West is difficult to answer. Lack of interest can hardly be the answer, as there is plenty of evidence for circulation of Rufinus and, later, the *Historia tripartita*.

Things might have been different if an authority such as Jerome had actually composed his projected church history (*Life of Malchus* 1). Instead, Jerome's chronicle turned chronicle writing into the preferred historiographical medium in Latin. Indeed, even the narrative history of Sulpicius Severus assimilates itself to that genre with its title, *Chronica*. If one sees ecclesiastical history as essentially a genre of controversy, that is, as a genre that reflects defense of orthodoxy, the greater doctrinal uniformity of the West may be another reason why it was little practiced – even if the argument would entail that Donatism should have been an impulse to writing church history in Africa. Finally, it has been suggested that Rome sought to legitimize itself by focusing on its foundation by St. Peter and, hence, did not submit itself to historical narrative (Kany 2007, p. 576; Blaudeau 2016, p. 129). Serial biography, as found in the *Liber pontificalis*, focused on the individual personality of each bishop and the way he preserved the heritage of St. Peter. At any rate, with the center offering no impulse, the genre was condemned to marginality.

With Greek, Syriac is the language in which most ecclesiastical histories are written. The genre was first received through translations from the Greek. In particular, Eusebius's *Ecclesiastical History* was translated already by the end of the fourth or the beginning of the fifth century. Socrates was translated too, by the end of the sixth century at the latest. Historiography directly written in Syriac started in that same century. The first ecclesiastical history is Pseudo-Zachariah, a compilation of a Syriac translation of Zachariah Scholasticus, a continuation until 560, and some texts on earlier history, even if it is uncertain if its original title was, indeed, *Ecclesiastical History* (568/569). At the end of the sixth century, church history was clearly popular: John of Ephesus finished his tripartite work ca. 589; there is the somewhat mysterious John called Glybo, who may have written under or just after Justinian I. In the eight and ninth centuries, we know of a group of historians from Edessa, including Theophilus of Edessa, Daniel of Tur Abdin, and Theodosius of Tell-Mahre. Edessa was an important place of culture, but our perspective is distorted, as these authors are all known through Dionysius of Tell-Mahre (patriarch 818–845), author of a chronicle and himself from Edessa (see, in general, Debié 2009, 2015). Dionysius himself divided his chronicle into two parts, an ecclesiastical and a secular one. This innovation permitted the integration into narrative history of church history and secular history, an integration that in practice had already existed in chronicles. The format was adopted by the famous chronicles of Syriac renaissance in the twelfth and thirteenth centuries.

All the works just referred to are West Syrian – that is, Miaphysite. It is likely that the output of ecclesiastical history was spurred by the progressive institutionalization of that church in this period, generating a need to distinguish oneself from the Chalcedonian Church. It has been traditional to argue that the East Syrians (so-called Nestorians) developed a different type of historiography, in that they did not adopt the traditional forms of chronicle writing and ecclesiastical historiography. Instead, their histories tend to be biographical, individual, or serial (Debié 2010). This view needs to be reconsidered. If the sixth-century work *History of the Holy Fathers Persecuted for the Truth* by Barhadbesabba d-Bet-'Arbaye (after 569) is indeed biographical in nature and is only later called a church history, it represents a format of martyrological stories that is known in all traditions. Serial biography, as represented in the *History of Arbela* (twenty-one biographies of the bishops of Arbela, after 544) was also known in the other traditions. More importantly, there is extensive evidence for ecclesiastical histories written by East Syrians in the seventh century, even if it is all fragmentary in nature: Alaha-Zekha (early seventh century); Micah of Beth Garmai; Gregory of Kaskar (early-middle seventh century); Meshiha Zekha (seventh century); Daniel Bar Maryam (middle of seventh century); Elias of Merw (seventh century). This continued into the 8th century with Bar Sahde (seventh to eighth century), Gregory of Shuster (eighth century), Simon Bar-Tabahe (middle of eighth century), Theodore bar Koni (end of eighth century), and, somewhat later in the ninth century, a certain Pethyon. If some of these works are cited by later authors for biographical information and therefore may have had a biographical order (such as Elias of Merw and Pethyon), others are clearly chronological and narrative in nature (Daniel Bar Maryam, Bar Sahde, and Simon of Bar-Tabahe). Indeed, some of these narratives went back quite a bit in time. Bar Sahde covered at least the post-Chalcedonian period, and Simon wrote against Chalcedon and thus probably started there too. Daniel Bar Maryam, in turn, started with Christ. This flurry can be understood as a response to the rise of the West Syrian Church at the end of the sixth century, which encroached on the eastern territories where the East Syrians had been living. The East Syrians felt compelled to respond to the concomitant rise in ecclesiastical histories on the West Syrian side. Another impulse may have been the conquest of the Persian Empire (where the East Syrians lived) by Islamic forces and the need to define one's own position in that new context: Self-definition became important in a context where one was being defined by new powers (see Fiey 1970, pp. 113–143). In the shifting sands of political history of the seventh century, history may have been as much a response to the rise of Islam as to an apocalypse.

Literary genres are shaped by tradition, in that authors follow earlier models and seek to imitate and emulate them. In that sense, Eusebius is, indeed, the founding father of the genre: His work was the impetus for the various traditions just surveyed. Imitation was never slavish; as we have seen, the genre was enriched with many forms that deviated from the Eusebian model. At the same time, the writing of church history was influenced by particular circumstances, which could be as varied as the desire to participate in controversy and the wish to celebrate the end of controversy. The genre was rooted in social reality in yet another way: It can be understood as one particular form of the social self-affirmation of religious groups. Hence, the creation of ecclesiastical history by Eusebius is a testament both to the increased institutionalization of the church and to his will to display the life of the church to a wider audience. The genre was strong in periods when West Syrians and East Syrians needed to establish their own identity vis-à-vis each other, the Byzantine Chalcedonian Church, and Islam. It disappears in the Byzantine Empire when the Church identifies fully with the state, but it is reinvented by Bede when he seeks to define the English in ecclesiastical terms. It will return to the front stage of Western literary history during the debates between Catholics and Protestants in the early modern period.

ACKNOWLEDGMENT

The research leading to these results has received funding from the European Research Council under the European Union's Seventh Framework Programme (FP/2007–2013)/ERC Grant Agreement n. 313153 and from the Flemish Research Fund.

REFERENCES

Editions and bibliographies for all the authors mentioned can be found in the database available at http://www.late-antique-historiography.ugent.be/database; see also Van Hoof, Lieve and Peter Van Nuffelen, ed. 2018. *Clavis Historicorum Tardae Antiquitatis*, Turnhout: Brepols. Syriac authors can also be accessed via Debié 2015.

Bausi, Alessandro and Camplani, Albert. (2013). New Ethiopic documents for the history of Christian Egypt. *Zeitschrift für antikes Christentum* 17: 195–227.

Bidez, Joseph, des Places, Édouard, Bleckmann, Bruno et al. (2013). *Philostorge. Histoire ecclésiastique*. Sources chrétiennes 564. Paris: Éd. du Cerf.

Blaudeau, Philippe. (2006). *Alexandrie et Constantinople, 451–491: De l'histoire à la géo-ecclésiologie*. Bibliothèque des écoles françaises d'Athènes et de Rome 327. Rome: École française de Rome.

Blaudeau, Philippe. (2016). Narrating papal authority (440–530): The adaptation of Liber Pontificalis to the Apostolic See's developing claims. In: *The Bishop of Rome in Late Antiquity* (ed. Geoffrey D. Dunn), 127–140. London: Routledge.

Bleckmann, Bruno and Stein, Markus. (2015). *Philostorgios. Kirchengeschichte. Kleine und fragmentarische Historiker der Spätantike* E7, 1–2. Paderborn: Ferdinand Schöningh.

Burgess, Richard W. (1999). *Studies in Eusebian and Post-Eusebian Chronography. Historia Einzelschriften 135.* Stuttgart: Steiner.

Cameron, Averil. (1998). Education and literary culture. In: *The Cambridge Ancient History. Vol. 13: The Late Empire A.D. 337–425* (ed. Averil Cameron and Peter Garnsey), 665–707. Cambridge: Cambridge University Press.

Cassin, Matthieu, Debié, Muriel, and Perrin, Michel-Yves. (2012). La question des éditions de l'Histoire ecclésiastique et le livre X. In: *Eusèbe de Cesarée: Histoire ecclésiastique, commentaire. Vol. 1: Etudes d'introduction* (ed. Sébastien Morlet and Lorenzo Perrone), 185–207. Paris: Les Belles Lettres.

Chesnut, Glenn F. (1986). *The First Christian Histories.* Macon, GA: Macon Mercer University Press.

Corke-Webster, James. (2013). *Violence and Authority in Eusebius of Caesarea's Ecclesiastical History.* Diss. University of Manchester.

Debié, Muriel. ed. (2009). *L'historiographie syriaque.* Études syriaques 6. Paris: Geuthner.

Debié, Muriel. (2010). Writing history as "histoires": The biographical dimensions of East Syriac historiography. In: *Writing "True Stories." Historians and Hagiographers in the Late Antique and Medieval Near East* (ed. A. Papaconstantinou), 43–75. Cultural Encounters in Late Antiquity and the Middle Ages 9. Turnhout: Brepols.

Debié, Muriel. (2015). *L'Écriture de l'histoire en Syriaque: Transmissions interculturelles et constructions identitaires entre hellénisme et Islam.* Late Antique History and Religion 12. Louvain: Peeters.

DeVore, David J. (2013). Genre and Eusebius' Ecclesiastical History: Prolegomena for a focused debate. In: *Eusebius of Caesarea: Traditions and Innovations* (ed. Aaron Johnson and Jeremy Schott), 19–50. Cambridge, MA: Harvard University Press.

Fiey, Jean Marie. (1970). *Jalons pour une histoire de l'Église en Iraq.* Louvain: Peeters.

Johnson, Aaron P. (2014). *Eusebius.* London: I.B. Tauris.

Kany, Roland. (2007). Tempora Christiana. Vom Umgang des antiken Christentums mit Geschichte. *Zeitschrift für Antikes Christentum* 10: 564–79.

Marincola, John. (1997). *Authority and Tradition in Ancient Historiography.* Cambridge: Cambridge University Press.

Markus, Robert A. (1975). Church history and the early Church historian. In: *The Materials, Sources and Methods of Ecclesiastical History,* Studies in Church History 11 (ed. D. Baker), 1–17. Oxford: Blackwell.

Meier, Mischa. (2004). Prokop, Agathias, die Pest und das "Ende" der antiken Historiographie. Naturkatastrophen und Geschichtsschreibung in der ausgehenden Spätantike. *Historische Zeitschrift* 278: 281–310.

Momigliano, Arnaldo. (1977). Pagan and Christian historiography in the fourth century A.D. In: *Essays in Ancient and Modern Historiography,* 107–127. Oxford: Blackwell.

Momigliano, Arnaldo. (1990). *The Classical Foundation of Modern Historiography.* Sather Classical Lectures 54. Berkeley: University of California Press.

Morgan, Teresa. (2005). Eusebius of Caesarea and Christian historiography. *Athenaeum* 93: 193–208.

Morlet, Sébastien. (2006). L'introduction de l'Histoire Ecclésiastique d'Eusèbe de Césarée (I, ii-iv): Étude génétique, littéraire et rhétorique. *Revue des études augustiniennes et patristiques* 52: 57–95.

Nau, François. (1915–1917). Une liste de chronographes. *Revue de l'Orient chrétien* 10: 101–103.

Sundermann, Werner. (1986). Studien zur kirchengeschichtliche Literatur der iranischen Manichäer I. *Altorientalische Forschungen* 13: 40–92.

Timpe, Dieter. (2001). *Römische Geschichte und Heilsgeschichte.* Hans-Lietzmann-Vorlesungen 5. Berlin: de Gruyter.

Van Hoof, Lieve, Manafis, Panagiotis, and Van Nuffelen, Peter. (2016). Hesychius of Jerusalem, Ecclesiastical history (CPG 6582). *Greek, Roman and Byzantine Studies* 56: 504–527.

Van Hoof, Lieve, Manafis, Panagiotis, and Van Nuffelen, Peter (2017). Philo of Carpasia, Ecclesiastical history. *Revue d'Histoire ecclésiastique* 112: 35–52.

Van Nuffelen, Peter. (2002a). La tête de l' "histoire acéphale." *Klio* 84: 125–40.

Van Nuffelen, Peter. (2002b). Gélase de Césarée, un compilateur du cinquième siècle. *Byzantinische Zeitschrift* 95: 621–640.

Van Nuffelen, Peter. (2004). *Un héritage de paix et de piété: étude sur les histoires ecclésiastiques de Socrate et de Sozomène.* Orientalia Lovaniensia analecta 142. Louvain: Peeters.

Van Nuffelen, Peter. (Forthcoming). Considérations sur l'anonyme homéen. In: *Les historiens grecs à l'état fragmentaire dans l'Antiquité tardive* (ed. Eugenio Amato).

Verdoner, Marie. (2010). Überlegungen zum Adressaten von Eusebs Historia Ecclesiastica. *Zeitschrift für Antikes Christentum* 14: 362–378.

Wallraff, Martin. (1997). *Der Kirchenhistoriker Sokrates: Untersuchungen zu Geschichtsdarstellung, Methode und Person.* Forschungen zur Kirchen- und Dogmengeschichte, 68. Göttingen: Vandenhoeck & Ruprecht.

Wallraff, Martin. (2015). Warum ist "Kirchengeschichte" in der Antike ausgestorben? In: *Geschichte als Argument? Historiographie und Apologetik* (ed. Martin Wallraff), 1–19. Studien der patristischen Arbeitsgemeinschaft 13. Louvain: Peeters.

Winkelmann, Friedhelm. (1966). *Untersuchungen zur Kirchengeschichte des Gelasios von Kaisareia.* Sitzungsberichte der Deutschen Akademie der Wissenschaften zu Berlin. Klasse für Sprachen, Literatur und Kunst. Berlin: Akademie.

Winkelmann, Friedhelm. (1991). *Euseb von Kaisarea. Der Vater der Kirchengeschichte.* Berlin: Akademie.

CHAPTER ELEVEN

Chronicles

R.W. Burgess

11.1 Introduction

One of the most distinctive and complex literary forms of late antiquity is that of chronicles. The chronology of the West in the fifth century is impossible without them, and for the entire empire from the beginning of the fourth to the first quarter of the seventh century they are invaluable and unequaled chronological and historical sources. And yet most historians know little or nothing about them, individually or as a genre, and find them extremely difficult to work with, not least because of the peculiar nature of Theodor Mommsen's editions and the lack of modern scholarship. Scholars of other late antique disciplines have for the most part simply ignored them. To make matters worse, the term "chronicle" can signify quite different things to scholars of different disciplines. So the topic is either a minefield or a quagmire, depending on how one wishes to look at it. Given this state of affairs, it will be most useful in the limited space of this chapter to provide a basic guide to the major late antique chronicles with a helpful bibliography. For everything else, as well as for the background to what appears here, I refer the reader to the first and, eventually, later volumes of *Mosaics of Time* (Burgess and Kulikowski 2013).

What must be made clear first, however, is the definition of "chronicle" employed here (see Burgess and Kulikowski 2013, pp. 1–62), since I shall not be discussing many of the works usually called or considered chronicles. A chronicle is a work in which the author considers the placing of events over a long period of time within their correct annalistic and chronological context to be of paramount importance. Consequently, each year is set out explicitly and distinctly from those before and after. Because of the wide chronological coverage brevity becomes the second defining characteristic. Tied to this need for brevity is the lack or minimal appearance of narrative intrusion, and so chronicles often have the appearance of anonymous repositories of facts with no explicit narrator to guide the reader, make didactic comments, or explain the causes, meanings, or lessons of events and actions. This brevity and the general lack of a narrative guide result in a paratactic structure that appears to coordinate or correlate unrelated events of vastly differing importance and that can also fail to make explicit important connections between and among a series of events. Chronicles so defined stretch for over three and a half thousand years, from the beginning of the second millennium BCE in Assyria and Babylonia to the modern period, the longest unbroken tradition of any historical genre in Western literature.

11.2 Consularia

Consularia are a subgenre of chronicles, and the earliest surviving late antique chronicles are the consularia of the fourth century. (This discounts the Greek chronicles of the third century that survive on papyrus [Burgess and Kulikowski 2013, pp. 90, 121, 313–315], which are simply copies and continuations of earlier Hellenistic chronicles and not products that are recognizably "late antique.") For the most part the consularia divide into two completely independent traditions: those related to the *Descriptio Consulum* and those related to the *Consularia Italica*. Of these, the former is the earliest.

Late antique consularia derive from the same tradition as the Latin epigraphic fasti and consularia of the early empire, most particularly the famous Fasti Ostienses. The near identical nature of both the earlier and the later texts shows that, in spite of the absence of evidence for consularia for more than one hundred years into the third century, from the end of the Fasti Ostienses to the beginning of the *Descriptio Consulum*, there must have been a continuous tradition of consularia from the reign of Augustus right through to the beginning of the seventh century (Burgess and Kulikowski 2013, pp. 35–57, 133–184).

Consularia are for the most part compilations of consular fasti, imperial proclamations, and accounts of local events such as earthquakes, disease, and celestial and meteorological phenomena. While there certainly was an original author who began a single text at the origin of each of these traditions, the traditions quickly ramified as later readers brought their copies up to date. Some traditions became particularly popular and were copied often, and they traveled widely across the empire. As a result, there is no single "author" or even "text" of such works, since that text was constantly being changed in ways that we cannot now see because of the fragmentary nature of our witnesses.

The *Descriptio Consulum* is a complex document based upon consular fasti from 509 BCE to 468 CE. It was originally compiled in Trier in ca. 342, with the compilation of a solid block of detailed and dated entries deriving from imperial proclamations and perhaps local calendars between 286 and 337 and a few less detailed entries between 340 and 342 that were added from local knowledge. It is also probable that the earlier material now found before 286 was also included at the time of the original composition: historico-literary entries, derived, it would seem, from an early Latin chronicle (112 BCE–19 CE); early Christian and martyrological entries (2 BCE–258 CE); and a random assortment of entries relating to imperial history at the end of the third century (261–284). The original text traveled from Trier to Rome (entries for the years 350–355), Constantinople (356–388.1, with a few earlier additions going back as far as 341.2, hence Mommsen's title of *Consularia Constantinopolitana*), Spain (388.2–395), Africa (398–405), and Rome (411–423). Different recensions of the Constantinopolitan text between 370 and 388 served as an important source for many later writers in Latin and Greek. Its unique preservation of many otherwise unknown or corrupt dates and unknown or poorly known events makes it of fundamental importance for the chronology of the fourth and early fifth centuries (Burgess 1993, pp. 175–245; *Chron. Min.* 1, pp. 199–247; Burgess 2000; Burgess and Kulikowski, forthcoming).

The *Consularia Italica* is the collective name, not for a surviving text, but for a tradition whose influences can be traced in over 20 later works in Latin and Greek, in Italy, Constantinople, and Alexandria from the fifth to the ninth centuries. The surviving witnesses show that it covered the period between 379 and 495, though it may originally have begun earlier. It would seem to have ended with references to the birth of the Antichrist in 493 and 495. The date of 379 suggests that its narrative was considered in some ways as a continuation of Jerome (below), even though its fasti begin with Julius Caesar. All the surviving witnesses to this tradition that are discussed below retain the original consularia format. The two other major witnesses do not: chapters 36–38 and 48–56 of the *Anonymi Valesiani pars posterior* and Agnellus's *Liber pontificalis ecclesiae Ravennatis* of ca. 850. It was originally compiled in Trier (like the *Descriptio*) and then Rome, but it was taken to Ravenna in the early fifth century, which seems to have been the home of the main tradition, though at least twice recensions were taken to Alexandria where they were translated into Greek. Theophanes's *Chronographia* of 814 is a witness to the earliest of these. The popularity of the *Consularia Italica* tradition in late antiquity and its immense importance today are both a result of the fact that it is unique in providing a detailed chronology for the western empire from the end of the fourth to the end of the fifth centuries. Without it our chronology for the emperors of this period would be even more opaque than that for the emperors of the third century (*Chron. Min.* 1, pp. 251–321; Holder-Egger 1876, pp. 215–368; *RE Suppl.* 1 (1903), pp. 296–298 (Hartmann); Muhlberger 1990, pp. 23–46; Burgess 2000; Burgess and Kulikowski, forthcoming).

The name *Consularia Vindobonensia* describes a recension of the *Consularia Italica* that extended that work from 496 to ca. 527. The only reasonably complete witnesses to this text are two separate recensions found in a single late fifteenth-century manuscript (Österreichische Nationalbibliothek 3416), called *priora* and *posteriora* by Mommsen, the *priora* (*CVpr*) extending from Caesar to 493 and the *posteriora* (*CVpost*) from Caesar to 539. The core of the work is fasti from ca. 44 BCE to the end, becoming consularia in 379, where frequent historical entries first begin to appear. The *CVpr* prefaces its fasti with a list of the seven kings. This common text is the best and most compete witness we have to the final version of the *Consularia Italica*. The *CVpost* is highly lacunose and much more corrupt than the *CVpr*, which is also lacunose between 403 and 455 and 493 to ca. 575 (*Chron. Min.* I, pp. 263–264, 274-334; Frick 1892, pp. 375–418; Holder-Egger 1876, pp 217–232, 238–247; Cessi 1916; Burgess 2000, 2012; Burgess and Kulikowski, forthcoming).

The *Excerpta Sangallensia* are an early witness to the complete *CVpr* tradition made by Bishop Walafrid Strabo in the 830s (Stiftsbibliothek, St. Gallen 878). They include consuls and historical entries relating to unusual natural phenomena such as earthquakes and plagues between 390 and 572, thus showing that the *CVpr* must originally have extended to ca. 575 (*Chron. Min.*1, pp. 298–336; Frick 1892, pp. 421–423; Holder-Egger 1876, pp. 232–247; Burgess 2012; Burgess and Kulikowski, forthcoming).

The *Consularia Scaligeriana* is the third part of the *Chronographia Scaligeriana*, usually called the *Excerpta Latina Barbari* or the *Barbarus Scaligeri*, a Latin translation made in Corbie in the 780s of an illustrated Greek chronograph compiled probably in Alexandria early in the reign of Justinian I (Bibliothèque nationale, Paris lat. 4884). The original consularia were a heavily augmented Greek translation of an earlier and less corrupt recension of the *CVpost*. The *Chronographia* is very closely related to the *Chronographia Golenischevensis* (below). Like the *Consularia Berolinensia*, *Consularia Marsibergensia*, and *Consularia Golenischevensia*, the consularia of this text were originally illustrated, though the surviving manuscript includes only blank spaces and a few captions. It exists for the years 44 BCE–99 CE and 296–387 (Schoene 1875, appendix VI, pp. 177–239 [still the best edition and the basis for the others]; Frick 1892, pp. lxxxiii–ccx, ccxxi–ccxxii, 184–371; *Chron. Min.* 1, pp. 274–298 [consularia only]; *RE* 6.2 [1909], pp. 1566–1576 [= Jacoby 1956, pp. 257–262]; Burgess 2000; Garstad 2012; Burgess 2013; Burgess and Kulikowski, forthcoming).

The *Consularia Golenischevensia* is known only from a single incomplete folium from the *Chronographia Golenischevensis*, an illustrated chronograph of the second or third quarter of the sixth century (often called the "Alexandrian World Chronicle") that survives in a small collection of broken papyrus fragments copied in the second half of the sixth century (Pushkin Museum of Fine Arts, Moscow 310/8). It is closely related to the *Consularia Scaligeriana* (above) and thus the *CVpost*. It only exists for the years 383–392 (Bauer and Strzygowski 1905; Burgess and Dijkstra 2013; Burgess and Kulikowski, forthcoming).

The *Consularia Hafniensia*, called the *Auctarium Havniense* by Mommsen, is preserved in a unique late twelfth-century Copenhagen manuscript (Copenhagen, Royal Library 454). In ca. 626 a recension of the *Consularia Italica* that is very closely related to the *Consularia Vindobonensia* and had been extended to 523 was interpolated into and after a copy of the chronicle of Prosper along with excerpts from the *Liber Pontificalis*, the chronicle epitome of Isidore, and other Gallic sources. The text for the years 458 to 473 is now missing. This text was continued with a short narrative account from the death of Theoderic, also heavily dependent on Isidore and a known continuation of Isidore, down to 619, with a concluding sentence to 626 and an interpolated date of 639/640 at the end. The text between 475 and 489 exists in duplicate and triplicate versions, the remnants of attempts by the original author (pre-626) to improve and flesh out the bare entries of the source into a narrative, as was done in the *Anonymus Valesianus*. As a result, the extra material in these expanded entries is highly suspect (*Chron. Min.* 1, pp. 266–271, 298–339; Holder-Egger 1876, pp. 259–268; Cessi 1922; Muhlberger 1984 [with translation]; Burgess and Kulikowski, forthcoming).

The *Consularia Marsiburgensia* occupies the lower half of a mid-eleventh-century parchment folium preserving three columns covering the years 411–413 (no consuls for 412); 421–423 (no consuls for 422); 427–429; 434–437; 439 (illustration only)–443; and 452–454 (Merseburg Cathedral Chapter House Library 202). This fragment is our purest and oldest witness to the *Consularia Italica* tradition and fills an important lacuna in the tradition. As noted above, many entries are illustrated with stereotypical drawings (Bischoff and Koehler 1939; Burgess and Kulikowski, forthcoming).

The *Paschale Campanum* is a continuation of the 466 continuation of the Vatican epitome of Prosper (Vatican Library, Reginae 2077, copied in 585). It is a combination of a recension of the *Consularia Italica* from 464 to 504 and an annotated Campanian recension of the Easter table of Victorius of Aquitaine from 464 to 566, to which was attached the preface to a completely different chronological work that covered Creation to 464. It was first compiled in 543, probably in Vivarium, and later extended many times down to 613. The most interesting entries concern the birth of the Antichrist (493 and 496) and two eruptions of Mount Vesuvius (505 and 512) (*Chron. Min.* 1, pp. 305–334, 492–493, 744–750; Troncarelli 1989; Burgess and Kulikowski, forthcoming).

The *Consularia Berolinensia* survives for the years 251–273, 306, 312–338, with 10 historical entries and four illustrations, written in two columns on one side of a single damaged piece of fifth/sixth-century parchment in Berlin. This is an odd text, since it is a Greek translation of two unrelated Latin traditions: consular fasti that are closely related to the precursor of the fasti found in the *Consularia Vindobonensia* and Prosper with historical entries that, for the most part, derive from a Greek translation of the *Descriptio Consulum*, whence, therefore, must come the illustrations (Lietzmann 1937; Burgess and Dijkstra 2012; Burgess and Kulikowski, forthcoming).

Cassiodorus, the famous author and statesman of the Italian Gothic court, wrote his consularia for presentation to the consul Eutharicus on 1 January 519. They cover the period from Creation to 519. Although it is always referred to as a chronicle, it is, in fact, minimalist consularia with a very short account of the period between Creation and 510 BCE appended to the beginning. The unique consular list, derived chiefly from Livy and Victorius of Aquitaine, has been lightly annotated in the manner of consularia with text from Jerome, Eutropius, Prosper, and a unique recension of the *Consularia Italica* also used by Paul the Deacon (*Chron. Min.* 2, pp. 111–161; Klaassen 2010).

The *Consularia Caesaraugustana* is a collection of excerpts covering the years 451–567, preserved only as notes copied no later than the early eighth century into the margins of a now lost manuscript of Victor of Tunnuna and John of Biclar (below). Although the style is similar to earlier consularia, the content does not derive from imperial proclamations, though the nature of the original text is difficult to determine since the excerptor was chiefly interested in Gothic history. It probably represents a later continuation of earlier consularia like the *Descriptio Consulum* (*Chron. Min.* 2, pp. 221–223; Cardelle de Hartmann 2001, 79*–80*, 115*–124*, 4–47, 61[entries in italics], 95–109; Burgess and Kulikowski, forthcoming).

11.3 Chronicles

All of what most readers would consider to be typical late antique chronicles are the direct descendants of Eusebius's *Chronici canones*.

The *Chronographia* and *Chronici canones* of Eusebius of Caesarea were a two-part chronological work presenting in volume 1 the raw material and sources for composing a chronology and in volume 2 the compilation and synthesis of that material into a universal chronicle covering the years 2016 BCE to 325 CE. This second volume marks the confluence of three distinct streams of Greek chronography: Hellenistic chronicles, Christian apologetic chronology, and *canones* (regnal lists), of which Claudius Ptolemy's *Royal Canon* is the most famous example. Strangely, it marks both the end of the Hellenistic chronicle tradition in Greek and the beginning of the late antique and medieval chronicle traditions in Latin and Syriac (see Burgess and Kulikowski 2013, pp. 99–131; Burgess, in press).

The *Canones* was not well received in the Greek world, chiefly because its columnar format required too much space and was therefore too expensive to maintain; because it was too complicated to copy accurately and was therefore open to corruption; and because its antimillenarian chronology went against the great tide of chronological thinking at the time. It was, for the most part, attacked and reworked, chiefly in the fourth century. In spite of this, its impact on later Greek chronography was enormous, since Eusebius's individual chronologies became the de facto standard against which all other chronologies were measured. In addition, its universal and compact nature spearheaded the shift away from full blown narrative history to the more abbreviated historical forms that dominated later Byzantine historiography. It had no imitators that we know of in Greek (Schoene 1866, 1875; Gutschmid 1889; Keseling 1927-28; Mosshammer 1979; Croke 1982; Adler 1992; Burgess 1997; Witakowski 1999–2000; Burgess 1999, pp. 21–109, 2006; Armenian translation: Karst 1911; Greek fragments of *Chronographia*: Cramer 1839, pp. 118–163).

Jerome produced his augmented and extended Latin translation of Eusebius's *Chronici canones*, in 380–381, in the lead-up to the Council of Constantinople. It seems to have become immediately popular. The *Descriptio Consulum* predates Jerome by about 40 years, and so it would seem that the West was already experimenting with chronicles and ready for the reintroduction of a Latin chronicle based on Hellenistic exemplars, a genre that appears to have been moribund in Latin since Nepos and Atticus in the first century BCE (Burgess and Kulikowski 2013, pp. 91–97; Cornell 2013, sections 33 and 45).

Jerome's major sources for his additions and continuation were (1) a compendium of Roman Republican history from the earliest inhabitants of Italy, used also by Eutropius; (2) Enmann's famous *Kaisergeschichte*; (3) a Constantinopolitan recension of the *Descriptio Consulum* to 370; (4) the *Continuatio Antiochiensis*, a Greek continuation of Eusebius down to 350 (Burgess 1999, pp. 113–305); (5) Suetonius's *De Viris Illustribus*; and (6) a similar work, covering famous writers of the reign of Constantine. There were also other nonhistorical sources, such as earlier patristic writings and contemporary ecclesiastical documents, as well as his own knowledge.

There are two standard editions of Jerome's *Chronici canones*: Rudolf Helm's of 1956 (the first edition of which originally had appeared in two handwritten volumes in 1913 and 1926) and John Knight Fotheringham's of 1923. Helm's edition is the most useful and easily cited, but Fotheringham's has a better text and is more attractive (Helm 1956; Fotheringham 1923; Schöne 1900 [out of date]; Helm 1929; Kelly 1975, pp. 72–75; Mosshammer 1979, pp. 37–73; Donalson 1996; Burgess 1999, pp. 90–98; Burgess 2002; Vessey 2010).

Prosper of Aquitaine, a well-known supporter of St. Augustine from Marseille or its environs, first composed a continuation of Jerome's *Chronici canones* in 433. Instead of attaching his continuation to the end of Jerome, as later chroniclers would, he composed a slightly augmented epitome of that work to take its place, adding a short account from Creation to the birth of Abraham. Mommsen's mistaken title of the chronicle as a whole (*Epitoma Chronicon*) is actually just a reference to this epitome in the manuscripts' preface. This continuation he himself continued in 445 and again in 455, the latter existing in two recensions and involving extensive revision to earlier material. There is no evidence for an edition of 451. Prosper shows the great influence of consularia in his substitution of Jerome's regnal years with consular dates.

Even though it is still often said that Prosper worked in Rome for Pope Leo, there is no credible evidence for any connection with Leo (Markus 1986, Salzman 2015), and errors of fact in the chronicle—e.g. the death of Valentinian and the date of the Council of Chalcedon, and his attack on Leo at the very end—show that he could not have been in Rome working for Leo.

The only modern edition is marred by Mommsen's belief that Prosper never revised his work and by his consequent failure to publish different texts for the two surviving editions. Prosper's chronicle was recommended along with Marcellinus's by Cassiodorus in his *Institutes*, and after Jerome it was the most popular and well known of all the late antique chronicles during the Middle Ages (*Chron. Min.* 1, pp. 343–485 [486–493, the continuations, for which see Burgess and Kulikowski, forthcoming]; Holder-Egger 1876, pp. 15–90; Valentin 1900, pp. 195–204, 411–441; *RE* 23.1 [1957], 880–997, esp. 894–896 [Helm]; Markus 1986; Muhlberger 1990, pp. 48–135; Hwang 2009 [biography]; translations: De Paor 1993, pp. 72–87 [very poor, from the *PL* edition]; Murray 2003, pp. 62–76 [excerpts]).

The anonymous *Gallic Chronicle of 452* is a continuation of Jerome, written in Valence or Marseille and attributed to Prosper in the manuscripts. It is a pessimistic account of the collapse of Gaul and the entire Roman Empire in the face of barbarian invasion and the spread of heresy, and, as such, it is a valuable and unique window into the events of and provincial mindset during the middle of the fifth century. There are three different groups of manuscripts, all descending from a single exemplar of the sixth or seventh century. With the exception of Sigibert of Gembloux, who used it as a major source for his famous chronicle, no medieval author presents any direct knowledge of this work (*Chron. Min.* 1, pp. 617–125, 646–662; Burgess 2001a; Holder-Egger 1876, pp. 91–20, 324–327; Muhlberger 1990, pp. 136–192; Murray 2003, pp. 76–85 [translation]).

As bishop of Aquae Flaviae in Gallaecia (modern Chaves in northern Portugal) Hydatius played a leading role in defending his city and territory against the depredations of the Sueves, having been sent to Gaul on an embassy to Aëtius in 431–432. He completed his chronicle in 468/469, and it begins in 379, in continuation of Jerome, with a typical account of the history of the Roman Empire. As the chronology advances, events in Spain begin to take center stage. It ends focused almost entirely on a decidedly isolated and battered post-imperial Gallaecia, thus making it the earliest extant example of post-imperial (and thus medieval) literature. The situation seemed so hopeless that Hydatius believed that the end of the world was approaching (in 482) and structured his work with an eye to demonstrating this. The chronicle was used by a number of later chroniclers, like the author of the *Gallic Chronicle of 511*, Isidore, Fredegar, and Sigibert (*Chron. Min.* 2, pp. 3–35; Burgess 1989; Muhlberger 1990, pp. 193–312; Burgess 1993; Cardelle de Hartmann 1994; Murray 2003, pp. 85–98 [translated excerpts]).

The *Gallic Chronicle of 511* is another anonymous Gallic continuation of Jerome, though like Prosper it follows only an interpolated epitome of Jerome. It was probably written in Arles and is attributed to Sulpicius Severus in the sole surviving thirteenth-century manuscript (Biblioteca Histórica Marqués de Valdecilla of the Universidad Complutense de Madrid 134). The text has been heavily epitomized (perhaps more than once), so it is difficult to say anything specific about the author or his purposes. Hydatius, Orosius, the *Gallic Chronicle of 452*, and a recension of the *Consularia Italica* are the most obvious surviving sources for the work, and they make up the bulk of the narrative before ca. 450. There is also evidence for the use of a now-lost chronicle of Arles and a source that parallels Marius of Avenches, Isidore, and the *Consularia Caesaraugustana*. After 450 the chronicle becomes more valuable as an independent witness to events in southern Gaul, northern Spain, and northern Italy (*Chron. Min.* 1, pp. 626–628, 632–666; Burgess 2001b; Holder-Egger 1875; Murray 2003, pp. 98–100 [translation from section 71]).

Marcellinus *comes*, an Illyrian courtier living in Constantinople, composed a continuation chronicle of Jerome, first to 518 and then to 534. As they did Prosper, consularia prompted him to abandon Jerome's chronological structure of regnal years, Olympiads, and years from the birth of Abraham for consuls, to which he added indictions. His major identifiable sources for the early part of his chronicle are Orosius, a recension of the *Descriptio Consulum* that continued down to the early years of the sixth century (a related source was used in the *Chronicon Paschale* to 468), a recension of the *Consularia Italica*, and Gennadius's De *Viris Illustribus*. The chronicle was recommended along with Prosper by Cassiodorus, and it was later used by Jordanes, early Irish chroniclers, and Bede (*Chron. Min.* 2, pp. 60–104; Croke 1995, 2001).

An unknown chronicler continued the second edition of Marcellinus's chronicle from 534 to at least 548, where the text breaks off in mid-sentence in the sole surviving sixth-century manuscript (Oxford, Auct. T. II. 26). Although Brian Croke believes that the continuator wrote in Constantinople, the author's sources of information and his focus are fundamentally Italian, and the manuscript is Italian as well, so there is nothing that prevents the work itself from being Italian (*Chron. Min.* 2, pp. 104–108; Croke 1995, pp. xxv, 45–52, 127–39; Croke 2001, pp. 216–236).

Marius, the bishop of Avenches in Switzerland (573–593), continued Prosper down to 581, though his work is little more than annotated (and not even fully or regularly annotated) fasti that offer frequent entries only from 553. Marius employed five identifiable written sources, of which the most important are a recension of the *Consularia Italica*; an Italian chronicle, or consularia, exhibiting parallels with the continuation of Marcellinus *comes*; and a Burgundian/Frankish chronicle exhibiting parallels with Gregory of Tours. The work survives in a single manuscript (British Library, Add. 16974), the same manuscript that contains the *Gallic Chronicle of 452* (*Chron. Min.* 2, pp. 232–239; Favrod 1993; Murray 2003, pp. 100–108 [translation]).

Victor, bishop of Tunnuna in Africa Proconsularis, lived during the second and third quarters of the sixth century and composed a chronicle that covers the years 444 to 565 as a continuation of a truncated version of the 455 edition of Prosper (Muhlberger 1986). He spent the last 25 or so years of his life in exile or prisons across the Mediterranean for his staunch support of the

Three Chapters, anathematized by Justinian in 543/544. His chronicle follows Prosper in using consulates down to 541 (from corrupt fasti), then post-consulates for 22 years, and then regnal years of Justinian for the last four years. His content focuses exclusively on imperial, papal, and patriarchal succession; events in Africa involving the Vandals; and, most especially, ecclesiastical affairs. His main source down to 518 (section 101) was the ecclesiastical history of Theodorus Lector, but he also used both historical works of Isidore and various ecclesiastical texts (*Chron. Min.* 2, pp. 165–206; Cardelle de Hartmann 2001, 7*–115*, 3–55; *ODB* 3, p. 2165).

John of Biclar was born in Lusitania, educated in Constantinople, and exiled to Barcelona for 10 years upon his return. He later founded a monastery in Biclar and was appointed bishop of Gerona between 589 and 592. He wrote his chronicle sometime after 604 (he knows of the death of Gregory in that year, section 81), even though the latest dated event is the Romano-Persian peace of 591. The chronicle is a continuation of Victor's and continues Victor's Byzantine regnal years, to which are appended Visigothic regnal years from 569. John's account was more influenced by Jerome's version of history and by consularia than by Victor, in that he presents a traditional political and military narrative, mostly of Spanish affairs, with few references to purely ecclesiastical matters other than papal succession and the floruits of local churchmen (*Chron. Min.* 2, pp. 165–77, 207–220; Cardelle de Hartmann 2001, 7*-94*, 124*-43*, 59–83, 110–148; Wolf 2011, pp. 1–9, 51–66; *ODB* 2, p. 1062).

11.4 Chronicles after the Sixth Century

In Latin the late Roman chronicle tradition ends with John in 591, though the *Paschale Campanum* does note the accession of Phocas in 602. A new independent tradition of chronicling had begun in Ireland in the sixth century but was not associated with the central European tradition until the middle of the seventh century and the resulting major recensions did not appear until ca. 740 and 911. Meanwhile, in the seventh and eighth centuries chronicling was picked up again in Kent and Northumbria, and these early texts were bound up in the new Frankish interest in chronicles that began in the eighth century and exploded at the beginning of the ninth in the Carolingian period (Burgess and Kulikowski 2013, pp. 1, 56, 184, 208–221, 237–239, 243–249). Throughout these years the well-known late antique chronicles described above were still being read and copied.

In the eastern empire, the chronicle in Greek virtually came to an end with Eusebius and whatever fourth-century continuators he may have had.

The next known chronicle, the *Chronicon Paschale*, was written 300 years later ca. 630. It is a unique genre-bending work that interpolates often lengthy excerpts from different narrative texts (particularly Malalas) into chronological underpinnings drawn from an epitome deriving ultimately from Eusebius (which begins numbering every year only from Abraham), with regnal years, Olympiads, *anni mundi*, and eventually indictions, and then a Greek translation of the *Descriptio Consulum*, with the addition of consuls (which mistakenly start in 440 BCE instead of 509) (Whitby and Whitby 1989; Treadgold 2007, pp. 340–348; *ODB* 1, p. 447). It had no imitators and there are no other known chronicles until the appearance of Theophanes's *Chronographia* in 814. The niche once held by chronicles in Greek historiography was replaced by universal breviaria and even shorter synopses, works that were brief but for the most part displayed no interest in chronology at all.

In the Near East Eusebius's chronicle prompted the adoption of the chronicle format in Syriac, starting as early as the beginning of the sixth century (the *Chronicle of Edessa*), and two epitomes of Eusebius's chronicle are preserved within other Syriac chronicles, one from around 640 and the other from 775. There is also the chronicle of James of Edessa, which was written at the end of the seventh century as a continuation of a "simplified" version of the *Chronici canones*. True chronicles continued to be composed in Syriac as late as the ninth century, and they, in turn, prompted Arabic and Armenian chronicles and chronographic histories that are beyond the purview of this chapter (Debié 2009, 2015).

ABBREVIATIONS

Chron. Min. = *Chronica Minora* 1–3. In: *Monumenta Germaniae Historica* 9, 11, 13 (ed. Theodor Mommsen). Berlin: Weidmann, 1892–1898.

ODB = *The Oxford Dictionary of Byzantium*. 3 vols. (ed. Alexander P. Kazhdan). Oxford: Oxford University Press, 1991.

RE = *Paulys Real-Encyclopädie der classischen Altertumswissenschaft*. 82 vols. (ed. Georg Wissowa et al.). Stuttgart: J.B. Metzler, 1894–1980.

RE Suppl. = Supplemental volumes of *RE*.

TTH = Translated Texts for Historians

REFERENCES

Adler, William. (1992). Eusebius' chronicle and its legacy. In: *Eusebius, Christianity, and Judaism* (ed. Harold W. Attridge and Gohei Hata), 467–91. Leiden: Brill.

Bauer, Adolf and Strzygowski, Josef. (1905). *Eine alexandrinische Weltchronik.* Denkschriften der kaiserlichen Akademie der Wissenschaften, Phil.-Hist. Klasse 51. Vienna.

Bischoff, Bernhard and Koehler, W. (1939). Eine illustrierte Ausgabe der spätantiken ravennater Annalen. In: *Medieval Studies in Memory of A. Kingsley Porter* 1 (ed. W.R.W. Koehler), 125–138. Cambridge, MA: Harvard University Press.

Burgess, R.W. (1989). *Hydatius: A Late Roman Chronicler in Post-Roman Spain.* PhD diss., University of Oxford.

Burgess, R.W. (1993). *The Chronicle of Hydatius and the Consularia Constantinopolitana: Two Contemporary Accounts of the Final Years of the Roman Empire.* Oxford: Clarendon.

Burgess, R.W. (1997). The dates and editions of Eusebius' *Chronici canones* and *Historia ecclesiastica. Journal of Theological Studies* n.s. 48: 471–504 = Burgess 2011, I.

Burgess, R.W. (2000). "Non duo Antonini sed duo Augusti": The consuls of 161 and the origins and traditions of the Latin consular *Fasti* of the Roman Empire. *Zeitschrift für Papyrologie und Epigraphik* 132: 259–90 = Burgess 2011, XV.

Burgess, R.W. (2001a). The Gallic chronicle of 452: A New critical edition with a brief introduction. In: *Society and Culture in Late Antique Gaul. Revisiting the Sources* (ed. Ralph W. Mathisen and Danuta Shanzer), 52–84. Aldershot: Ashgate.

Burgess, R.W. (2001b). The Gallic chronicle of 511: A new critical edition with a brief introduction. In: *Society and Culture in Late Antique Gaul. Revisiting the Sources* (ed. Ralph W. Mathisen and Danuta Shanzer), 85–100. Aldershot: Ashgate.

Burgess, R.W. (2002). Jerome explained: An introduction to his *Chronicle* and a guide to its use. *Ancient History Bulletin* 16: 1–32 = Burgess 2011, III.

Burgess, R.W. (2006). A chronological prolegomenon to reconstructing Eusebius' *Chronici canones*: The evidence of Ps-Dionysius (the *Zuqnin Chronicle*). *Journal of the Canadian Society for Syriac Studies* 6: 29–38 = Burgess 2011, II.

Burgess, R.W. (2011). *Chronicles, Consuls, and Coins, Historiography and History in the Later Roman Empire.* Farnham: Ashgate.

Burgess, R.W. (2012). The chronograph of 354: Its manuscripts, contents, and history. *Journal of Late Antiquity* 5: 345–396.

Burgess, R.W. (2013). The date, purpose, and historical context of the original Greek and the Latin translation of the so-called *Excerpta Latina Barbari. Traditio* 68: 1–56.

Burgess, R.W. (In press). The origin and development of early Christian and Byzantine universal historiography. In: *Chronicles as Literature* (ed. S. Mariev). Byzantinisches Archiv 34. Berlin: De Gruyter.

Burgess, R.W. and. Dijkstra, Jitse H. F. (2012). The Berlin "Chronicle" (*P. Berol.* inv. 13296): A new edition of the earliest extant late antique *Consularia. Archiv für Papyrusforschung* 58: 273–301.

Burgess, R.W. and Dijkstra, Jitse H. F. (2013). The "Alexandrian World Chronicle," its *Consularia* and the date of the destruction of the Serapeum (with an Appendix on the List of *Praefecti Augustales*). *Millennium* 10: 39–113.

Burgess, R.W. and Kulikowski, Michael. (2013). *Mosaics of Time: The Latin Chronicle Traditions from the First Century BC to the Sixth Century AD. Vol 1: A Historical Introduction to the Chronicle Genre from Its Origins to the High Middle Ages.* Turnhout: Brepols.

Burgess, R.W. and Kulikowski Michael. (Forthcoming). *Mosaics of Time: The Latin Chronicle Traditions from the First Century BC to the Sixth Century AD. Vol. 2: The Earliest Chronicles and the Consularia Traditions.* Turnhout: Brepols.

Burgess, R.W. with the assistance of Witakowski, Witold. (1999). *Studies in Eusebian and Post-Eusebian Chronography.* Stuttgart: Steiner.

Cardelle de Hartmann, Carmen. (1994). *Philologische Studien zur Chronik des Hydatius von Chaves.* Stuttgart: Steiner.

Cardelle de Hartmann, Carmen. (2001). *Victoris Tunnunensis Chronicon cum reliquiis ex Consularibus Caesaraugustanis et Iohannis Biclarensis Chronicon.* CCSL 173A. Turnhout: Brepols.

Cessi, Roberto. (1916). Studi sulle fonti dell'età Gotica e Longobarda I. "Fasti Vindobonenses." *Archivio Muratoriano* 17–18: 293–405.

Cessi, Roberto. (1922). Studi sulle fonti dell'età Gotica e Longobarda II. "Prosperi Continuatio Hauniensis." *Archivio Muratoriano* 22: 585–641.

Cornell, T. J. (2013). *The Fragments of the Roman Historians.* Oxford: Oxford University Press.

Cramer, John Anthony. (1839). *Anecdota graeca e codd. manuscriptis bibliothecae regiae Parisiensis* 2. Oxford: Oxford University Press.

Croke, Brian. (1982). The originality of Eusebius' chronicle. *American Journal of Philology* 103: 195–200.

Croke, Brian. (1995). *The Chronicle of Marcellinus.* Sydney: Australian Association for Byzantine Studies.

Croke, Brian. (2001). *Count Marcellinus and His Chronicle.* Oxford: Oxford University Press.

Debié, Muriel. ed. (2009). *L'historiographie syriaque.* Études syriaques 6. Paris: Geuthner.

Debié, Muriel. (2015). *L'écriture de l'histoire en syriaque: Transmissions interculturelles et constructions identitaires entre hellénisme et islam.* Late Antique History and Religion 12. Leiden: Peeters.

de Paor, Liam. (1993). *Saint Patrick's World: The Christian Culture of Ireland's Apostolic Age.* Blackrock and Dublin: Four Courts.

Donalson, Malcolm Drew. (1996). *A Translation of Jerome's Chronicon with Historical Commentary.* Lewiston, NY: Mellen.

Favrod, Justin. (1993). *La chronique de Marius d'Avenches (455–581).* 2nd ed. Lausanne: Faculté des lettres de l'Université de Lausanne.

Fotheringham, John Knight. (1923). *Eusebii Pamphili Chronici canones, Latine uertit, adauxit, ad sua tempora produxit S. Eusebius Hieronymus.* London: Humphrey Milford.

Frick, Karl. (1892). *Chronica minora* 1. Leipzig: Teubner.

Garstad, Benjamin (2012). *Apocalypse. Pseudo-Methodius. An Alexandrian World Chronicle.* Dumbarton Oaks Medieval Library 14. Cambridge, MA: Harvard University Press.

Gutschmid, Alfred von. (1889). Untersuchungen über die syrische Epitome der Eusebischen Canones. In: *Kleine Schriften von Alfred von Gutschmid* 1 (ed. Franz Rühl), 483–529. Leipzig: Teubner.

Helm, Rudolf. (1929). *Hieronymus' Zusätze in Eusebius' Chronik und ihr Wert für die Literaturgeschichte.* Philologus Supplementband 21, Heft 2. Leipzig: Dieterich.

Helm, Rudolf. (1956). *Die Chronik des Hieronymus. Hieronymi Chronicon.* 2nd ed. Eusebius Werke 7, GCS. Berlin: Akademie.

Holder-Egger, Oswald. (1875). *Über die Weltchronik des sogenannten Severus Sulpitius und südgallischen Annalen des fünften Jahrhunderts: eine Quellenuntersuchung.* Göttingen: Gebrüder Hofer.

Holder-Egger, Oswald. (1876). Untersuchungen über einige annalistische Quellen zur Geschichte des fünften und sechsten Jahrhunderts. *Neues Archiv,* 1: 15–120, 215–368.

Hwang, Alexander Y. (2009). *Intrepid Lover of Perfect Grace: The Life and Thought of Prosper of Aquitaine.* Washington, DC: Catholic University of America Press.

Jacoby, Felix. (1956). *Griechische Historiker.* Stuttgart: A. Druckenmüller.

Karst, Josef. (1911). *Die Chronik aus dem Armenischen übersetzt mit textkritischem Commentar.* Eusebius Werke 5: GCS 20. Leipzig: Akademie.

Kelly, J.N.D. (1975). *Jerome. His Life, Writings, and Controversies.* London: Duckworth.

Keseling, P. (1927–1928). Die Chronik des Eusebius in der syrischen Überlieferung. *Oriens Christianus* 23: 23–48, 223–41; 24 (1928): 33–56.

Klaassen, Michael. (2010). *Cassiodorus' Chronica: Text, Chronography, and Sources.* PhD diss., University of Pennsylvania.

Lietzmann, Hans. (1937). Ein Blatt aus einer antiken Weltchronik. In: *Quantulacumque. Studies presented to Kirsopp Lake by Pupils, Colleagues and Friends* (ed. Robert P. Casey, Silva Lake, and Agnes K. Lake), 339–48. London: Christophers.

Markus, R. A. (1986). Chronicle and theology: Prosper of Aquitaine. In: *The Inheritance of Historiography, 350–900* (ed. C. Holdsworth and T. P. Wiseman), 31–43. Exeter: Exeter University Publications.

Mosshammer, Alden A. (1979). *The Chronicle of Eusebius and Greek Chronographic Tradition.* Lewisburg, PA: Bucknell University Press.

Muhlberger, Steven. (1984). Heroic kings and unruly generals: The "Copenhagen" continuation of Prosper reconsidered. *Florilegium* 6: 50–95.

Muhlberger, Steven. (1986). Prosper's *Epitoma chronicon*: Was There an Edition of 443? *Classical Philology* 81: 240–44.

Muhlberger, Steven. (1990). *The Fifth-Century Chroniclers: Prosper, Hydatius, and the Gallic Chronicler of 452.* Leeds: Francis Cairns.

Murray, A. C. (2003). *From Roman to Merovingian Gaul: A Reader.* Peterborough, ON: Broadview.

Salzman, Michele Rene. (2015). Reconsidering a relationship: Pope Leo of Rome and Prosper of Aquitaine. In: *The Bishop of Rome in Late Antiquity* (ed. Geoffrey D. Dunn), 109–25. Farnham: Ashgate.

Schoene, Alfred. (1866). *Eusebi Chronicorum libri duo II: Eusebi Chronicorum canonum.* Berlin: Weidmann.

Schoene, Alfred. (1875). *Eusebi Chronicorum libri duo I: Eusebi Chronicorum liber prior.* Berlin: Weidmann.

Schöne, Alfred. (1900). *Die Weltchronik des Eusebius in ihrer Bearbeitung durch Hieronymus.* Berlin: Weidmann.

Treadgold, Warren. (2007). *The Early Byzantine Historians.* Basingstoke/New York: Palgrave Macmillan.

Troncarelli, F. (1989). Il consolato dell'Anticristo. *Studi Medievali* 3rd series, no. 30: 567–592.

Valentin, L. (1900). *Saint Prosper d'Aquitaine: Étude sur la littérature latine ecclésiastique au cinquième siècle en Gaule.* Paris: Alphonse Picard et fils.

Vessey, Mark. (2010). Reinventing history: Jerome's chronicle and the writing of the post- Roman West. In: *From the Tetrarchs to the Theodosians: Later Roman History and Culture, 284–450 CE* (ed. Scott McGill, Cristiana Sogno, and Edward Watts), 265–289. Cambridge: Cambridge University Press.

Whitby, Michael, and Whitby, Mary (1989). *Chronicon Paschale, 284–628 AD.* TTH 7. Liverpool: Liverpool University Press.

Witakowski, Witold. (1999–2000). The chronicle of Eusebius: Its type and continuation in Syriac historiography. *ARAM* 11/12: 419–437.

Wolf, Kenneth Baxter. (2011). *Conquerors and Chroniclers of Early Medieval Spain.* 2nd ed. TTH 9. Liverpool: Liverpool University Press.

CHAPTER TWELVE

Epideictic Oratory

Alex Petkas

A late antique individual's life was punctuated by publicly experienced occasions. Some were cyclical or regularly occurring: They included birthdays, arrivals, departures of important persons such as governors and emperors, contests and feasts, often in honor of God or gods, saints, heroes, or rulers. Others were theoretically unique, such as marriages, deaths, disasters, and victories. Which events one participated in, and the degree to which one could participate, varied greatly depending on social status, location, and gender; urbanites had many more such events to choose from than their rural counterparts. All of these occasions could be augmented by public speeches composed for and delivered at the event – the more important the occasion, the more likely a speaker would be slotted into the agenda. Prose speeches in this era took over many of the ceremonial and ritual roles of poetry from earlier periods (Pernot 2015, pp. 15–16). Thus while the conventions of this "epideictic" oratory drew on the millennium-old tradition of *paideia* and had important precedents in the classical age of the fifth and fourth century BCE Greek *poleis*, the genre achieved an unprecedented flowering in the highly ceremonialized imperial Roman world, especially in the Greek-speaking East (Pernot 2015, pp. 1–28; both judicial and deliberative rhetoric remained important as well, and central in teaching: Webb 2003; Heath 2004).

A Companion to Late Antique Literature, First Edition.
Edited by Scott McGill and Edward J. Watts.
© 2018 John Wiley & Sons, Inc. Published 2018 by John Wiley & Sons, Inc.

12.1 What Do We Mean by "Epideictic"?

The term "epideictic" (*epideixis*, "a display," with the related verb *epideiknusthai*, "to make a display") out of context might suggest a staggeringly broad range of discourse (Burgess 1902 takes such an approach). Aristotle was the first to associate the genre of epideictic rhetoric specifically with praise and blame; he additionally claims its point of reference as the present (whereas judicial addresses the past and deliberative the future; *Rhetoric* 1358b). This schema – which we might reframe as evaluative discourse with reference to the present occasion – is still useful for identifying many of the salient features of late antique epideictic, and we will follow it in this chapter; despite the fact that epideictic in many ways breaks down into a set of discrete subgenres, it was unified enough that it could also be treated as a single category by late antique practitioners and theoreticians – for example, Menander Rhetor (see below).

It is helpful to be aware of some related and occasionally interchangeable terms. *Encomium* is the most common word for describing the extended praise of individuals; it is often treated by the handbooks as a smaller unit within an entire epideictic speech. *Panegyric* etymologically refers to a festival (*panegyris*) and thus by extension to the sort of speech delivered there (such as Isocrates's *Panegyricus*) (on terminology: Russell 1998, pp. 19–21; Pernot 2015, pp. 70–71); while often used as a synonym for epideictic by modern scholars, the word was more often used in its more focused sense by ancient authors. For many reasons, praise is much more common than blame in the practice of epideictic. (For invective see Flower 2013).

A treatment this brief of a topic this vast cannot hope to be comprehensive. My main objectives will be to give an overview of the subject of late antique epideictic, indicate some exciting recent developments in the field, and provide some illustrative examples. We will thus leave aside many forms of speech and writing that might fit the category as laid out above. Imperial panegyrics, perhaps the highest-stakes form of epideictic rhetoric in late antiquity, are distinctive enough to deserve their own separate chapter in this volume. I will therefore focus on aspects of the genre other than its role in negotiating power between ruled and rulers or among the ruling classes – and thus I will bypass, too, the praise of imperial governors and officials, which can be argued to have more in common with imperial panegyric than, say, with festal orations (compare the *basilikos logos* with the *prosphonetikos* at Menander (II) 368 and 414.31, respectively). Julian's fascinating and idiosyncratic *Misopogon* is composed in the form of an epideictic speech (an inverted "praise of city"; Marcone 1984; Gleason 1993), but it falls outside of our scope because of its imperial quality. I also will not be concerned with verse epideictics (both of praise and blame) such as are found among the poems of Claudian in Latin. While here the comparison with prose epideictic, even in Greek, is illuminating, nevertheless such poetry is indebted enough to the traditions of Latin epic and satire to merit separate treatment (Long 1996, pp. 65–105; Ware 2012).

These two omissions make the focus of this essay overwhelmingly Greek; besides the (imperial) *Panegyrici Latini*, there are far fewer surviving examples of prose epideictic in Latin from late antiquity. This is not merely an accident of transmission. The epideictic genre was seen by Cicero as primarily a Greek phenomenon, the one exception being the funeral oration performed in the senate house (*De Orat* 2.341); he lists no examples of Roman epideictic in his *Brutus*. Quintilian echoes Cicero's genealogical judgment, though he observes that prose epideictic has become quite fashionable in his own day (*Inst.* 3.7; there are, of course, many Silver Latin poetic examples; see Peirano 2012, pp. 117–172). Isidore of Seville in part reproduces the earlier Roman bias when criticizing panegyric as a wicked Greek invention by which orators flatter rulers with specious lies (*Etymologies* 6.8.7), although professing suspicion of false and empty speeches is, in fact, a very ancient topos within Greek epideictic itself (e.g. Thucydides 2.35). There are, nonetheless, a few other extant late antique Latin epideictics such as Ambrose's funeral oration for his brother Satyrus (Savon 1980; McCauley et al. 1953). The genres of biography and hagiography draw much from the epideictic tradition but also deserve separate treatment. Syriac literature seems for the most part to be only indirectly affected by the Greek epideictic tradition until the later Middle Ages (Watt 1989, 1993 for Antony of Tagrit). Our chronological focus is primarily on the fourth century, which stands out for the quantity, variety, and innovativeness of its surviving epideictic speeches.

12.2 Topoi

In attempting to understand late antique epideictic, we are aided in particular by a set of rhetorical treatises most likely from the late third century. These include two texts on epideictic attributed to the sophist Menander of Laodicea (third century CE), usually collectively referred to as "Menander Rhetor" I and II (below often as "M. R."). They were almost surely written by different authors (Russell and Wilson 1981, pp. xxxiv–xl) and the first of the two is particularly unlikely to have actually come from Menander

(Heath 2004, pp. 127–131). In addition to these there are the beginning sections "on epideictic speeches," from a larger rhetorical treatise probably from around the same period, falsely attributed to Dionysius of Halicarnassus (hereafter "Dionysius"; translation (based on Radermacher's text) in Russell and Wilson 1981, pp. 362–381). The first Menandrian treatise organizes the speeches by the *subject* of praise; treatise II organizes encomia by *occasion*. "Dionysius" follows the same occasion-based approach as Menander II. This method of categorization by occasion type has no equivalent in the treatises dedicated to the deliberative and judicial genres: Encomium here is seen no longer as an abstract rhetorical form, but rather as a social practice, or set of social practices, embodied in concrete circumstances (Pernot 2015, p. 20).

Whether our fourth century epideictic authors actually possessed and referred to copies of these works, or had been exposed to them in their rhetorical training, is difficult to say with confidence, but many parallels with extant epideictics suggest that at the very least these treatises reflect trends prevalent in late antiquity. Nonetheless, it should be kept in mind that the more talented a rhetor was, the less dependent he was likely to be on topoi. Moreover, a quality rhetorical education emphasized sensitivity and a critical stance toward textbook formulae (Heath 2004, pp. 217–254; Menander II.430.7–8).

12.3 Some Social Aspects of Epideictic

Pure "display" was an important feature of high imperial Greek rhetorical culture, and this continued into the now increasingly so-called Third Sophistic (Fowler and Quiroga Puertas 2014). For young elite men attending school, an important part of rhetorical education involved learning to emulate examples both living and dead (Libanius, *Or.* 1.23; see Cribiore 2007, pp. 138–141). It was standard academic practice to attend the lectures not just of one's own chosen teacher but of other sophists in the city as well (Libanius, *Or.* 1.16), and these were often simply model speeches. While the lectures were often referred to as *epideixeis*, they could also treat, besides "epideictic" in our sense, judicial and deliberative declamations (drawn from historical or fictional situations); students would then learn to produce their own examples in imitation (Cribiore 2001, pp. 231–238). Even if the occasion or theme (*hypothesis*) was fictional, the stakes for teachers were real: Failure to regularly impress even their own students could mean "a risk of being scorned and overlooked by the lads as they flutter away" to other teachers, as Synesius remarks in his humorous and unflattering portrayal of the life of professional sophists in the *Dio* (12–14, esp. 14.2). In his student days in Athens, Libanius felt the inverse of this pressure: He incurred the anger of his school when he, unimpressed, failed to clamor and applaud his own teacher's speeches (*Or.* 1.17).

There were many consequential fields for epideictic action beyond the classroom. From the earlier, high imperial period, there is abundant inscriptional evidence for contests at civic festivals and Panhellenic games, at which prizes were awarded for prose encomia (see Wörrle 1988). Festal orations (*panegyric* proper), treated below, were not always formally competitive. On the other hand, Libanius's autobiography vividly records the intensely competitive atmosphere at Constantinople of public rhetoric contests, which do not seem to be necessarily associated with religious festivals. He records one instance of a Cappadocian sophist at Constantinople who, as a result of an impressive speech in one single competition, was installed in an imperially sponsored chair of rhetoric by recommendation of the city council (*Or.* 1.35).

This rhetorical, epideictic culture played a determinative role in the development of the nascent Christian homiletic discourse. It provided the social and intellectual context for the consumption of highly stylized, extended speeches pertaining to ethically or socially normative themes; it also reinforced a traditional vocabulary of praise and blame based on examples drawn from a traditional repertoire (Cameron 1991, pp. 73–88). But even though we have extensive knowledge of the oral culture of late antiquity, we must never forget, when dealing with extant examples of epideictic, that what we have are texts and not verbatim transcripts of oral performances. Extant epideictic speeches are a literary genre purporting to imitate or record social acts; similar things could be said, mutatis mutandis, about much of Greek and Latin poetry. The historian must thus be careful before inferring from a written speech what was actually said on a particular occasion; and the literary scholar should take note both of an epideictic text's performative possibilities and its potential literary ambitions. We possess many of the works that we do precisely because their authors in one way or another hoped and ensured that they would transcend the often ephemeral circumstances that they purport to address, and this often involved revising an originally delivered speech. Though this fact may sometimes cast doubt on the strict "historicity" of texts, it can also be seen to enhance their complexity and depth. At any rate, an author's license in revising was not unlimited.

I will first offer a more extended treatment of a single epideictic speech, and then go on to treat other forms more briefly.

12.4 An Epithalamium

Himerius, sophist and teacher of rhetoric in Athens (fl. mid 340s–mid 360s), wrote an *epithalamios logos* for his former student Severus. Menander and "Dionysius" both address this genre of "wedding speech" (II.339.11; 269 Radermacher), which had its origins in the "wedding poem" (*epithalamium*) of which many famous earlier examples are extant both in Latin and Greek (e.g. Theocritus 18; Catullus 62, 64). Himerius's piece is strikingly close at points to the lighthearted advice of Menander – much more so than to the moralizing "Dionysius" (Russell 1979; Penella 2007 (who also provides a translation)). Nonetheless he executes this performance for Severus and his bride with his own personal touch and sensitivity to the specific situation.

He begins with a proem (9.3–6), in which he touches on the mythic and historical origins of the genre of the current speech. Apollo turned to wedding songs after he had won great victories playing the lyre; similarly, Lesbian Sappho positioned herself in a soon-to-be couple's bedroom, gathered the young maidens, and summoned Aphrodite "after the contests." Now Himerius takes up the same duty. Through this mythic figuration he contrasts the lighthearted and joyful world of wedding rhetoric with the agonistic contests for which he and his students normally train: The lyric contests of the past here represent the sophistic performances and contests of his day ("It is time for me, too, to be done with serious music so that I may dance along with the young girls in honor of Aphrodite" [9.3]). He conceives of his project, here more vividly than elsewhere, as a fundamentally poetic one.

Next comes the *thesis* section, which according to the handbook guidelines is supposed to argue that marriage is a good thing (M. R. II.400.29). Himerius begins, fittingly, with the origin of the universe (9.7). The cosmogonic union of God and Nature is the first event in a long series of famous marital couplings: Ocean and Tethys, the Danube and the Black Sea, the Rhine and the Atlantic. The two great aforementioned rivers arise at the same source, but Eros divided them and sent them chasing after different lovers. Himerius leaves implicit, but obvious, the fact that the god responsible for this happy provincial event is also the god who gave the future Romans their northern border.

Geographical texturing is, in fact, one of the more striking features of this *epithalamios*. The groom was a native of Athens, who had been set up with a noble wife from a distant Thracian city named after Philip II of Macedon (either Philippopolis or (probably) Philippi; Penella 2007). An ecumenical marriage between an outsider and someone from what was still the conceptual center of the civilized world for many Greeks – especially the small but entrenched local elite of Athens (Watts 2006, pp. 48–78) – deserved an ecumenical treatment. Thus while in the *thesis* section Himerius does highlight, after the rather "cosmic" Danube and Rhine, some more local lover-rivers, such as the Boeotian Enipeus and the Attic Ilissus, in the following "praise of the families" section he pans back out. Needing a glorious example with which to compare the youthful love of the couple, he aptly adduces Philip II himself and Olympias, the mother of Alexander – who fell in love with the young king upon seeing him at the Mysteries of Samothrace (but contrast Plutarch, *Alexander* 2.2). He goes on to praise the royal Thracian lineage of the bride's family, describing where their city lies (west of the Bosporus, near the Scythians, with the Aegean lying to the south). Then Himerius (himself originally from Bithynia) having earlier pointed out that the story (trite by then) of Athenian autochthony is a myth (9.9), elaborates on the noble and non-Athenian origin of the groom's family: They originally came from the province of Diospontus (the name had actually been "Helenopontus" since the reign of Constantine). Thus the orator deftly turns a potential point of weakness or anxiety for the young couple into an object of praise: Such outsiders, he implies, do not debase but ennoble the stock of the city. This integrative act of rhetoric incidentally shows that knowledge of localized traditions of myth and ancestry was still vibrant and very useful in the popular culture of late antiquity; enthusiasm for it is widely attested in contemporary epideictic (e.g. Libanius, *Antiochikos* (= *Or*.11)).

While his praise of the bride in the final section is woven with elegant studs of Sappho and Anacreon, he warms to the conclusion with an elaborate *paraleipsis*: "If I had a poetic nature such that I could freely let my tongue loose," he would have summoned the Muses from their home in Athens (*not* Boeotia, *pace* the poets) and the Nereids from the sea and would have led a chorus of Nymphs, Dryads, Satyrs, Pan, Dionysus, and others. But he restrains himself. Despite suggesting above that he does not have a poetic nature, he proceeds rather to demonstrate the opposite, rounding off this *paraleipsis* with brief wedding ode "such as I would have provided *if* a song had been needed." The piece that follows is not in verse but is so poetic in language that editors have suspected a lost fragment of Sappho under it (Bergk *PLG* 133). Whether or not there is a Lesbian *Vorlage* here, the audience is left with a sense that the orator has not, in fact, unleashed his full potential, but that the nuptial feast has nonetheless received what was "needed" – in this case, rhetorical brilliance under firm and cool control, and respect for the aesthetic virtue of *to prepon* (appropriateness) with respect to *kairos* (occasion).

Himerius, in borrowing diction from the poets and keeping to a reasonable time limit, is following the advice he gives in the "explanatory comment" (*protheoria*) for the speech (directly preceding it in the MSS). This brief preface gives some guidance, both to those who would use his speech as a model and to more general reading audiences, as to the nature of the type of speech in question and the criteria of success. He suggests that readers decide for themselves whether the *epithalamios* that he composed achieved what it set out to do, and if it has (which he also suggests), then it is a better guide to the *techne* of composing a speech than a *protheoria* could be – in other words, that it is a model worthy of emulation (Penella 2007, p. 10, on *protheoriai*). Himerius seems to have gone through the process of editing *Oration* 9, which presumably he did, in fact, deliver in some form. But the preservation in writing of this speech highlights for us the double aspect of epideictic's aim to imbue often quotidian events with diachronic significance. First, the speaker connects the particular present event to timeless, universal examples via comparisons and, second, he tries to pass on the event to future memory. So also the classical epideictic genre, from its earliest prose instances like Isocrates's *Evagoras* to such poetic forebears as Pindar's epinicians, sought not just to compare the glorious past to the (often allegedly even more glorious) present, but also to add the *hypothesis* under consideration (whether person or thing or event) to this very repertoire of meaningful examples – in a sense, to turn the present into history. Himerius, by writing down and publishing his *epithalamios*, did this quite literally for Severus's wedding. Yet (assuming a correspondence between the text and the prior verbal utterance), by glorifying the nobility of the families, the cosmic significance of Eros, and the worthiness of the bride, and by offering a rare display of learning and verbal beauty, he had already endeavored to persuade the attendant guests that they were at an event which was unique, worth remembering, and good.

12.5 Monody

Menander II, with good reason, ascribes the origins of the *monodia* to Homer, who has Andromache, Priam, and Hecuba pronounce monodies of Hector in the *Iliad* (434.10–15; *Iliad* 22.416–436, 477–514; 24.725–745, 748–759; see Alexiou 1974/2002). The purpose of this kind of speech, he explains, is to lament and express pity (434.19; *threnein kai katoiktizesthai*). Yet his instructions suggest that the successful monodist does not simply perform this emotional expression but perhaps chiefly *provokes* it in his bereaved audience: "You should use *apostrophe*:...O splendid and distinguished family – up until this day! What treasure do you possess like that you have lost?" (435.30–436.2; he advises a similar address to the city at

434.30). The orator is instructed to share in the grief as well. This is not a tasteless dwelling upon misfortunes but rather can be conceived of as a call for communal catharsis, building on an exchange of emotion between orator and audience.

Although Menander's topoi only explicitly envision the lament of individuals, the genre naturally could be extended to lament destroyed cities. Upon the destruction by earthquake of Nicomedia, where he spent some of his best professional years, Libanius composed a stirring monody that takes cues from his rhetorical predecessor Aelius Aristides (Karla 2007; Libanius had and admired a portrait of him (*Ep.* 1534)). The piece was first delivered in front of only four close friends before the written version of it was circulated much more widely (*Ep.* 33). His treatment of the event in certain letters describe the oration and its performance as having a curative effect both for him and his audience. The monody thus helps the bereaved overcome grief, partly, it seems, by vividly portraying the glorious city (61.7–10) and the disaster that strikes it (61.14–15). As the orator closes he expresses a desire to fly to the city and witness its ruin – though it would be horrifying, "the lover finds some consolation in throwing himself upon his beloved who lies dead" (61.23; trans. in Cribiore 2015). But his vivid ekphrasis has in a small way already allowed the audience some contact with fallen Nicomedia through his *logos*.

Monody could be a deeply personal affair as well: Himerius composed a moving example on the death of his own son Rufinus (*Or.* 8), which focuses intensely on the father's grief. He performs a monodic ekphrasis of the city of Athens, describing the many places that he will never visit again because they are filled with (formerly) happy memories of his lost son (8.14–19). Rufinus had died in Athens when Himerius was in Boeotia, preventing him from attending the funeral. He seems to reflect on the inability of words to replace actual presence at 8.9: "I am wrapping you in words, my child, since I have been prevented from wrapping you in a shroud" (see 8.19). It has been argued that the orator was in exile (see Penella 2007, p. 22). If so, his speech may signal an openness to being invited back and restored to Athens. Could this expression of grief thus allow everyone involved to effect a face-saving restoration? In any event, this surprisingly subtle speech is on the whole quite faithful to Menander II's recommendations for structuring the monody. Yet it is precisely in observing Himerius's subtle departures from convention that we can see the ways in which he introduces themes more pertinent to himself than to the mourned (Watts 2015). It seems that we have much yet to appreciate about the creative and nuanced ways in which late antique authors communicated through highly formalized rhetorical channels.

12.6 Epitaphios

The funeral oration of Pericles (*Thucydides* 3.34–46) was the most famous original example of the classical Greek form of *epitaphios* (prose eulogy) (M.R. II.418; "Dionysius" 277; see Synesius, *Dio* 1.13). By the Roman period, however, what had originally been one form was generally distributed among the monody, *epitaphios logos*, and *paramythetikos* (speech of consolation). According to Menander (II) and actual late antique practice, the *epitaphios* was a form designated for some time after the death of the *laudandus*. Thus, while including some emotional lamentation (M. R. II.419.11–420.9), the speech was to include many of the topoi of a typical praise encomium (Russell and Wilson 1981, pp. 331–332). Libanius first composed his brief monody for Julian and later followed it with the much longer funeral oration (see Felgentreu 2007, Watts 2014).

Most of our late antique examples are epitaphs of individuals rather than of groups. Gregory of Nazianzus's *epitaphios* on Basil of Caesarea (*Or.* 43) is one of the most famous. It is very instructive to compare it with the eulogy delivered by the brother of the departed, Gregory of Nyssa, as the differing way each orator treats his relationship to Basil in his speech reveals much about the impact Christianity had on the culture of friendship, as David Konstan (2000) has shown. Nazianzen's more traditional approach allows for ample depiction of his own intense relationship with the man (e.g. 43.14–22), while Nyssen's explicit eschewing of the topoi of family, country, and so forth as "worldly" (*PG* 46.816A–B) signals that his version of *epitaphios* has already taken a major stride in the direction of hagiography – Basil was not simply virtuous but, even from childhood, as otherworldly as a true saint should be (789B). Both eulogies compare Basil favorably with holy figures from both Old and New Testaments (Nyssen, 789D, 792A; Nazianzen, 43.70–76), much as Isocrates praised Evagoras as surpassing Trojan War heroes in excellence (*Evag.* 65). The purpose of this Christianized traditional trope (M. R. II.420.31) is again not just sheer hyperbole but part of fashioning the deceased as a new moral paradigm for present and future generations of the church. Epideictic is in such a way the vehicle by which Gregory of Nazianzus presents Basil as a *nomos empsychos* for posterity (43.80).

12.7 Festal Oration

Whether they were celebrated on the small scale of a hamlet or deme or boasted the attendance of something as large as the entire Greek world (conceptually), religious festivals in the ancient Mediterranean were events central to the articulation and reinforcement of group identity (Iddeng 2012, for overview and investigative methodology). Through the Roman era festivals had, thus, become one of the main vehicles for propagating a self-conscious Hellenism in the urban centers of the eastern Mediterranean. These celebrations of Greek culture had as their forebears gatherings that had since the Archaic period been (alongside the symposium) one of the original contexts for performance and consumption of Greek literature – the world of rhapsodes, drama, dithyrambs, and so forth (see Hesiod *Works and Days* 654–657; MacDougall 2015, pp. 12). For this reason, the intertextual nexus pertaining to festivals was unusually dense and could be activated to subtle or striking effect by a skilled rhetor such as Gregory of Nazianzus (this subject has recently received an illuminating full length study: MacDougall 2015). Late antique "panegyric" speeches, depending on the needs of the rhetorical situation, could heavily involve other forms of epideictic. Thus for the Sminthiac Oration (to Apollo at Alexandria Troas) Menander's topoi devote much space to praising the god (437.6), but Libanius's *Antiochikos* (*Or.* 11), delivered presumably at the Antiochean Olympic games at Daphne, in substance is primarily a long "praise of a city" (see M. R. I.346.27); despite the original Elean Olympics being banned in 392, the Antiochene counterpart seems to have continued into the sixth century (Webb 2008, p. 35). Himerius addresses his oft-cited *Oration* 47 to Basilius on the occasion of that governor's visit to the Panathenaic games in the early 380s, and he uses most of his space praising this "friend of the Muses" before moving on to a rhetorical mimesis of the Panathenaic procession (on which see MacDougall 2015, pp. 48–51).

One guiding objective of the *panegyrikos logos* that is more or less present in all of these is to make manifest to the audience the deeper significance of the event that they attend. This is especially clear in Gregory of Nazianzus's festal orations (*Or.* 1, 38–41, 45; Harrison 2008), where, so claims the orator, the real purpose of the gathering is *theoria*, contemplation of the divine – both "theology" and "economy" (e.g. *Or* 38.8). The concept of *theoria* had originally denoted honorary spectatorship at religious festivals by delegations from other *poleis*, before being turned into a metaphor for the highest aspirations of philosophy in the classical period, especially in Plato (Nightingale 2004). Thus Gregory reinserts the goal of contemplative *theoria* into the literal setting of ritual spectatorship, which had originally given birth to the metaphor. Despite the fact that Christian orators, including Gregory, frequently contrasted the new religion's own festivals (optimistically) as more spiritual, in contrast to riotous body-oriented pagan festivals, the tradition of seeking the philosophical essence of the *panegyris*, or *heortē*, is quite old. Gregory walks a path well-trodden by Dio Chrysostom, who in his speech at Olympia urged the attendants to contemplate the true meaning of the famous statue of Zeus by Pheidias (*Or.* 12). In such a way Nazianzen speaks about festivals like any proper pagan sophist should (MacDougall 2015, pp. 19–26, 103–112). The performance and experience of this tradition of discourse is, thus, one of the major points of continuity between classical and Christian Mediterranean culture and will surely be a rewarding subject for further study.

12.8 Pure Sophistry?

Another subset of epideictic not so well represented in surviving late antique literature but nonetheless important is the paradoxical encomium, in which a sophist demonstrates his talent by taking up a theme so inglorious as to seem impossible, such as Helen, the fly, salt, or Thersites (Gorgias, Lucian, Polycrates (lost), Libanius (Gibson 2008, p. 229)). This genre was, since the fifth century BCE, widely admired and reviled – we may infer the former from evidence of the latter. Imperial rhetoricians took it up with renewed vigor (for ancient sources Burgess (1902, p. 157–166) is still a very useful starting point). Paradoxography, though less clearly tied to occasion than the above types, most provokes the characterization of epideictic as literature for literature's sake – whether that is good or bad depends on one's perspective (and either way it is an oversimplification – Pernot 2015, p. 69; Webb 2003). We owe antiquity's most elaborate, extended, and successful example to Synesius of Cyrene in his *Praise of Baldness*, which also preserves an extended fragment of the lost speech of Dio to which it responds, the *Praise of Hair*. The *Encomium calvitii* stands out for its sustained engagement with more serious philosophical doctrines (e.g. 7.1, 8.1); the bald head is, of course, closer to the shape of the heavenly bodies (9–11). But this philosophical stance has influenced the literary aspects as well: Much of the treatise's humor comes from its insistent repudiation of sophistic trifles and deception – Synesius disavows *prooimia* in the middle of his own *prooimion* (4.3). Addressing a philosophically educated audience through this irony, he invites the reader to examine and critique his arguments, as well as question the relationship between the authorial voice and the historical author (Seng 2012). This is an important interpretive strategy to keep in mind for other, less ironic specimens of epideictic rhetoric as well. It has recently been argued that Synesius wrote the treatise not as a youthful showpiece, as earlier scholarship generally held, but rather after his more "serious" treatises *On Dreams* and *Dio*. In the latter text he unironically defends the usefulness of lighter literary fare for serious philosophers; thus this encomium may be part of a wider literary program (Seng 2012). Erasmus mentions this *Encomium* as an important precedent for his *Praise of Folly* in that text's prefatory epistle to Thomas More.

12.9 Conclusion

At first glance, late antique epideictic can occasionally seem like a bewilderingly trite exercise in tired formalities. But the evidence suggests that this cultural discourse was, in fact, an object of intense excitement and fanfare for ancient audiences, who were after all exposed to much more of it than even most modern experts could boast (or tolerate). When approached with sensitivity to the generic constraints and historical context, as well as with imaginative sympathy, these texts can come to life with meaning, nuance, and even beauty. Recent work has emphasized how the study of epideictic literature has much more to teach us about, among other things, the history of emotions in late antiquity (Cribiore 2013, pp. 89–95) and the mechanics of popular morality (Pernot 2015, pp. 91–100) – for unlike many philosophical and polemical texts, most epideictic rhetoric is pronounced by some sort of authorized representative of the community addressed and aims to refresh consensus around principles that, in theory, the audience already accepts. Epideictic *does* aim at persuasion (Webb 2003), and what is at stake is generally the values that a culture holds dearest. These are never as sturdy and unanimously accepted as encomiasts like to portray them, and this is precisely why many people looked to orators to insist upon them. In an era of cultural shifts and social upheavals such as the late antique Mediterranean world, it is possible that epideictic rhetoric had never before been so consequential.

ADDENDUM

I have not dealt here with the "school" of Gaza (especially Procopius and Choricius), which is an exciting area of development for the history of epideictic and late antique rhetoric more broadly, particularly in the wake of a project to publish new editions of all the works of the Gazan rhetors in the Collection des Universités de France (Budé) series (beginning with Procopius [Amato et al., 2014; see also the collected volume by Amato, Thénevet and Ventrella 2014]).

REFERENCES

Alexiou, Margaret. (1974). *The Ritual Lament in Greek Tradition.* London: Cambridge. (2nd ed. 2002, rev. Dimitrios Yatromanolakis and Panagiotis Roilos. Lanham, MD: Rowman & Littlefield.)

Amato, Eugenio, Thénevet, Lucie, and Ventrella, Gianluca. ed. (2014). *Discorso pubblico e Declamazione scolastica a Gaza nella tarda antichità.* Bari: Edizioni di Pagina.

Amato, Eugenio, Corcella, Aldo, Ventrella, Gianluca et al. (2014). *Discours et Fragments: Procope de Gaza.* 2014. Paris: Belles Lettres.

Burgess, Theodore. (1902). *Epideictic Literature.* Chicago: University of Chicago Press.

Cameron, Avril. (1991). *Christianity and the Rhetoric of Empire.* Berkeley: University of California Press.

Cribiore, Raffaella. (2001). *Gymnastics of the Mind: Greek Education in Hellenistic and Roman Egypt.* Princeton, NJ: Princeton University Press.

Cribiore, Raffaella. (2007). *The School of Libanius in Late Antique Antioch.* Princeton, NJ: Princeton University Press.

Cribiore, Rafaella. (2013). *Libanius the Sophist: Rhetoric, Reality, and Religion in the Fourth Century.* Ithaca: Cornell University Press.

Cribiore, Raffaella. (2015). *Between City and School: Selected Orations of Libanius.* Liverpool: Liverpool University Press.

Felgentreu, Fritz. (2007). Aufbau und Erzähltechnik im *Epitaphios* auf Kaiser Julian: Zur Kompositionskunst des Libanios. In: *Theatron: Rhetorische Kultur in Spätantike und Mittelalter* (ed. Michael Grünbart), 53–68. Berlin: De Gruyter.

Flower, Richard. (2013). *Emperors and Bishops in Late Roman Invective.* Cambridge: Cambridge University Press, 2013.

Fowler, Ryan and Quiroga Puertas, Alberto. (2014). A prolegomenon to the Third Sophistic. In: *Plato in the Third Sophistic* (ed. Ryan Fowler), 1–25. Boston: De Gruyter.

Gibson, Craig. (2008). *Libanius' Progymnasmata: Model Exercises in Greek Prose Composition and Rhetoric.* Atlanta: Society of Biblical Literature.

Gleason, Maud. (1993). Festive satire: Julian's *Misopogon* and the New Year at Antioch. *Journal of Roman Studies* 24: 106–119.

Harrison, Nonna Verna. (2008). *St. Gregory of Nazianzus: Festal Orations.* 2008. Crestwood, NY: St. Vladimir's Seminary Press.

Heath, Malcolm. (2004). *Menander: A Rhetor in Context.* Oxford: Oxford University Press.

Iddeng, Jon W. (2012). What is a Graeco-Roman festival? A polythetic approach. In: *Greek and Roman Festivals: Content, Meaning and Practice* (ed. J. Rasmus and Jon W. Iddeng). Oxford: Oxford University Press.

Karla, Grammatiki. (2007). Die Klage über die zerstörte Stadt Nikomedeia bei Libanios im Spiegel der Mimesis. In *Theatron: Rhetorische Kultur in Spätantike und Mittelalter* (ed. Michael Grünbart), 141–156. Berlin: De Gruyter.

Konstan, David. (2000). How to praise a friend: St. Gregory of Nazianzus' funeral oration for St. Basil the Great. In: *Greek Biography and Panegyric in Late Antiquity* (ed. Thomas Hägg and Philip Rousseau), 160–179. Berkeley: University of California Press.

Long, Jacqueline. (1996). *Claudian's In Eutropium, or How, When, and Why to Slander a Eunuch*. Chapel Hill: University of North Carolina Press.

MacDougall, Byron. (2015). *Gregory of Nazianzus and Christian Festival Rhetoric*. PhD diss., Brown University.

McCauley, Leo P., Sullivan, John J., McGuire, Martin R.P. et al. (1953). *Funeral Orations: Saint Gregory Nazianzen and Saint Ambrose*. New York: Fathers of the Church.

Marcone, Arnaldo. (1984). Un panegirico rovesciato. Pluralità di modelli e contaminazione letteraria nel *Misopogon* giuleaneo. *REAug* 30: 226–239.

Nightingale, Andrea. (2004). *Spectacles of Truth in Classical Greek Philosophy: Theoria in Its Cultural Context*. Cambridge: Cambridge University Press.

Peirano, Irene. (2012). *The Rhetoric of the Roman Fake*. Cambridge: Cambridge University Press.

Penella, Robert. (2007). *Man and the Word: The Orations of Himerius*. 2007. Berkeley: University of California Press.

Pernot, Laurent. (2015). *Epideictic Rhetoric*. Austin: University of Texas Press.

Russell, Donald. (1979). Rhetors at the wedding. *Proceedings of the Cambridge Philological Society* 25:104–117.

Russell, Donald. (1998). The panegyrists and their teachers. In *The Propaganda of Power: The Role of Panegyric in Late Antiquity* (ed. Mary Whitby), 17–52. Leiden: Brill.

Russell, Donald and Wilson, Nigel. (1981). *Menander Rhetor: Edited with Translation and Commentary*. 1981. Oxford: Clarendon.

Savon, Hervé. (1980). La première oraison funèbre de saint Ambroise (*De excessu fratris* I) et les deux sources de la consolation chrétienne. *REL* 58: 370–402.

Seng, Helmut. (2012). An den Haaren herbeigezogen. Sophistische Argumentation im *Encomium calvitii*. In: *Synesios von Kyrene: Politik, Literatur, Philosophie* (ed. Helmut Seng and Lars Martin Hoffman), 125–143. Turnhout: Brepols.

Ware, Catherine. (2012). *Claudian and the Roman Epic Tradition*. Cambridge: Cambridge University Press.

Watt, John. (1989). Syriac panegyric in theory and practice. *Le Muséon* 102: 271–298.

Watt, John. (1993). Grammar, Rhetoric, and the Enkyklios Paideia in Syriac. *Zeitschrift der Deutschen Morgenländischen Gesellschaft* 143: 45–71.

Watts, Edward. (2006). *City and School in Late Antique Athens and Alexandria*. Berkeley: University of California Press.

Watts, Edward. (2014). The historical context: The rhetoric of suffering in Libanius' *Monodies, Letters*, and *Autobiography*. In: *Libanius: A Critical Introduction* (ed. Lieve van Hoof), 39–58. Cambridge: Cambridge University Press.

Watts, Edward. (2015). Libanius and the personalization of monody. In: *Shifting Genres in Late Antiquity* (ed. Geoffrey Greatrex), 319–324. Farnham: Ashgate.

Webb, Ruth. (2003). Praise and persuasion: Argumentation and audience response in epideictic oratory. In: *Rhetoric in Byantium* (ed. Elizabeth Jeffreys), 127–135. Aldershot: Ashgate.

Webb, Ruth. (2008). *Demons and Dancers: Performance in Late Antiquity.* Cambridge, MA: Harvard University Press.

Wörrle, Michael. (1988) *Stadt und Fest im kaiserzeitlichen Kleinasien: Studien zu einer agonistischen Stiftung aus Oinoanda.* Munich: Beck.

CHAPTER THIRTEEN

Panegyric

Roger Rees

In quantitative terms, surviving late antique imperial panegyric can be charted as follows: In late antique Greek the major panegyrical works in prose are the *Vita Constanini* (Cameron and Hall 1999) and *Laus Constantini* (Drake 1976) by Eusebius; *Orations* 1–3 by Julian; various speeches by Libanius, notably *Or.* 12, 13, 59 (Wiemer 1995; Van Hoof 2014); *Or.* 1–19, 34 by Themistius (Vanderspoel 1995; Hägg and Rousseau 2000; Heather and Moncur 2001); and late antique Greek verse panegyrics that are almost completely lost (Cameron 1965, p. 471; 1970, p. 254). In late antique Latin, the major panegyrical works in prose are the *XII Panegyrici Latini* (*PanLat*) collection (Nixon and Saylor Rodgers 1994; Rees 2012a); *Or.* 1–3 by Symmachus, now fragmentary (Pabst 1989; Callu 2009); Ausonius's consular *gratiarum actio* (Green 1991); and Ennodius's panegyric to Theodoric (MacCormack 1975). In verse the key texts are the hexameter panegyrics by Claudian (Cameron 1970; Ware 2012), Sidonius Apollinaris, Merobaudes, Priscian, and Corippus (Schindler 2009; Gillett 2012). We also have references to other panegyrical works now lost, such as, among many others, Fronto's consular *gratiarum actio* (1.110 Haines); a speech to the emperor Gallienus (Pernot 2015, p. 16); speeches that preceded Libanius's to Julian in 363 (*Autobiog.* 128 – see below); Libanius's to Gallus (*Autobiog.* 91, 97), to the prefect Strategios (*Autobiog.* 111–112), and to Valens (only half of which was delivered – *Autobiog.* 144); Symmachus's speech to the usurper Magnus Maximus in 388 (*Ep.* 2.31 postscript; Sogno 2006, pp. 70–73; Rees 2010, pp. 20–21); Augustine's

---

A Companion to Late Antique Literature, First Edition.
Edited by Scott McGill and Edward J. Watts.
© 2018 John Wiley & Sons, Inc. Published 2018 by John Wiley & Sons, Inc.

rather vague mention of his preparation to deliver a panegyric (*Conf.* 6.6.9); various references to Greek works in Philostratus's *Lives of the* Sophists and to Greek verse panegyrics by poets such as Theotimus and Diphilus (Cameron 1965, pp. 477–478); a speech an orator was putting aside for later (*PanLat* XI[3]1.3); and Eusebius's reference to other speeches delivered in praise of Constantine on the occasion of the 30th anniversary of his accession (*LC* 1.1; Burgess 1902; MacCormack 1981, p. 9; Pernot 2015, p. 19). The loss of some of these speeches, such as Symmachus's to Maximus, was no doubt deliberate; the reverse scenario, such as when Libanius denied having addressed a panegyric to the usurper Procopius (*Autobiog.* 163–165), could also come about. Political reputations could be won and lost by addressing – or not addressing – a panegyric.

This record of survival and loss tells us that panegyric was a popular late antique form in both Greek and Latin, in prose and verse, and in Christian and pagan contexts. In addition, not from references but from extrapolation from the surviving material, we can reasonably surmise a great deal more that has not reached us; an anonymous orator of 307, speaking at an imperial wedding, says that imperial benefactions to the state can be praised on "many occasions of different times" (*PanLat* VII[6]1.2 *multis occasionibus diversorum temporum*). From the speeches of thanksgiving for the consulship by Claudius Mamertinus (*PanLat* III[11]) and Ausonius, for example, we can confidently assume that every year each new consulship was marked with a panegyric, continuing a tradition that went back to the earlier empire. If, alternatively, the emperor himself was consul, it seems he would hear panegyrics to celebrate that (Libanius *Or.* 12; Claudian *PanIIICon*, *PanIVCon*, *PanVICon*; Dewar 1996).

Perhaps with a little less conviction but, nonetheless, a degree of confidence, from the evidence of *PanLat* X(2) delivered in Trier in 289 on the occasion of Rome's birthday (21 April), we can imagine that such celebrations took place every spring in many or most cities, at least in the western empire. Other annual occasions can be factored in, such as imperial birthdays (*PanLat* XI[3]), and other "occasional" celebrations such as imperial victories (*PanLat* VIII[4], XII[9], IV[10]), marriages (*PanLat* VII[6]), and accession anniversaries (*PanLat* IV[10], Themistius *Or.* 15, Eusebius *Laus Constantini*). Many late antique emperors were notably itinerant, and the tradition came into being of each new town on his travels receiving him with an *adventus* speech, such as Aelius Aristides *Or.* 17 and 21 and Libanius *Or.* 13. We also know that in certain cases the absence of the addressee/*laudandus* was not a serious obstacle to the delivery of a panegyric. These include the Dyarchic and Tetrarchic speeches that were not delivered before the full imperial college but address it directly nonetheless (Rees 2002, pp. 12–19); an address by Nazarius to Constantine in his absence (*PanLat* IV[10]3.1); Themistius *Or.* 6, which is addressed to the brothers Valens and Valentinian, although Valentinian was not present; Libanius *Or.* 59, addressed to Constantius and Constans although Constans was not present; and Themistius's speech of 363, addressed to Julian who was in Antioch (Watts 2015, pp. 117–118). Panegyric is not limited exclusively to praise of the emperor – the ancient evidence attests regular rhetorical praise of other dignitaries, such as Strategios, of gods, places, and concepts – but imperial panegyric is well represented in our late antique sources and was clearly a recognized form (Burgess 1902; Pernot 2015).

That such panegyrics were delivered in great number finds further confirmation in the survival from late antiquity of educational resources designed specifically to offer instruction in rhetorical composition, particularly in epideictic ("display"), which since classical Greek times was considered the third (and least significant) subdivision of rhetorical type, after forensic and deliberative (see Chapter 12 in this volume.) Epideictic is itself subdivided into praise and blame. In popular perception, ancient and modern, where forensic rhetoric was a due part of judicial culture and deliberative rhetoric drove good political practice, epideictic rhetoric was of and for itself. Surviving instruction in it from late antiquity includes the *progymnasmata* of Libanius, who was professor of rhetoric in Antioch, and texts by Theon, Hermogenes, Aphthonius, and Nicolaos (Pernot 1993, 2015; Gibson 2008).

The most instructive text for appreciation of imperial panegyric, however, is the *Basilikos Logos* treatise of Menander Rhetor, the only surviving ancient text to offer specific advice on the subject matter for a panegyric to the emperor; the text is organized chronologically starting from the honorand subject's birth and childhood, then thematically, based on his virtues in war and peace. This Greek treatise dates to the late third century (Russell and Wilson 1981). If the origins and distribution of the work remain matters for speculation, nonetheless it attests an appetite – a societal need – for instruction in epideictic oratory, which can in turn be understood as an index of the high frequency of panegyrical speeches in late antiquity. In sum, we have a substantial corpus of panegyrical literature from late antiquity, but we can be sure it represents only a fraction of what there once was. This survival record is probably best attributed to Sabine MacCormack's often quoted characterization of panegyric's "in-built obsolescence" (1975, p. 159); according to this, once delivered, a typical panegyric had discharged its primary function and had no realistic claim to a longer shelf life. In turn, it follows from this that the panegyrics that have survived are, by definition, exceptional – Donald Russell makes the point that apart from some of the *Panegyrici Latini* collection, the speeches we have are by known men of letters, who saw to the publication and distribution of their work themselves (1998, p. 17). For example, although the speeches themselves do not survive, various references in the letters of Fronto attest the preservation in the Acts of the Senate in Rome of consular *gratiarum actiones*, available for consultation and enjoyment in future decades (1.p.110, 126–128 Haines; Rees 2011, pp. 175–176). So, too, in his *Or.* 12.2, Libanius, apparently casually, speaks of his present and later audience – in the latter case, a readership (see also Libanius *Ep.* 818; Pliny *Pan.* 4.1; *PanLat* II[12]47.6).

Generally, it is difficult to identify post-delivery revisions in panegyrics, and the academic orthodoxy, perhaps a little too easily accepted, is to assume they survive as delivered (Nixon 1983). The most notable and certain exception is Pliny's *Panegyricus*, a revised and elaborated version of the speech he gave (*Ep.* 3.13 and 18; Roche 2011). Libanius has a revealing anecdote about how the Praetorian Prefect Strategios commissioned 10 copyists to help broaden the readership of a panegyric Libanius had delivered in his honor: Libanius's rival Acacius bribed one of the copyists to make suitable changes and additions to the speech, to his own [Acacius's] advantage; this information was leaked, and Acacius was sentenced to a punishment (although in the end he was spared) (*Autobiog.* 112–114). A persuasive case has recently been made that after its original delivery at Rome, Themistius published a significantly revised version of his *Or.* 3 (Vanderspoel 2012). But even in the case of that speech, the orator took care to convey in the written version classical oratory's standard impression of a "live" transcript.

Precursors to late antique Latin panegyric are easily identified: To start with prose, Cicero's *Pro lege Manilia* and his Caesarian speeches were important protopanegyrics; so, too, Seneca's *De Clementia* (Morton Braund 1998; 2009); Pliny's *Panegyricus* of 100 CE, his only oratory to survive, later to be anthologized at the head of the *Panegyrici Latini* was a watershed publication (Roche 2011); and in Latin verse, among other possibilities, we can point to the *Panegyricus Messallae*, *Laus Pisonis*, Horace *Odes* IV, Martial books 8 and 9, and Statius *Silvae* (1.1, 1.6, 4.1, 2, 3) (Rees 2012b). Much earlier, the Greeks had pioneered epideictic rhetoric, in the *epitaphios logos* ("funeral speech") tradition (Loraux 1986) and in accounts of near-contemporary individuals, such as in Isocrates's *Evagoras* and Xenophon's *Agesilaus*; Greek verse praise included epinician lyric through to Theocritus's *Idylls*. In the Second Sophistic, Greek epideictic oratory flourished, as it was systematically taught in schools of rhetoric (Pernot 1993).

In sum, although late antique political culture was an environment in which panegyric could prosper, it would be wrong to see it as an exclusively *late* literary form. If there was not a bigger empire in the later third century than there had been before, there were at least more urban populations, including provincial capitals, more schools of rhetoric, and, during some administrations at least, more emperors; also there were more occasions on which panegyrics were an appropriate part of the ceremonial. A brief comparison between the *fasti* of the Republican period and the calendar of Philocalus from the mid-fourth century bears this out – by late antiquity the rhythms of urban society were largely dictated by occasions relating to the imperial family. When in 100 CE Pliny said that part of the challenge he faced in addressing a speech to Trajan was that the tradition of oratorical praise-giving was already tired and suspect (*Ep.* 3.13.2), it seems that he was essentially referring to the practice of consular *gratiarum actiones*. No doubt there were exceptions, but it seems that Pliny was working within a norm where oratorical praise-giving was most closely identified with the hardy perennial of a consul's speech. By late antiquity, the panegyrical calendar would have been busier – and, of course, not simply in Rome.

A composite picture of the circumstances in which a typical prose panegyric was delivered in late antiquity possibly risks capturing the particular context of none, but it might give a worthwhile sense of the major features: a town hall, forum, theater, or basilica in a provincial city; a crowd consisting of the local political class, including town councillors and office-bearers from the provincial government; the emperor, perhaps, or his representative; if the emperor was present, his bodyguard and other military personnel, plus a retinue of courtiers; and the orator, sometimes only one of several waiting his turn to deliver a speech, in which he would trace the contours of accepted oratorical practice that he had learned from his time as a student in a school of rhetoric and, perhaps, now even taught himself as a professor. An orator speaking in Trier in 311 details the pressure he felt in such a context (*PanLat* V[8]9.3). In Greek centers, it seems there was often a competitive (*agonistic*) element to the performance of speeches, with each orator trying to outdo his fellows: Libanius explains how orators could earn money, reputation, and career advancements by success in competition (*Autobiog.* 37–42; Pernot 2015, pp. 14–15). Just as an orator might weave a personal petition into a speech that essentially articulated the loyalty and ambition of his city, so, too, in a competitive environment in particular, he might risk some stylistic adventure to help his work linger longer in the audience's memory than might otherwise be the case. If this scenario and its many variations were being played out in a range of provincial cities, late antique panegyrics must have, indeed, been generated in great quantities.

It seems likely, then, that late antiquity was richer in Greek and Latin panegyric than earlier periods were. The Aristotelean rhetorical taxonomy, which had epideictic oratory (that is, the rhetoric of praise and blame) as a distant third behind the giants of forensic and deliberative oratory, continued to be reprised by Greek and Latin theorists, but, in fact, by late antiquity the balance had altered. Laurent Pernot has recently observed that "the epideictic genus, which started as rhetoric's poor relation, became under the Roman Empire its most esteemed and prominent" (Pernot 2015, pp. 9–10). Given the survival record, it is difficult to evaluate with any precision the proportion of late antique epideictic oratory relative to its forensic and deliberative counterparts, but its rise seems to have coincided with their corresponding demise. Pernot attributes this development to the consolidation over time of a society with an emperor at its heart, to the increasingly aristocratic character of urban centers (where panegyric was performed), and to the spread of a formal education system that promoted epideictic rhetoric. We might also note that a good deal of surviving panegyric from late antiquity resists tidy classification as purely "epideictic." In fact, many speeches clearly fulfil a practical political function. Some might request tax breaks from the emperor, or his munificence toward the city, or his ongoing commitment to military resources in the region. Certain orators, meanwhile, used the opportunity to phrase a more personal request, such as career positions for themselves or their family. This ambassadorial or probouleutic function invested panegyric with a more meaningful communicative capacity than the ancient textbooks suggest (Hostein 2012). And this communication could work the other way too: As well as this "communication ascendante," by which an orator used the vehicle of panegyric to inform or petition the emperor, Guy Sabbah noted the form's "communication descendante," by which an orator could be primed by the imperial court to include information for the benefit of the citizen audience (Sabbah 1984; Ando 2000, pp. 126–128). The most conspicuous example of this is the announcement in the panegyric of 310 (*PanLat* VI[7]2.2) that Constantine's ancestry went back to Claudius Gothicus II – such a claim must surely have had the backing of the court, or even have been their initiative. By late antiquity, panegyrics – greater in number than before – could serve many functions at the same time.

One function assigned to late antique panegyric throughout its history has a dark cast: The form stands as a tool of deceitful flattery. Famously, critiques of panegyric's dishonesty date to the period. If we take a lead from Lactantius in the early fourth century, we find a highly sensitive situation. Lactantius criticizes pagan poets for raising their ancestors to the status of gods and likens that practice to the delivery of mendacious praise to kings: *sicut faciunt qui apud reges, etiam malos, panegyricis mendacibus adulantur. quod malum a Graecis ortum est: quorum levitas, instructa dicendi facultate et copia, incredibile est quantas mendaciorum nebulas excitaverit* ("they are just the same, those who adulate kings – even bad ones – with dishonest panegyrics. This evil came from the Greeks: It is unbelievable what clouds of lies their fickleness has roused, informed by their facility and capacity to speak" *Div. Inst.*1.15.13). Lactantius's racist overtones were reprised by Isidore, Bishop of Seville, in the seventh century, in his definition of "panegyric": *panegyricum est licentiosum et lasciviosum genus dicendi in laudibus regum, in cuius conpositione homines multis mendaciis adulantur. quod malum a Graecis exortum est, quorum levitas instructa dicendi facultate et copia incredibili multas mendaciorum nebulas suscitavit* ("panegyric is the licentious and lascivious genre of speaking in praise of kings, in the composition of which men give praise through many lies. This evil came from the Greeks, whose fickleness, informed by an incredible facility and capacity to speak, raised many clouds of lies" *Etymologiae* 6.8.7).

Isidore's association of panegyric with Greek culture should not give the impression that the form was unfamiliar in the Latin west at the time and might, rather, be characterized as an outspoken extension (via Lactantius in particular) of the aggressive denunciation of the form as Greek that featured variously in the late republic and early empire. Isolated remarks in late republican and early imperial evidence suggest an identification of panegyrical discourse as Greek rather than Roman (i.e. Latin); for example, the anonymous *Rhetorica ad Herennium* 3.15 insists that opportunities for panegyric were infrequent in Roman society. Cicero, meanwhile, distinguishes Roman custom from the Greek: *nos laudationibus non ita multum uti soleremus* ("we are not used to employing *laudationes* that much" *De Oratore* 2.341). This attitude was to be echoed in the pages of Quintilian, who claimed that Roman deployment of praise-discourse was geared toward practical affairs: *sed mos Romanus etiam negotiis hoc munus inseruit* ("but Roman practice has even woven this task into business matters" *Inst. Orat.* 3.7.1–2; Pernot 2015, p. 9). The word *panegyricus* is Greek, originally an adjective describing a public gathering (which, itself, is revealing of the contexts in which such literature was performed) (Russell 1998, pp. 19–21; Rees 2010, 23). The term *panegyricus* is not common in classical or late Latin – the cases of Lactantius and Isidore are exceptional rather than the norm – and other late antique examples may still carry unwanted traces of Greek cultural association (although, perhaps, late antiquity's increased familiarity with the form rendered some relevant terminology acceptable). For example, except in its titles and marginalia, which may all postdate late antiquity, the *Panegyrici Latini* collection nowhere features the word *panegyricus*, and its earliest instance of the Latinate term *laudatio* occurs in Nazarius's speech of 321, to be reprised by Pacatus Drepanius in 389 (*PanLat* IV[10]2.9, 6.1, 34.2; II[12]2.2; Rees 2010, p. 23). (*Panegyricus* was not Pliny's name for his speech, which is first attested in the fifth century.) Was literary praise hesitant to name itself? Perhaps, but despite this cautious commitment to the terminology of praise-giving, the very fact of a late fourth-century collection of Latin epideictic oratory is an index of the growing acceptability of imperial panegyric in the west. Dyed-in-the-wool Hellene Libanius wrote allusively but regretfully of the preference of some students of rhetoric to go to Italy to receive instruction in Latin rather than in Greek (*Autobiog.* 214, 234).

But there are also some sterling examples of Greek–Latin crossovers, such as Themistius's Greek oration to Constantius delivered in Rome in 357 (*Or.* 3) and the consular *gratiarum actio* of Claudius Mamertinus delivered to Julian in Constantinople in 362, in Latin (*PanLat* III[11]); the following year saw Julian himself as consul, an appointment celebrated in Antioch with three speeches, the first in Latin, followed by two in Greek (including Libanius's *Or.* 12). Notable, too, is the interest in Themistius of known western notables such as Symmachus and Vettius Agorius Praetextatus (Vanderspoel 1995, pp. 24–25). Most conspicuously, perhaps, the fact that Greek-speaking Claudian wrote imperial panegyrical hexameters in Latin leaves the aggressive disavowal by Lactantius and Isidore of literary praise-giving as part of their own self-definition looking like a distinctive but maverick cultural pose. Claudian shows no reticence when later recalling (in verse) his first foray into panegyric (in 395): *Romanos primum bibimus te consule fontes/et Latiae cessit Graia Thalia togae* ("I first drank the Roman waters when you were consul, and my Greek Muse gave way to the Latin toga" *Carm. Min.* 41. 13–14; Wheeler 2007; Sánchez-Ostiz 2014 and Gualandri 2014).

Nonetheless, the strain of anti-Greek racism aside, the moral opprobrium that Lactantius and Isidore cast echoes down through the centuries. Augustine's damning characterization of his own panegyrical output hinges precisely on the question of the absence of truth and reliability: *pararem recitare imperatori laudes, quibus plura mentirer et mentienti faueretur ab scientibus* ("I was preparing to declaim praise to the emperor, in which I would tell many lies and win favor as a liar from those who knew" *Confessiones* 6.6.9). Panegyric is seen to tell lies, and everybody seems to have known it. No doubt it was this that led many of the practicing historians of the day to shun its rhetoric (Ammianus Marcellinus 31.16.9; Eutropius *Brev.*10.18.3; Festus *Brev.* 30; Lucian *De Hist. Conscrib.* 38–41). And also, amid the untrustworthiness of imperial panegyric and the formulaic character that was the product of the political climate, the rise of ceremonial and rhetorical education, perhaps inevitably a sense of ennui often attaches to it, akin to that of the narrator of Juvenal's first *Satire* (1–21). Although some texts refer fleetingly to their addressee's reaction to the words they are hearing (e.g. *PanLat* X[2]4.4, VI[7]14.1, II[12]44.3, Libanius *Or.* 45.11), within reasonable limits, one wonders how often an emperor actually paid much attention to what was said. Even a request such as that of the orator of 310 that his sons be given opportunity within the imperial administration might hardly have caused Constantine to prick up his ears (*PanLat* VI[7]23.1–2). An exception in the sources is a full account of an emperor's response to a speech detailed in Libanius's *Autobiography*. Libanius records Julian's reaction to his speech of 1 January 363:

> I spoke last, with the Emperor himself thinking that as many people as possible would gather; they said that in his care for his attendant, Hermes touched each member of the audience with his wand so that no word of mine would pass without its share of admiration. The Emperor accomplished this, first by mentioning his pleasure at my style, then by his tendency to get to his feet, then (when he could not restrain himself even when trying his hardest) he leapt from his seat, opened his cloak out fully with hands outstretched (*Autobiography* 129).

Julian's alleged enthusiasm no doubt prompts a degree of scepticism in Libanius's readers, but given that Julian was late antiquity's cerebral emperor, an educated, literary man and, in fact, the author of surviving panegyrics himself, it is plausible that he was both qualified and interested in the form. Even so, he was probably in the minority.

Since late antiquity was a period in which panegyric seems to have thrived and some commentators of the time were ready in their condemnation of it, the form has easily been appropriated as evidence in academic and popular models of late antique decline. It is quite clear that Edward Gibbon is referring to panegyric – probably, in fact, the *Panegyrici Latini* – when he interrupts his narrative of the reign of Diocletian with observations famously critical of creative arts and says, "A languid and affected eloquence was still retained in the pay and service of the emperors, who encouraged not any arts except those which contributed to the gratification of their pride or the defence of their power" (Gibbon 1776–1789, chapter 13). Panegyric has regularly and easily been assimilated into a narrative of aesthetic, moral and political decline in late antiquity. Central to this is designation of panegyric as *propaganda* (for example, Cameron 1970, Rodríguez Gervás 1991, Whitby 1998) – part of a centralized, systematized program of political communication. This underlying assumption has shaped much of the scholarship to have addressed panegyric, although often in more or less nuanced and sophisticated ways. But in general perception, and despite the enormous range and depth of surviving material, neatly exemplified by Eusebius's spiritual, Christian, Greek, prose *Laus Constantini* and Claudian's Virgilian, pagan, Latin, hexameter panegyrics at the fourth century's end, the material is really only beginning to experience an equivalent to the enlightened and sympathetic reception that has characterized approaches to Augustan poetry in recent decades. That particular body of literature has been rightly enshrined as canonical, despite the pressures exerted by the patronage that allowed it to come into being. That is not to say there was no difference between Augustan patronage of high literature via the offices of Maecenas and the relationships between the late imperial court and its prose and verse panegyricists. But historically scholarship has been quick to champion the literary achievement of Augustan poets and to denounce the efforts of late antique panegyric. One response to Gibbon would be to confront his model of decline with the pithy claims of two of Virgil's greatest critics: from the fourth century, Servius's prefatory statement of Virgil's intention, *Homerum imitari et Augustum laudare a parentibus* ("to imitate Homer and praise Augustus from his forefathers"), and from the twentieth century, David West's forthright assertion that "the *Aeneid* is successful panegyric" (1991).

REFERENCES

Ando, Clifford. (2000). *Imperial Ideology and Provincial Loyalty in the Roman Empire*. Berkeley: University of California Press.

Burgess, Theodore. (1902 [Reprint 1980]). *Epideictic Literature*. Chicago: University of Chicago Press.

Callu, Jean-Pierre. (2009). *Symmaque: Tome 5. Discours-Rapports*. Paris: Belles Lettres.

Cameron, Alan. (1965). Wandering poets: A literary movement in Byzantine Egypt. *Historia* 14, 470–509.

Cameron, Alan. (1970). *Claudian. Poetry and Propaganda at the Court of Honorius*. Oxford: Oxford University Press.

Cameron, Averil and Hall, Stuart. (1999). *Eusebius. Life of Constantine*. Oxford: Oxford University Press.

Dewar, Michael. (1996). *Claudian: Panegyricus de sexto consulatu Honorii Augusti*. Oxford: Oxford University Press.

Drake, Hal. (1976). *In Praise of Constantine: A Historical Study and New Translation of Eusebius' Tricennial Orations*. Berkeley: University of California Press.

Gibbon, Edward. (1776–1789). *The History of the Decline and Fall of the Roman Empire*. London: Strahan and Cadell.

Gibson, C.A. (2008). *Libanius's Progymnasmata: Model Exercises in Greek Prose Composition and Rhetoric*. Atlanta, GA: Society of Biblical Literature.

Gillett, Andrew. (2012). Epic panegyric and political communication in the fifth-century West. In: *Two Romes: Rome and Constantinople in Late Antiquity* (ed. Lucy Grig and Gavin Kelly), 265–290. Oxford and New York: Oxford University Press.

Green, Roger. (1991). *The Works of Ausonius.* Oxford: Oxford University Press.

Gualandri, Isabella (2013 [2014]). Claudian: from Easterner to Westerner. *Talanta* 45: 115–130.

Hägg, Tomas and Rousseau, Philip. ed. (2000). *Greek Biography and Panegyric in Late Antiquity.* Berkeley: University of California Press.

Haines, C.R. (1919–1920) *Fronto. Correspondence.* 2 vols. London and Cambridge MA.

Heather, Peter and Moncur, David. (2001). *Politics, Philosophy, and Empire in the Fourth Century: Select Orations of Themistius.* Liverpool: Liverpool University Press.

Hostein, Antony. (2012). *La Cité et l'Empereur. Les Éduens dans l'Empire roman d'après les* Panégyriques latins. Paris: La Sorbonne.

Loraux, Nicole. (1986). *The Invention of Athens: The Funeral Oration in the Classical City.* Cambridge, MA: Harvard University Press.

MacCormack, Sabine. (1975). Latin prose panegyrics. In: *Empire and Aftermath, Silver Latin II* (ed. Thomas Dorey), 143–205. London: Routledge.

MacCormack, Sabine. (1981). *Art and Ceremony in Late Antiquity.* Berkeley: University of California Press.

Morton Braund, Susanna.(1998). Praise and protreptic in early imperial panegyric. In: *The Propaganda of Power: The Role of Panegyric in Late Antiquity* (ed. Mary Whitby), 53–76. Leiden: Brill.

Morton Braund, Susanna. (2009). *Seneca De Clementia.* Oxford: Oxford University Press.

Nixon, Ted. (1983). Latin panegyric in the Tetrarchic and Constantinian period. In: *History and Historians in Late Antiquity* (ed. Brian Croke and Alanna Emmett), 88–99. Sydney: Pergamon.

Nixon, Ted and Saylor Rodgers, Barbara. (1994). *In Praise of Later Roman Emperors. The Panegyrici Latini.* Berkeley: University of California Press.

Pabst, Angela. (1989). *Symmachus: Reden.* Darmstadt: Wissenschaftliche Buchgesellschaft.

Pernot, Laurent. (1993). *La rhétorique de l'éloge dans le monde gréco-romain.* Paris: Institut d'Etudes Augustiniennes.

Pernot, Laurent. (2015). *Epideictic Rhetoric: Questioning the Stakes of Ancient Praise.* Austin: University of Texas.

Rees, Roger. (2002). *Layers of Loyalty in Latin Panegyric, AD 289–307.* Oxford: Oxford University Press.

Rees, Roger. (2010). Words of praise in Roman politics. *Millennium* 7: 9–28.

Rees, Roger. (2011). Afterwords of praise. In: *Pliny's Praise. The* Panegyricus *in the Roman World* (ed. Paul Roche), 175–188. Cambridge: Cambridge University Press.

Rees, Roger, ed. (2012a). *Latin Panegyric.* Oxford: Oxford University Press.

Rees, Roger. (2012b). The modern history of the *Panegyrici Latini.* In: *Latin Panegyric* (ed. Roger Rees), 3–48. Oxford: Oxford University Press.

Roche, Paul. ed. (2011). *Pliny's Praise. The* Panegyricus *in the Roman World.* Cambridge: Cambridge University Press.

Rodríguez Gervás, Manuel J. (1991). *Propaganda política y opinión pública en los Panegíricos Latinos del Bajo Imperio*. Salamanca: Universidad de Salamanca.
Russell, Donald. (1998). The panegyrists and their teachers. In: *The Propaganda of Power. The Role of Panegyric in Late Antiquity* (ed. Mary Whitby), 17–50. Leiden: Brill.
Russell, Donald and Wilson, Nigel. (1981). *Menander Rhetor: Edited with Translation and Commentary*. Oxford: Clarendon.
Sabbah, Guy. (1984). De la rhétorique à la communication politique: Les *Panégyriques latins*. *BAGB* 43: 363–88.
Sánchez-Osta, Alvaro (2013 [2014]). Lucretius, Cicero, Theodorus: Greek Philosophy and Latin eloquence in Claudian's encomiastic imagination. *Talanta* 45: 97–114.
Schindler, Claudia. (2009). *Per carmina laudes. Untersuchungen zur spätantiken Verspanegyrik von Claudian bis Coripp*. Berlin: Walter de Gruyter.
Sogno, Cristiana. (2006). *Q. Aurelius Symmachus: A Political Biography*. Ann Arbor: University of Michigan.
Van Hoof, Lieve. ed. (2014). *The Cambridge Companion to Libanius*. Cambridge: Cambridge University Press.
Vanderspoel, John. (1995). *Themistius and the Imperial Court*. Ann Arbor: University of Michigan Press.
Vanderspoel, John. (2012). A tale of two cities: Themistius on Rome and Constantinople. In: *Two Romes: Rome and Constantinople in Late Antiquity* (ed. Lucy Grig and Gavin Kelly), 223–240. Oxford and New York: Oxford University Press.
Ware, Catherine. (2012). *Claudian and the Roman Epic Tradition*. Cambridge: Cambridge University Press.
Watts, Edward. (2015). *The Final Pagan Generation*. Berkeley: University of California Press.
West, David. (1991). *Virgil: The* Aeneid. London. Penguin.
Wheeler, Stephen. (2007). More Roman than the Romans of Rome. Vergilian (Self-) Fashioning in Claudian's *Panegyric for the Consuls Olybrius and Probinus*. In: *Texts and Culture in Late Antiquity: Inheritance, Authority, and Change* (ed. David Scourfield), 97–134. Swansea: Classical Press of Wales.
Whitby, Mary. ed. (1998). *The Propaganda of Power: The Role of Panegyric in Late Antiquity*. Leiden: Brill.
Wiemer, Hans-Ulrich. (1995). *Libanios und Julian. Studien zum Verhältnis von Rhetorik und Politik im vierten Jahrhundert n. Chr*. Munich: C.H. Beck.

CHAPTER FOURTEEN

Epic Poetry

Mary Whitby* and Michael Roberts

14.1 Greek Epic

Among Greek texts the very definition of epic is problematized in late antiquity by a pervasive and innovative syncretism that drew beneath the umbrella of epic forms that elsewhere existed independently, in particular those associated with rhetorical education, such as the *ethopoiea* (speech in character), *ekphrasis* (detailed and vivid description), and paraphrase, but also elements from pastoral, tragedy, and the novel. In addition, the epic hexameter is challenged by extended iambic poems, in the innovative oeuvre of Gregory of Nazianzus and later in the iambic panegyrics of George of Pisidia. It has been cogently argued (Agosti 2012, pp. 377–378) that all late antique poetry was composed for performance, whether before a private gathering or in a more public arena: hence epic and occasional poetry also merge. And major Greek poets collapse cultural boundaries, most notably Nonnus, who composed both a Hellenic *Dionysiaca* and a verse paraphrase of the Gospel of John; others import Orphic or Neoplatonic elements (the *Argonautica* and *Lithica*, Colluthus, John of Gaza). Several authors (Gregory of Nazianzus, Christodorus, Paul the Silentiary) composed poems in more than one genre (epic, epigram), further confronting standard distinctions. Finally, we know (through papyrus finds, entries in ancient handbooks) of much that is

* M.W. is grateful to Gianfranco Agosti for corrections and additional bibliography. She regrets that it has not been possible to take systematic account of bibliography published after 2015.

incomplete or lost, often other works by extant poets (Miguélez Cavero 2008; Agosti 2012) – evidence that can only be touched on here. These issues must form a backdrop to any assessment of the extant corpus. The material may be broadly classified as mythological, panegyrical or occasional, didactic, and Christian (biblical, hagiographical, religious).

14.1.1 Mythological Epic

Following the massive works of Nestor of Laranda (lipogrammatic *Iliad*) and his son Pisander (*Heroic Theogamies* in 60 books) in the Severan period (Ma 2007), mythological epic continued vibrant. Under the tetrarchs, Soterichus of Oasis wrote works entitled *Calydoniaca*, *Bassarica*, and *Ariadne* (Miguélez Cavero 2013a, p. 80 n. 206), but they are entirely lost. Quintus of Smyrna, of whom nothing certain is known, wrote his 14-book *Posthomerica* during the third century, after Oppian (176–180 CE), probably before Triphiodorus (ca. 300). It deals with events in the Trojan War between the *Iliad* and the *Odyssey*, material also treated in the poems of the so-called Epic Cycle, which were probably lost about this time. Quintus ostentatiously identifies himself with Homer in the delayed proem of book 12 (306–313), but recent scholarship (Baumbach and Bär 2007; Carvounis 2008; Bär 2009; MacIver 2012a, 2012b) foregrounds his nuanced redefinition, for example, through engagement with Hesiod and the didactic tradition, Callimachus, and perhaps Virgil (hotly debated), as well as with tragedy and ancient scholia, and by imposing Stoic ethics.

Two short poems by Egyptians that sit on either side of Nonnus also treat Trojan topics. Triphiodorus's *Capture of Troy* (691 lines) belongs between the mid-third and early fourth centuries (Miguélez Cavero 2013a, pp. 4–6, 72–74). The poet develops Demodocus's song of the Wooden Horse (*Odyssey* 8.499–520), drawing on Homeric exegesis, Hesiod's account of Pandora, and rhetorical techniques (*ekphrasis* of the horse, apostrophe), as well as on the language of Pindar, tragedy, and the Alexandrians, including Lycophron. His relationship to the Epic Cycle and Virgil's *Aeneid* is more ambivalent (Miguélez Cavero 2013a). Colluthus's *Rape of Helen* (394 lines) renegotiates traditional models and confronts late antique Christian and Neoplatonic culture and poetry (Claudian in particular), often undercutting audience expectations. A strong visual, even voyeuristic, element integrates him into performative contexts, quite possibly pantomime (Jeffreys 2006, Magnelli 2008, Paschalis 2008, Prauscello 2008, Cadau 2015). Musaeus *grammatikos* (scholar and teacher), writing before Colluthus, chose the tragic love of Hero and Leander as the theme of his 343-line epyllion, which is pervaded by imagery of light and darkness, perhaps a Neoplatonic allegory (Kost

1971; Gelzer 1975, pp. 316–322). Two hundred lines are devoted to the lovers' first meeting and their dialogue, the latter uncharacteristic of Nonnus, with whom, however, Musaeus has linguistic affinities. Musaeus also explicitly alludes to the vicissitudes of Odysseus's homecoming, as well as to Achilles Tatius (Hopkinson 1994, pp. 136–139) and to contemporary Christian poetry (Gelzer 1975, pp. 297–302).

Of Claudian's brief Greek *Gigantomachy*, composed perhaps 390–395 (Cameron 1970, pp. 6–18; Mulligan 2007) or 400–402 (Livrea 1998), only the prologue (1–17) and the last 60 lines survive: sixty-eight lines are missing from the middle (Ludwich 1897, p. 166). The prologue indicates a performative, probably competitive, context before a crowd, in an extended navigational metaphor, arguably Neoplatonic, while the description of Aphrodite (43–54) and other vignettes have much that anticipates Nonnus (Whitby 1994, pp. 126–128), for whom, of course, Gigantomachy was also a theme (*Dionysiaca* 1–2, 48). The richness and diversity of Nonnus's massive and multifaceted 48-book "biography" of Dionysus, written in the mid-fifth century, is only now emerging, thanks to new commentaries and unparalleled scholarly enthusiasm (e.g. Shorrock 2011; Spanoudakis 2014a, 2014b; Accorinti 2016). Not only did Nonnus perfect the technical refinement of the classical hexameter (Whitby 1994; Agosti and Gonnelli 1995; Magnelli 2016), but he plundered his literary predecessors so as to embed in his epic the full gamut of classical genres (epic, pastoral, didactic, novelistic) and modes (tragic, comic, satiric, rhetorical), while also capturing the animated intellectual Christian/Hellenic polemic of contemporary Alexandria.

The Orphic *Argonautica* (1376 lines), plausibly dated to the later fifth century (Vian 1987, pp. 45–47), engages agonistically with Apollonius Rhodius, amplifying, rewriting, and foregrounding the figure of Orpheus, perhaps drawing on a pre-Apollonian Orphic text (Nelis 2005). With unprecedented "generic consciousness" the narrator explicitly moves from didactic to epic, in a sophisticated negotiation of literary traditions (Hunter 2005). Written by a convinced pagan, it confronts the contemporary Christianization of pagan relics, but, like Musaeus' poem, it is not necessarily allegorical (Agosti 2008a; Cecchetti 2013, contra Schelske 2011).

14.1.2 Panegyrical Poetry

By their very occasional context, panegyrical poems are prone to perish, as attested by many fragments on papyri (Miguélez Cavero 2008, pp. 33–79). We might single out, for example, from the beginning and end of our period, an encomium to Diocletian that has links with the prescriptions preserved in

Menander Rhetor (Agosti 2002b; Miguélez Cavero 2008, pp. 44–45) and the much-derided poems for local worthies by Dioscoros of Aphrodito (mid-sixth century), who, however, owned an impressive library (Fournet 1999; Agosti 2008b; Miguélez Cavero 2008, pp. 225–226). A whole category, the verse *patria* celebrating individual cities, has all but disappeared, but there were many, often written by Egyptians – Claudian, Nonnus, Christodorus of Coptus and others (Cameron 2004, pp. 330–331 = 2016, pp. 165–166; Miguélez Cavero 2008, pp. 63–65); some were explicitly Christian (Fournet 2003; Whitby 2013, pp. 212–213). And both panegyrics and *patria* were written in iambics as well as hexameters (Cameron 2004, 336-37 = 2016, pp. 170–171; Agosti 2012, p. 366).

A papyrus dated around 400 preserves parts of 82 lines from three separate sections of a *Blemmyomachy*, a Homerizing poem celebrating the victorious campaign of Germanus. Its attribution to Olympiodorus of Thebes (Livrea 1978) is attractive but perhaps implausible (Whitby 1994, pp. 128–129; 2013, pp. 215–216; Miguélez Cavero 2008, pp. 59–61). Controversy about authorship has also surrounded the four distinct poems, two of them encomia, preserved in *PVindob gr.* 29788 A–C, (Miguélez Cavero 2008, pp. 72–74), but Livrea has recently reiterated his view (Livrea 1979, 2014) that all are the work of the pagan Pamprepius (440–484), whose colorful career ended when he was beheaded, following Illus's failed revolt against Zeno (Cameron 2007, pp. 35–36 = 2016, pp. 155–157; Agosti 2012, pp. 368–369).

From the next century, three ekphrastic poems describing works of art and architecture represent a different kind of celebratory poem. We do not know the occasion for which Christodorus of Coptus, who flourished under Anastasius (491–518), composed his description of the statues in the baths of Zeuxippus in Constantinople, now preserved as the second book of the *Palatine Anthology*, but its length of around 400 lines, comparable with his contemporary Colluthus's *Rape of Helen* (whose Trojan theme it shares), suggests that it was intended for a celebratory performance (Tissoni 2000; Jeffreys 2006; Kaldellis 2007; Bär 2012; Whitby 2018). Two iambic passages (A1–25, B1–4) show that John of Gaza's *ekphrasis* of a cosmic painting in the winter baths at Gaza (or perhaps Antioch) was performed in two sections of similar length in a rhetorical presentation or competition (Renaut 2005). This poem, written before 526 and the only example from Gaza of an epic in the style of Nonnus, draws on Neoplatonic ideas of ascent to the divine (Gigli Piccardi 2005, 2014; Lauritzen 2011, 2014, 2015). Paul the Silentiary's 1029-line *ekphrasis* of the church of Hagia Sophia in Constantinople was presented, also in two sections, shortly after Christmas 562 as part of the celebration of Justinian's restoration of his church following its partial collapse after an earthquake. Notes in the manuscript indicate a ceremonial setting, in which the audience moved from the imperial palace to the episcopal palace, with emperor and patriarch both presiding (Whitby 1985; Macrides and Magdalino 1988; Bell 2009); a 304-line description of the *ambo* was subsequently presented separately.

The last great imperial panegyrist was George of Pisidia, whose iambic poems celebrated Heraclius's Persian campaigns that led to victory in 628. Some are brief exclamatory celebrations, such as the lines improvised on the occasion of Heraclius's restoration of the True Cross to Jerusalem. Other longer narrative pieces, such as that on Heraclius's first Persian campaign, were delivered in several sittings (Whitby 2002).

14.1.3 Didactic

After a dynamic period from Hadrian (Dionysius Periegetes: Lightfoot 2014) to Marcus Aurelius (Oppian of Cilicia: Kneebone 2008, forthcoming) and Caracalla (Pseudo-Oppian: Whitby 2007a), secular didactic poetry veered toward the abstruse. Framed as a conversation in a Theocritean setting, the 774-line Orphic *Lithica* (Giannakis 1982; Halleux and Schamp 1985) is a sophisticated exposition of the magical and therapeutic properties of 30 stones. Lines 68–74 probably refer to the death in 372 of Julian's teacher, the Neoplatonic philosopher and theurgist Maximus of Ephesus (Hopkinson 1984; Livrea 1992; Zito 2012a, 2013, p. 173), while Maximus himself is almost certainly the author of the extant astrological poem *On Undertakings* (περὶ καταρχῶν: Livrea 1992, 205; Zito 2012b), describing the influence of the moon on human initiatives. Parts of the poem on astrology *Apotelesmatika* (*Influences*), attributed to the Egyptian Manetho, may also date to this period (Livrea 1992, p. 206; Agosti 2012, p. 365; second or third century: Hopkinson 1994, p. 205). At any rate, [Manetho] was read by Gregory of Nazianzus (Simelidis 2009, p. 47) and George of Pisidia, who was attracted by the lexical rarities of book 4 and saw [Manetho] as representative of the didactic genre (Whitby 2014). Indeed, didactic took on a new role in Christian poetry, above all in the poems of Gregory of Nazianzus, discussed in the next section.

14.1.4 Christian Poetry (see also chapter 16 in this volume)

Our view of Christian poetry in this period has changed fundamentally since the publication (1984, 1999) of the fragmentary poems in the Bodmer papyrus, the so-called *Codex of Visions* (*P.Bodm.* 29–37), a collection of nine mid fourth-century poems (preserved in a codex dated ca. 400), eight in hexameters, one (*To the Just*) elegiac, totaling more than 700 lines. They include ethopoeic presentations of the sacrifice of Isaac and the episodes of Cain and Abel but are dominated by the initial 343-line *Vision of Dorotheus*, which recounts the speaker's vision of reckoning and redemption in the court of heaven, using the technical terminology of Byzantine officialdom. These texts, thematically and stylistically homogeneous but self-consciously varied in form, were found near Panopolis in Egypt and were probably assembled for the edification of an ascetic Christian community (e.g. Agosti, 2002a, 2015; Miguélez Cavero 2008, pp. 61–63, 218–223; 2013b).

The importance of Julian's Schools Edict (362 CE) as a catalyst for Christian poetry such as the lost biblical paraphrases of Apollinarius (Kaster 1988, pp. 242–243; McLynn 2014) is now usually downplayed in favor of the view that educated Christians naturally adopted classical meters (Agosti 2001; contra Simelidis 2009, pp. 25–27). Certainly the most cogent witness is the 17 000 verses (Simelidis 2009, p. 7) of Gregory of Nazianzus (ca. 330–390). Gregory's poems are highly original in numerous ways: they range over different genres, including didactic (on the Christian life), epistolary, and hymns, but also break new ground in handling theological and autobiographical material on an epic scale, the latter in a crafted self-representation (McLynn 1998a, 1998b; Cameron 2007, pp. 30–31; Whitby 2008, p.80). Hexameters and iambics are used interchangeably for poems on similar topics: Gregory's contemporary Amphilochius also wrote a 337-line didactic iambic poem for young Christians, *To Seleucus*. The hexameters challenge contemporary metrical practices (Agosti and Gonnelli 1995; Cameron 2004, pp. 333–339=2016, pp. 168–172), yet are suffused with profound knowledge of rhetorical techniques and secular literary texts, subtly but pointedly redeployed, alongside lexical originality (Whitby 2008; Simelidis 2009). Gregory's poetry was also much read, both in schools and by intellectuals, and hence highly influential (Demoen 2009). This corpus still awaits a full modern critical edition and, therefore, systematic evaluation. The religious poetry of George of Pisidia (early seventh century) primarily in iambics, but with one hexameter poem *On Human Life* (Whitby 2014), may be seen as following in Gregory's footsteps. The major work is a *Hexaemeron* (1864lines) that explores the marvels of God's creation, in particular mankind (Gonnelli 1998), while shorter poems inveigh against heresy (*Contra Severum*) and reflect on the difficulties of living a Christian life. George, too, is highly original, in particular in weaving complex recurring imagery as a vehicle for religious thought.

The mid-fifth century saw a remarkable explosion of biblical poetry in three roughly contemporary figures. A paraphrase of the Psalms, incorrectly attributed to Apollinarius, was dedicated to Marcian, probably *oikonomos* of

Hagia Sophia in Constantinople, by a poet of Egyptian origin. It follows its stichic model quite closely, but a recent evaluation argues that its author is subtler and more original than was hitherto believed (Faulkner 2014). The Empress Eudocia, wife of Theodosius II, composed (lost) verse paraphrases of the Octateuch, admired by Photius (*Bibl.* cods. 183–184), and surviving centos that redeploy Homeric lines and half-lines to tell the Gospel story, contextualized in the Old Testament scheme of God's plan for mankind. In addition, Eudocia composed a verse hagiography of St. Cyprian of Antioch, substantially extant, that utilized three independent prose texts from the fourth century. This work draws innovatively on Homer and later poets but, like Gregory, is metrically idiosyncratic (Sowers 2008, 2018; Whitby 2007b, 2013; Cameron 2016, 73–76). It should be set alongside the lost hexameter *Life of Apollonius of Tyana* by Soterichus of Oasis, and Marinus's metrical version of his *Life of Proclus* (Agosti 2009). Finally, Nonnus's *Paraphrase of the Gospel of John* enormously expands the biblical model, drawing on Cyril of Alexandria's recent commentary and other exegesis (Simelidis 2016), as well as the synoptic gospels, to create a deeply original work, part of whose purpose was to highlight similarities between his two heroes, Dionysus and Christ (Spanoudakis 2007, 2013, 2014b).

14.1.5 Conclusion

Greek epic responded with vitality and flexibility to the shifting dynamics of this period, encompassing the impact of Neoplatonic and Christian ideologies (Hernández de la Fuente 2015), creating the space for an explicitly Christian didactic and accommodating to changing metrical needs, both through the stringency of the Nonnian hexameter and the use of iambics. Recurrent allusion to Hesiod is a further sign of didactic self-consciousness. Christian and Hellenic, poetry and prose, engage in a dialogue that precludes exclusiveness. And the importance for poetry of Egypt – including Alexandria – long recognized, cannot be overstated (Cameron 1965 = 2016, pp. 1–35; 2007 = 2016, pp. 147–162; Agosti 2014).

14.2 Latin Epic

The generic landscape of late Latin poetry looks very different from that of classical antiquity. Love elegy, satire, and drama are barely represented, at least in surviving works; only the epigram and the epic, understood as extended narrative poetry in hexameters, continue to flourish. But in subject matter and compositional practices the epics produced in the period show striking innovations that distinguish them from their classical predecessors. The works of the period fall into five categories: on the secular side, panegyric and mythological epics; on the Christian side, biblical, hagiographical, and allegorical epics. Of these five categories only the mythological conforms broadly to classical models in its subject and treatment. Within late antiquity a number of these subgenres of epic established their own traditions, building on or playing off against earlier examples. In what follows I will consider each of these subgenres.

14.2.1 Panegyrical Epic

The Egyptian poet Claudian, active in Rome 394–404, is the first exponent of the Latin panegyrical epic whose work survives. His corpus includes six verse consular panegyrics, including poems for the emperor Honorius's third, fourth, and sixth consulships and for the consulship of his patron Stilicho (in three books). He also wrote two historical epics, on the campaigns against the African warlord Gildo (*De bello Gildonico*) and, in 401–402, against the Visigothic leader Alaric (*De bello Getico*). Although the titles of these last two works indicate a desire to distinguish them from the overtly panegyrical consular poems, in practice, as has often been observed, both categories of compositions show the same mixture of praise and narrative. The topical organization of panegyrics accommodates a large element of narrative, especially in the praise of a subject's virtues, while Claudian's narration in his historical epics serves to convey praise of his patron, i.e. of Stilicho. Both categories of poems combine accounts of contemporary events with praise and are frequently treated as functionally indistinguishable in respect of genre (Hofmann 1988; Kirsch 1989, pp. 51–92; Schindler 2009, pp. 59–172).

The epic nature of Claudian's poems derives from his use of the hexameter and of epic idiom, as well as from his frequent employment of formal and compositional features characteristic of the genre (e.g. developed similes, ekphrases, battle narratives). He forgoes, however, any divine machinery governing human events of the kind found in traditional classical epic. The gods and goddesses who appear in Claudian's poems are largely personifications of geographical entities: rivers, cities, or countries. Their role is often to represent human interests and to appeal to human agents for relief. They serve to generalize and elevate to a higher level the perils that the subjects of the panegyrics will relieve or the wishes they will satisfy. Speeches in general play a large part in Claudian's panegyrical epics, along with passages of description. The narrator in his poems, unlike the practice in traditional epics, is not an objective recorder of events, but is engaged as a partisan of the person praised. Claudian's invectives, too, against the eastern ministers

Rufinus and Eutropius (both in two books) combine epic elements and praise of Stilicho with disparagement and denunciation of their subjects.

Claudian's example found imitators in the mid-fifth century. Flavius Merobaudes, a literary and military figure active at the court of Valentinian III, composed a panegyric, now only partially preserved, for the consulship in 446 of Flavius Aetius, chief Roman general in the West, combining narrative and praise after the Claudianic manner (Schindler 2009, pp. 173–181). The poem innovates by including a dialogue between two divine agents of evil who plan to throw the world into disorder.

Also in the tradition of Claudian are three panegyrics of Sidonius Apollinaris, the major Gallo-Roman literary figure of the mid-fifth century (Schindler 2009, pp. 181–215). He wrote poems for the consulships of his father-in-law Flavius Eparchius Avitus (456), elevated to the purple in the previous year, and of the emperor Anthemius (468); his panegyric for Majorian (458) also celebrated a recently elevated emperor. The poems combine passages of direct praise, often following the traditional schemata, with narrative, predominantly of military action. As in Claudian, divinities personifying cities, countries, and rivers play a large role, but typically divine action remains separated from the human sphere. The gods themselves may play the role of secondary narrator, recounting the actions of the subjects of the poems.

A group of poems composed in Latin, but in the eastern half of the empire, while combining narrative and praise, deviates significantly from the model of Claudian. The grammarian Priscian wrote a poem on the emperor Anastasius in the early years of the sixth century, divided between praise of his achievements in war and peace, framing the work in a context of Christian devotion that finds no parallel in the earlier western tradition (Schindler 2009, pp. 215–226). In the middle of the century Flavius Cresconius Corippus, a *grammaticus* from North Africa, was the author of two poems: the *Iohannis*, in eight books, on the North African campaigns of the Byzantine general Johannes Troglita in 546–548, and the *In laudem Iustini Augusti minoris*, on the events surrounding the accession and consulship of Justin II (Zarini 2003; Schindler 2009, pp. 228–309). The first poem dates to 549/550, the second to 566/568. Already the length of the *Iohannis* points to its distinction from the western tradition, with a fuller development of the historical narrative, elaborated according to the compositional and thematic norms of ancient epic, especially Virgil and Lucan, and amounting to what has been called the first Christian historical epic. While the intent to praise remains present, the topical structure of the rhetorical panegyric plays, at most, a minimal role. The *In laudem Iustini* goes its own way again, giving a central role to description of court ceremonial as an index of the imperial majesty of its subject.

14.2.2 Mythological Epic

Claudian's *De raptu Proserpinae* (last years of the fourth century) is the sole representative of mythological epic from Latin late antiquity. It tells the familiar story of the abduction of Proserpine, from Pluto's threat to throw the world into disorder if he does not receive a wife to Ceres's setting out to search the world for her daughter. The poem is in three books, but incomplete. A fourth book recounting Ceres's search and its outcome was never written. Despite the traditional subject matter and poetic idiom, the composition is quite untraditional in the predominance of speeches and description, with very little in the way of action (Fo 1982, pp. 97–115).

Other late antique poets wrote on mythological subject matter, but rarely at any length. An exception may be made for the North African poet Blossius Aemilius Dracontius (late fifth century), whose *Romulea*, as his minor poems are conventionally titled, includes compositions on Hylas, the abduction of Helen, and Medea, ranging from 163 to 655 lines in length. His *Orestis tragoedia*, in 974 hexameters, separately transmitted, covers the subject matter of Aeschylus's trilogy, though incorporating a variety of sources.

14.2.3 Biblical Epic

The first epic poem of late antiquity marked a profound break from its classical antecedents. The *Evangelium libri quattuor* (*ELQ*) of the Spanish priest Gaius Vettius Aquilinus Juvencus takes its subject from the Gospels, primarily following Matthew, but with supplements from the other Gospels, especially Luke and John (Roberts 1985, Green 2006, pp. 1–134). Composed in or around the year 329 and containing a dedication to the emperor Constantine, it recasts the biblical text, recounting "Christ's life-bringing actions" (*Christi vitalia gesta*, *Pr*, 19) in a Virgilian idiom designed to appeal to an educated readership. Juvencus follows closely the biblical narrative, employing the paraphrastic procedures of abbreviation, amplification, and occasionally transposition. The effect, in Reinhart Herzog's formulation (1975, pp. 99–154), is to throw into relief those elements that promote Christian edification while downplaying or eliminating details alien to a Roman readership.

Juvencus's poem begins with a preface that formulates for the first time a Christian poetics. In it he makes clear that he understands his poem to be an epic by comparing his own work on the salvific actions of Christ with those of Homer and Virgil, whose subjects are the deeds of men. In language and turns of phrase the *ELQ* is strikingly Virgilian, and it maintains an epic elevation of tone. Thematic and compositional elements traditional to epic do not play a large role, however: Extended similes are rare – this is true of biblical epic generally – as are extended descriptive passages, with the exception of a storm description (a theme also found in the other New Testament poets, Sedulius and Arator). The history of biblical poetry in late antiquity involves the increasing incorporation of exegetical material, allegorical and spiritual interpretations, into the poetic text. In Juvencus such exegesis is rarely overt, though recent scholarship has detected evidence of familiarity with the biblical commentaries of Origen.

In the third quarter of the fourth century the female poet Faltonia Betitia Proba turned again to biblical subject matter, this time in the form of a cento, narrating events from the Old Testament (especially the Creation and Fall) and the life of Christ in language derived entirely from Virgil (Herzog 1975, pp. 14–51; Schottenius Cullhed 2015). Despite arousing the disapproval of Jerome, her poem was to enjoy great popularity. Modern reception has similarly been divided. But critical distaste for the cento as a literary form has increasingly given way to a more nuanced understanding of the technical resourcefulness and interpretative subtleties of Proba's poem.

By the second quarter of the fifth century, when the Italian poet Caelius Sedulius wrote his New Testament epic, the five-book *Paschale carmen*, Christian biblical exegesis had taken a firm hold in the West. His poem, also on the life and miracles of Christ, was more selective than Juvencus's treatment, concentrating in its central books (3 and 4) on the miracle stories (Roberts 1985; Springer, 1988; Green 2006, pp. 135–250). (Book 1 is introductory, including Old Testament miracles.) Sedulius's Christian involvement in the narrative leads him to frequently interject his own responses to it, eliciting its moral and spiritual content and using epigrammatic point to emphasize the miraculous in Christ's actions. His poem intensifies a tendency, already evident in Juvencus, to break up the narrative into individual pericopes, thereby reflecting the nature of the biblical text but also conforming to the practices of late Latin poetry more generally.

The final important poet of Latin New Testament epic in the period, Arator, wrote his *Historia apostolica*, on the Acts of the Apostles, in mid-sixth-century Rome (Deproost 1990; Green 2006, pp. 251–350). (It received a public reading there in 544.) His work, in two books, the first devoted to the apostle Peter and the second to Paul, both protectors of the city, struck a welcome chord at a time of great insecurity. Arator's poem continues the trend toward incorporating exegetical material into the biblical subject matter; in structure the work alternates between narrative and interpretation, though often with the latter predominating. At times it has the nature of a versified commentary or sermon.

The Latin New Testament poets were widely read and studied in the Middle Ages. Old Testament epic, however, lacked canonical status (Herzog 1975, pp. xix–xxxiii). The earliest poem, the pseudonymous *Heptateuchos*, from early in the fifth century, recounts the events of the first seven books of the Bible, though there is some evidence that it was once more extensive (Herzog 1975, pp. 52–154; Roberts 1985). It generally sticks close to the biblical text, recasting it in a Virgilian idiom, though passages of sacred law are typically much abbreviated, and it shares a tendency with Juvencus to remove specifically Jewish references from the text.

The *Alethia* ("Truth") of Claudius Marius Victorius probably dates to the second quarter of the fifth century. It recounts in three books the events of Genesis from the Creation to the destruction of Sodom and Gomorrah, though a fourth book may be lost (Martorelli 2008; Cutino 2009). Again there is a strong interpretative/exegetical element to Marius Victorius's epic. He breaks new ground by introducing digressions with a pronounced Lucretian flavor on the evolution of human culture and society.

The latest (last decade of the fifth century) and most important of the Old Testament epics is the *Spiritual History* (*De spiritalis historiae gestis*) of the bishop of Vienne, Alcimus Ecdicius Avitus. Avitus devotes three books to a continuous account of the Creation, Fall, and Expulsion from Paradise; book 4 tells the story of the Flood and book 5 the exodus from Egypt and crossing of the Red Sea (Roberts 1985). His poem traces the salvation history of humankind, from the Fall and its consequences to the figural promise of redemption embodied in the narratives of the Flood and Red Sea. Of all the biblical poets Avitus has most in common with the norms of traditional epic. Old Testament epic was always receptive to set-piece descriptive passages, for instance of Paradise and the Flood. Avitus goes one better and also recasts the biblical account of the encounter of the Egyptians and Israelites at the Red Sea as a traditional battle narrative of the kind familiar from epic.

14.2.4 Hagiographical Epic

The life and miracles of Martin of Tours, as described by Sulpicius Severus in his *Life of St. Martin* and in books 2 and 3 of his *Dialogues*, form the subject of two hagiographical epics written a century apart (Labarre 1998; Roberts 2002). Both show the influence of Sedulius's *Paschale carmen*, with its treatment of Christ's life and miracles, and both serve in part to promote the interests of the church and the bishop of Tours. Paulinus of Périgueux, the author of the earlier poem, probably in the 460s, follows Sulpicius's narrative in his first five books, but includes a sixth based on a dossier of Martin's posthumous miracles provided to him by the bishop, Perpetuus; Venantius

Fortunatus dedicates to Gregory of Tours his Martin poem, in four books, dating to between 563 and 566. Despite their common subject matter and indebtedness to Sedulius, the two poems are different in nature; Paulinus's poem often has something of the quality of a sermon, Fortunatus's of a collection of epigrammatic meditations on Martin's life. Both show the tendency to break up the narrative into distinct compositional units characteristic too of the New Testament epic.

14.2.5 Allegorical Epic

In the last years of the fourth and the first years of the fifth century the writer Aurelius Prudentius Clemens created a body of Christian poetry that marked him out as the supreme Christian poet of late antiquity. His most influential poem, the *Psychomachia*, "Battle of/in/for the Soul," pits personified virtues and vices in epic-style combat for the human soul (Gnilka 1963; Mastrangelo 2008). The poem culminates in the construction of the temple of the soul, now purged of vices. Prudentius combines the typical epic language of battle narratives with personifications as combatants, building on the prevalence of such figures in contemporary literature and art and their traditional use in epic. The account of the temple with which the poem ends has some features of the ekphrasis of a work of art, though in its elaborate architecture and rich decoration its main inspiration is the book of Revelation. As is characteristic of much of Prudentius's poetry, and building on the multiple levels of Christian exegesis, Prudentius's narrative is capable of a variety of senses, not just psychological but also at times ecclesiological and eschatological.

14.2.6 Conclusion

The epic poetry of Latin late antiquity is rich and varied; it encompasses, at a conservative estimate, 23 different poems. They represent the continued capacity of the classical, and more particularly Virgilian, epic tradition to inspire imitation but also constitute a spectrum of creative reworkings of the genre that in many cases struck a powerful chord with a medieval readership.

REFERENCES

Accorinti, Domenico. ed. (2016). *Brill's Companion to Nonnus of Panopolis*. Leiden and Boston: Brill.

Agosti, Gianfranco. (2001). L'epica biblica nella tarda antichità greca: Autori e lettori nel IV e V secolo. In: *La scrittura infinita. Bibbia e poesia in età medievale e umanistica* (ed. Francesco Stella), 67–104. Florence: SISMEL.

Agosti, Gianfranco. (2002a). I poemetti del codice Bodmer e il loro ruolo nella storia della poesia tardoantica. In: *Le Codex des Visions* (ed. André Hurst and Jean Rudhardt), 73–114. Recherches et Rencontres 18. Geneva: Librairie Droz.

Agosti, Gianfranco. (2002b). *POxy* 4352, fr. 5.II.18–39 (Encomio a Diocleziano) e Menandro Retore. *Zeitschrift für Papyrologie und Epigraphik* 140: 51–58.

Agosti, Gianfranco. (2008a). Reliquie argonautiche a Cizico. Un'ipotesi sulle Argonautiche orfiche. In: *Incontri triestini di filologia classica X* (ed. Lucio Cristante and Ireneo Filip), 17–36. Trieste: Edizioni Università di Trieste.

Agosti, Gianfranco. (2008b). Il ruolo di Dioscoro nella storia della poesia tardoantica. In: *Les Archives de Dioscore d'Aphrodité cent ans après leur découverte. Histoire et culture dans l'Égypte byzantine. Actes du colloque international (Strasbourg 8–10 décembre 2005)* (ed. Jean-Luc Fournet and Caroline Magdelaine), 33–54. Paris: De Boccard.

Agosti, Gianfranco. (2009). La *Vita di Proclo* di Marino nella sua redazione in versi. Per un'analisi della biografia poetica tardoantica. *CentoPagine* 3: 30–46.

Agosti, Gianfranco. (2012). Greek poetry. In: *The Oxford Handbook of Late Antiquity* (ed. Scott Fitzgerald Johnson,) 361–392. Oxford: Oxford University Press.

Agosti, Gianfranco. (2014). Greek poetry in late antique Alexandria: Between culture and religion. In: *The Alexandrian Tradition: Interactions between Science, Religion and Literature* (ed. Luis Arturo Guichard, Juan Luis García Alonso and María Paz de Hoz), 287–312. Bern: Peter Lang.

Agosti, Gianfranco. (2015). Poesia greca nella (e della?) Biblioteca Bodmer. *Adamantius* 21: 86–97.

Agosti, Gianfranco and Gonnelli, Fabrizio. (1995). Materiali per la storia dell'esametro nei poeti cristiani greci. In: *Struttura e storia dell'esametro greco* (ed. Marco Fantuzzi and Roberto Pretagostini), 1: 289–434. Rome: Giardini.

Bär, Silvio. (2009). *Quintus Smyrnaeus "Posthomerica" 1: Die Wiedergeburt des Epos aus dem Geiste der Amazonomachie. Mit einem Kommentar zu den Versen 1–219.* Hypomnemata 183. Göttingen: Vanderhoeck and Ruprecht.

Bär, Silvio. (2012). "Museum of words": Christodorus, the art of *ekphrasis* and the epyllic genre. In: *Brill's Companion to Greek and Latin Epyllion and its Reception* (ed. M. Baumbach and S. Bär), 447–471. Leiden and Boston: Brill.

Baumbach, Manuel and Bär, Silvio. ed. (2007). *Quintus Smyrnaeus: Transforming Homer in Second Sophistic Epic.* Berlin and New York: De Gruyter.

Bell, Peter N. (2009). *Three Political Voices from the Age of Justinian: Agapetus, Advice to the Emperor, Dialogue on Political Science, Paul the Silentiary, Description of Hagia Sophia.* Translated Texts for Historians 52. Liverpool: Liverpool University Press.

Cadau, Cosette. (2015). *Studies in Colluthus' Abduction of Helen.* Memnosyne Supplements 380. Leiden: Brill.

Cameron, Alan. (1965 [rev. ed. 2016]). Wandering poets: A literary movement in Byzantine Egypt. *Historia* 14: 470–509.

Cameron, Alan. (1970). *Claudian: Poetry and Propaganda at the Court of Honorius.* Oxford: Clarendon.

Cameron, Alan. (2004 [rev. ed. 2016]). Poetry and literary culture in late antiquity. In: *Approaching Late Antiquity: The Transformation from Early to Late Empire* (ed. Simon Swain and Mark Edwards), 327–354. Oxford: Oxford University Press.

Cameron, Alan, (2007 [rev. ed. 2016]). Poets and pagans in Byzantine Egypt. In: *Egypt in the Byzantine World, 300–700* (ed. Roger S. Bagnall), 21–46. Cambridge: Cambridge University Press.

Cameron, Alan, (2016). *Wandering Poets and Other Essays on Late Greek Literature and Philosophy.* Oxford: Oxford University Press.

Carvounis, Katerina. (2008). Transforming the Homeric models: Quintus' battle among the gods in the *Posthomerica.* In: *Signs of Life? Studies in Later Greek Poetry* (ed. Katerina Carvounis and Richard Hunter), 60–78. Ramus Critical Studies in Greek and Roman Literature. Victoria, Australia.

Cecchetti, Valentina. (2013). Review of Schelske 2011. *Prometheus,* n.s. 2: 299–302.

Cutino, Michele. (2009). *L'Alethia di Claudio Mario Vittorio: La parafrasi biblica come forma di espressione teologica.* Rome: Institutum Patristicum Augustinianum.

Demoen, Kristoffel. (2009). Poétique et rhétorique dans la poésie de Grégoire de Nazianze. In: *Actes du colloque Doux remède. Poésie et poétique à Byzance (EHESS 24–26 février 2006)* (ed. Paolo Odorico, Panagiotis Agapitos, and Martin Hinterberger), 47–66. Paris: De Boccard.

Deproost, Paul-Augustin. (1990). *L'apôtre Pierre dans un épopée du VIe siècle.* Paris: Études Augustiniennes.

Faulkner, Andrew. (2014). Faith and fidelity in Biblical epic: The *Metaphrasis Psalmorum,* Nonnus and the theory of translation. In: *Nonnus of Panopolis in Context: Poetry and Cultural Milieu in Late Antiquity,* Trends in Classics, supp. vol. 24 (ed. Konstantinos Spanoudakis), 195–210. Berlin and Boston: De Gruyter.

Fo, Alessandro. (1982). *Studi sulla tecnica poetica di Claudiano.* Catania: Tringale.

Fournet, Jean-Luc. (1999). *Hellénisme dans l'Égypte du VIᵉ siècle. La bibliothèque et l'œuvre de Dioscore d'Aphrodité.* 2 vols. Institut français d'archéologie orientale. MIFAO 115: Cairo.

Fournet, Jean-Luc. (2003). Théodore, un poète chrétien alexandrin oublié. L'hexamètre au service de la cause chrétienne. In: *Des Géants à Dionysos: Mélanges de mythologie et de poésie grecques offerts à Francis Vian* (ed. Domenico Accorinti and Pierre Chuvin), 521–39. Alessandria: Edizioni dell'Orso.

Gelzer, Theodor. ed. (1975). Musaeus: *Hero and Leander* (trans. Cedric Whitman), 289–389. Cambridge, MA: Harvard University Press.

Giannakis, Georgios. ed. (1982). *ΟΡΦΕΩΣ ΛΙΘΙΚΑ.* Ioannina: Ioannina University.

Gigli Piccardi, Daria. (2005). ΑΕΡΟΒΑΤΕΙΝ: L'ecfrasi come viaggio in Giovanni di Gaza. *Medievo Greco* 5: 181–199.

Gigli Piccardi, Daria. (2014). Poetic inspiration in John of Gaza: Emotional upheaval and ecstasy in a Neoplatonic poet. In: *Nonnus of Panopolis in Context: Poetry and Cultural Milieu in Late Antiquity,* Trends in Classics, supp. vol. 24 (ed. Konstantinos Spanoudakis), 403–419. Berlin and Boston: De Gruyter.

Gnilka, Christian. (1963). *Studien zur Psychomachie des Prudentius.* Wiesbaden: Harrassowitz.

Gonnelli, F. ed. (1998). Giorgio di Pisidia, Esamerone. Pisa: Edizioni ETS.

Green, Roger P. H. (2006). *Latin Epics of the New Testament: Juvencus, Sedulius, Arator.* Oxford: Oxford University Press.

Halleux, Robert and Schamp, Jacques. ed. (1985). *Les Lapidaires grecs.* Paris: Les Belles Lettres.

Hernández de la Fuente, David. (2015). Poetry and philosophy at the boundaries of Byzantium (5th–7th Centuries): Some methodological remarks on the Nonnians. In: *New Perspectives on Late Antiquity in the Eastern Roman Empire* (ed. Ana de Francisco Heredero, David Hernández de la Fuente, and Susana Torres Prieto), 81–100. Newcastle-upon-Tyne: Cambridge Scholars.

Herzog, Reinhart. (1975). *Die Bibelepik der lateinischen Spätantike: Formgeschichte einer erbaulichen Gattung.* Munich: Fink.

Hofmann, Heinz. (1988). Überlegungen zu einer Theorie der nichtchristlichen Epik der lateinischen Spätantike. *Philologus* 132: 101–159.

Hopkinson, Neil. (1984). Review of Giannakis 1982. *Classical Review* 34: 19–22.

Hopkinson, Neil. (1994). *Greek Poetry of the Imperial Period: An Anthology.* Cambridge: Cambridge University Press.

Hunter, Richard. (2005). Generic consciousness in the Orphic *Argonautica.* In: *Roman and Greek Imperial Epic* (ed. Michael Paschalis), 169–192. Heraklion: University of Crete.

Jeffreys, Elizabeth. (2006). Writers and audiences in the early sixth century. In: *Greek Literature in Late Antiquity: Dynamism, Didacticism, Classicism* (ed. Scott Fitzgerald Johnson), 127–139. Aldershot and Burlington VT: Ashgate.

Kaldellis, Anthony. (2007). Christodorus on the Statues of the Zeuxippos Baths: A New Reading of the Ekphrasis. *Greek, Roman and Byzantine Studies* 47: 361–383.

Kaster, Robert A. (1988). *Guardians of Language: The Grammarian and Society in Late Antiquity.* Berkeley: University of California Press.

Kirsch, Wolfgang. (1989). *Die lateinische Versepik des 4. Jahrhunderts.* Berlin: Akademie.

Kneebone, Emily. (2008). ΤΟΣΣ' ΕΔΑΗΝ: The poetics of knowledge in Oppian's *Halieutica.* In: *Signs of Life? Studies in Later Greek Poetry* (ed. Katerina Carvounis and Richard Hunter), 32–59. Ramus Critical Studies in Greek and Roman Literature. Victoria, Australia.

Kneebone, Emily. (Forthcoming). Monograph on Oppian's *Halieutica.*

Kost, Karl Heinz. ed. (1971). *Musaios. Einleitung, Text, Übersetzung und Kommentar.* Bonn: Bouvier.

Labarre, Sylvie. (1998). *Le manteau partagé: Deux metamorphoses poétiques de la Vie de saint Martin chez Paulin de Périgueux (Ve s.) et Venance Fortunat (VIe s.).* Paris: Études Augustiniennes.

Lauritzen, Delphine. (2011). *Exegi monumentum*: l'*ekphrasis* autonome de Jean de Gaze, *Byzantinoslavica* 69: 61–79.

Lauritzen, Delphine. (2014). Nonnus in Gaza. The expansion of modern poetry from Egypt to Palestine in the early sixth century CE. In: *Nonnus of Panopolis in Context: Poetry and Cultural Milieu in Late Antiquity*, Trends in Classics, supp. vol. 24 (ed. Konstantinos Spanoudakis), 421–433. Berlin and Boston: De Gruyter.

Lauritzen, Delphine (2015). *Jean de Gaze, Description du tableau cosmique*. Paris: Les Belles Lettres.

Lightfoot, Jane. ed. (2014). *Dionysius Periegetes: Description of the Known World*. Oxford: Oxford University Press.

Livrea, Enrico. ed. (1978). *Anonymi fortasse Olympiodori Thebani Blemyomachia (P. Berol. 5003)*. Meisenheim am Glan: A. Hain.

Livrea, Enrico. ed. (1979). *Pamprepii Panopolitani Carmina (P. Gr. Vindob. 29788 A–C)*. Leipzig: Teubner.

Livrea, Enrico. (1992). Review of Halleux and Schamp (1985). *Gnomon* 64: 204–211.

Livrea, Enrico. (1998). La chiusa della *Gigantomachia* greca di Claudiano e la datazione del poemetto. *Studi Italiani di Filologia Classica* 16: 194–201.

Livrea. Enrico. (2014). The last pagan at the court of Zeno: Poetry and politics of Pamprepius of Panopolis. In: *New Perspectives on Late Antiquity in the Eastern Roman Empire* (ed. Ana de Francisco Heredero, David Hernández de la Fuente, and Susana Torres Pieto), 1–30. Newcastle-upon-Tyne: Cambridge Scholars.

Ludwich, Arthur. ed. (1897). *Eudociae Augustae, Procli, Lycii, Claudiani carminum graecorum reliquiae*. Leipzig: Teubner.

Ma, John, (2007). The worlds of Nestor the poet. In: *Severan Culture* (ed. Simon Swain, Stephen Harrison, and Jaś Elsner), 83–113. Cambridge: Cambridge University Press.

MacIver, Calum. (2012a). *Quintus Smyrnaeus' Posthomerica: Engaging Homer in Late Antiquity*. Leiden: Brill.

MacIver, Calum. (2012b). Representative bees in Quintus Smyrnaeus' *Posthomerica*. *Classical Philology* 107: 53–69.

McLynn, Neil. (1998a). The other Olympias: Gregory Nazianzan and the family of Vitalian. *Zeitschrift für Antike und Christentum* 2: 227–246.

McLynn, Neil. (1998b). A self-made holy man: The case of Gregory Nazianzen. *Journal of Early Christian Studies* 6: 463–483.

McLynn, Neil. (2014). Julian and the Christian professors. In: *Being Christian in Late Antiquity: A Festschrift for Gillian Clark* (ed. Carol Harrison, Caroline Humfress, and Isabella Sandwell), 120–136. Oxford: Oxford University Press.

Macrides, Ruth and Magdalino, Paul. (1988). The architecture of *ekphrasis*: Construction and context of Paul the Silentiary's poem on Hagia Sophia. *Byzantine and Modern Greek Studies* 12: 47–82.

Magnelli, Enrico. (2008). Colluthus' "Homeric" Epyllion. In: *Signs of Life? Studies in Later Greek Poetry* (ed. Katerina Carvounis and Richard Hunter), 151–172. Ramus Critical Studies in Greek and Roman Literature. Victoria, Australia.

Magnelli, Enrico. (2016). The Nonnian hexameter. In: *Brill's Companion to Nonnus of Panopolis* (ed. Domenico Accorinti), 353–370. Leiden and Boston: Brill.

Martorelli, Ugo. (2008). *Redeat verum: Studi sulla tecnica poetica dell' Alethia di Mario Claudio Vittorio*. Stuttgart: Franz Steiner.

Mastrangelo, Marc. (2008). *The Roman Self in Late Antiquity: Prudentius and the Poetics of the Soul*. Baltimore: Johns Hopkins University Press.

Miguélez Cavero, Laura. (2008). *Poems in Context: Greek Poetry in the Egyptian Thebaid, 200–600 AD*. Berlin and New York: De Gruyter.

Miguélez Cavero, Laura. (2013a). *Triphiodorus, The Sack of Troy: A General Study and a Commentary*. Berlin and Boston: De Gruyter.

Miguélez Cavero, Laura. (2013b). Rhetoric for a Christian community: The poems of the *Codex Visionum*. In: *The Purpose of Rhetoric in Late Antiquity: From Rhetoric to Exegesis* (ed. Alberto J. Quiroga Puertas), 91–121. Tübingen: Mohr Siebeck.

Mulligan, Bret. (2007). The poet from Egypt? Reconsidering Claudian's eastern origin. *Philologus* 151: 285–310.

Nelis, Damian. (2005). The reading of Orpheus: The Orphic *Argonautica* and the epic tradition. In: *Roman and Greek Imperial Epic* (ed. Michael Paschalis), 169–192. Heraklion: University of Crete.

Paschalis, Michael. (2008). The *Abduction of Helen*: A reappraisal. In: *Signs of Life? Studies in Later Greek Poetry* (ed. Katerina Carvounis and Richard Hunter), 136–150. Ramus Critical Studies in Greek and Roman Literature. Victoria, Australia.

Prauscello, Lucia. (2008). Colluthus' pastoral traditions: Narrative strategies and bucolic criticism in the *Abduction of Helen*. In: *Signs of Life? Studies in Later Greek Poetry* (ed. Katerina Carvounis and Richard Hunter), 173–190. Ramus Critical Studies in Greek and Roman Literature. Victoria, Australia.

Renaut, Delphine. (2005). Les declamations d'*ekphraseis*: Une réalité vivante à Gaza au VIe siècle. In: *Gaza dans l'Antiquité tardive. Archéologie, rhétorique et histoire* (ed. C. Saliou), 197–220. Cardo 2. Salerno: Helios.

Roberts, Michael. (1985). *Biblical Epic and Rhetorical Paraphrase in Late Antiquity*. Liverpool: Cairns.

Roberts, Michael. (2002). Venantius Fortunatus's life of Saint Martin. *Traditio* 57: 129–187.

Schelske, Oliver. (2011). *Orpheus in der Spätantike. Studien und Kommentar zu den Argonautica des Orpheus*. Berlin and New York: de Gruyter.

Schindler, Claudia. (2009). *Per carmina laudes: Untersuchungen zur spätantiken Verspanegyrik von Claudian bis Coripp*. Berlin: De Gruyter.

Schottenius Cullhed, Sigrid. (2015). *Proba the Poet: The Christian Virgilian Cento of Faltonia Betitia Proba*. Leiden: Brill.

Shorrock, Robert. (2011). *The Myth of Paganism: Nonnus, Dionysus and the World of Late Antiquity*. Bloomsbury, London: Bristol Classical Press.

Simelidis, Christos. ed. (2009). *Selected Poems of Gregory of Nazianzus (I.2.17; II.1.10, 19, 32)*. Hypomnemata 177. Göttingen: Vandenhoeck and Ruprecht.

Simelidis, Christos. (2016). Nonnus and Christian literature. In: *Brill's Companion to Nonnus of Panopolis* (ed. Domenico Accorinti), 289–307. Leiden and Boston: Brill.

Sowers, Brian P. (2008). Eudocia: The making of a Homeric Christian. PhD diss., University of Cincinnati.

Sowers, Brian.P. (2018). *In Her Own Words: The Life and Poetry of Aelia Eudocia*. Center for Hellenic Studies. Cambridge, Massachusetts: Harvard University Press.

Spanoudakis, Konstantinos. (2007). Icarius Jesus Christ? Dionysiac Passion and biblical narrative in Nonnus' Icarius Episode (Dion. 47, 1–264). *Wiener Studien* 120: 35–92.

Spanoudakis, Konstantinos. (2013). The resurrections of Tylus and Lazarus in Nonnus of Panopolis (*Dion.* XXV, 451–552 and *Par.* Λ). In: *Le voyage des légendes. Hommages à Pierre Chuvin* (ed. Delphine Lauritzen and Michel Tardieu), 191–208. Paris: CNRS.

Spanoudakis, Konstantinos. ed. (2014a). *Nonnus of Panopolis in Context: Poetry and Cultural Milieu in Late Antiquity*, Trends in Classics, supp. vol. 24. Berlin and Boston: De Gruyter.

Spanoudakis, Konstantinos. ed. (2014b). *Nonnus of Panopolis, Paraphrasis of the Gospel of John XI*. Oxford Early Christian Texts. Oxford: Oxford University Press.

Springer, Carl. (1988). *The Gospel as Epic in Late Antiquity: The Paschale Carmen of Sedulius*. Leiden: Brill.

Tissoni, Francesco. ed. (2000). *Cristodoro. Un introduzione e un commento*, Hellenica 6. Alessandria: Edizioni dell'Orso.

Vian, Francis. ed. (1987). *Les Argonautes Orphiques*. Paris: Les Belles Lettres.

Whitby, Mary. (1985). The occasion of Paul the Silentiary's *ekphrasis* of S. Sophia. *Classical Quarterly* 35: 215–228.

Whitby, Mary. (1994). The evolution of the Nonnian style. In: *Studies in the Dionysiaca of Nonnus* (ed. Neil Hopkinson), 99–155. Cambridge Philological Society Supplement 17. Cambridge: Cambridge Philological Society.

Whitby, Mary. (2002). George of Pisidia's presentation of the Emperor Heraclius and his campaigns: Variety and development. In: *The Reign of Heraclius (610–641): Crisis and Confrontation* (ed. Gerrit J. Reinink and Bernard H. Stolte), 157–173. Leuven, Paris, Dudley MA: Peeters.

Whitby, Mary (2007a). The *Cynegetica* attributed to Oppian. In: *Severan Culture* (ed. Simon Swain, Stephen Harrison, and Jaś Elsner), 125–134. Cambridge: Cambridge University Press.

Whitby (2007b). The Bible Hellenized: Nonnus' *Paraphrase* of St John's Gospel and "Eudocia's" Homeric centos. In: *Texts and Culture in Late Antiquity: Inheritance, Authority, and Change* (ed. J.H.D. Scourfield), 195–231. Swansea: Classical Press of Wales.

Whitby, Mary. (2008). "Sugaring the pill": Gregory of Nazianzus' advice to Olympias (*Carm.* 2.2.6). In: *Signs of Life? Studies in Later Greek Poetry* (ed. Katerina Carvounis and Richard Hunter), 79–98. Ramus Critical Studies in Greek and Roman Literature. Victoria, Australia.

Whitby, Mary. (2013). Writing in Greek: Classicism and compilation, interaction and transformation. In: *Theodosius II: Rethinking the Roman Empire in Late Antiquity* (ed. Christopher Kelly), 195–218. Cambridge: Cambridge University Press.

Whitby, Mary. (2014). A learned spiritual ladder? Towards an interpretation of George of Pisidia's hexameter poem *On Human Life*. In: *Nonnus of Panopolis in*

Context: Poetry and Cultural Milieu in Late Antiquity, Trends in Classics, supp. vol. 24. (ed. Konstantinos Spanoudakis), 435–457. Berlin and Boston: De Gruyter.

Whitby, Mary. (2018). Christodorus of Coptus on the statues in the baths of Zeuxippus at Constantinople: Text and context. In: *Nonnus of Panopolis in Context II: Poetry, Religion, and Society* (ed. Herbert Bannert and Nicole Kröll), 271–288. Leiden and Boston: Brill.

Zarini, Vincent. (2003). *Rhétorique, poétique, spiritualité: La technique épique de Corippe dans la Johannide*. Turnhout: Brepols.

Zito, Nicola. (2012a). Massimo di Efeso e *I Lithica* orfici. *Rivista di Filologia e di Istruzione Classica*, 140: 134–166.

Zito, Nicola. (2012b). Sull'autore del poemetto Περὶ καταρχῶν attribuito a Massimo di Efeso. *Eikasmos* 23: 259–276.

Zito, Nicola. (2013). Per una rilettura del 'secondo prologo' dei *Lithici orfici*. In: *Le voyage des légendes. Hommages à Pierre Chuvin* (ed. Delphine Lauritzen and Michel Tardieu), 161–173. Paris: CNRS.

CHAPTER FIFTEEN

Epigrams, Occasional Poetry, and Poetic Games

Bret Mulligan

We have cultivated a healthy skepticism toward talk of cultural renaissance and rejuvenation, terms that often reveal more about the vagaries of cultural transmission and the aesthetic priorities of the critic than about the reality of a past culture glimpsed through that ever-hazy distant mirror. Yet when one surveys the breadth, multiplicity, and richness of poetic composition in late antiquity, one is hard pressed to resist those old categories. Greek and Latin, high and low, Christian and secular, reactionary and revolutionary, center and periphery, in East and West, on stone and vellum – wherever one casts the eye, one spies poetry. A surge of creative interest and poetic capacity began in the early decades of the fourth century; crested in the first half of the fifth, and then ebbed until, by the mid-seventh century, this moment had passed and something else had emerged. Here we will survey the broad vistas of short-form poems, minor poetic genres, and occasional verse produced during later antiquity. Many of these are little poems about little things – artwork in baths, an epitaph for a pet bird, a silver dish. But small or minor need not make mean or trite: These were also significant works inscribed on monumental architecture and works of greater or lesser scale delivered to the temporal and spiritual masters of the world with keen purpose and real consequence. By necessity, our approach will be panoptic, and we will not spare a favorite device of late antique verse: the list. Strict chronology and the linguistic divide will often be deprioritized, not because these

---

A Companion to Late Antique Literature, First Edition.
Edited by Scott McGill and Edward J. Watts.
© 2018 John Wiley & Sons, Inc. Published 2018 by John Wiley & Sons, Inc.

are unimportant (and indeed others have begun to tell these tales, e.g. Dihle 1994) but because it is better here to seek connections and commonalities, as there is so very much to discover.

The *Oxford Classical Dictionary* would once say of late antique epigram that "to know their models is to despise them" (s.v. "Epigram"). But scholars in recent decades have exposed the crafty methods by which late antique poets selected, fragmented, epitomized, redacted, and supplanted prestigious texts. Nowhere is this clearer than with the cento ("patchwork"), in which phrases and whole lines extracted from Homer or Virgil were recombined into a new narrative whole (McGill 2005). Some centos aimed to delight. In the *Cento nuptialis*, Ausonius notoriously repurposed Virgil into a lurid account of a wedding night. Other centos possessed didactic purpose, refashioning secular texts in service of Christian truth. Pomponius's *Versus ad Gratiam Domini* (early fifth century) draws on Virgilian phrases to Christianize *Eclogue* 1: This Tityrus is saved by the Christian God rather than by Octavian (cf. Endelechius's Christian fantasy on *Ecl.* 1)! Jerome grumpily dismissed centos as "childish and like the scams of charlatans" (*Epist.* 53.7). But Faltonia Betitia Proba's 694-line mix of Old and New Testament stories was an instant hit in the mid-fourth century. In the early sixteenth century it was still in the curriculum, alongside Juvencus, Lactantius, Prudentius, and Sedulius. The longest extant cento was composed in Greek by the Empress Eudocia, wife of Theodosius II. Her cento, which she claims was begun by another, is a biblical history from Genesis to the time of Christ, in 2344 Homeric lines. Centos could also serve the occasion. Eudocia was said to have included a centonic passage in her encomium of Antioch. Centos, although born from epic, could be miniaturized, as in a nine-verse Christian epitaph from Anatolia or the Greek epigrams on Hero and Leander (*AP* 9.381) and Echo (9.832). Such texts demand that they be approached analytically, fragmented through the act of commentary, as their contextual implications are decoded as part of the reinterpretation of traditional texts and genres. They are quintessentially *metaliterary* works that draw attention to themselves as textual, written, and (re-)written objects (Formisano 2007).

The acute awareness of textuality displayed by the centonists was one strand of a poetics focused on the intense, thoughtful manipulation of word and form (Charlet 1988). If figural poetry arose in the scholastic environment of Hellenistic Alexandria, its late antique apogee was intensely political. Optatianus dedicated 20 intricate poems to Constantine on the anniversary of his succession in 325/326 CE, in the hope that the emperor would repeal his exile. Optatianus's ingenious acrostic and figural poems – in which meandering, often polymetric *versus intexti* trace shapes: a palm tree, an altar, a ship – carried the day (Squire 2017). Politics dance behind Fortunatus's most involuted figural composition, whose cruciform *versus intexti* form an embedded second poem in support of Radegund's efforts to secure a piece of the true cross (5.6). Fortunatus also saw fit to publish a poetic "failure," a figural poem whose complexity trumped Fortunatus's ability – or patience (2.5; cf. the quasihexameter acrostic for the fourth-century Numidian banker L. Praecilius Fortunatus, *CLE* 512). At a time when poetry was predominantly sonic, sequential, and performative, figural poems gained their special currency from the private construction of visual meaning rooted in the multisequential reconfiguration of the minute building blocks of language into new forms.

Figural poems may be the most intricate manifestation of late antiquity's intense interest in the making and remaking of literary texts, but the same spirit (and audience preference) animates a slew of poems that work within strict patterns of meter, syllable, and letter. Textual play was an important motif for the Vandal epigrammatist Eugenius and his compatriot Flavius Felix, whose 12 rectilinear hexameters embed not only an acrostic but a mesostich and telestich (*AL* 205 SB). Christians were especially invested in such acrostic play: Of 86 acrostic epitaphs, 13 are datable to the fourth century, of which all but one are Christian. The sarcophagus of Bassa preserves an exemplar of this type, in which an epitaph replaces one of the expected iconographic scenes (*ICUR* 5.14076). The acrostic, *Bassae suae/Gaudentius*, yokes the two hexametric columns: the first extolling Bassa's virtues and her ascent to heaven; the second a consolation for Gaudentius in Bassa's voice. The nun Taurina inscribed an epitaph for her four beloved aunts, in which the first letter of each competent hexameter line spells out the names of the deceased (*CLE* 1.748). In a lighter vein, we find echoing distichs (*AL* 25–68) in which the first half of the hexameter repeats at the end of the pentameter, as well as longer *versus echoici* by the Constantinian poet Pentadius on fortune, spring, and Narcissus (*AL* 259). The *Latin Anthology* also includes several serpentine couplets on Virgilian characters (*AL* 33, 36, 38, 47, 65). Ausonius composed a rhopalic prayer, in which the first word has one syllable, the second two, the third three, and so forth. Ausonius could compose simple epigrammatic riddles – for example, *Technop.* 13, which poses 15 questions and answers, each with a monosyllable at the end of the verse. But his *Griphus* on the number three, which began as a frivolity over dinner in Trier and was subsequently sent as an epistolary gift to Symmachus, is fiendishly obscure. Among more traditional riddlers of late antiquity, the best known is the fifth-century poet Symphosius, whose 100 riddles, each in hexametric tercets, influenced the tradition of the Medieval Latin verse riddle.

Paraphrase was the most familiar form of textual manipulation. Although the mode had its origin in ethopoeia and school exercises, the urge to manipulate familiar texts continued into adulthood, manifestations of elite *otium*, in which poems known by heart were recast in amusing ways. There was a craft to condensing Virgilian *Eclogues* or books of the *Georgics* or *Aeneid* into tetrastichs, pentastichs, hexastichs, or single lines (*AL* 2, 2a SB; 591–602, 653–654, 634 R, 653 R), in iteratively paraphrasing Virgil's epitaph (*AL* 507–518 555–566 R), and in reworking a Virgilian kernel – whether in condensing Dido's indictment of Aeneas (*A.* 4.365–387) into a tetrastich (Ennodius *Dictio* 28) or expanding her speech to 150 lines with a helping of Ovid's *Heroides* (*AL* 71 SB), or in mashing up similar passages to destabilize the image of the Virgilian hero (*AL* 214). Virgil was by far the most popular source and field for paraphrastic literary play. But other prestigious texts could so serve. The 89-hexameter *Verba Achillis in Parthenone* (*AL* 189 SB) draws on Statius for an ethopoeia in which Achilles justifies his decision to reject his feminine disguise on Scyros only to be confronted by an anonymous interlocutor who questions whether his glory is worth Thetis's grief. The 106 epigrams of Prosper of Aquitaine, which paraphrase the teachings of Augustine in simple verse, reveal a different kind of textual manipulation, directed not toward sacred texts but toward Christian education.

Letters of the alphabet provided a ready-made structure for text-focused poets and readers. Some of these are explicitly playful, such as Ausonius's *Epigr.* 85, in which initial letters of Greek names spell out a lewd act, or the work of the anonymous seventh-century Scottish poet who fancied hexameter riddles on the letters of the alphabet. But Christian hymnody, doubtless inspired by the Psalms, routinely favored alphabetic composition. An alphabetic acrostic spans the 24 strophe *Maiden Song* in loose, nonclassical iambs that the early fourth-century Greek martyr Methodius appended to the end of his prose *On Virginity*. Augustine's rare foray into verse also took the form of a plain-spoken abecedarius, a "Psalm" against the Donatists that employs the end-rhymed triads found in Semitic poetry (Bastiaensen 2007). A generation after Augustine, Sedulius brought the abecedarius into the fold of classical prosody with a celebrated hymn in iambic dimeters.

Ausonius had composed his pornographic cento as part of a playful, private literary competition with the emperor Valentinian. But many late antique poets were called to compose and perform public poetry for (and against) figures at the center of temporal and ecclesiastical power, often on a tight schedule. In the autumn of 399, Claudian stood before the grandees of the imperial court in Milan, set to renew his assault on his patron's nemesis, Eutropius, in 602 savage hexameters. But recently news had arrived that the eunuch consul had been sacked. Thus Claudian used his elegiac preface to reframe his attack on the "unmanned tyrant" (2 *pr. Eutr.* 21) into a broader critique of the East's inability to rule itself. Many public performances were more strictly celebratory. In 544 Arator recited his two-book paraphrase of *Acts* in the Church of San Pietro in Vincoli before an audience that included Pope Vigilius. Paulus Silentarius regaled the elite of Constantinople with his 887-hexameter description of Hagia Sophia and a 275-hexameter account of its singer's pulpit during the reconsecration ceremony on 6 January 563. Such occasional poems, rooted in spectacular public ceremonies, created an audience in their moment and became a vehicle for the propagation of individual and collective memory.

Occasional poetry enabled successful poets to acquire wealth and other forms of social capital. Ausonius, the son of a country doctor, rode his intellectual talents to chairs of grammar and rhetoric in Bordeaux and from there to the imperial court and eventually the consulship (379 CE). The rivalrous cities of the East created a ready market for ambitious, professional poets – many from the thriving, literary communities of Upper Egypt – who traveled the eastern Mediterranean composing and performing learned accounts of cities, encomia for and invectives against local dignitaries, epithalamia for high officials, grander martial epics for victorious generals, and other occasional modes of poetry. Most of the "wandering poets" who plied their literary trade in the fourth and fifth centuries – Helladius of Antinupolis, Hermesias, Horapolon, Andronicus – are mere names to us: Their poems, which drew on the intense interest in local antiquities during this period, only rarely won readers outside the honored city.

The paltry remains of Greek occasional poems belie their abundance, reach, and importance, as poetry often served a practical purpose in the later empire. Since these poems are almost entirely lost, the literary scene must be reconstructed from passing references, the odd quotation, and later encyclopedic mentions. Epistolary collections offer a particularly insightful view of contemporary literary networks. When Libanius's friend Heraclianus seeks a recommendation, he suggests that Diphilus will sing his praises – for a price. Libanius warns another friend that Dorotheus will praise those who pay and lampoon those who don't (*Ep.* 1517). Palladas inveighs against his rivals who work for pay (*AP* 11.291). But poets did not shy from saying that their Muse was for sale. Corippus mentions his salary in the preface to his encomium of Justin II. Diodorus of Aphrodito ends his encomium for John with a direct appeal for payment! But the best of these poets did not go begging for scraps from their patrons' tables. John the Lydian was paid the going rate of one *solidus* per line for a panegyric on the praetorian prefect Zoticus. One assumes the emperor paid better. Victors of poetic competitions in Oxyrhynchus were granted exemption from taxes. Claudian and Pamprepius won brides in prominent and wealthy families. While some received rewards for specific poems – Icarius was appointed *comes Orientis* after delivering a panegyric to Theodosius – others leveraged their poetic service into political connections that led to wealth, titles (Claudian, Dioscorus), and even positions at court (Corippus), ambassadorships (Olympiodorus), and a place in the upper echelons of politics. Risks attended on fame and fortune. Cyrus of Panopolis leveraged the favor of Eudocia, the highly literate wife of Theodosius II, to the city and praetorian prefectures and, thence, the consulship in 441, only to be exiled by the jealous emperor.

This vibrant market attracted literary talent from the West. Corippus, after the success of his *Iohannis* (an eight-book hexametric account of the Byzantine war against the Berbers), traveled to Constantinople, where he performed his Latin panegyric for Anastasius and Justin II (*In laudem Iustini*). Although the smaller market and Latinity of the less urbanized West limited the opportunities for Greek poets, a few did make the jump. Eunapius mentions a certain Eusebius, whose poetry was suited to flattering Roman aristocrats (Athenians had found him bothersome [*VS* 493]). The most successful of these wandering poets was Claudian, an Alexandrian who traveled to Italy ca. 395 CE. His reputation must have preceded him. His first commission was to commemorate the dual consulships of two scions of the powerful Anici family. First before the aristocrats of Rome and, then, before the courtiers of Milan, Claudian pioneered a new hybrid form of epicizing panegyric that fused the goals of encomium with the narrative integrity of epic (Ware 2012). Nearly all of Claudian's occasional verse praised the child emperor Honorius or his regent, Stilicho – or attacked their rivals in the East. While Claudian wove a stable of imagery, personifications, and tropes into a coherent representation of the imperial court for an elite audience in the West, Constantinople doubtless waged its own poetic war. Eusebius Scholasticus and Ammonius wrote epics on the revolt of Gainas, who had been Stilicho's proxy. Theotius composed verse panegyrics for Anthemius, the successor of Claudian's reviled Eutropius, and Synesius of Cyrene observes that he was only one of many poets to support Anthemius's successor, Aurelian.

Claudian's example was much imitated in the following century. The Spanish poet and general Merobaudes won a statue in the Forum of Trajan for his praise of Aetius, the Stilicho-figure at the court of Valentinian III. Merobaudes's work survives only in a tattered palimpsest, but his adherence to the thematic and stylistic path set by Claudian is unmistakable. Like Claudian, he also composed minor poems for Aetius and his circle: ekphrastic epigrams (e.g. of imperial mosaics) and birthday and baptismal poems, including one in hendecasyllables for Aetius's son. A generation later Sidonius Apollinaris continued the project of large and small poems devoted to political patrons and friends, although without Claudian's luck: The objects of

Sidonius's praise – Anthemius, Majorian, Avitus – quickly fell. In addition to his eight panegyrics and 16 other significant poems, many smaller works are embedded within his letters. Well into the early sixth century poets continued to mix encomiastic and minor verse. Florentinus composed a brief eulogy for the Vandal king Thrasamund (d. 523) as well as mythological, erotic, satirical, and protreptic poems. Priscian joined two Greek authors, the poet Christodorus of Coptus and the orator Procopius of Gaza, in praising Anastasius's campaigns against the Isaurians.

Claudian's innovations also spurred the popularity of encomiastic wedding song. Thirteen (of 17 extant) epithalamia date from late antiquity, many by the period's best-known poets. In 398 Claudian had been tasked with securing public support for the marriage of the child emperor Honorius to Maria, the young daughter of his regent, Stilicho. Four lyric fescennine poems mingle praise of Stilicho with modest descriptions of conjugal sex. But it was Claudian's epithalamium – 341 hexameters prefaced by 11 elegiac couplets – that established a new template for late antique wedding song. Drawing from Statius's epithalamium for his friend Stella (*Silv.* 1.2), which augmented the style of the genre by bringing the mythological and human worlds into dialogue in sensuous praise of the newlyweds, Claudian turned his praise toward the families of the newlyweds and his patron (see also, *carm. min.* 25; *app.* 5). Although most late antique epithalamia reveal a mutual debt to Statius and Claudian, the occasional nature of the poems also yields important differences of tone, style, and purpose. Sidonius's two epithalamia are devoted almost entirely to ekphrases set in the divine world with short codas devoted to the wedding. Luxorius leveraged Ausonius's saucy praise of Gratian and Constantia for his centonic epithalamium for Frigus (perhaps the Fridamal addressed in two of his epigrams [*AL* 299–300 SB]). Dracontius composed two epithalamia after his imprisonment by King Gunthamund (*Rom.* 6–7). Fortunatus uncharacteristically incorporates a mythological apparatus in a lengthy epithalamium for Sigibert and Brunhild (6.1), illustrating how fixed and durable the expectations for the genre had become.

Composing epithalamia for devout Christians required further modifications. When Julian wed Titia, Paulinus of Nola, himself an ascetic convert to Christianity, rejected the genre's mythological trappings (*carm.* 25.9–10) and converted personal encomium into a protreptic for a virtuous "chaste partnership" (191). Echoes of Paulinus's poem appear in an early fifth-century Gallic poem, the *Carmen ad uxorem*, in which a husband urges his wife to follow him in his devotion to a chaste marriage. In this fascinating poem, the author displays a deep knowledge of Christian and secular literature, as the 16-verse opening in anacreontics that recalls Claudian's fescennines leads to elegiac praise of the inner harmony of chaste marriage as a shield against the socioeconomic chaos of post-invasion Gaul. Polymetry also plays a strategic role in Ennodius's epithalamium for Maximus (388 V). Ennodius, while recognizing the higher virtue of chastity, had to encourage a reluctant Maximus to embrace the conjugal duties of his terrestrial marriage. Thus an opening invocation of spring's bounty in elegiacs (cf. Gregory of Nazianzus) evolves into an invocation of the Muses (trochees), the appearance of Venus (appropriate Sapphics), and a call to action by her unnamed son (suitably protreptic hexameters; on late antique polymetry, see Consolino 2017). In the end Venus will claim her due, but only because the natural order and Ennodius's good-natured audience demand it (hendecasyllables). A different sort of wedding work deserves passing mention: the nine-book, prosimetric allegory "On the Marriage of Philology and Mercury" by Martianus Cappella. In between the opening elegiac hymn to Hymnaeus that fuses the epithalamic with the philosophic and his concluding iambic lament that old age has attenuated his Muse, Martianus interlaces dense, metaphorical poetry into his Menippean encyclopedia.

The most enduring form of late antique encomiastic poetry is Christian hymn. The simple, engaging iambic dimeters set in four-line stanzas that Ambrose composed to entertain the crowd during the occupation of Milan's Arian church in 386 set the standard for subsequent Latin hymns. But Latin hymnody had its birth a generation before when Hilary of Poitiers, inspired by liturgical song during his banishment in the East, composed anti-Arian hymns in classical forms. By late antiquity, Greek liturgical song had a long tradition that had emerged from the conventions of Semitic verse. Latin authors, in contrast, repurposed classical modes and meters (although we also encounter hymns in free psalmic prose by Marius Victorinus, Augustine, and the fourth-century *Psalmus Reponsorius*). The Ambrosian tradition was advanced by notable authors like Sedulius, Ennodius, and especially Fortunatus, whose trochaic *Pange lingua* and iambic *Vexilla regis* continue to be sung during Holy Week. Latin hymnody in this mode flourished for centuries, long after other classicizing forms evanesced. In contrast, the withering of pagan festivals diminished and then occulted the need for traditional hymns, although Orphic and Neoplatonic hymns continued to be composed in the fifth century.

Many antique poets during this period composed in multiple genres, cultivating a literary eclecticism and appealing to divergent audiences. In the East Agathias (d. 582) is best known for the roughly 100 spirited, elegant epigrams that he published together in a *Cycle* of contemporary poets; it would become one of the building blocks of the *Greek Anthology*. Agathias also continued Procopius's history (in prose) and composed a collection of erotic myths, the *Daphniaca*, in nine hexametric books (now lost). A similar eclecticism prevails among his contemporaries. Epigrams in Nonnian style by Christodorus of Coptus, describing 80 statues in Zeuxippus's gymnasium, survive. Christodorus also composed *patria*, historical epic, and hexameter poems on the disciples of the Neoplatonic philosopher Proclus. Although most of Claudian's near 10 000 lines support the political program of Stilicho and Honorius, he began mythological epics on the gigantomachy and the abduction of Proserpina, and composed more than 50 short poems on a diverse range of subjects, including exotic animals, sexual deviants, literary criticism, friendship, scenic vistas, statues, Christ, tourist traps, royal gifts, scientific curiosities, and more (we also find a few poems in Greek by Claudian and spurious poems by less accomplished poets). Even more varied in scale and genre are the compositions by Ausonius. Alongside prose works – prefaces to poetic works, a panegyric for Gratian, and letters to friends, including Paulinus of Nola – we find commemoratory works for his family (*Parentalia*) and his predecessors in Bordeaux (*Professores*); an epigrammatic cycle for a comely German slave (*Bissula*); strange works like the *Cupido cruciatus* (a lengthy description of a painting); scholastic works on the calendar, myth, geography, and the most difficult questions a teacher could face; translations from Greek; a smattering of Christian poems (e.g. the *Versus Paschales*); and his longest work, the *Mosella*, an encomiastic description of the idyllic, florid Gallic river in 483 "divine" hexameters (according to Symmachus in a letter to the poet). Although the majority of his poems were composed in hexameters and elegiacs, Ausonius was equally dexterous in lyric meters: His *Ephemeris*, an account of the bureaucrat's day, uses different meters for each of the day's different tasks. Through Ausonius's many poems there emerges a detailed picture of his career, town, teachers, students, friends, frenemies, and family – his wife was a poet too and wove her poems into tapestries (*Epigr*. 27–29).

The late antique impulse to explain one's poetic practices in prose preface and proemic verse is reflected in an abundance of autobiographical poetry. When Justinian summoned the African bishop Verecundus to Constantinople, Verecundus attempted to win favor by composing a verse apologia, a *lamentabile carmen* according to Isidore. Paulinus of Pella, a descendant of Ausonius, composed the remarkable, autobiographical *Eucharisticos*, which recounts in 616 hexameters how, after a good education in Bordeaux and an advantageous marriage in 396, he lost his worldly fortune and domestic tranquility to a series of personal and geopolitical disasters, a crucible that confirmed his faith. Ausonius's contemporary, Gregory of Nazianzus, was remarkable not only for the diverse abundance of his Greek verse but also for the rich inner portrait of his poetic ambitions. Although eclipsed as a theologian, epistolographer, and orator by contemporaries, as a poet Gregory holds the field, composing 17 000 verses in nearly 400 poems, most in the last decade of his life after he resigned as Patriarch of Constantinople. He wrote theological poems on dogmatic and moral topics, epitaphs, epigrams, and poems on himself and his circle, all in classicizing hexameters, elegiacs, iambics, and lyrics. These poems testify to Gregory's vast erudition and his confidence in his own innovations, both great (treating familiar topics in unexpected forms) and small (purposefully admitting unpoetic words and quantities). Gregory's poems convey a nuanced portrait of his beliefs, affections, and moods. While delivering spiritual instruction, he repeatedly returns to the question of why he wrote poetry in lengthy poems in elegiacs (*Laments on the Suffering of His Own Soul*), hexameters (*Things Concerning Himself*), and iambics (*On His Life*, in 1949 iambic trimeters). For Gregory, poetry disciplined his thought and expression, while its sweetness would soften the bitterness of his instruction and soothe him in his old age. But Gregory also had a larger purpose in mind: the supplanting of the pagan canon with a new raft of poetry that extolled and defended the faith. The variety and immensity of his corpus were not incidental to this aim.

Prudentius, a Spaniard who held administrative positions under Theodosius I, was the first Latin poet since Horace to craft a significant lyric corpus (nearly 10 000 lines). With deft virtuosity, Prudentius aimed to create a new canon of Christian Latin poetry that could stand alongside the pagan classics. Within the collected edition that Prudentius published in 405 were hymns for the daily round and Christians festivals (*Cathemerinon*) and gory accounts of martyrdom in Horatian lyrics (*Peristephanon*), a didactic meditation on original sin in iambics (*Hamartigenia*), and the first overtly Christian allegorical poem (*Psychomachia*), as well as polemic, didactic, and ekphrastic works in hexameters, including 49 tetrastichs describing the paintings in a church (cf. Paulinus's description of a like-decorated church [*Carmen* 27] and Rusticus Elpidius's hexametric triplets). In Vandal Spain, Dracontius, a senator with legal training, produced a compendium of epithalamia, dedicatory poems, and mythological poetry. He also composed small paraphrastic poems: *In laudibus Dei*, a three-book account of creation, sin, and salvation; the *Satisfactio*, a penitential poem in Ovidian elegiacs that sought forgiveness from God (and the Vandal king); and the *Orestes*, a sympotic dialogue in 974 hexameters.

Nearly two centuries after Prudentius, Fortunatus self-consciously sought to write himself into this emergent Christian canon (Roberts 2009). His 11 books of verse epistles, hymns, and various congratulatory and occasional poems (including panegryics for Merovingian kings and an account of a trip on Moselle) effortlessly fused classical and Christian modes of poetic expression in diverse forms and meters. Standing above these was Fortunatus's masterwork, his four-book hagiography of Saint Martin of Tours. Such confident, classicizing, Christian poetry had a bravura inception. Near the end of Constantine's reign, the anonymous Gallic poet of the *Laudes Domini* visited his wife's tomb. When the tomb burst opens, she beckoned him to the beyond. Over the next 114 stately hexameters – and with dashes of Virgil, Ovid, Horace, and Lucretius – the poet intertwines accounts of local miracles with biblical cosmology, building to a prayer that Christ protect Constantine, the greatest emperor by virtue of his conversion. Early on we also catch hints of Christian allegorical poetry, *The Phoenix*, whose 85 elegiac couplets have been ascribed (not without considerable debate) to the Constantinian author Lactantius (Roberts 2017). Although the poem lacks overt Christian references, it is often recognized as an early allegory of Man's Fall and Redemption.

The fourth and early fifth centuries experienced a dramatic renewal of epigram in both the Latin West and the Greek East. The aesthetic trends that animate late antique poetics would seem to make inevitable a turn to the epigrammatic: passion for ekphrastic and epideictic composition both in subject and style; preference for the commingling of genres and tones that accompany Alexandrian *Kleinwerk*; fondness for juxtaposition and paradox; and, especially, the fragmentation and subordination of narrative in favor of a refined focus on the individual episode. After the high imperial trio of Strato, Ammianus, and Lucian, Greek epigram found sporadic practitioners during the third century. But the fourth century witnessed poetic production and creativity of a greater magnitude. Gregory of Nazianzus repurposed traditional epigram into the service of Christian panegyric. Elegant erotic compositions by Rufinus and the barbed epigrams of Palladas – who in turn rejected erotic themes, insulted his fellow *grammatici*, complained about his students, and peevishly lamented paganism's eclipse – serve as the vanguard of an epigrammatic revival that experienced its full flowering during the reigns Anastasius I and Justinian.

Outstripping even this literary resurgence, Greek epigraphical poetry proliferated from the fourth century onwards. Often these inscribed epigrams were minor affairs, whether personal – e.g. a fragmentary epigram dedicating a dining couch to the martyr Trophimus (*AP* 1.18) – or commemorating moments of high social significance – e.g. the couplet that commemorates the removal of pagan imagery from Hagia Sophia (1.1). But verse inscriptions could also be monumental in every sense of the word. Among the modest Christian inscriptions of the first book of the *Greek Anthology* lurks a monster: 76 Nonnian hexameters commemorating Anicia Juliana's renovation of the Church of St. Polyeuctus originally built by Eudocia

(Whitby 2006). Because of its scale, the poem was long thought to be a literary epigram in praise of Juliana masquerading as a dedicatory inscription. But excavations in 1960 revealed that the poem, inscribed in letters 11 cm high, dominated over 250 square meters of the church's nave and narthex. Eudocia, herself an ambitious poet, as we have seen, also commemorated buildings in verse. A 17-verse hexameter fragment of her dedication is inscribed on the bath complex at Hammat Gader. This epigraphic habit continued well into the sixth century when 19 epigrams describing the bas-relief scenes of filial love towards mothers were added to the Pergamene Temple of Apollonis in Cyzicus (*AP* 3). The faltering meter of these poems attests both to the enduring popularity of verse inscriptions and the accelerating breakdown of classical prosody during this period.

In the mid-sixth century, a circle of epigrammatists emerged in Constantinople: Agathias, Paulus Silentarius, Julian Aegyptus, Macedonius, and Leontinus, along with Christodorus, Marianus, Theaetetus, Damocharis, and others (Rapp 2005). These poets engaged hoary themes: eros, ekphrasis, courtesans, and freaks. They adored charioteers: 54 poems inscribed in the Hippodrome survive. They praised and blamed contemporaries: Julian on the usurper Hypatius (7.591–592) and the grammarian Theodorus (7.594); Agathias on Joanna the chanteuse (7.612). They commemorated the dead in poems poignant (e.g. 7.583, for a mother and infant who died during childbirth; 7.589, for Eustorgius, a 17-year-old law student) and jocose (7.204–205, Agathias sacrifices his cat à la Polyxena after it decapitated his pet partridge). They had their special interests: Julian added eight ekphrases to the corpus on Myron's cow (67.738–739, 793–798); Paul composed the most sensuous erotics of the group; Leontius specialized in pithy poems on the paintings of dancers that lined the streets of Constantinople (16.283–288; cf. Agathias 5.297). Some drew from the full tradition of epigram; others looked to the recent past (e.g. Agathias's reworking of erotic epigrams by Rufinus and Fronto (5.218 and 220~5.41 and 43)). Still others favored particular *veteres*, like Macedonius's imitations of Leonidas of Terentum or the dueling riffs on Posidippus by Agathias and Julian (9.359~5.302, 9.446). If the themes of these Justinianic epigrammatist were traditional, their language showed the irresistible urge to apply the grandiose linguistic, stylistic, and metrical features of Nonnus to minor poetry, occasionally even incorporating half-lines from Nonnus into their poems (9.619 Agathias~*D.* 13.220). Their preference for Nonnian superabundance is evidenced by their fondness for neologisms, erudite detail, and, above all, a scale that is alien to traditional epigram. Only Leontinus shows a preference for the four-verse standard, while Agathias was at ease offering a languid 20-line account of Nicostratus's philosophizing (11.354).

Latin epigram had suffered a deep senescence after Martial. But as the fourth century unwound, epigram reemerged as a node of readerly interest and compositional energy. To the first half of this century, we might assign Pentadius's echoing couplets and several poems by Tiberianus, the governor of Gaul in 355. But it was in the second half of the fourth and early fifth centuries that Latin epigram flourished with the work of Ausonius, Claudian, Probinus, Naucellius, and the other epigrammatists of the *Epigrammata Bobiensia*, an uneven farrago of 72 epigrams and short elegies. Enthusiasm for Latin epigram would proliferate in the fifth century, in Avianus's 42 elegiac fables and Prosper's distichic maxims, through Sidonius's experimental *longa*, and eventually culminating in the eclectic epigrammatic collections of Luxorius, the most Martialian of late antique epigrammatists, and Ennodius, who composed short poems in a Claudianic mode and also embedded poems within prose à la Sidonius. In the sixth century, we encounter two peculiar elegists. Maximianus, a friend of the philosopher-politician Boethius who interlaced his *Consolatio* with short poems, composed six lengthy, artful elegies in which love serves as a pivot to considerations about mortality and the hardships of senility. Around the same time, Eucheria, a Gallo-Roman aristocrat from Provence and (perhaps) recipient of letters and poems from Fortunatus, cast her savage rejection of a low-born man who dared court her in a long series of elegiac adynata – the longest such catalog in Latin poetry.

Epigram, born in the memorialization of the dead, regained its role in commemoration, renovation, and ideological appropriation during late antiquity. Approximately one in five of the *carmina epigraphica Latina* date from this period, yielding a corpus of over 425 poems, three-quarters of which are epitaphic. In 384, Vettius Agorius Praetextatus, one of the beloved lions of the old Roman aristocracy, passed away on the eve of his consulship. On three sides of a marble statue base was carved a wonderful funerary poem in iambic senarii that appears to have been composed by Praetextatus and his wife, Fabia Aconia Paulina. Two sides preserve Praetextatus's praise of his wife, a virtuous *matrona* and devotee of the old religion. On the third, Paulina praises her husband's career, his character, and his literary achievements. Her 41-line poem ends with a poignant (albeit expected) lament:

> Everything is gone now...
> But still blessed, because I am yours
> And was, and after death soon will be. (*CIL* 6.1779)

Epigraphic poems are one of the few venues in which we can hear the voices of female poets. Around 355 "mournful Constantia" composed a brief, classicizing epitaph for her Christian husband (*AL* 660 B*). Anicia Fultonia Proba, granddaughter of the centonist, may have composed the verse epitaph in 24 elegiac couplets for her husband, Petronius Probus, who dedicated to Theodosius a collection of poems by himself, his father, and grandfather (his sons continued the family hobby). A remarkable example of joint composition is found on the Dalmatian estate of Pelagia and Licinianus, *quaestor* and friend of Sidonius. The couple takes turns praising a spring and its resident nymph in epigrams of 10 and six lines respectively (*CIL* 3.1894). We also find many poems by men in memory of their wives: a hexametric diptych for Agape (*ILCV* 2392); seven Lucretian and Virgilianizing lines for Julia Modesta (ca. 320; *Ann. Epigr.* 1948, 107); Laberius's polymetric cycle of four epitaphs for his wife Bassa (*CLE* 1559; cf. *CLE* 2152, for M. Aurelius Timavius).

Paulina and Praetextatus's poem of mutual commemoration was erected by order of the Senate in the ancient epicenter of Roman political life, the Forum. The same year saw the passing of Pope Damasus, who during his papacy had created a new form of Christian commemoration by composing allusive, dynamic epigrams to accompany his restoration of Christian buildings on the periphery of the city. Jerome, who composed hexametric epitaphs for Paula, approved of his efforts – he was "elegant in composing verse" (Jer. *De Vir*. 103) – and his poems influenced the style and poetic programs of the most important Christian authors of the next generation: Paulinus and Prudentius. The richness of Christian epitaphic verse is on display in the Coemeterium of Saint Agnes on the Via Nomentana. The site was monumentalized in the 340s by Constantia, who commemorated her patronage in 14 hexameters. Damasus added a 10-verse epigram during his renovation of the site. But Agnes's shrine contained no fewer that 22 other verse inscriptions, most of which are private epitaphs, including one for the fifth-century senator and panegyricist Flavius Merobaudes (*CIL* 6.31983 *ICUR* 8.21048).

Constantia's inscription was just one component of a pro-regime "public relations campaign waged through the inscription of Latin verse" that included epigrams in the Vatican Basilia, the 24-hexameter poem carved into Constantius's obelisk in the Circus Maximus that yoked his *gestae* with the the stone's miraculous journey to Rome, and the epitaph inscribed on the magnificent sarcophagus of Junius Bassius (Trout 2015, p. 41). After this mid-century imperial peak, Latin verse inscriptions became more a vehicle for upwardly mobile provincials than state propaganda. It is in this context that we can understand the verse commemorations of Claudian, Merobaudes, and Sidonius erected in the Forum of Trajan, as well as the numerous quasi-epitaphic works of Ausonius and Ennodius (Kelly 2013). Commemoration in verse could also take a more grandiose form: e.g. the *Life of Proclus* by the late-fifth-century Neoplatonic philosopher Marinus or Eudocia's fragmentary epyllion on the martyrdom of St. Cyprian; Avitus's 666-line poem lauding the virginity of his deceased sister, Fuscina (cf. Damascius's encomium for the wife of Hermesias); and the hagiographies of Martin by Fortunatus and (the less-gifted) Paulinus of Petricordia.

In appreciating the different aesthetic principles that animated late antique authors and their audiences, we should not forget that practical concerns often motivated the composition of verse. The purpose may be slight: a memento shared between friends, as were many of the small poems by Ausonius or Claudian. But minor poetry was also yoked to didactic purpose. Stobaeus preserves 73 lines of a Greek didactic poem by Naumachius that counseled Christian women how best to behave in life and marriage. Poets might explicate the duality of Christ's nature (the 137-hexameter *De Iesu Christo Deo et Homine*) or embellish the story of Christ's crucifixion and resurrection through an account of his harrowing of hell in the 108 hexameters of the *Triumphus Christi heroicus*, whose Pluto attempts to rally his demonic troops, only to see them submit to Christ. Christian poets also sought to ease anxiety during the tumultuous fifth century. Orientius, Bishop of Auch, used just over 1000 classicizing elegiac lines to instruct the faithful how they could strive towards heaven in the deteriorating world of early-fifth century Gaul. The *De Providentia Divina* tackles the question of why the faithful and sinful were alike afflicted by the barbarian invaders. Paulinus of Béziers crafts a hexametric dialogue in which an abbot and two monks, one of whom has recently traveled through a devastated Gaul, discuss moral decline, drawing heavily on satirical reproaches of women. The pagan poet Rutilius Namatianus was notoriously in a less-forgiving mood recounting his sad departure from Rome ca. 417 and his journey through the ruined landscape of Italy and Gaul. We also find a category of poems that straddle the line between hexameter didactic and polemic. Prosper documents and condemns the Semipelagians in his *De ingratiis*, a theological treatise in 1002 lines. The pseudo-Tertullian *Carmen adversus Marcionitas* attacks heretical doctrines; the 122-hexameter *Carmen contra paganos* takes aim at Praetextatus, anti-Christian politician and translator of Greek philosophy and verse (Cameron 2011, p. 318). The plain style of these poems further suggests that their audience was not primarily among the cultural elite. In contrast, Prudentius's *Apotheosis* infuses polemics against heresies into an elegant didactic poem on the Trinity, while his two books of his *Contra Symmachum* rehearse the long-settled controversy over the Altar of Victory. The most-read didactic work is also the shortest and least Christian: The *Disticha Catonis*, a pseudographic collection of ca. 130 hexametric couplets attributed to Cato Censorius (or Uticensis) but dating from the late third to fourth century, propounds a generally Stoic approach to life and its troubles.

Traditional didactic topics endure in longer form as well, as the surviving hymnic proem to a didactic poem on marine life and the iambic works by the senator Avienius, Symmachus's friend and translator of Aratus's *Phaenomena*, attest. Avienius's works engaged the antiquarian interests of the senatorial class of the later fourth century (the set that provides the personages for Macrobius's *Saturnalia*). This antiquarian interest and choice of meter were also manifest in the East. Helladius of Antinupolis composed a didactic encyclopedia, a *Chrestomathia* or "Things Worth Knowing," on linguistic, literary, and antiquarian topics in four books of iambic trimeters. If the audience for antiquarian didactics was predominantly aristocratic and learned, Christian authors, too, turned to iambic poetry as a vehicle for more popular education. In a papyrus we discover an anapestic abecedarius instructing the reader on good Christian living. Amphilochius, a friend of Gregory Nazianzus, lays out in a scant 337 iambs a program for how Christians should interact with the secular world.

In the colonization of genres by iambic meters, we witness a piece of the progressive breakdown of the old hierarchies and categories that had dominated Latin and Greek poetic composition since the Hellenistic period. By the end of the sixth century, most poets had put aside the old meters (Agosti 2001). The Celtic poet Columba more or less followed classical grammar, but his language (a fusion of biblical and ecclesiastic Latin with odd words also seen in the prosimetric *Hisperica famina*) and form (rhythmic, rhyming abecadarii) mark his hymns as decidedly non-Classical. For Greeks, the increasing turn to iambic verse acknowledged the shift in Greek pronunciation that had long since decoupled its quantities from the old meters. The increasing regimentation of the hexameter – Nonnus admitted only nine patterns of the hexameter; Paulus Silentarius only six – was a rearguard action, an attempt to match classical quantitative rhythm with contemporary tonal accent. The iambic epic, panegyric, and epigrams of George of Pisidia (early seventh) often stand as the signpost that we have left the classicizing world of late antiquity and embarked fully into the Byzantine milieu. Indeed, we might seem to have crossed into a new world when we read George's *Hexameron*, a 1894-verse account of the Creation in the 12-syllable iambics that would dominate Byzantine verse. (Michael Psellus, the great 11-century intellectual, would rank George above Euripides!) But even George composed his *On Human Life* and *On the Vanity of Life* in Nonnian hexameters. There always seems to be a further candidate for the last "last poet of antiquity." A generation after Columba, the talented Celtic poet Columban would still compose quantitative poetry, including an epistle in adonics and the spirited *Song of the Oar* in hexameters. A generation later still, Eugenius II, Bishop of Toledo, supplemented Dracontius's *Satisfactio* and composed around 100 epigrams in simple but correct Latin steeped in the new canon of late antique Christian poets. Although his prosody often lapses from classical standards, there is a sense that these are not missteps taken in ignorance but, like the lapses of Gregory three centuries before, conscious decisions to slough off moribund strictures. Instead of a decisive break with the past or threshold crossed, we face the conundrum of the ship of Theseus. The sweep of late antique minor and occasional poetry reveals the tenacious endurance of the old forms alongside the new until at last, we observe something that in many essential ways remains the same – yet is undeniably different.

REFERENCES

Agosti, Gianfranco. (2001). Late antique iambics and *Iambikè Idéa*. In: *Iambic Ideas* (ed. Alberto Cavarzere, Antonio Aloni, and Alessandro Barchiesi), 219–248. Lanham, MD: Rowman and Littlefield.

Bastiaensen, A.A.R.(2007). Biblical poetry in Latin liturgical texts. In: *Poetry and Exegesis in Premodern Latin Christianity* (ed. Willemien Otten and Karla Pollmann), 265–274. Leiden: Brill.

Cameron, Alan. (2011). *The Last Pagans of Rome*. New York: Oxford University Press.

Charlet, Jean-Louis. (1988). Aesthetic trends in late Latin poetry (325–410). *Philologus* 132: 74–85.

Consolino, Franca Ela. (2017). Polymetry in late Latin poems: Some observations on its meaning and functions. In: *The Poetics of Late Latin Literature* (ed. Jas Elsner and Jesús Hernández Lobato), 100–124. New York: Oxford University Press.

Dihle, Albrecht. (1994). *Greek and Latin Literature of the Roman Empire*: New York: Routledge.

Formisano, Marco. (2007). Towards an aesthetic paradigm of late antiquity. *Antiquité Tardive* 15: 277–284.

Kelly, Gavin. (2013). Sidonius and Claudian. In: *New Approaches to Sidonius Apollinaris* (ed. Johannes A. van Waarden and Gavin Kelly), 171–192. Leuven: Peeters.

McGill, Scott. (2005). *Virgil Recomposed: The Mythological and Secular Centos in Antiquity*. New York: Oxford University Press.

Rapp, Claudia. (2005). Literary culture under Justinian. In: *The Cambridge Companion to the Age of Justinian* (ed. Michael Maas), 376–397. New York. Cambridge University Press.

Roberts, Michael. (2009). *The Humblest Sparrow*. Ann Arbor, MI: University of Michigan Press.

Roberts, Michael. (2017). Lactantius's *Phoenix* and late Latin poetics. In: *The Poetics of Late Latin Literature* (ed. Jas Elsner and Jesús Hernández Lobato), 373–390. New York: Oxford University Press.

Trout, Dennis. (2015). *Damasus of Rome: The Epigraphic Poetry*. New York: Oxford University Press.

Squire, Michael. (2017). POP art: The optical poetics of Publilius Optatianus Porfyrius. In: *The Poetics of Late Latin Literature* (ed. Jas Elsner and Jesús Hernández Lobato), 25–99. Oxford: Oxford University Press.

Ware, Catherine. (2012). *Claudian and the Roman Epic Tradition*. New York: Cambridge University Press.

Whitby, Mary. (2006). The St Polyeuktos epigram (*AP* 1.10): A literary perspective. In: *Greek Literature in Late Antiquity: Dynamism, Didacticism, Classicism* (ed. Scott Fitzgerald Johnson), 159–188. New York: Routledge.

CHAPTER SIXTEEN

Christian Poetry

Laura Miguélez-Cavero and Scott McGill

In the second book of his *Epistles* (*Ep.* 2.9.4), the fifth-century CE bishop and writer Sidonius Apollinaris describes a library he encountered while visiting the estates of two friends. In the library devotional works were placed in an area for women and rhetorical works in an area for men. The latter comprised Christian and non-Christian authors who resembled one another in their *scientia* or "artistic skill," and who were similar in their style although their doctrines differed (*in causis disparibus dicendi parilitatem*): "Here was read Augustine, there Varro, here Horace, there Prudentius" (*hinc Augustinus hinc Varro, hinc Horatius hinc Prudentius lectitabantur*).

Sidonius's account reflects a significant innovation in late antiquity: the development of Christian poetry, that is, poetry on Christian subject matter and thought, represented by Prudentius in *Ep.* 2.9.4, within the broader field of Christian literature. As Sidonius understood when he noted the disparities in *causae* and when he distinguished Horace from Prudentius (*hinc… hinc*), Christian content is an obvious line of demarcation between Christian and classical verse. With that content came new poetic forms as well as new purposes and functions for poetry. Authors were committed not only to Christian truth but also to Christian edification and exegesis, and they sought to celebrate and advance Christianity, including, at times, in specific devotional settings. At the same time, there is a far deeper connection between Christian and classical poetry than that which Sidonius identifies when he notes the similar styles and *scientia* of the authors in the library. Most Christian poetry in late antiquity was inextricably bound to the classical

---

A Companion to Late Antique Literature, First Edition.
Edited by Scott McGill and Edward J. Watts.
© 2018 John Wiley & Sons, Inc. Published 2018 by John Wiley & Sons, Inc.

Greek and Latin literary past. This is because Christian poetry developed within Greco-Roman culture and took much from it. The poetry was hybrid verse that blended classical literature with the Bible, with Christian doctrine and thought, and with Christian ideas about what poetry was and did. Responses to the classical tradition were varied, and they show dependence and independence, continuity and distance, accommodation and polemics, descent and dissent (Roberts 1989, pp. 122–131; Shorrock 2011, pp. 45–46, Elsner and Hernández Lobato 2017, pp. 3–16). The relationship manifests itself in a range of ways: Christian authors recurrently situate themselves and their work against their classical forebears; resist and reject elements of classical/pagan culture and literature in their poetics, even as they fuse the Christian and classical in their texts; modify and renew classical literary genres, thus adapting classical modes of expression and representation to Christian subjects (and vice versa); incorporate classical patterns of thought into their texts; echo classical language; and imitate specific classical models.

16.1 Greek Christian Poetry

16.1.1 Christian Poetics

Constantine's accession to the throne does not seem to have had an immediate effect on the composition of Greek poetry. On the contrary, when the Emperor Julian passed a series of laws that de facto banned Christians from teaching classical literature or philosophy on the grounds that they could not uphold with faith the contents of their teaching (*CTh* 13,3,5 = *CIust* 10,53,7; Iul. *Epist.* 42, with Banchich 1993), according to two late antique historians (Socrates *HE* 3.16.1–5; Sozom. *HE* 5.18), a certain Apollinaris of Laodicea produced paraphrases of the books of the Old Testament, imitating Homer and the tragedians. Nothing remains of this enterprise, if it really occurred (Agosti 2001a, pp. 70–71), but Julian's monopolization of classical culture seems to have caused learned Christians to realize the need to make explicit their right to operate within the classical tradition.

Thus Gregory of Nazianzus (Van Dam 2002, pp. 189–202; McLynn 2006) championed in several speeches a cultural resistance to Julian's policies and his right to enjoy classical literature (*Or.* 15 and 4, esp. 4.103–4, differentiating Hellenic people and Hellenic religion, and 4.108 on poetry). Other Christian notables were more cautious: Basil of Caesarea recommended in his *Ad adulescentes* (Van Dam 2002, pp. 181–188) traditional classical studies (including the reading of Homer) as preliminary to the study of Christian texts.

The at least theoretical concern with the harming of Christian souls in contact with immoral poetry spurred a creative middle way: the composition of poetry on Christian topics in classical style. This implied the double compositional challenge of bringing classical tradition closer to Christianity and effectively transforming Christianity to look and sound classical. Additionally, poetry could be used to advance spiritually Christian believers and lukewarm converts, and as a means of learned seduction of non-Christians, with the complete conversion of society in mind.

A late antique description of the poetic middle way can be found in Gregory's justification of his writing of poetry in *On His Own Verses* II.1.39, lines 34–57 (McGuckin 2006; Milovanovic-Barham 1997). His first reason is to control his prolixity (poetry required more work than prose), which implies a Christian ascetics of the word, a serious poetic intent, in opposition to playful compositions on classical topics. Secondly, his poetry is written for the sake of (Christian) youth and those who enjoy literature, leading them toward the good and sweetening the harsh aspects of the Christian commandments, that is, as a substitute for other (non-Christian) types of poetry, and with a spiritual intent on the part of poet and reader. The third reason is linked to the second: Gregory writes because the *xenoi* (lit. "the strangers" – both "pagans" and "heretics" – Simelidis 2009, pp. 25–27) should not necessarily be better skilled in *logoi* (words). This opens up the Christian competition with classical authors and an orthodox (anti-heretical) approach. Poetry is also a consolation for Gregory's old age, and he compares his poetry with a swan's final brilliant song, his verses being for him as important as his speeches. Finally, he invites the wise to enter his mind through his poetry (2.1.39, lines 58–59), contrasting poetry as a means to portray his "real" inner Christian soul and the sophistic appearances he assumes in his speeches, a frequent basis for the evaluation of his career (especially in Constantinople).

16.1.2 Liturgy

Following the tradition of the classical world, hymns were at the center of Christian worship as noted in early Christian writings (Eph. 5:19–20, Col. 3:16; McGuckin 2008; Brucker 2014). The few second- and third-century extant hymns suggest that formal variety (prose, rhythmic prose in which accents are loosely regulated, different metrical forms) was the norm (Löhr 2014; Leonhard 2014). These include *P.Oxy.* 1786, a hymn with musical notation, written in a quantitative meter; the anapaestic hymn to Christ preserved by Clement of Alexandria (*Paedagogus* 3.12.101); and the iambic hymn to Christ, bridegroom of the Church, cited by Methodius of Olympus at the end of his *Banquet*.

From the fourth century we have Gregory of Nazianzus (see above and infra) and Synesius of Cyrene (370–413), whose nine hymns in ionic meter illustrate his knowledge of Neoplatonic philosophy and classical culture as much as his Christian beliefs (Amande 2008; Di Pasquale Barbanti 2008; Roques 2007). The creative culmination of the genre is Romanos the Melodist (sixth century CE), who composed liturgical hymns in Justinian's Constantinople. His *kontakia* (a proem followed by a series of strophes in the same rhythm, each ending with the same refrain; the initial letters of the line form an acrostic) adapted the biblical narrative to the events of the liturgical calendar, supplying additional details to inscribe the final composition in the general economy of salvation (Krueger 2004, pp. 159–188).

16.1.3 Other Spiritual Uses of Poetry

Oracles in verse (Busine 2005a) were popular in the eastern part of the empire from at least the second century CE. Because of their focus on theological reflection about the nature of god, the function of the traditional gods, and the immortality of the soul, verse oracles popularized a "theological *koine*," a pool of poetic expressions to describe the divine acceptable to worshippers of all creeds. These oracles came to circulate in collections (Busine 2005b) that Christian writers often quote as an external confirmation of their faith (Busine 2005a, pp. 373–431).

A Christian oracular tradition came into being under the authority of the Sibyl. The *Oracula Sibyllina* include a number of Christian books that draw on the tradition of the oracular hexameter. Books 1–2 review the history of the human race over 10 generations, from the creation of the world and of man to the end of the world and the Day of Judgment (Lightfoot 2007). Book 6 is a hymn (28 verses) and books 7–8 are frequently cited by Lactantius.

The *Codex Visionum* (*P.Bodmer* 29–38), a papyrus codex dated to the turn of the fifth century, preserves some poems not extant elsewhere (Hurst and Rudhardt 2002; Miguélez-Cavero 2013; Agosti 2015), which were copied as tools for personal and community instruction as well as meditation. For their composition a number of classical and Christian elements were combined in a novel way: basic forms of classical rhetoric (comparison, paraphrase, ethopoeia), biblical narratives (*On Abraham, Words of Cain, Words of Abel*); standard Christological themes (*[Eulogy] of the Lord Jesus, The Lord to Those Who Suffer*); some frequent topics on Christian conversion (*Speech to the Righteous*); and the generic forms of visionary literature (*Vision of Dorotheus*).

16.1.4 Gregory of Nazianzus (Late 320s–390)

As the author of 17 000 lines, Gregory was the most prolific Christian poet of antiquity. The Maurist edition (Paris, 1778–1840), reprinted by J.P. Migne in his *Patrologia Graeca*, vols. 37–38 (Paris, 1858–1862), organized his poems in four sections: dogmatic (I.1.1–38), moral (I.2.1–40), self-referential (II.1.1–99), and referring to others (II.2.1–8). These sections, however, do not reflect the variety and innovative quality of Gregory's production: He operated in different meters (Agosti and Gonnelli 1995, pp. 359–409) and transformed a number of preexisting genres with a Christian twist to enhance the spiritual advancement of a broad audience.

Gregory composed a number of devotional texts (Daley 2006, pp. 165–78), including hymns (I.1.30, 33), and prayers (I.1.35, 37 and II.1.3, 24–26, 74). He also tried his hand at biblical paraphrase (I.1.20–27; Palla 1989), reducing the biblical accounts to the most essential details, perhaps to help in memorizing the Scripture.

As for didactic poetry, the *Poemata Arcana* (I.1.1–5, 7–9; Sykes 1970; Daley 2012) describe central revealed truths of the Christian faith. Although the formal influence of the Homeric hymns is visible (Faulkner 2010), they have been mostly read as Gregory's attempt to create a Christian version of classical didactic poetry of the philosophical type (Sykes 1985; Moreschini and Sykes 1997, pp. 57–60): where earlier didactic forms inform and entertain, the *Poemata* seek the involvement of the reader and try to exact from him or her a confession of faith (Meinel 2009).

The *Carmina quae spectant ad alios* (II.2.1–8) is a series of verse epistles (Demoen 1997), each addressed to a particular person to deal with a concrete "pastoral" problem, but with a potential wider readership in mind. Thus, no. 6, "To Olympias," on her marriage, focuses on the general necessity of *sophrosyne* (Whitby 2008), and 7, "To Nemesianus," explains the principles of Christianity and attacks paganism at first sight in order to convert the dedicatee, although the text is suitable for a broader pagan audience.

Book 8 of the *Palatine Anthology* gathers 256 epigrams by Gregory, mostly epitaphs (with more than one poem dedicated to the same subject, e.g. 52 to Gregory's mother), and some on funerary matters (e.g. against tomb desecrators: Floridi 2013; Palla and Moroni 2013). The composition of Christian poetic epitaphs illustrates to what point Christianity had permeated the local establishment of Cappadocia at the time (McGuckin 2006, p. 204).

Gregory also composed polemical poems (Agosti 2001b, pp. 221, 231–233), both the more general moral(izing) diatribe (I.2.10 *On virtue*; I.2.25 *On wrath*; I.2.27 *On true nobility*; I.2.35 *On Philosophical Poverty*) and invectives on individuals and groups (I.2.28 *Against the Rich*; II.1.12–13 against improper bishops; II.1.40–41 and II.1.11.750–1037 against Maximus).

Finally, Gregory is well known for his "autobiographical" poems (II.1.1–99), including *On His Own Affairs* (II.1.1), *On His Own Life* (II.1.12), and *On His Own Verses* (II.1.39). Gregory gives poetic voice to a wider literary trend of personal apology and philosophical reflection (e.g. Augustine's *Confessions*), as a means to legitimize his position (McGuckin 2001; Elm 2015). As instances of authoritative recording of events, these poems are similar to historiographical writings, but for their focus on the divine they also seek to transform historiography into a form of devotion (Abrams Rebillard 2012).

16.1.5 Christian Epics

The fifth century saw the full emergence of epic poetry as a Christian genre (Agosti 2001a; Whitby 2007, 2016). Books of the Bible were redrafted in Homeric hexameters, either reusing the existing lines (cento, i.e. a "patchwork" of Homeric lines) or writing verses anew (paraphrase). These poets hoped to claim parity with the classical tradition by "conquering" the genre with the highest cultural prestige, and presenting the Bible in an attractive way to the learned. The adherence to both the Bible text and Homeric principles of composition is praised in programmatic passages, in a double take on religious and poetic orthodoxy (Nodes 1993, pp. 9–20; Agosti 2001a; Faulkner 2014).

In the East the cento is linked to the Empress Eudocia (ca. 400–460; Agosti 2001a, pp. 74–85; Sowers 2008). She says that she corrected and expanded for publication a first edition of the *Homerocentones*, composed by a certain bishop Patricius (Usher 1998). The two prefaces present the poem as aiming at the diffusion of the Christian message (*AP* 1.119.3–4) and at pleasing God (praef. line 1). The prefaces also show concern with the harmony of the lines (praef. 6, 14), fidelity to Homer (praef. 8–9), and attainment of fame (praef. 36–38).

Eudocia is the presumed author, too, of *The Martyrdom of St. Cyprian*, a paraphrase in verse of a prose hagiography on the conversion of Cyprian, a magician from Antioch (Sowers 2008, pp. 164–268). Regarding paraphrases of the Bible, the *Paraphrase of the Psalms* attributed to Apollinaris was composed between 450 and 470 (Agosti 2001a, pp. 85–92; De Stefani 2008). The Psalmic metaphrast opens his poem with a *protheoria*, in which he claims that his poetic version of the Psalms recovers the beauty of the meter lost in the prosaic Greek translation of the Hebraic poems (lines 18–23) and claims to do so "so that the others too will know that every language proclaims Christ King" (Met. Ps. Pro. 32–33). "Others" has been taken to refer to the pagans (Agosti 2001a, p. 89). The metaphrast then explains (52–104) how the Holy Spirit reestablishes one single world language accessible to all, as when it appeared as tongues of fire on the Apostles, whose words were then heard by all peoples (after *Acts* 2:2–11).

The *Paraphrase of the Gospel of John* (21 books, one per chapter of the gospel), was written in the central decades of the fifth century by Nonnus of Panopolis (Accorinti 2016, pp. 28–32). The *Paraphrase* follows strictly the sequence of events of the Gospel text and expands individual details with elements imported from theological exegesis, especially from the *Commentary of the Gospel of St. John* by Cyril of Alexandria (Franchi 2016; Simelidis 2016), and with different forms of literary embellishment in epic style (e.g. expressions of time, epic epithets, brief descriptions of places).

16.1.6 Buildings and Poetry

The construction of churches and other buildings by Christian patrons led to inscriptions in verse celebrating their achievement. Thus, the first book of the *Palatine Anthology* gathers 123 epigrams (Waltz 1928, pp. 3–47), mostly copied from inscriptions engraved on monuments to preserve the memory of their builders or restorers (1–18 from monuments of Constantinople and its outskirts; 21–30 from churches, on Christ the Savior) or to explain the subject matter of a painting (32–94 – including cycles on the Nativity, 37–42; and on passages of the Gospels, 44–56). One of the most celebrated is *AP* 1.10, praising Anicia Juliana for building the church of St. Polyeuktos in Constantinople in the 520s (Whitby 2006; Agosti 2008b, pp. 689–692).

The celebration of the euergetic activities of the powerful was not restricted to inscriptions. Paul the Silentiary wrote the *Description of St. Sophia*, which was read aloud as part of the celebrations of the reopening of the church in the final days of 562 or the first days of 563. Paul addresses the Emperor Justinian and the patriarch Euthychius in two iambic proems and then focuses on the description itself. He also composed a supplementary *Description of the Ambo of St. Sophia*, and a number of mainly erotic epigrams. Paul's language and descriptive techniques are similar to those found in other celebratory descriptions (Whitby 2003a).

John of Gaza (Lauritzen 2015–2016) wrote a poetic description, too, entitled *Tabula Mundi*, but in this case on a painting that supposedly adorned a bathhouse: The personifications of physical elements and principles are governed by the Cross and the Trinity and the Ether crowning the World for its victory over Nature. The Christian intellectuals active in Gaza in late antiquity had made a considerable effort to assimilate Neoplatonic traditions of the description of the cosmos (Champion 2014), and John gave them poetic form.

16.1.7 Coda

Late Antique Greek Christian poetry comes to an end with the transition from classical to Byzantine accentuated metrics: The last poem in classical metrics is the *De vita humana* written in the first decades of the seventh century by George of Pisidia (Whitby 2003b, 2014). Most of the sociocultural elements that enabled the production of the poems listed in this chapter disappear gradually in the sixth century. There are, however, surprising discoveries, such as Dioscorus. A notary from Aphrodito, a small village halfway between Lycopolis and Panopolis, in Upper Egypt, Dioscorus kept a library with copies of the Homeric poems and Menander and composed encomia on local dignitaries under the double inspiration of Christian faith and classical culture (Fournet 1999; Agosti 2008a). Dioscorus spoke Greek and Coptic, had enjoyed a classical education and traveled to Constantinople, and composed a number of poems in classical meters, including different types of encomia and epithalamia.

16.2 Latin Christian Poetry

While Latin Christian poetry stretches back to the idiosyncratic *Instructiones* and *Carmen apologeticum* of the probably third-century CE Commodian, its history begins in earnest in the Age of Constantine with two poems. (I pass over Publilius Optatianus Porfyrius, who incorporates Christian imagery and content into his collection of figure poems but works more with non-Christian matter, including panegyric of Constantine.) One is the anonymous *Laudes Domini*, likely written between 317 and 324 (Salzano 2000, 2007, pp. 57–79; Schierl 2009). The 148-line hexameter text tells the miraculous story of a dead woman in the land of the Aedui who moved her hand to welcome her newly deceased husband as he was placed beside her in their joint tomb. The miracle, related briefly (7–31), is attributed to Christ (34–35), whom the narrator praises for the bulk of the poem; the prevailing purpose is to promote belief in the Resurrection and Christ's ability to grant eternal life. But the *Laudes* is not simply a Christian poem; it is also in fundamental ways a classicizing one. Meter, stylistic features (including rhetorical figures), and linguistic echoes all link the work to the classical tradition. Its project is to put the elements of classical verse in the service of communicating faith (Salzano 2000, p. 25). A concluding prayer to Christ (143–148) to grant Constantine victory and success and to reward him with children equal to him squarely places this transformational poem in a transformational time, when Christianity was no longer persecuted by an emperor, but was professed by him – and the prayer for Constantine's children is a prayer that this may continue after him. The concluding lines claim legitimacy and authority for the faith and, thus, for the Christian *Laudes* by indicating that Christianity was now the imperial religion and by establishing Jesus's power as a source for the emperor's.

The second Constantinian poem is Juvencus's *Evangeliorum libri IV* (ca. 329), the first Christian epic poem in the Western tradition. Juvencus recast the Gospel story, with Matthew his main source, as a four-book, roughly 3200-line hexameter epic. Presumably aiming to appeal to educated cultural elites (McGill 2016, pp. 23–24), Juvencus discovered a way of bringing together the authority of ancient epic and Christian edification, while also transforming epic by using it to treat a new kind of heroism, new world-historical events, and a new set of cultural values. Striking is the confidence of this vanguard figure. In the 27-line preface to his poem, Juvencus casts himself as an epic inheritor of Homer and Virgil, but he sets himself apart from them and above them by proclaiming the truth of his poem, as opposed to the lies that they narrate (9–20). This is the first instance of the topos in Christian poetics in which authors contrasted Christian truth with pagan lies (Klopsch 1980, pp. 9–12; Mastrangelo 2016, p. 43). The topos enabled a Christian author to carve out new literary space for himself, even as he reused and updated classical genres, conventions, themes, and language. Juvencus hopes, moreover, that his truthful poem about "the life-giving deeds of Christ" (*Christi vitalia gesta*; 19) will save him at the Second Coming and grant him eternal life (21–24). This is a variation on the classical theme that poetry grants immortality to an author; now, however, the prize is personal salvation as a Christian (Witke 1971, pp. 200–202). Juvencus gives new weight to the practice of writing poetry. His work is an expression of his faith – hence his call at the close of his preface to the Holy Spirit and the River Jordan for inspiration (25–27), an invocation that, like the truth/lies dichotomy, anticipates a later topos in Christian poetics (Mastrangelo 2016: p. 43). Yet it is also, he hopes, a way of receiving faith's ultimate reward.

Later in the fourth century, a more eccentric narrative poem with biblical content appeared. This was the *Cento Probae*, likely written by Faltonia Betitia Proba in the middle of the century, perhaps in the early 360s (Bazil 2009; Schottenius Cullhed 2015). The cento is a work made up of discrete lines and segments of lines taken from Virgil's *Eclogues*, *Georgics*, and *Aeneid* and recombined to produce a new narrative text. Proba's is the first of four Christian Virgilian centos to survive from antiquity; there are, in addition, 12 centos on mythological and secular topics. After an introduction that combines original verses with centonic lines (1–55), Proba reuses Virgil to narrate parts of Genesis and Exodus (56–332) and the Gospel story of Christ

(333–688) and, then, closes with a brief conclusion (689–694). In her introduction (23), the author programmatically states, "I will say that Virgil sang/prophesied the pious gifts of Christ" (*Vergilium cecinisse loquar pia munera Christi*). The verb *cano* not only echoes *Aen*. 1.1 but also appears to signal a peculiar form of allegory, in which Christian content is present in Virgil's verses and just needs a centonist's rearranging to bring it out; *cano* in the sense of "prophesy" – a meaning that Proba gives the word later in her work (343) – makes the point provocatively. This is in line with the patristic idea that Christian doctrine and the Christian view of the world extended into the past pagan world and its literature. Christianity was, in a sense, always there, and thus it has a claim to priority. In addition, because of the cento form she uses, Proba stakes a direct claim to the cultural authority enjoyed by Virgil even as she powerfully appropriates that authority by using his verses to relate Christian subject matter. This is to ground the text in the past and to invest it with the weight of literary history while also breaking from the classical tradition – a tension animating most ancient Christian poetry, including the fourth-century *Triumphus Christi heroicus* (Salzano 2007, pp. 127–151), a kind of Christian epyllion in 108 hexameter lines on the Crucifixion and Resurrection, but with an account of Christ's descent into hell that remakes the classical epic katabasis.

The *Cento Probae* is the *ne plus ultra* of linguistic reuse; as such, it exaggerates the very wide practice in Christian Latin poetry of recasting the language of classical models (Thraede 1962, 1034–1041; Herzog 1975, 185–211; Pelttari 2014; Mastrangelo 2016; Kaufmann 2017). Christian poetry differed from classical verse in its religious commitment and intent as well as its hermeneutic turn: Texts expounded Scripture and doctrine and also interpreted the world through a Christian lens (Herzog 1989, pp. 32–33). But it retained extensive verbal ties to the classics through intertextuality, in which Christian authors participated in the same linguistic and poetic codes as their classical predecessors, and through imitation/allusion. It is difficult to generalize about the topic, because of the very large number of examples. What is clear, however, is that imitation and allusion are productive and varied forces in Christian Latin verse. There is inevitably a gap between a Christian narrative and a classical/pagan one when Christian writers fit their source material to new religious content and commitments. But it is reductive to think only in terms of a conflict model. *Kontrastimitation*, in which the content of the imitating text is set in opposition to and, in a sense, "corrects" its antecedent (Thraede 1962, pp. 1039–1041), is widespread. Yet very many examples also exist of ornamental imitation, which demonstrates that Christian authors could freely adapt and assimilate classical material without a polemical edge, as well as of imitation where the subject matter of the source work complements and fills out Christian content.

Classical language is pervasive in fourth-century Christian verse inscriptions that appeared in Rome. The earliest such inscription dates to the 340s at the basilica of St. Agnes. Constantina, the daughter of Constantine, had funded the construction of the basilica, and a 14-line dedicatory inscription in hexameters commemorates her deed. The poem contains classical phrasing (e.g. *Tartaream* [8], *caeca nocte* [11]) as well as debts to specific models (e.g. *summi fastigia tecti* [6], from Virgil, *Aen.* 2.302). Constantina's is one of a handful of verse inscriptions in Rome connected to the Constantinian dynasty; the poems imply the appeal of monumental classicizing verse for imperial messaging (Trout 2016, pp. 81–88). But the epigraphic habit extended much wider in late antiquity among Christians and non-Christians alike (see Chapter 15 in this volume; Trout 2016, pp. 90–95). Pride of place must go to Pope Damasus (ca. 305–384; papacy 366-384). Damasus composed epigraphic epigrams, most inscribed in the script of Filocalus, for different spots around Rome and elsewhere, notably the tombs of martyrs (Trout 2015a). By definition, they helped to Christianize public space in the fourth century; at the same time, some inscriptions Christianized Roman identity by recalibrating traditional virtues of the ideal Roman citizen and soldier and assigning them to martyrs and, in one instance (*Epig. Dam.* 20), by seeming to replace the Dioscuri with Peter and Paul as divinities of the city of Rome (Curran 2012, pp. 341–43). Because the epigrams contain pervasive echoes of Virgil, especially the *Aeneid*, they Virgilianize Christian space as well. No matter how much individuals recognized the Virgilian material, extensive traces of his poetry were inscribed on stone for public viewing; accordingly, Virgil shaped the experience of the Christian sites, even for those members of the public who were unaware of his presence.

Damasus is possibly the author of another Christian poem, the *Carmen contra paganos*. Stylistic considerations, notably the absence of the word *et* from Damasus's epigrams and the *Carmen* and similar phrasing in each, make the attribution of the *Carmen* to Damasus plausible, though far from certain (Cameron 2011, pp. 308–17; Trout 2015a, pp. 26–38). The poem is a 122-line hexameter invective directed at an unnamed pagan prefect; Alan Cameron (2011, pp. 273–307, 318–319) convincingly argues that the prefect is Vettius Agorius Praetextatus, and that the poem was written soon after his death in 384 to counter the public grief occasioned by his death. The *Carmen* is one of four polemical hexameter works against paganism from around the same time; the others are Prudentius's *Contra Symmachum* (see infra) and the anonymous *Carmen ad quendam senatorem* and *Carmen ad Antonium* (Trout 2015b). The poems each give individual expression, with ample classical diction, to a satiric impulse to criticize and lampoon paganism. The satire defines Christians against the pagan Other and elevates them above it. This is not necessarily a reflection of a broad culture war between Christianity and paganism, whether experienced directly or remembered. Instead, Prudentius and the anonymous poets, like the author of the *Carmen contra paganos*, were likely responding to the actions of specific individuals and to specific events (Barnes 1976; Cameron 2011, pp. 325–326). The *carmina* also suggest a felt need to use satires of paganism to articulate what it was to be a Christian for the Christian elite and to work to establish an identity as an in-group in contrast to pagans (Trout 2015b).

The fourth century also saw the emergence of Latin hymnody, represented especially by the bishops Hilary of Poitiers (?315-367) and Ambrose of Milan (ca. 337–397). The two composed their hymns in classicizing quantitative meters (although Ambrose also has strong accentual patterns) for liturgical use (Palmer 1989, pp. 58–67; Fontaine et al. 1992; den Boeft 2007). Ambrose's hymns, in eight stanzas of four lines and in the iambic dimeter acatalectic meter, have a brevity and rhythm particularly suitable to congregational performance. He appears to have introduced to western churches the practice of regular hymn-singing by the whole congregation (Palmer 1989, p. 62; Richardson 2016, p. 7). Augustine (*Conf.* 9.7) states that the innovation began when Justina, the mother of the emperor Valentinian II and an adherent of Arianism, was persecuting Ambrose; his congregation kept guard for him in the church, and to keep them from succumbing to exhaustion or depression, the decision was made to have them sing hymns. The strongly anti-Arian Ambrose later used hymns to put forward orthodox views on the Trinity as well as to present other Christian teaching.

With Hilary and Ambrose, a picture continues to emerge of the growth of Christian Latin poetry in the 300s. The very end of that century through roughly the first half of the 400s constitutes the late antique Golden Age for Latin Christian verse. A good deal of the corpus dates to this time. It includes the work of two of the most important and accomplished poets of late antiquity. The first is Paulinus of Nola (ca. 354–431), the Gallic aristocrat turned ascetic Christian. Verse epistles he exchanged with his teacher and friend Ausonius offer compelling glimpses into the disruptive effects of Paulinus's conversion to a rigorous brand of Christianity (Amherdt 2004, Rücker 2012). Both men struggle to determine what Paulinus's Christian turn means for their friendship, which was grounded in a shared commitment to classical culture. The second poet is Prudentius, mentioned above (348 to after 405). In an autobiographical preface to his poetry, Prudentius relates that he had a successful bureaucratic career but has devoted his old age to saving his soul by serving God, including by writing Christian poetry. Prudentius thus defines his poetry by his and its religious commitment and, similar to Juvencus, connects it to his personal salvation.

Paulinus and Prudentius each illustrate a salient feature of the poetry of their age: the proliferation of poetic forms. In addition to his verse epistles, Paulinus wrote 13 *natalicia* for St. Felix, or poems celebrating the anniversary of Felix's death in Nola; paraphrases of the Psalms; an epithalamium; a propemptikon; a consolation; protreptic pieces; and verse inscriptions (Green 1971; Trout 1999). Prudentius, meanwhile, composed six texts (seven if a short *Epilogus* is counted) along with the *Contra Symmachum*: two collections of hymns, one on martyrs (*Peristephanon*) and one of songs for the day, for fasting, for burial of the dead, and for Christmas and Epiphany (*Cathermerinon*; O'Daly 2012; Richardson 2016); two poems on doctrine (*Apotheosis* and *Hamartigenia*; Malamud 2011); an allegorical epic on the fight between the virtues and vices (*Psychomachia*; Gnilka 1963; Mastrangelo 2008); and 48 epigrams, each of four lines, on scenes from the Bible, possibly to accompany church paintings (*Dittochaeon*).

Other works that appear in the period include biblical epics (both New Testament and Old Testament; see Chapter 14 in this volume) and a Christian bucolic, Endelechius's *De mortibus boum*. (*De Iesu Christo deo et homine*, in 137 hexameters, probably dates as well to this time; it is a doctrinal poem, dealing with the double nature of Christ [Salzano 2007, pp. 103–125].) These texts join with the poetry of Paulinus and Prudentius to reveal a second widespread feature of this Golden Age of Christian verse: its generic fluidity, as exemplified by the "mixing" or "crossing" of genres. (On Prudentius, see Fontaine 1980, pp. 1–23.) Endelechius's work is notable in this regard: It is partly a bucolic poem based on Virgil's first *Eclogue* but contains a lyric meter (second asclepiads) and incorporates a plague narrative in the tradition of Virgil's *Georgics* (Schierl 2016). In mixing, dissolving, and remaking inherited genres, poets of the period reflect a broader trait of late antique literature. Late antiquity on the whole was a time of significant generic innovation, as old forms were updated and hybridized and new forms were developed, often by crossing or eroding traditional categories (Pollmann 2001; Young 2004; Fuhrer 2013; Elsner and Hernández Lobato 2017, p. 15).

Endelechius offers a striking example of Christian, and Christianizing, engagement with the classical literary tradition. In Endelechius's poem, the cattle of Tityrus, a character taken from Virgil's first *Eclogue* and, thus, representative of Latin bucolic, are saved from a plague because he made the sign of the cross over them. Another good example from the period is Prudentius's *Psychomachia*. The poem transforms epic models of battle and widely imitates Virgil, but also presents an optimistic vision of triumphant Christianity, culminating in a concluding image of the temple of the soul. The temple illustrates the victory of virtue over vice and anticipates the eschatological glory that awaits believers (Roberts 2008, p. 634).

Several poets of the age, including Prudentius, also address Roman history through the lens of Christian belief and thought. Thus Prudentius offers a teleological view of history in his *Contra Symmachum*, a work in two hexameter books (667 lines and 1132 lines, respectively) on the (resolved) controversy over the removal of the Altar of Victory from the Roman senate house in the early 380s. In the poem, the Roman Empire is seen as a necessary condition for the spread of Christianity and for salvation history. A set of texts, meanwhile, responds to the unrest and devastation caused by the incursions of Germanic tribes into Gaul in the early fifth century (cf. McLynn 2009). Three are the *Commonitorium*, ascribed to Orientius, the *Ad coniugem*, and the *Carmen de providentia Dei*, attributed by some scholars to Prosper. The poems deal in different ways with how a Christian should respond to the parlous times, offering defenses of God's guidance over the universe and advocating concern for the inner life rather than for the outer world (Fielding 2014, 569–585). In addition, a 110-line hexameter dialogue entitled the *Epigramma Paulini* (attributed, probably mistakenly, to Paulinus of Béziers) features three speakers, one of whom (Salmon) tells another (Thesbon) that he has journeyed through Gaul after it was ravaged by the Alans, Vandals, and Sarmatians. The focus of the text, however, lies less upon that violence than upon the moral decline of the age among both men and women, which is lamented in satiric strains, and which is contrasted with Christian piety and, it seems, monastic life. Like Endelechius's poem, the *Epigramma Paulini* is modeled on Virgil's first *Eclogue* but transforms classical pastoral by adapting it to Christian content and concerns. The poem also remakes *Eclogues* 1 by prominently featuring acerbic satire and concomitant social criticism (including criticism of women's preference for reading about Virgil's Dido over reading the bible; 76–77) within its Virglian pastoral frame (Chiappiniello 2009).

Later in the fifth century (in or around 460), Paulinus of Pella deals with the unrest in Gaul in the period and his personal losses on account of it in his *Eucharisticos*, a 616-line hexameter poem ostensibly of Thanksgiving to God, but filled with bitter lament. Paulinus is one of a handful of significant Latin Christian poets active after the mid-fifth century. Three others are Dracontius (ca. 455–ca. 505), from Vandal North Africa; Ennodius (473/474–521), bishop of Pavia; and Venantius Fortunatus (ca. 530–ca. 600/609), from northern Italy and later living in Merovingian Gaul. (I bypass Arator and Avitus, treated in Chapter 14 of this volume.) The spread of the authors exemplifies the geographic diversity that marks all late antique verse. Dracontius wrote poetry on mythological and secular subjects and on Christian matter; his *De laudibus Dei*, in three books of hexameters, claims to provide knowledge of divine wrath and mercy (Arweiler 2007; Tommasi Moreschini 2010). (This is a fitting topic for the poet, who produced the poem when trying to secure release from imprisonment by the Vandal Gunthamund.) Ennodius likewise wrote non-Christian and Christian verse. Among the latter are 13 hymns (at least one of which may be spurious); a cycle of poems on bishops of Milan; epigraphic and ekphrastic pieces on Christian topics; and a few scoptic epigrams on Christian figures (Kennell 2000; Urlacher-Becht 2014). Venantius Fortunatus is the author of the famous hymns *Pange lingua* and *Vexilla regis*, as well as of a four-book hagiographic epic on the life of Martin of Tours (Roberts 2009) – also the subject of a poem by Paulinus of Périgueux, probably from the 460 s. Venantius's *Vita sancti Martini* is "the last epic of antiquity" (Roberts 2001), with epic scope, encoding, and coloring; with a focus on the heroic deeds of the Christian Saint; and with features (e.g. narrative fragmentation, a strong tendency toward the ekphrastic and epigrammatic) that, along with its Christian content, define it as a new-model epic for late antiquity. Fortunatus himself offers a partial history of late antique Christian Latin poetry when, at the start of his epic (1.10–25), he lists his literary predecessors, all of whom are Christian, including Juvencus, Orientius, Prudentius, Paulinus of Nola, and the biblical epicists Sedulius, Arator, and Avitus.

ACKNOWLEDGMENT

* Laura Miguélez-Cavero should like to thank the editors of this volume and Mary Whitby for their help with her part of the chapter.

REFERENCES

Abrams Rebillard, Suzanne. (2012). Historiography as devotion: *Poemata de seipso*. In: *Re-reading Gregory of Nazianzus. Essays on History, Theology, and Culture* (ed. Christopher Beeley), 125–142. Washington, DC: Catholic University of America Press.

Accorinti, Domenico. (2016). The poet from Panopolis: An obscure biography and a controversial figure. In: *Brill's Companion to Nonnus of Panopolis* (ed. Domenico Accorinti), 11–53. Leiden: Brill.

Agosti, Gianfranco. (2001a). L'epica biblica nella tarda antichità greca: Autori e lettori nel IV e V secolo. In: *La scrittura infinita. Bibbia e poesia in età medievale e umanistica*, (ed. Francesco Stella), 67–104. Tavarnuzze: Edizioni del Galluzzo.

Agosti, Gianfranco. (2001b). Late antique iambics and *iambikè idéa*. In: *Iambic Ideas: Essays on a Poetic Tradition from Archaic Greece to the Late Roman Empire* (ed. Alberto Cavarzere, Alessandro Barchiesi, and Antonio Aloni), 217–254. Lanham, MD: Rowman & Littlefield.

Agosti, Gianfranco. (2008a). Il ruolo di Dioscoro nella storia della poesia tardoantica. In: *Les archives de Dioscore d'Aphrodité cent ans après leur découverte* (ed. Jean-Luc Fournet), 33–54. Paris: De Boccard.

Agosti, Gianfranco. (2008b). Epigrammi lunghi nella produzione epigrafica tardoantica. In: *Epigramma longum: Da Marziale alla Tarda antichità* (ed. Alfredo Morelli), 663–692. Cassino: Università degli Studi di Cassino.

Agosti, Gianfranco. (2015). Poesia greca nella (e della?) biblioteca Bodmer. *Adamantius* 21: 86–97.

Agosti, Gianfranco and Gonnelli, Fabrizio. (1995). Materiali per la storia dell'esametro nei poeti cristiani greci. In: *Struttura e storia dell'esametro greco* (ed. Marco Fantuzzi and Roberto Pretagostini), 1.289–434. Roma: Gruppo Editoriale Internazionale.

Amande, Carlotta. (2008). Tradizione classica e cristianesimo negli *Inni* di Sinesio di Cirene: La sfera della prassi. In: *Motivi e forme della poesia cristiana antica tra scrittura e tradizione classica*, 435–442. Roma: Institutum Patristicum Augustinianum.

Amherdt, David. ed. (2004). *Ausone et Pauline de Nole: Correspondence*. Berne: Peter Lang.

Arweiler, Alexander. (2007). Interpreting cultural change: Semiotics and exegesis in Dracontius' *De laudibus Dei*. In: *Poetry and Exegesis in Premodern Latin Christianity: The Encounter between Classical and Christian Strategies of Interpretation*. Supplements to Vigilae Christianae 87 (ed. Willemien Otten and Karla Pollmann), 147–172. Leiden, Boston: Brill.

Banchich, Thomas. (1993). Julian's School Laws: Cod. Theod. 13.3.5 and Ep. 42. *The Ancient World* 24: 5–14.

Barnes, Timothy David. (1976). The historical setting of Prudentius' *Contra Symmachum*. *American Journal of Philology* 97: 373–386.

Bazil, Martin. (2009). *Centones christiani: Métamorphoses d'une forme intertextuelle dans la poésie latine chrétienne de l'Antiquité tardive*. Paris: Études Augustiniennes.

Brucker, Ralph. (2014). "Songs", "Hymns", and "Encomia" in the New Testament. In: *Literature or Liturgy? Early Christian Hymns and Prayers in Their Literary and Liturgical Context in Antiquity* (ed. Clemens Leonhard and Hermut Löhr), 1–14. Tübingen: Mohr Siebeck.

Busine, Aude. (2005a). *Paroles d'Apollon: Pratiques et traditions oraculaires dans l'Antiquité tardive (IIe-VIe siècle)*. Leiden: Brill.

Busine, Aude. (2005b). Gathering sacred words: Collections of oracles from pagan sanctuaries to Christian books. In: *Selecta Colligere II. Beiträge zur Technik des Sammelns und Kompilierens griechischer Texte von der Antike bis zum Humanismus* (ed. Rosa Maria Piccione and Matthias Perkams), 39–55. Alessandria: Edizioni del Orso.

Cameron, Alan. (2011). *The Last Pagans of Rome*. Oxford: Oxford University Press.
Champion, Michael. (2014). *Explaining the Cosmos: Creation and Cultural Interaction in Late-Antique Gaza*. Oxford: Oxford University Press.
Chiappiniello, Roberto. (2009). *Feminei furores*: Prudentius' *Harmartigenia* and the *Epigramma Paulini*. *Vigiliae Christianae* 63: 169–188.
Curran, John. (2012). Virgilizing Christianity in late antique Rome. In: *Two Romes: Rome and Constantinople in Late Antiquity* (ed. Lucy Grig and Gavin Kelly), 325–344. Oxford: Oxford University Press.
Daley, Brian. (2006). *Gregory of Nazianzus*. London: Routledge.
Daley, Brian. (2012). Systematic theology in Homeric dress. In: *Re-Reading Gregory of Nazianzus. Essays on History, Theology, and Culture* (ed. Christopher Beeley), 3–12. Washington, DC: Catholic University of America Press.
Demoen, Kristoffel. (1997). Gifts of friendship that will remain forever. *Jahrbuch der Österreichischen Byzantinistik* 47: 1–11.
Den Boeft, Jan. (2007). *Cantatur ad delectationem*: Ambrose's lyric poetry. In: *Poetry and Exegesis in Premodern Latin Christianity: The Encounter between Classical and Christian Strategies of Interpretation*. Supplements to Vigilae Christianae 87 (ed. Willemien Otten and Karla Pollmann), 81–97. Leiden, Boston: Brill.
De Stefani, Claudio. (2008). La *Parafrasi di Giovanni* di Nonno e la *Metafrasi dei Salmi* dello Pseudo-Apollinare. In: *Nonno e i suoi lettori* (ed. Sergio Audano), 1–16. Alessandria: Edizioni del Orso.
Di Pasquale Barbanti, Maria. (2008). Elementi neoplatonici nella dottrina trinitaria di Sinesio di Cirene: *Inni* I, II e IX. In: *Motivi e forme della poesia cristiana antica tra scrittura e tradizione classica*, 413–433. Rome: Institutum Patristicum Augustinianum.
Elm, Susanna. (2015). Apology as autobiography: An episcopal genre? Emperor Julian, Gregory of Nazianzus, Augustine of Hippo. In: *Spätantike Konzeptionen von Literatur* (ed. Jan Stenger), 41–56. Heidelberg: Universitätsverlag Winter.
Elsner, Jaś, and Jesús Hernández Lobato. (2017). Introduction: Notes towards a poetics of late antique literature. In: *The Poetics of Late Latin Literature* (ed. Jaś Elsner and Jesús Hernández Lobato), 1–22. Oxford: Oxford University Press.
Faulkner, Andrew (2010). St. Gregory of Nazianzus and the classical tradition: The "Poemata Arcana" qua Hymns. *Philologus* 154: 78–87.
Faulkner, Andrew. (2014). Faith and fidelity in Biblical epic. The *Metaphrasis Psalmorum*, Nonnus, and the theory of translation. In: *Nonnus of Panopolis in Context* (ed. Konstantinos Spanoudakis), 195–210. Berlin and Boston: De Gruyter.
Fielding, Ian. (2014). Physical ruin and spiritual perfection in fifth-century Gaul: Orientius and his contemporaries on the "landscape of the soul." *Journal of Early Christian Studies* 22: 569–585.
Floridi, Lucia. (2013). The epigrams of Gregory of Nazianzus against tomb desecrators and their epigraphic background. *Mnemosyne* 66: 55–81.
Fontaine, Jacques. (1980). *Études sur la poésie dans l'occident chrétien: Esquisse d'une histoire de la poésie latine chrétienne du IIIe au VIe siècle*. Paris: Études Augustiniennes.

Fontaine, Jacques, Charlet, J.-L., Deléani, S. et al. ed. (1992). *Ambroise de Milan: Hymnes*. Paris: Éditions du Cerf.

Fournet, Jean-Luc. (1999). *Hellénisme dans l'Égypte du VIe siècle: la bibliothèque et l'œuvre de Dioscore d'Aphrodité*. Le Caire: Institut Français d'Archéologie Orientale.

Franchi, Roberta. (2016). Approaching the "spiritual gospel": Nonnus as interpreter of John. In: *Brill's Companion to Nonnus of Panopolis* (ed. Domenico Accorinti), 240–256. Leiden: Brill.

Fuhrer, Therese. (2013). Hypertexts and auxiliary texts: New genres in late antiquity? In: *Generic Interfaces in Latin Literature: Encounters, Interactions, and Transformations* (ed. Theodore D. Papanghelis, Stephen J. Harrison, and Stavros Frangoulidis), 79–92. Berlin and Boston: De Gruyter.

Gnilka, Christian. (1963). *Studien zu* Psychomachie *des Prudentius*. Wiesbaden: O. Harrassowitz.

Green, Roger (1971). *The Poetry of Paulinus of Nola: A Study of His Latinity*. Collection Latomus 120. Brussels: Latomus.

Herzog, Reinhart. (1975). *Die Bibelepik der lateinischen Spätantike: Formgeschichte einer erbaulichen Gattung*. Munich: Wilhelm Fink.

Herzog, Reinhart. (1989). Einführung in die lateinische Literatur der Spätantike. In: *Restauration und Erneuerung: Die lateinische Literatur von 284 bis 374 n. Chr.* (ed. Reinhart Herzog), 1–44. Handbuch der lateinischen Literatur der Antike, vol. 5. Munich: C.H. Beck.

Hurst, André and Rudhardt, Jean. (2002). *Le Codex des visions*. Geneva: Droz.

Kaufmann, Helen. (2017). Intertextuality in late Latin poetry. In: *The Poetics of Late Latin Literature* (ed. Jaś Elsner and Jesús Hernández Lobato), 149–175. Oxford: Oxford University Press.

Kennell, Stefanie A.H. (2000). *Magnus Felix Ennodius: A Gentleman of the Church*. Ann Arbor: University of Michigan Press.

Klopsch, Paul (1980). *Einführung in die Dichtungslehren des lateinischen Mittelalters*. Darmstadt: Wissenschaftliche Buchgesellschaft.

Krueger, Derek. (2004). *Writing and Holiness: The Practice of Authorship in the Early Christian East*. Philadelphia: University of Pennsylvania Press.

Lauritzen, Delphine. (2015–2016). Sur l'identité de Jean de Gaza: Grammatikos et notable. *Revue des Études Tardo-Antiques* 5: 177–210.

Leonhard, Clemens. (2014). Which hymns were sung in ancient Christian liturgies? In: *Literature or Liturgy? Early Christian Hymns and Prayers in Their Literary and Liturgical Context in Antiquity* (ed. Clemens Leonhard and Hermut Löhr), 175–194. Tübingen: Mohr Siebeck.

Lightfoot, Jane L. (2007). *The Sibylline Oracles: With Introduction, Translation, and Commentary on the First and Second Books*. Oxford: Oxford University Press.

Löhr, Hermut. (2014). What can we know about the beginnings of Christian hymnody? In: *Literature or Liturgy? Early Christian Hymns and Prayers in Their Literary and Liturgical Context in Antiquity* (ed. Clemens Leonhard and Hermut Löhr), 157–174. Tübingen: Mohr Siebeck.

Malamud, Martha A. (2011). *The Origin of Sin: An English Translation of the Hamartigenia.* Ithaca, NY: Cornell University Press.

Mastrangelo, Marc. (2008). *The Roman Self in Late Antiquity: Prudentius and the Poetics of the Soul.* Baltimore, MD: Johns Hopkins University Press.

Mastrangelo, Marc. (2016). Toward a poetics of late Latin reuse. In: *Classics Renewed: Reception and Innovation in the Latin Poetry of Late Antiquity* (ed. Scott McGill and Joseph Pucci), 25–45. Heidelberg: Universitätsverlag Winter.

McGill, Scott. (2016). *Juvencus' Four Books of the Gospels: Evangeliorum libri Quattuor.* London: Routledge.

McGuckin, John A. (2001). Autobiography as apologia. *Studia Patristica* 37: 160–177.

McGuckin, John A. (2006). Gregory: The Rhetorician as Poet. In: *Gregory of Nazianzus: Images and Reflections* (ed. Jostein Børtnes and Tomas Hägg), 193–212. Copenhagen: Museum Tusculanum.

McGuckin, John A. (2008). Poetry and hymnography (2): The Greek world. In: *The Oxford Handbook of Early Christian Studies* (ed. Susan Ashbrook Harvey and David G. Hunter), 641–656. Oxford: Oxford University Press

McLynn, Neil. (2006). Among the Hellenists: Gregory and the Sophists. In: *Gregory of Nazianzus: Images and Reflections* (ed. Jostein Børtnes and Tomas Hägg), 213–228. Copenhagen: Museum Tusculanum.

McLynn, Neil. (2009). Poetic identity and political crisis in early fifth-century Gaul. *Journal of Late Antiquity* 2: 60–74.

Meinel, Fabian. (2009). Gregory of Nazianzus' "Poemata arcana": *Arreta* and Christian persuasion. *Cambridge Classics Journal* 55: 71–96.

Miguélez-Cavero, Laura. (2013). Rhetoric for a Christian community: The poems of the *Codex Visionum.* In: *The Purpose of Rhetoric in Late Antiquity: From Performance to Exegesis* (ed. Alberto Quiroga Puertas), 91–121. Tübingen: Mohr Siebeck.

Milovanovic-Barham, Celica. (1997). Gregory of Nazianzus' *Ars Poetica* (In suos versus: carmen 2.1.39). *Journal of Early Christian Studies* 5: 497–510.

Moreschini, Claudio and Sykes, D.A. (1997). *St. Gregory of Nazianzus: Poemata arcana.* Oxford: Clarendon Press.

Nodes, Daniel Joseph. (1993). *Doctrine and Exegesis in Biblical Latin Poetry.* Leeds: Francis Cairns.

O'Daly, Gerard. (2012). *Days Linked by Song: Prudentius'* Cathemerinon. Oxford: Oxford University Press.

Palla, Roberto. (1989). Ordinamento e polimetria delle poesie bibliche di Gregorio Nazianzeno. *Wiener Studien* 102: 169–85.

Palla, Roberto and Moroni, Maria Grazia. (2013). Gli epigrammi di Gregorio Nazianzeno contro i violatori di tombe. In: *Dulce Melos* 2 (ed. Victoria Zimmerl-Panagl), 33–66. Pisa: ETS.

Palmer, Anne-Marie. (1989). *Prudentius on the Martyrs.* Oxford: Clarendon.

Pelttari, Aaron. (2014). *The Space That Remains: Reading Latin Poetry in Late Antiquity.* Ithaca, NY: Cornell University Press.

Pollmann, Karla. (2001). The transformation of the epic genre in Christian late antiquity. *Studia Patristica* 36: 61–75.

Richardson, Nicholas. (2016). *Prudentius' Hymns for Hours and Seasons: Liber Cathemerinon.* London: Routledge.

Roberts, Michael. (1989). *The Jeweled Style: Poetry and Poetics in Late Antiquity.* Ithaca, NY: Cornell University Press.

Roberts, Michael. (2001). The last epic of antiquity: Generic continuity and innovation in the *Vita Sancti Martini* of Venantius Fortunatus. *Transactions of the American Philological Association* 131: 257–285.

Roberts, Michael. (2008). Poetry and hymnography (1): Christian Latin poetry. In: *The Oxford Handbook of Early Christian Studies* (ed. Susan Ashbrook Harvey and David G. Hunter), 628–640. Oxford: Oxford University Press

Roberts, Michael. (2009). *The Humblest Sparrow: The Poetry of Venantius Fortunatus.* Ann Arbor: University of Michigan Press.

Roques, Denis. (2007). Les *Hymnes* de Synésios de Cyrène: Chronologie, rhétorique et réalité. In: *L'hymne antique et son public* (ed. Yves Lehmann), 301–370. Turnhout: Brepols.

Rücker, Nils. (2012). *Ausonius an Paulinus von Nola: Textgeschichte und literarische Form der Briefgedichte 21 und 22 des Decimus Magnus Ausonius.* Göttingen: Vandehoeck & Ruprecht.

Salzano, Aniello. (2000). Laudes Domini: *Introduzione, testo, traduzione e commento.* Naples: Arte Tipografica.

Salzano, Aniello. (2007). *Agli inizi della poesía christiana latina: autori anonimi dei secc. IV-V.* Salerno: Edisud Salerno.

Schierl, Petra. (2009). *Tu casti rectique tenax*: Gottes-und Kaiserlob in den *Laudes Domini.* In: *Lateinische Poesie der Spätantike: Internationale Tagung in Castelen bei Augst, 11.–13. Oktober 2007* (ed. Henriette Harich-Schwarzbauer and Petra Schierl), 129–158. Schweizerische Beiträge zur Altertumswissenschaft 36. Basel: Schwabe.

Schierl, Petra. (2016). A preacher in Arcadia? Reconsidering Tityrus Christianus. In: *Classics Renewed: Reception and Innovation in the Latin Poetry of Late Antiquity* (ed. Scott McGill and Joseph Pucci), 241–264. Heidelberg: Universitätsverlag Winter.

Schottenius Cullhed, Sigrid. (2015). *Proba the Prophet: The Christian Virgilian Cento of Faltonia Betitia Proba.* Mnemosyne Supplements 378. Leiden: Brill.

Shorrock, Robert. (2011). *The Myth of Paganism: Nonnus, Dionysus, and the World of Late Antiquity.* London: Bristol Classical Press.

Simelidis, Christos. (2009). *Selected Poems of Gregory of Nazianzus: I.2.17; II.1.10, 19, 32: A Critical Edition with Introduction and Commentary.* Göttingen: Vandenhoeck & Ruprecht.

Simelidis, Christos. (2016). Nonnus and Christian literature. In: *Brill's Companion to Nonnus of Panopolis* (ed. Domenico Accorinti) 289–307. Leiden: Brill.

Sowers, Brian. (2008). *Eudocia: The Making of a Homeric Christian.* PhD diss., University of Cincinnati.

Sykes, Donald. (1970). The *Poemata Arcana* of St Gregory Nazianzen. *Journal of Theological Studies* 31: 32–41.

Sykes, Donald. (1985). Gregory Nazianzen as didactic poet. *Studia Patristica* 16: 433–437.

Thraede, Klaus. (1962). Epos. *Reallexikon für Antike und Christentum* 5: 983–1042.

Tommasi Moreschini, Chiara O. (2010). Roman and Christian history in Dracontius' *De Laudibus Dei*. In: *Studia Patristica, Vols. XLIV-XLIX: Papers Presented at the Fifteenth International Conference on Patristic Studies Held in Oxford 2007* (ed. J. Baun, A. Cameron, M. Edwards, and M. Vinzent), 303–308. Louvain: Peeters.

Trout, Dennis. (1999). *Paulinus of Nola: Life, Letters, and Poems*. Berkeley: University of California Press.

Trout, Dennis. (2015a). *Damasus of Rome: The Epigraphic Poetry. Introduction, Texts, Translations, and Commentary*. Oxford: Oxford University Press.

Trout, Dennis. (2015b). Napkin art: *Carmina contra paganos* and the difference satire made in fourth-century Rome. In: *Pagans and Christians in Late Antique Rome* (ed. Michele Renée Salzman, Marianne Sághy, and Rita Lizzi Testa), 213–231. Cambridge: Cambridge University Press.

Trout, Dennis. (2016). Poetry on stone: Epigram and audience in Rome. In: *Classics Renewed: Reception and Innovation in the Latin Poetry of Late Antiquity* (ed. Scott McGill and Joseph Pucci), 77–95. Heidelberg: Universitätsverlag Winter.

Urlacher-Becht, Céline. (2014). *Ennode de Pavie: chantre officiel de l'Église de Milan*. Paris: Études Augustiniennes.

Usher, Mark. (1998). *Homerocentones Eudociae Augustae*. Stuttgart and Leipzig: Teubner.

Van Dam, Raymond. (2002). *Kingdom of Snow: Roman Rule and Greek Culture in Cappadocia*. Philadelphia: University of Pennsylvania Press.

Waltz, P. (1928). *Anthologie Palatine, Tome I (Livres I–IV)*. Paris: Belles Lettres.

Whitby, Mary. (2003a). The vocabulary of praise in verse celebration of 6th-century building achievements: *AP* 2, 398-406, *AP* 9, 656, *AP* 1, 10 and Paul the Silentiary's *Description of St Sophia*. In: *Des géants à Dionysos: Mélanges de mythologie et de poésie grecques offerts à Francis Vian* (ed. Domenico Accorinti and Pierre Chuvin), 593–606. Alessandria: Edizioni del Orso.

Whitby, Mary. (2003b). George of Pisidia and the persuasive word: Words, words, words... In: *Rhetoric in Byzantium* (ed. Elizabeth Jeffreys), 173–186. Aldershot: Ashgate.

Whitby, Mary. (2006). The St. Polyeuktos Epigram (*AP* 1, 10): A literary perspective. In: *Greek Literature in Late Antiquity: Dynamism, Didacticism, Classicism* (ed. Scott Johnson), 159–187. Aldershot: Ashgate.

Whitby, Mary. (2007). The Bible Hellenized: Nonnus' *Paraphrase* of St. John's Gospel and '"Eudocia's" Homeric centos. In: *Texts and Culture in Late Antiquity: Inheritance, Authority, and Change* (ed. J.H.D. Scourfield), 195–231. Swansea: Classical Press of Wales.

Whitby, Mary. (2008). "Sugaring the pill": Gregory of Nazianzus' advice to Olympias (*Carm.* 2.2.6). *Ramus* 37: 79–98.

Whitby, Mary. (2014). A learned spiritual ladder? Towards an interpretation of George of Pisidia's hexameter poem *On Human Life*. In: *Nonnus of Panopolis in Context* (ed. Konstantinos Spanoudakis), 435–457. Berlin and Boston: De Gruyter.

Whitby, Mary. (2016). Nonnus and Biblical epic. In: *Brill's Companion to Nonnus of Panopolis* (ed. Domenico Accorinti) 215–239. Leiden: Brill.

Witke, Charles. (1971). *Numen Litterarum: The Old and the New in Latin Poetry from Constantine to Gregory the Great*. Mittellateinische Studien und Texte 5. Leiden: Brill.

Young, Frances. (2004). Classical genres in Christian guise; Christian genres in classical guise. In: *The Cambridge History of Early Christian Literature* (ed. Frances Young, Lewis Ayres, and Andrew Louth), 251–258. Cambridge: Cambridge University Press.

CHAPTER SEVENTEEN

Prosimetra

Joel C. Relihan

17.1 Introduction

How are we to interpret late antique literary works with classical affiliations when they are compounded of integrated prose and verse? My *Ancient Menippean Satire* (1993) defined a classical genre and traced its evolution and ultimate Christianization in late antiquity: The mixture of prose and verse, seen as fundamentally indecorous, served a cause of authorial auto-irony. But Menippean satire is only a subset of prosimetric phenomena, which go far beyond classical temporal boundaries. Peter Dronke (1994), considering a wide range of medieval prosimetry, Latin and vernacular, found in classical truth-testing models formal inspirations and theoretical lineages for medieval biographical and autobiographical texts. Here, the multiplicities of identity find expression in, because they are uncovered by, the *contrasting* habits of prose and verse. Writing about oneself in two modes is a heuristic exercise; prose and verse suggest that one's component parts may not be integrated.

Bernhard Pabst (1994) found a different sort of unity in late classical and medieval prosimetric texts. For Pabst their combination of instruction and moralizing highlights a complementary reality: The moral authority that can be easily assigned to the elevated status of verse. (See Witke 1996 for an introduction to Pabst's exhaustive medieval catalogue of prosimetric texts.) Ingrid De Smet (1996), writing on humanist texts, largely charted the influence of Seneca's *Apocolocyntosis* as a model for both political and academic criticism. The essays contained in Joseph Harris and Karl Reichl

(1997) considered prosimetrum in new, more theoretically rigorous ways, and they investigated prosimetry as a range of phenomena in world literature across classical, biblical, Icelandic, African, Irish, Persian, and Chinese texts, though humanist Latin texts are not discussed.

A student of prosimetric texts in late antiquity would do well to start with these five books. But there has been no comprehensive, universal literary history either of Menippean satire (best is Koppenfels 2007) or of prosimetrum (Orth 2000 brings some aspects of medieval prosimetrum up to date). Late antique texts can be more fully integrated into such a still-unwritten history by considering what are the traditions that these texts, like all Menippean satires, seek to subvert (see Relihan 2017, pp. 340–342). What I will propose here is a new way to think about prose and verse in late antique texts by contrasting Menippean satires and commentary traditions in their various approaches to the defense of authoritative authors and their critique of intellectual traditions.

My starting point is Boethius's *Consolation*. Just as Menippean satire does not define prosimetrum, so, too, *Consolation* does not define Menippean satire. The *Consolation* is an extraordinary text, in every sense of the word, and its outsize medieval influence should not lead us to think by default that it defines a predictable practice: As John Marenbon (2014) says, speaking in general terms, Boethius is paradigmatic of nothing. Studies of the influence of *Consolation* as a prosimetric text are of three sorts. Foremost is the study of its themes, either as they relate to antecedent texts (Relihan 2007b) or as they relate to the texts of the twelfth century (see the dissertation of Goddard 2011 and, now, the introductions to Wetherbee's translations of Alan of Lille's *Complaint of Nature* [2013] and Bernardus Silvestris's *Cosmographia* [2015]). There is an increasing acceptance of the view that I put forward in my study *The Prisoner's Philosophy* (2007b) that *Consolation* tests the limits of the authority figure, and that reflections of this are found throughout the later allegorical traditions (Wetherbee 2009). There is also the study of its prosimetric qualities per se (on the medieval side, see especially Johnson 2009), in which the regular alternation of prose and verse, its very ordering and elaborate patterning, exhibits the order of the universe (Blackwood 2015). But it is also a consolation, and, as such, it is tailored to the unique needs of its unique narrator; it is an exhortation to rise above history and circumstance, to accept the "philosopher's challenge" and so find truth in the abstract and atemporal realms (Donato 2013).

By demonstrating the extraordinary ways in which *Consolation* exploits verse and how it stretches the boundaries of Menippean satire, the chapter will be able to define better what it is that Menippean satire does as a prosimetric genre; in the process, it will help to define, in contrast to that genre, other prosimetric traditions. In what follows I do not intend to create a list of texts and summaries of contents or to elaborate a universal typology of prosimetra (to borrow the term from Ziolkowski 1997, p. 48). Rather, I will offer as topics for future research a schematic series of arguments and assertions, both historical and literary, about the growth of prosimetrum from a popular mode of narrative to a universalizing mode of thought, in which prose plus verse, on the one hand, is positive, because it seeks to include everything and so sum up in an era of cultural change the traditions of the past, and, on the other hand, is subversive, because it seeks to destabilize this combination of contrasting modes of thought; about the struggle of sophisticated authors simultaneously to embrace and to keep at arm's length the provocative and popular form that is prosimetrum; about the contrast between verse conceptualized as authoritative and moral, and verse exploited as a mocking intrusion; and ultimately, about the different functions of prosimetrum, both in defense of authoritative texts and in critique of authoritative genres.

17.2 Popular Origins of Mixed-Meter Satire

At this point I will jettison the word "prosimetrum," a twelfth-century term for a medieval phenomenon, and use "prosimetra" to refer not to a single genre but to the broad range of texts, genres, and experiments in which verse and prose make competing claims upon a text and its interpretation, including learned symposia (Plutarch, Athenaeus, Macrobius), Lucianic dialogues and fictions, and popular prose, such as the *Alexander Romance* and *Apollonius, King of Tyre*. The "other genre" of satire that Quintilian claims as Roman (*Institutes* 10.1.93), the one that is not the hexametric form that Lucilius finally settles on in his own poetic evolution, is the satire of mixed meter. Varro is said on this account to add prose to the mixed-meter form (Freudenberg 2013). It is good to remember, then, that mixed-meter satire is the metrical substratum of Menippean satire; we should not allow the example of Boethius to mislead us into thinking that Menippean satire is *alternating* prose and verse. Further, mixed-meter satire is popular in origin, as the scurrility of Seneca's *Apocolocyntosis* would suggest, whose every joke and insult can be explained in reference to the person and personality of Claudius (Bonandini 2010).

The *Caesars* of Julian the Apostate, subtitled *Saturnalia* and written in Greek, is modeled on *Apocolocyntosis* and provides a bridge from Seneca to Boethius. But the most prominent and influential complex of prosimetric texts in late antiquity are all in Latin and on the academic end: Menippean satire, particularly as practiced by Boethius and Martianus Capella (the encyclopedic fantasy of *The Marriage of Philology and Mercury*, for its conservative championing of rhetorical over practical arts, see Formisano 2013, p. 210), though Fulgentius (the trivializing encyclopedia *Mythologies*; see now Hays 2013) and Ennodius (the minor *Educational Exhortation*) stake their claims as well. The genre has, therefore, something of a renaissance in late antiquity, but also a reimagining. Varro's *Menippean Satires*, the distant model, have brought in their train Varronian encyclopedism, evident even in Athenaeus's *Deipnosophists*, where the host Larensius states his affiliation to the Menippean Varro (4.160c; Jacob 2013, p. 20). Textbook learning, coupled with extensive use of verse, now embraces a sort of psychological introspection performed in the presence of *authority*. This transforms a genre whose historical roots are more clearly glimpsed in backward-looking Lucian. But this is our question: How did a popular mode become the vehicle for such sophisticated and philosophical fictions? There is more at work in this transformation than the importation of Varro the polymath into Varro the satirist in late antiquity. In fact, the great changes in prosimetra – in form, in topic, and in outlook – can be traced to another event in the literary history of the second century. The contrast between Pseudo-Lucian's *Ass* and the *Golden Ass* of the forward-looking Apuleius will prove instructive, documenting a parallel shift from social satire to auto-ironic fantasy, where the author/narrator reserves for himself a reality and a heaven beyond his text.

Consolation's practice will show us a path to this second-century answer. A proper evaluation of means and ends in *Consolation* begins by admitting that Boethius the author was guilty as charged. Boethius chose *Consolation* to be a sort of confession. He did want to be emperor; he admits as much in his political manifesto in book 1.4. James O'Donnell 2008 is emphatic: "Theoderic was not merely paranoid: he had a real enemy. Boethius wanted to be emperor himself – or, more precisely, he wanted to be Plato's philosopher king" (pp. 166–167). After this first step we can start to evaluate the function of prose and verse in this confession by seeing it as the end point of a trio of prosimetric texts that look at emperors and the universe in increasingly introspective ways, a Menippean line to be traced from *Apocolocyntosis* through *Caesars* to *Consolation*. Seneca's attack on Claudius asks, "Where does *he, who used to be emperor*, fit in the cosmic order?" Its poetry is diverse and irregular: There are poetic tags in Greek and in Latin and a half-dozen poems, mostly hexameters (one in fulsome praise of Nero), one in comic senarii, one in anapests. But when, in Greek, the emperor Julian adapts Seneca with a more Lucianic aesthetic (restrained verse, the presence of Silenus, a *concilium deorum* that has become more a parodied symposium), the question becomes, "Where do *I, who am emperor*, fit with my predecessors in the cosmic order?" Like Seneca, Julian is a person in his fantasy, more at the edges than in the middle; like

Seneca, he receives the cosmic vision from an external source; unlike Seneca, he ponders his own position in the world. Julian laughs at all his predecessors and has a separate heaven reserved for himself; Mithras is his separate god. Boethius asks, "Where do *I, who wanted to be emperor*, fit into the cosmic order?" Julian writes an encapsulated history of Rome, a comic compendium, verse modestly deployed; Boethius is not writing a history of philosophy but an account of himself, and *Consolation*'s verses, of extraordinary proportions and depth, are a crucial element in Boethius's presentation of his own relation to philosophy and to the universe – this is a world away from Seneca and Julian.

17.3 The Extraordinary Verses of *Consolation*

Consolation as a literary genre mirrors consolation as a human endeavor: Each must be tailored to the individual who is addressed. The twists and turns of Philosophy's arguments reflect her accurate understanding of the difficult task at hand, reminding the sixth-century philosopher of the nature of sixth-century philosophy (Donato 2013). But the text of *Consolation* does not describe the unbroken history of philosophy and does not describe the prisoner as a sixth-century philosopher: The text mentions Plato, schismatic Hellenistic philosophers, and Roman philosophical martyrs (1.3.9). If Boethius the author had a Platonic longing to be the philosopher-king, our prisoner is appealing not to the unbroken chain of philosophy but to its origins: He longs to return to the beginnings. Antonio Donato's theme is that Philosophy wants the prisoner to rise to the philosopher's challenge – to rise above the things of earth and find his value in the context of eternal realms. The political manifesto of 1. 4 represents to Philosophy the sorts of things that the prisoner ought to leave behind if he wants to be free; he has exiled himself from his true home, she says (1.5.3–5). But the plot structure of *Consolation* is a stubborn reality: Philosophy says, "Let's rise up," at the beginnings of books 4 and 5 (4m.1; 5.1.4–5), and the prisoner says, "No." The final view of the *Consolation* is not the prisoner's view of the ordered universe but rather the divine view of a providential world; the prisoner's punishment is revealed as providential, and acceptance of that revelation is where his consolation lies, not in union/reunion with God. The prisoner had been offered the freedom of eternity, but finds himself accepting his place within the world of time, the failed philosopher-king. This is what Eleanor Johnson (2013, pp. 136 and following), calls "the consolation of temporality."

Donato (2013) is right: Philosophy herself makes a conscious and consistent attempt to take the prisoner's personal, historic, individual, grounded experience and to universalize it. This strips the prisoner of his particularities in order to make him abstract and eternal. Indeed, poetry is the primary medium by which she does so, because the poems are where we find at their most concentrated her exhortations to look up. The abstract beauty of the poems has often proved seductive. Peter Glassgold (1994, p. 15) claims that *Consolation*'s prose merely offers "a dramatic framework for the poetry's philosophical lyricism, which seeks in translation a language transcending time, echoing and reechoing Boethius's dream of the eternal ideal." James Harpur (2007, p. 9 and back jacket) offers a "coherent poetic sequence" in which "the poems gain from the protracted intensity of poetic imagination carried over, uninterrupted, poem by poem." They are imagined as reaching a sort of moral crescendo. Seth Lerer's introduction to David Slavitt's translation of the complete *Consolation* asks the first-time reader not to worry too much about doctrine or history in the shaping of the text (Slavitt 2008, p. xv): "Instead, the reader should savor the resonances of its verse: from the ruefulness of its opening meters in Book I, through the power of its natural descriptions in Book II, the purview of its cosmology in Book III, the affecting retellings of the tales of mythic heroes in Books III and IV, to the knowing serenity in Book V." These poems constitute a *vade mecum*, a tale of personal relevance, an emotional journey from sorrow to serenity reenacted by the reader, not the particular tale of the prisoner reconstituted by the reader.

Poetry is a medium that belongs primarily to Philosophy. Of the 39 poems in the five books of *Consolation*, arranged 7 + 8 + 12 + 7 + 5, only three are composed and delivered by the prisoner (1 m.3, 1 m.5, and 5 m.3; the opening poem is the dictation he took from the Muses), and only two of those are substantial (1 m.5, 5 m.3). The first book begins with a poem and ends with one, while all the other books begin with prose. Every book ends with a poem, except for the last book, where the absence of a final poem has always been a problem, often seen as a sign of the physical incompleteness of the book. There is, then, a curious symmetry between the first book and the last: The first has one poem too many; the last one too few (6 + 1, 8, 12, 7, 6-1). In fact, book 1 begins with a poem that shouldn't be there (the dictated poem, a dismal false start) and book 5 ends with a poem that isn't there. These bookends of *Consolation* are themselves statements about the proprieties and limitations of poetry: What is said in verse lies between what shouldn't have been said and what cannot be said; the prisoner plays poet only in books where the structure is interrupted.

The poetry of *Consolation* attempts to have meaning without reference to speakers, and it tries to be universal; that is, it tries to find truths beyond the specific physical circumstance of the prisoner. *Poetry is not an emotional medium that stands in contrast to the rationality of prose and to discursive thought, but an abstract medium that stands in distinction to the physical circumstance of the prisoner.* Part of poetry's pattern is that it serves as a medium that suppresses the history and the experience of the prisoner. This reveals much about Boethius the author's view of the nature of poetry. In *Consolation*, poetry cannot tell a life story, it cannot record personal experience, it is built only for the abstract, and this is its *failing*. When one compares Boethius to Maximian, the poet who most immediately uses him and his *Consolation*, the great gulf between them becomes apparent. Maximian in his great *Third Elegy* can, in fact, write about his dealings with Boethius, in which Boethius the teacher takes Philosophy's role and Maximian the student takes the prisoner's role, and as a poet he can make Boethius's life part of his, Maximian's, own life story (Relihan 2007b, pp. 101–107).

So why write poetry at all? Poetry puts to the test Philosophy's claim to the total understanding of human life and thought. The *Consolation*'s aggressive reliance on alternating prose and verse is a constant reminder of the two worlds that it lives in. Boethius the author has offered his own experience not as the subject of poetry but as the objection to poetry. The reversion of the prisoner to prayer (see Murton 2015), and Philosophy's turning to the public audience of those whose politics put the prisoner in prison, is part of this package: Poetry tries to be universal, and Boethius writes a self-consolation in which he makes his peace with the world, in which he finds his consolation by resisting Philosophy's call for forgetting himself.

17.4 Literary Shifts in the Second Century

The glimpse of eternity and the return to earth is a Menippean staple and is easily visible in Lucian: The truth is at your feet, not in the sky. The narrator's view of himself from on high, on the other hand, is unique; so is the use of verse, a protreptic to abandon the earth and embrace a view of eternity that the narrator fights against. Boethius has his prisoner measure himself *against* eternity, and verse functions as an emblem of eternity.

This is not merely poetry's clichéd insistence upon its ability to confer immortality on the poet. Poetry's role as adversary has been acquired over time. Consider *Satyricon*, which should be dated to the second century (Henderson 2010). Here we clearly have a sort of auto-ironic humor in the form of rogue academics who range through an immoral world as immoral agents, bemoaning declining standards while writing in a form that is itself a challenge to the high styles of serious literature: Their form belittles their pretensions and is in contrast to their lives. A different approach appears in the popular fictions, Greek and Latin, in which verse composition is employed: *Apollonius King of Tyre* and *The Alexander Romance* (Dronke 1994, pp. 70–75). Verse-in-prose as a popular medium suggests that there are conflicts in some prosimetric authors between a desire to be innovative, to break boundaries, to parody the conventions of literature, and caution in the presence of a popular medium. This tension is most clearly seen in Lucian, who is at pains to call himself an innovator because he made dialogue neither prose nor verse but a Hippocentaur (*Bis Acc.* 33) – yet his own practice shows a surprising conservatism. His use of verse is sparing, just as his willingness to involve himself in his own name in his fictions and fantasies is quite restrained.

So *Satyricon* raises the possibility of academic auto-irony, and Lucian demonstrates the nervousness with which a highly literate author chooses to deploy a generic innovation. All authors who deal in prose and verse are aware that *poetry judges the author*. The involvement of an author as a character in prosimetra is problematic, and calls for caution. Neither Petronius nor Lucian is using his medium for a consideration of the psychology or personality of his own self as author. To invoke Gian Biagio Conte's famous title, Petronius is the "hidden author." Seneca and Julian have kept themselves at the periphery of their pieces. But Boethius is shown to reject this call for caution. He does so spectacularly, far beyond the auto-ironic examples of Fulgentius, a would-be scholar who is schooled by his Muse and revealed as a fool, or Martianus Capella, whose Muse upbraids him at the end for making a mess of the Seven Liberal Arts.

But what pushes verse into the realm of transcendence? What has intervened is Apuleius's *Golden Ass*. Its language is influential in late classical prosimetry, though it is not prosimetric itself; the decisive element is its conclusion, when the narrator is revealed to be the man from Madauros, who has a personal salvation under the tutelage of the goddess Isis. Apuleius provides a crucial moment in the history of Menippean satire, fashioning an inward, introspective turn that leads to the theme of the two worlds (Weinbrot 2005). On the one side stands the world in which the author lives and which he can describe; on the other rests the world that he believes in but cannot describe because it exists beyond the bounds of reasonable communication (Relihan 2007a, pp. xxii–xxvi). Apuleius takes the Greek *Metamorphoseis*, a sort of romance if we may judge by the *Onos*, makes it over as an anti-romance, and in so doing changes the nature and history of Menippean satire. Indeed, after Apuleius, Lucian's brand of Menippean satire is out of date. *The Golden Ass* turns away from the Roman and contemporary social world to contemplate an alternate reality, individual, abstract, and abstracted from this world – an inward turn of romance, which is not about identity lost and found in the context of family and society but about identity lost and found internally – and it is this turning away from the world that is so strangely reflected in *Consolation*.

In the context of individuals set against eternity, verse plays a universalizing role. It represents tradition, summarizes culture, and speaks as the embodiment of history and authority. This distinction between text and tradition is important and proves to be useful to an understanding of late classical prosimetra. The prisoner's Muse-dictated opening poem in *Consolation* shows his distance from true traditions. But *Consolation*, an amalgam of arguments, of Cynic, Stoic, Platonic, Aristotelian, even Augustinian approaches, working on the prisoner through twists and turns, problems and conundrums and achieving a consolation tailored to our unique political philosopher, does not have the status of a textbook. This is important. Consider again the *Apocolocyntosis–Caesar –Consolation* triad, in which *Caesars* stands out as a comic textbook, an encapsulated Roman history, above which floats Julian himself, better than his predecessors and worthy of a separate heaven with Mithras, not this comic Olympus of wrangling unworthies. The comic Olympus appears in Martianus Capella as well, the less-than-glorious destination for Philology's ascent, after she has glimpsed the Unknown Father at the edge of the universe (2.200–6), once she has jettisoned her knowledge – prayer in the form of nonsense syllables, beyond the realm of discursive thought. Here, too, we have a book, an encyclopedia, composed by an author whose frame for it suggests its less-than-ultimate value. Menippean satire is a medium in which authors can both create textbooks and criticize them in a fantasy setting or, in the case of Boethius, play with the notion of authority itself.

17.5 The Evidence of Sympotic Literature

Satyricon, Lucian, and Apuleius illustrate a range of second-century options for keeping an author separate from the world he describes and the medium he uses to describe it. But there is a related shift in the history of symposium as well, a genre that becomes and remains highly prosimetric, though not with the regularity, or poetic invention, of Menippean texts. Plutarch's first-century *Table Talk* can be read as a sort of serious intellectual biography: The author reflects on the learned men who helped to shape him into the author that he has now become (König 2011). How different this is from Athenaeus's *Deipnosophists*, where scholars by their command of the minutiae of comic texts show themselves to be comic themselves, where the sympotic has become both playful and encyclopedic (Jacob 2013). Lucian's spectacles of philosophical hypocritical symposiasts are barely related to this genial work.

Yet when Macrobius attempts to create a similar gathering, and where he might have license for levity given that the occasion is the *Saturnalia*, which gives his book its title, he is more modest and much more restrained. Macrobius's *Saturnalia* isn't really about Macrobius himself and, despite Evangelus and some of the other trappings of the Plato-dominated genre, it isn't an exercise to any degree in humor at the expense of intellectuals, and Macrobius's authorship of the text is not nearly so important as Athenaeus's authorship of his (Jacob 2013, pp. 9–12).

The point most worth making in this regard is that this learned symposium is defending an author: Virgil. The speakers are not comic, even if Evangelus can be dastardly; they do not create their own poetry. Macrobius's innovations lie in his *Commentary on The Dream of* Scipio, which, according to Julieta Cardigni (2013), is its own *narratio fabulosa* by which Scipio is established both as ideal Roman and as ideal reader. In either case, defense of a text is serious business. There are, in other words, countervailing forces that can force prosimetry into respectability. Consider also Fulgentius. His prosimetric *Mitologiae* is a textbook, and as a Menippean satire it makes fun of the scholar who thinks that he understands the true meanings of classical myths: Satire comes to set him straight, dispenses with his services, and proceeds in three books to wring any profundity out of mythology by a series of breezy allegorizations. The text parodies the textbook. On the other hand, the *Allegorical Content of Virgil* makes fun of Fulgentius the author in many of the same ways but is not prosimetric: Here Fulgentius is defending the authoritative Virgil, and prosimetrum is out of consideration (Relihan 1993, pp. 158–161).

17.6 Conclusion: Two Pre-Boethian, Two Post-Boethian Traditions

In the history of Menippean satire, the crucial late classical innovation is the exploitation of encyclopedic content. This should not be thought of as a Varronian addition to the genre so much as its appropriate topic in a textbook age. Menippean satire, itself subversive of intellectual systems, helps us to identify what is the chief intellectual system of its time. The increasingly ordered aggregation of human learning into systems, into handbooks, has a valuable function: "Encyclopedic learning had a long association with the portrayal of communal learning and shared ethical virtues in classical literature" (Bjornlie 2015, p. 292). Menippean satire in this age is a critique of the notion of cultural patrimony. Prosimetry has become a vehicle for amassing everything (in which prose with verse establishes universality) and criticizing everything (in which prose with verse establishes dissonance).

The two most complex prosimetric texts of late antiquity are Julian's *Caesars* and Boethius's *Consolation*, at opposite ends of the prosimetric spectrum. The ways in which they and their authors align is instructive (Relihan 2005). I would like to emphasize the congruity of their pride: Julian is the only worthy emperor in the history of the Roman Empire, and for him is reserved a separate heaven and a separate salvation under the tutelage of the god Mithras; Boethius through his prisoner represents himself as the last Roman poet, the last true patriot, the last true philosopher. Both see history as focused on themselves and ending with themselves. Julian came to his *Caesars* in the course of a wide-ranging literary career, at once satiric, belletristic, philosophical, and protreptic. *Caesars* does not bear that much weight in Julian's oeuvre, and it is certainly lightweight in comparison to *Consolation*.

Caesars lies at the intersection of many traditions, each of which thinks of prose with verse in a different way, though all point to some understanding of the mixture representing a universalization of literature and of experience, a way to move from the particular, the historical, and the earthbound to the universal, the abstract, and the celestial. *Caesars* shows a development of the mixed-meter, political, naming-names tradition of Latin satire; it shows the Varronian encyclopedic strain of Menippean satire; as a parody of a symposium, it belongs to Lucianic traditions of humor; in its sparing use of verse, it shows Lucian's nervousness concerning the popular nature of prose with verse; and as Saturnalian writing, specifically following in Seneca's footsteps, it plays with the seriousness of the social order in its critique of both cultural and literary traditions. It is encyclopedic in a way that *Consolation* is not; it does not expose Julian to criticism in the way that *Consolation* exposes Boethius.

The defense of text vs. critique of tradition allows us another valuable insight into the nature of Menippean satire. Menippean satires do not actively parody an existing book; rather, they create the books that they parody. What is *Caesars* but a new textbook of Roman history played for laughs? Or the *Marriage of Mercury and Philology* but a new handbook in which handbook learning is put in its place? Cardigni (forthcoming) sees *Marriage* as a parody of Apuleius's *Cupid and Psyche*. When Mercury wants a bride, he does not get his bride of choice: Sophia is unsuitable, Mantice is unavailable, and Psyche has already been taken. Martianus's *Marriage*, which does not include an actual marriage, is emphatically not the reunion of soul and source; the textbook arts are a substitute for what might have been. Boethius's *Consolation* is too complex for this sort of categorization – *Consolation* is not a philosophy handbook squinted at through some ironic lens but philosophy in a new way. Boethius, who spent a lifetime as a translator, interpreter, and commentator, was first and foremost a defender of texts; when he came to write *Consolation*, he took the opportunity to become a critic of traditions, and prose and verse served him in a number of ways, ways that are ultimately too personal for us to explain as universal laws of a genre.

Late antiquity is not best known for its humor; it is only in texts that we can call Menippean that sophisticated comic play resides, and that is humor at the expense of educational and interpretive systems (Shanzer 2002, pp. 25–26). But if we are now comfortable in saying that late antiquity is a period of intellectual and literary innovation, where we can speak of "Postmodern Late Antiquity/Late Antique Postmodernity" (Elsner and Hernández Lobato 2017, pp. 20–22), or speak approvingly of its recognition that words may not communicate as much as silence can (a "Poetics of Silence;" Hernández Lobato 2017), we can appreciate Menippean satire both as an intellectually subversive genre and as an inspiration for other works that, although not prosimetric per se, latch onto its auto-ironic criticism of traditions. Boethius as a formal and intellectual inspiration is most prominent in the twelfth-century Renaissance, in Alain of Lille and Bernardus Silvestris, but this line of influence has died out. The true, vital Menippean line of influence in the late classical period extends not through Boethius but through Martianus Capella to the seventh-century Virgilius Maro Grammaticus (Latin grammar made fantastic, and Latin grammarians made ridiculous; see Law 1995) and the *Cosmographia* of the early eighth-century Aethicus Ister. Aethicus Ister, drawing on the Grammaticus and other sources, writes in the person of St. Jerome, who claims to edit, translate, and comment on the cosmographical work of an unknown pagan philosopher Aethicus the Istrian. Its narrative includes verse passages, fantastic geography, and humor at the expense of saints, philosophers, and exegetes (see Herren 2011; Dronke 1994, pp. 14–19 is still insightful). Literarily, he anticipates the modern Menippean satires that work by footnotes, parodying their own texts, a tradition from *Dunciad* to Flann O'Brien to Nabokov's *Pale Fire* to David Foster Wallace (Zetzel 1995); "for the twenty-first century literature has become the last refuge of an encyclopaedism that can be taken seriously" (West 2013, p. 500). If Menippean satire is going to parody the book, it needs to write that book first.

ACKNOWLEDGMENT

I am pleased to thank a number of colleagues who helped guide, revise, and redirect my prosimetric thoughts (though not this chapter) over a long stretch of years: Ann Astell, Stephen Blackwood, H. Christian Blood, Bracht Branham, Jeffrey Henderson, A.M. Juster, Megan Murton, Karen Ní Mheallaigh, Joseph Pucci, Eileen Sweeney, and, at the end, Julieta Cardigni, who let me see in draft form her work on Martianus Capella as a parody of *Cupid and Psyche*.

REFERENCES

Bjornlie, Shane. (2015). The rhetoric of *Varietas* and epistolary encyclopedism in *Variae* of Cassiodorus. In: *Shifting Genres in Late Antiquity* (ed. Geoffrey Greatrex and Hugh Elton), 289–303. London: Routledge.

Blackwood, Stephen. (2015). *The Consolation of Boethius as Poetic Liturgy*. Oxford: Oxford University Press.

Bonandini, Alice. (2010). *Il contrasto menippeo: Prosimetro, citazioni e commutazione di codice nell'Apocolocyntosis di Seneca. Con un commento alle parti poetiche.* Labirinti 130. Trento: Università degli Studi di Trento.

Cardigni, Julieta. (2013). *El comentario como género tardoantiguo: Commentarii in Somnium Scipionis de Macrobio*. Colección Saberes. Buenos Aires: Facultad de Filosofía y Letras, Universidad de Buenos Aires.

Cardigni, Julieta. (Forthcoming). *Fandis tacenda farcinat*: Discourse and Silence in Martianus Capella's *De nuptiis Mercurii et Philologia*.

De Smet, Ingrid A.R. (1996). *Menippean Satire and the Republic of Letter, 1581–1655*. Genève: Librairie Droz S.A.

Donato, Antonio. (2013). *Boethius's* Consolation of Philosophy *as a Product of Late Antiquity*. London: Bloomsbury Academic.

Dronke, Peter. (1994). *Verse with Prose from Petronius to Dante: The Art and Scope of the Mixed Form*. Cambridge, MA: Harvard University Press.

Elsner, Jaś and Hernández Lobato, Jesús. (2017). Introduction: Notes toward a poetics of late antique literature. In: *The Poetics of Late Latin Literature* (ed. Jaś Elsner and Jesús Hernández Lobato), 1–22. Oxford: Oxford University Press.

Formisano, Marco. (2013). Late Latin encyclopaedism: Towards a new paradigm of practical knowledge. In: *Encyclopaedism from Antiquity to the Renaissance* (ed. Jason König and Greg Woolf), 197–215. Cambridge: Cambridge University Press.

Freudenburg, Kirk. (2013). The afterlife of Varro in Horace's *Sermones*: Generic issues in Roman satire. In: *Generic Interfaces in Latin Literature: Encounters, Interactions and Transformations* (ed. Theodore D. Papanghelis, Stephen J. Harrison, and Stavros Frangoulidis), 297–336. Trends in Classics – Supplementary Volumes 20. Berlin: De Gruyter.

Glassgold, Peter. trans. (1994). *Boethius: The Poems from* On the Consolation of Philosophy, *Translated out of the Original Latin into Diverse Historical Englishings, Diligently Collaged by Peter Glassgold*. Los Angeles: Sun & Moon.

Goddard, Victoria. (2011). *Poetry and Philosophy in Boethius and Dante*. PhD diss., Centre for Medieval Studies, University of Toronto.

Harpur, James. trans. (2007). *Boethius: Fortune's Prisoner: The Poems of Boethius's The Consolation of Philosophy*. London: Anvil Press Poetry.

Harris, Joseph and Reichl, Karl. ed. (1997). *Prosimetrum: Crosscultural Perspectives on Narrative in Prose and Verse*. Cambridge: D. S. Brewer.

Hays, Gregory. (2013). Fulgentius the mythographer? In: *Writing Myth: Mythography in the Ancient World* (ed. Stephen M. Trzaskoma and R. Scott Smith), 309–333. Leuven: Peeters.

Henderson, Jeffrey. (2010). The *Satyrica* and the Greek novel: Revisions and some open questions. *International Journal of the Classical Tradition* 17: 483–496. doi: 10.1007/s12138-010-0215-2

Hernández Lobato, Jesús. (2017). To speak or not to speak: The birth of a "poetics of silence" in late antique literature. In: *The Poetics of Late Latin Literature* (ed. Jaś Elsner and Jesús Hernández Lobato), 278–310. Oxford: Oxford University Press.

Herren, Michael W. ed., trans., and comm. (2011). *The Cosmography of Aethicus Ister*. Turnhout: Brepols.

Jacob, Christian. (2013). *The Web of Athenaeus* (trans. Arietta Papaconstantinou). Hellenic Studies 61. Center for Hellenic Studies. Cambridge, MA: Harvard University Press.

Johnson, Eleanor. (2009). Chaucer and the Consolation of *prosimetrum*. *Chaucer Review* 43: 455–472. doi: 10.1353/cr.0.0024

Johnson, Eleanor. (2013). *Practicing Literary Theory in the Middle Ages: Ethics and the Mixed Form in Chaucer, Gower, Usk, and Hoccleve*. Chicago: University of Chicago Press.

König, Jason. (2011). Self-promotion and self-effacement in Plutarch's *Table Talk*. In: *The Philosopher's Banquet: Plutarch's* Table Talk *in the Intellectual Culture of the Roman Empire* (ed. Frieda Klotz and Katerina Oikonomopoulou), 179–203. Oxford: Oxford University Press.

Koppenfels, Werner von. (2007). *Der andere Blick oder Das Vermächtnis des Menippos. Paradoxe Perspektiven in der europäischen Literatur*. Munich: C.H. Beck.

Law, Vivien. (1995). *Wisdom, Authority and Grammar in the Seventh Century: Decoding Virgilius Maro Grammaticus*. Cambridge: Cambridge University Press.

Marenbon, John. (2014). Boethius' unparadigmatic originality and its implications for medieval philosophy. In: *Boethius as a Paradigm of Late Ancient Thought* (ed. Thomas Böhm, Thomas Jürgasch, and Andreas Kirchner), 231–244. Berlin: De Gruyter.

Murton, Megan. (2015). Praying with Boethius in *Troilus and Criseyde*. *Chaucer Review* 49: 294–319. doi: 10.5325/chaucerrev.49.3.0294

O'Donnell, James. (2008). *The Ruin of the Roman Empire*. New York: Harper Collins.

Orth, Peter. (2000). *Hildeberts Prosimetrum De Querimonia und die Gedichte eines Anonymus: Untersuchungen und kritische Editionen*. Wiener Studien Beiheft 26. Vienna: Verlag der Österreichischen Akademie der Wissenschaften.

Pabst, Bernhard. (1994). *Prosimetrum: Tradition und Wandel einer Literaturform zwischen Spätantike und Spätmittelalter*. 2 vols. Ordo: Studien zur Literatur und Gesellschaft des Mittelalters und der frühen Neuzeit 4/1–2. Cologne: Böhlau.

Relihan, Joel. (1993). *Ancient Menippean Satire*. Baltimore: Johns Hopkins University Press.

Relihan, Joel. (2005). Late arrivals: Julian and Boethius. In: *The Cambridge Companion to Roman Satire* (ed. Kirk Freudenburg), 109–122. Cambridge: Cambridge University Press.

Relihan, Joel. trans. (2007a). *Apuleius: The Golden Ass*. Bloomington, IN: Hackett.

Relihan, Joel. (2007b). *The Prisoner's Philosophy: Life and Death in Boethius's Consolation*. Notre Dame, IN: University of Notre Dame Press.

Relihan, Joel C. (2017). Prose satire. In: *A Guide to Neo-Latin Literature* (ed. Victoria Moul), 340–357. Cambridge: Cambridge University Press.

Shanzer, Danuta. (2002). Laughter and humor in the early medieval Latin West. In: *Humour, History and Politics in Late Antiquity and the Early Middle Ages* (ed. Guy Halsall), 25–47. Cambridge: Cambridge University Press.

Slavitt, David, trans. (2008). *Boethius: The Consolation of Philosophy*. Introduction by Seth Lerer. Cambridge, MA: Harvard University Press.

Weinbrot, Howard D. (2005). *Menippean Satire Reconsidered: From Antiquity to the Eighteenth Century*. Baltimore: Johns Hopkins University Press.

West, William. (2013). Irony and encyclopedic writing before (and after) the Enlightenment. In: *Encyclopaedism from Antiquity to the Renaissance* (ed. Jason König and Greg Woolf), 482–503. Cambridge: Cambridge University Press.

Wetherbee, Winthrop. (2009). The *Consolation* and medieval literature. In: *The Cambridge Companion to Boethius* (ed. John Marenbon). Cambridge: Cambridge University Press.

Wetherbee, Winthrop. ed. and trans. (2013). *Alan of Lille: Poetic Works*. Dumbarton Oaks Medieval Library 22. Cambridge, MA: Harvard University Press.

Wetherbee, Winthrop. ed. and trans. (2015). *Bernardus Silvestris: Poetic Works*. Dumbarton Oaks Medieval Library 38. Cambridge, MA: Harvard University Press.

Witke, Charles. (1996). Review of Pabst 1994. *Journal of Medieval Latin* 6: 226–232.

Zetzel, James E.G. (1995). Review of Law 1995. *Bryn Mawr Classical Review* 95.10.23.

Ziolkowski, Jan. (1997). The prosimetrum in the classical tradition. In: *Prosimetrum: Crosscultural Perspectives on Narrative in Prose and Verse* (ed. Joseph Harris and Karl Reichl), 45–65. Cambridge: D.S. Brewer.

CHAPTER EIGHTEEN

Philosophical Commentary

Han Baltussen

18.1 Background

Among the written forms of ancient philosophical discourse, the philosophical commentary was a relatively late arrival. The earliest Greek philosophers are partially preserved in the traditional poetic language of Homer using hexameter lines, as seen in the fragments of Parmenides, Xenophanes, and Empedocles – a sign of the strongly oral culture they lived in. Prose was used later, perhaps by Anaximander in the mid-sixth century BCE (fr. 12B.1 DK), but certainly by Heraclitus in the late sixth century (fr. 1 DK = Sextus Empiricus, *Against the Mathematicians* VII.132). Yet even their prose style echoes the imagery and thought patterns of oral culture, which was characterized by mnemonic techniques (meter and formulaic language) and metaphor to facilitate memorization and depth of expression. In other words, at first *writing* philosophy was not an aim in itself but intended to support the oral presentation of ideas. Further oral interaction and polemic (Tarrant 1996 suggests they are like protreptic sound bites) was not far behind and stimulated reflection on language as a vehicle for ideas. We may well begin by clarifying two aspects of the genre: its origin and its nature.

The question of when commentary arose has no clear answer. Early exegetical activities can be identified in the earliest polemics of the first philosophers as well as the more sophisticated close readings of texts in the late fifth and early fourth centuries BCE (Baltussen 2007; Cherniss 1977). A striking example is Plato's *Protagoras*, in which Socrates engages in the interpretation of a

---

A Companion to Late Antique Literature, First Edition.
Edited by Scott McGill and Edward J. Watts.
© 2018 John Wiley & Sons, Inc. Published 2018 by John Wiley & Sons, Inc.

poem by Simonides and makes use of hermeneutical moves that betray an existing practice of exegesis (*Protag.* 347a): Thus he claims to know the author's intention (*boulēsis*), uses grammatical arguments to prove his point, and investigates the hidden meaning of the poem. The dialogue also reveals two further instances of hermeneutical principles (which are implicit): The one focuses on the importance of authorial consistency (341e1–2) that would eventually find expression in the phrase "clarifying Homer from Homer" (Schäublin 1977, based on Porphyry, *Quaest. Homericae* p. 297, 16–17 [ed. Schrader]; cf. Mansfeld 1994; Sluiter 2000; Baltussen 2004, 2007); the other principle assumes the importance of an overall purpose of the poem, rather than just focusing on individual words or phrases (see esp. Baltussen 2004, and compare Yunis 2003, Kahn 2003). Even if we allow for an element of parody in Plato's representation of these practices, it had to contain certain realistic features to be plausible and credible to his audience.

A further important question is this: What counts as commentary? One obvious fact about commentary, whether ancient or modern, is its "reactive" and second-order nature, that is, a commentary needs a base text to *comment on*. On closer inspection, this requirement turns out to be fulfilled only when the text is considered worthwhile to engage with in the first place. And while scholars are not fully agreed on when exactly the philosophical commentary arose, it is clear that "worthwhile" in this case must mean that the text(s) commented on contained an important message *and* had authority. These two requirements needed very special circumstances to give rise to commentary: It required a *canon* and the *tools* to undertake textual exegesis (on informal beginnings, see Baltussen 2007). We can observe this in a formal sense from the first century BCE onward, when clear evidence survives in the Peripatetic tradition: The rise of exegetical comments on Aristotle's *Categories* (Griffin 2015). The Anon. *Commentary on Plato's Theaetetus,* on a papyrus dated to 150 CE, may be an exception to some extent, but its creation date is not certain (late first century BCE possible). Informally, earlier writings may have consisted of comments on a particular work, but only then the two other requirements were in place. In support of this broad outline we may quote Alexander of Aphrodisias, who ca. 200 CE looked back at the earlier centuries and noted that, before his time, philosophical engagement was less bookish and certainly not aimed at writing commentary (*In Top.* 27,12–16):

> This kind of speech was customary among the older philosophers, who set up most of their classes in this way — not with reference to books, since at the time there were not yet any books of this kind. After a thesis has been posited, they trained their aptitude at finding argumentative attacks by producing attack arguments about this thesis, establishing and refuting the position through what is approved. (Sellars 2006, pp. 29–30)

It should be stated at the outset, however, that "commentary" in the philosophical tradition is quite different from how we often conceive of it today. Modern scholarship tends to have a primary concern with meticulous philological comments on words, phrases, sentences, and the historical or cultural context; philosophers developed a style of exegesis that aimed at clarifying the writings of the great pioneers of Greek philosophy Plato and Aristotle, but with a focus on ideas and doctrine.

By the second century CE both these factors (language and philosophy) had become contributing elements in the new genre of philosophical exegesis. Their expansive notes arose for mostly two reasons: First, a linguistic one (Sedley 1997), derived from the need to clarify texts considered important that were written in language no longer well understood, and second, a pedagogical one, designed to enhance the philosophical instruction by a teacher. Such learned notes could take different formats, but the most common type was what we would now call "running commentary," which was both scholarly and philosophical (Baltussen 2008, pp. 14–15). Once established, the running commentary became common, lasting into the Middle Ages.

18.2 Commentary and Exegesis

We should now turn to the central focus of this chapter, the ancient philosophical commentary from late antiquity and its most typical "literary" forms. I will distinguish *formal commentary* (a narrow literary product of a literate culture) from *exegesis* (broadly understood as any interpretative act, whether positive, polemical, or implicit). The question of origin becomes less important when we realize that commentary was a second-order exegetical activity that emerged from a slow process of debate and exegesis – an evolving format of texts commenting on other texts. In other words, commentaries were primarily meta-texts with pedagogical and ideological purpose.

The period in which full-blown commentary became a dominant form of doing philosophy falls between 300 and 700 CE. These centuries saw scholarly and complex exegetical writings originate primarily (though not exclusively) in the educational context of late Platonism, which brought a style of reading Plato initiated by Plotinus (205-270 CE). Late Platonists had a vested interest in Plato and his works and were convinced that Plato's wisdom revealed the preferred philosophical wisdom. In the preceding centuries two schools of thought had come out on top in the competitive world of ideas: Platonism and Stoicism. Now the philosophical discourse was influenced by both as well as by Aristotelian ideas. As we will see, Plotinus illustrates this new situation well in his reading of Plato *and* Aristotle, while certain Stoic terminology had already become *lingua franca* among philosophers (Gatti 1996). Plotinus's followers created writings that contained increasingly more learned notes (*hypomnēmata, sungrammata, scholai*) in a cumulative process that also strengthened their increasingly bookish approach to intellectual endeavors. But their primary purpose was usually to clarify in great detail the words and thoughts of Plato (and Plotinus), whose writings were considered authoritative, covering everything from natural philosophy to theology and metaphysics. Thus Iamblichus (ca. 245–325 CE, see esp. Dillon 1987) introduced the idea of a singular objective (*skopos*) for each work studied, which would streamline the interpretive process and encourage exegetes to think in terms of the overall thematic consistency of a work. This idea is already found in the *Protagoras*, when Socrates discusses the Simonides poem (Baltussen 2004). This approach led to distinguishing discrete points to be discussed with any author, the so-called isagogical issues (Westerink 1962; Hadot 1978; Mansfeld 1994). In the process they made use of other authors (most famously Aristotle) for the purpose of clarifying and shoring up Plato's system, with the surprising result that the views of Plato and Aristotle came to be regarded as harmonious (Baltussen 2008).

In short, the motivation, format, and origin of ancient philosophical commentaries are very different from modern commentary. They share the same scholarly nature, an eye for detail, and responsiveness to their place in a long-standing tradition. They also have a range of formats and variable levels of technicality, both of which have long stood in the way of a balanced treatment in modern scholarship. It is fair to say that the ancient philosophical commentary evolved over a long period of time and only has become visible to the historian's probing eye at a time when it had already developed a near-mature form (200 CE) as the "running commentary" in the works of Alexander of Aphrodisias. Literary analysis of the ancient philosophical commentary has been rather sparse, even if the past three decades have seen major progress in the evaluation of their philosophical value and impact (Sorabji 1990). The next section pays particular attention to this aspect by focusing on the form of these unwieldy and complex works.

18.3 Forms of Commentary

The work of Plotinus offers an important milestone in late antique exegesis. His innovative style of philosophizing is highlighted by his biographer Porphyry, our main source on Plotinus's inspired and inspiring style of interpreting Plato and Aristotle (*VPlot* 14). We should think of his classes as the locus for close teacher–pupil interactions, characterized by reading texts together (*sunanagnōsis*). It is this triangulated dynamic of teacher, students, and texts (base texts and previous commentaries) that sets the agenda for future authors of commentaries. His interpretive comments on Plato, Aristotle, and other thinkers are not (formal) commentary in the strict sense, but his critical engagement with texts shares a particular attitude with the later commentators, typified by a self-conscious positioning within a tradition and a sense of the new building on the old. According to Porphyry, he had "compactly incorporated" (*katapepuknōtai*) Aristotle's *Metaphysics* within his doctrines (*VPlot* 14). Porphyry leaves no doubt about the importance of books of earlier commentaries in Plotinus's teaching. A list of writers he used includes Severus, Gaius, Numenius, and Alexander of Aphrodisias (*VPlot* 14.3), which shows how strongly text-based his style of philosophical enquiry was. But Plotinus was not commenting on the text for the sake of clarifying the text, but was using it as a jumping-off point to develop his own philosophy.

As his student and biographer, Porphyry marked a further important stage in the history of later Greek philosophy. Plotinus's classes had become an encouraging environment for exegetical activities on "canonized" texts, and Porphyry instigated a curious reversal of chronology, making Aristotle's work the introduction to Plato. Thus commentary on both authors became the preferred mode of philosophical education. Andronicus (ca. 50 BCE) had already made this work the starting point for studying Aristotle, in particular for logic and demonstration (Griffin 2015, pp. 32–39). This approach to the two scholarchs of related, but distinct, philosophical persuasions was based on the idea that their views could be brought into harmony (*sumphōnia*), which is not to be confused with complete agreement (Gerson 2005; Karamanolis 2006). This was not completely new: A rapprochement of Plato and Aristotle had started with the philosopher Antiochus (ca. 125–ca. 68 BCE, head of the Fourth Academy), and the choice of Aristotle's *Categories* as a starting point for the philosophical curriculum can be traced back to Andronicus (mid-first century BCE). But Porphyry's initiative made the *Categories* a formal starting point in the curriculum. He set an example by writing two commentaries on the work, and many later Platonists followed suit, as we can read in Simplicius's commentary on the *Categories* (ed. Kalbfleisch 1907), which incorporates materials from previous works now lost. Clearly, then, commentary was a product of teaching practices, but their exegesis was intended to be philosophical, not merely philological.

The works known to us, but not all extant, take several different forms, characterized by several different formats: word-by-word commentary, longer essays, problem-oriented discussion, and commentary on part of a text or on a complete text. These could coexist and at times go hand in hand.

The range of formats taken by commentaries composed between 100 and 800 CE suggests that it took some time for a fixed form to crystallize out of the different attempts to offer clarifications to the Platonic and Aristotelian corpus (Plato's works probably formed the earliest corpus in a strong sense). The works can vary in length, in how much text they propose to cover, in exegetical approach, and in how much their exegesis is confined to clarification or constitutes a springboard for broader philosophical musings.

In line with these criteria of (in)completeness, I have divided them into *four* broad groups:

18.3.1 Discursive Evaluations: Essays and Short Lectures

This is the type of writing in which "commentary" only applies very loosely, since these writings typically arise from a passage. But there is clearly a text at the center of the discussion, and hence exegesis will occur: A prime example is Plotinus, whose style of discussing Plato, Aristotle, and other philosophers extracts short phrases or sentences and offers a very idiosyncratic and syncretistic interpretation. He was much read in subsequent centuries, as is clear from quotations inside and outside the Platonist tradition (Klitenic Wear 2013, p. 149, argues that Plotinus was known even in Christian circles of Alexandria). Porphyry tells us that Plotinus would often read a passage and interpret it on the spot (*VPlot.* 14.4). He would read Plato, Aristotle, and Alexander of Aphrodisias in conjunction and expand on their philosophical position to construct his own interpretation. Remarkably, the written version of his thoughts was put to paper only very late in his life (between 253 and 275 CE; Porph. *VPlot.* 4–6), so they are in a way a more developed philosophically than one would expect, yet also still quite fresh due to their dynamic and impressionistic style. It may be relevant to remember that Plotinus was an Egyptian whose Greek is not particularly elegant and also not flawless. Porphyry notes that he often had to correct the orthography of the text (*VPlot.* 8; 19; 39–40). Other examples in this group are the essays of Simplicius embedded in his *Commentary on Aristotle's Physics* (book 4), in which he elaborates on place and time, taking Aristotle as his springboard. The essays are self-contained accounts of the late Platonist positions and are strongly influenced by his teacher Damascius (ca. 458– after 538), for instance, his *Corrollaries on Place and Time* (Urmson 1992; Athanassiadi 1999).

18.3.2 Paraphrase and Summary

Another form used by the commentators consisted of a paraphrase of the text under scrutiny (*paraphrasis*), or a summary (*epitomē*). We only have two clear examples for this type of work among late Platonists, and both date to the early sixth century CE: one by Priscian (*Epitomē of Theophrastus' On Sense Perception*) and one by Simplicius (*Epitomē of Theophrastus' Physics*). The term *epitomē* is here to be understood as a compressed rendering of the content in its main points, not a close summary that follows the text in linear fashion. Priscian's work survives (translated by Huby 1997), but for Simplicius's *epitomē* we only have a few snippets in self-references (mainly in his commentary on Aristotle's *Physics*, book 1). We should not forget that the Peripatetics also wrote summaries and synopses of Aristotle's works (e.g. of the *Physics*, as Simplicius reports *in Phys.* 6.2–3: *tōn spoudaiotatōn autou mathētōn…kephalaia autēs kai sunopseis poioumenōn*). We also have Themistius's paraphrases of Aristotle, but he is not a Platonist.

18.3.3 Partial or Selective Comments

In this type we may include selective notes on Aristotle's *Categories* like those by Lucius and Boethus (first century BCE), as recorded by Simplicius in his *Commentary on Aristotle's* Categories 1,18–19. It may have its earliest predecessor in Krantor's comments on Plato's *Timaeus*, which did not cover the whole work (Proclus *in Plat. Tim.* I. 76. 1–2, who calls him *exēgētēs*).

18.3.4 Fuller "Running" Commentary, Usually Covering a Whole Work

Commentary as a continuous set of notes to explain words, phrases, sentences, and overall outlook and aim of a work starts as partial commentary (as mentioned under 18.3.3). Its overall structure is often determined by a set of questions that arose from classroom discussions: These would address the purpose or objective (*skopos*) of the work, its utility (*chrēsimon*), its position in the corpus (*taxis*), whether it was genuine (*gnēsion*), what its main sections were (*kephalaia*), and which part of philosophy it belonged to (*meros*) (Mansfeld 1994, pp. 10–11). Clearly these are all useful topics to consider when examining a work of Aristotle or Plato: They became known as *schēmata isagogica*, "introductory figures."

A few examples may be useful. The earliest example of a "running" commentary is probably the so-called *Anonymous Commentary on (Plato's) Theaetetus* (*Anon. in Tht.*), also dated to the first century BCE (Bastianini and Sedley 1995). Simplicius (ca. 480–540 CE) reports that the Peripatetic Boethus of Sidon (*in Cat.* 1.18, based on Porphyry) wrote a "word-by-word exegesis" on the *Categories* in the first century BCE (*in Cat.* 30.2). Next, one could point to the commentaries of Aspasius and Alexander of Aphrodisias, in the mid- to late second century CE.

Good examples of Aristotelian commentators who lived during the so-called Second Sophistic (ca. 100–250, when intense study of the "Classics" from the golden era of Athens occurred), are Aspasius and Alexander of Aphrodisias. About Aspasius we know very little, except that he wrote a commentary on Aristotle's ethics (Alberti and Sharples 1999). Alexander, holder of the Chair of Peripatetic philosophy, was the designated exegete of Aristotle in Athens (Sharples 1987; Rashed 2011). It was one of four chairs set up by emperor Marcus Aurelius in the 160s CE (Philostr., *Lives of Sophists* 566). Recently a newly discovered inscription revealed his full name and that of his father (Chaniotis 2004a, 2004b). The most important feature of his commentaries is the meticulous attention to detail and the continuous reflection on almost every aspect of the arguments and language of Aristotle's writings. He typically reads Aristotle in a way that can be labeled "creative exegesis:" a manner of reinterpreting passages that allows for shifts in meaning over time of important concepts. Alexander also regularly expresses disagreement with Aristotle but often attempts to preserve Aristotle's integrity by reworking certain views so as to make them consistent with the overall system.

Thus the running commentary of this period exhibits a kind of meta-narrative that closely follows a base text of a philosopher, who is seen as an authority. Its scholarly nature and particular format now seem all too familiar. Its scholarly nature arose in the context of teaching activity and because the teachers consciously attached considerable authority to the lecture notes and to comments of previous teachers. This circumstance created a two-pronged approach to explicating texts: attention to the text itself as well as attention to existing exegeses (a fuller argument is presented in Baltussen 2016).

Apart from these broad groupings, there are exceptional cases among the Platonists that cannot be pigeonholed so easily. Some, in fact, will fit two or three categories. A peculiar case of a polemical commentary on a whole work is Plutarch's *Adversus Colotem*, an attempt to provide a refutation of the Epicurean Colotes, who attacked a great number of earlier Greek philosophers (see esp. Kechagia 2011). Special mention should be made of Galen of Pergamum, the philosopher-physician, who wrote commentaries on Hippocrates with a philosophical bent (Smith 1979). Porphyry wrote philosophical essays as well as an extensive *Categories* commentary, the now-lost *Ad Gedalium*, and a shorter *Commentary by Questions and Answers* (Strange 1992; *in Cat.* [preface] 1.1–2.29). He used Alexander of Aphrodisias and also Iamblichus, whose commentary he tries to boil down to its essentials (*in Cat.* 3.2–10). There is also Hierocles's commentary on the *Golden Verses of Pythagoras* (ca. 430 CE). A most unusual work, Proclus's *Platonic Theology*, also deserves our attention, although it cannot be covered comprehensively here (Dodds 1963). This work explicates Plato's metaphysics by systematically proving that reality is a unity (One). It further shows that within this reality there are only three true causes: gods, intellects, and souls. The content of this work is closely tied to the works of Plato, yet its philosophical tendencies and terminology are clearly Proclus's. The resulting format is one of organizational and exegetical rigor with a dual doctrinal connection to the object text: dependence in so far as it aims to clarify Plato; independence by the way in which it develops its argument through a series of propositions, which suggest mathematical rigor and systematization not found in Plato himself.

All in all, the ancient philosophical commentary proves to be a very dynamic genre, incorporating within it a variety of formats and styles. The early stage (first century BCE) may well have been due to the "revival" of Aristotelian philosophy and was geared towards explicating the corpus, but the main period of the running commentary took shape in a new era of philosophy, in which the curriculum of the Platonists set the agenda for the extensive works we can now consult in the German edition of the *Commentaria in Aristotelem Graeca* (*CAG*), published by the Berlin Academy under the general editor Hermann Diels between 1882 and 1909 – some 15 000 pages of late antique Greek.

The variable formats clearly show how much they tended to arise organically in the context of teaching, and not always as an author's deliberate choice. There is, however, one important point to be noted: While the works of Alexander of Aphrodisias were the most influential in the way they illustrated what detailed and sophisticated commentary could be like, the Platonist commentaries after Plotinus added a stronger philosophical agenda to the genre by using this format as a vehicle for doing philosophy. So while their starting point would often be a text of Plato or Aristotle, they would as a rule expand on the philosophical aspects to clarify their own interpretation. Sometimes this would lead to readings that strike us as forced, or they would add "digressions" to the text in which they expounded their specific ideas on a subject.

18.4 Techniques and Strategies

With the rise of longer exegetical works in philosophy, interpretive activity continued to include deciding on the meaning of a philosophical text in light of doctrinal positions and their supporting arguments. But while known techniques remained in use, commentators increasingly made use of polemic in order to establish their own philosophical position in opposition to others.

Ideally such choices would be made in a dispassionate way, judging the arguments and relevant information on their own merit. In reality the critical assessment of arguments more often than not included a critique of particular views of individuals as one step in the right direction for developing one's own views. Plotinus already had to engage in a "war of words" against contemporaries, in particular the Gnostics:

> But we have addressed what we have said so far to our own intimate pupils [*gnōrimous*], not to the Gnostics (for we could make no progress towards convincing them) so that they may not be troubled by these latter, who do not bring forward proofs [*apodeixeis*] – how could they? – but make arbitrary, arrogant assertions. Another style of writing would be appropriate to repel those who have the insolence to pull to pieces [*diasurein*] what godlike men of antiquity have said nobly and in accordance with truth. (*Enn.* ii.9.10.12-14; trans. Armstrong 1966)

His awareness of different styles in expressing and defending one's views is clear as is the rather lively manner of debate. Another famous example concerns the acrimonious debate about the eternity of the world between Simplicius and his contemporary Philoponus. Although they never met, Simplicius's arguments are clearly *ad hominem*.

Apart from such matters of mode and style, it stands to reason that the authors of commentaries had developed tools to do what they wanted to do. We now know much more about the terminology related to exegesis, ranging from marginal annotation (*paratithesthai*) to clarifying notes (*scholia*) and commentaries (*hypomnêmata*) (Mansfeld 1994). Many of these exegetical techniques had previously been developed in Alexandria by Homer scholars, who started comparing versions of the text and tested the overall consistency of the style and content. These continued to be used and refined. For instance, in his comments to Aristotle's *Physics* 3 (*in Phys.* 395.20–21) Simplicius indicates how he is alert to textual problems but also determined not to let these get in his way:

> It should be known that at many places there are different readings in the text of this book [*en pollois khoriois diaphoros hē graphē toutou pheretai tou bibliou*]. But we must move to the discussion of the text passage by passage [*epi ta kata meros tēs lexeōs*]. (trans. Urmson 2001)

This is one of several comments in which we can see his methodical agenda, his thorough knowledge of the text, and the determination to produce a continuous exegesis. This gradual progression through the text is one good reason to assume his commentaries have a didactic motive. While short passages of the text are often interspersed between the passages of exegesis (which could have been added later), one can easily follow the text of Aristotle in the paraphrastic style of the commentaries, and the referencing forward and backward in both texts (that is, Aristotle's and Simplicius's) shows Simplicius's astounding control of both narratives. Moreover, the comment seems to prove that the division of distinct books was already established, even if the larger subdivision of thematic units was still disputed, as with the *Physics*, which was divided by some as "five books *On Natural Principles*, and three *On Motion*" (*in Phys.* 6.5–10 Adrastus; cf. 801.13–16 "Aristotle and the associates of Aristotle" 1358.8–9), while others adhere to a four–four division (e.g. Porphyry, at Simpl. *in Phys.* 802.8–11). Simplicius expresses surprise over this but confirms that Porphyry used a "division of the eight books, as the four books from the fifth to the eighth coming after constitute the treatise on motion and is entitled idiosyncratically *On Motion*" (McKirahan 2001, n. 558).

18.5 Defining the Commentator

It is a remarkable fact about this long exegetical tradition that no explicit definition of the commentator's task is found before the sixth century CE. The best description of the task of the commentator is found in Simplicius *in Cat.* 7.23–32, where he outlines his criteria for the Aristotelian exegete (trans. Wildberg 2005):

> The worthy exegete of Aristotle's writings [*ton axion tōn Aristotelikōn sungrammatōn exēgētēn*] must not fall wholly short of the latter's (S1) greatness of intellect [*megalonoia*]. He must also have (S2) experience overall of what the Philosopher has written [*empeiros*], and must be (S3) a connoisseur of Aristotle's stylistic habits [*epistēmōn*]. (S4) His judgement must be impartial [*krisin adekaston*], so that he may neither, out of misplaced zeal, (4.1) seek to prove something well said to be unsatisfactory, nor…(4.2) should he obstinately persist in trying to demonstrate that [Aristotle] is always and everywhere infallible, as if he had enrolled himself in the Philosopher's school.

The definition may be read as both aspirational (must be "worthy," *axios*) and prescriptive ("must not fall short," etc.), while the main features also illustrate how comprehensively the prerequisites cover exegetical skills, close familiarity with the base text, and a balanced judgment. This last point does not mean that impartiality was always reached, but it certainly played a role in their considerations.

Half a century later an important testimony shows how Simplicius's definition of an exegete influenced the commentators after him. Simplicius's important description of the ideal commentator may be compared to that of "Elias" (late sixth century CE), who at *in Cat.* 122–123 (*CAG* vol. 18.1) displays clear echoes of Simplicius's injunctions. Little is known about this "Elias" except that his name is associated with certain commentaries from the second half of the sixth century (Wildberg 2005, pp, 326–327). There are, however, also some intriguing elaborations that aim to clarify this task further, mixing these with brief historical or literary observations, so that the commentator's role becomes even clearer as a result of further commentary on it. But there are also subtle additions and shifts of emphasis (S1, S2, etc., refer to the parallels in Simplicius):

> The commentator should be both commentator [*exēgētēs*] and scholar [*epistēmōn*=S4] at the same time. It is the task of the commentator to (E1) unravel obscurities in the text [lit. "unfolding," *anaptuxis*]; it is the task of the scholar to (E2) judge (=S4) what is true and what is false, or what is sterile and what is productive [*krisis tou alēthous kai tou pseudous*]. He must (E3) not assimilate himself [*summetaballesthai*] to the authors he expounds, like actors on the stage who put on different masks because they are imitating different characters. When expounding Aristotle he must not (E4.1) become an Aristotelian (=S4.2) and say there has never been so great a philosopher, when expounding Plato he must not (E4.2) become a Platonist and say there has never been a philosopher to match Plato. He must not (E5) force the text at all costs [*mē ek pantos tropou biazesthai*] and say that the ancient author [*arkhaios*] whom he is expounding is correct in every respect; instead he must repeat to himself at all times "the author is a dear friend, but so also is the truth, and when both stand before me the truth is the better friend." (trans. Wildberg 2005, p. 327)

These general points of agreement between the two texts strongly suggest a connection: They share the emphasis on clarity (E1), judgment (E2), and avoiding bias if possible (E3). But the passage has a few additional observations of interest, including two precedents as examples of why one might be encouraged to take the problem of excessive partiality into account (emphasis mine):

> He must not (E6) sympathize with a philosophical school (=S4.1-2), *as happened to Iamblichus*, who out of sympathy for Plato is condescending in his attitude to Aristotle and will not contradict Plato in regard to the theory of ideas. He must not (E7) be hostile [*mē antipaschein hairesei*] to a philosophical school *like Alexander* [of Aphrodisias was]. The latter, being hostile to the

immortality of the intellectual part of the soul, attempts to twist in every way the remarks of Aristotle in his third book on the immortality of the soul which prove that it is immortal (cf. E5). The commentator must know the whole of Aristotle (=S2) in order that, having first proved that Aristotle is consistent with himself [*sumphōnon...heautōi*], he may expound Aristotle's works by means of Aristotle's works. He must know the whole of Plato in order to prove that Plato is consistent with himself [*sumphōnon...heautōi*], and *make the works of Aristotle an introduction to those of Plato*. (trans. Wildberg 2005, p. 327)

The comments on actors, Iamblichus, the truth, consistency, and bias are illuminating and very similar to Simplicius's requirements. The final comment also confirms the late Platonist approach – fixed by Porphyry and ahistorical in our eyes – that Aristotle serves as introduction to the ideas of Plato (see above on Porphyry, who made this standard in the school practice). But the demand for impartiality is here applied to both Aristotelians and Platonists, a significant extension compared to Simplicius.

18.6 Conclusion

This brief overview of the literary forms of the ancient philosophical commentary has adopted a definition of "literary" in the specific sense of "relating to a well-developed genre of writing." In its mature form the commentary used by the late Platonists is clearly an incredibly rich and multilayered mode of exegesis, with added philosophical qualities as shown in excurses, elaborations, and creative reinterpretations of the text. I have used Simplicius's commentaries as a particularly good example of this "culture of the commentary" (the phrase is Sluiter's 2000, p. 200). It is even likely that his comprehensive approach eclipsed large parts of the tradition.

Apart from a slowly evolving form (or format), the genre also developed a sense of self-awareness in two particular ways. Early on commentators became aware of their exegetical predecessors, which meant that the activity of explaining the central primary text also required taking earlier clarifications into account. This would, of course, add a certain complexity to the exegesis. Secondly, the writers of commentary reflected on their work and offered methodological considerations on the requirements for good commentary. Some emphasized criteria such as clarity, a broad knowledge of the author under scrutiny, and awareness of one's ideological preferences ("bias"). But it has also become clear that these works were not explaining and interpreting the text as a purpose in itself, but as a result of an educational system that used this exegetical format as a serious platform for *doing* philosophy and considering life choices. Contemplating the world by way of evaluative exegesis of the great thinkers of old was a philosophical activity and a way of life.

REFERENCES

Alberti, Antonina A. and Sharples, R.W. ed. 1999. *Aspasius: The Earliest Extant Commentary on Aristotle's Ethics*. Berlin: De Gruyter.

Armstrong, A.H. (1966). *Plotinus. Enneads*. Cambridge MA/London: Harvard University Press.

Athanassiadi, Polymnia. 1999. *Damascius: The Philosophical History*. Athens: Agape.

Baltussen, Han. (2004). Plato *Protagoras* 340–48: Commentary in the making? In: *Philosophy, Science and Exegesis in Greek, Latin and Arabic Commentaries* (ed. P. Adamson, H. Baltussen, and M.W.F. Stone), 21–35. BICS Supplements, London: ICS.

Baltussen, Han. (2007). From polemic to exegesis: The ancient philosophical commentary. In: *Genres in Philosophy* (ed. Jonathan Lavery). *Poetics Today* 28.2: 247–281.

Baltussen, Han. (2008). *Philosophy and Exegesis in Simplicius: The Methodology of a Commentator*. London: Duckworth.

Baltussen, Han. (2016). Philosophers, scholars, exegetes. The ancient philosophical commentary from Plato to Simplicius. In: *Classical Commentaries* (ed. Christina S. Kraus and Christopher Stray), 173–194. Oxford: Oxford University Press.

Bastianini, Guido and Sedley, David N. ed. (1995). Anonymous, *Commentarium in Platonis Theaetetum*. In: *Corpus dei papiri filosofici greci e latini*, vol. 3 (ed. Guido Bastianini and David N. Sedley), 227–562. Florence: Olschki.

Chaniotis, Angelos. (2004a). Epigraphic evidence for the philosopher Alexander of Aphrodisias. *Bulletin of the Institute of Classical Studies* 47: 79–81.

Chaniotis, Angelos. (2004b). New inscriptions from Aphrodisias (1995–2001). *American Journal of Archaeology* 108: 377–416.

Cherniss, Harold. (1977). Ancient forms of philosophic discourse. In: *Harold Cherniss, Selected Papers* (ed. L. Tarán), 14–35. Leiden: Brill.

Dillon, John. (1987). Iamblichus of Chalcis. *Aufstieg und Niedergang der Römischen Welt* II.36.2: 862–909.

Dodds, E.R. 1963. *Proclus. Elements of Theology*. 2nd ed. Oxford: Clarendon.

Gatti, Maria Luisa. (1996). Plotinus: The Platonic tradition and the foundation of Neoplatonism. In: *Cambridge Companion to Plotinus*, (ed. Lloyd P. Gerson), 10–37. Cambridge: Cambridge University Press.

Gerson, Lloyd P. (2005). *Aristotle and Other Platonists*. Ithaca, NY: Cornell University Press.

Griffin, Michael J. (2015). *Aristotle's Categories in the Early Roman Empire*. Oxford: Oxford University Press.

Hadot, Ilsetraut. (1978). *Le problème du néoplatonisme Alexandrin: Hiéroclès et Simplicius*. Berlin: De Gruyter.
Huby, Pamela M. (1997). *Priscian: Theophrastus on Sense Perception*. London: Duckworth.
Kahn, Charles H. (2003). Writing philosophy: Prose and poetry from Thales to Plato. In: *Written Texts and the Rise of Literate Culture in Ancient Greece* (ed. Harvey Yunis), 139–161. Cambridge: Cambridge University Press.
Karamanolis, George. (2006). *Plato and Aristotle in Agreement? Platonists on Aristotle's Philosophy from Antiochus to Porphyry*. Oxford: Oxford University Press.
Kechagia, Eleni. (2011). *Plutarch Against Colotes: A Lesson in History of Philosophy*. Oxford: Oxford University Press.
Klitenic Wear, Sarah. (2013). Another link in the golden chain: Aeneas of Gaza and Zacharias Scholasticus on Plotinus *Enn.* 4.3. *Greek, Roman, and Byzantine Studies* 53: 145–165.
Mansfeld, Jaap. (1994). *Prolegomena: Questions to Be Settled Before the Study of an Author or a Text*. Leiden: Brill.
McKirahan, Richard. trans. (2001). *Simplicius, On Aristotle's Physics 8.6–10*. London: Duckworth.
Rashed, Marwan. (2011). *Alexandre d'Aphrodise, Commentaire perdu à la Physique d'Aristote, livres IV–VIII*. Berlin: De Gruyter.
Schäublin, Christoph. (1977). *Homerum ex Homero. Museum Helveticum* 34: 221–227.
Sedley, David N. (1997). Plato's Auctoritas and the rebirth of the *Commentary* tradition. In: *Roman Aristotle* (ed. Jonathan Barnes and Miriam Griffin), 110–129. Oxford: Oxford University Press.
Sellars, John. (2006). *Stoicism*. Chesham: Acumen/Berkeley: University of California Press.
Sharples, R.W. (1987). Alexander of Aphrodisias: Scholasticism and innovation. *ANRW II* 36.2: 1176–1243.
Sluiter, Ineke. (2000). The dialectics of genre: Some aspects of secondary literature and genre in antiquity. In *Matrices of Genre: Authors, Canons and Society* (ed. Mary Depew and Dirk Obbink), 183–203. Cambridge, MA: Harvard University Press.
Smith, Wesley. (1979). *The Hippocratic Tradition*. Ithaca, NY: Cornell University Press.
Sorabji, R.R.K. ed. (1990). *Aristotle Transformed*. Ithaca, NY: Cornell University Press.
Strange, S. (1992). *Porphyry. On Aristotle Categories*. London: Duckworth.
Tarrant, Harold. (1996). Orality and Plato's narrative dialogues. In: *Voice into Text: Orality and Literacy in Ancient Greece* (ed. Ian Worthington), 129–147. Leiden: Brill.
Urmson, J.O. trans. (1992). *Simplicius. Corollaries on Place and Time*. London: Duckworth.

Urmson, J.O. trans., with Peter Lautner. (2001). *On Aristotle Physics 3*. London: Duckworth.

Westerink, L.G. (1962). *Anonymous Prolegomena to Platonic Philosophy*. Amsterdam: North-Holland.

Wildberg, Christian. (2005). Philosophy in the age of Justinian. In: *The Cambridge Companion to the Age of Justinian* (ed. Michael Maas), 316–340. Cambridge: Cambridge University Press.

Yunis, Harvey. ed. (2003). *Written Texts and the Rise of Literate Culture in Ancient Greece*. Cambridge: Cambridge University Press.

CHAPTER NINETEEN

Biblical Commentary

Marie-Pierre Bussières

19.1 Introduction

The late antique practice of composing commentaries in order not only to compile and circulate knowledge but also to create it has increasingly attracted scholars in recent years (Lössl and Watt 2011, p. 2). Among the wealth of commenting literature produced in antiquity, biblical commentary represents a large corpus, long studied with the purpose of understanding the history of dogma. Little attention has been paid to the form, or rather forms, commentaries took, as they have not been perceived as cultural texts with didactic aims of their own (Shuttleworth Kraus 2002, pp. 6–7). This tendency has been recently partially addressed (Pollman 2009; Rousseau 2013). If it is true that a postclassical text is consciously written with the admission that it needs to be read against the framework imposed by tradition (Pelttari 2014, p. 49), the practice of commentary is a literary act "inasmuch as it effects a new reading of the reference text" (Pelttari 2014, p. 28), which is the primary purpose of exegesis. Commenting, therefore, leaves the realm of technical literature and enters that of letters.

Occasionally, biblical commentary is labeled as a literary genre (Geerlings 2000, p. 199; Pollman 2009, p. 268), but, when it has been so labeled, function rather than defining formal characteristics determine the genre. "Commenting literature" seems, therefore, a more fitting designation, rather than the traditional "commentary," which gives the impression of generic uniformity. Commenting literature evokes a larger categorization that includes scholia;

hypomnemata; treatises; running commentaries; collections of chapters, with or without a prologue to the commented text (Mejor 2004); and even letters (Teske 2004). This perspective speaks directly to the goal of this volume, as the necessity to interpret the Bible engaged late antique authors to make use of many diverse literary forms.

For many commentators, exegetical activity was not merely pedagogical, pastoral, or polemical, but a literary pursuit appropriate for men of erudition. Emerging from various traditions that shared the same purpose of making a text meaningful for their readers, commentaries, in varying guises, constitute a large part of the body of literary production of late antique Christian authors.

Perhaps nothing shows the range of approaches authors took when commenting on Scripture better than a sample of the collection of texts treating the book of Genesis (Pollmann 2009, p. 258; Young 1997, pp. 54–62). These run from a protreptic work of the second century in Greek to a Latin paraphrase of the Old Testament composed in Gaul in the fifth century. This chapter will focus on works explaining one verse, Genesis 1:26: "Then God said, 'Let us make man in our image, after our likeness; and let them have dominion'" (Revised Standard Version), in order to show how different the forms of Biblical commentary could be. The texts will include Theophilus of Antioch's *To Autolycos*, Origen's *Homilies on Genesis*, Basil of Caesarea's and Ambrose of Milan's *Ninth Homily on the Creation*, Ambrosiaster's *Question 45: On the Image*, Augustine of Hippo's *Literal Interpretation of Genesis*, and Cyprian of Gaul's *Heptateuchos*. Together these authors will show how explanations of the same biblical text were fashioned and refashioned in ways suited to particular occasions and audiences, and with literary devices that suited the various authors' voices.

19.2 Origins and Development

While the explanation of the Bible has been a preoccupation of the Christian movement from its inception (Fürst 2011, pp. 14–16; Waszink 1979, pp. 17–18), it was first used as an argument in texts of other genres, and it was not until the third century that authors produced works that had exegesis as their primary function. Christian authors borrowed from a host of preexisting practices of explaining a reference text, but it is as yet unclear whether their primary models derived from the grammatical commentaries on epics and tragedies (ter Haar Romeny 2004, p. 163), the philosophical commentaries on Platonic and Aristotelian texts (Fürst 2011, p. 16; Mansfeld 1994, pp. 10–19), or rabbinic exegesis (Dorival 2000, pp. 169–81). All these practices, however, likely played some part in the different manifestations of biblical commenting literature (Geerling 2000, pp. 201–202). Because all these types of texts shared the common purpose of interpreting another work, it is not surprising that they could draw upon and combine a range of didactic methods. Some authors, however, sought to distinguish biblical exegesis from other forms of commentary. Ambrose of Milan, for example, thought that the search for spiritual meaning alone distinguished the commentary of the grammarians from exegesis (*Ep.* 8.55.1; CSEL 82/1, 43). Ambrose, who is here referring to homilies, exemplifies how commentary is a classification of "professional determinacy" (Vessey 2002, p. 56), in which commenting with the aim of spiritual elevation constitutes the deciding element in the work's categorization.

Exegetes were, of course, well aware of the differences of forms required by various approaches to the text. Origen remarked in his *Commentary on the Gospel of John* that some problems cannot fit into a running commentary and would require specially dedicated treatises (πραγματεία [study], *Joh.* 10.16.88, or συγγραφή [writing], *Joh.* 10.17.96; SC 157, 436, 440). He established a basic distinction between the nonthematic commentary and the thematic treatise. Nonthematic commenting literature has two general types: the line-by-line extensive commentary and the collection of notes on disconnected passages (Snyder 2000, p. 75). From a formal perspective, both allow segmentation of exegesis. In the range of disconnected notes, the collection of question and answer is the dominant form from the fourth century on. Whether this form is closer to (or even derives from) the *scholia* (Geerlings 2000, p. 202) or not (Volgers and Zamagni 2004) remains unanswered. Jerome, who titled such a collection *Hebraic Questions on Genesis* but referred to it as short commentaries (*quaestionum hebraicarum in Genesin commentariolos* [*Ep.* 155.2; CSEL 88, 132]), showed that he considered his work to have taken on a hybrid form, between *scholia* and *commentarius* (Kamesar 2001, pp. 94–96). This is a reminder, if indeed one is needed, that the definition of literary categories is not as conveniently delineated as we would wish. Moreover, "interpretation permeated practically every other literary genre…every mode of communication" in Christian late antiquity (Pollman 2009, p. 259). In that respect, it may be true that the Christian conception of the role of literature changed some authors' approach to writing (Fontaine 1988, pp. 65–68). Therefore, trying to impose formal codification on commenting literature would reduce to a mere practice a vast body of texts more loosely unified by their exegetical intent.

19.3 About Literature

If we agree that "all writing from ancient Christianity belongs to literary history in a general way, but all writing is not literature" (Alexandre 1997, p. 166), one could conclude that the broken sequence of line-by-line commentaries aims at speed in finding the passage commented upon and holds mainly practical, exegetical, dogmatic, or catechetical merits, but no artistic originality. The form would be disregarded on account of the reverence of the matter (Kugel 1998, pp. 14–19; Basser 2008, p. 37) and on account of the example of the Scriptures themselves.

The adoption by Christian authors of the Platonic opposition between artifice of words and truth-bearing actions (*Phaedr.* 272d–e) both exonerated the literary awkwardness of the Scriptures and encouraged a Christian reading of the Scriptures focused on content. Truth and inspiration became the mark of eloquence and divine essence, but, nonetheless, men of letters were still not satisfied with the Scriptures' simplicity and "writers interested in rhetoric found rhetoric in the Scriptures and started a tradition of commentary and teaching on their artfulness" (Ambrose, *Ep.* 8.55.1; CSEL 82/2, 77). For fear of a taint of artifice, however, some writers elaborated a self-conscious argumentation about writing literature (or not) in the act of interpretation: "My task," said Jerome, "is to explain obscure passages," not to bring pleasure of an aesthetic nature to the reader. (*Gal.* 3 *prol.*; CCSL 77A, 158. Cf. Cain 2011, p. 101; Pelttari 2014, pp. 16–17.) Jerome further warned that his commentaries were not the place to look for eloquence. Such a protest is not so much an apology (Pelttari 2014, p. 17) as an indicator. For Jerome's expression in this text and in at least three other instances (*Eph., prol.*; PL 26, 469, *Ep.* 29.1; CSEL 54, 233, *Helu.* 16; PL 23, 210) *eloquentiam quaerere*, "to look for eloquence," was plucked right from Cicero (*Top.* 85; *2Ver.* 1.29) and was most likely destined to bring an echo of the Arpinate to the ear of the reader. In case the allusion was missed, the great orator's name was then explicitly mentioned along with those of Demosthenes, Polemon, and Quintilian, a statement of literary ambition in the guise of propriety.

Commentators frequently invoked notions of literary self-consciousness and framed their work as a conversation among equals. In a letter to the bishop Justus of Lyon, Ambrose rejoiced at the thought that they should devote their "conversation in absence to the interpretation of the heavenly word." For what, asked Ambrose, is more conducive to friendship than conversation on holy subjects (*Ep.* 1.1.1; CSEL 82/1, 3)? Without a doubt, the bishop meant that Christianity cemented a friendship, but, in the circles of literate society, conversation on literary matters constituted an activity practiced in the company of friends among men of equal quality (Johnson 2000, 2009). Ambrose was consciously building a collection of exegetical epistles (cf. *Ep.* 6.32.7; CSEL 82/1, 228) that combined the tradition of epistolary collections containing discussions of literary substance with his preoccupation for scriptural explication.

Techniques of interpretation were introduced early on in forms of writing other than a running commentary, as we will observe in the second section of this chapter, through the works of Theophilus of Antioch, Origen, Basil of Caesarea, Ambrose of Milan, Ambrosiaster, Augustine and Cyprian of Gaul.

19.4 Survey

We can now turn from a general discussion of the perception of Biblical commentary as literature to a survey of the range of approaches authors took. To do this, we will focus on a cross section of "commentaries" on Genesis 1:26 that run chronologically from the second to the fifth century.

At the end of the second century, Theophilus of Antioch wrote *To Autolycos*, a protreptic treatise with a strong polemical flavor. In response to the assumption that the Scriptures were worthless on account that they carried no flourishes (*Aut.* 1.1; SC 20, 59), he retorted that, on the contrary, the Scriptures possessed the ultimate gift of speech. While the Creation is for man an inexpressible reality, he said, the Scriptures captured it in a single sentence, as God said: "Let us make man" (Gen 1:26; *Aut.* 2.18; SC 20, 144). Theophilus derided the idea that God is calling for help when using the plural in "Let us make," and he explained that God is talking to his Logos and his Sophia (*Aut.* 2.15 and 18; SC 20, 144, 146). Their presence explains both plurals: "let us make" and "our image." The example of Athena, presented in exercises of hymns to the gods (*laudes deorum*) in schools of rhetoric as Zeus's Wisdom, may have inspired Christians to represent a wise and eloquent God (Grant 1959, pp. 41–43). Even a superficial reading of *To Autolycos* reveals a practiced and eloquent style, using brief cola, indirect questions, exclamations, enumerations, and popular etymologies to fight commonplace battles against the Greek pantheon, in a recognizable tradition of judicial eloquence. (On the ties between apologetic and judicial eloquence, see Dorival 2001; Humfress 2007, pp. 135–150). Theophilus's incisive defense of Christianity, then, also echoes the courtrooms in its form and tone. His exegesis, however, serves his larger apologetic purpose.

It is believed that homilies destined for Christian sympathizers and the baptized are distinct from the written commentary only when delivered orally (Dorival 2000, p. 181). If Rufinus's translation of Origen's *Homilies on Genesis* is remotely faithful to the stenographic notes taken during their oral rendering (cf. Eusebius, *Hist.* 6.36.1), the audience must have needed to pay close attention in order to follow his explication of Genesis 1:26. Origen's interpretation develops out of a tapestry of citations and allusions to various passages of the Scriptures. Most of these allusions must have passed unnoticed in an oral delivery, and it would have likely been more challenging to read his commentary alongside a complete scriptural apparatus than to follow it aurally. Nevertheless, on account of the numerous citations that form the commentary itself, Origen's homily bears a rather professorial tone. It falls somewhere between a running commentary and a text that retained a quality of immediacy.

By contrast, Basil of Caesarea's *Hexameron* captures this quality of literary immediacy more effectively. Over the course of his nine homilies on creation, Basil offered a sustained explanation of the narrative of creation in which he occasionally utilized devices to capture the attention of his audience. In the *captatio benevolentiae* of the ninth homily, for example, he introduced the metaphor linking feast/fast to speech in an allusion to the fast of Lent. He reminds the assembly that in church they feed not only on words, λόγοι, but also on the Logos itself by asking them, "How did you find this morning's meal of words?" (*Hex.* 9.1, SC 26bis, 478), a reference both to the homily and to the Eucharist. Further questions more deeply involved the audience, encouraging it to meditate along with the bishop and adopt his explication of the Scriptures. Throughout the work, then, Basil frequently invited the audience to ponder with him on the meaning of the text.

Despite his claim that sciences are the worthless expression of a maddened wisdom (*Hex.* 9.1, SC 26bis, 482), Basil developed at length a rationale for the creation of animals that combines Aristotelian ideas with teachings from the New Testament. Here, too, he sought to engage his listeners with a rhetorical objection: "We have learned what the nature of beings belonging to us is, but we ignore what we are" (*Hex.* 9.6, SC 26bis, 512). Basil thus awakens the disengaged attention of the listener who had remained idle during the long exposition on animals. The sentence then signalled the transition to the exegesis of "Let us make man."

It is here that we reach his treatment of Genesis 1:26. The bishop opens and closed his explanation of Gen. 1:26 with a touch of polemic against those who think that God speaks to himself or to angels who participated in the Creation (an interpretation found in the Old Testament apocryphal *Jub.* 3:4; also Philo, *Op. mun.* 72). Basil refuted the former with a touch of irony: "What worker would talk to himself when setting to task, while being alone with his tools?" (Hex. 9.6; SC 26bis, 515). Parallels with daily life were another common technique used in the homily, an approach recommended later by Augustine to keep the attention of a wider audience (Aug., *Cat. Rud.* 13.19; CCSL 46, 142–143). Basil's homily continued with an explanation that looked to grammar: The plural ("Let us make") indicates that the Creator was not the only person present. This other person, the Scripture tells us, was the Son.

The varied levels of sophistication of Basil's audience (*Hex.* 3.1; SC 26bis, 190) did not deter him from refuting the Anomeans' error, denying that the

Son shares an equal nature with the Father, with a grammatical answer provided by the divine eloquence of the Scripture. Since man is made "in our image," the plural "our" and the singular "image" establish that there is one nature shared by more than one person. Angels cannot have the same image as their Creator because only the Son is born from God and not created by God. Basil's last question, "Don't you recognize in the Son his similarity with the Father, which he holds from his nature?" (*Hex.* 9.6, SC 26bis, 520–522), sent the audience home pondering the logical implications of his reasoning. If the Son shares God's nature, he must be his equal. If the Son is God's equal, the phrase "Let us make man in our image" then represents both the Father and the Son, because the Son participates in the act of creation. Basil thus encouraged his flock to weigh the theological implications of the Creation narrative, exhorted them to feast on his words as they went back home, and warned them against false beliefs. Biblical exegesis took with the bishop of Caesarea the guise of deliberative oratory.

Ambrose of Milan, who crafted Latin adaptations of Basil's homilies on the Creation, envisaged his sermons not as mere commentary but as a literary activity. In a letter to Simplicianus, Ambrose wrote about his predication in terms of imitation by implying that he had in the past emulated other renowned writers: "I will not," he wrote, "imitate some great exegete, but myself, as I go back to my habits and not some other great ones" (*Ep.* 2.7.2; CSEL 82/1, 44). This is a good way to understand his approach to the *Hexameron*. Although Ambrose borrowed most of the argumentation and allusions from Basil, his rhetorical strategy is quite different from that of his model. In the sixth homily, while he acknowledged his audience's fatigue (*Hex.* 6.1.1, CSEL 32/1, 204), Ambrose did not appeal to his listener with the sort of engaging questions Basil used. He used Basil's rhetorical objection "When will we learn about what concerns us?" (*Hex.* 6.2.3, CSEL 32/1, 205) to introduce his discussion of the creation of animals, instead of a transition from it. Thereafter most of Basil's questions disappear from Ambrose's text. While Basil's text abounded in philosophical references and knowledge of natural history, Ambrose's prose is laden with allusions to Sallust and evocations of or quotations from Virgil, Ovid, or Horace. Ambrose's written version of his sermon offers a full display of elegant writing, but it is not concerned with engaging the audience in reflection without providing all the answers.

More and more collections in the fourth and fifth centuries of explanations of the Scriptures came, not in the form of thematic or line-by-line exegesis of passages, but in the form of questions and answers. Many of these lack a preface (Geerlings 2000, pp. 203–204), as if they were envisaged by their author not as a literary piece requiring proper presentation but as a useful tool for consultation that did not pretend to have any literary cohesion. One such text is Ambrosiaster's *Questions on the Old and the New Testament*. Preceded by *capitula* for quick consultation in the manuscript tradition, it does not contain an explanatory preface. The composite character of the collection is further emphasized by the fact that, in one of its two versions (cf. Bussières 2007 on the dual tradition of the collection), it includes a series of developments announced by a theme instead of by a question. Such is the case of *Question 45: On the Image*, which answers an implicit interrogation, "How is man the image of God?" and comments on Genesis 1:26–28. With an anti-Arian argument, Ambrosiaster stated that the plural "Let us make" does not include the angels, as the angels and God cannot have the same image; for in order to have the same image, it is necessary to have the same nature. Therefore, the plural refers to the Father, the Son and the Holy Spirit. Ambrosiaster proceeded at a fast pace, each sentence serving as predicate for the next:

> Therefore the image of the three is one, because whether Father, Son, or Spirit, God is one. For this reason, man was made one in one god's image. Man is God's image in that, as God, from whom all heavenly things exist, is unique in heaven, similarly man is unique on earth, from whom all men have their carnal origin. (*Qu. test.* 45.2, CSEL 50, 82)

This is obviously the explanation Ambrosiaster favored, yet he next embarked on the refutation of a second interpretation. Some say, he wrote, that mankind is made in the image of God because God created man (*homo*) to rule over animals. But if mankind rules over the animals, the woman rules too. To Ambrosiaster, this raised a question: Would she, too, be in God's image? This is insane, he answered. Woman cannot be made in God's image because we know for a fact that she is under the dominion of man (*vir*) (*Qu. test.* 45.3; CSEL 50, 82–83). Ambrosiaster's short chapter thus closes on what not to think, without any recapitulation of the correct interpretation. This organization may seem peculiar because of its argumentative implication. Indeed, it goes against the rules of persuasion to close with the refutation of a point after its demonstration. This shows that Ambrosiaster was more preoccupied with countering errors than he was with developing a theology. Set in the context of perceived disorder brought on by the enthusiasm for female asceticism within Roman society (Hunter 2007, p. 128), Ambrosiaster's insistence on woman's submission to man is hardly surprising. The organization of the text is, therefore, not the product of Ambrosiaster's lack of sophistication or a lack of knowledge about oratorical technique. *Question* 45 could, instead, represent a deliberate use of exegesis so as to make a plea for social order in response to a contemporary issue vexing Ambrosiaster's milieu or church. With the matter settled, it is not until the last chapter of the collection that the place of woman in creation resurfaces (*Qu. test.* 127: *On Adam and Eve*; CSEL 50, 399–416, cf. Hunter 1989, 1992). Collections of disconnected exegeses thus allow for freedom that was lacking in the running commentary, where the line-by-line structure obliged authors to refrain from developing thematic excurses or long digressions, as was pointed out by Origen (*Joh.* 10.17.88; SC 157, 436).

Another interpretation of "let us make" in Genesis 1:26 appears in Augustine's unfinished *Literal Interpretation of Genesis*. Augustine developed his thought strictly according to reason, as befitted a man trained in dialectic (*Gen. ad lit.* 16; CSEL 28/1, 502). The very enunciation "Let us make" illustrates the importance of the Logos, Augustine argued, because speaking is not separate from making. This very example of verbal performance would have resonated with people trained in rhetoric. The active voice of *faciamus* also enhances the excellence of man's creation. Unlike man, other elements or creatures of the cosmos were created in the passive voice and, therefore, with less involvement from God. In addition, the plural form proves that the Son participated in the Creation. Man was thus made in the image of the Trinity, for he is a spiritual being made by God along with the Son.

Augustine acknowledged that his exegesis relied heavily on logic. "In order that we may not seem to be making this point by reason alone," Augustine wrote, "we should use the authority of the Apostle James" (*Gen. ad lit.* 16; CSEL 28/1, 502); he then introduced the scriptural quotation, upon which the treatise is left interrupted and unfinished. This abrupt interruption and Augustine's precaution to introduce the quotation makes it look as though the author was not yet at ease with using the Scriptures as proof and felt he ran off course from his logic-driven explanation.

Biblical epics sit at the other end of the spectrum from the running commentary. They have definition issues of their own, as scholars do not agree on whether they are a genre, a subgenre of epic poetry, a versified form of exegesis, or even literature at all (Green 2007, pp. 74–75; cf. Pelttari 2014, p. 10, Dinkova-Brunn 2007, p. 317). As the author reworks Scripture in epic form, however, he or she codified and rendered recognizable interpretations of the biblical text that might not be clearly stated in the original account. These paraphrases stand out in commenting literature because they tell the biblical stories at the same time as they explain them, thereby creating and embedding new meanings for the biblical text. Jerome captured the essence of the practice well when he spoke of Juvencus's poetical endeavor: "He explicated in verses the story of our savior the Lord" (*Ep.* 70.5; CSEL 54, 708). As such, biblical epics constitute "exegetical narratives" (Levinson 2004, pp. 498–501), a denomination that emphasizes the literary mindset of their authors. These poems vary in the level and overtness of their exegetical content (Roberts 1985, p. 39).

The fifth-century *Heptateuchos* attributed to Cyprian of Gaul shows a high tendency of embedding commentary into narrative in its treatment of Genesis. It says that, when the divine power had created livestock, he noticed that a ruler (*rectorem*) of the worldly things was missing. God then said out loud (*memorat*), "Let us make man perfectly similar to our images" (*nostris faciamus in unguem vultibus adsimilem*; *Hept.* 1.26–27; CSEL 23, 2), so that "he rule over the whole universe" (*regnet toto orbe*; *Hept.* 1.26; CSEL 23, 2). Cyprian added that once he saw him made (*formatum*) in his likeness (*effigie sua*; *Hept.* 1.32; CSEL 23, 2), God instilled sleep in man in order to create woman from his rib. Creation of man and woman, then, is told in just about 10 hexameters (*Hept.* 1.26–35; CSEL 23, 2).

Poetica licentia allowed Cyprian to neither explain the plural "Let us make" nor to specify to whom God speaks (*memorat*) nor even to indicate to his readers what was meant when they read God referring to "our images" (*nostris vultibus*). "Let us make" and "our," which were cause for scandal in prose, had in epic language an acceptable resonance as poetic plurals. They needed no more elaboration than the nonbiblical plural "images." Although Cyprian undoubtedly believed the similitude of man to God resided in his figure (*vultibus nostris* 1.26–27; *effigie sua*, 1.32; CSEL 23, 2), the use of *rectorem defore* allows us to conclude that he also understood man's image to be destined to rule the entire universe (*toto in orbe*) as *rector*, just as God governs the universe, including man. We have seen Ambrosiaster vehemently reject this interpretation, although it is not new: Philo called God the "director of all things" (πάντων ἡγεμών) (*Op. mun.* 75), borrowing the image from Plato (*Phaedr.* 246e). In classical epic, the epithet *rector* applied to leaders (Caesar in Lucan, *BC* 1.359, *Romani maxime rector*; a ship pilot at 5.515, *rectorem dominumque*) or Jupiter (Virgil, *Aen.* 8.572, *maxume rector*; Ovid, *Met.* 2.60 and Lucan, *BC* 2.4, *rector Olympi*). Used in the singular form by Christian authors, it not infrequently referred to God (e.g. Cyprian, *Ad Dem.* 5, *mundi dominus et rector*; CCSL 3A, 37) and in the plural form to bishops (certainly influenced by Sir. 33:19, *rectores ecclesiae*) or demons (*rectores mundi tenebrarum*, borrowed from Paul, Eph. 6:12), but it never designates man inside creation. In Cyprian's verses *rector* has a familiar ring for a learned audience, referring at the same time to (the supreme) God and to the heroic leader. The epic imagery rendered recognizable the figure of a man destined by his God to rule, but it also made palatable the representation of God speaking in the plural form. Cyprian's biblical paraphrase reveals a rhetoric that is "both epic and homiletic" (Deproost 2001, p. 450, on Arator's *Historia Apostolica*), narrative and exegetical.

19.5 Conclusion

The exegesis of Genesis 1:26, because of God's act of enunciation, gave ancient authors an occasion to expound upon their love of the spoken word. Their artistic consciousness made them depart from a more technical type of commenting literature – à la a grammarian's commentary – to use interpretation in ways that varied in purpose, length, form, and tone. There are, however, some similarities in approaches across this creative landscape, in that even authors who professed or pretended to neglect the *ars* made good use of it, some in a show of learning, others with literary ambition.

The instrumental use of interpretation in Theophilus's protreptic treatise is not too far from the ad hoc explication of Ambrosiaster in that it goes to the point and is trenchant in tone, but the two exegeses have nothing in common from a formal perspective. Theophilus's explication is a type of proof, but Ambrosiaster's exists for its own sake. Speaking in church, Ambrose consciously imitates Basil's homily, but his rhetoric delivers the conclusions, while Basil's engages the audience to participate in finding them. Despite the imitation in the points of argumentation, the organization and delivery of ideas differ starkly between the two. As for Origen, he appears to offer an exercise of "commenting the Bible with the Bible," to paraphrase the Aristarchean maxim. The exercise of the running, exhaustive commentary was also an exhausting one, as the example of Augustine shows when, after embarking on a philosophical debate on creation, he stopped short, as if this argumentative mode did not leave space for the scriptural proof. Poetical paraphrases, meanwhile, present the Scriptures with varying degrees of (implicit or overt) commentary, and Cyprian, in fact, delivered them to the reader fully interpreted.

Each of these forms of commenting literature has an artistic quality that we do not find, for instance, in the contemporary grammarians who produced commentaries of literary texts.

REFERENCES

Alexandre, Monique. (1997). Les écrits patristiques grecs comme corpus littéraire. In: *Les Pères de l'Église au XXe siècle: Histoire—littérature—théologie. "L'aventure des Sources chrétiennes,"* 163–187. Paris: Cerf.

Basser, Herbert W. (2008). What makes exegesis either Christian or Jewish? In: *The Reception and Interpretation of the Bible in Late Antiquity* (ed. Lorenzo DiTommaso and Lucian Turcescu), 37–53. Leiden, Boston: Brill.

Bussières, Marie-Pierre. (2007). Le public des *Questions sur l'Ancien et le Nouveau Testament* de l'Ambrosiaster. *Annali di storia dell'esegesi* 24: 229–247.

Cain, Andrew. (2011). Jerome's Pauline commentaries between East and West: Tradition and innovation in the commentary on Galatians. In: *Interpreting the Bible and Aristotle in Late Antiquity: The Alexandrian Commentary Tradition between Rome and Baghdad* (ed. Josef Lössl and John W. Watt), 91–110. London: Ashgate.

Deproost, Paul-Augustin. (2001). De la lettre au sens ou la poésie comme exégèse (À propos d'un livre sur le poète Arator). *Latomus* 60: 446–455.

Dinkova-Bruun, Greti. (2007). Biblical versifications from late antiquity to the middle of the thirteenth century. In: *Poetry and Exegesis in Premodern Latin Christianity* (ed. Willemien Otten and Karla Pollmann), 315–342. Leiden: Brill.

Dorival, Gilles. (2000). Exégèse juive et exégèse chrétienne. In: *Le commentaire entre tradition et innovation* (ed. Marie-Odile Goulet-Cazé), 169–181. Paris: Vrin.

Dorival, Gilles. (2001). L'apologétique grecque des premiers siècles. *Connaissance Hellénique* 88: 16–22.

Fontaine, Jacques. (1988). Comment doit-on appliquer la notion de genre littéraire à la littérature latine du IVᵉ siècle? *Philologus* 132: 53–73.

Fürst, Alfons. (2011). Origen: Exegesis and philosophy in early Christian Alexandria. In: *Interpreting the Bible and Aristotle in Late Antiquity: The Alexandrian Commentary Tradition between Rome and Baghdad* (ed. Josef Lössl and John W. Watt), 13–32. London: Ashgate.

Geerlings, Wilhelm. (2000). Les commentaires patristiques latins. In: *Le commentaire entre tradition et innovation* (ed. Marie-Odile Goulet-Cazé), 199–211. Paris: Vrin.

Grant, Robert M. (1959). Scripture, rhetoric and theology in Theophilus. *Vigiliae Christianae* 13: 33–45.

Green, Roger P.H. (2007). The *Euangeliorum Libri* of Juvencus: Exegesis by stealth? In: *Poetry and Exegesis in Premodern Latin Christianity* (ed. Willemien Otten and Karla Pollmann), 65–80. Boston: Brill.

Humfress, Caroline. (2007). *Orthodoxy and the Courts in Late Antiquity*. Oxford: Oxford University Press.

Hunter, David G. (1989). *On the Sin of Adam and Eve*: A little-known defense of marriage and childbearing by Ambrosiaster. *Harvard Theological Review* 82: 283–299.

Hunter, David G. (1992). The paradise of patriarchy: Ambrosiaster on woman as (not) God's image. *Journal of Theological Studies* 43: 447–469.

Hunter, David G. (2007). *Marriage, Celibacy, and Heresy in Ancient Christianity: The Jovinianist Controversy*. Oxford: Oxford University Press.

Johnson, William A. (2000). Toward a sociology of reading in classical antiquity. *American Journal of Philology* 121: 593–627.

Johnson, William A. (2009). Constructing elite reading communities in the high empire." In: *Ancient Literacies: The Culture of Reading in Greece and Rome* (ed. William A. Johnson and Holt N. Parker), 320–330. Oxford: Oxford University Press.

Kamesar, Adam. (2001). Ambrose, Philo, and the presence of art in the Bible. *Journal of Early Christian Studies* 9: 73–103.

Kugel, James L. (1998). *Traditions of the Bible: A Guide to the Bible as It Was at the Start of the Common Era*. Cambridge, MA: Harvard University Press.

Levinson, Joshua. (2004). Dialogical reading in the rabbinic exegetical narrative. *Poetics Today* 25: 497–528.

Lössl, Josef and Watt, John W. ed. (2011). *Interpreting the Bible and Aristotle in Late Antiquity: The Alexandrian Commentary Tradition between Rome and Baghdad.* London: Ashgate.

Mansfeld, Jaap. (1994). *Prolegomena: Questions to Be Settled before the Study of an Author or a Text.* Leiden: Brill.

Mejor, Mieczyslaw. (2004). Review of *Der Kommentar in Antike und Mittelalter. Beitrage zu seiner Erforschung* by Wilhelm Geerlings, Christian Schulze. *Bryn Mawr Classical Review* 2004.03.24.

Pelttari, Aaron. (2014). *The Space that Remains: Reading Latin Poetry in Late Antiquity.* Ithaca, NY: Cornell University Press.

Pollman, Karla. (2009). Exegesis without end: Forms, methods, and functions of biblical commentaries. In: *A Companion to Late Antiquity* (ed. Philip Rousseau), 258–269. Chichester, Malden: Blackwell.

Roberts, Michael. (1985). *Biblical Epic and Rhetorical Paraphrase in Late Antiquity*, Liverpool: Francis Cairns.

Rousseau, Philip. (2013). Homily and exegesis in the patristic age: Comparisons of purpose and effect. In: *Purpose of Rhetoric in Late Antiquity: From Performance to Exegesis* (ed. Alberto J. Quiroga Puertas), 11–29. Tübingen: Mohr Siebeck.

Shuttleworth Kraus, Christina. (2002). Reading commentaries/commentaries as reading. In: *The Classical Commentary: Histories, Practices, Theory* (ed. Roy K. Gibson and Christina Shuttleworth Kraus), 1–27. Leiden: Brill.

Snyder, H. Gregory. (2000). *Teachers and Texts in the Ancient World. Philosophers, Jews and Christians*, London: Routledge.

ter Haar Romeny, Bas. (2004). Question-and-answer collections in Syriac literature. In: *Erotapokriseis: Early Christian Question-and-Answer Literature in Context* (ed. Annelie Volgers and Claudio Zamagni), 145–163. Leuven: Peeters.

Teske, Roland. (2004). Augustine of Hippo and quaestiones et responsiones literature. In: *Erotapokriseis: Early Christian Question-and-Answer Literature in Context* (ed. Annelie Volgers and Claudio Zamagni), 127–144. Leuven: Peeters.

Vessey, Mark. (2002). From cursus to ductus: Figures of writing in late antiquity (Augustine, Jerome, Cassiodorus, Bede). In: *European Literary Careers: The Author from Antiquity to the Renaissance* (ed. Patrick Gerard Cheney and Frederick A. de Armas), 47–103. Toronto: University of Toronto Press.

Volgers, Annelie, and Claudio Zamagni, eds. (2004). *Erotapokriseis: Early Christian Question-and-Answer Literature in Context.* Louvain: Peeters.

Waszink, Jan Hendrick. (1979). Tertullian's principles and methods of exegesis. In: *Early Christian Literature and the Classical Intellectual Tradition: In honorem Robert M. Grant* (ed. William Richard Schoedel, Robert Louis Wilken, and Robert McQueen Grant), 17–31. Paris: Beauchesne.

Young, Frances M. (1997). *Biblical Exegesis and the Formation of Christian Culture.* Cambridge: Cambridge University Press.

CHAPTER TWENTY

Christian Theological Literature

Josef Lössl

20.1 Some Preliminary Remarks: "Christian," "Theological," "Literature"

The title of this chapter is problematic, and not just as a whole ("Christian Theological Literature"); its various components ("Christian," "theological," "literature"), too, as well as partial combinations such as "Christian theological," "theological literature," and "Christian literature" require clarification as to how they might be understood and how they might inform an enquiry such as the one offered in this chapter. I will, therefore, begin with a brief discussion of these questions and then offer a brief historical outline of Christian theological literature in late antiquity, roughly from the mid-third to the end of the fifth century, focusing mainly on the Greco-Latin cultural sphere.

"Christian," to begin with, is here not merely a denominational label, as in the distinction between, for example, Christian and Jewish or Christian and "pagan," whatever the latter category may denote; it is also a cultural marker. It denotes "absence" of Classical learning (Chin 2008, p. 152). What does this mean? Perhaps a brief example might help to explain: Writing in the late 390s, Augustine of Hippo reports that as a student of classical rhetoric in Carthage in the early 370s he was repelled by the "low" (*indigna*) style of the Christian Bible, because it apparently lacked the "prestige" (*dignitas*) of Ciceronian Latin (*Conf.* 3.5.9). In other words, the Christian literary product

---

A Companion to Late Antique Literature, First Edition.
Edited by Scott McGill and Edward J. Watts.
© 2018 John Wiley & Sons, Inc. Published 2018 by John Wiley & Sons, Inc.

did not reflect the degree of classical learning that he, as an educated user, would have expected from a piece of literature.

It is sometimes argued that in the Greek sphere the clash between classical and Christian literary culture was less severe (Vessey 2008, p. 46). Even there, however, Christian authors, including those, like Athanasius, who disassociated themselves from "classical education," still aspired to (and achieved!) a classical style (Stead 1976, pp. 121–137). But Christians could not simply claim that style as their own. It originally came with a non-Christian ("pagan") content. The clash, therefore, was not just one of style but also one of doctrine and way of life. Pagans, such as the emperor Julian in the early 360 s, tried to claim both for themselves and to relegate Christian culture, including literature, to a lower cultural stratum, where according to Augustine's testimony Christians might indeed have found themselves, if they had had to confine themselves merely to the literary outputs of their own tradition. During that period, therefore, Christians tried to produce a "classicizing" literature of their own (cf. Markschies 2009, pp. 70–72). At the same time they protested against their exclusion from the study of pagan literature (cf. Wilson 1975).

At any rate, "Christian" literature, at least until the end of the fourth century, was quite distinct from "literature" as commonly understood at the time, namely, the products of the classical tradition. In fact, the Latin word *litteratura* (which translated the Greek γραμματική [τέχνη]) was used by Christian authors to refer specifically to non-Christian (i.e. "pagan") "literature" (cf. Jerome, *Ep.* 52.2.1; Augustine, *Civ.* 6.6; Vessey 2008, p. 53).

Thus Christian literature began in a certain sense as "nonliterature." In order to be accepted or recognized as literature it first had to imitate the classical style, which is to some extent what it did in late antiquity. Later, when it found to its own, "humble" (*humilis*), style, as in the later works of Augustine or Jerome, it initiated the tradition of a new type of literature, which also characterized a whole new epoch, that of Medieval and Byzantine literature (Auerbach 1953, 1965; Curtius 1953; Vessey 2008).

When (also in the late 390 s) Jerome embarked on compiling his work *De viris illustribus* (or *De scriptoribus ecclesiasticis*), a "catalog" of Christian authors beginning with the apostle Peter and culminating in himself, he bemoaned that unlike classical literature, Christianity had not yet developed a literary canon, that might have guided his selection (Halton 2010, p. 1). His main source for the period before the fourth century was Eusebius's *Church History*. In hindsight, *De viris illustribus* itself is now sometimes labeled the first "history of Christian theological literature" (Quasten 1983, pp. 1–2) and thought of as introducing such a canon. But this (modern) use of the expression "Christian theological literature" only highlights further its problematic nature (cf. Vessey 2008, pp. 42–43).

What was "Christian" for Jerome? Interestingly, it seems not to have been synonymous with "orthodox" (against Vessey 2008, p. 43). *De viris illustribus* includes not only orthodox authors – later called "[Church] Fathers" (cf. Vincent of Lérins, *Comm.* 27–28; Vessey 2008, p. 43) – such as Athanasius or Ambrose, but also "heresiarchs," such as Bardaisan, Novatian, and Eunomius, and even Jews, such as Philo of Alexandria (Ceresa-Gastaldo 1988, pp. 96, 126, 176, 220). Nor did Jerome exclude the Bible from his canon of early Christian theological literature. Saint Paul and the putative authors of the four canonical New Testament Gospels are listed in his catalog as well as, for example, Juvencus, who more than two hundred years after they were first written in humble Koine Greek "rewrote" the Gospels in classical Latin hexameters; or Dexter, an imperial official, who according to Jerome wrote a universal chronicle; or Marius Victorinus, a Roman professor of rhetoric, who converted to Christianity very late in his life and yet wrote several biblical commentaries and theological treatises (Ceresa-Gastaldo 1988, pp. 190, 206, 228).

Thus "Christian," for the period concerned (ca. 250–500), is not coextensive with "orthodox" or "theological," let alone clerical. It refers to a cultural tradition that, as a whole, differs from ancient Classical culture, but that was in itself a hugely diverse phenomenon. At the same time, it is true that during that period a "Christian orthodox" tradition began to emerge, which began to exclude heretical movements, and this tradition as a whole began to be "theologically" grounded, as will be shown below. Interestingly, it was often heretics who initiated theological reflection (Edwards 2009). "Theology," to be sure, must here be understood very differently from the way it has come to be understood since the Middle Ages, as a scholastic discipline with philosophy as her handmaiden. In this latter sense there was no theology in early Christianity. Rather, the Christian literary culture that Jerome's *De viris illustribus* reflects emerged as a "sideline" of ancient classical culture, embedded as it was in the context of higher schools of (literary) grammar and rhetoric—i.e. precisely the γραμματικὴ τέχνη mentioned earlier, which Jerome identified as the source of the development of classical *litteratura*.

It is these "schools" to which we must look as the birth place of early Christian theological literature. Despite Christian suspicion toward pagan education, early Christians were massively involved in higher education, at least from the second century onward (Markschies 2009). As they developed their teaching from this context, they styled it as a type of philosophy (Löhr 2010). Christians thus had a considerable part in that widespread and profound educational movement called "Second Sophistic," with its ideal of a rounded *paideia* (Lechner 2011), which extended so far into late antiquity that some have begun to speak of a "Third Sophistic" dominated by Christian literature and its main producers, church teachers and leaders (Quiroga Puertas 2007). This is why this process has also been referred to as a move "from 'Sophistopolis' to 'Episcopolis'" (Quiroga Puertas 2007).

Late antique Christian theological literature was thus scholastic in the sense that it originated from a school context, but its scholasticism was based on the study not of a certain type of Aristotelian logic but of literary grammar and rhetoric (Kaster 1988; Chin 2008). Almost all late antique Christian theological writers were at least trained in these disciplines; Many of them were actually teachers, and the genres of Christian theological literature were those of the late antique literary canon or derived thereof.

The fact that there were genres the live context of which was the church as a community of worship, such as prayers, hymns, creeds, and similar forms, merely underlines the above observation; for as literature such forms are transmitted only in a scholastic or school context, in works formed or at least informed by authors who were active as teachers and/or leaders (cf. Markschies 2009, pp. 136–210).

One remarkable, common feature of all Christian theological literature was that it was "hermeneutical." It had not yet itself become canonical, nor had the process of the biblical canon formation been fully completed yet. But from the second century onward the culture of Christian theological literature was, in the words of Reinhart Herzog, one of "global hermeneutics," in which the world was explained with reference to normative texts rather than represented by normative texts (Herzog 1989, p. 33). In the mid-second century Lucian of Samosata was still able to mock Christians for writing sacred books and commenting on them at the same time (Lucian, *Peregr.* 11). From the third century onward no new "sacred books" of this kind were admitted to Christian theological discourse. Whatever was written from then on in terms of theological literature referred back to the books of the Old and New Testament. One dominant genre that emerged in the process of this development was the biblical commentary, the origin of which coincided with that of the philosophical commentary among Aristotelians and Platonists (see Lössl and Watt 2011).

But it would be wrong to reduce late antique Christian theological literature to biblical commentary. As Thomas Graumann (2009) has pointed out, new forms of canonical literature emerged in the fourth and fifth centuries – for example, the Nicene Creed, accompanied by a multitude of hermeneutical literature, treatises, letters, canons, memoranda, minutes of church synods and councils, and others. Graumann described this process as "conduct of theology," the "playing out" of (rhetorical) theological performance in the arena of councils, synods, and other types of meetings (e.g. at imperial courts or in worship), the forms of oral and written communication this involved and the forms of literature produced in this process. Again, traditional approaches to the study of literature may ask if we can speak here of "literature" at all, yet for a study of Christian theological literature in late antiquity, which is concerned less with aesthetically defined, "finished" products than with the *culture* in which these products emerged (Vessey 2008, p.57), they will be of the utmost interest.

20.2 Approaching Late Antiquity: The Emergence of Christian Theological Literature

In classical antiquity the word "theology" had an ambiguous ring. "Theologians" were basically "mythologizers," authors such as Homer or Hesiod, who explained natural events and processes in mythological terms. This is how the expression is used, for example, by Aristotle (e.g. *Mete.* 353a35) in a disparaging fashion. But elsewhere Aristotle also concedes that the question of the nature and origin of the universe as a whole can only be addressed through what amounts, ultimately, to a form of "theology" (*Met.* 983b27-32). Aristotle seems here to refer to Plato, who sometimes addressed transcendental questions through myths. In late antiquity, the rationalizing exegesis of (the Homeric and Hesiodic) myths became a central activity of (especially Platonic) philosophy (Lamberton 1986; Brisson 2004), and although Christian theologians vehemently distanced themselves from their pagan counterparts by claiming their religion to be essentially different, their techniques of interpreting the biblical narratives and the core doctrines of their religion bore a striking resemblance to those employed by pagan philosophers and sophists. The cultural context from which this tradition emerged was, as already mentioned, that of the schools of grammar, rhetoric, and philosophy in the Roman Empire from the second century onward.

The beginnings of Christian theological writing in this sense thus predate late antiquity. They go back to the second century. In terms of theological (doctrinal) content, the main problem with which they were grappling could be summarized as follows (see Lössl 2010, pp. 159–163): "How can Christians claim to believe in and worship only one God, and yet claim at the same time that the man Jesus Christ is also God?" Christian writers addressed this question (a) by formulating their own positions (in a rational and "confessional" way) and (b) by demarcating their own positions against those of pagan, Jewish, and also other Christian opponents (so-called heretics). The earliest form in which this kind of theological writing was cast was the apology (see Vessey 2008, p. 50 with reference to Overbeck 1882, p. 423).

The early Christian apology of the second century, as represented, for example, by authors such as Quadratus, Aristides, Justin Martyr, or Athenagoras, was in some sense a continuation of Jewish apology, which emerged from the "war of books" between Greek and barbarian cultures during the Hellenistic age (Droge 1989, p. 7). Although they do not constitute a literary genre as such and are not exclusively Christian (cf. Edwards, Goodman, and Price 1999), apologies contain (besides other things) the first substantial pieces of Christian theological writing and were continued from the mid-second century until long into late antiquity (Fiedrowicz 2006). Their importance lies in their interaction with pagan, Jewish, and heretical ideas and their reflection of a wider cultural-intellectual trend at the time toward a more "monotheistic" outlook in philosophically informed types of religion (Edwards 2004; Potter 2004, pp. 173–214; Trapp 2007; Mitchell and van Nuffelen 2010; van Nuffelen 2011).

It was in the late second and early third century, with authors such as Clement of Alexandria and Tertullian, that Christian theological writing reached a new point of departure. Seminal works from this period (ca. 220–250) include the *Refutatio [= elenchos] omnium haeresium*, also known as *Philosophoumena*, traditionally attributed to Hippolytus (cf. Moreschini and Norelli 2005, I, pp. 232–239, also on the question of the author's identity), and Origen's *De principiis* (*Peri archōn*) and *Contra Celsum*. David Potter has called the *Refutatio* "a truly astonishing book" (2004, p. 211). Although only partially extant, its vast scope can still be appreciated. It demarcates what the author perceives as the true Christian doctrine from all heresies, which are demonstrated to derive from Greek philosophy and ancient pagan (including Egyptian, Babylonian, Persian and South Asian) religion. It is exceedingly learned and draws on a vast amount of earlier sources on philosophy and the history of religions. Ironically, this makes the *Refutatio* less a source for Christian theology than for all that its author refutes as not being Christian theology.

Origen's *De principiis*, written around the same time (mid-220s) and also only extant in fragments, is a very different work. It, too, is in some sense apologetic. It refutes the view that the Christian faith is superstitious, irrational, and uneducated. But it does so positively, by demonstrating the main tenets of the Christian faith, that is, belief in one God, creation, divinity of Christ, incarnation, Holy Spirit, Trinity, and salvation, as a set of coherent, systematic teachings derived, by way of a very specific exegetical method (not unlike that of the Neoplatonic philosophers), from the biblical writings (Crouzel and Simonetti 1978–1984). *De principiis* is also of importance for the reception and repeated condemnation of Origen's teachings in late antiquity (in 400 and 553; cf. Clark 1992; Hombergen 2001; Perczel 2001).

Its precise content is disputed, because it is only extant in fragments and a Latin translation (by Rufinus), which were used and partially distorted by accusers as well as defenders of Origen. In the course of these controversies, Origen became also accused of preparing the way for the Arian heresy, although it was he who in *De principiis* 1.2.2/9 first coined one of the main tenets of the Nicene faith: That God Father and Son were co-eternal in the sense "that there was no time when the Son was not" (cf. Dünzl 2007, pp. 35–40; Lössl 2010, pp. 170–171; Ramelli 2012).

Contra Celsum is apologetic in a way similar to Hippolytus's *Refutatio*. It gives a lot of space to a work by the pagan philosopher Kelsos entitled *True Teaching* (*Alēthēs logos*), dating from the late 170s. It cites this work almost in its entirety, refuting it in turn. Yet this refutation consists not only of negative polemic but also of a positive theology centered on the figure of Jesus Christ, Logos and Son of God and focus of the biblical prophecies and the life of the Christian church. The latter, according to Origen, has created a new cultural reality and replaced the old social and political order subscribed to by Kelsos (Moreschini and Norelli 2005, I, pp. 290–293).

Origen's lifetime (ca. 186–254) was divided between Alexandria (until 231) and Antioch, Athens, and Caesarea in Palestine, where he lived until his death in 253/254. One of his heirs in the latter city was Eusebius, whose *Church History*, as already mentioned, was one of the main sources for Jerome's *De viris illustribus*. Caesarea was a center of early Christian learning that radiated across the crisis of the third century into the revival period of the Tetrarchy and that also saw the renewal of higher (rhetorical) education across the empire, as manifest, for example, in the *Latin Panegyric* of Eumenius, which attests to the reestablishment of a rhetorical school in Gaul (Nixon and Rodgers 1994, pp. 145–177). During this period, especially under the new regime of the emperor Constantine, there emerged also a new breed of Christian theological writers creating new types of Christian theological literature.

Among the first of these, leaving aside Eusebius, were Arnobius and his pupil Lactantius. Both were professors of rhetoric and wrote in the early fourth century, Arnobius in Africa and Lactantius in Nicomedia and later in Trier, where he seems to have remained until his death around 325. Lactantius's main work, the *Divinarum institutionum libri vii*, is clearly modeled on Quintilian's *Institutionis oratoriae libri xii*, a comprehensive handbook of rhetoric. Lactantius's *Divine institutes* is aimed at demonstrating in a systematic and comprehensive way the exclusive and unique truthfulness (*veritas*) of the Christian religion (*religio*) against the entirety of the pagan cultural setup (Moreschini and Norelli 2005, I, pp. 399–402). Lactantius was already able to draw substantially on earlier Latin Christian writers such as Tertullian and Cyprian of Carthage and to demonstrate that Christian intellectual culture was a force to be reckoned with.

Around the same time as Lactantius wrote his *Divine institutes*, i.e. some time within the first two decades of the fourth century, Eusebius too wrote two works of monumental scope, the *Praeparatio evangelica* in 15 books and the *Demonstratio evangelica* in 20 books: the first to demonstrate the superiority of the biblical (Jewish) over the classical (pagan) tradition; the second to show that the Christian Gospel and church tradition was the appropriate fulfillment of the former.

Together with Origen's *De principiis* these and similar works formed the basis and core of Christian theological writing in late antiquity.

20.3 The "Long Fourth Century": Toward an Orthodox Theology of the "Fathers"

One aspect that must not be overlooked in the works of Lactantius and Eusebius is their new outlook on history under the impression of the coming to power of the emperor Constantine in 312 in the Latin West and in 324 in the Greek East. This impression, and the questions it raised with regard to Christian loyalties were still resonating a century later, especially after the sack of Rome in 410, in, for example, Augustine's *De civitate dei* (*City of God*) and Orosius's *Historiarum adversus paganos libri vii* (*Seven Books of Histories against the Pagans*) both written within a decade of 410: Was a Christian Roman Empire the last word in history, as Orosius stipulated (van Nuffelen 2012), or was Rome merely one worldly regime among many more to come before the end-time, as Augustine surmised (O'Daly 1999)?

But regardless of a new historical outlook in Christian theology, Constantine's coming to power had also a more immediate impact on the making of Christian theological literature. For Constantine immediately (from 313 in the west and from 324 in the east) summoned (!) bishops to meet in synods and councils to make decisions regarding doctrine and governance (see Brennecke 2007, pp. 25–48). This also resulted in new forms of theological literature and new ways in which this kind of literature was produced and transmitted. "Creeds," for example (cf. Graumann 2009, pp. 543–547; Kinzig and Vinzent 1999; Kelly 1972), confessional statements of faith, had existed in the early church before, but the Nicene Creed, produced by the Council of Nicaea held in 325, turned out to be of a different category. As its opponents continued trying to refine its wording and produced numerous further creeds (Hahn 1897), its defenders elevated it and the council that produced it to canonical status (Athanasius, *De synodis*

13.2-4; Graumann 2009, p. 545). The literature produced in the process – letters, treatises, acts, canons, commentaries, histories, even poems – forms the core of what until today remains Orthodox, or Patristic, Christian theological literature, both in Greek and in Latin (for "Patristic" as "relating to the Fathers of the Church," see Graumann 2009; a historical overview is provided by Hanson 1988; conciliar texts are collected in Schwartz and Straub 1914–1984).

While the Creed itself was not produced by an individual author but reflects the position of those who confess to it both individually and collectively, many individual authors can be identified in the fourth and fifth centuries who produced theological literature attacking and defending a variety of positions related to the Creed or systematically extrapolating and commenting on its main tenets, such as God, the Trinity, the nature and Incarnation of Christ, the Holy Spirit, the Church and Salvation. It is this kind of literature that could be more narrowly defined as "theological" during this period. Some of the main authors (and works, in so far as they are extant) include Arius (*Thalia*), Asterius (*Syntagmation*), Athanasius (*Contra Arianos, Contra gentes, De incarnatione*), Apollinaris of Laodicea (who wrote many works that were later attributed to Athanasius), Hilary of Poitiers (*De synodis, De Trinitate*, the latter also known as *Contra Arianos* or *De fide*), Marcellus of Ancyra (whose thought is chiefly known from works against him), Gregory of Nazianzus (*Orationes*, better known as "Theological Orations"), Basil of Caesarea (*De spiritu sancto, Hexaemeron*), Gregory of Nyssa (*Hexaemeron, Contra Eunomium*), Marius Victorinus (works against Arius and on the Trinity) and Ambrose of Milan (*Explanatio symboli, De sacramentis, De mysteriis*), to name but a few (see Moreschini and Norelli 2005, II, pp. 20–56, 81–135, 236–288).

Nicaea was only a starting point. The "Nicaeno-Constantinopolitan" version of the Creed, which is still recited in Orthodox churches today, was only finalized at the Council of Constantinople in 381. Neither Nicaea nor Constantinople settled the Christological questions, which were addressed again at Ephesus (in 431 and 449) and Chalcedon (in 451). This process produced another credal formula, the "Formula of Chalcedon," and another wave of theological literature with major authors such as Cyril of Alexandria, Nestorius, and Theodoret of Cyr (Moreschini and Norelli 2005, II, pp. 536–571). Other authors from this period include Diodore of Tarsus, John Chrysostom, Theophilus of Alexandria, Theodore of Mopsuestia, Synesius of Cyrene, Augustine of Hippo (many works on grace; *De Trinitate*), Jerome of Stridon, Epiphanius of Salamis (*Panarion*), Nemesius of Emesa (*De natura hominis*), and poets such as Prudentius and Paulinus of Nola. Extensive collections of liturgical and canonical material are also extant from this period (literature in Moreschini and Norelli 2005, II, pp. 146–200, 296–347, 362–409).

An important feature of this period (from ca. 320 to 451 and beyond) is that it immediately began to produce its own reception process. This involved the emergence not only of canonical forms such as Creeds and credal formulae such as the formula of Chalcedon, as mentioned already, but also of major, quasicanonical, figures, "Church Fathers," as mentioned above, whose theological works were seen as canonical in elaborating on the Orthodox faith that was embodied in those Creeds and formulae. There are several such "Fathers" or groups of them, who fulfill different roles. Athanasius of Alexandria, for example, became a heroic symbol of the struggle against the Arian heresy and of the establishment of the Nicene faith, and this happened within less than a century (Graumann 2003). His works *De synodis* and *Contra Arianos* provided the standard account of how the latter was achieved and what its basic tenets were. Interestingly, this happened despite the fact that some of Athanasius's theological positions (especially his use of the word *hypostasis* in *Contra Arianos*) lent themselves to misinterpretations, which brought him into close association with more heterodox theologians such as Marcellus of Ancyra and Apollinaris (Moreschini and Norelli 2005, II. pp. 34–35).

A generation later, Basil of Caesarea, Gregory of Nazianzus, and Gregory of Nyssa were credited with developing and exploring the trinitarian formula "one *ousia* and three *hypostaseis*," in view of the Nicaeno-Constantinopolitan Creed. They enjoy until today a reception as "Cappadocian Fathers" (cf. Meesters 2012; Louth 2004; Lienhard 1999; Zizioulas 1995), Gregory of Nazianzus as author of the *Theological Orations*, Basil as author of *De spiritu sancto*, and both Basil and Gregory of Nyssa as authors of works *Contra Eunomium*. Because of differences in their theological outlook, which modern Patristic study has brought ever more sharply into focus, treatment of them as a homogeneous theological entity is today widely called in question (Louth 2004, p. 291; Ayres 2004, p. 2; Ludlow 2007, p. 2). But the phenomenon of a group of Church Fathers and their literary works assuming such canonical status can be understood against the background of the emergence in the fourth and fifth centuries of new canonical forms that characterized the late antique Church of the Fathers (see Barnes 1998). Reception of the "Cappadocian" formula can already be observed, for example, in Augustine's *De Trinitate* in the early fifth century.

In the fifth century it was Cyril of Alexandria who assumed towering status as a Church Father in the East, especially in the context of the Nestorian controversy and in the run-up to and reception of the Council of Chalcedon, while Augustine of Hippo assumed a similar status in the Latin West against the background of the Donatist and the Pelagian controversies (Graumann 2009, pp. 551–554). In addition, Augustine also stands out as the author of *De Trinitate*, one of the greatest and most influential works of Christian theology in late antiquity and arguably of any age (see Kany 2007).

20.4 Consolidation and Reception toward the End of Late Antiquity

To some extent Cyril and Augustine also represent a dying breed of late antique Christian theological writers. With the Orthodox parameters now established through the councils and the Fathers, later theologians were restricted in the way they could produce new forms and content. A lot of the activity now consisted in analyzing, systematizing, abridging, and commenting on the great literature of the fourth and fifth centuries or on continuing or readdressing the controversies of that period, especially in the East.

This can be said, for example, of the writings of Prosper Tiro, Leo the Great, John Cassian, Salvian of Marseilles, and Vincent of Lérins, whom we mentioned earlier as one of the first theologians defining the concept of "Church Father" (see Moreschini and Norelli 2005, II, pp. 410–480). These authors wrote in a West (Africa, Spain, Gaul, Italy) over which the Roman Empire rapidly lost control and that was increasingly shaped by barbarian kingdoms. In the sixth century authors like Boethius, Cassiodorus, Gregory the Great and Isidore of Seville already lived in a post-Roman age (Moreschini and Norelli 2005, II, pp. 483–535).

In the East, during the same period, the scene was dominated by controversies following the Council of Chalcedon and literature produced in their context (e.g. the works of Severus of Antioch), by historiography (e.g. works by Gelasius of Cyzicus, Zacharias Rhetor, or John Malalas), spiritual and hagiographic writing (Isidore of Pelusium, Cyril of Scythopolis), and exegetical works (e.g. Cosmas Indicopleustes).

For theology in the narrower sense two figures emerge who are representative both in their attitude to the past and in their importance for the future: Boethius and Pseudo-Dionysius (Moreschini 2014; Lössl 2014; Stang 2012).

Boethius lived in the first few decades of the sixth century in Italy under the Ostrogothic ruler Theoderich. His works *De fide catholica*, *Contra Eutychen et Nestorium*, *De sancta Trinitate* and *De hebdomadibus* stand for his program: He theologically explores the Creed and its most profound doctrine, the Trinity, and he takes up a position in support of the Chalcedonian formula against heretics such as Eutyches (a Miaphysite) and Nestorius.

He also develops new methods of philosophical analysis based on a study of Aristotelian logic and, thus, prepares the way for medieval scholasticism. At the same time, in his last work, the *Consolatio Philosophiae*, he expresses once more the tension between classical and Christian culture which so characterized Christian intellectual life in late antiquity.

In the Greek (and Syriac) East there appeared in the first decades of the sixth century a set of theological writings (the four treatises *De divinis nominibus*, *De caelesti hierarchia*, *De ecclesiastica hierarchia*, and *De mystica theologia* and 10 letters) that were attributed to Dionysius the Areopagite, who according to Acts 17:34 had converted to Christianity in response to Saint Paul's preaching on the Areopagus in Athens. In reality, the writings represent an adaptation of Proclean Neoplatonism to late antique Christian doctrine and appear to try and reconcile Chalcedonian and Miaphysite Christology. However, Christological doctrine is not the guiding interest of Pseudo-Dionysius, but the question of whether and how God can be known. The answer given is that we cannot know God as "he really is," but only God's positive (kataphatic) and negative (apophatic) attributes, or "names," as revealed in Scripture and through mystical illumination.

As in the case of Boethius, Christian theological writing was here influenced by the philosophy of late antique Aristotelian and Platonist commentators. The result was both a summing up of late antique Christian theology and a new point of departure. Pseudo-Dionysius, for example, influenced the work of the seventh-century theologian Maximus the Confessor. Moreover, from the ninth century onward it was translated several times into Latin and influenced such important medieval theologians as John Scotus Eriugena, Richard of St. Victor, and Thomas Aquinas.

20.5 Summary and Conclusion

In conclusion: When approaching the Christian theological literature of late antiquity several aspects should first be considered. "Christian" may denote not only theological content but also literary form. In the first instance "Christian" is "not classical" (or "pagan"). During late antiquity Christian literature can be "classicizing," or it can be departing from the classical model and developing a "humble" style. As other literature in late antiquity, Christian literature, too, may best be studied in the context of the literary rhetorical school culture from which it emerged. This may grant better access both to the main authors of this literature and to its major forms. In terms of content the central early Christian theological problem was how to claim credibly to be monotheistic when at the same time confessing Christ as God.

Most late antique Christian theology deals in one way or other with this question. The earliest literary form in which all problems hinted at so far were addressed was the apology. The second-century apology in its many different manifestations can, therefore, perhaps be considered the earliest form of Christian theological writing.

In the third century Christian theological literature experienced a boost in the work of Origen, who not only wrote biblical commentaries but also worked on theological principles (e.g. *De principiis*). The fourth and fifth centuries saw the emergence of a more structured canonical framework with the Nicene Creed and an emerging canon of Church Fathers and their works. Athanasius and Cyril of Alexandria in the Greek East and Augustine of Hippo in the Latin West were singled out as such authors.

Toward the end of late antiquity theological authors such as Boethius and Pseudo-Dionysius referred back to the fourth/fifth-century framework (doctrines of the Trinity and Christ). But by adapting late antique ("pagan") philosophical elements (e.g. Aristotelian logic in Boethius's case, Proclean epistemology and metaphysics in Pseudo-Dionysius's) and keeping to relatively simple form and language, they also prepared the way for a strong medieval reception.

REFERENCES

Auerbach, Erich. (1953). *Mimesis: The Representation of Reality in Western Literature* (trans. Willard R. Trask). Princeton, NJ: Princeton University Press.

Auerbach, Erich. (1965). *Literary Language and Its Public in Late Latin Antiquity and in the Middle Ages* (trans. Ralph Manheim). Princeton: Princeton University Press.

Ayres, Lewis. (2004). *Nicaea and its Legacy: An Approach to Fourth-Century Trinitarian Theology*. Oxford: Oxford University Press.

Barnes, Michel René. (1998). The fourth century as trinitarian canon. In: *Christian Origins: Theology, Rhetoric and Community* (ed. Lewis Ayres and Gareth Jones), 47–67. London: Routledge.

Brennecke, Hanns Christof. (2007). *Ecclesia est in re publica. Studien zur Kirchen- und Theologiegeschichte im Kontext des Imperium Romanum*. Berlin: De Gruyter.

Brisson, Luc. (2004). *How Philosophers Saved Myths. Allegorical Interpretation and Classical Mythology* (trans. Catherine Tihanyi). Chicago, IL: University of Chicago Press.

Ceresa-Gastaldo, Aldo. ed. (1988). *Gerolamo. Gli uomini illustri, De viris illustribus*. Florence: Nardini.

Chin, Catherine. (2008). *Grammar and Christianity in the Late Roman World*. Philadelphia: University of Pennsylvania Press.

Crouzel, Henri and Simonetti, Manlio. (1978–1984). *Origène. Traité des principes.* 5 vols. Sources chrétiennes 252, 253, 268, 269, 312. Paris: Cerf.

Curtius, Ernst Robert. (1953). *European Literature and the Latin Middle Ages* (trans. Willard R. Trask). Princeton, NJ: Princeton University Press.

Droge, Arthur J. (1989). *Homer or Moses? Early Christian Interpretations of the History of Culture.* Hermeneutische Untersuchungen zur Theologie 26. Tübingen: Mohr Siebeck.

Dünzl, Franz. (2007). *A Brief History of the Doctrine of the Trinity in the Early Church* (trans. John Bowden. London: Continuum.

Edwards, Mark. (2004). Pagan and Christian monotheism in the age of Constantine. In: *Approaching Late Antiquity. The Transformation from Early to Late Empire* (ed. Simon Swain and Mark Edwards), 211–234. Oxford: Clarendon.

Edwards, Mark. (2009). *Catholicity and Heresy in the Early Church.* Farnham: Ashgate.

Edwards, Mark, Goodman, Martin, and Price, Simon. ed. (1999). *Apologetics in the Roman Empire: Pagans, Jews and Christians.* Oxford: Oxford University Press.

Fiedrowicz, Michael. (2006). *Apologie im frühen Christentum. Die Kontroverse um den christlichen Wahrheitsanspruch in den ersten Jahrhunderten.* 3rd ed. Paderborn: Schöningh.

Graumann, Thomas (2003). Kirchliche Identität und bischöfliche Selbstinszenierung: Der Rückgriff auf "Athanasius" bei der Überwindung des nachephesinischen Schismas und in Kyrills Propaganda. In: *Literarische Konstituierung von Identifikationsfiguren in der Antike* (ed. Barbara Aland, Johannes Hahn, and Christian Ronning), 195–213. Tübingen: Mohr Siebeck.

Graumann, Thomas. (2009). The conduct of theology and the "Fathers" of the Church. In: *A Companion to Late Antiquity* (ed. Philip Rousseau), 539–555. London: Blackwell.

Hahn, August. (1897). *Bibliothek der Symbole und Glaubensregeln der alten Kirche.* 4th rev. and enl. ed. Breslau: Morgenstern.

Halton, Thomas P. (2010). *St. Jerome. On Illustrious Men.* Washington, DC: Catholic University of America Press.

Hanson, R.P.C. (1988). *The Search for the Christian Doctrine of God. The Arian Controversy, 318–381.* Edinburgh: T & T Clark.

Herzog, Reinhart. (1989). Einführung in die lateinische Literatur der Spätantike. In: *Restauration und Erneuerung: Die lateinische Literatur von 284 bis 374 n. Chr.* Handbuch der lateinischen Literatur der Antike, vol. 5. (ed. Reinhart Herzog), 1–44. Munich: Beck.

Hombergen, Daniel. (2001). *The Second Origenist Controversy.* Studia Anselmiana 132. Rome: Sant'Anselmo.

Kany, Roland. (2007). *Augustins Trinitätsdenken. Bilanz, Kritik und Weiterführung der modernen Forschung zu De* Trinitate. Tübingen: Mohr Siebeck.

Kaster, Robert. (1988). *Guardians of Language: The Grammarian and Society in Late Antiquity.* Berkeley, CA: University of California Press.

Kelly, J.N.D. (1972). *Early Christian Creeds.* 3rd ed. London: Longman.

Kinzig, Wolfram and Markus Vinzent. (1999). Recent research on the origin of the Creed. *The Journal of Theological Studies* 50: 535–559.

Lamberton, Robert. (1986). *Homer the Theologian: Neoplatonic Allegorical Reading and the Growth of the Epic Tradition*. Berkeley: University of California Press.

Lechner, Thomas. (2011). Very Sophisticated? – Mission und Ausbreitung des Christentums in der Welt der Zweiten Sophistik. *Millennium* 8: 51–86.

Lienhard, Joseph T. (1999). *Ousia* and *Hypostasis*: The Cappadocian Settlement and the theology of "one hypostasis." In: *The Trinity: An Interdisciplinary Symposium* (ed. Stephen T. Davis, Daniel Kendall, and Gerald O'Collins), 99–121. Oxford: Oxford University Press.

Löhr, Winrich. (2010). Christianity as philosophy: Problems and perspectives of an ancient intellectual project. *Vigiliae Christianae* 64: 160–188.

Lössl, Josef. (2010). *The Early Church: History and Memory*. London: Continuum.

Lössl, Josef. (2014). An inextinguishable memory: Pagan past and presence in early Christian writing. In: *Being Christian in Late Antiquity. A Festschrift for Gillian Clark* (ed. Carol Harrison, Caroline Humfress, and Isabella Sandwell), 74–89. Oxford: Oxford University Press.

Lössl, Josef and Watt, John. ed. (2011). *Interpreting the Bible and Aristotle in Late Antiquity. The Alexandrian Commentary Tradition between Rome and Baghdad*. Farnham: Ashgate.

Louth, Andrew. (2004). The Cappadocians. In: *The Cambridge History of Early Christian Literature* (ed. Frances Young, Lewis Ayres, and Andrew Louth), 289–301. Cambridge: Cambridge University Press.

Ludlow, Morwenna. (2007). *Gregory of Nyssa: Ancient and (Post)modern*. Oxford: Oxford University Press.

Markschies, Christoph. (2009). *Die kaiserzeitliche christliche Theologie und ihre Institutionen*. Tübingen: Mohr Siebeck.

Meesters, Albert C. (2012). The Cappadocians and their trinitarian conceptions of God. *Neue Zeitschrift für systematische Theologie und Religionsphilosophie* 54: 396–413.

Mitchell, Stephen and van Nuffelen, Peter. ed. (2010). *One God: Pagan Monotheism in the Roman Empire*. Cambridge: Cambridge University Press.

Moreschini, Claudio. (2014). *A Christian in Toga. Boethius: Interpreter of Antiquity and Christian Theologian*. Göttingen: Vandenhoeck & Ruprecht.

Moreschini, Claudio and Norelli, Enrico. ed. (2005). *Early Christian Greek and Latin Literature. A Literary History* I–II (trans. Matthew J. O'Connell). Peabody, MA: Hendrickson.

Nixon, C.E.V. and Rodgers, Barbara Saylor. (1994). *In Praise of Later Roman Emperors. The Panegyrici Latini*. Berkeley: University of California Press.

O'Daly, Gerard. (1999). *Augustine's City of God. A Reader's Guide*. Oxford: Oxford University Press.

Overbeck, Franz. (1882). Über die Anfänge der patristischen Literatur. *Historische Zeitschrift* 12: 417–72.

Perczel, István. (2001). The anti-Origenist anathemas of 553: To what did they refer? In: *The Sabaïte Heritage in the Orthodox Church from the Fifth Century to the Present* (ed. J. Patrich), 261–282. Leuven: Peeters.

Potter, David. (2004). *The Empire at Bay, AD180–395*. London: Routledge.

Quasten, Johannes. (1983). *Patrology. Vol. 1: The Beginnings of Patristic Literature*, Allen, TX: Christian Classics.

Quiroga Puertas, Alberto. (2007). From Sophistopolis to Episcopolis: The case for a third Sophistic. *Journal for Late Antique Religion and Culture* 1: 31–42.

Ramelli, Ilaria L.E. (2012). Origen, Greek philosophy, and the birth of the trinitarian meaning of *Hypostasis*. *Harvard Theological Review* 105: 302–350.

Schwartz, Eduard and Straub, Johannes. (1914–1984). *Acta Conciliorum Oecumenicorum* I–IV. Berlin: De Gruyter.

Stang, Charles. (2012). *Apophasis and Pseudonymity in Dionysius the Areopagite: "No Longer I."* Oxford: Oxford University Press.

Stead, Christopher. (1976). Rhetorical method in Athanasius. *Vigiliae Christianae* 30: 121–137.

Trapp, Michael. (2007). *Philosophy in the Roman Empire: Ethics, Politics and Society*. Aldershot: Ashgate.

Van Nuffelen, Peter. (2011). *Rethinking the Gods. Philosophical Readings of Religion in the Post-Hellenistic Period*. Cambridge: Cambridge University Press.

Van Nuffelen, Peter. (2012). *Orosius and the Rhetoric of History*. Oxford: Oxford University Press.

Vessey, Mark. (2008). Literature, patristics, early Christian writing. In: *The Oxford Handbook of Early Christian Studies* (ed. S. Ashbrook Harvey and D.G. Hunter), 42–65. Oxford: Oxford University Press.

Wilson, N.G. (1975). *Saint Basil on the Value of Greek Literature*. London: Duckworth.

Zizioulas, John D. (1995). The doctrine of the Holy Trinity: The significance of the Cappadocian contribution. In: *Trinitarian Theology Today* (ed. Christoph Schwöbel), 44–60. Edinburgh: T & T Clark.

CHAPTER TWENTY-ONE

Sermons

Jaclyn Maxwell

In the century following the reign of Constantine, bishops gained greater prominence in their communities, rising numbers of educated men entered the clergy, Christian communities grew, and the competition among Christian sects intensified. All of these factors heightened the importance of sermons in Christian worship and increased expectations regarding the skills that went into their composition and presentation. Although only a fraction of the sermons preached in late antiquity have been preserved, the number of surviving texts is staggering: around 900 from John Chrysostom alone, and more than 500 by Augustine – the largest collections of Greek and Latin sermons – in addition to the collections of sermons by numerous other preachers from cities across the Roman Empire (Olivar 1991; Dunn-Wilson 2005).

In order to understand the significance of the sermons for their authors and intended audiences, the texts must be studied within the social context of preaching in this period. Ecclesiastical careers were often built on one's reputation for eloquence, which can be seen in the particularly dramatic case of John Chrysostom. John Chrysostom was chosen as the new bishop of Constantinople based on his renown as a preacher. The church historian Socrates Scholasticus describes him as being known for his irritability and arrogance among his peers, but he was able to win over large numbers of laypeople with his preaching (*H.E.* 6.3). Later, when he faced enemies within the clergy and imperial household, he remained popular in the city because of his sermons: "The people nevertheless continued to regard him with love and veneration, on account of his valuable discourses in the church, and therefore

---

A Companion to Late Antique Literature, First Edition.
Edited by Scott McGill and Edward J. Watts.
© 2018 John Wiley & Sons, Inc. Published 2018 by John Wiley & Sons, Inc.

those who sought to traduce him, only brought themselves into contempt" (*H.E.* 6.4). Socrates goes on to testify that people of his own day, several decades after Chrysostom's death, could easily understand this dynamic because they could read the texts for themselves – Chrysostom had published some sermons and others had been recorded by shorthand writers (*H.E.* 6.4).

Although John Chrysostom was an exceptionally famous preacher and an influential bishop, the importance of his sermons in his own day as direct communication with his congregation and their subsequent preservation and circulation point to broader developments in Christian leadership and culture in late antiquity. Members of the educated elite were joining the clergy and utilizing their rhetorical skills to educate their followers in Christian doctrine and ethics, and, in many cases, they competed with other sects for the laity's support. In addition to reaching their immediate audience, particularly impressive sermons were recorded and circulated, providing models for preachers who did not have the benefit of a formal rhetorical education.

In late antiquity, preachers mostly addressed people who already considered themselves Christians and focused on deepening their understanding of Christian doctrine, answering their questions, and rebuking them for their errors. Although "being preached at" holds negative connotations today, there is a great deal of evidence that dynamic preachers were in high demand. Late antique church leaders produced some of the first systematic biblical commentaries in the form of sermons, while also addressing specific issues related to their times, including theological controversies and the Christianization of social norms and daily life. Sermon collections from this period were preserved as models for later generations of preachers, which meant that these writers (speakers) were influential in both their own time periods and beyond (Bailey 2010).

This chapter will address some of the key issues related to sermons in late antiquity – their relationship to earlier sermons and to other types of literature from this period, their connections to classical rhetorical training, the ways in which preachers aimed to teach and persuade their listeners, and the nature of the preacher's audience. Rather than recounting the content of certain collections of sermons and their contributions to biblical exegesis and the formation of doctrine, the chapter will focus on sermons as a form of communication that bridged the world of intellectuals with the rest of society.

21.1 Origins of Sermons

The style, content, and function of late antique sermons developed from a variety of earlier forms of religious instruction that can be traced back to the New Testament. The Gospels and Acts of the Apostles provide the earliest examples of Christian missionary preaching and also glimpses of preaching as scriptural commentary, reflecting Jewish practices of the time (e.g. Luke 4:17). Although the form and context of the apostles' missionary work differed from sermons that would later become part of the liturgy, an early form of preaching was considered essential for new believers: "Faith comes from hearing the message, and the message is heard through the word about Christ" (Rom. 10:17) (Olivar 1991, pp. 31–36; Fitzmyer 1989, pp. 22–26; Stewart-Sykes 2001, pp. 3–23).

In contrast to Paul's famous address at the temple of Artemis in Ephesus, apostolic preaching did not usually take the form of public speeches. Instead, explanations of the Christian message and discussions of its ethical implications took place in environments similar to synagogues and in Hellenistic philosophical schools, drawing on both cultures' approaches to the study of texts (Stowers 1984; Fitzmyer 1989, pp. 27–28; Stewart-Sykes 2001, pp. 39–87). In the decades following the apostles' missions, Christians continued to gather in private, teaching a form of catechism to new members as well as giving additional instruction for baptized Christians. As more effort shifted from proselytizing to instructing the converted, teachers emphasized commentary on the Scriptures and exhortations regarding behavior rather than the basic proclamation of their message (Dodd 1960, pp. 7–8). Alistair Stewart-Sykes (2001, pp. 79–80) describes the development from the less-structured practice of prophecy in the earliest gatherings into discussions of the meaning of prophecies and, later on, to sermons that explained the scriptures and their implications for the lives of their listeners, a process he describes as involving "scholasticization" and "synagogalization." The inclusion of scriptural commentary into the liturgy would guarantee the importance of preaching in later Christian communities, as well as its important role in the responsibilities of Christian authorities.

By the mid-second century, sermons followed the reading of scriptures and preceded the prayers and offerings in the liturgy (Justin Martyr, 1 *Apol.* 66). From around the same time, the anonymous text 2 Clement, with its focus on repentance and resurrection, and a few other texts provide the earliest evidence of sermons or sermon-like discourses (Stewart-Sykes 2001, pp. 174–239; Lienhard 1989, p. 37). Origen's oeuvre from the 230s to the 250s provides the first substantial collection of sermons by a Christian teacher addressing his community. His sermons differ from his scriptural commentaries primarily in their length – the timing of the liturgy and the congregation's attention span meant that there was limited time for speaking, whereas written commentaries had no such constraints (Lienhard 1989, pp. 39–40).

Origen's sermons were aimed at educating Christians about their religion rather than at proselytizing nonbelievers. He spoke to catechumens and baptized Christians with varying levels of interest in or knowledge of complicated theological matters (Hällström 1984). His sermons focused on each day's reading from Scripture, providing both literal and spiritual meanings along with ethical implications. Origen also expressed his concern about the congregation's lack of attention and poor attendance and refers to complaints about his preaching (Lienhard 1989, pp. 44–46). Despite the later condemnation of some of Origen's theological positions, his commentaries and sermons provided models for influential preachers and theologians in the fourth century.

21.2 Sermons as a Genre

By the fourth century the basic features of Christian preaching and its role in the liturgy were well established: The preacher (usually the bishop) presented a combination of scriptural commentary and moral exhortation out loud to his listeners. But within these parameters, sermons did not adhere to one particular stylistic pattern and could serve additional functions, such as polemic against rivals or as hagiography. Moreover, the style of a sermon could vary considerably: For example, Syriac sermons were composed in verses meant to be chanted (Mayer 2008, p. 570). Although this chapter has been using the term "sermon," patristic authors used various terms to refer to pastoral instruction, sometimes distinguishing the commentary on biblical texts as homilies and more formal discussions as sermons, but in many cases using the terms "homilia" or "logos" or in Latin, "tractatus" and "sermo" interchangeably (Olivar 1991, pp. 487–514; Cunningham and Allen 1998, pp. 1–2).

Despite the wide range of addresses referred to in this chapter as sermons, most of these texts exhibit certain features linked to their original presentation to listeners: short clauses, rhetorical questions, fictional dialogues or debates, conversational phrasing or tone, and various indications of ex tempore composition such as digressions, repetition, non sequiturs, abrupt endings, and very specific exhortations related to the time and place of the original preaching (Oberhelman 1991, p. 111; Cunningham 1995, p. 24; Hill 1998, pp. 313–316). Extensive evidence that most sermons were extemporaneous rather than composed for recitation can be found within the sermons themselves and also in other texts that describe preaching in this period (Deferrari 1922; Hartney 2004, pp. 37–39). In general, in addition to these aspects of oral presentation, sermons were also usually limited in length, but even this could vary. In the case of John Chrysostom's homilies on the Psalms, these texts were too long for the liturgy but still show signs of oral presentation, leading Charles Hill (1998, p. 308) to identify them as presentations at church gatherings later in the day, after the main assembly.

In addition to drawing on Jewish traditions of scriptural commentary, Christian preaching was also influenced by the Cynic-Stoic diatribe, which focused on ethical issues and often took the form of a fictional dialogue in order to engage listeners (Uthemann 1998, p. 143; Oberhelman 1991, pp. 109–110). Although the extent of Cynic-Stoic influence has been the subject of debate, it is clear that sermons shared a lot in common with pagan traditions of textual commentary in their rhetorical style and interest in ethical teachings. A key difference, though, was that the preachers reached audiences much broader than the circles of learned men.

The distinction between sermons and scriptural commentaries is especially difficult to define. Contrary to the assumption that learned scriptural commentaries and sermons addressed different audiences and did so with different styles and concerns, Philip Rousseau (2014, pp. 14–15) highlights the overlap between these types of texts. In addition to sharing many of the same concerns and topics, some sermons were revised by their authors or by later editors into the format of scriptural commentaries. For example, all of Ambrose's surviving works are revised sermons (Oberhelman 1991, p. 101). The relationship between sermons and exegetical commentaries is especially clear in Augustine's *Expositions of the Psalms*, a series that includes sermons presented to his listeners as well as other texts that were written in the style of homilies but not presented as such (Rousseau 2014, p. 24; Olivar 1991, p. 933). Ultimately, the fact that the same men wrote commentaries and presented sermons (which usually included some amount of scriptural exegesis) meant that the content tended to be similar and the texts themselves might serve in more than one context.

21.3 The Influence of Classical Rhetoric

In late antiquity, bishops were increasingly drawn from upper-class families, whose sons were trained in the schools of grammarians followed by advanced study with rhetoric professors (Rapp 2005, pp. 172–207; Elm 2012). Eloquence played a key role in the self-presentation of the elite and prepared them to represent their communities as local officials and as legal advocates (Kaster 1988; Gleason 1995). As preachers who aimed to keep the attention of their listeners, they used their rhetorical skills to inculcate orthodox belief and promote Christian behavior and to compete with rival Christian sects. The most influential bishops of this time, including John Chrysostom, Ambrose, and Augustine, were trained in rhetoric and had prepared for careers in law courts or teaching rhetoric when they entered the clergy. The influence of the rhetoric schools reached well beyond these famous cases, which can be seen in Jerome's *On Illustrious Men*, a collective biography of learned Christians written as a response to pagan accusations that Christians were uneducated. In this text eloquence is an important aspect of being "illustrious," and several bishops and preachers are noted for having started off as rhetoric teachers (*De vir. illust.* 67, 71, 101). The historian Socrates also describes the career of Ablabius, an orator who continued to teach rhetoric even after he was ordained as the Novatian bishop of Nicaea (*H.E.* 7.12). Socrates also refers to two provincial bishops who raised money for their sees by preaching in Constantinople, which was possibly a widespread practice (*H.E.* 6.11; Van Nuffelen 2015, pp. 209–212). These examples illustrate the overlap between the worlds of the orators and preachers of the time.

Part of the demand for well-trained and persuasive speakers stemmed from ongoing theological controversies: If one group had representatives making a good case for its interpretation of doctrine, then rival groups had to counter with their own attacks and defense. Theodoret describes how Flavian, bishop of Antioch, taught his priests to make theological arguments:

> [Flavian] did not himself preach at the services of the church, but furnished an abundant supply of arguments and scriptural thoughts to the preachers, who were thus able to aim their shafts at the blasphemy of Arius…Discoursing alike at home and abroad, he easily rent asunder the heretics' nets and showed their defenses to be mere spiders webs. (Theod. *H.E.* 4.22; trans. NPNF [Nicene and Post-Nicene Fathers] series 2, vol. 3, p. 127)

The use of rhetorical training was a display of privilege and cultural authority, but it was also a practical matter: Preachers needed to use these techniques to attract and maintain the loyalty of their congregations. People in late antique cities encountered rhetorical speaking in various contexts – it was central to their entertainment, their courts, education, and politics (Maxwell 2006, pp. 42–64). When adapting classical rhetoric for Christian contexts, preachers introduced new elements of style that were based on a Christian ideal of a simple style, or *sermo humilis*, based on biblical language and geared toward teaching ordinary Christians (Auerbach 1965, pp. 27–66). This combination of styles became more standardized in the fourth-century treatises that offered advice to preachers regarding the useful elements of classical rhetoric within a distinctively Christian approach to teaching.

21.4 Advice about Sermons

Despite concerns about rhetorical education's links to pagan culture, most Christian authors recognized this as an essential skill for communicating with the laity. The influence of Second Sophistic rhetorical style is evident throughout Greek and Latin texts from this time (Oberhelman 1991; Ameringer 1921; Campbell 1983). But there were pitfalls to avoid – overindulgence in rhetorical embellishment and the temptation to seek popularity with listeners. Ambrose, Augustine, and John Chrysostom wrote treatises offering advice to preachers to help them address their congregations effectively while avoiding these missteps. Ambrose was well known for his eloquence, but he expressed concern about the potential for rhetoric to mislead the laity. In his *De officiis* (380s), he advised preachers to use the Bible as their stylistic model and stressed the importance of keeping their audiences' attention. Ambrose recommended that sermons should be the right length (neither too long nor too short) and should also strike a balance in tone and style, neither "soft or effete" nor "coarse or uncouth" (*De off.* 1.19.84). Elsewhere, Ambrose stressed a key difference between preaching and other types of oratory. In contrast to an orator who might aim for a prize or public acclaim, for a preacher, the salvation of the listeners and the speaker was at stake (Graumann 1997, p. 590).

In the final book of *On Christian Doctrine*, Augustine offered his own advice to preachers, recommending that they should aim "to teach, to delight, and to persuade"(4.17.34). Because of their subject material and audience, preachers should break certain conventions of classical oratory: Instead of following Cicero's instructions to use a low, middle, or high style, depending on the importance of the topic, preachers should consider all of their subjects to be of the highest importance. Modeling their speech after the examples of Paul's letters and those of other Christian authors, they should use different levels of style for teaching and persuasion whenever necessary (4.18.35–4.32.50). According to Augustine, preachers could embellish their sermons if they had the right motives: "Not in a spirit of ostentation but wisely, not content only with the aim of charming our listener, but rather concerned to use it to help him to the good of which we wish to persuade him" (4.25.55; Roberts 1989, pp. 125–130). Augustine advised preachers to gauge their audiences' response in order to learn whether or not their sermons were successful: Applause was good, but tears were better: "They indicated by applause that they were being taught or pleased, but tears indicated they were persuaded" (4.24.53). The goals and methods of a preacher had much in common with the orator, but they were supposed to be driven by different motives and aiming for very different, serious goals, while somehow avoiding the old ambitions of pleasing the listeners and receiving acclaim as speakers.

Jerome makes a similar point about the desired response to a sermon when giving advice to a young priest: "Let the tears of those who hear you sound your praises." He warns against verbosity and overreliance on style rather than substance:

> Reeling off words and speaking briskly to win admiration from the unwashed masses are the ploys of ignorant men. The shameless man often explains what he does not know, and after convincing others he asserts for himself a possession of knowledge. (*Ep.* 52.8; trans. Cain 2013, p. 47)

Showing off rhetorical skill was not just in bad taste; it was also a cause for suspicion. Jerome implies that relying on style rather than on substance could be an intentional way to mislead the laity: "There is nothing as easy as deceiving the illiterate rabble with a slick style of speaking, for whatever they do not understand they admire all the more" (*Ep.* 52.8; trans. Cain 2013, p. 47; cf. Rousseau 1998, p. 393).

Overall, this advice about preaching aimed to steer Christian authors toward the development of a new approach to eloquence when addressing a heterogeneous group of listeners, with the *sermo humilis* as their ideal (Auksi 1995, pp. 164-170; Kaster 1988, pp. 83–84; MacMullen 1966). But striving for a plain style was not simple for educated men: The advocates for the Christian plain style did not always follow their own advice. They condemned their rivals for seeking popularity and profit from their eloquence, but they continued to draw on these skills themselves. Peter Van Nuffelen (2015, p. 203) has noted that despite their protests to the contrary, bishops knew that rhetorical skill was the key to their popularity with the laity and the respect from their peers, "even when such ambitions were covered under the cloak of humility." The contradiction between a stated wish for simplicity and the actual use of rhetorical techniques was a part of the larger cultural transition that brought together conflicting elements of the classical world and Christianity, which put educated men in the strange position of denouncing education (Kaster 1988, pp. 77–89; Oberhelman 1991, pp. 121–124; Hartney 2004, p. 50; Cameron 1997, p. 27).

John Chrysostom's advice to preachers in his treatise *On the Priesthood* centered on the congregation's reactions to sermons. He describes the laity as eager for entertainment: "The power of eloquence is more desired in church than when professors of rhetoric are made to contend against each other" (*De sac.* 5.1). In this context, preachers should avoid seeking popularity by ignoring both positive and negative feedback. Despite his concerns about preachers being treated as public orators,

Chrysostom himself had become famous as an eloquent speaker, earning his nickname "Goldenmouth."

Although he was one of the most famous preachers of the time, he was clearly uncomfortable with his own popularity. In one of his sermons, he discussed how easily an acclaimed orator could think too highly of himself. Applause was a dangerous temptation (*Hom, in Acts* 30):

> Many take a deal of pains to be able to stand up in public, and make a long speech: and if they get applause from the multitude, it is to them as if they gained the very kingdom (of heaven); but if silence follows the close of their speech, it is worse than hell itself, the dejection that falls upon their spirits from the silence! (trans. NPNF series 1, vol. 11, p. 193)

He then uses the first person plural for the perspective of the vainglorious speaker:

> This has turned the Churches upside down, because both *you* desire not to hear a discourse calculated to lead you to compunction, but one that may delight you from the sound and composition of the words, as though you were listening to singers and minstrels and *we* too act a preposterous and pitiable part in being led by your lusts, when we ought to root them out. (trans. NPNF series 1, vol. 11, p. 193)

He compares this situation to a father who allows his unhealthy child to eat as much cake as he pleases, against the doctor's orders, because he does not want him to cry. In the preacher's case, he finds himself busy trying to please his listeners and receive their applause. Chrysostom confesses that he is guilty of this:

> Believe me, I speak not other than I feel – when as I discourse I hear myself applauded, at the moment indeed I feel it as a man (for why should I not own the truth?): I am delighted, and give way to the pleasurable feeling…(trans. NPNF series 1, vol. 11, p. 193)

He suggests setting a rule against applause during the sermon, only to have his suggestion met with…applause: "What means that noise again? I am laying down a rule against this very thing." After he goes into more detail about the importance of silence for learning, he pleads, "I will not be tempted by praise and honor, or to delight you…it should be quiet like a painter's studio…How now? Applauding again?" (*Hom in Acts* 30; Olivar 1991, pp. 834–867). This fascinating example of an eloquent speaker rejecting (or claiming to reject) applause provides another glimpse of how the transformation of culture and values played out in complicated ways.

21.5 The Preachers and their Audiences

Whom were the preachers addressing in these sermons? As we have seen, the preachers themselves as well as the church historians remarked on the popular enthusiasm for sermons and for individual preachers. But the sermons themselves, as they have been preserved, often appear to be more complex or more tedious than what we imagine the ordinary, uneducated Christian laity might have clamored for. In his work on this question, Ramsay MacMullen emphasizes the economic, social, and cultural gulf between educated preachers and ordinary Christians and argues that sermons were meant for upper-class Christians. Moreover, most of the population lived in the countryside and often did not speak Greek or Latin (MacMullen 1966, 1989). Even in the case of the urban Christians, MacMullen argues, the devotion of ordinary Christians was geared more toward the martyrs' shrines than the churches (MacMullen 2009, pp. 14–32, 104–111). Moreover, sermons focus on the problems and concerns of the wealthy rather than on the poor, and wealthier people were the ones who had leisure time that could be spent at church. When "the poor" are mentioned, in many cases it is clear that the relatively poor, the non-rich, are meant rather than the destitute (Brown 2012, pp. 342–347).

Countering this view, Wendy Mayer (1998) and others (Rousseau 1998; Maxwell 2006) have interpreted late antique sermons as addressing a broader audience. Although the wealthy do receive a disproportionate amount of attention, numerous sermons provide evidence of the diversity of urban Christian congregations. For example, John Chrysostom's 34 homilies on Hebrews refer to the presence of the following groups in the congregation: baptized and unbaptized Christians, men and women, ascetics, rich widows, married women, the wealthy, the moderately wealthy, and the poor. The congregation included the literate and illiterate, some who lacked knowledge of Scriptures, some who were learning, others who were not, and some who were distracting themselves and others by laughing and chatting. In some cases Chrysostom remarked about the presence of a large crowd or especially low attendance (Allen 1996, pp. 408–415). A similar analysis of the audience in sermons by the bishop Quodvultdeus of Carthage shows that he preached in the 430s to a congregation of Berber-Punic artisans, farmers, fishermen, and wealthy people (Finn 1997, p. 49).

Although it is true that workers had less free time, there are indications that they still attended church and that the preachers were aware of their time constraints. John Chrysostom recognized that many Christians had work to do following church: "Let each one leave the church and take up his daily tasks: one hastening to work with his hands, another hurrying to his military post, and still another to his position in government" (*Catech.* 8.17;

Mayer 1998, p. 132). Basil of Caesarea also described the pressure on him to accommodate his sermons to his congregation's needs: "Many artisans, employed in manual labors and who earn just enough at their daily work to provide for their own nourishment, are surrounding me and obliging me to be brief, so I will not keep them too long from their jobs" (*Hex.* 3.1).

MacMullen's caveats about linguistic divides and the numbers of people who could fit into any given church are important, but, at the same time, the advice they gave about preaching (see above) points to the broad appeal of sermons, and, at times, late antique authors directly describe the popularity of sermons. In his treatise *On the Priesthood*, Chrysostom remarks, "Do you not know what a passion for sermons has burst in upon the minds of Christians nowadays?" (*De sac.* 5.8). Gregory of Nazianzus makes a similar comment in a more negative tone, suggesting that the people of Constantinople wanted a crowd-pleasing bishop rather than a serious and virtuous one: "They are not seeking priests, but rhetors" (*Or.* 42.24). Gregory of Nyssa corroborates this view in his remarks about the widespread participation in theological discussions in Constantinople, which, he claimed, included food and clothing vendors, moneylenders, and bath attendants (*De deitate*, 120–121; cf. Gr. Naz. *Or.* 27.2). In these cases, late antique authors seem to be describing urban congregations as excessively enthusiastic about sermons and theological discussions. As Richard Lim (1995, pp. 149–180) has demonstrated, church authorities began to discourage public discussions of certain theological questions because it was too easy for controversy to arise. Moreover, the moral exhortations found in many sermons addressed issues that were broadly relevant to Christians of any social level who were aiming to live according to their religion's teachings. Sermons were one part of an exchange of knowledge and values across social and cultural lines taking place in this period; these instructions, along with the liturgy, Christian artwork, and visits to pilgrimage sites all played a role in transforming the worldviews of the laity (Cameron 1997, pp. 31–33).

21.6 Shorthand Writers and the Preservation of Sermons

Only a fraction of the sermons presented in late antiquity were preserved – even in the case of Augustine, we only have around 10% of the sermons he gave during his long career (Brown 2012, p. 339; cf. Müller 2012, p. 301). The sermons that survive were recorded by shorthand writers, *notarii*, and sometimes edited by the preacher before circulation (Deferrari 1922, pp. 105–109; Lienhard 1989, p. 39; Liparov-Chicheren

2013). In other cases, sermons were dictated and sent as letters to be read out loud in church (Deferrari 1922, pp. 101–103). Augustine kept shorthand transcripts of his sermons in an archive, which he cataloged in response to requests from other bishops (Müller 2012, pp. 299–304). Members of the congregation could also take their own notes: Gregory of Nazianzus remarks (negatively) on scribes "seen and unseen" (*Or.* 42.26; Hill 1998, p. 304). Sermons from preachers known for their eloquence and theological insight were preserved and used as models (or crib sheets) for later preachers. Socrates Scholasticus refers to John Chrysostom's sermons being available in the form that he published and also from the notes taken by shorthand writers. He states that both versions convey the preacher's eloquence and persuasiveness (*H.E.* 6.4). Socrates's description of the bishop Atticus, who became bishop of Constantinople soon after John Chrysostom was sent into exile, provides additional insight into the process of shorthand writing and preservation of sermons. Atticus started off by reciting sermons he had memorized beforehand and then later became confident enough to preach extemporaneously. Despite this progress, "His discourses, however, were not such as to be received with much applause by his auditors, nor to deserve to be committed to writing" (Soc. *H.E.* 7.2). This seems to have been the fate of the majority of sermons preached during this time.

As we have seen, the key difference between commentaries and sermons was the oral presentation of biblical exegesis and exhortation to listeners, in contrast to written treatises meant for a small circle of literate friends. In some cases, sermons had an afterlife as written texts and reached additional audiences of readers. Some of these readers then modeled (or cribbed) their own sermons from the texts. Augustine endorsed the practice of other preachers doing this if they were not rhetorically gifted: They could "take something eloquently and wisely written by others, memorize it, and offer it to the people in the person of the author" (*Doc. Chr.* 4.29.62). Later, in the sixth century, Caesarius of Arles took the process a step further by drawing on collections of sermons by Augustine, Ambrose, and others and composing sermons to share with bishops in Gaul, Italy, and Spain (Bailey 2010).

REFERENCES

Allen, Pauline. (1996). The homilist and the congregation: A case study of Chrysostom's homilies on Hebrews. *Augustinianum* 36: 397–421.

Ameringer, Thomas E. (1921). *The Stylistic Influence of the Second Sophistic on the Panegyrical Sermons of St. John Chrysostom.* Washington, DC: Catholic University of America.

Auerbach, Erich. (1965. repr. 1993). *Literary Language and its Public in Late Latin Antiquity and in the Middle Ages* (trans. Ralph Manheim). Princeton: Princeton University Press.

Auksi, Peter. (1995). *Christian Plain Style: The Evolution of a Spiritual Ideal.* Montreal: McGill-Queen's University Press.

Bailey, Lisa Kaaren. (2010). *Christianity's Quiet Success: The Eusebius Gallicanus Sermon Collection and the Power of the Church in Late Antique Gaul.* South Bend, IN: University of Notre Dame Press.

Brown, Peter. (2012). *Through the Eye of a Needle: Wealth, the Fall of Rome, and the Making of Christianity in the West, 350–550 AD.* Princeton, NJ: Princeton University Press.

Cain, Andrew. (2013). *Jerome and the Monastic Clergy: A Commentary on Letter 52 to Nepotian, with an Introduction, Text, and Translation,* Supplements to Vigiliae Christianae 119. Leiden: Brill.

Cameron, Averil. (1997). Christianity and communication in the fourth century: The problem of diffusion. In: *Aspects of the Fourth Century: Proceedings of the Symposium Power & Possession: State, Society, and Church in the Fourth Century A.D.* (ed. H.W. Pleket and A.M.F.W. Verkoogt), 23–42. Leiden: Agape.

Campbell, James. (1983). *The Influence of the Second Sophistic on the Style of the Sermons of St. Basil the Great,* Cleveland, OH: J.T. Zubai.

Cunningham, Mary. (1995). Andreas of Crete's homilies on Lazarus and Palm Sunday: The preacher and his audience. *Studia Patristica* 31: 22–41.

Cunningham, Mary and Allen, Pauline. ed. (1998). *Preacher and Audience: Studies in Early Christian and Byzantine Homiletics,* Leiden: Brill.

Deferrari, Roy J. (1922). St. Augustine's method of composing and delivering sermons. *American Journal of Philology* 43.2: 97–123; 43.3: 193–219.

Dodd, C.H. (1960). *The Apostolic Preaching and Its Developments.* New York: Harper & Brothers.

Dunn-Wilson, David. (2005). *A Mirror for the Church: Preaching in the First Five Centuries.* Grand Rapids, MI: Eerdmans.

Elm, Susanna. (2012). *Sons of Hellenism, Fathers of the Church: Emperor Julian, Gregory of Nazianzus, and the Vision of Rome.* Transformation of the Classical Heritage 49. Berkeley: University of California Press.

Finn, Thomas. (1997). Quodvultdeus: Preacher and the audience. The homilies on the Creed. *Studia Patristica* 31: 42–58.

Fitzmyer, Joseph. (1989). Preaching in the apostolic and subapostolic age. In: *Preaching in the Patristic Age: Studies in Honor of Walter J. Burghardt, S.J.* (ed. David Hunter), 19–35. New York: Paulist.

Gleason, Maud W. (1995). *Making Men: Sophists and Self-Presentation in Ancient Rome.* Princeton, NJ: Princeton University Press.

Graumann, Thomas. (1997). St. Ambrose on the art of preaching. In: *Vescovi e Pastori in Epoca Teodosiana.* XXV Incontro di studiosi dell'antichità cristiana, Roma, 8–10 maggio, 1996, Studia Ephemeridis "Augustinianum," 58.2, 587–600. Rome: Institutum Patristicum Augustnianum.

Hällström, Gunnar af. (1984). *Fides Simpliciorum according to Origen of Alexandria*. Commentationes Humanarum Litterarum 76. Helsinki: Societas Scientiarum Fennica.

Hartney, Aideen. (2004). *John Chrysostom and the Transformation of the City*. London: Duckworth.

Hill, Charles. (1998). Chrysostom's homilies on the Psalms: Homilies or tracts? In: *Prayer and Spirituality in the Early Church* (ed. Pauline Allen, Raymond Canning, and Lawrence Cross), 301–317. Queensland: Centre for Early Christian Studies.

Kaster, Robert. (1988). *Guardians of Language: The Grammarian and Society in Late Antiquity*. Berkeley: University of California Press.

Lienhard, John. (1989). Origen as homilist. In: *Preaching in the Patristic Age: Studies in Honor of Walter J. Burghardt, S.J.* (ed. David Hunter), 36–52. New York: Paulist.

Lim, R. (1995). *Public disputation, power, and social order in late antiquity*. Berkeley: University of California Press.

Lipatov-Chicheren, Nikolai. (2013). Preaching as the audience heard it: Unedited transcripts of patristic homilies. *Studia Patristica* 44: 277–297.

MacMullen, Ramsay. (1966). A Note on *Sermo Humilis*. *Journal of Theological Studies* 17: 108–112.

MacMullen, Ramsay. (1989). The preacher's audience (AD 350–400). *Journal of Theological Studies* 40: 503–511.

MacMullen, Ramsay. (2009). *The Second Church: Popular Christianity AD 200-400*. Writings from the Greco-Roman World Supplement Series 1. Atlanta, GA: Society of Biblical Literature.

Maxwell, Jaclyn. (2006). *Christianization and Communication in Late Antiquity: John Chrysostom and his Congregation in Antioch*. Cambridge: Cambridge University Press.

Mayer, Wendy. (1998). John Chrysostom: Extraordinary preacher, ordinary audience. In: *Preacher and Audience: Studies in Early Christian and Byzantine Homiletics* (ed. Mary Cunningham and Pauline Allen), 105–137 Leiden: Brill.

Mayer, Wendy. (2008). Homiletics. In: *The Oxford Handbook of Early Christian Studies* (ed. Susan Ashbrook Harvey and David Hunter), 565–583. Oxford: Oxford University Press.

Müller, Hildegund. (2012). Preacher: Augustine and his congregation. In: *A Companion to Augustine* (ed. Mark Vessey), 297–309. Malden, MA: Blackwell.

Oberhelman, Steven. (1991). *Rhetoric and Homiletics in Fourth-Century Christian Literature: Prose Rhythm, Oratorical Style, and Preaching in the Works of Ambrose, Jerome, and Augustine*. Atlanta, GA: Scholars Press.

Olivar, Alejandro. (1991). *La Predicación Cristiana Antigua*. Barcelona: Herder.

Rapp, Claudia. (2005). *Holy Bishops in Late Antiquity: The Nature of Christian Leadership in an Age of Transition*. Transformation of the Classical Heritage 37. Berkeley: University of California Press.

Roberts, Michael. (1989). *The Jeweled Style: Poetry and Poetics in Late Antiquity*. Ithaca, NY: Cornell University Press.

Rousseau, Philip. (1998). "The preacher's audience": A more optimistic view. In: *Ancient History in a Modern University. Vol. 2: Early Christianity, Late Antiquity and Beyond* (ed. T.W. Hillard, R.A. Kearsley, C.E.V. Nixon, and A.M. Nobbs), 391–400. Grand Rapids, MI: Eerdmans.

Rousseau, Philip. (2014). Homily and exegesis in the patristic age: Comparisons of purpose and effect. In: *The Purpose of Rhetoric in Late Antiquity* (ed. Alberto J. Quiroga), 11–29. Studien und Texte zu Antike und Christentum 72. Tübingen: Mohr Siebeck.

Stewart-Sykes, Alistair. (2001). *From Prophecy to Preaching: A Search for the Origins of the Christian Homily*. Supplements to *Vigiliae Christianae* 59. Leiden: Brill.

Stowers, S.K. (1984). Social status, public speaking and private teaching: The circumstances of Paul's preaching activity. *Novum Testamentum* 26: 59–82.

Uthemann, K.-H., (1998). Forms of communication in the homilies of Severian of Gabala: A contribution to the reception of the diatribe as a method of exposition. In: *Preacher and Audience: Studies in Early Christian and Byzantine Homiletics* (ed. Mary Cunningham and Pauline Allen), 139–177. Leiden: Brill.

Van Nuffelen, Peter. (2015). A war of words: Sermons and social status in Constantinople under the Theodosian dynasty. In: *Literature and Society in the Fourth Century AD: Performing Paideia, Constructing the Present, Presenting the Self* (ed. Lieve Van Hoof and Peter Van Nuffelen), 201–217. Mnemosyne Supplements: Monographs on Greek and Latin Language and Literature 373. Leiden: Brill.

CHAPTER TWENTY-TWO

Travel and Pilgrimage Literature

Jan Willem Drijvers

Sidonius Apollinaris, prominent member of the provincial aristocracy in Gaul and later bishop of Clermont-Ferrand, arrived in the city of Rome late in 467. In response to a request of his friend Heronius, Sidonius reports in a letter about his journey from Lyon to the Eternal City (*Epist.* 1.5). Leaving Lyon Sidonius had the privilege of traveling by the public post service (*cursus publicus*); he stopped regularly at friends' houses along the way. After having crossed the Alps he went down to Ticinum (Pavia), where he embarked on a river boat. Sailing downstream on the river Po, he first reached Cremona and then continued to Ravenna, the imperial residence. He presents an impression of the latter city focusing on the large quantities of imported foodstuff and the polluted water conditions. After having crossed the Rubicon, he continued his journey via Rimini and Fano and then continued on the Via Flaminia to Rome. During the latter part of his journey Sidonius suffered from fever and fear of bad drinking water. Having arrived at his destination he offered thanks "at the triumphal thresholds of the Apostles," i.e. at the Basilicas of St. Peter and S. Paolo fuori le Mura, before entering the city (Fournier and Stoehr-Monjou 2014).

Although the letter is highly rhetorical and has an antiquarian imprint as well as reminiscences of Horace's journey from Rome to Brindisi (*Satire* 1.5), it gives a nice and probably trustworthy impression of traveling conditions in the late Roman Empire. These conditions seem to have been not very dissimilar from the circumstances in the early empire. What differs, however, is that in late antiquity there seems to have been a deeper sensitivity for geography than in the centuries before (Traina 2013, 2015) and that we have more

---

A Companion to Late Antique Literature, First Edition.
Edited by Scott McGill and Edward J. Watts.
© 2018 John Wiley & Sons, Inc. Published 2018 by John Wiley & Sons, Inc.

testimonies of travel and physical movement than we do from the earlier centuries of the empire. Possibly there was also an intensification of both travel itself and of travel narratives, which could be explained, at least partly, by the introduction of Christian religious travel in the early fourth century. Seeing and interacting with holy places and objects, encountering holy men, and participating in religious festivals became a significant motivation for traveling for the increasing number of Christians. The Christianization of travel is also a distinguishing marker of late antique travel literature in comparison with that of earlier periods.

This chapter discusses a variety of late antique writings about travel, with a particular focus on texts about Christian pilgrimage to the Holy Land. The letter of Sidonius demonstrates that traveling is closely associated with representations, both real and imaginary, of geographical space and the Christianization of the cosmos (Johnson 2014, p. 394).

The late Roman Empire was a very mobile society. People traveled for numerous reasons – commerce, government affairs, religion, education, military business, migration; they made use of the elaborate system of roads and the available modes of transport such as wagons, horses, and boats (Leyerle 2009; Dietz 2005, pp. 11–42). Although it is not easy to define travel literature as a genre, at least three kinds of texts can be characterized as specific travel literature: the *itinerarium*, the *periplous*, and the *periegesis*. Furthermore, reflections of journeys and travel can be found in a variety of texts such as letters, historical accounts, and the *vitae* of holy men and women. Travel and geography are not easily separated categories in late antique literature. Therefore travel narratives, geographical texts, and maps will all be reviewed in this chapter.

22.1 Letters

Epistolography had developed into a prominent literary art in late antiquity. We possess a large collection of letters that give insight into many aspects of late antique life. Some of them, such as the letter of Sidonius Apollinaris summarized above, provide information about modes of travel, routes, landscape, and aspects of a geopolitical and geohistorical kind. Synesius of Cyrene's *Letter* 5, dated 396/397 and addressed to his brother Euoptius, presents a dramatic account of Synesius's sea journey from Alexandria to his home town of Cyrene. The ship on which Synesius had embarked had a crew consisting of Jews and peasants who had hardly any experience in handling the ship. Apart from Synesius, there were some 50 passengers aboard, a third of them women, who were separated from the men by a screen. Among the men were soldiers. Soon after its departure the ship was overtaken by a heavy storm and was nearly shipwrecked on the reefs. Even though the Jewish skipper stopped steering the ship because of the Sabbath, the vessel made it to a deserted shore. After the storm had calmed down, the vessel took to the sea again but was soon struck by another storm. Eventually the passengers and the crew made it to a coast where they were amply provisioned by women whose men had gone away on commercial business. Synesius concludes the letter by advising his brother never to trust himself to the sea.

Obviously the line between fact and fiction in the letter is not clear, and this makes the historicity of the unfortunate journey doubtful. Synesius has enriched his account with many comic and tragic tropes as well as with Homeric elements. There are also reminiscences of Paul's sea journey from Caesarea to Rome (Acts 27:1–44). This makes the letter very much a literary construct appreciative of older epic, tales of sea journeys in Greek novels, and biblical stories (Johnson 2014, p. 396) while simultaneously presenting practical information about sea travel.

Jerome's *Letter* 108, written on the occasion of the death of Paula in Bethlehem in 404 and addressed to her daughter Eustochium, is of a nature other than that of the letters of Sidonius and Synesius since it is, in essence, the narrative of a religious journey. Jerome describes the journey of Paula, an extremely wealthy woman from a prominent Roman senatorial family, from Rome to Bethlehem. After she was widowed, she decided not to remarry and to dedicate her life to the Christian faith. Around 386 she departed from Ostia by ship and arrived in Antioch by way of Cyprus. From there she traveled southwards to the Holy Land, where she visited numerous holy places from both the Old and the New Testament (Hunt 1984, pp. 171–172; Dietz 2005, pp. 126–132). Jerome describes all of this but pays particularly close attention to her sojourns at Jerusalem and Bethlehem. After a journey through Egypt, where she paid visits to the many holy men who were living in the monastic communities there, she settled in Bethlehem and founded a double monastery in the city. Her journey as described by Jerome occurs in an exclusive Christian context. She visits biblical holy sites, laments Jesus's suffering and death at Jerusalem when she is shown the Cross, and stays at monasteries and in the residences of bishops. Because Jerome's purpose was not to write an all-embracing travel account but a report of Paula's visit to the biblical places (*Epist.* 108.8.1), the letter does not, for instance, provide information about travel conditions, apart from the fact that Paula traveled in a group of virgins (and probably with a substantial entourage). It also says little about the hazards of travel. In that respect one of the letters (*Epist.* 2.5–7) of the Greek church father Gregory of Nyssa is more illuminating. He warns his readers, that is, monks and virgins who wanted to see the sacred sites in the Holy Land, about the dangers of travel and, in particular, all the lurking (sexual) passions. These were profound because men and women did not travel separately, women needed help getting on and off their mounts, and the servants in hostels and inns were indiscriminate.

22.2 Religious Travel

Religious travel was not specific to Christian monotheism. In Greco-Roman polytheistic society people traveled, for example, to honor the gods by attending religious festivals, to visit oracles and healing sanctuaries, or to get initiated into a cult (Elsner and Rutherford 2005; Harland 2011). Leaders or founders of cults toured around for missionary reasons in order to promote and diffuse the cult of their deity on the religious market (Stark 1996) just like the apostles who traveled to gain adherents for the Jesus movement.

Paula was neither the first nor the last aristocratic lady who embarked on a pilgrimage to the Holy Land. She was preceded by Melania the Elder, who settled and founded a monastery in Jerusalem and would be followed by, inter alia, Poemenia, Melania the Younger, and the empress Eudocia (Dietz 2005, pp. 107–153). A few years before Paula made her religious journey through Palestine and Egypt, Egeria had come to the Holy Land. She stayed in Jerusalem for about three years (381–384), from where she made various trips to holy places. The account of her travels, written for her fellow sisters and only preserved fragmentarily, is a fascinating report about the expanding Christianization of the landscape and traveling in a religious context. She visited places like the Thebaid in Egypt (where many holy men lived), the Galilee, Mt. Nebo, Carneas, the Jordan River, and Mt. Sinai (Maraval 1982; Wilkinson 1999). On her return journey she made a detour to Edessa, which by the end of the fourth century had become an important center of religious tourism because letters of Jesus from his correspondence with King Abgar of Edessa were preserved there. From Edessa she traveled on to Seleucia in Isauria to visit St. Thecla's martyrium (Davis 2001). Her account ends with her arrival in Constantinople. Whether she continued her journey from there to Aquitania or Galicia whence she probably came is uncertain.

When Egeria and Paula made their pilgrimages the number of holy sites in the Holy Land had increased considerably since the time that the emperor Constantine (306–337) had ordered churches to be constructed at sites related to Christ's life and crucifixion. In Bethlehem the Church of the Nativity was built and in Jerusalem the Church of the Holy Sepulcher at the supposed spot of Golgotha and Jesus's tomb. Another one had been built on the Mount of Olives (Eusebius, *VC* 3.25–43). At least by the beginning of the fourth century, but probably somewhat earlier, an interest arose in the religious geography of the Holy Land by linking biblical places to their geographical location, of which the *Onomastikon* (On the Place-Names in the Holy Scriptures) by Eusebius is the first literary evidence (Freeman-Grenville 2004; Stenger 2015). At the end of the fourth century this topographical index of biblical sites was translated into Latin and extended by Jerome under the title *Liber locorum*. Interest in biblical topography is also expressed in the *Topography of the Holy Land* by Theodosius from around 518 (Geyer and Cuntz 1965, 1.115–125). Earlier, around the middle of the fifth century, a letter ascribed to Eucherius, bishop of Lyon, reflects a similar interest in the significance of the topography of Judaea and Palestine (Geyer & Cuntz 1965, 1.237–243). Later Adomnán (before 683) and Bede (ca. 702) consulted Eucherius's letter for their works on the holy places. The city of Jerusalem was at the center of Eucherius's and Theodosius's biblical geography. Apart from holy sites and relics, Eucherius conveys an interest in living holy men and women and their monasteries, thereby expressing attentiveness for both the Christian past and the present (Johnson 2014, p. 401).

The new Christian passion for the geographical identification of holy sites (Markus 1994; Sotinel 2005) and the imperial interest in Palestine shown by the emperor Constantine and his mother Helena, who had visited the region in 327/328 (Drijvers 2011, pp. 137–143), were a great stimulus for Christian religious travel in late antiquity. Increasing numbers of pilgrims traveled from all over the Roman Empire and beyond to the Holy Land. They also visited other sites, such as martyr's graves, the holy men living in the Egyptian and Syrian deserts, and the shrines of living saints (e.g. that of Symeon Stylites close to Aleppo). With this travel they sought to deepen their faith and come close to the divine at these tangible testimonies of the Christian faith. The earliest existing pilgrim's report of this sort is the *itinerarium* by the anonymous Bordeaux pilgrim who traveled to Jerusalem in 333.

22.3 Itineraries

Itineraria were road maps presenting details for a given route that included cities, villages, and other stops along the way as well as the distance between them. The land itinerary seems to be a principally Roman phenomenon (Salway 2001, p. 26) since all of them are in Latin apart from the Greek account of Theophanes (see below). There were written itineraries and graphic ones. The *Antonine Itinerary* (Cuntz 1929, pp. 1–85; Löhberg 2010), probably compiled in the version as we have it at the end of the third century but in all likelihood going back to early imperial times, is the most elaborate provincial and maritime itinerary now preserved (Salway 2001, pp. 39–43). It encompasses a series of itineraries and is based on the Roman network of roads and the provincial system; it serves to chart journeys from one place to another and back. The itinerary was evidently a successful and hands-on way of presenting geographical information for use of travel and transport (Brodersen 2001, 14). *Itineraria* predominantly describe routes over land, but sea and river routes are not excluded. However, charts for navigating on sea and rivers seem not to have existed in antiquity (Salway 2004).

Since the itinerary is a linear narrative and can be accessed at random points to start a journey, new data and routes could be easily included in the text. In late antiquity it was probably available in codex form, which made it easier to consult and use en route. The genre of the *itinerarium* has been drawn on to argue that the Roman worldview was "hodological" and that Romans perceived geographical space principally not by shapes but by the lines of the itineraries. Based on the itineraries, Romans could create a mental map of geographical space (Whittaker 2004, pp. 63–87).

Late antique Christian narratives of religious travel follow the format of the *itinerarium*, and the Bordeaux pilgrim was the first to adopt it. The traveler from Bordeaux must have been a person of some importance since she/he was allowed to make use of the transport facilities of the *cursus publicus* (Kolb 2001; Lemcke 2016). The Bordeaux pilgrim traveled overland from Bordeaux to Palestine noting the stopping places and the mileage between them. On average the traveler journeyed 24 miles per day. Occasionally she/he notes points of Christian and other interest. Upon arriving in Jerusalem she/he mentions, among other things, Sion, the Siloam pool, Golgotha, Christ's tomb, the praetorium of Pontius Pilate, and the churches built by Constantine. Her/his information reads as a topography of the city and is a testimony of the Christianization of the city's urban space. Jerusalem is the most important halting place for the traveler from Bordeaux and her/his *itinerarium* is "a work of remarkable ideological innovation" (Elsner 2000, p. 194) signifying the new Christian Constantinian empire of which Jerusalem was the religious focal point. Jerusalem as capital of the world of late antique Christendom is also at the center of the itinerary of the Piacenza pilgrim. Apart from the now traditional sites in and around Jerusalem, in Judaea, and Mt. Sinai, he also traveled to Suras at the Euphrates in order to honor St. Sergius and St. Bacchus, who suffered martyrdom there, as well as to Haran since it was considered the birthplace of Abraham.

The Bordeaux pilgrim, Egeria, Paula, and the Piacenza pilgrim are just a small representation of the many religious travelers who visited Jerusalem and the other biblical sites in the Holy Land in late antiquity (Maraval 1985). On the one hand, their pilgrim's narratives were not only personal impressions of their contacts with the Christian past and present at holy sites but also functioned as guide books for others who made similar journeys, because they contained practical information about stopping places, distances, locations, and hostels. On the other hand, these travel narratives could and did function to make a pilgrimage in the mind instead of a real one for those who were not able to make the physical journey.

The memoranda of Theophanes's itinerary preserved in the Archive of Theophanes from the early fourth century (Matthews 2006) represents a special case. The archive contains a variety of papyri concerning the undertakings of Theophanes, a wealthy gentleman from Hermopolis in the Thebaid in Egypt. These include financial records, household inventories, building documents, and personal papers as well as an account of his voyage from Hermopolis to Syrian Antioch and back ca. 320. This protracted but not uncommon journey – many people must have made this and similar trips – took about a year. Theophanes's account of what most probably was a business trip provides valuable information about the conditions of traveling in the late Roman Empire. It details, among other things, stopping places along the Via Maris, the diet en route, and the daily expenditures on a variety of items such as food, wine, oil, firewood, fodder for pack animals, and the use of bathhouses.

22.4 Maps

The Christianization of the landscape is not only conveyed in pilgrims' narratives but also in the sixth-century Madaba map, a floor mosaic in the church of St. George in Madaba in Jordan. It contains the oldest cartographic impression of the Holy Land and presents a rather detailed representation of the urban landscape of sixth-century Jerusalem (Donner 1992).

The itinerary of Theophanes, as well as other *itineraria adnotata*, shows a fashioning of conception of space that is also reflected in maps, or *itineraria picta* (Vegetius, *De re militari* 3.6). The third-century leather shield from Dura Europos (found in 1922) fits well into this category of *itineraria picta* and into cartographical thinking, even though it had a decorative and not a practical purpose. It presents stations along a coastal route in the northern Black Sea and the distances between them as well as pictures of ships (Dilke 1985, pp. 120–122; Brodersen 2001, pp. 14–16). It is, however, imaginable that illustrated itineraries have existed for practical use. The best known example of an *itinerarium pictum* is without doubt the unique *Tabula Peutingeriana*, named after its one-time owner Konrad Peutinger (1465–1547). It is the best example of what comes close to a modern-day map, although we should realize that, if the Romans had maps, these were completely unlike contemporary scale maps because of an entirely different Roman conception of geographical space (on maps see Dilke 1985). The multicolored copy of the *Tabula Peutingeriana* dates from ca. 1300 (e.g. Albu 2014), but most likely goes back to a late antique original. Its dimensions are extreme: 672 cm long and 33 cm high. It consists of 11 segments stretching from the Atlantic Ocean to India and depicts a detailed plotting of land routes, that is, a linear representation of place names and figures of distance. Apart from the network of roads that is at the base of the map, it shows mountains, rivers, seas, and islands. Cities, imperial capitals, hostels, and baths are indicated by pictorial symbols of various kinds. The map seems to be a representation of the entire road network and topographical organization of the late Roman world (Johnson 2014, p. 5), and appears to be based on written itineraries (Salway 2001, p. 47). Because Rome is at the center of the map, this is most likely an impression of the *orbis Romanus*, the inhabited world under Roman control. The foreshortened (north–south) and elongated (east–west) Peutinger map, which, for instance, shows the Mediterranean Sea as a narrow strip of water and Italy as wholly horizontal, cannot have had any practical use and was, like the Dura Europos shield, of a decorative nature. It has been suggested that the original was part of a scheme for a public space, in particular an imperial palace from the Tetrarchic period (Talbert 2010, pp. 142–157).

22.5 Periegeseis and Periploi

The *oikoumenè*-based perception of space as displayed in the Peutinger map is challenged by the literary geographies of the *periegesis* and *periplous*. A *periegesis* was a descriptive journey – in prose or in verse – around a place or an area or even the known world. The best known is that of Dionysius Periegetes, who composed a *periegesis* in Greek of just under 1200 hexameters in Alexandria in the time of Hadrian (117–138). It is an exquisite specimen of ancient geography, but, like many works of geography in the Greco-Roman world, it is evidence that the elite's view of the geography of the world was very much a literary one. Dionysius's text was not meant for practical use. Instead, as a composition of didactic poetry it was learned and studied in schools. The work was still very much en vogue and widely read in late antiquity. Its popularity was such that it was at least twice translated into Latin prose, first in the fourth century by Avienus, whose translation is known by the title *Descriptio orbis terrae* (Van de Woestijne, 1961), and then, some 200 years later, by Priscian, a grammarian working in Constantinople (Van de Woestijne 1953).

Like the *periegesis*, the *periplous* is Greek in origin. A *periplous* is a circumnavigation or a description of a coastal voyage. *Periploi* are like *itineraria* lists of routes, ports, river mouths, coastal markers, peoples, and occasionally references to myths. The earliest *periploi* date from Greek classical times, but the genre was still very much alive in late antiquity. We have the *Ora maritima* of the fourth-century senator Rufus Festus Avienus, which describes the coastline from Marseille to Cadiz (Murphy 1977). Rutilius Claudius Namatianus (fl. fifth century) describes a coastal voyage from Rome to Gaul undertaken in 416 in a poem (in elegiac meter) known as the *De reditu suo* (Doblhofer 1972–1977). Marcianus, who came from Heraclea Pontica, wrote around the year 400 a *Periplus maris exteri* (Periplous of the Outer Sea, i.e. the Ocean) in two books (Müller 2010, pp. 515–562). The work, which inter alia uses Ptolemy's *Geography* as a source, is now incomplete and the distances between the coastal stopping places and significant geographical markers are given in stades (Dilke 1985, pp. 141–143). *Periploi* could also be mixed with other literary forms, such as novels or historical works. Ammianus Marcellinus's description of the Black Sea (*Res gestae* 22.8) is essentially a *periplous* (Drijvers 1998).

Periegeseis and *periploi* could have a practical use, but they also are clearly literary in character. Like the *itineraria*, they seem to reflect the late antique fervor for cataloguing the world (Racine 2010, pp. 29–76, 133–147) while organizing and systematizing knowledge in an encyclopedic form (Formisano 2012, pp. 512–520). The *Expositio totius mundi et gentium*, by an anonymous author and dated to the mid-fourth century, is perhaps the best example of this (Rougé 1966). The text focuses on the *mare nostrum* and its periphery and presents a description of provinces, cities, and peoples from the far east to the west. Cities like Antioch, Alexandria, Carthage, and Rome are elaborately described, but the descriptions of places become increasingly fantastical and mythical as they extend into places on the periphery of the *oikoumenè* (Romm 1992). Like Theophanes mentioned above, the author of the *Expositio* was probably a merchant, an identification supported by his reporting on the commercial possibilities within the Roman Empire (Rougé 1966, pp. 27–47). Other examples of the late antique dedication of systematizing knowledge are the *Notitia dignitatum*, the *Notitia urbis Constantinopolis*, *Laterculus Veronensis*, and the *Notitia Galliarum* (Seeck 1876).

Two centuries later, during the reign of Justinian, another merchant and later monk by the name of Cosmas wrote about his travel experiences in the Red Sea, the Persian Gulf, and the Indian Ocean on his way to India (hence his epithet Indicopleustes). Cosmas Indicopleustes possibly came from Alexandria, but, if he did not, this was at least the city where he settled after his travels. He then became a monk and wrote his *Christian Topography* (Walska-Conus 1968–1973). This elaborate work, which is in essence a *periplous*, presents a wealth of geographical, cosmological, and natural historical information about the eastern regions beyond the borders of the empire. It is, however, also a Christian polemical text since it denies the sphericity of the universe. Cosmas argues against his second-century fellow Alexandrian Ptolemy that the world is flat instead of spherical and that it was formed after the Mosaic tabernacle: He imagined the world as a box covered by a canopy with the sun turning around a mountain standing in the center. Even among Christians Cosmas's worldview was not influential and did not have many adherents, though his travel narrative remained striking enough for the text to live on.

22.6 Historiography

The historiographical work of Ammianus Marcellinus shows clearly the interdependence between historical and geographical descriptions. His *Res gestae* contains several geographical digressions. Apart from the one on the Black Sea mentioned above, there are excursuses on the eastern provinces of the Roman Empire, the Boden Lake, Gaul, Persia, Egypt, and Thrace (Feraco 2004, 2011). The lost books of the *Res gestae* also contained geographical digressions, and it has been suggested that together these digressions presented the complete *oikoumenè*. In antiquity there was no clear distinction between history and geography, and descriptions of the physical world were often an integral part of historical narratives. Since the pioneering work of Herodotus, geography and history were mutually dependent in a way that was still the case in late antiquity as the historical writings of, for instance, Orosius, Jordanes, Procopius, and Isidore of Seville demonstrate (Merrills 2005). However, historical accounts provide geographical and travel information not only in digressions but also in reports about military expeditions or journeys of emperors and high officials. These reports can give practical evidence about routes and geographical circumstances, such as mountain ranges, the course and navigability of rivers, their crossing points, and many other such details.

22.7 *Vitae*

One might not immediately think of Christian biographic and hagiographic writings (*vitae*) about holy men and women as travel accounts, but many of these texts certainly merit such consideration. Holy men and women made a mental journey by ultimately making the decision to renounce the world and dedicate their life to God, and many also undertook physical journeys to the Egyptian or Syrian desert or to the Holy Land. Some of them remained in these locations, choosing an anchoritic life, settling in monasteries, or adopting other forms of religious coenobitism. Apart from monks living in monasteries or anchorites in the desert, there were the so-called wandering monks, who did not live under monastic rule. They either wandered perpetually as beggars, teachers, or religious enthusiasts or journeyed from monastery to monastery with their traveling interrupted by short stays of only a few days at a time (Caner 2002; Dietz 2005, pp. 88–105). A prominent example of a wandering monk is Barsauma whose Syriac *vita* presents his journeys through the eastern provinces in the first half of the fifth century and can, therefore, be seen as a travel narrative. He visited, for instance, Jerusalem four times, the last time to expel the Jews who had taken over the Temple Mount, allegedly with the consent of the empress Eudocia. Together with his gang of monks, Barsauma did not refrain from intimidating behavior in association with verbal and physical violence in converting pagans, Jews, and Samaritans to Christianity (Hahn and Menze forthcoming). In contrast to Barsauma's violent travels stand the peaceful journeys of John Moschus some two centuries later, as described in his *Spiritual Meadow* (Wortley 2010). John, a monk at the Theodosius monastery in Jerusalem, traveled to, among other sites, the Jordan River, Cilicia, Cyprus, Antioch, the Sinai desert, Alexandria, Antioch, Thessaloniki, and Rome before probably ultimately settling in Constantinople. He took this trip to observe diverse monastic practices, and his account of his trip contains many tales of religious practices and miracles.

The culture of movement in late antiquity was diverse, and this diversity is reflected in the late Roman travel literature, which essentially organized and archived geographical knowledge of the *oikoumenè*, or parts of it, in textual genres (Johnson 2016). People traveled for many reasons and made use of a variety of transportation, as they did in the early empire. The Christianization of Mediterranean society brought a new dimension and framework to the culture of traveling and to geographical thinking about space. Christian travel developed into a significant and distinguishing feature in late antiquity, which then generated a new dynamism that expanded the scope and power of travel literature.

REFERENCES

Albu, Emily. (2014). *The Medieval Peutinger Map: Imperial Roman Revival in a German Empire*. Cambridge: Cambridge University Press.

Brodersen, Kai. (2001). The presentation of geographical knowledge for travel and transport in the Roman World: *Itineraria non tantum adnotata sed etiam picta*. In: *Travel and Geography in the Roman Empire* (ed. Colin Adams and Ray Laurence), 7–21. London: Routledge.

Caner, Daniel. (2002). *Wandering, Begging Monks: Spiritual Authority and the Promotion of Monasticism in Late Antiquity.* Berkeley: University of California Press.

Cuntz, O. (1929). *Itineraria Romana.* Vol. 1: Itineraria Antonini Augusti et Burdigalense, nos, 1–75 (terrestrial), 76– 85 (maritime). Leipzig: Teubner.

Davis, Stephen J. (2001). *The Cult of Saint Thecla: A Tradition of Women's Piety in Late Antiquity.* Oxford: Oxford University Press.

Dietz, Maribel. (2005). *Wandering Monks, Virgins and Pilgrims: Ascetic Travel in the Mediterranean World, AD 300–800.* University Park, PA: Pennsylvania State University Press.

Dilke, O.A.W. (1985). *Greek and Roman Maps.* Baltimore, MD: Johns Hopkins University Press.

Doblhofer, Ernst. (1972–1977). *Rutilius Claudius Namatianus, De reditu suo sive Iter Gallicum.* Vol. 1: Einleitung, Text, Übersetzung, Wörterverzeichnis. Vol. 2: Kommentar. Heidelberg: Winter.

Donner, Herbert. (1992). *The Mosaic Map of Madaba.* Kampen: Kok Pharos.

Drijvers, Jan Willem. (1998). Ammianus Marcellinus on the geography of the Pontus Euxinus. *Histos. The Online Journal of Ancient Historiography* 2: 268–78. http://research.ncl.ac.uk/histos/documents/1998.11DrijversAmmianuson PontusEuxinus268278.pdf (accessed 21 Nov 2017).

Drijvers, Jan Willem. (2011). Helena Augusta, the Cross and the myth: Some new reflections. *Millennium. Yearbook on the Culture and History of the First Millennium C.E.* 8: 125–174.

Elsner, Jas. (2000). The *Itinerarium Burdigalense*: Politics and salvation in the geography of Constantine's empire. *Journal of Roman Studies* 90: 181–195.

Elsner, Jas and Rutherford, Ian. ed. (2005). *Pilgrimage in Graeco-Roman and Early Christian Antiquity: Seeing the Gods.* Oxford: Oxford University Press.

Feraco, Fabrizio. (2004). *Ammiano geografo: La digressione sulla Persia (23,6).* Naples: Loffredo Editore.

Feraco, Fabrizio. (2011). *Ammiano geografo: Nuovi studi.* Naples: Loffredo Editore.

Formisano, Marco. (2012). Late antiquity, new departures. In: *The Oxford Handbook of Medieval Latin Literature* (ed. Ralph J. Hexte and David Townsend), 509–534. Oxford: Oxford University Press.

Fournier, Mauricette and Stoehr-Monjou, Annick. (2014). Cartographie géo-littéraire et géo-historique de la mobilité aristocratique au Ve siècle d'après la correspondence de Sidoine Apollinaire: Du voyage official au voyage épistolaire. *Journal belge de géographie*, 2. http://belgeo.revues.org/12689 (accessed 4 June 2015).

Freeman-Grenville, G.S.P. (2004). *Palestine in the Fourth Century A.D.: The Onomasticon of Eusebius of Caesarea.* Jerusalem: Carta.

Geyer, P. and O. Cuntz. (1965). *Itineraria et alia geographica.* 2 vols. Corpus Christianorum Series Latina 175–176. Turnhout: Brepols.

Hahn, Johannes and Menze, Volker. ed. (Forthcoming). *The Wandering Holy Man: The Life of Barsauma, Christian Asceticism and Religious Conflict in Late Antique Palestine.* Berkeley: University of California Press.

Harland, Philip A. ed. (2011). *Travel and Religion in Antiquity.* Studies in Christianity and Judaism 21. Waterloo: Wilfrid Laurier University Press.
Hunt, E.D. (1984). *Holy Land Pilgrimage in the Later Roman Empire AD 312-460.* Oxford: Oxford University Press.
Johnson, Scott F. (2014). Real and imagined geography. In: *The Cambridge Companion to the Age of Attila* (ed. Michael Maas), 394–413. Cambridge: Cambridge University Press.
Johnson, Scott F. (2016). *Literary Territories: Cartographical Thinking in Late Antiquity.* Oxford: Oxford University Press.
Kolb, Anne. (2001). Transport and communication in the Roman state: The *cursus publicus.* In: *Travel and Geography in the Roman Empire* (ed. Colin Adams and Ray Laurence), 95–105. London: Routledge.
Lemcke, Lucas. (2016). *Imperial Transportation and Communication from the Third to the Late Fourth Century. The Golden Age of the* cursus publicus. Collection Latomus 353. Brussels: Éditions Latomus.
Leyerle, Blake. (2009). Mobility and the traces of empire. In: *A Companion to Late Antiquity* (ed. Philip Rousseau), 110–123. Malden, MA: Wiley Blackwell.
Löhberg, Bernd. (2010). *Das "Itinerarium provinciarum Antonini Augusti": Ein kaiserzeitliches Straßenverzeichnis des Römischen Reiches: Überlieferung, Strecken, Kommentare, Karten.* 2 vols. Berlin: Frank & Timme.
Maraval, P. (1982). *Journal de Voyage. Itinéraire d'Égérie.* Sources Chrétiennes 296. Paris: Les Éditions du Cerf.
Maraval, P. (1985). *Lieux saints et pèlerinages d'Orient. Histoire et géographie. Des origines à la conquête arabe.* Paris: Les Éditions du Cerf.
Markus, Robert A. (1994). How on earth could places become holy? Origins of the Christian holy places. *Journal of Early Christian Studies* 2: 257–271.
Matthews, John. (2006). *The Journey of Theophanes, Travel, Business, and Daily Life in the Roman East.* New Haven, CT: Yale University Press.
Merrills, A.H. (2005). *History and Geography in Late Antiquity.* Cambridge: Cambridge University Press.
Müller, Karl. (1855/2010). *Geographici Gracei Minore,* vol. 1. Cambridge: Cambridge University Press.
Murphy, J.P. (1977). *Rufus Festus Avienus: Ora Maritima or Description of the Seacoast from Brittany round to Massilia.* Chicago: Ares.
Racine, Félix. (2010). *Literary Geography in Late Antiquity.* PhD diss., Yale University.
Romm, James S. (1992). *The Edges of the Earth in Ancient Thought.* Princeton, NJ: Princeton University Press.
Rougé, Jean. (1966). *Expositio totius mundi et gentium.* Sources Chrétiennes 124. Paris: Édition du Cerf.
Salway, Benet. (2001). Travel, *itineraria* and *tabellaria.* In: *Travel and Geography in the Roman Empire* (ed. Colin Adams and Ray Laurence), 22–66. London: Routledge.
Salway, Benet. (2004). Sea and river travel in the Roman itinerary literature. In: *Space in the Roman World: Its Perception and Presentation* (ed. Richard Talbert and Kai Brodersen), 43–96. Münster: LIT.

Seeck, Otto. (1876). *Notitia Dignitatum: Accedunt Notitia urbis Constantinopolitanae et Laterculi provinciarum*. Berlin: Weidmann.
Sotinel, Claire, (2005). Les lieux de culte chrétien et le sacré dans l'Antiquité tardive. *Revue de l'histoire des religions*, 222.4: 411–434; repr. as Places of Christian worship and their sacralization in late antiquity. In: Claire Sotinel. 2010. *Church and Society in Italy and Beyond*, 1–19. Farnham: Ashgate/Variorum.
Stark, Rodney. (1996). *The Rise of Christianity. A Sociologist Reconsiders History*. Princeton: Princeton University Press.
Stenger, Jan R. (2015). Eusebius and the representation of the Holy Land. In: *Brill's Companion to Ancient Geography: The Inhabitated World in Greek and Roman Tradition* (ed. Serena Bianchetti, Michele R. Cautadella, and Hans-Joachim Gehrke), 381–398. Leiden: Brill.
Talbert, Richard J. A. (2010). *Rome's World: The Peutinger Map Reconsidered*. Cambridge: Cambridge University Press.
Traina, Giusto. (2013). Mapping the world under Theodosius II. In: *Theodosius II: Rethinking the Roman Empire in Late Antiquity* (ed. Christopher Kelly), 155–171. Cambridge: Cambridge University Press.
Traina, Giusto. (2015). Mapping the new empire: A geographical look at the fourth century. In: *East and West in the Roman Empire of the Fourth Century: An End to Unity?* (ed. Roald Dijkstra, Sanne van Poppel, and Daniëlle Slootjes), 49–62. Leiden/Boston: Brill.
Van de Woestijne, Paul E.K. (1953). *La Périégèse de Priscien*. Brugge: De Tempel.
Van de Woestijne, Paul E.K. (1961). *La* Descriptio orbis terrae *d'Avienus*. Brugge: De Tempel.
Walska-Conus, Wanda. (1968–1973). *Cosmas Indicopleustès. Topographie chrétienne*. 3 vols. Sources Chrétiennes 141, 159, 197. Paris: Éditions du Cerf.
Wilkinson, John. (1999). *Egeria's Travels: Newly Translated with Supporting Documents and Notes*. 3rd ed. Warminster: Ares and Phillips.
Whittaker, C.R. (2004). *Rome and Its Frontiers: The Dynamics of Empire*. London: Routledge.
Wortley, John. ed. and trans. (2010). *John Moschos. The Spiritual Meadow*. Piscataway, NJ: Cistercian.

CHAPTER TWENTY-THREE

Biography, Autobiography, and Hagiography

Sarah Insley and Jeanne-Nicole Mellon Saint-Laurent

23.1 Introduction

Late antiquity was a fertile period for the writing and reading of *Lives*, both as independent texts and embedded within larger works, spurred largely by the changing fortunes of Christianity from the beginning of the fourth century. Indeed, it is no exaggeration to say that the related literary forms of autobiography, biography, and hagiography – especially the last of these – enjoyed a period of intense attention and innovation in the Mediterranean world in the period. In addition, recent advances in scholarship make this a rewarding time in which to focus on these three interrelated traditions. While premodern biography and autobiography have received less systematic scholarly attention than other literary forms, this is changing with respect to the classical period and late antiquity (see, e.g., Hägg 2012; Marasco 2011; McGing and Mossman 2006; Urbano 2013). Likewise, hagiographical scholarship has traditionally focused on the collection, classification, and editing of hagiographical texts and less on their theoretical interpretation. This is hardly surprising given the complexity of the literary tradition and the difficulty of establishing a critical corpus of texts with which to work. In recent decades, however, hagiography, too, has become a subject of renewed and invigorating scholarly consideration. This is beginning to reward the application of new critical methodologies and a more sophisticated appreciation of hagiography's centrality to its late antique

---

A Companion to Late Antique Literature, First Edition.
Edited by Scott McGill and Edward J. Watts.
© 2018 John Wiley & Sons, Inc. Published 2018 by John Wiley & Sons, Inc.

historical and cultural context (for a recent guide to advances in the field with bibliography, see Efthymiadis 2011–2014 and Harvey 2008).

Though autobiography, biography, and hagiography were related and mutually productive literary forms in late antiquity, all three present unique critical difficulties. Not least is the fact that they can only loosely be considered "genres," or distinct literary forms, at all. Tomas Hägg has noted as much with respect to ancient biography:

> I do not regard [it] as a literary genre with a strong identity or developmental force of its own. It owes much of its vitality and topicality to its parasitic dependence on cognate literary forms and to contemporary cultural fashions. (2012, p. 380)

As will be shown below, the same can certainly be said of autobiography and hagiography in late antiquity, so that it is perhaps best to follow the recommendation of M.J. Edwards and Simon Swain (1997) and focus on "autobiographical, biographical, and hagiographical writing" in this period, rather than upon three discrete forms with clearly demarcated characteristics and conventions.

For example, when referring to "autobiography" in late antiquity, are we to consider only free-standing texts in which the subject is ostensibly a roughly chronological narrative of the author's life, such as Augustine's *Confessions* and Gregory of Nazianzus's *De vita sua*, or should we also include any text in which authorial self-representation is a primary aim? Likewise, it is now generally agreed that "hagiography" should be thought of as a discourse found in a variety of literary forms, both prose and verse, whose subject is the life, acts, and/or sayings of a holy person (Van Uytfanghe 1993; Hinterberger 2014). This idea necessarily affects our classification and interpretation of hagiographical literature. Finally, while "biography" is a recognizable classical form from about the fifth century BCE (Momigliano 1993; Hägg 2012), beginning in the late third and fourth centuries CE it is frequently difficult to discern where "biography" ends and "hagiography" begins (see, e.g., Cox 1983; Hägg 2011; Hägg and Rousseau 2000).

What is clear, however, is that biographical and autobiographical writing underwent significant development in late antiquity, and that experimentation with these forms contributed, in particular, to the evolution of Christian hagiographical writing in this period. Late antique hagiography thus draws as much on the classical literary tradition in both Greek and Latin (biography, panegyric, romance, etc.) as it does upon Judeo-Christian forms such as Scriptural narrative, apocryphal acts, and martyr passions. And, while biography and autobiography were very much the arena of élite Greco-Roman authors and intellectuals, hagiography, by contrast, became the domain of a more varied writing and reading public. The form seems to have encouraged the development of a literary vernacular in Greek and Latin and also enjoyed considerable success among Coptic, Syriac, and, later, Arab Christian audiences.

In this chapter, we will necessarily be limited to a very brief and partial sketch of these three interrelated forms. Although it is impossible to be comprehensive, we will, nonetheless, attempt to provide a general overview of life-writing in late antiquity. We begin with autobiographical and biographical traditions in the Greek- and Latin-speaking Mediterranean and then proceed to offer a general account of the emergence of hagiography, focusing primarily on the Syriac tradition in order to give a more holistic impression of the writing of *Lives* in late antiquity. Because of the multiplicity and diversity of texts, each section will be organized around a few exempla that we feel best represent the creativity and hybridity of late ancient *Lives*. Our intention is thus to offer a basic outline of late ancient biographical writing in its various forms.

23.2 Autobiography

"Autobiography" in the modern sense – namely, an ostensibly complete, chronological narrative of the author's life from birth to the moment of composition, particularly as regards the explication of his/her private life – did not exist in antiquity (for issues of generic classification, see Niggl 2005). The period did give rise to exciting developments in what we might term "spiritual" autobiographical writing, in which the author's religious identity is explored at length. Still, of the three literary forms we are considering, autobiography remains the least represented both in terms of late antique literary history and in modern scholarship. With respect to the latter, the primary study for both the classical period and late antiquity remains Georg Misch's two-volume *History of Autobiography in Antiquity* (1951; see also Momigliano 1993, p. 18 for comment), with the recent addition of three edited collections (Baslez, Hoffmann, and Pernot 1993; Marasco 2011; Reichel 2005). With the exception of studies of individual texts – notably the substantial bibliography on Augustine and the *Confessions* (see, e.g., Brown 2000; O'Donnell 1992, 2005; Quinn 2002; Vessey 2012) – there is comparatively little systematic consideration of autobiographical forms in classical and late antiquity, rendering this an exciting field for future research.

From the outset it is important to remember that, as with both biography and hagiography, autobiographical writing in the classical period and late antiquity was largely devoted to the representation of the author as a public persona – in which sense we can, with Marasco 2011, refer to much of it as "political" autobiography. Libanius, for example, wrote a lengthy autobiographical narrative of his fortunes and misfortunes over the course of his career. Composed in at least two stages, beginning in 374 and then revised until 392, his "autobiography" stands in final form at 279 chapters, and was transmitted at the head of his rhetorical corpus as *Oration* 1 (Norman 1965). The emperor Julian's corpus also contains substantial autobiographical writing, including the satirical self-portrait in the *Misopogon*, addressed to the citizens of Antioch after his ill-received stay in the city in 361–362, and the *Letter to the Athenians*, in which he defends his installation as Augustus and impending campaign against Constantius.

With the unique developments in Christian autobiographical literature, however, a new focus on the author's spiritual trajectory – and the resulting tension between the demands of his spiritual and public lives – provides a new focus for self-representation in late antiquity. For example, in Latin, in addition to Augustine, we should also note the *Eucharisticon* of Paulinus of Pella, an autobiographical poem of thanksgiving to God in the midst of the author's misfortunes, written ca. 460 (Evelyn White 1921, pp. 293ff). Nonetheless, even in Christian autobiographical writing of this sort, we shall be disappointed if we expect a portrait of the author as a private individual to emerge: he remains for the most part defined by his social status, his selected models, and his role as a public figure, whether that be in society at large or specifically within the church as a bishop or theologian. Although Augustine, for example, tells us much about his life in the first nine books of the *Confessions*, his experiences are refracted through the lens of his ultimate reception into the Catholic Church and his concomitant rejection of the Manichean religion with its view on creation and its understanding of the human person. When we consider all 13 books of Augustine's *Confessions* together, the main subject is not Augustine himself but rather the Trinitarian God in whom he comes to believe and in whom he longs to rest (O'Donnell 2005, pp. 63–86; Fredriksen 2012).

Rapid changes within the Christian Church and the evolving role of Christianity in late ancient society facilitated the development of new autobiographical forms among Christian intellectuals. The first extended example of Christian autobiographical writing thus fuses classical literary forms with Christian self-expression. Between his retirement from public life in 381 and his death ca. 390, Gregory of Nazianzus penned more than 15 000 lines of poetry spread across nearly 100 poems (White 1996, p. xxv). Because much of this material is about himself, these poems may be considered autobiographical in nature, if not entirely in form. They range in length from a few lines to nearly 2000. They include epigrams, an epitaph, and poems that could be classed as quasi-tragedies, and they display a range of meters, including iambic trimeter, elegiac couplets, and hexameter, replete with full epic dialect (Tuilier and Bady 2004). The overall effect of this calculated experimentation with classical poetry is, broadly, to inscribe the author within the Greek traditions of epic and tragedy while simultaneously using classical verse forms to legitimize his status as a Christian leader and intellectual.

At about 1950 lines, Gregory's *De vita sua* (Εἰς τὸν ἑαυτοῦ βίον) provides the most complete autobiographical narrative, beginning with his childhood and ending with his retirement from public life in 381 (Jungck 1974). In this, as in his other lengthy autobiographical poems (e.g. *De rebus suis* [Περὶ τῶν καθ' ἑαυτόν]), Gregory's focus is largely on his misfortunes in public life. The decision to concentrate his autobiographical narrative on his personal suffering also informs Gregory's choice of verse over prose. By serving as a remedy to suffering and as a source of enjoyment for himself and others, verse is best suited to his aims (see *Poem* II.1.39 in White 1996, pp. 2–9). Similarly, in addition to what might be termed "free-standing" autobiographical texts like the *De vita sua*, Gregory's orations, notably *Oration* 42 (the "Farewell Address to the Bishops") and *Oration* 43 (the *epitaphios* on Basil of Caesarea), involve lengthy autobiographical excurses, frequently with an apologetic tone (see Elm 2000; McLynn 1998).

At this juncture, a word should also be said about other types of embedded autobiographical narrative, such as the inclusion of the author's *vita/βίος* at the conclusion of biographical and hagiographical collections. *The Lausiac History* of Palladius, for example, includes the author's own *βίος* as its final chapter (see Krueger 2004, pp. 106–109). In like manner, Jerome, an author who uses various literary forms as part of an extended project of self-fashioning (Cain 2009), leaves the last word to himself in his *De viris illustribus*, inscribing his own corpus among those of *literati* past and present. Finally, current scholarship on late antique liturgical poetry, focusing in particular on the sixth-century hymns of Romanos the Melode, highlights the importance of autobiographical writing in a wider variety of literary forms. Derek Krueger's recent assessment of self-representation in Romanos, examining the performance of a penitential Christian subjectivity in first-person passages in these liturgical texts, opens up new horizons in the study of late ancient autobiographical writing (Krueger 2014). We can thus see the degree to which autobiographical discourse was developing as an innovative and multiform means of authorial self-expression in the late antique period. This will reward systematic study in the future.

23.3 Biography

It is generally agreed that biography is one of the more difficult forms to classify and assess, not least because it is so closely aligned with historiography and epideictic oratory in both classical and late antiquity (Hägg 2012;

Hägg and Rousseau 2000). In the late antique period, the added difficulty of distinguishing between biography and hagiography – particularly in the fourth century, when both underwent significant innovation in the hands of Christian authors – renders late ancient biography a challenging and exciting field of study (see, e.g., Cox 1983 and the response of Dillon 2006). Because any overview of biography in late antiquity of necessity must be selective, this section will focus on the biographical writings of Eusebius of Caesarea, which we feel best represent the major characteristics and features of the form in the period.

Eusebius is currently the subject of critical reassessment and is becoming much better appreciated for the innovation and creativity of his literary achievement (Inowlocki and Zamagni 2011; Johnson and Schott 2013). While he is known primarily as a historiographer and scriptural commentator, Eusebius's biographical writings, which include his four-book *Life of Constantine* (hereafter *VC*; Winkelmann 1975) and the life of Origen embedded in book six of *The Ecclesiastical History* (hereafter *HE*; Bardy 1952–1958), best highlight his spirit of literary experimentation. Both texts have been the subject of thoughtful discussion in recent decades, and both are perfectly representative of the developments in biographical writing that occurred in late antiquity, but three representative features of these two works underscore the unique nature of late antique biography: (1) the "hybrid," multiform nature of biographical writing; (2) the use of biography as a tool for communal and self-definition; and (3) the ethical purpose of biography to produce ideal models for individual behavior rather than "objective" or "complete" accounts of the subject's life.

In discussions of the *VC* as a literary text, the question of its genre is frequently emphasized (see, e.g., the main outline of the discussion in Barnes 1990; Cameron 1997). At the outset of their translation and commentary, Averil Cameron and Stuart Hall (1999, p. 1) note, "While the work certainly has biographical elements, it is better described as an uneasy mixture of panegyric and narrative history," highlighting the difficulty of classifying a text that otherwise seems to resist categorization. Yet if we read the *VC*, and likewise the life of Origen embedded in *HE* 6, in light of studies of ancient biography as a "parasitic" genre comfortably existing at the boundaries of historiography and panegyric (as suggested by Hägg 2012), these texts are immediately recognized as examples of late ancient biographical writing par excellence. In fact, we might neatly describe the life of Origen as – both literally and figuratively – existing at the confluence of biography and historiography, just as the *VC* emerges from epideictic rhetoric. Both texts thus allow us to see Eusebius as a biographer working at the intersection of the literary forms of historiography, apologetics, and panegyric, all of which he had already mastered. They also allow us to observe the process by which a Christian intellectual actively negotiated and adapted classical literary forms to suit the particular needs of his contemporary context.

With regard to the use of biography for individual and communal self-definition, Arthur Urbano (2013) highlights the ways in which biographical narratives were employed in the context of competition between philosophical schools and religious groups in late antiquity. As such, the life performs an apologetic function by using the portrait of its founder both to make implicit arguments for the superiority of a particular "school" and to erect a model of individual excellence intended to shape the intellectual activity and ethical behavior of readers/disciples. In the *life* of Origen and, on a grander scale, in the *VC*, we can trace precisely this process of communal and self-definition at work. Eusebius's account of Origen, embedded at a key point within his universalizing account of Christian history, functions both as an *apologia* for the subject and as an argument for a Christian intellectual ideal representing the natural marriage of secular *paideia*, scriptural exegesis, and heroic leadership within the Christian community.

By contrast, whereas Origen is rooted in the age of the martyrs, which Eusebius draws in epic proportions throughout the *HE*, the *VC* uses the person of the emperor to define a uniquely Christian imperial ideology that harmonizes with Eusebius's reading and writing of history. Just as Constantine's reign represents the culmination of history for Eusebius (see *HE* 10), his biographical delineation in the *VC* grandly combines the language and themes of Christian panegyric with Eusebius's particular historiographical method and elements of ethical biography in a way that allows Eusebius to work out a Christian political theology through the person of the ideal emperor (see also Schott 2008). Both texts thus actively define Christian community at various levels: at that of the individual, of the "school" or intellectual circle, and finally, within the context of the empire at large, of the grand sweep of teleological history.

These texts additionally represent the ethical aim of late ancient biography to produce ideal conduct in its readers. A consistent theme in *Lives* both in the classical and late ancient Mediterranean is indeed that the text itself should be endlessly productive. The image created by the author should shape the behavior and actions of its audience. As such, the categories of "fact" and "fiction" – or, in late antique terms, of "truth" and "falsehood" – are delineated in a manner at odds both with modern tastes and definitions and with the perceived aims of historiography. Patricia Cox (1983), for example, illustrates how Eusebius's account of Origen is flexible rather than rigid in its definition of "truth." The opening sections of the *VC* likewise illustrate this flexibility. In *VC* 1.11, Eusebius announces that he will omit the stuff of history in his account of Constantine in order to record an image of the "life beloved of God" – an unexpected goal in imperial biography (*VC* 1.11.1). And yet this allows Eusebius the space to interpret liberally the *life* of Constantine. It does not provide a factual record of an historical figure but rather edifies and shapes the lives of his readers, while creating a standard to be applied to future emperors. This emphasis on ethics, self-definition, and innovation of biographical discourse through engagement with a variety of literary forms characterizes the spirit of late antique biography.

23.4 Hagiography

As mentioned above, hagiography as a form is actually "multiform" – i.e. the term applies to texts in a variety of literary forms in both prose and verse (encomia; *Lives*; miracle collections; martyr passions; *apophthegmata*, or "sayings" collections; hymns; and so forth; see Hinterberger 2014). In this section we will focus on *lives* and martyr *passions* in the Syriac tradition in order to illustrate the functions and forms of hagiographical writing in late antiquity beyond the Greek- and Latin-speaking Mediterranean (Fiey 2004; Binggeli 2012).

In 360, Athanasius of Alexandria composed the first extended hagiographic narrative, *The Life of Antony of Egypt* (βίος καὶ πολιτεία; PG 26: 835–936; Athanasius/Gregg 1980). This text became a "best-seller" in the late antique world, and its form was canonized as the literary exemplar for describing the life of a saint. It was translated into several ancient languages, including Latin, Coptic, and Syriac. Athanasius describes Antony as an illiterate yet economically privileged Egyptian youth who heard the call to radical Christian discipleship. Following the instructions of Jesus (Luke 18:22), Antony sells all his possessions and flees his life of comfort to live in the desert in order to embrace a life of ascetic devotion: constant prayer, renunciation of food and sex, poverty, and solitude. He isolates himself in a cave, where demons assault him. Yet he emerges radiant and transformed, the intersection of the human and divine. Subsequent late antique hagiographers imitated Athanasius's narrative structure that depicted (1) the saint's childhood; (2) conversion; (3) asceticism; (4) miracles; (5) extraordinary death; and (6) communal commemoration. Hagiographers projected their own agenda onto the lives of the saints whom they described, telling us as much about themselves as they did about the saint whom they memorialized. Hagiographic prologues, for example, are often spaces for encounters between the hagiographer, the saint commemorated, the reader, and the divine. The hagiographer guides his audience in the interpretation of the story he has written and asks for their prayers in exchange for the gift of his story.

The stories of the penitent harlots (Ward 1986) comprise another hagiographic narrative type. These tales feature women of "loose" sexual mores who undergo radical changes of heart to follow Christ. In the story of Pelagia of Antioch (*AMS* VI, 616–649; Brock and Harvey 1998, pp. 40–62), for instance, we meet a prostitute who adorns herself in jewels, provocative clothing, and perfumes, as she parades the streets of Antioch with her entourage of fellow performers. She is struck with a desire to cast off her way of life, however, and converts to Christianity. She becomes a transvestite monk: "Pelagion." She gains many disciples, and only at her death do people realize her sex. These narratives idealized the possibility of sanctification for any person with a changed heart. Both *Antony* and *Pelagia* enjoyed widespread popularity throughout the late antique world and were received in many cultural and linguistic traditions.

23.5 Monastic Tales

Hagiography magnified both individual ascetic superstars and monastic communities. The Greek-speaking world learned of the feats of the Syrian monks through Theodoret of Cyrrhus's *History of the Monks of Syria* (Theodoret/Price 1998). He likens the theatrical and even extreme Syrian monastic practices to disciplined athletic training camps for wrestlers, and he portrays Syrian monks according to the patterns of Greek hagiography. One of the monks whom Theodoret describes was Simeon the Stylite (d. 451), and stories about Simeon circulated in Greek and Syriac (*AMS* 4:507–644; Doran 1992). Simeon stands on a pillar with arms outstretched as a sign of his devotion to God. He mediates in both heavenly and temporal affairs, an embodiment of the joining of heaven and earth (Brown 1971). In Syriac imagination, the ideal bishop was also formed by the disciplines of monasticism. We see this in the hagiography of Rabbula, a fifth-century bishop of Edessa (*AMS* 4:396–450). He combined monastic training with pastoral tenderness and concern for the poor and sick of his city (Doran 2006).

Syrian monks also wrote hagiography to affiliate their monasteries with others in both the Syriac-speaking world and Egypt. Hagiographic traditions attribute the founding of many monasteries in Mesopotamia to disciples of the legendary ascetic, Mar Awgin. (*AMS* III: 476–480), a pearl diver from Clysma (in Egypt) who became a monk at the monastery of Pachomius. According to tradition, Awgin and some disciples left Egypt and built monasteries throughout Mesopotamia. This imagined link between the monks of Egypt and Mesopotamia was mythologized in hagiographies describing founders who traced their roots to Awgin (Fiey 2004).

In the sixth century, with the gradual separation of the Miaphysite church from the Chalcedonian Church, the Syriac-speaking Miaphysites composed hagiography describing the deeds of those who became pillars of the nascent Syrian Orthodox church. One of the most important collections of Syriac hagiographic texts is John of Ephesus's *Lives of the Eastern Saints* (PO 17:1–304; PO 18: 513–698; PO 19:153–282; Harvey 1990; Saint-Laurent 2015). His stories commemorate ascetics who lived in northern Mesopotamia in monasteries near the city of Amida. The Empress Theodora championed the cause of the Miaphysites, and Syrian Orthodox hagiographic traditions remember her as a saint and daughter of a Syrian Orthodox priest (Harvey 2001).

Syriac Christians of the area of Tur Abdin (modern-day southeast Turkey) produced many hagiographies honoring the monastic heroes of the area, including the Trilogy of Lives (Sts. Samuel, Simeon, and Gabriel) connected to the monastery of Qartmin, or Mor Gabriel (Palmer 1990; Tannous 2012). Tur Abdin became the cradle of Syrian Orthodox monasticism, and devotion to local saints was a vital part of Christian life in this region. After the coming of Islam in the seventh century, Syriac hagiographies like the *Life of Simeon of the Olives* provide important insights to early interactions between Christians and Muslims (Tannous 2012).

23.6 Martyr Texts

Syriac martyr *Passions* shared a number of features with their Greek and Latin counterparts. These include an account of virtues of the saints, their arrest, dialogues with a judge, tortures, deaths, and burials, as well as the distribution or enshrining of their relics after death. The passion of the Edessan martyrs Shmona, Guria, and Habib, two laymen and a deacon, circulated shortly after their death (during the Diocletianic persecution) when their shrine became a center of pilgrimage. The *Acts of Sharbel, Babai*, and *Barsamya* describes the martyrdom of a former pagan priest, his sister, and an early bishop of Edessa. This fictionalized story set in the reign of Trajan belongs to a fifth-century collection of texts designed to add eminence to Edessa's Christian lineage (Burkitt [1913] 2007).

The *Vita* of Febronia of Nisibis (*AMS* V, 573–615; Brock and Harvey 1998, pp. 152–76) is a romance that idealizes the life of a virtuous monastic scholar, Febronia, who lived in a convent in Nisibis in the fourth century during the persecution of the emperor Diocletian (the *Vita* dates to the sixth century, however). Febronia's beauty attracts the attention of the Romans, who attack Nisibis and arrest Christians there. Febronia is ultimately martyred for her refusal to marry a pagan. Her torturers humiliate her with sexualized brutality. When Febronia dies, her martyrdom is identified as a betrothal to Christ. The *Life of Febronia* is unique among hagiographies because it was purported to have been written by a woman, a sister from Febronia's convent. The story takes a special interest in showing the spiritual friendships and sisterhood present in Febronia's community (Harvey 1996). Her story circulated in Greek and Latin translation; her cult spread to Constantinople and as far as southern Italy and Sicily (Saint-Laurent 2012).

The Acts of the Persian martyrs comprise a large body of texts whose literary accounts are similar to counterparts in the Greek- and Latin-speaking world (Brock 2009; Smith 2014). The heroes are idealized as virtuous, courageous, eloquent imitators of Christ, and they withstand brutal torture at the hands of their Sasanian Zoroastrian accusers. These texts show knowledge of Zoroastrian religious practices and were a genre for monks and Christian elites in Sasanian Persia to craft a prestigious Christian lineage for themselves vis-à-vis the Christians in the Byzantine Empire (Payne 2015; Walker 2006).

23.7 Conclusion

We have attempted to present an overview of the development of biographical, autobiographical, and hagiographical texts in the late antique period and to show their significance within the canon of late antique literature. The application of critical methodologies to the study of these texts has generated fresh insights and an increased appreciation for their literary complexity as well as for their historical importance in attesting to the symbols and values that were meaningful for those who wrote and promoted them.

Writing portraits of the self or other persons was an enterprise that developed with a particular vitality in the late antique period, and this process, often presented as an act of spiritual devotion, produced a variegated corpus of autobiographical, biographical, and hagiographical texts. In these we observe how authors demonstrated continuity with the biblical and classical past through literary allusion, typology, and mimesis of rhetorical formulae and narrative conventions. Yet they also broke from these forms in moments of pronounced discontinuity. The malleable nature of these evolving genres gave authors room for experimentation as they crafted, idealized, and mythologized memories of themselves or holy persons. These texts circulated among the literate, who then proclaimed them orally in the context of feast days and the liturgy, thus preserving and protecting their subjects from oblivion.

REFERENCES

Athanasius, Saint. (1980). *The Life of Antony and the Letter to Marcellinus* (trans. Robert Gregg). New York: Paulist.

Bardy, Gustave. (1952–1958). *Eusèbe de Césarée. Histoire ecclésiastique*. 3 vols. Paris: Éditions du Cerf.

Barnes, Timothy. (1990). Panegyric, history, and hagiography in Eusebius' *Life of Constantine*. In: *The Making of Orthodoxy: Essays in Honour of Henry Chadwick* (ed. Rowan Williams), 94–123. Cambridge: Cambridge University Press.

Baslez, Marie-Françoise, Hoffmann, Philippe, and Pernot, Laurent. ed. (1993). *L'invention de l'autobiographie d'Hésiode à Saint Augustine: Actes du deuxième colloque de l'Equipe de recherche sur l'hellénisme post-classique*. Paris: Presses de l'Ecole normale supérieure.

Binggeli, André. ed. (2012). *L'hagiographie syriaque*. Études Syriaques 9. Paris: Geuthner.

Brock, Sebastian P. trans. (2009). *History of the Holy Mar Ma'in, with a Guide to the Persian Martyr Acts*. Persian Martyr Acts in Syriac: Text and Translation. (ed. Adam Becker). Piscataway, NJ: Gorgias.

Brock, Sebastian P. and Harvey, Susan Ashbrook. trans. (1998). *Holy Women of the Syrian Orient*. Updated ed. Berkeley: University of California Press.

Brown, Peter. (1971). The rise and function of the Holy Man in late antiquity. *Journal of Roman Studies* 61: 80–101.

Brown, Peter. (2000). *Augustine of Hippo: A Biography*. 2nd ed. Berkeley: University of California Press.

Burkitt, Francis C. ([1913] 2007). *Euphemia and the Goth with the Acts of Martyrdom of the Confessors of Edessa, Shmona, Guria, and Habib*. London: Williams and Norgate. Reprint. Piscataway, NJ: Gorgias.

Cain, Andrew. (2009). *The Letters of Jerome: Asceticism, Biblical Exegesis, and the Construction of Christian Authority in Late Antiquity*. Oxford: Oxford University Press.

Cameron, Averil. (1997). Eusebius' *Vita Constantini* and the Construction of Constantine. In: *Portraits: Biographical Representation in Greek and Latin Literature of the Roman Empire* (ed. M.J. Edwards and Simon Swain), 145–174. Oxford and New York: Oxford University Press.

Cameron, Averil and Hall, Stuart G. (1999). *Eusebius: Life of Constantine*. Oxford: Clarendon Press.

Cox, Patricia. (1983). *Biography in Late Antiquity: A Quest for the Holy Man*. Berkeley: University of California Press.

Dillon, John. (2006). Holy and not so holy: On the interpretation of late antique biography. In: *The Limits of Ancient Biography* (ed. Brian McGing and Judith Mossman), 155–168. Swansea: Classical Press of Wales.

Doran, Robert. trans. (1992). *Lives of Simeon Stylites*. Kalamazoo, MI: Cistercian.

Doran, Robert. trans. (2006). *Stewards of the Poor: The Man of God, Rabbula, and Hiba in Fifth-Century Edessa*. Kalamazoo, MI: Cistercian.

Edwards, M.J. and Swain, Simon. ed. (1997). *Portraits: Biographical Representation in Greek and Latin Literature of the Roman Empire.* Oxford and New York: Oxford University Press.

Efthymiadis, Stephanos. ed. (2011–2014). *The Ashgate Research Companion to Byzantine Hagiography.* 2 vols. Farnham, UK and Burlington, VT: Ashgate.

Elm, Susanna. (2000). A programmatic life: Gregory of Nazianzus' Orations 42 and 43 and the Constantinopolitan elites. *Arethusa* 33: 411–427.

Evelyn White, Hugh. ed. and trans. (1921). *Ausonius.* 2 vols. London: William Heinemann.

Fiey, J-.M. (2004). *Saints syriaques.* (ed. L. Conrad). Studies in Late Antiquity and Early Islam 6. Princeton, NJ: Darwin.

Fredriksen, Paula. (2012). The *Confessions* as autobiography. In: *A Companion to Augustine* (ed. Mark Vessey), 87–98. Chichester and Malden, MA: Wiley-Blackwell.

Hägg, Tomas. (2011). The life of St Antony between biography and hagiography. In: *The Ashgate Research Companion to Byzantine Hagiography.* 2 vols (ed. Stephanos Efthymiadis), 17–34. Farnham, UK and Burlington, VT: Ashgate.

Hägg, Tomas. (2012). *The Art of Biography in Antiquity.* Cambridge: Cambridge University Press.

Hägg, Tomas and Rousseau, Philip. ed. (2000). *Greek Biography and Panegyric in Late Antiquity.* Berkeley: University of California Press.

Harvey, Susan Ashbrook. (1990). *Asceticism and Society in Crisis: John of Ephesus and the Lives of the Eastern Saints.* Berkeley: University of California Press.

Harvey, Susan Ashbrook. (1996). Sacred bonding: Mothers and daughters in early Syrian hagiography. *Journal of Early Christian Studies* 4: 27–56.

Harvey, Susan Ashbrook. (2001). Theodora the "Believing Queen": A study in Syriac historiographical tradition. *Hugoye: Journal of Syriac Studies* 4: 209–234.

Harvey, Susan Ashbrook. (2008). Martyr passions and hagiography. In: *The Oxford Handbook of Early Christian Studies* (ed. Susan A. Harvey and David G. Hunter), 603–627. Oxford: Oxford University Press.

Hinterberger, Martin. (2014). Byzantine hagiography and its literary genres. Some critical observations. In: *The Ashgate Research Companion to Byzantine Hagiography.* 2 vols (ed. Stephanos Efthymiadis), 25–60. Farnham, UK and Burlington, VT: Ashgate.

Inowlocki, Sabrina and Zamagni, Claudio. ed. (2011). *Reconsidering Eusebius: Collected Papers on Literary, Historical, and Theological Issues.* Leiden: Brill.

John of Ephesus. (1923–1925). *The Lives of the Eastern Saints.* (ed. and trans. E.W. Brooks), PO 17:1–304; PO 18: 513–698; PO 19:153–282. Paris: Firmin-Didot.

Johnson, Aaron and Schott, Jeremy. ed. (2013). *Eusebius of Caesarea: Traditions and Innovations.* Washington, DC: Center for Hellenic Studies.

Jungck, Christoph. (1974). *Gregor von Nazianz De vita sua: Enleitung, Text, Übersetzung, Kommentar.* Heidelberg: Winter.

Krueger, Derek. (2004). *Writing and Holiness: The Practice of Authorship in the Early Christian East.* Philadelphia: University of Pennsylvania Press.

Krueger, Derek. (2014). *Liturgical Subjects: Christian Ritual, Biblical Narrative, and the Formation of the Self in Byzantium*. Philadelphia: University of Pennsylvania Press.

Marasco, Gabriele. (2011). *Political Autobiographies and Memoirs in Antiquity: A Brill Companion*. Leiden: Brill.

McGing, Brian and Mossman, Judith. ed. (2006). *The Limits of Ancient Biography*. Swansea: Classical Press of Wales.

McLynn, Neil. (1998). A self-made Holy Man: The case of Gregory Nazianzen. *Journal of Early Christian Studies* 6: 463–483.

Misch, Georg. (1951). *A History of Autobiography in Antiquity*. 2 vols. Cambridge, MA: Harvard University Press.

Momigliano, Arnaldo. (1993). *The Development of Greek Biography*. Cambridge, MA: Harvard University Press.

Niggl, Günter. (2005). Zur Theorie der Autobiographie. In: *Antike Autobiographien: Werke, Epochen, Gattungen* (ed. Michael Reichel), 1–13. Cologne: Böhlau.

Norman, A.F. (1965). *Libanius' Autobiography (Oration 1): The Greek Text Edited with Introduction, Translation, and Notes*. London: Oxford University Press.

O'Donnell, James. (1992). *Augustine: Confessions*. 3 vols. New York: Oxford University Press.

O'Donnell, James. (2005). *Augustine: A New Biography*. New York: Ecco.

Palmer, Andrew. (1990). *Monk and Mason on the Tigris Frontier: The Early History of Tur Abdin*. Cambridge: Cambridge University Press.

Payne, Richard E. (2015). *A State of Mixture: Christians, Zoroastrians, and Iranian Political Culture in Late Antiquity*. Berkeley: University of California Press.

Quinn, John M. (2002). *A Companion to the Confessions of St. Augustine*. New York: P.Lang.

Reichel, Michael. ed. (2005). *Antike Autobiographien: Werke, Epochen, Gattungen*. Cologne: Böhlau.

Saint-Laurent, Jeanne-Nicole. (2012). Images de femmes dans L'hagiographie Syriaque. In: *L'hagiographie syriaque*. Études Syriaques 9. (ed. André Binggeli), 201–224. Paris: Geuthner.

Saint-Laurent, Jeanne-Nicole Mellon. (2015). *Missionary Stories and the Formation of the Syriac Churches*. Berkeley: University of California Press.

Schott, Jeremy M. (2008). *Christianity, Empire, and the Making of Religion in Late Antiquity*. Philadelphia: University of Pennsylvania Press.

Smith, Kyle. trans. (2014). *Martyrdom and History of Blessed Simeon Bar Sabbaʿe*. (ed. Adam Becker). Persian Martyr Acts in Syriac: Text and Translation 3. Piscataway, NJ: Gorgias Press.

Tannous, Jack. (2012). L'hagiographie Syro-Occidentale à la période islamique. In: *L'hagiographie syriaque*. Études Syriaques 9. (ed. André Binggeli), 225–245. Paris: Geuthner.

Theodoret of Cyrrhus. (1988). *A History of the Monks of Syria*. (trans. Richard M. Price). Kalamazoo, MI: Cistercian.

Tuilier, André and Bady, Guillaume. ed. (2004). *Saint Grégoire de Nazianze. Oeuvres poétiques 1, 1: Poèmes personnels II. 1, 1–11.* (trans. Jean Bernardi). Paris: Belles Lettres.

Urbano, Arthur P. (2013). *The Philosophical Life: Biography and the Crafting of Intellectual Identity in Late Antiquity.* Washington DC: Catholic University of America Press.

Van Uytfanghe, Marc. (1993). L'hagiographie: Un "genre" chrétien ou antique tardif? *Analecta Bollandiana* 111: 135–188.

Vessey, Mark. ed. (2012). *A Companion to Augustine.* Chichester and Malden, MA: Wiley Blackwell.

Walker, Joel. (2006). *Legend of Mar Qardagh: Narrative and Christian Heroism in Late Ancient Iraq.* Berkeley: University of California Press.

Ward, Benedicta. (1986). *Harlots of the Desert: A Study of Repentance in Early Monastic Sources.* Kalamazoo, MI: Cistercian.

White, Carolinne. (1996). *Gregory of Nazianzus: Autobiographical Poems.* Cambridge: Cambridge University Press.

Winkelmann, Friedhelm. (1975). *Eusebius Werke, Band 1.1: Über das Leben des Kaisers Konstantin.* Berlin: Akademie.

CHAPTER TWENTY-FOUR

Epistolography

Cristiana Sogno and Edward J. Watts

Until relatively recently letters and letter collections have represented some of the least appreciated late antique literary innovations. Given the extensive use that many historians have made of individual late antique letters over the past century, it is perhaps surprising to call them underappreciated. Letters have indeed been mined for information, but scholars have tended to think of late antique letters as discrete documents that capture a genuine conversation between figures. Consequently, scholars have read letters in isolation, as relatively uncomplicated sources that lack the digressions and literary artifice of classical historiography. In recent years, however, the literary complexity of late antique epistolography has become far better appreciated. Not only have we come to see how the individual letters can serve as literary monuments to the skill and creativity of their authors, but the collections to which they belong often represent creative literary works in which characters develop and themes unfold in specifically designed ways. The late antique letter collection, then, does not represent simply the stack of papers found on someone's desk when he or she died. It is instead a complicated and very deliberately organized literary document often designed to use the author's literary interactions with others to define and develop a specific literary persona (e.g. Beard 2002; Gibson 2012). At the same time, as we shall argue below, the macrotextual dimension of the letter collection does not always necessarily depend on the intentionality of its author.

Although some of the pioneering work on the literary aspects of letter collections has focused on earlier assemblages of the letters of Cicero and

---

A Companion to Late Antique Literature, First Edition.
Edited by Scott McGill and Edward J. Watts.
© 2018 John Wiley & Sons, Inc. Published 2018 by John Wiley & Sons, Inc.

Pliny, there can be little doubt that late antiquity represents the golden age of ancient letter collections. There are more surviving Greek and Latin letters and letter collections from the period between 355 and 415 than there are from the previous thousand years. These include massive collections of figures like Isidore of Pelusium (the author of over 2000 surviving letters), Libanius (over 1500 extant letters), and Symmachus (over 900 letters), as well as far smaller collections from figures like Aeneas of Gaza or Ausonius. In all, however, more than 30 substantial collections of literary letters survive from late antiquity (Sogno, Storin, and Watts 2016). This cannot be attributed simply to an accident of transmission. Moreover, after the publication of letter collections slows in the early seventh century, nothing like the rate of production and preservation of letter collections found in late antiquity occurs again until the later medieval period.

This essay explains why late antiquity became a golden age for the production and preservation of literary letter collections. It has three parts. First, it considers the nature of a literary letter collection and the particular characteristics of later Roman society that incentivized the production and dissemination of these texts. Second, it examines the literary creativity involved in producing letter collections that developed a particular identity for their author. Late antique authors had some earlier, classical models of collected letters from which they could take inspiration, but their projects pushed far beyond the limits set by these earlier exemplars in ways that demonstrated remarkable literary creativity. The final section of the chapter then looks at how late antique authors brought similar innovative genius to the individual letters that they composed. This will show the degree to which letter collections as well as the individual letters within them embody the late antique authorial tendency to push against and experiment with classical literary templates in exciting and creative ways.

24.1 Letter Collections in the Later Roman World

The idea of the letter collection as a deliberately organized text remains somewhat controversial in some circles. This is on some level understandable because not all late antique letter collections fit the same mold. Some, like the collection of Paulinus, are early modern creations (Trout 2016), while others, like the seemingly ever-expanding corpus of letters of Augustine, are modern assemblages (Ebbeler 2016). Many late antique collections also do not now appear in their original order. From the Renaissance forward, editors have tended to reorganize, anthologize, or simply disassemble collections that ancient authors took care to put together in specific ways (Gibson 2012), that mostly disregarded and tended to obscure the chronology of the letters. There is little doubt that this kind of early modern and modern editorial violence was inspired by a specific historiographical bias that tended to regard letters as raw and unmediated sources for history rather than as literary artifacts in their own right. Even though the view of epistolography as a lesser form of historiography is a demonstrably ancient idea, the chronological bias of Renaissance authors seems to have been inspired by Cicero's letters, which are exceptionally rich in historical information but were never prepared by their author for publication. The main cause for the editorial approach described above has been an almost exclusive focus on the microlevel of the individual letter and the historical information that could be gleaned from it. Only recently has the macrolevel of the collection attracted scholarly attention. The concept of "macrotext," which was developed by Italian semioticians in the 1970s and used by Maria Corti to study Italo Calvino's collections of short stories (Corti 1975; Viti 2014), seems to be an especially powerful hermeneutical tool for studying letter collections. Even when, or especially when, the identity of the editor is uncertain, and the history of the collection remains unknowable, the tension between the macrotextual dimension of the collection and the microtextual reality of the single letter opens up new perspectives for the study of letter collections as a novel and specifically late antique literary form/genre. As Marco Formisano has recently argued (Formisano 2016a, 2016b), the macrotext represents a textual formation that bears a different and potentially opposite meaning from that conveyed by the microtext read in isolation.

Some collections have managed to preserve their original order in modern editions. Seven of the nine books of Symmachus's letters were organized by addressee, and later editors seem to have been mostly respectful of the original order, not only because it was easily understood to be deliberate, but also because the lack of historical information made it especially challenging to reorganize the collection chronologically (Sogno 2016). Similarly, in the later fifth century, Sidonius Apollinaris made explicit at the outset of his collection that he was following Symmachus and, ultimately, Pliny in creating a coherent collection made up of units designed to fit together in a certain way (Gibson 2013; Harries 1994). Later copyists and editors understood this project, too, and tended to respect Sidonius's work by preserving the integrity of the collection as he had designed it (Mratschek 2016). Many collections were not so fortunate, however. One must work hard to reconstruct the original manuscript order of the letters of Gregory Nazianzus because their modern edition has reorganized them chronologically (Storin 2012). There are problems even when the critical edition follows the manuscript order, because some of the best-known translations of letter collections frequently do not. Although the modern critical edition of Libanius's 1546 letters preserves the organization found in the best manuscripts, recent translations have preferred to read the letters in chronological order, with each translator choosing selections of letters based on their thematic or historical importance (Van Hoof 2016).

Something important is lost when we do this. In the case of Libanius, his collection of letters contains three chronologically distinctive tranches. Although all three batches of letters illustrate the prominence, influence, and wit of Libanius, each of them features a different cast of characters and a slightly different set of themes. The largest group, which contains letters 19–839 and covers the years between 355 and 363, begins with a letter from the winter of 358/359 that Libanius sent to the prefect Anatolius in the midst of a dispute about whether Libanius praised people disingenuously (Van Hoof 2016). This letter falls in the middle of the collection chronologically, but Libanius has clearly chosen it to introduce his readers to Anatolius not as the firm friend Libanius believed him to be in 355 but as the shady character he had become by 358. This was a deliberate act of literary foreshadowing made possible only because the letters to Anatolius appear in the collection out of chronological order.

This introductory letter did more than establish Anatolius's character. It also allowed Libanius to sketch out the literary character that he would himself project across the collection. The charge that Libanius disingenuously praised people was potentially a biting one, but Libanius's response to it is powerful and compelling. It had to be. The rest of this batch of letters is full of praises of friends and, in *Letter* 19, Libanius catalogs many of the types of praises he offers throughout the larger collection along with explanations of why they are justified. *Letter* 19, then, not only foreshadows the development of Libanius's relationship with Anatolius; it provides a set of literary guidelines that readers can use to appreciate Libanius's fuller literary achievements across 821 letters – and to do it on the terms that Libanius himself set.

One sees a similar process unfold in the other two tranches of Libanian letters. Letters 840–1112, a group written between 388 and 393 and presumably published after Libanius's death by a literary executor, begin with a letter to the praetorian prefect and consul Flavius Eutolmius Tatianus. In this letter Libanius demonstrates his strong friendship with Tatianus, a figure who had been left in de facto charge of the East while Theodosius marched west to fight a civil war, and also proclaims the exoneration of Libanius from charges that he had supported Magnus Maximus in his recent revolt. Libanius then casts himself as a loyal and influential elder statesman, a persona he will inhabit across the mini-collection. Something similar happens in *Letter* 1113, the introduction to the batch of 429 letters that document Libanius's activities between the death of Julian in 363 and the revolt of Procopius in 365. The letter is addressed to Caesarius, the vicar of Asia, and mentions that it, too, was composed in the presence of Celsus, the governor of Syria. Not only does it show Libanius's continued importance after the death of Julian, but it also presents Libanius's effective and compelling defense against a charge that he has been a negligent correspondent. Like the letter to Anatolius from 358/359, *Letter* 1113 displays Libanius's distinctive ability to turn charges of epistolary misconduct against his accusers and, in so doing, use a letter to seize control of the social dynamics of a relationship. This again sets the tone for the larger collection by introducing the prominent cast of characters it will feature and the sorts of displays of literary authority that Libanius will make through these letters.

Libanius was not the only author to strategically arrange the letters in his collection in order to define a specific literary identity. Many other authors in late antiquity used collections of letters to showcase a certain literary persona they wished to claim. Jerome, for example, seems to have used small collections of letters to advertise his unique combination of biblical expertise and ascetic training to potential literary patrons in Rome (Cain 2009). The Cyrenean philosopher Synesius used his letter collection to present himself as a political and intellectual go-between whose writings and social activities joined the cosmopolitan worlds of Constantinople and Alexandria to the backward and isolated Libyan hinterland (Petkas forthcoming). It is then no surprise that letters seeking the literary blessings of the Constantinopolitan sophist Nicander and the Alexandrian philosopher Hypatia on two of Synesius's most famous texts bookend his collection (Watts 2017).

Certain aspects of late Roman society made late antiquity a particularly fertile period for the sort of literary self-definition engaged in by authors like Libanius, Jerome, and Synesius. The authors of the famous letter collections of the late republic and early empire had been prominent men of affairs like Cicero and Pliny, men whose actions and authority resonated across the Mediterranean. They lived, however, in an empire where only a small group of Italian elites could claim this sort of ecumenical influence. By the turn of the fourth century, the nature of the empire had changed. The dramatic expansion of citizenship in the third century and the tremendous growth of the imperial bureaucracy in the decades spanning the turn of the fourth century meant that more Romans than ever before could aspire to a level of influence like that of Pliny. Late antiquity saw provincial elites like Libanius, men of middling curial rank like Augustine, and even failed bureaucrats like Jerome aspire to a level of Mediterranean-wide influence that their ancestors could never imagine. The Mediterranean world of late antiquity offered everyone from pagan Italian aristocrats like Symmachus to Christian landholders in isolated provinces like Synesius an opportunity to grab fame and fortune on an imperial stage.

The letter collection represented a perfect vehicle for displaying the unique sets of attributes that defined the influence of such figures. The trappings of tradition on which it drew gave a timeless, old-Roman quality to the authority that these new elites claimed, but the collection also afforded them plenty of scope to reimagine and reinvent the ways in which they defined themselves. Only in a collection of letters could Synesius make the case that he was an uncompromising devotee of philosophy who served as a civic and ecclesiastical leader in Cyrenaica and had strong connections with leading intellectuals in Alexandria and Constantinople. Similarly, only a letter collection could preserve, demonstrate, and disseminate the breadth of the teachings given by the abbots Barsanuphius and John, two monks who communicated with the ascetics under their charge and the laity under their influence exclusively by letter (Hevelone Harper 2016). And, as the anti-Chalcedonian hierarchies of Egypt and Syria struggled to survive persecutions under Justinian, the collected letters of Severus of Antioch defined for the community an exemplar of principled episcopal resistance at a moment of deep communal crisis.

24.2 Innovation and the Late Antique Letter Collection

Late antique letter collections often served to define the public persona of the figure who authored their contents, but they succeeded in doing so because they were often sophisticated literary creations specifically designed to function in the literary, social, and religious milieus of the later Roman world. This was, of course, not a late antique innovation. Pliny had already chosen epistolography over historiography to acquire literary immortality. He found the genre to be profoundly flexible, enabling him to dabble in the writing of a micro-history within individual letters and to experiment with other mechanisms of self-representation. Indeed, one could argue that Pliny's discovery of the (auto)biographical potential of the letter collection had escaped even Cicero. Cicero had no doubt contemplated the possibility of publishing his own letters, but, when Lucceius declined his request to write a panegyrical monograph on Cicero's consulship, Cicero resorted to writing a poem rather than a carefully selected correspondence. As recent studies have shown (Hoffer 1999; Marchesi 2008; Gibson and Morello 2012), Pliny's letter collection, long considered dull because of an unfair and uninformed comparison with Cicero's, is a highly sophisticated and polished literary creation, a true *labor limae*. In the preface to his collection, Pliny explains his rationale for rearranging the letters in a corpus, and his savvy in exploiting the possibilities that the epistolary genre affords cannot be overemphasized.

Pliny's successful experiment in self-representation and his exploitation of the macrotextual dimension of the letter collection were embraced and imitated by Sidonius Apollinaris, who explicitly cites Pliny as a model. In fact, the arrangement of Pliny's collection into nine books of "personal" letters addressed to individuals and a book of "official" letters addressed to the emperor Trajan was thought for a long time to have provided the model for late antique collections such as those of Ambrose and Symmachus. Recent studies have taken a more nuanced view (Nauroy 2016; Sogno 2016; Salzman and Roberts 2011). Even though the editors of late antique collections arranged their collections with the same thoughtfulness and sophistication as Pliny, they did not resort to mere mechanical imitation of the actual arrangement. They also did not exactly replicate Pliny's themes. Instead, even in collections of letters by senatorial figures whose social standing resembled that of Pliny, one can see a sort of productive engagement with that second-century text in which Pliny's model is consciously adapted and refined to reflect the specific circumstances of late antique elite life.

It is, then, no exaggeration to say that the letter collection was (re)invented in late antiquity. The sheer number of collections that survive, the number of different approaches their editors take, the level of sophistication their organization shows, and the interest in experimentation both at the macrolevel of the collection and the microlevel of the individual letter all point to a tremendous creative energy directed toward the fashioning of letter collections. But what, precisely, was a letter collection in late antiquity?

The word "collection" evokes the activity of an editor and his or her choice to arrange an existing correspondence or (in the case of fictional letters) to create a body of letters with a specific literary purpose in mind (Hodkinson 2007). The notion is clear enough, but it also points to a problem. Not all and, in fact, not even the majority of late antique letter collections were edited by the author of the letters. There is a wide spectrum of options. At one end of the spectrum we have the letter collection of Sidonius Apollinaris, carefully arranged by Sidonius himself and with a programmatic letter detailing the rationale for the arrangement as well as Sidonius's epistolary models. At the other extreme we have the collections of Augustine or Paulinus of Nola, which were put together by later editors. And in between these two extremes, we have cases like the letter collection of Symmachus, which was organized by Symmachus himself but published by his son after his death and, in all likelihood, supplemented by a sixth-century editor who added additional books of letters (8–10) on the model of Pliny's collection. Each of these is a letter collection, but none of them is a product of the same process of literary creativity.

24.3 Innovation in the Individual Letter

The appeal of the late antique letter collection came not just from the characters and themes it developed so effectively on the macrolevel. The individual letters that made up the collection could also show incredible literary creativity precisely because the letter as a literary construction could be built from any kind of content. Some were short poems written in verse, others described long fictional situations not unlike a segment of an ancient novel, many were written for the specific purpose of recommending the carrier of the letter, and still more were filled with quite serious meditations on consequential events in the world. A letter collection could serve as a kind of literary curio cabinet that displayed an author's ability to do all of these things, and this characteristic may explain the growing appeal and popularity of such an "elastic" genre.

The generic ambiguity of the letter invited experimentation, and several late antique letter writers did play with conventions and manipulated, with varying degrees of success, epistolary conventions to achieve their goals. Libanius, for example, blended epistolary forms in ways that enabled him to deploy his devastating wit against correspondents who charged him with being a negligent friend. In a letter from 392 that Libanius wrote to the retired military official Firminus (*Ep.* 1048, discussed in Watts 2015, pp. 197–198), he begins the letter with what seems to be an apology for neglecting to answer a number of letters Firminus had previously sent. The letter then takes a dramatic, whiplash-inducing turn near its halfway point. Libanius transforms his apology into a counterattack by writing, "You should have looked for some other reason" for my silence other than a failure to be a good friend. Libanius goes on to tell Firminus about the death of his son and the devastating effect that it supposedly had on Libanius. Finally, Libanius concludes by telling Firminus that, if he had been a true friend, he would have written a monody for Libanius's son rather than an insensitive letter of blame. Letters like these became such instant classics that, not even two decades after Libanius's death, Eunapius (*VS* 496) would remark that his letters "are filled with such grace and sarcastic wit and an elegance that pervades all of his writings."

Not all experiments were as successful. Augustine, for example, tried to pursue a new and bold course of action by "inventing" the letter of correction

(Ebbeler 2012). A (poor) substitute for a visit, letters had been conceived traditionally as a conversation *in absentia*, and the expectation of a regular exchange of letters that had prompted the request of Firminus mentioned above was the basis of *amicitia* in the much wider and more global world of late antiquity. For late Roman senators like Symmachus, *amicitia* was idealized as the communion and commonality (*unanimitas*) of thoughts, feelings, and interests and, in practice, depended upon a willingness to "scratch each other's backs." Augustine, however, tried to promote the ideal of corrective friendship by writing letters to rebuke or correct the errors of his friends. As the example of Libanius shows, letters of rebuke existed before Augustine, and Epicurean circles promoted a similar ideal of friendly correction, but Augustine's ideal of epistolary correction was modeled upon the example of Paul (2 *Galatians*). Augustine, then, tried (but failed) to Christianize this aspect of the epistolary culture of late antiquity. Even though Augustine promoted the ideal of a mutually beneficial friendship in which both correspondents are morally bound to correct each other, the letters that survive show only Augustine in the role of "corrector." There is also no evidence that any of his attempts at correction were actually successful (though, on the importance of remembering how incomplete and therefore misleading the epistolary record is, see Ebbeler 2016). Unlike Libanius's letter of blame, Augustine's letters of correction did not become instant classics and failed to inspire imitators among his contemporaries. In the longue durée, however, his corrective letters can be seen as "as a late antique prequel to the institutionalized penitential practices of medieval Christianity" (Ebbeler 2012, p. 230). Augustine's experiment is ultimately a testimony to the richness, liveliness, and inventiveness of late antique epistolary culture.

At the other end of the spectrum, we find the proverbial *brevitas* of Symmachus's letters, which was as much admired by earlier readers of the letters like Alain de Lille as it was reviled by the nineteenth-century editor of the Symmachan corpus, Otto Seeck. That stylistic tendency, too, can be seen as an innovation within the very restrictive limits imposed by Symmachus on himself because of his love of tradition (*amor consuetudinis*). Even though the correspondence of Symmachus does not contain the same programmatic letters that distinguish Pliny's and Sidonius's collection, Symmachus quite clearly places himself within the tradition of senatorial epistolography that saw in Cicero its ultimate model (Sogno 2014). Neither the political situation nor the highly codified epistolary etiquette would have allowed a fourth-century Roman senator to write the kind of openly political letters that Cicero wrote (indeed, it is unclear whether Cicero would have published his letters without any changes since the purpose of a letter between "friends" of a certain social standing was never meant to inform, as Cicero himself acknowledges). The contrast with Pliny, who also blamed the decline of epistolography on the changed political circumstances, but whose letters delight because of the variety of themes explored, has been detrimental to Symmachus. It may very well be that Symmachus wrote little because he had nothing to say, but, given his reputation for eloquence, it is equally possible that Symmachus's choice of *brevitas* was due not to a lack of intellect but to a precise stylistic choice (Sogno 2016). Unlike Augustine, who tried to transform epistolary practice and mores, Symmachus operated within the narrow confines and strict etiquette of traditional senatorial epistolography, which he set out to distill and preserve for posterity.

24.4 Conclusion

Neither the writing of individual literary letters nor the assembly of letter collections was a late antique invention. Authors working in both Greek and Latin had exemplars to which they could turn and established rules they were expected to follow, but they also understood that these rules allowed considerable scope for literary creativity. A letter could be a miniature history or a poem or even a fantastic travel narrative. It could contain expressions of genuine emotion, acts of brutal sarcasm, or lists of unadorned information. But, most importantly, a letter provided an author with a framework that nevertheless offered him the freedom to creatively express himself.

While the individual letter offered small tableaux on which an author could sketch literary scenes, the letter collection offered an expansive landscape on which an author could construct his own three-dimensional literary identity. Not only was the collection a display space in which the artist could hang his literary sketches, but it could also serve as a careful sculpture of the public persona of the artist himself. A carefully assembled letter collection was a dynamic thing that showed the evolution of relationships and the emergence of character traits far better than any other genre could. It defined an author not just by the words he deployed and the deeds he performed but by the personalities of the men and women with whom he interacted. Late antique authors, their immediate literary heirs, and their later admirers appreciated that skillfully edited letter collections could even bend time in ways that redefined relationships and emphasized certain aspects of individual personae. These experimentations were usually subtle enough that scholars seeking to find chronological signposts or looking to pull "facts" out of late antique letters do not realize what the collection on which they depend was actually designed to do. But late antique, Carolingian, and Byzantine audiences fully appreciated the creative achievements evident in a potent individual letter and a carefully organized letter collection. Modern scholars are only now appreciating why late antique letters and letter collections genuinely merited such great esteem.

REFERENCES

Beard, Mary. (2002). Ciceronian correspondences: Making a book out of letters. In: *Classics in Progress: Essays on Ancient Greece and Rome* (ed. T.P. Wiseman), 103–144. Oxford: Oxford University Press.

Cain, Andrew. (2009). *The Letters of Jerome: Asceticism, Biblical Exegesis, and the Construction of Christian Authority in Late Antiquity*. Oxford: Oxford University Press.

Corti, Maria. (1975). Testi o macrotesto? I racconti di Marcovaldo in I. Calvino. *Strumenti Critici* 9, 182–197.

Ebbeler, Jennifer. (2012). *Disciplining Christians: Correction and Community in Augustine's Letters*. Oxford: Oxford University Press.

Ebbeler, Jennifer. (2016). The letter collection of Augustine of Hippo. In: *Late Antique Letter Collections: A Critical Introduction and Reference Guide* (ed. Cristiana Sogno, Bradley K. Storin, and Edward Watts), 239–253. Berkeley: University of California Press.

Formisano, Marco. (2016a). Reading dismemberment: Vitruvius, Dinocrates, and the Macrotext. *Arethusa* 49: 145–159.

Formisano, Marco. (2016b). La fabula Aristaei, l'aneddoto di Dinocrate e il macrotesto. In: *Apis Matina: Studi in onore di Carlo Santini* (ed. Aldo Setaioli), 306–318. Trieste: Edizioni Università di Trieste.

Gibson, Roy. (2012). On the nature of ancient letter collection. *Journal of Roman Studies* 102: 56–78.

Gibson, Roy. (2013). Pliny and the letters of Sidonius: From Constantius and Clarus to Firminus and Fuscus. In: *Pliny in Late Antiquity* (ed. Bruce J. Gibson and Roger Rees). *Arethusa* 46: 333–355.

Gibson, Roy and Morello, Ruth. (2012). *Reading the Letters of Pliny the Younger: An Introduction*. Cambridge: Cambridge University Press.

Harries, Jill. (1994). *Sidonius Apollinaris and the Fall of Rome AD 407–485*. Oxford: Clarendon.

Hevelone Harper, Jennifer. (2016). The letter collection of Barsanuphius and John. In: *Late Antique Letter Collections: A Critical Introduction and Reference Guide* (ed. Cristiana Sogno, Bradley K. Storin, and Edward Watts), 418–432. Berkeley: University of California Press.

Hodkinson, Owen. (2007). Better than speech: Some advantages of the letter in the Second Sophistic. In: *Ancient Letters. Classical and Late Antique Epistolography* (ed. Ruth Morello and Andrew D. Morrison), 283–300. Oxford: Oxford University Press.

Hoffer, Stanley E. (1999). *The Anxieties of Pliny the Younger*. Oxford: Oxford University Press.

Marchesi, Ilaria. (2008). *The Art of Pliny's Letters: A Poetics of Allusion in the Private Correspondence*. Cambridge: Cambridge University Press.

Mratschek, Sigrid. (2016). The letter collection of Sidonius Apollinaris. In: *Late Antique Letter Collections: A Critical Introduction and Reference Guide* (ed. Cristiana Sogno, Bradley K. Storin, and Edward Watts), 309–336. Berkeley: University of California Press.

Nauroy, Gérard. (2016). The letter collection of Ambrose of Milan. In: *Late Antique Letter Collections: A Critical Introduction and Reference Guide* (ed. Cristiana Sogno, Bradley K. Storin, and Edward Watts), 146–160. Berkeley: University of California Press.

Petkas, Alex. (Forthcoming). The place of philosophy: Landscapes and audiences of the works of Synesius of Cyrene. PhD. diss., Princeton University.

Salzman, Michele and Roberts, Michael. ed. and trans. (2011). *The Letters of Symmachus, Book 1*. Atlanta: Society of Biblical Literature.

Sogno, Cristiana. (2014). The ghost of Cicero's letters: Epistolography and historiography in senatorial letter-writing. *Journal of Late Antiquity* 7: 201–222.

Sogno, Cristiana. (2016). The letter collection of Quintus Aurelius Symmachus. In: *Late Antique Letter Collections: A Critical Introduction and Reference Guide* (ed. Cristiana Sogno, Bradley K. Storin, and Edward Watts), 175–189. Berkeley: University of California Press.

Sogno, Cristiana, Bradley K. Storin, and Edward Watts, eds. (2016). *Late Antique Letter Collections: A Critical Introduction and Reference Guide*. Berkeley: University of California Press.

Storin, Bradley K. (2012). The letters of Gregory Nazianzus: Discourse and community in late antique epistolary culture. PhD diss., Indiana University.

Trout, Dennis. (2016). The letter collection of Paulinus of Nola. In: *Late Antique Letter Collections: A Critical Introduction and Reference Guide* (ed. Cristiana Sogno, Bradley K. Storin, and Edward Watts), 254–268. Berkeley: University of California Press.

Van Hoof, Lieve. (2016). The letter collection of Libanius of Antioch. In: *Late Antique Letter Collections: A Critical Introduction and Reference Guide* (ed. Cristiana Sogno, Bradley K. Storin, and Edward Watts), 113–130. Berkeley: University of California Press.

Viti, Alessandro. (2014). Macrotesto: Original conceptualization and possible extensions. In: *Cycles, Recueils, Macrotexts: The Short Story Collection. Interférences littéraires/Literaire interferenties* 12: 105–117.

Watts, Edward. (2015). *The Final Pagan Generation*. Berkeley: University of California Press.

Watts, Edward. (2017). *Hypatia: The Life and Legend of an Ancient Philosopher*. Oxford: Oxford University Press.

CHAPTER TWENTY-FIVE

Pseudepigraphy

Javier Martínez

25.1 Introduction

"Pseudepigrapha" is a general term given to works whose stated authorship is false or spurious: The name that appears in the title of a text, its body, or recorded tradition does not reflect the actual author (Speyer 1971, p. 13). The term itself, meaning "falsely attributed," is a Greek compound formed by the stem *pseud–*, "false," and the noun *epigraphē* with the sense of "ascription." Initially the term carried no negative connotations regarding the text's deceptive intent: A drinking-song might be attributed (rightly or wrongly) to Anacreon as readily as, even now, a proverb to Solomon or a witticism to Oscar Wilde (Martínez 2012). The scholarly term pseudepigrapha is quite broad in scope and implies certain historical ambiguities: Extant pseudepigraphical texts include a considerable number that might properly be considered as literary forgeries, but it is not uncommon to find the term used to describe pseudonymous works or as a simple label to indicate the problematic character of a text within a larger canon (Peirano 2012, p. 1). Because of this definitional vagueness, the attempt to establish guidelines that permit definition and classification of questionable texts has been a salient concern of many modern studies of pseudepigrapha and literary forgeries, ranging from the monumental work of Wolfgang Speyer (1971) and the influential guidelines established by Metzger (1972) to more recent studies by Baum (2001, 2013) or Ehrman (2014).

The typology of pseudepigrapha has been detailed in an exemplary manner by Baum (2001), who distinguishes between primary pseudepigrapha, those whose author deliberately appends a false name to the text, and secondary, where various factors might attach the wrong author's name to a work in the course of transmission. Baum offers two other useful criteria: whether the ascription is deliberate or not and whether it is intentionally or unintentionally deceptive. In addition to these criteria, a host of additional classifications and definitions can be adduced, because of the complexity of pseudepigraphy as a phenomenon: We must consider not just questions of authorship and authenticity but also various related phenomena such as parody, plagiarism, interpolations and alterations, commissioned texts, and ghostwriting. Despite the broad variety of texts that qualify as pseudepigrapha, it is necessary to stress that, in antiquity, no deliberate forgery was considered innocent or legitimate (Mülke 2008). From our modern perspective we have to agree with Grafton (1990, p. 37): "The only reason to assume that most earlier forgers were more innocent is our own desire to explain away a disquieting feature of the past."

25.2 Origins of Pseudepigrapha in Antiquity

The concept of authorship in Greek culture first develops in the sixth century BCE. With the popularization of books and the emergence of the book market in Athens in the fifth century BCE, the concept of authorship became tied to the question of authority. A philosophical treatise produced by Plato or Aristotle would hold more sway because of a perceived external authority on the subject, as would a medical text with Hippocrates's name on it. The phenomenon of pseudepigraphy thus accompanies the spread of books as medium of knowledge transmission, not only because of the ease with which in antiquity a *titulus* could be lost, changed accidentally, or "corrected," but also because the deliberate promotion of false authorship under the guise of real authority might serve a host of purposes, such as gaining political or religious advantage, securing readership, economic gain, or simply the settling of personal grudges. In Greek literature references are found very early to the dubious authenticity of documents and authors, with questions regarding works circulating under the name of the mythical Orpheus, Musaeus, and Linus (Plato *Rep.* 2.364b). In some instances, forgers are referred to by name, as with the case of Onomacritus in the sixth century BCE (Herodotus 7.6; "the first known commissioned forger" [Martínez 2011]).

The initial conceptualization and systematization of literature as carried out by Aristotle and his school had to deal with such questions of authorship as a matter of course: in some cases, their conclusions persist. However, it was not until the Hellenistic era when a more rigorous, almost scientific study of literature began to develop effective methods for these questions (Quintilian *Inst.Or.* 1.4.3). Hellenistic scholarship made authentication of texts central and essential, developing what modern classical scholarship would term *Echtheitskritik*. By the middle of the third century BCE in Alexandria, the Library of the Museum started to apply classifications, distinguishing between genuine works (γνήσια) and spurious (νόθα) or doubtful ones (ἀμφίβολα, ἀμφιδοξούμενα or ἀμφιβαλλόμενα). This methodological basis of literary and grammatical study developed in Hellenistic Alexandria would exert an enormous influence on all subsequent scholarship: From antiquity to the present day, critics have inherited and applied their methods with little modification.

Greek education was based on imitation of canonical models. As education became systematized, starting in the fourth century BCE on into the Hellenistic period, schools of rhetoric began to arise in the Greek and Latin worlds, developing and spreading their educational methods and texts. The writing exercises employed in the Hellenistic educational system, called *progumnásmata*, instructed students to imitate established authors as a means of learning how to write prose. Depending on the level of difficulty required by the teacher, students might be asked to paraphrase or expand upon existing texts or to refute or prove a given proposition while employing appropriate rhetorical style. Since the aim was faithful imitation of the model, students might produce speeches or letters that qualified almost as a pastiche or that bore obvious affinity with the original model.

From this arose, within a *hic et nunc* creative framework, works that might later be considered pseudepigrapha, but that were composed without any intent to deceive: These were school exercises. The influence of this type of pseudepigrapha was limited, as such works generally do not have any extra-literary purpose, are limited to certain genres, and are usually recognizable by their lower technical and stylistic quality. But this educational method in itself provided the essential skills to anyone who might wish to employ them for other purposes as well: In this sense, the schools of rhetoric in the ancient world doubled as involuntarily schools of literary forgery.

The establishment of scholarly canons had a larger cultural effect: If a text was proven to be the product of pseudepigraphy, it would often be neglected or destroyed. In consequence, a great deal of pseudepigraphical writing is only known by secondary references or citations. In modernity, a similar process occurred again, as works that had been copied, transmitted, and studied for centuries were largely condemned to oblivion when their spuriousness was demonstrated: Scholarly interest in reprinting or commenting upon the *Epistles of Phalaris* plummeted after Richard Bentley demonstrated (1697) that the text was not the work of an authentic philosopher-king (whose reputation for cannibalism and burning his subjects alive tended to eclipse observations on his prose style in antiquity) but an obvious forgery.

In recent decades, however, an interest in pseudepigraphy as a phenomenon in its own right has led to renewed approaches to such texts that have survived the vicissitudes of transmission, as offering a different sort of value, which might give us insight into the original context in which they were composed. Contemporary scholars focus their attention on whether pseudepigraphy should be regarded as a literary tool rather than a mere act of forgery, and examine the justifications offered by ancient authors regarding the use or rejection of pseudepigrapha (Baum 2013, p. 11). Pseudepigraphical works could be also regarded as "creative supplements" that might inform our approach to canonical texts or fill literary gaps (Peirano 2012, pp. 10–16). Similarly, they might be understood as a rhetorical tool for the development of argumentation within a specific discipline, like theology (Wessel 2001, 2012, building off Gray's [1988] "act of progress").

25.3 Late Antique Pseudepigrapha

Pseudepigrapha began to proliferate increasingly in the third century and their dissemination picked up speed from the fourth century onwards, seemingly prompted by the religious controversies that arose after Christianity had become the official religion of the Roman Empire. The rising prominence of forgeries and false ascriptions in the religious realm did not lessen their presence in virtually every genre, and in virtually every language, of the empire and beyond. To get a better sense of the breadth and variety of pseudepigrapha in late antiquity, it is worth enumerating some of the texts and common varieties encountered.

25.3.1 *Medical, Technical, and Similar Texts*

The authority held by some famous or great writers provides the obvious reason why certain corpora attract a great deal of spurious or pseudonymous texts with little resemblance to the authentic works they are attached to. Some of these texts seem designed to establish their own validity under the name of a recognized authority, while others seek to supplement the existing authority by treating subjects that might have been dealt with by a certain writer but were not; still others are mere accretion to a corpus with similar themes.

The *Corpus Hippocraticum* offers a useful example: From Hellenistic times it had already existed as a canonical collection, yet this did not prevent new and spurious material from being added in late antiquity well into the medieval period (van der Eijk 2016, p. 22). New pseudo-Hippocratica appeared as well around the fourth century, including *On the Generation of Man and the Seed*, *On the Formation of Man*, and *On the Pulse and the Human Temperament* (Jouanna 2008, 2012, p. 355). The obvious rationale for these pseudo-Hippocratic texts was to validate the content of new texts by ascribing them to an established authority (Nutton 2004; Jouanna 2012, p. 359). Consequently, numerous medical texts, including *On the Humors* by Pseudo-Galen, the anonymous *On the Constitution of the Universe and of Man*, and the *Isagoge Saluberrima* of Pseudo-Soranus, appear to have been forged during the renaissance of Greek medicine in sixth-century Alexandria (Jouanna 2012, p. 249).

All of these established medical authors, however, were ripe for pseudepigraphy seemingly at any time. To Galen were attributed a broad variety of medical works (Thorndike 1963); false attributions, likewise, were attached to comparable authors like Soranus, in the case of *Quaestiones medicinales*, or like Thessalus, in the case of *De virtutibus Herbarum*, a curious treatise on botanical astrology of uncertain date (Nutton 2004, 269; ní Mheallaigh 2014b). In the fourth century the author of a *Herbarium* invoked the authority of Apuleius. An anonymous neo-Pythagorean treatise from the mid-fourth century, meanwhile, the *Theologumena arithmeticae*, was attributed to Iamblichus, possibly through confusion with an actual treatise that he promised to write at the end of his *On the Arithmetical Introduction of Nicomachus* (125.15).

Spurious names appear recurrently in a range of other texts as well. Thus Gargilius Martialis (mid-third century) is transmitted as an appendix to the *Mulomedicina* of Vegetius (Fischer 2000); Pseudo-Thessalus has a treatise that claims Hermes Trismegistus as its author; and the fourth-century Kyranides, with more magical than medical content, show how accretions of alchemical discussion were transmitted repeatedly under spurious names (ní Mheallaigh 2014a, p. 164). Indeed, alchemy and occult studies became a particular rich ground for the generation of pseudepigrapha, as texts were assigned and reassigned to famous and prestigious historical or mythical characters (Suárez 2014), even as these texts did little more than rehash existing material within larger and more comprehensive corpora (Johnson 2006, p. 191). Among alchemical writings – which we can follow from extant papyri regarding Greco-Egyptian alchemy (ca. 300 CE) down into medieval manuscripts – the oldest texts include historical attributions, like Democritus and Cleopatra, and obviously mythical ones like Hermes and Isis. Texts were also attributed to similarly famous names in later periods, such as Synesius (fourth century), Olympiodorus (sixth century) and Stephanus of Alexandria (seventh century), as were various poems ascribed to Heliodorus, Theophrastus, Archelaus, and others (Mertens 2006, p. 208). Other examples are the fourth-century treatise known as *Lithica*, detailing in hexameters the wondrous properties of certain stones, attributed to Orpheus (Gager 1992, p. 239), and Olympiodorus's commentary on Zosimus's *On Activity*, which clearly invokes the prestige enjoyed by the Neoplatonic philosopher (Wildberg 2008). There is further evidence of treatises attributed to Justinian and Heraclius, which are no longer extant (Mavroudi 2006, p. 73).

Aristotle represents the most noteworthy example of a famous name that generated extraordinary amounts of pseudepigrapha: by late antiquity, during the vogue for all sorts of alchemical, astrological, magical, and occult treaties, the ascription of such writings to Aristotle is relatively common (Thorndike 1922). A pseudo-Aristotelian letter of uncertain date somehow became one of the most influential writings of the Middle Ages: Known as the *Secretum Secretorum*, the work purports to contain the esoteric knowledge of Aristotle. The text itself grows through accretion as it becomes transmitted; in the eighth century an Arabic translation further expanded and altered it (Williams 2003, pp. 28–30).

Many other texts related to Aristotle are dubiously attributed, like the three commentaries on him that are transmitted under the name of Elias (Wildberg 2016). The attributions of some texts have been questioned only in relatively recent times, like the commentary *De Anima*, formerly attributed to Simplicius, but probably a work by Priscian of Lydia (Blumenthal 2000).

25.3.2 *Historical Texts, Itineraries, et alia*

Historical pseudepigrapha purporting to treat events long before written history emerges as a genre. Thus the claim by two pseudepigraphical fictions of pseudo-documentary character on the Trojan War that they were eyewitness histories was widely accepted throughout the Middle Ages and the Renaissance (Prosperi 2016). Dares of Phrygia is the name attached to the Latin *De Excidio Troiae*: The exact date of composition, and whether it was based on a Greek original, is unknown. The *Ephemeris Belli Troiani* by Dictys of Crete was based on an original Greek version of uncertain date (probably in the late first century); the extant Latin text, a translation by Lucius Septimius ("the Latin Dictys"), is probably from the fourth century (Merkle 1989, pp. 263–291; Gainsford 2012). On this same topic, there also exists an anonymous *Excidium Troiae*, datable between the fourth and sixth century.

The *Itinerarium Alexandri* is a fourth-century work based on the history of Arrian but also on the *Romance of Alexander* by Pseudo-Callisthenes, a work of no historical reliability from the third century and best described, perhaps, as fan-fiction about Alexander the Great. Authorship of the *Itinerarium* is ascribed to Julius Valerius, whose name also appears as the Latin translator of Pseudo-Callisthenes, suggesting a possible confusion by homonymy (Fox 1997). The *Cosmography* of Aethicus Ister, probably written in the early eighth century, is a highly problematic text that (despite the title) offers another sort of enigmatic itinerary and is presented as the work of St. Jerome (Herren 2011). The work bears obvious similarities to the anonymous *Ravenna Cosmography* from the late sixth century (Dillemann and Janvier 1997). The *Blemyomachia* offers history in the form of an epic poem (fourth or fifth century), of which only fragments are preserved; it was traditionally and wrongly attributed to Olympiodorus of Thebes (Kanavou 2015). The popular school reader *Disticha Catonis* (or *Dicta Catonis*), an anonymous hexametrical collection (late third century) is attributed to M. Porcius Cato, whose historical reputation as a moral authority presumably prompted the ascription.

Among historical pseudepigrapha, one of the most interesting and debated texts is the *Historia Augusta*, a modern name given to a work of unknown title and authorship, probably composed around 400 (Meckler 2016). The work relates extravagantly fictionalized biographies of Roman emperors from the years 117 to 284 and presents itself as a compilation of individual texts by six authors. But closer examination reveals these six historians to have impossible chronologies, allusive or joking names, and a uniformity of style that leads scholars currently to regard it as the work of a single writer.

25.3.3 Christian Texts

Pseudepigrapha take on a different character when the phenomenon of literary forgery is used to alter a canon of existing works and applied to theological or religious texts. In late antiquity, literary forgery arises to a much greater extent with religious texts than with any other kind: The phenomenon is clearly generated by internal debates within religious communities and because of the specific dynamics of textual production for religious texts. The authority that emanates from canonical texts or authors vested with prestige could be used to validate or legitimize spurious and forged texts in order to refute specific ideas or else claim them for orthodoxy. The phenomenon of pseudepigrapha in this context becomes enormously complex, as questions arise simultaneously regarding forgery and authenticity, where the moral and religious implications for the forger, as well as the theological problem of canonicity, elevate the subject of textual authentication above matters of mere pedantry (Baum 2013, p. 12; Ehrman 2014, pp. 149–153). Although Speyer (1971) hypothesized a category of "genuine religious pseudepigrapha" for works that emerged from authentic mythological or religious tradition and received a mythic ascription nontendentiously, the most recent studies adduce documentation to show that all ancient religious pseudepigrapha were in some way tendentious, and there was no such thing as innocent ancient pseudepigrapha (Baum 2001, 2013; Mülke 2008; Ehrman 2014, pp. 36, 149–153). Speyer (1971) offers an impressive and systematic investigation of motives for pseudepigrapha, while Ehrman (2014) provides a very detailed study of about 50 Christian forgeries from the first four centuries (149–548). Though most false attributions and forgeries appear to result from theological quarrels and controversies, where specific texts or ecclesiastical policies must be legitimized, forgery appears to result from a complex concatenation of different intentions. This presents a phenomenon vastly more complex than in the previous cases, where religion was not a factor.

It is noteworthy, however, that in this period we find direct testimony from forgers explaining their reasons for fabricating texts. Salvian of Marseille (ca. 440) writes an explanation letter to his bishop after been suspected for writing a pamphlet under the under the name of Timothy (Haefner 1934). At the Third Council of Constantinople in 680, Macarius of Antioch contrived to have forged letters of Vigilius inserted in the Acts of the Second Council of Constantinople (553); when confronted with the evidence by the Council, his uncanny answer was recorded (ACO Ser, II.2.2, 650). Anastasius Sinaites appears to us as both critic and forger; he describes how he produced successfully a florilegium against monophysites (*Tomus ad Leonem*, CPG 5938), although he acknowledges his own handling as "wicked" (πανοῦργον, PG 89: 180C).

The classical pedagogical method in grammar and rhetoric was studied and adopted by Christians. Very soon, from the middle of the second century, Christian scholars flourished: Justin Martyr (died 165), Tertullian (ca. 160–ca. 240), Origen (184–254) and Eusebius of Caesarea (ca. 260–339) applied the inherited philosophical and philological methodology to their theological discussions, which necessarily included an examination of pseudepigrapha (Grafton and Williams 2006). The interminable disputes of the patristic writers led to the sharpening of scholarly tools; as a consequence, forgers had to become more skillful, as Grafton (1990) has demonstrated.

Ehrman (2014, p. vii) handles the texts with a very effective topical division regarding chronology, demonstrating that forgery is inevitably an immediate product of its own time and circumstances. For example, "forgeries which attack Paul's person and message" (Ehrman 2014, pp. 239–282, esp. 312) are found in the Pseudo-Clementine *Recognitions* (ca. 310) and *Homilies* (360–380), both based on a Christian novel from the early third century.

"Anti-Jewish forgeries" (Ehrman 2014, pp. 323–366, esp. 344) such as the *Didascalia Apostolorum* were common from the beginning of the tradition.

The *Didascalia* (early fourth century) claims to have been written by the apostles: Its original Greek version is lost but a complete Syriac version has been preserved. The *Acts of Pilate* (fourth century) are supposedly written by the Rabbi Nicodemus and thus are sometimes referred to as the *Gospel of Nicodemus*; Latin, Coptic, Syriac, Armenian, and Georgian versions exist for the text, which was extremely popular during Middle Ages. The work may have been written as a counterforgery to delegitimize a previous *Acts of Pilate*, mentioned by Eusebius. This anti-Christian and slanderous work has not been preserved, but apparently it caused a great commotion earlier in the fourth century, during the reign of Diocletian's successor Maximinius Daia, who was, like his predecessor, an opponent of Christians and who ordered that the original forged *Acts of Pilate* be taught in schools. Similar examples are provided by the *Anaphora Pilati* (late fourth century) and several letters purporting to be written by or addressed to Pontius Pilate.

"Forgeries that deal with the organization and leadership of the Church" (Ehrman 2014, pp. 367–406) in this period mainly take the form of "church orders" like the *Apostolic Constitutions* (fourth century), which claims to have been written by the apostles: The text even warns its readers to beware of forgeries. The work was put together from other documents, such as the *Didascalia*, mentioned above, the anonymous *Didache*, and the *Apostolic Tradition*, wrongly attributed to Hippolytus, along with 85 "apostolic canons."

The Edict of Milan (313) would occasion further proliferation of pseudepigrapha, as the periodic systematic purges or anathemata issued (Speyer 1981, pp. 142–14) to preserve orthodoxy necessitated hiding certain beliefs, but also hiding the existence of banned texts. At the Council of Nicaea (325) the teachings of Arius were anathematized: His works as well as those of Porphyry were condemned. Following the imposition of Nicene orthodoxy (383), Theodosius gave the order that the writings of the Eunomians be burned. Under Theodosius II the Council of Ephesus (431) had sanctioned the works of Nestorius, but in 435 Theodosius ordered the burning of Nestorian books. The resilience of Nestorian Christological views and the continued appeal of Nestorian teachings forced the banning of his "heretical" works again, at the Councils of Chalchedon (451) and Constantinople (553). In Constantinople, Arius, Eunomius, Macedonius, Apollinaris, Eutyches, and Origen were also anathematized. The Council at Trullo (691) banned pagan practices and commanded the burning of forged martyrologies, a Christian apologetic genre that proliferated beginning in the early third century with numerous extant examples of both nonpseudepigraphic forgeries (for third-person narratives) as well as pseudepigraphic forgeries narrated in the first person such as the *Martrydom of Polycarp* (mid-third century?).

Any religious faction that was interested in perpetuating their teachings and writings in the face of official opposition had to comply with orthodoxy or else disguise their texts by using pseudepigraphical methods. Consequently, forged writings abounded in this period, but not many of the texts survived the persecution of heretics. One of the most skilled sources of forgery in this period were the Apollinarians, highly specialized interpolators (Tuilier 1987, p. 590), whose altered versions of the works of Athanasius would be used by Cyril in his theological writings. The pseudo-Athanasian formula "one incarnate nature of God the Word" was one of their interpolations that became sanctioned by later theologians and would eventually prompt the resolutions in the Council of Chalcedon (451) that led ultimately to the schism of the eastern churches.

Among the forgeries arising from "later theological controversies" (Ehrman 2014, pp. 455–480) are the *Abgar Correspondence* (end of the third century), purporting to be a letter from the ruler of Edessa to Jesus, complete with Jesus's written reply, which has a rather charming formal epistolary style. The work was Christian anti-Manichean propaganda written by a threatened orthodox minority.

The aforementioned Pseudo-Clementine *Recognitions* and *Homilies*, combining anti-Pauline polemic with Arian savior, also date from this later period, as do the six Pseudo-Ignatian letters (late fourth century) whose forger added them to the seven originals, which contained heavy interpolations by him. This forger, an otherwise-unknown Julian, was well versed in the language of these texts and also very industrious: He apparently also produced the *Apostolic Constitutions* and a *Commentary on Job* attributed (falsely) to Origen.

The purpose of these forgeries is still debatable, as they may have had multiple polemical targets and purposes, even as they demonstrate some evidence of the forger's own theological agenda. Outside of internal disputes concerning orthodoxy, the apologetic forgeries also appeared frequently as a means of defending the faith from non-Christian adversaries. The aforementioned *Acts of Pilate* are a good example of this type.

Because of the formal and rhetorical nature of letters in antiquity, epistolography has been particularly dogged by questions of authenticity (Neil and Allen 2015). Forged letters (like those of Phalaris) were particularly common, and among religious pseudepigrapha examples include the mentioned correspondence of Abgar of Edessa with Jesus Christ or of Herod Antipas with Pontius Pilate and later the Letters of Paul and Seneca (mid-fourth century). In their attempt to create some organic connection between the Roman Empire and Christianity, these works resemble the extant *Oracula Sibyllina*, with heavy interpolation by Christians (who create book 6 and perhaps 7 at the end of the fourth century). Other forged Christian texts have different purposes and include many writings attributed to John Chrysostom (Aldama

1965) and the treatise *De virginitate* attributed to Eusebius (mid-fourth century) as well as a similarly titled treatise appearing under the name of Basil of Caesarea; the *Paraphrase of the Psalms* attributed to Apollinarius the elder (fifth century); and numerous apocalyptic texts that appeared in the seventh century under the authoritative names as Pseudo-Methodius, and Pseudo-Athanasius (Alexander and Abrahamse 1985).

All kinds of pseudepigrapha are found in Syriac (Lied 2012) and Coptic texts. The latter are by far the most affected by this phenomenon. Besides the later forgeries attributed to the successors of Pachomius, Theodore, and Horsiesi and the Pseudo-Shenoute, we find the regular attributions to prominent church fathers of the fourth and fifth centuries increasing especially in the seventh and eighth centuries. It seems to be a mere routine of ascribing texts of doubtful origin to a single previous period and one homogenous literary school, but probably also because of some kind of authorial inhibition against publishing *in propria persona* (Orlandi 1991, pp. 1456–1458, 2016).

At the end of this period (and especially from the ninth century onward), the wealth and institutional power of the church gave new motives for forgery, establishing rights and property of the church itself, as we can see with the Le Mans Forgeries (mid-ninth century, Goffart 1966) and the Pseudo-Isidorian Decretals (mid-ninth century). The latter are a compilation of diverse fraudulent and authentic materials dating from the fourth century onwards (Zechiel-Eckes 2001), which contains the oldest known version of the *Donatio Constantini* forged in the mid-eighth century (Fried 2007). The *Donation of Constantine* was fabricated mainly in order to establish church ownership of the Lateran Palace and subsequently rights to the city of Rome itself (Lieu 2012).

One of the most interesting and influential (up to modern times!) forgeries of this period is the corpus of Pseudo-Dionysius the Aeropagite (late fifth century, called *Corpus Areopagiticum* or *Corpus Dionysiacum*), written by an unknown person but attributed to Paul's Athenian convert (mentioned in *Acts* 17:34): starting with Eusebius, various different attributions were proposed (*EH* 3.4.11). The works are the product of a highly trained intellectual who was well acquainted with the contemporary Neoplatonic school of Athens and seem intended to provide (or "forge") a Neoplatonic intellectual structure for the orthodox doctrines of Christianity (Klitenic and Dillon 2007; a pagan Neoplatonist is proposed by Louth 2009). The authority of Pseudo-Dionysius was already recognized in 532 in a convocation that was assembled by Justinian, where the work would be authenticated along with Athanasius, Cyril, and Gregory Thaumaturgus. The forgery was still regarded as wholly authentic by both opposing sides in the Sixth Ecumenical Council in Constantinople (680), which ironically had been termed the council of "antiquaries and paleographists" (von Harnack 1990, 2: p. 433).

REFERENCES

Aldama, José Antonio de. (1965). *Repertorium pseudochrysostomicum.* Paris: Centre national de la recherche scientifique.

Alexander, Paul Julius and de Abrahamse, Dorothy. (1985). *The Byzantine Apocalyptic Tradition.* Berkeley: University of California Press.

Baum, Armin D. (2001). *Pseudepigraphie und literarische Fälschung im frühen Christentum. Mit ausgewählten Quellentexten samt deutscher Übersetzung.* Tübingen: Mohr Siebeck.

Baum, Armin D. (2013). Authorship and pseudepigraphy in early Christian literature: A translation of the most important source texts and an annotated bibliography. In: *Paul and Pseudepigraphy* (ed. Stanley E. Porter and Gregory P. Fewster), 11–63. Leiden: Brill.

Bentley, Richard. (1697). *A Dissertation upon the Epistles of Phalaris, Themistocles, Socrates, Euripides, and Others, and the Fables of Æsop.* London: Leake.

Blumenthal, Henry J. ed. (2000). *Simplicius: On Aristotle's "On the Soul 3.1–5", The Ancient commentators on Aristotle.* Ithaca, NY: Cornell University Press.

Dillemann, Louis, and Yves Janvier. (1997). *La cosmographie du Ravennate.* Brussels: Latomus.

Ehrman, Bart D. (2014). *Forgery and Counterforgery: The Use of Literary Deceit in Early Christian Polemics.* Oxford: Oxford University Press.

Eijk, Philip van der. (2016). On "Hippocratic" and "non-Hippocratic" medical writings. In: *Ancient Concepts of the Hippocratic* (ed. Lesley Dean-Jones and Ralph M. Rosen), 15–47. Leiden: Brill.

Fischer, Klaus-Dietrich. (2000). Pseudo-Gargilius Martialis, *Curae boum.* In: *Nouvelle histoire de la littérature latine.* Tome 4. *L'âge de transition: De la littérature romaine à la littérature chrétienne, de 117 à 284 après J.-C.* (ed. Klaus Sallmann), 311. Turnhout: Brepols.

Fox, R.J. Lane. (1997). The itinerary of Alexander: Constantius to Julian. *Classical Quarterly* 47 (1): 239–252.

Fried, Johannes. (2007). *Donation of Constantine and Constitutum Constantini: The Misinterpretation of a Fiction and Its Original Meaning.* Berlin & New York: De Gruyter.

Gager, John G. (1992). *Curse Tablets and Binding Spells from the Ancient World.* New York: Oxford University Press.

Gainsford, Peter. (2012). Diktys of Crete. *Cambridge Classical Journal* 58: 58–87.

Goffart, Walter A. (1966). *The Le Mans Forgeries: A Chapter from the History of Church Property in the Ninth Century.* Cambridge, MA: Harvard University Press.

Grafton, Anthony. (1990). *Forgers and Critics: Creativity and Duplicity in Western Scholarship.* Princeton, NJ: University Press.

Grafton, Anthony and Williams, Megan Hale. (2006). *Christianity and the Transformation of the Book: Origen, Eusebius, and the Library of Caesarea.* Cambridge, MA: Harvard University Press.

Gray, Patrick. (1988). Forgery as an instrument of progress: Reconstructing the theological tradition in the sixth century. *Byzantische Zeitschrift* 81: 284–89.

Haefner, Alfred. (1934). A unique source for the study of ancient pseudonymity. *Anglican Theological Review* 16: 8–15.

Harnack, Adolf von. (1990). *Lehrbuch der Dogmengeschichte*. 3 vols. Reprint of the 4th ed. (1909). Tübingen: J.C.B. Mohr (Paul Siebeck).

Herren, Michael W. (2011). *The Cosmography of Aethicus Ister: Edition, Translation, and Commentary*. Turnhout: Brepols.

Johnson, Scott Fitzgerald. (2006). *The Life and Miracles of Thekla: a Literary Study*. Washington, DC: Center for Hellenic Studies.

Jouanna, Jacques. (2008). La postérité de l'embryologie d'Hippocrate dans deux traités pseudohippocratiques de la médecine tardive: *Sur la formation de l'homme et Sur la génération de l'homme et de la sémence*. In: *L'embryon: Formation et animation* (ed. Luc Brisson, Marie-Hélène Congourdeau, and J.L. Solère), 15–41. Paris: J. Vrin.

Jouanna, Jacques. (2012). *Greek Medicine from Hippocrates to Galen: Selected Papers*. Leiden: Brill.

Kanavou, Nikoletta. (2015). Notes on the *Blemyomachia* (*P.Berol.* 5003 + *P.Gen.* inv. 140 + *P.Phoib.* fr. 1a/6a/11c/12c). *Tyche* 30: 55–60.

Klitenic, Sarah and Dillon, John M. (2007). *Dionysius the Areopagite and the Neoplatonist Tradition: Despoiling the Hellenes*. Aldershot and Burlington, VT: Ashgate.

Lied, Liv Ingeborg. (2012). The reception of the pseudepigrapha in Syriac traditions: The case of 2 *Baruch*. In: *"Non-Canonical" Religious Texts in Early Judaism and Early Christianity* (ed. Lee Martin McDonald and James H. Charlesworth), 52–60. London: T & T Clark.

Lieu, Samuel N.C. (2012). Constantine in legendary literature. In: *The Cambridge Companion to the Age of Constantine* (ed. Noel Emmanuel Lenski), 298–322. Cambridge: University Press. doi: 10.1017/CCOL0521818389.014

Louth, Andrew. (2009). The reception of Dionysius up to Maximus the Confessor. In: *Re-Thinking Dionysius the Areopagite* (ed. Sarah Coakley and Charles M. Stang), 43–53. Chichester: Wiley Blackwell.

Martínez, Javier. (2011). Onomacritus the forger, Hipparchus' scapegoat? In: *Falsificaciones y falsarios de la Literatura Clásica* (ed. Javier Martínez), 217–226. Madrid: Ediciones Clásicas.

Martínez, Javier. (2012). Prefacio/Foreword. In: *Mundus vult decipi: Estudios interdisciplinares sobre falsificación textual y literaria* (ed. Javier Martínez), 9–16. Madrid: Ediciones Clásicas.

Mavroudi, Maria V. (2006). Occult science and society in Byzantium: Considerations for future research. In: *The Occult Sciences in Byzantium* (ed. Paul Magdalino and Maria Mavroudi), 39–95. Geneva: La Pomme d'Or.

Meckler, Michael. (2016). Comparative approaches to the *Historia Augusta*. In: *Splendide Mendax: Rethinking Fakes and Forgeries in Classical, Late Antique, and Early Christian Literature* (ed. Edmund P. Cueva and Javier Martínez), 205–215. Groningen: Barkhuis.

Merkle, Stefan. (1989). *Die Ephemeris belli Troiani des Diktys von Kreta*. Frankfurt am Main: P. Lang.

Mertens, Michèle. (2006). Graeco-Egyptian alchemy in Byzantium. In: *The Occult Sciences in Byzantium* (ed. Paul Magdalino and Maria Mavroudi), 205–230. Geneva: La Pomme d'Or.

Metzger, Bruce M. (1972). Literary Forgeries and canonical pseudepigrapha. *JBL* 91 (1): 3–24.

Mülke, Markus. (2008). *Der Autor und sein Text: die Verfälschung des Originals im Urteil antiker Autoren.* Berlin: De Gruyter.

ní Mheallaigh, Karen. (2014a). *Reading Fiction with Lucian: Fakes, Freaks and Hyperreality.* Cambridge: Cambridge University Press.

ní Mheallaigh, Karen. (2014b). Reading the fraudulent text: Thessalus of Tralles and the Vook of Nechepso. In: *Fakes and Forgers of Classical Literature: Ergo decipiatur!* (ed. Javier Martínez), 179–186. Leiden: Brill.

Neil, Bronwen and Allen, Pauline. (2015). *Collecting Early Christian Letters: From the Apostle Paul to Late Antiquity.* Cambridge: Cambridge University Press.

Nutton, Vivian. (2004). *Ancient Medicine.* London: Routledge.

Orlandi, Tito. (1991). Literature, Coptic. In *The Coptic Encyclopedia* (ed. Aziz Suryal Atiya), 1450–1460. New York: Macmillan.

Orlandi, Tito. (2016). Coptic. In: *The Oxford Handbook of the Literatures of the Roman Empire* (ed. Daniel L. Selden and Phiroze Vasunia). Oxford: Oxford University Press.

Peirano, Irene. (2012). *The Rhetoric of the Roman Fake: Latin Pseudepigrapha in Context.* Cambridge: Cambridge University Press.

Prosperi, Valentina. (2016). The Trojan War: Between history and myth. In: *Splendide Mendax: Rethinking Fakes and Forgeries in Classical, Late Antique, and Early Christian Literature* (ed. Edmund P. Cueva and Javier Martínez), 93–111. Groningen: Barkhuis.

Speyer, Wolfgang. (1971). *Die literarische Fälschung im heidnischen und christlichen Altertum: Ein Versuch ihrer Deutung.* Munich: Beck.

Speyer, Wolfgang. (1981). *Büchervernichtung und Zensur des Geistes bei Heiden, Juden und Christen.* Stuttgart: A. Hiersemann.

Suárez de la Torre, Emilio. (2014). Pseudepigraphy and magic. In: *Fakes and Forgers of Classical Literature: Ergo decipiatur!* (ed. Javier Martínez), 243–262. Leiden: Brill.

Thorndike, Lynn. (1922). The Latin Pseudo-Aristotle and medieval occult science. *JEGP* 21: 229–258.

Thorndike, Lynn. (1963). The Pseudo-Galen, *De Plantis. Ambix* 11: 87–94.

Tuilier, André. (1987). Remarques sur les fraudes des Apollinaristes et des Monophysites: Notes de critique textuelle. In *Texte und Textkritik: eine Aufsatzsammlung* (ed. Jürgen Dummer and Johannes Irmscher), 581–590. Berlin: Akademie.

Wessel, Susan. (2001). Literary forgery and the monothelete controversy: Some scrupulous uses of deception. *Greek, Roman, and Byzantine Studies* 42: 201–220.

Wessel, Susan. (2012). Theological argumentation: The case of forgery. In: *The Oxford Handbook of Late Antiquity* (ed. Scott F. Johnson), 916–934. Oxford: Oxford University Press

Wildberg, Christian. (2008). Olympiodorus. *The Stanford Encyclopedia of Philosophy* (ed. Edward N. Zalta). http://plato.stanford.edu/archives/fall2008/entries/olympiodoru (accessed 3 July 2016).

Wildberg, Christian. (2016). Elias. *The Stanford Encyclopedia of Philosophy* (ed. Edward N. Zalta). http://plato.stanford.edu/archives/fall2016/entries/elias (accessed 3 July 2016).

Williams, Steven J. (2003). *The Secret of Secrets: The Scholarly Career of a Pseudo-Aristotelian Text in the Latin Middle Ages*. Ann Arbor: University of Michigan Press.

Zechiel-Eckes, Klaus. (2001). Pseudoisidorische Dekretalen. In: *Lexikon der Kirchengeschichte* (ed. Bruno Steimer), 1345–1349. Freiburg: Herder.

CHAPTER TWENTY-SIX

Legal Texts

Charles N. Aull

26.1 Introduction

The most striking difference between the legal texts that the Roman Empire produced in its first three centuries and those of the later empire are their legislative styles. Emperors of the early and high empires commanded; later Roman emperors persuaded (Cohen and Lendon 2010). Scholars have long been aware of this evolution, but too little attention has been given to the fact that as legal texts evolved in late antiquity they began to take on the distinct characteristics of other literary genres. This is most noticeable in how legal texts echoed imperial panegyric, ceremonial speeches given in praise of Roman emperors. Legal texts and panegyric utilized comparable diction, prose rhythms, and rhetorical strategies. Consequently, the emperor's own speech in late antiquity came to sound very similar to ceremonial speech about the emperor.

The following discussion sets out to trace some of the details of these similarities by exploring several characteristics of late antique legal texts and comparing them to imperial panegyric. It begins with an overview of the different forms that legal texts could take in late antiquity and discusses some of the major problems that past scholars have encountered with them. It then parses a small sample of laws from the fourth century and compares them to features commonly found in late antique panegyric. Collectively, this chapter will serve as a starting point for how one might think about late antique legal texts as literary forms. At the same time, it highlights the

---

A Companion to Late Antique Literature, First Edition.
Edited by Scott McGill and Edward J. Watts.
© 2018 John Wiley & Sons, Inc. Published 2018 by John Wiley & Sons, Inc.

Roman government's embrace of late antiquity's creative literary spirit and underscores the existence of a complex imperial discourse that functioned to shape perceptions of the Roman emperor.

26.2 Legal Texts in Late Antiquity: Forms and Problems

The emperor's word carried the weight of law in the Roman world. For this reason, one may consider a letter from the emperor responding to a specific question from a provincial governor, general, or bishop to be as much a legal text as a sweeping imperial edict carved into stone or bronze. All such texts can be placed in the category of "imperial legislation," which serves as the primary focal point of this study.

The two most important sources for our knowledge of late antique imperial legislation are the *Theodosian* and *Justinianic Codes*, massive compilations of Roman law made at the order of their respective emperors – Theodosius II and Justinian I – in the fifth and sixth centuries. Theodosius II commissioned the legal code that would bear his name in the year 429 with the intention of codifying Roman legal principles throughout the empire's western and eastern halves. The undertaking took close to a decade to complete. The code covered laws issued by Roman emperors from 312 to 438 and touched on various topics, such as taxation, military and veterans issues, and religion, just to name a few. The compilers included in the codex what Theodosius called general laws, legislation that pertained to specific issues but had broad applicability. Such laws took the form of imperial edicts, letters from the emperor to the Roman Senate, and letters from the emperor to imperial administrators in the provinces. Excluded from the codex were private rescripts, letters from the emperor responding to legal questions from private citizens. Private rescripts made up the bulk of two nonextant legal codes that preceded the *Theodosian Code*: the *Codex Gregorianus* and the *Codex Hermogenianus*, both of which date to the reign of Diocletian (284–305) and were named after their editors. While far from being in perfect condition, the vast majority of the *Theodosian Code* has survived into the present day. Roughly 2700 of what was originally 3250 texts are extant (Matthews 2000, pp. 65–70; Dillon 2012, pp. 15–27). The authoritative modern edition of the code is that edited by Theodore Mommsen and published in 1905. Clyde Pharr published an English translation of the entire code in 1952.

The *Justinianic Code* proved more ambitious. First commissioned by Justinian I in 527, it was meant to synthesize all active imperial legislation, including laws contained in previous legal codes as well as laws produced in the interim between 438 and 528. This involved compiling laws, editing them, removing contradictions, and solving inherent legal and textual conflicts. A first edition of the code, which does not survive, was produced in 529. From that point on, it legally superseded all previous Roman law codes. A second edition was published five years later to incorporate legislation pursued by Justinian's administration between the time of the first edition and 534. This second edition survives. In between the time of the first and second editions, Justinian commissioned two other works that served as companions to each other and the code itself. One is known as the *Institutes*, essentially a legal textbook; the other is known as the *Digest*, a collection of classical Roman juristic writings. Historians and classicists refer to all three of these works collectively as the *Corpus Iuris Civilis* (or just *Corpus Iuris*). Sometimes considered part of the *Corpus Iuris* are laws enacted by Justinian after 534 known as *Novellae*. The *Corpus Iuris* as a whole is estimated to contain more than a million words (Honore 1993, pp. 29–38; Robinson 1997, pp. 43–45). An edition of the *Justinianic Code* produced by Paul Kruger in 1877 remains preeminent in Roman legal scholarship. Bruce Frier has recently edited an authoritative three-volume translation of the code.

Despite the centrality of the *Theodosian* and *Justinianic Codes* to the study of Roman law and late antique legal literature, students and scholars could benefit from a more inclusive conceptualization of legal texts in late antiquity. Just as legal texts today might include an Act of Congress, an executive order from the President, or an opinion from the Supreme Court, legal texts in late antiquity could come in many different forms. Two sources from the fourth and sixth centuries offer examples of the diverse forms that legal texts in late antiquity could take.

The first is a slab of limestone from the North African city of Timgad. Around 360, the Roman administration in North Africa etched into the stone prices for litigating in the court of the Roman governor of Numidia. For example, the inscription states that it cost a plaintiff X amount to register the case with the court. It would then cost Y amount to have an attorney present the case and then Z amount to issue a summons for a defendant or to actually have the judgment enforced (assuming the case was decided in the plaintiff's favor). The inscription, often known as the *Ordo Salutationis*, was erected in the middle of the city. As a historical document, it underscores the exclusiveness of access to litigation in late antiquity. One study of the inscription argued that litigation fees in the court of Numida equaled close to what was needed for a peasant family of four to survive on for a full year (Kelly 2006, p. 140). A harsh reality no doubt, but the *Ordo* was, like the *Theodosian* and *Justinianic Codes*, a strategic attempt by the Roman imperial government – the emperor – to codify and establish procedure. Fascinatingly, legal texts like the *Ordo* that stood prominently and permanently in city centers were probably ones with which many everyday Romans were most familiar.

A second source that shows the different forms that legal texts in late antiquity could take is the *Variae*. This collection of 468 documents was penned by a government official named Cassiodorus, who worked in the administrations of the Ostrogothic king Theodoeric and his successors throughout the first half of the sixth century. Cassiodorus held several high-level positions in the Ostrogothic administration, many of which required him to serve as something of a spokesperson or as a legal draftsman. At some point in the mid-sixth century, he collected and edited the documents he wrote on behalf of the Ostrogothic government and published them in 12 books. Most of the books include letters that Cassiodorus wrote in the name of Theoderic and his successors. They touched on various diplomatic, administrative, and legal issues and were addressed to recipients such as the Roman Senate, the Eastern Roman Empire, kings of other western states, and officers of the Ostrogothic kingdom. Two other books consist largely of stock language used for making government and honorary appointments, unique legal texts in their own right. The final two books include letters that Cassiodorus wrote in his own name as an Ostrogothic official. It should be noted that the *Variae* are considerably different from the massive imperial archives discussed above. The primary purpose of the *Variae*, unlike that of the *Theodosian* and *Justinianic Codes*, was not legal clarification or codification. In fact, Cassiodorus may have been thinking very little about legal issues when he began the process of compiling and editing documents for the *Variae*. Instead, it has been argued, he may have envisioned the work primarily as a vehicle for self-fashioning and presenting an idealized portrayal of the Ostrogothic government. These goals, in turn, may have informed how Cassiodorus curated and edited his source materials (Bjornlie 2016). Nonetheless, the *Variae* should be viewed as an archive of late antique legal texts as much as the *Theodosian* and *Justinianic Codes* are, although the original motivations behind the creation of these archives should not be forgotten.

Just as legal texts could take many different forms in late antiquity, they have survived in different ways, too, and were preserved for various reasons and purposes. In addition to massive compilations like the *Theodosian* and *Justinianic Codes*, we have smaller archives of extant legal texts such as the *Collectio Avellana*, the *Fragmenta Vaticana*, and the *Collectio Sirmondiana*. The *Collectio Avellana* is a collection of roughly 250 ecclesiastical documents that include letters from emperors from the time of Valentinian I to Justinian. It was compiled sometime in the mid-sixth century and offers a unique window into church–state relations in late antiquity. The *Fragmenta Vaticana* consists of writings from Roman jurists and imperial legislation from the western empire in the early fourth century. Less than 20% of the original archive is believed to have survived, and little is known of its scope, organizational principles, or purpose. The *Collectio Sirmondiana*, like the *Collectio Avellana*, has a religious focus and features a small group of imperial laws from the fourth and fifth centuries. It takes its name from the Jesuit scholar Jacques Sirmond, who first edited and published the laws in 1631 as an appendix to an edition of the *Theodosian Code*. There are also numerous legal texts preserved on stone and on papyrus, some of which carry exceptional historical and legal significance. For example, the *Edict on Maximum Prices*, established by the emperor Diocletian, has survived largely in the form of fragmented stone inscriptions from the eastern Mediterranean. In some instances, legal texts have even come down to us through literary works. Several legal texts purportedly authored by the emperor Constantine, for instance, are presented in the works of Eusebius of Caesarea, a fourth-century bishop who wrote a history of Constantine's reign.

Scholars face difficult questions when it comes to the history and transmission of extant late antique legal texts. Why did late antique compilers choose the laws that they chose? Where and what were their original source materials? To what extant have extant legal texts been edited or modified? Can we trust the presentation of legal texts in literary sources? Here is not the place to address all of these questions. The answers, after all, are often unique to particular collections and texts. But the thorny issue of how the texts in the *Theodosian Code* – which form the backbone of the discussion that follows in the next section – were edited presents an illustrative example of the types of problems with which historians grapple when it comes to late antique legal texts. It also has a direct bearing on how we read and interpret legal texts.

To understand the nature of the editing problem with the *Theodosian Code*, one must first understand the Roman government's legislative production model. The starting point of any piece of new legislation was the emperor himself and his closest legal advisers, an inner circle often known nowadays as the imperial consistory. After the consistory formulated a basic policy framework or solution to a particular problem, it was the job of an official called the quaestor to craft the actual language and text of the law. Quaestors worked with teams of legal experts and were often expected to be widely knowledgeable of legal matters, but other skill sets could come into play and even outweigh expertise in law. Perhaps the most illuminating example of the varied backgrounds of quaestors can be seen in the Emperor Valentinian's appointment of Decimus Magnus Ausonius in 375. Ausonius had minimal legal expertise when he took the job. Instead, his background was largely in rhetoric and poetry. (The involvement of individuals like Ausonius in the drafting of imperial legislation helps to explain some of the stylistic features of late antique legal texts discussed later in this chapter.) The drafting process likely involved a good deal of back-and-forth between the quaestor's office and the consistory and would conclude only with the emperor's permission. From there, the text would be sent out to the appropriate officials in the provinces. It was at this point in the process that most Romans in late antiquity came into contact with imperial law. Officers in the provincial administration were responsible for ensuring that the law was read aloud in places such as city councils or churches and that the law was publicly displayed in a visible and prominent location (Matthews 2000, pp. 168–199; Watts 2015, pp. 47–48).

The texts of the laws that survive in legal compilations like the *Theodosian Code* are likely different from what Romans saw and heard in their local communities and from what actually emanated from imperial centers. How different has been a fundamental question for scholars of late antique legal texts. Theodosius II gave the editors of the *Theodosian Code* leeway to truncate and prune legal texts. This involved removing preambles and lengthy imperial titles as well as language deemed superfluous. Only what the editors determined to be the legally meaningful portions of a text were to be left unspoiled (Honore 1998, pp. 143–44). Theodosius commanded this: "the words themselves…insofar as they pertain to the matter at hand, are to be preserved" (*CTh.* 1.1.5).

But how closely did the editors follow these instructions? Quite closely, it turns out. John Matthews, in a critical study of the codex, examined the procedures of the editors by comparing the truncated versions of texts in the *Code* to other versions that are believed to have come down to us largely unaltered. Matthews showed that, on the one hand, the "words themselves" were not always preserved perfectly verbatim. In addition to the removal of introductions and titles – which Theodosius sanctioned and encouraged – light editing of the substantive portions of legal texts does appear to have happened. On the other hand, most of the substantive sections of the texts that survive offer by-and-large faithful, if not exact, reflections of the original texts (Matthews 2000, pp. 121–167). Ultimately, what this means for how we read imperial legislation is that we should approach late Roman laws both as the products of imperial consistories and, by extension, as the actual utterances and words of late Roman emperors (cf. Dillon 2012, pp. 83–84). Understanding this point is foundational to appreciating the literary and political import of imperial legislation in late antiquity.

26.3 Language and Style in Late Antique Imperial Legislation

A sample of imperial legislation from the fourth century illustrates several of the stylistic features that characterized these types of legal texts in late antiquity. Our first text dates to 324. Issued by the emperor Constantine, it lays down procedures for reporting bureaucratic malfeasance. In a study of Constantinian legislation, John Dillon offers an insightful reading of this law, arguing that its real goals were communicative. Through this edict Constantine articulated to the empire his vision of good government and the ideal relationship between subject and emperor (Dillon 2012, pp. 97–104). The text is a powerful piece of rhetoric, but what makes it work is its careful attention to language and syntax.

The extant portion of the edict opens with a fast-paced sequence of lists and mimicking sounds:

> If there is anyone of any position, station, or rank who believes that he can truthfully and unmistakably prove anything against any of my judges, companions, friends, or palace staff, which does not seem to have been done honestly and justly, let him fearlessly and confidently approach and address me.

> *Si quis est cuiuscumque loci ordinis dignitatis, qui se in quemcumque iudicium comitum amicorum vel palatinorum meorum aliquid veraciter et manifeste probare posse confidit, quod non integer adque iuste gessise videatur, intrepidus et securus accedat, interpellet me.* (CTh. 9.1.4)

Constantine's listing of his administrators presents a carefully arranged sequence of words with similar sounding endings. *Iudicium* and *comitum* work together and are accented by the *quemcumque*, while *amicorum*, *palatinorum*, and *meorum* conclude the sequence. Most interesting about this sentence is the way that it comes to a halt once it reaches its main cause, the crux of the text where Constantine finally provides clear instruction. No less than four subordinate clauses precede it, each with varying degrees of complexity. The main clause itself consists simply of two adjectives, two verbs, and an object, Constantine himself, placed not before the verb *interpellet*, where we might expect it, but instead afterwards.

The rhythm of the text continues into the next series of sentences and plays on the placement of *me* in the last sentence. It begins with "I myself will hear everything; I myself will judge, and, if it should be proven, I myself will avenge myself" (*ipse audiam omnia, ipse cognoscam et si fuerit comprobatum, ipse me vindicabo*). The repeating of *ipse* ("myself") is impossible to miss, though more hidden is the inverted parallelism of *me ipse* which leads into the sentence and *ipse me* which closes it. The same word begins and ends the next clause, giving the word itself greater emphasis. An English translation can hardly hope to replicate it: "Let him speak untroubled and let him speak confidently" (*dicat securus et bene conscius dicat*).

The rapidity calms down in the final lines, but the complexity and parallelisms continue:

> If he proves it, as I said, I will avenge myself upon him, who has deceived me up to this time with false integrity. That man who makes known and proves the crime, however, I will increase his rank and wealth.
>
> *Si probaverit, ut dixi, ipse me vindicabo de eo qui me usque ad hoc tempus simulata integritate deceperit, illum autem qui hoc prodiderit et conprobaverit, et dignitatibus et rebus augebo.*

Here is a third appearance of the *ipse me* combination and a reappearance of the phrase "*ipse me vindicabo.*" Note also the parallel relative clauses, which compare the administrator, who deceives (*deceperit*), to Constantine's subject, who exposes the crime and proves it (*prodiderit et conprobaverit*). Both clauses occur within the confines of a loose chiastic structure – a sort of cross-stitching – set up by the first person verbs *vindicabo* and *augebo*.

As Dillon argued, Constantine used this law to communicate his vision of good government and how he wanted Romans to perceive the role of the emperor in their lives. The sophisticated way this text was written helped Constantine achieve this goal in several ways. Constantine's government, for example, is one centered on proof. He emphasized this through the frequent use of verbs such as *probare* and *comprobare* and underscored them with syntax. Similarly, the law stresses Constantine's full control over the empire. The repetition of first-person pronouns and verbs makes clear that Constantine hears his subjects' concerns and that he responds to them. But ultimately what makes this text work in the way that it does is Constantine's mastery of language and syntax. The text's persuasiveness and larger message would have been lost without this.

Constantine did not reserve this style of speech exclusively for when he wanted to communicate with his subjects on a mass scale. Extant legal texts give the impression that he spoke in this manner frequently, regardless of context, audience, or subject matter. A letter that he wrote to an imperial official in 319 provides an apt example. In this text, Constantine laid out the proper method for executing individuals convicted of parricide:

> If anyone should hasten the fate of a parent, or a son, or of any relative whatsoever with the result that it be known by the name of parricide, regardless of

whether he had done this in secret or out in the open, let him meet neither the sword, nor fire, nor any other customary punishment.

si quis in parentis aut filii aut omnino affectionis eius, quae nuncupatione parricidii continetur, fata properaverit, sive clam sive palam id fuerit enisus, neque gladio, neque ignibus, neque ulla alia solenni poena subiugetur... (*CTh.* 9.15.1)

Constantine makes ample use of repetitive structures and language in these lines. The simplicity bred by repetition is offset by the poetic phrase *fata properaverit*, literally "to hasten fate." One finds close variations on this expression in classical texts such as Seneca's *Hercules Furens* (867), Ovid's *Metamorphoses* (10.31), and the poetry of Propertius (2.28.25). The text, thus, layers its clarity with poetic complexity.

The next line morbidly utilizes mimetic syntax: "but sewed into a leather sack and confined within its deadly closeness, let him mingle with the company of serpents" (*sed insutus culeo et inter eius ferales angustias comprehensus serpentum contuberniis misceatur*). The syntactical structure of *insutus culeo* and *inter...comprehensus* plays on the nature of the actions that Constantine prescribes. Just as the offender is to suffer confinement (among other things), so, too, do the very words that mandate his punishment.

Constantine concludes this section of the law by instructing that the convicted party be thrown into the sea – snakes and all:

As the nature of the region will determine, he is to be thrown either into a nearby sea or into a river, so that while still alive he may begin to lose every enjoyment of the elements, and so that the heavens may be taken from him while living, and the earth while dead.

ut regionis qualitas tulerit, vel in vicinum mare vel in amnem proiiciatur, ut omni elementorum usu vivus carere incipiat, ut ei coelum superstiti, terra mortuo auferatur

These two lines showcase syntactical features seen elsewhere in the text such as the repetition of similar phrases, but they also reveal some of Constantine's syntactical range. This is particularly noticeable in the final clause. We have seen before Constantine's fondness for chiastic syntax. Here, however, the syntax is interlaced. *Coelum superstiti* is juxtaposed with *terra mortuo*, interweaving an unmistakable, and haunting, comparison between polar opposites – heaven and earth and life and death.

Just as Constantine's edict on bureaucratic corruption showed that he utilized rhetorical and elegant speech when communicating key messages on a mass scale, his letter from 319 shows that he used this same form of speech when discussing meaner topics in a more private context. Constantine sought to persuade his subjects through high diction and sophisticated syntax regardless of audience or subject matter.

Constantine was far from being the only later Roman emperor to have done this. A cursory glance through extent legal texts from the fourth century suggests that, to some degree or another, all later emperors spoke and legislated in this elevated style. In 369, for instance, Valentinian and Valens used a style similar to Constantine's in a letter to a praetorian prefect, informing him that legal and administrative fees – like the ones listed on the Timgad inscription – are not to be charged on days of imperial celebration:

> Whenever the joys of happy announcements are made known to provincials and when any message is disseminated throughout the world, whether these are the illustrious victories of our soldiers or the slaughter of our enemies or our triumphs or those consulships, which we hold ourselves or impart to someone, are announced.
>
> *siquando faustorum nuntiorum gaudia provincialibus intimantur quotiensque quid per terrarum orbem disseminatur, seu militum illustres victoriae seu strages hostium aut nostri triumphi perferuntur vel hi quos geremus aut deferimus consulatus.* (*CTh.* 8.11.3)

Like Constantine, the emperors display a fondness for repetition and variation as well as for alliteration. They also make frequent use of bracketing and chiastic structures.

We can see another example in a letter from Theodosius I to a general in 391, instructing him not to allow soldiers to urinate or defecate in local drinking supplies:

> When the whole multitude of the legions halts upon the green banks of the rivers, by our farseeing authority we decree this: that no one at all may defile the common drinking supply with filthy excrement in the streams; nor while hurriedly washing the sweat off of horses may anyone offend the public gaze by appearing in the nude and thus mix drinking with filth and shock those who are looking onward. But instead, let him go far away from the view of all to the lower parts of rivers.
>
> *cum supra virentes fluminum ripas omnis legionum multitudo consistit, id provida auctoritate decernimus, ut nullus omnino inmundo fimo sordidatis fluentis commune poculum polluat neve abluendo equorum sudore deproperus publicos oculos nudatus incestet atque ita et turbido potum caeno misceat et confundat aspectum, sed procul a cunctorum obtutibus in inferioribus partibus fluviorum.* (*CTh.* 7.1.13)

A clever pattern is at work in this text. The first clause interweaves its words. But a terse main clause, in which the emperor invokes his "farseeing authority," suddenly intervenes and changes the flow to a more standardized Latin syntax (*ut ... polluat*) and takes advantage of similar sounding endings: *omnino inmundo fimo sordidatis fluentis*. Shortly into the following clause, the syntax flips again, this time to a chiastic structure (*deproperus publicos oculos nudatus*), which is succeeded by a second instance of interweaving (*turbido potum caeno misceat*) and then a return to chiastic structure (*cunctorum obtutibus in inferioribus partibus fluviorum*). The law offers an impressive piece of syntactical craftsmanship and shows that even the subject of human excrement merited the emperor's eloquence.

These latter two examples confirm what we saw before with Constantine's legislation. Regardless of context, addressee, or subject matter, emperors in late antiquity spoke and legislated in a lofty and elevated manner. They regularly utilized complex syntax, elevated diction, and poetic language. These were key features not only of the late antique legislative style but also of the Roman emperor's majestic and persuasive style of speaking.

26.4 Legal Texts and Panegyric

A handful of passages from late antique panegyrics demonstrates that the way later emperors spoke in imperial legislation echoed the way that Romans spoke about the emperor in ceremonial contexts. An anonymous panegyric for the emperor Constantius Chlorus delivered in the late third century offers a concise example:

> In this type of oratory, I perceived how much care, how much labor, and how much reverence there is even when I was engaged in the daily exercise of instructing youths. For although I am not able to do justice, in speaking, to the early accomplishments of your father and uncle in restoring the state, I am, nevertheless, able to assess them by counting.
>
> *Quo in genere orationis, quanta esset cura, quantus labor, quam sollicita veneratio, sensi etiam cum in cotidiana illa instituendae iuventutis exercitatione versarer. Quaevis enim prima tunc in renascentem rem publicam patris ac patrui tui merita, licet dicando aequare non possem, possem tamen vel censere numerando.* (*Pan. Lat.* 8.1.2)

The passage opens with the alliteration of *quo...quanta...quantus...quam*. More alliteration comes in the fast-paced line *renascentem rem publicam patris ac patrui*. The passage ends with a textbook example of chiasmus: *dicando aequare non possem, possem tamen vel censere numerando*. All of these same features appeared in the legal texts of the fourth-century emperors that we examined previously.

A passage from Claudius Mamertinus's panegyric for the emperor Julian in 362 (*Pan. Lat.* 3.14.3) offers a second example. While praising the emperor's industry and mobility, he wrote, "But our emperor adds to time what he extracts from his own leisure. He gives nothing to sleep, nothing to food, nothing to leisure" (*sed imperator noster addit ad tempus quod otio suo detrahit. Nihil somno, nihil epulis, nihil otio tribuit*). There is a noticeable bracketing effect in the placement of *addit* and *detrahit* in the first line. But more importantly, this is followed by the repetition of *nihil...nihil...nihil*, which is as unmistakable as the repetition of *ipse* that we saw in Constantine's edict from 324.

A third illustrative example can be found in a passage from Symmachus's second panegyric for Valentinian I, which dates to the late 360s. The passage displays a range of syntax and variation comparable to what we saw in Theodosius's letter to Richomer. It begins with a series of parallel structures:

> It harmonizes with your glory, it harmonizes with your skillful vigilance and cares that you enjoy praise in the camp and forum equally. No arts are silent; no industry is languid. Our voices have leisure for laws; our arms for borders.
>
> *congruebat hoc gloriae tuae, congruebat vigillis curisque sollertibus, ut campi pariter ac fori laude fruereris. Nullae artes silent, nulla friget industria: vacant ora legibus, arma limitibus.* (*Or.* 2.30)

The structural theme of these lines is a parallel ABAB arrangement. *Congruebat...sollertibus* introduces this theme. It is continued loosely by *ut campi...fruereris* and more closely by *vacant...limitibus*. Only the line featuring the repetition of *nulla* deviates from this structure, placing *friget* where the listener might expect *industria*. The next few lines in the passage follow a very different type of structural order: "Silence to great accomplishments is an enemy. What is glory, if there is silence? You have as many witnesses as the talents you have set free" (*silentium magnis rebus inimicum est: quid est gloria, si tacetur? Habes tot testimonia quot ingenia liberasti*). As the lines *silentium...inimicum* and *habes...liberasti* reveal, the parallel syntax of the first part of the passage has given way to a preference for chiastic structures. By switching structural styles so suddenly, Symmachus took his audience on a sort of syntactical tour in much the same way that Theodosius did in his letter to the general. The intention in each case was to overwhelm the listener by demonstrating a mastery of language and syntactical range.

The three passages above provide us with a sense of how similarly legal texts and panegyric must have sounded to Roman audiences in late antiquity. Both genres display a preference for some of the same rhetorical devices, techniques, and syntactical structures. Consequently, whether the words of the emperor himself were being read aloud in a town center or a trained orator spoke about an emperor in a theater, Romans could expect to be persuaded by a similar cocktail of complex prose rhythms and refined language and syntax.

26.5 Conclusion

The interconnections between legal texts and panegyric that this study illustrates make two important points about later Roman government and late antique literature. First, they stress the fact that Roman government and the emperor were not absent from the robust and creative literary activity of late antiquity. Rather, the manner in which emperors and their imperial consistories experimented with style and syntax and engaged with other literary genres such as panegyric demonstrates the government's participation in this activity. Second, the relationship between legal texts and panegyric underscores the existence of a late antique imperial discourse that must have shaped how Romans perceived their emperor. Late Roman government encouraged all Romans to view the emperor as a divine being, who spoke persuasively, authoritatively, and with unrivaled sophistication (Brown 1992; Kelly 2004). Panegyric acknowledged and reflected these attributes by describing the emperor as such and by speaking about him in a fittingly rhetorical and elevated manner. But, as this study has argued, imperial legislation actually put these attributes on display and showed them in action. In short, panegyric made the case for the emperor's majesty and grandeur. Legal texts helped prove it.

The above discussion is a cursory attempt to sketch out some of the more interesting similarities between legal texts and panegyric in late antiquity. A full study of the relationship between late antique legal texts and panegyric would include numerous other legal sources, especially epigraphic texts and the laws of emperors from the fifth and sixth centuries, which would show the continuation of the legislative style that the emperors of the fourth century pioneered. Another direction in which to take this conversation would be an examination of how the parallels between legal texts and panegyric evolved from earlier imperial history. The interconnections that this chapter has sought to highlight appear to be uniquely late antique and can likely be attributed to the governmental changes ushered in by Diocletian and Constantine. But that does not mean that earlier traces are impossible or even unlikely. A comparison of first and second century legal texts to Pliny's panegyric for the emperor Trajan could possibly reveal precedent for the stylistic nexus of legal texts and panegyric in late antiquity. A third direction would be a study of other late antique literary genres that influenced the authors of legal texts—especially letters, secular and ecclesiastical histories, and sermons. As with many of the literary forms discussed in the volume, the authors of legal texts in late antiquity appear to have expanded traditional generic boundaries and felt free to experiment and innovate. Undoubtedly, this involved far more stylistic overlap and generic borrowing than what this brief study has been able to show.

NOTE

All translations are the author's.

REFERENCES

Bjornlie, Shane. (2016). The letter collection of Cassiodorus. In: *Late Antique Letter Collections: A Critical Introduction and Reference Guide* (ed. Cristiana Sogno, Bradley K. Strorin, and Edward Watts), 433–448. Berkeley: University of California Press.

Brown, Peter. (1992). *Power and Persuasion in Late Antiquity: Towards a Christian Empire*. Madison: University of Wisconsin Press.

Cohen, D.A. and J.E. Lendon. (2010). Strong and weak regimes: Comparing the Roman Principate and the medieval Crown of Aragon. In: *The Roman Empire in Context: Historical and Comparative Perspectives* (ed. Johann P. Arnason and Kurt A. Raaflaub), 85–110. Malden, MA: Wiley Blackwell.

Dillon, John. (2012). *The Justice of Constantine: Law, Communication, and Empire*. Ann Arbor, MI: University of Michigan Press.

Honore, Tony. (1993). Justinian's Codification: Some reflections. *Bracton Law Journal* 25: 29–38.

Honore, Tony. (1998). *Law in the Crisis of Empire, 379–455 AD*. Oxford: Oxford University Press.

Kelly, Christopher. (2006). *Ruling the Later Roman Empire*. Cambridge: Cambridge University Press.

Matthews, John. (2000). *Laying Down the Law: A Study of the Theodosian Code*. New Haven, CT: Yale University Press.

Robinson, O.F. (1997). *The Sources of Roman Law: Problems and Methods for Ancient Historians*. New York: Routledge.

Watts, Edward. (2015). *The Final Pagan Generation*. Berkeley: University of California Press.

CHAPTER TWENTY-SEVEN

Handbooks, Epitomes, and *Florilegia*

Marietta Horster and Christiane Reitz

27.1 Introduction and General Remarks

… decem…libros…ad unum epitomae coegi, quod tibi misi, ut et facilius invenires quid quaereres, et apta semper materiis exempla subiungeres.

I have compressed 10 books in a one-book-epitome that I sent to you so that you can more easily find what you are looking for, and always add appropriate examples to your subject matter.

These are the words of Julius Paris, who in the late fourth century dedicated his epitome of the *Facta et Dicta memorabilia* by Valerius Maximus to one Licinius Cyriacus. According to his *dedicatio*, Paris has made the voluminous text easier to handle by epitomizing it into one volume (*facilius invenires* – so that you can more easily find). The text is therefore more useful to the reader (in this case probably the orator Licinius, who needs appropriate examples [*apta exempla*] for his speeches).

The compression, storage, and organization of knowledge are hotly debated subjects in our contemporary information era, too. The changes in media and the development of technologies have given rise to at least three different strategies for dealing with information, especially with literary products: (1) Unlimited storage, unlimited production, and unlimited access to texts by digitalization and online publications. This assumes that

---

A Companion to Late Antique Literature, First Edition.
Edited by Scott McGill and Edward J. Watts.
© 2018 John Wiley & Sons, Inc. Published 2018 by John Wiley & Sons, Inc.

there exists a worldwide community of responsible and sophisticated producers and of responsible and educated consumers, who are willing and able to find the texts and information they are looking for. (2) Reworking, reshaping, and selecting texts with unlimited access. The approach here is to provide a community of readers with a selection from the unlimited mass of texts and information. Selected items are meant to be accessible to everybody. By excerpting and reshaping huge quantities of text into consumer-friendly versions, new texts emerge. These are shorter, easily found, and ready at hand for consumers who have less time, who may take less pleasure in the search, and who, perhaps, have less education and less interest in deeply pursuing subjects real or fictional. (3) Critiquing, rejecting, or neglecting technological advances in the reading, writing, and storing of texts and information. Changes in reading and in mnemonic abilities brought on by information overload are criticized (see e.g. Carr 2010) and the pros and cons of digital editions are discussed (Ziolkowski 2011, on technocriticism and technomania in classical, medieval, and modern philology).

From the imperial period onward, books in the form of papyrus rolls were slowly replaced by parchment codices, that is, leaves bound together in book form. Important as this material change is for other contexts, mainly liturgical ceremonies, this was not a general media revolution: The production of many consumer-friendly, and often (though not always) shorter texts during late antiquity was not necessarily a consequence of this change in the materiality of texts (contra Piccione 2003). As a matter of course, the change of material and form was connected to changes in the material conditions for the storage and accessibility of texts. The accessibility and production of new texts were linked to the existence of many larger and smaller libraries (Cameron 1998). In the west there was a tendency toward decentralization, and different important centers cultivating letters and learning developed around monasteries and the residences of notables, emperors, and kings; but in the east, the main actor was the palace at Constantinople and its think-tank-dominated intellectual activities. The notion of "clarity and uniformity over controversy and diversity" dominated the "rule-based culture" of the Greek imperial bureaucracy and intellectual climate (Harries 2013, pp. 195; see also König and Whitmarsh 2007). The many existing monasteries, provincial capitals, and bishops' seats seem to have been of secondary rank compared to Byzantium, with consequences for the dissemination of literature (see Reitz 2005). This had an evident influence on the differences in the production and proliferation of literature in the eastern and western empire (Rapp 2005; Kruse 2015), and the *translatio* and reception of shortened texts into the Latin Middle Ages and the Greek Byzantine period.

As well as changes in media, shifts in the arrangement of books, and the localization of centers of knowledge during late antiquity, another current explanation (Herzog 1989; Eigler 2003; Banchich 2007) for the increase in condensed texts and collections of excerpts is that literature had lost its eminent political role in elite communication and in society as a network of common, canonical references. Furthermore, as the social, political, and cultural contexts of the pagan roots of classical texts seemed irrelevant or were even unknown in the contemporary culture of the *literati*, citations and excerpts could be presented as a stock of educated knowledge, detached from their original literary and historical context. Finally, it has been argued that rhetoric played a less important role in late antique society, and that late antique textual production, though diversified, was characterized by an "anti-rhetorical bookish mode" (Formisano 2012, p. 516).

These rather diverse modern interpretations and explanations for the increase in various modes of shortened texts reflect multifaceted ancient attitudes and make it likely that there was more than one reason to write and use abbreviated versions of texts (*epitomai*) or to collect excerpts that could be rearranged into *florilegia* and other collections. Yet preserving the tradition, albeit in an abbreviated and differently arranged manner, is a strong motivation behind the increased production of collective and condensed works. Late antique members of intellectual circles, from pagan senators in Rome to the monks and bishops in Cappadocia and Egypt, seem to have been well aware that the transmission of texts and of knowledge was fragile and at risk (see below). The desire to fight against this and to preserve the literature and ideas of the past is shared by pagans and members of the Christian church. It is notably illustrated in the demand for new editions and commentaries of canonical texts, such as Servius and Donatus for Virgil and Porphyrio for Horace, to name only the most prominent examples.

The various mechanisms and intellectual processes of collecting, reassembling, and abbreviating texts were by no means new and were not a phenomenon of late antique culture alone (Galdi 1922; Opelt 1962). Abbreviating and epitomizing is attested as early as the fourth century BCE. Historians such as Theopompus and Philochorus and philosophers such as Theophrastus and Epicurus published works in the fourth century BCE under the title *epitomai*. In addition, summaries of historical texts (Schepens and Schorn 2010), hypotheses of drama (von Möllendorff 2010; Mossman 2010), and précis of philosophical writings became an important part of Hellenistic and Roman literary culture (cf. Cicero, *Brut.* 15, on the practice of excerpting and epitomizing). Further examples of the abbreviating impulse are the verse summaries of Roman comedy (Sulpicius Apollinaris's of Terence) and the abbreviation of Livy's voluminous history as early as the first century CE;

however, the well preserved *epitome*, the *Periochae* of Livy was probably created only in the early fourth century (Chaplin 2010; Horster 2016), as were many other historical writings of the pagan past (Sehlmeyer 2009). Macrobius's *Saturnalia*, meanwhile, follows a tradition already in place in the second century CE (cf. Aulus Gellius and Athenaios), namely that of learned discussions at a banquet; authors working in that tradition amassed information on a huge variety of subjects in encyclopedic form. So, too, when Isidore of Seville in the sixth century compiled masses of etymological material, he was following his predecessor Varro (116–127 BCE) (Henderson 2007; Cardelle de Hartmann 2016). To create such encyclopedic compilations, a significant amount of excerpting, cutting down of information, and abbreviating was necessary.

To compose précis was a part of general education and rhetorical training (Cameron 1998). Yet abbreviation also figured in other educational contexts. When, again in the sixth century, Cassiodorus in his monastery at Scolacium organized a library and scriptorium and collected the texts for his *Institutiones*, his activity sprang mainly from the wish to preserve for posterity as much of the historical and literary tradition as possible. First he wanted to collect money so that he and Pope Agapetus of Rome would be able to install Christian schools in the city of Rome. But their plan failed because of the wars and violence in Italy. Undaunted, Cassiodorus chose another path:

> I was moved by divine love to devise for you, with God's help, these introductory books to take the place of a teacher. Through them I believe that both the textual sequence of Holy Scripture and also a compact account of secular letters (*saecularium litterarum compendiosa notitia*) may, with God's grace, be revealed. These works may seem rather plain in style since they offer not polished eloquence but basic description (*sed relatio necessaria*). But they are of great use as an introduction to the source both of knowledge of the world and of the salvation of the soul (*utilitas vero inesse magna cognoscitur, quando per eos discitur unde et salus animae et saecularis eruditio provenire monstratur*)...For learning taken from the ancients in the midst of praising the Lord is not considered tasteless boasting. (Cass. *Inst.* 1 praef.1; trans. Halporn 2004, pp.105–106)

As Cassiodorus demonstrates, the producers of abbreviated texts sometimes saw the need to justify themselves – and their readers. Another such justification is the topos of the important and hard-working magistrate or emperor who, pressed for time, has to rely on all kinds of shortened texts (cf. e.g. Pliny the Elder and Aulus Gellius). This argument finds striking expression in Eutropius's introduction to his *Breviarium ab urbe condita*. The emperor Valens (364–378) is said never to have had a proper education. Therefore, he does not know the names behind the stories, the *exempla* of Roman *virtus*. But because of his paramount Romanness, he follows his predecessors in virtue instinctively, due to his natural disposition and out of divine inspiration:

> *Res Romanas ex voluntate mansuetudinis tuae [Valens] ab urbe condita ad nostram memoriam, quae in negotiis vel bellicis vel civilibus eminebant, per ordinem temporum brevi narratione collegi strictim, additis etiam his, quae in principum vita egregia extiterunt, ut tranquillitatis tuae possit mens divina laetari prius se inlustrium virorum facta in administrando imperio secutam, quam cognosceret lectione.* (Eutr. Brev. 1 praef.)

> In keeping with the wish of your Clemency I have gathered in a brief narrative, in chronological sequence, the conspicuous achievements of the Romans, whether in war or in peace. I have also concisely added those topics which appeared exceptional in the lives of the emperors, so that your Serenity's divine mind may rejoice that it has followed the actions of illustrious men before it learned of them from reading. (trans. Bird 1993, p. 1)

An abbreviated version (*brevi narratione*) of these *exempla* and *facta* will give Valens pleasure and educate him about things that he had, by nature, already known.

27.2 New Genres and Christianity?

The increasing tendency toward "condensed texts" can be broadly ascribed to the changing intellectual climate of late antiquity, in which an already existent "world of words" was used to establish a new kind of metaliterary framework for reading and writing. Christianity was a crucial part of that changing climate. Danuta Shanzer (Shanzer 2009) claims that the Bible and noncanonical biblical texts, as well as the exegesis and paraphrase of the Scriptures, created a new textual framework in late antiquity. The Scriptures were the reference and the guide for texts written by the Church Fathers, for hagiography and martyr acts, for biblical epic and other Christian poetic forms, and for the narrative of a teleological Christian history of salvation ("church history"). Christian and pagan literary forms merged (Ronnenberg 2015). Biblical epic is an example: Juvencus, for instance, situated himself in the tradition of Homer and Virgil while also distinguishing his poetry from theirs. So pagan texts and practices were adapted rather than rejected. Likewise, Christian epicists reworked the Bible, by treating only selections of its content (thereby shortening the model text), by rearranging the sequence of its narrative, and by adapting individual scenes (or pericopes), including through both abbreviation and amplification (Roberts 1985).

Most Christian authors included in their texts pagan literary material drawn from a wide range of subjects and genres (cf. Cassiodorus, cited above); they ennobled their texts with the authority of the pagan literary tradition. There is no secure evidence that the cultural and moral claims of erudite Christians programmatically excluded parts of the literary tradition and, thereby, the values of the pagan past. The selection process of citations and excerpts followed other strategies. Among these, the physical arrangement of the available texts and the choice of material for, e.g. the *florilegia*, may seem rather simple. Christians integrated the earlier tradition and often made use of fragmented pagan texts. This fragmentation of pagan history and the perception of the remoteness of the reality behind it, of its lived experience, made it easy to integrate the former pagan literary world into the Christian world vision. The masterful and virtuoso reuse and even recreation of pagan texts was common practice, as can be seen also in the flourishing genre of the cento (see McGill 2005; Bažil 2009; Formisano and Sogno 2010). Faltonia Betitia Proba's fourth-century *cento Vergilianus* was the first to create a Christian cosmos out of Virgil's *Aeneid* by "singing" a condensed version of the creation of the world and the life of Christ in 693 lines (cf. Schottenius Cullhed 2015; Warner 2005, pp. 139–145 on "Virgil the Evangelist" from the fourth to the seventeenth century).

To explain the more or less versatile techniques of rearrangement, incorporation, and composition of late antique texts, it is often presumed that the transformation of the pagan world into the new, Christian context demanded a parallel process of cultural adaptation as well as new forms of textual production. But a large variety of *breviaria* and *epitomai* already existed in the pagan literary tradition. It may often be doubted whether it is necessary to identify a motive altogether different from the desire for easy and reliable access to information. The same method has, in fact, become common practice for modern readers living in the information era. However, the transformation of the pagan canon and its elements into other literary forms – partly expanding, partly abbreviating their sources – did accelerate in late antiquity, and it added new content and new genres to the Christian textual corpus. Thus social, religious, and political contexts played important roles, but there was no programmatic act set in motion by Christianity and the exponents of the new faith at a certain date. Moral implications might perhaps influence the treatment of a text where real historical characters are concerned, but they did not apply to transmission in general. Over centuries, the technique of systematizing knowledge and of providing new, more easily manageable forms for the chosen material remained the same. The increased number of condensed versions of all kinds of source texts from the fourth century may be remarkable, but it is only with the success of excerpt collections (Ihm 2001) like *florilegia, sententiae,* or the judicial *Digesta* and the flourishing of abbreviating forms of Christian poetry, including the Christian cento, that new modes seem to have been created within the already existing tradition. The selection process of the core texts, however, did not spring from a fixed ideology and did not follow a firm Christian plan. Few condensed texts were commissioned by the emperors – for example, the *Itineraria* dedicated to Constantius II in 346 or Vegetius's *Epitoma Rei militaris* (around 380; see Banchich 2007, p. 307). The emperors were not in the vanguard of literary production and of the trend toward condensation. Even Justinian's important judicial collections of the sixth century were rooted in the systematized organization and presentation of excerpts of the material law that the great jurists Gaius, Ulpian, Papinian, Paulus, and Modestinus of the late second and early third century had started. The Law of Citations (*Lex citationum*) issued by the western emperor Valentinian III in 425 (*CTh* 1.4.3) reflected the need to permit reference to earlier texts, even if the originals were lost. Second-hand arguments via paraphrases and verbatim citations were allowed only if approved by the authority of the five jurists named above (Harries 2013). This law expresses an awareness of how fragile and endangered the tradition and survival of texts were.

27.3 The Range of Abbreviated and Condensed Texts

During the fifth and sixth century, the full range of intellectual and textual approaches to the literary pagan and Christian world became more easily accessible and available to the interested reader. In addition to the texts based on a single source, this systematization of knowledge took place via the encyclopedic combination of excerpts, *hypotheseis,* summaries, and reviews. All these techniques were used in the compositions of some authors. Among those writing in Latin, one might name Martianus Capella (*De nuptiis Philologiae et Mercurii,* first half of the fifth century), Macrobius (*Saturnalia,* early fifth century), Cassiodorus (*Institutiones divinarum et saecularium litterarum,* early sixth century), Isidore of Seville (*Etymologiae sive Origines,* sixth century), and Ennodius (*Paraenesis didascalica,* late fifth century). Those writing in Greek included, for example, Stobaeus (*Eclogae, Florilegium,* fifth century) and, much later, Photius (*Bibliotheca,* ninth century). They all respected the traditional aspects of encyclopedic writing, namely *utilitas* and *ordo* (cf. Codoñer 1991; Formisano 2013). But they are also testimony to imagination, creativity, and fluidity beyond such functional categories, as they crossed the boundaries of subject matter (König and Woolf 2013). By choosing and arranging examples from a large reservoir of possible options, these emerging encyclopedic texts became exemplary in their own right and served as models for late antique, medieval, and Byzantine authors.

Less numerous and at the other pole of literary accomplishment are simple lists, being visually traceable, hierarchical arrangements of the written word. Lists present another attempt to give ordered access to the world of knowledge. The need for listing, too, is a phenomenon not peculiar to late antiquity, and it forms the basis for many cultural conditions and requirements in different ages (Asper 2007). Both methods – the encyclopedic approach as well as the bare list – dissociate the chosen part from its former context; they thus deconstruct and dehistoricize both its content and its form.

The methodological difficulty in reconstructing these processes of dissociation and reassociation is evident. The obstacle to detecting and describing the working principles and central issues of an epitomator is, in most cases, the absence of the original text. But even without the presumed original, the methods of textual criticism may permit us to deduce that different texts sprang from the same source: An identical or similar choice of words or phraseology, identical mistakes, and the sharing of a similar order are visible signs. These observations may then lead to the assumption of a hitherto unknown source-text behind the existing abbreviated versions. This was the case with the "Enmannsche Kaisergeschichte" of the late nineteenth century. It is supposed to be the basis for the epitomators Aurelius Victor (ca. 361); Eutropius (ca. 369); Jerome's chronicle (ca. 380/381); and other authors (Burgess 2005; Bleckmann 1997).

Florilegia, breviaria, and encyclopedias, then, were already a well-established and commonly practiced form for dealing with huge bulks of text and information. The techniques of abbreviating and rearranging were at hand when the need arose to reshape the world of information into a Christian context and to appropriate the philosophy and wisdom of the past into the present. This is a persuasive but not comprehensive explanation, because the same strategies were used by the pagan elite for pagan literary production, which continued into the fifth century. In the Latin-speaking part of the Roman Empire, in centers of Neoplatonic learning in Greece, and in some places in the Eastern Empire, these pagan authors as well Christians continued to compile and excerpt, to select and rearrange texts (Brown 2011).

Philosophical treatises, historiography, grammar, medical and legal texts, but also letters, laudatory oratory, biography, sayings of famous people, drama, and epic poetry – probably no subject and no literary genre from the late classical period was excluded from excerpting, summarizing, and compiling (Opelt 1962; van Rossum-Steenbeek 1997a and 1997b; Dickey 2007; Dubischar 2010). It was not the writing and compositional techniques, but rather new forms and contents of texts as well as the quantity of condensed texts, especially of sayings, *florilegia*, and chronicles, that created a new literary framework in late antiquity which differed from previous periods. Without doubt, the importance of various forms of shorter and compiled texts in the last centuries of antiquity is reflected in the survival of masses of medieval and Byzantine manuscripts with *breviaria*, *epitomai*, excerpt-collections, *florilegia*, *sententiae*, chronicles, and encyclopedias.

27.4 Handbook and *Florilegium*

An important *genus* of short-form text was the learned person's literary handbook. From the fourth century BCE on, these handbooks were focused on a specific subject, as is Varro's *De lingua latina* (first century BCE). Many "technical" treatises and lexica were based on extracts of their predecessors, combining paraphrases, citations, and summaries, as in Vegetius, *Epitoma rei militaris* (fourth century), the many legal compendia of late antiquity, and the impressive 70 (or 72) volumes of the *Collectiones medicae* of Oribasius (fourth century; van der Eijk 2010).

It has been observed that such handbooks follow various different principles of organization. In the Arabic tradition, the arrangement, even when the subject matter is similar, is very far from the Latin and Greek tradition, which at some point begins to make use of the alphabet (Overwien 2003), though not universally. Is it therefore possible to hypothesize that some of the organizing principles were devised independently in connection with specific handbooks? For example, the early Byzantine encyclopedic lexicon *Suda* (tenth century) does not seem to have an immediate predecessor. It has an alphabetic order and no specific subject-focus, whereas most of the known texts in integrating genres had a general overall topic or organized the broader contents under subject headings.

An example of the nonalphabetical, specific collection are, in the early imperial period, the *Fabulae* of Hyginus Mythographus, a reference work containing genealogies of deities and heroes, in 220 different short myths/stories (*fabulae*) and several lists (*indices*) of words, names, and places. The same Hyginus or a namesake composed the handbook *De astronomia* (or *Poeticon astronomicon*), which contained many excerpts, short summaries, etymologies, and lists. The main difference between these more-focused texts and the fourth-century *Chrestomathoi* of Helladius (in four books, composed in iambic meter) is obvious, even though we know his work only through the compilation of Photius: Helladius's *Chrestomathoi* seems to present a rather arbitrary choice of noteworthy things and examples explaining orthography, etymology, grammar, and the correct usage of words (forms of address, politeness, euphemisms, compliments, irony). The evolving mixture of notes on different subject matters and anecdotes about famous persons is not always transparent in aim and meaning. This is, at least, the impression we get from Photius, so that Helladius's work could be associated with the tradition of "Buntschriftsteller" seen in Aulus Gellius's *Noctes Atticae* and the "table talk" of Plutarch.

The *Florilegia* in the Greek and Latin tradition (Ihm 2001) usually followed in their content and organizing principles the same two formats: either thematic chapters (as in the *Sacra Parallela*) or alphabetical order, as determined by first words (as in the *Florilegium Marcianum* of the early ninth century [?]) or by authors' names (*Gnomica Basileensia*). Sometimes both methods were combined; thus an alphabetical order of chapters would be internally organized by subject matter, as in the early Byzantine *Florilegium Laurentianum*. In addition, these collections organize quotations into a hierarchy. The Old Testament is usually separated from quotations from the New Testament, and the Scriptures are then followed by quotations from patristic literature, which precede those from pagan texts. Subcategories might exist: for example, the excerpts from male philosophers first, followed by those from women (*Apophthegmata Vindobonensia*), and poets' *verba* first, followed by quotations from prose authors, as in Orion's *Antholognomicum* of the fifth century. Even though the *Corpus Parisinum* seems to have no such ordering principle, Gerlach (2003) assumes that the three main structural devices (author, subject, alphabet) still existed in the earlier *florilegia* integrated into the *Corpus*, but were artificially hidden in the later text.

Another example in which the ordering principles are less obvious is the anthology by Johannes Stobaeus (fifth century). It contains excerpts from more than 500 authors with a focus on philosophy and ethics, taken from poetry, history, oratory, philosophy, and medical authors (Bowie 2010). One might characterize Stobaeus's anthology as philosophical paraliterature. The new text, with its combination of citations, excerpts, compilation, and apothegms, and with its innovative organization by intertitles, created an original and hitherto unknown way for the reader to understand philosophy in a Stobaean manner (Konstan 2011; Searby 2011). This approach enabled the reader to forgo the individual philosophical treatises, each introducing a different philosophical school. Instead, the collection offered a well-organized repository of knowledge from which the fifth-century reader might make his choice. According to Rosa Piccione (2002, p. 169), Stobaeus set about instructing his audience by creating a "general inventory of the logically ordered world." His interpretation had a focus on "order" and thereby intensified the educational aspect.

Different didactic aims underlie Antiochus of Palestine's early seventh-century compilation known as the *Pandects of Holy Scripture*, in 130 chapters. The historical context for the book was quite dramatic, as Antiochus tells his reader: In 619, Ancyra was destroyed by the Persians, and the monks in the nearby monastery were forced to take refuge in other monasteries. As they could not manage to take all the books of the monastery library with them, the abbot Eustathius asked Antiochus to compile all the important texts into one. Even if Antiochus had a sharp intellect and was a quick reader and writer, this ambitious compilation could hardly have been the result of a life-threatening situation. In fact, the story is a telling metaphor for the process of collecting and storing knowledge that would otherwise be threatened with destruction: The collection serves as a refuge for texts and their content, protecting them from danger and preserving them from loss. The *Pandects* combine texts of early Christian authors with those of the Bible and create a list of moral sayings from the early prophets to the Church Fathers, organized under thematic headings. The last chapter, with a list of heretics, is an integral part of a text composed with the aim of becoming an authoritative guide to the "dos and don'ts" of a theologically and politically unstable world.

The threat of theological dissent was also the background of the *Breviarium causae Nestorianorum et Eutychianorum collectum* by Bishop Liberatus of Carthage in the mid-sixth century (Blaudeau 2015), even though he himself stated that writing was for him a distraction from the fatigue of traveling (as an ambassador of the African bishops to Rome). While writing about the two heresies of Nestorianism and Eutychianism, Liberatus was probably indirectly criticizing the schism and persecutions in the wake of Justinian's dealing with the "Three Chapters" (Leppin 2010; Keough 2011). The subject of theological authority and the right faith connects Liberatus to Procopius of Gaza (ca. 465–525), author of the *Eclogarum in libros historicos Veteris Testamenti epitome* for the book of Genesis. Procopius combines the *catena* tradition (though without mentioning the excerpted or cited predecessors) with a selection of lines from Genesis (Metzler 2015). Like Antiochus's text, Procopius's selection creates religious priorities and a hierarchy of theological and patristic thinking. Other Christian compilations include the two short versions of the martyrdom of Perpetua, which were created at an unknown date. These "Acta" had at least one more source than the main text of the *Passio Perpetuae*, as textual criticism has made evident (Kitzler 2007).

27.5 Other Forms of Compilation

Encyclopedism was another manifestation of the condensing impulse in late antiquity (although it was not exclusive to it; cf. e.g. the *Historia naturalis* of Pliny the Elder [23–79 CE]). As the intellectual concept of an all-embracing, universal, deeper knowledge of why and how things human and divine exist, encyclopedism is opposed to the selectivity and eclecticism of the etymologies and handbooks of the time. Encyclopedism seeks to unify knowledge, whereas other forms select from the universal cosmos of knowledge.

The aim of presenting masses of alternative, different, and even opposing explanations for the main questions concerning the visible world, mankind, God, and heaven, in combination with other physical, philosophical, and theological subjects, does not always lead to a reduction in the complexity of content or to a text in short form. The erudite Constantinopolitan patriarch Photius in the ninth century structured his *Bibliotheca* (Library) neither by content nor by alphabetical order nor by any other detectable system. He presents 279 reviews and book-summaries (epitomes) of varying length (Schamp 2010). His reviews probably lean on two types of predecessor: Alexandrian *hypotheseis* and the Alexandrinian *pinakes*, as the following example may illustrate. Photius's introduction to Memnon's work (FGrH 434) and his concluding remarks after summarizing the books give an idea of his working method:

> We read the historical work of Memnon from the ninth book to the sixteenth book. This history sets out to describe the noteworthy things which happened in Heracleia Pontica. It lists the tyrants of Heracleia, their character and deeds, the lives of the other [distinguished citizens], the manner of their death, and the sayings which were associated with them. (trans. Smith 2004)

There follows the epitome of Memnon's history. Photius then concludes with this:

> This history is intelligent and written in a plain style, with attention to clarity. It avoids digressions, except if its purpose necessitates the inclusion of some external events; and even then, the digression does not last for long, but concentrating on what is essential it returns neatly to the main course of the narrative. It uses a conventional vocabulary, though there are a few unusual words. We have not found a copy to read of the first eight books, or of anything after the sixteenth book. (trans. Smith 2004)

Products with less stylistic aspirations than Photius's eloquent summaries and reviews are chronicles and the *notitiae*. Some of these were bare lists, mainly produced to serve administrative needs, but they obviously circulated in copies as well. The so-called *Notitia dignitatum* (which had been originally two lists) is one such example; it explains in its first sentence what it is about: *notitia dignitatum continet omnium tam civilium quam militarium dignitatum utriusque imperii occidentis orientisque* (the list of dignitaries contains all civilian and military positions of both the eastern and the western parts of the empire). The following indices reflect the status of the structure and administration of the empire after 395 to 425–433. Though adorned with illustrations at the chapters' headings, the lists are simple and plain in wording and present the "skeletal elements of the administrative structure" of the Greek East and the Latin West (Brennan 1996, p. 149).

More complex but similar in its "subliterary" presentation and form is Jerome's *Chronicon*, based on Eusebius's early fourth-century Greek chronicle, but reworked and with additions up to the year 378. In his preface he describes his work thus:

> And so from Ninus and Abraham to the captivity of Troy it is a simple translation from the Greek (*pura Graeca translatio est*): from Troy to the twentieth year of Constantine many things are added or modified (*nunc addita, nunc mixta sunt plurima*), which we have carefully excerpted from Tranquillus and the other illustrious historians (*quae de Tranquillo, et caeteris illustribus historicis curiosissime excerpsi[mus]*): but from the aforementioned year of Constantine down to the sixth consulate of the Emperor Valens and second of the Emperor Valentinian, it is totally my own (*totum meum est*). (Jer. *Chron.*, praef. 4)

Jerome's chronicle is at the same time *interpretatio, imitatio,* and a new creation. The combination of various techniques in composing these texts (excerpts, additions, translations, completely new parts) form the basis not only of extended lists and chronicles but also of *breviaria* and *epitomai*, as some of their authors make explicit in their prefaces.

27.6 Epitome – the Transformation of Texts into a New and Condensed Form

A specific form of epitome is the condensation and abbreviation of literary texts, including poetry. Various influences triggered the need for such texts as the *Periochae Homeri Iliadis et Odyssiae* ascribed to Ausonius (fourth century). But in the *Ilias Latina*, a short version of the Homeric *Iliad* in 1070 hexameters, we have an example of an epitome of Homer that dates much earlier (ca. 68). This Latin *Iliad* from the Neronian period can be considered a rhetorical exercise that became a key text for the Middle Ages in the non-Greek-speaking part of Europe (Reitz 2007). The prose summaries of Pseudo-Ausonius, on the other hand, may already announce the decline of an audience that was equally familiar with Latin and Greek. They provide the reader of Homer with a guide through the long text. But the awareness that the Homeric epics and the history of Troy were part of an important cultural heritage generated not only these but also other texts. Thus the *Ephemeris belli Troiani* (fourth century) in Latin purports to be a translation of an earlier Greek version (itself, it is claimed, a translation of a Phoenician text) that gives an account of the Troy saga; the work is said to be a diary of the war from the mythical Greek hero Dictys Cretensis. Aligned with the *Ephemeris* as a piece of pseudepigraphy connected to the Trojan War, though with differences from that text in style, selection, and composition, is the account of the destruction of Troy supposedly told by the Trojan priest, Dares (fifth or sixth century); again, the claim (perhaps true) is that this is a Latin translation of a Greek source-text. These condensed accounts of events around the Trojan War (the term "novel"' does not seem appropriate for these texts) rely on their Homeric pre-text, but in the course of events they substitute for the original.

As already mentioned, such abbreviated texts (*breviaria, epitomai*) were already widespread during the Roman imperial period, such as Galen's medical auto-epitome, Justin's short history of Philip II, or Florus's *Epitome* in two books (*de T. Livio Bellorum omnium annorum DCC*, first–second century). These traditions were continued by the late antique Metz epitome on Alexander the Great (late fourth century with later additions), the epitomes of Valerius Maximus's *Facta et dicta* by Julius Paris, Januarius Nepotianus (fourth/fifth century), and Titius Probus (presumably fifth century), the epitome of Sallust's histories by Julius Exuperantius (fourth/fifth century), and the extremely short compilation of 1000 years of the history of the Roman people by Rufius Festus. The source of this fourth-century *Breviarium de brevario rerum gestarum populi Romani* is still disputed. Another example of a later historiographical condensation is Jordanes's (sixth century) epitome of Cassiodorus's *History of the Goths*. Short histories in the tradition of the imperial biographies include Aurelius Victor's *Liber de Caesaribus* or *Historiae abbreviatae* (fourth century), the anonymous *Epitome de Caesaribus* (fourth century), and Eutropius's *Breviarium ab urbe condita* in 10 books that ended with the year 369. They also include short Christian church histories like that of Epiphanius Scholasticus, who composed a *Historiae Ecclesiasticae Tripartitae Epitome* in Latin, based on the Greek church histories of Socrates Scholasticus, Sozomen, and Theodoret.

Theological treatises were also subject to epitomizing. Like the medical author Galen, Lactantius (ca. 250–320) saw the need for a shorter version of his own work, the *Institutiones divinae*, and described the technique and its consequences in the preface to the dedicatee (ep. pr. 2–3):

> *faciam quod postulas, etsi difficile videtur ea quae septem maximis voluminibus explicata sunt, in unum conferre.*
>
> I will do as you wish though it seems difficult to bring the content of seven voluminous books together in just one.

He continues with a warning that the argument might become unclear (*brevitate ipsa minus clarum* [by its very briefness less clear]), but underlines the goal of his effort: *diffusa substringere et prolixa breviare* (to draw together what was diffuse and to shorten what was prolix). But although Lactantius addressed his audience in the preface, we cannot assume that his approach is representative for audiences in late antiquity. The question of the implied readership has been debated as vehemently as the question of sources. Sehlmeyer (2009) assumes that historical *breviaria* were written for members of a less-well-informed magistrature and bureaucracy who had to keep up as quickly and easily as possible with the cultural background expected of persons in high office. But, as demonstrated above, there have been various suggestions about the question of audiences from the Roman imperial period on. Most often we will have to refrain from attributing a special target readership to the new formats. More important is the overall cultural and pragmatic context, wherever it can be reconstructed. Sometimes the readers are explicitly informed in programmatic statements about the intended audience and purpose of a work. Whether such statements are part of the commonplace formula in prologues and epilogues is difficult to decide. Nevertheless, we have to keep in mind that, irrespective of such authorial comments, the creators of *epitomai* bring a literary intention to their work and engage consciously with the new form.

27.7 Conclusion

We have seen that there are various reasons for the development and flourishing state in late antiquity of the diverse genres that can be subsumed under the term "condensed texts." Reading and using an organized library becomes more common. In addition, the Christian worldview leads to dehistoricization. This applies not only to the previous, pagan history but also to the history of the Christian world because of its teleological framework, in which man-made history is secondary and under the authority of God's will. In this changing intellectual context, readers were conscious of the vulnerability of transmission processes. The need for a reliable repertoire of references arose. These references are provided in the formats that have been discussed here: *epitomai*, handbooks, and *florilegia*. They, in particular, form the intellectual cosmos that preserved and organized, and sometimes reorganized, the treasury of knowledge and wisdom that tradition had entrusted to the cultural elites in late antiquity. Condensing a longer text can also be a means of evading or of obliquely addressing controversial topics, such as Christian dissent. The end of antiquity and the reorganization of the political and religious world meant, ironically, that these shifting and unstable products of condensing, compiling, and collecting texts consolidated and formed repositories of knowledge for centuries to come.

NOTE

Translations are by the authors unless otherwise noted.

REFERENCES

Asper, Markus. (2007). *Griechische Wissenschaftstexte. Formen, Funktionen, Differenzierungsgeschichten*. Stuttgart: Franz Steiner.

Bird, Harold W. (1993). *The* Breviarum ab urbe condita *of Eutropius, the Right Honourable Secretary of State for General Petitions: Dedicated to Lord Valens Gothicus Maximus & Perpetual Emperor*. Liverpool: Liverpool University Press.

Banchich, Thomas M. (2007). The epitomizing tradition in late antiquity. In: *A Companion to Greek and Roman Historiography* (ed. John Marincola), 305–311. 2 vols. Malden, MA: Blackwell.

Bažil, Martin. (2009). *Centones Christiani. Métamorphoses d'une forme intertextuelle dans la poésie latine chrétienne de l'Antiquité tardive*. Paris: Études Augustiniennes.

Blaudeau, Philippe. (2015). Adapter le genre du bréviaire plutôt qu'écrire une histoire ecclésiastique? Autour du choix retenu par Liberatus. In: *Shifting Genres in Late Antiquity*. (ed. Geoffrey Greatrex and Hugh Elton), 69–80. Farnham: Ashgate.

Bleckmann, Bruno. (1997). Überlegungen zur Enmannschen Kaisergeschichte und zur Formung historischer Traditionen in tetrarchischer und konstantinischer Zeit. In: *Historiae Augustae Colloquium Bonnense* (ed. Giorgio Bonamente and Karl Rosen), 11–37. Bari: Edipuglia.

Bowie, Ewen. L. (2010). Stobaeus and early Greek lyric, elegiac and iambic poetry. In: *Condensing Texts – Condensed Texts*. (ed. Marietta Horster and Christiane Reitz), 587–617. Stuttgart: Franz Steiner.

Brennan, Peter. (1996). The *Notitia Dignitatum*. In *Les littératures techniques dans l'antiquité romaine* (ed. Claude Nicolet), 147–178. Entretiens Fondation Hardt 42. Geneva: Fondation Hardt.

Brown, Peter. (2011). Concluding remarks. In: *Pagans and Christians in the Roman Empire: The Breaking of a Dialogue (IVth-VIth century A.D.)* (ed. Peter Brown and Rita Lizzi Testa), 599–608. Vienna: LIT.

Burgess, Richard W. (2005). A common source for Jerome, Eutropius, Festus, Ammianus, and the *Epitome de Casearibus* between 358 and 378, along with further thoughts on the date and the nature of the *Kaisergeschichte*. *Classical Philology* 100: 166–192.

Cameron, Averil. (1998). Education and literary culture. In: *Cambridge Ancient History 13: The Late Empire, A.D. 337–425* (ed. Averil Cameron and Peter Garnsey), 665–707. Cambridge: Cambridge University Press.

Cardelle de Hartmann, Carmen. (2016). Wissensorganisation und Wissensvermittlung im ersten Teil von Isidors Etymologiae (Bücher I-X). In: *Exzerpieren – Kompilieren – Tradieren. Transformationen des Wissens zwischen Spätantike und Frühmittelalter* (ed. Stephan Dusil, Gerald Schwedler, and Raphael Schwitter), 85–104. Berlin: De Gruyter.

Carr, Nicholas. (2010). *The Shallows: What the Internet Is Doing to our Brains*. New York: Norton.

Chaplin, Jane D. (2010). The Livian *Periochae* and the last republican writer. In: *Condensing Texts – Condensed Texts* (ed. Marietta Horster and Christiane Reitz), 451–468. Stuttgart: Franz Steiner.

Cordoñer, Carmen. (1991). De l'antiquité au moyen age: Isidore de Seville. In: *L'encyclopédisme. Actes du colloque de Caen 12–16 janvier 1987* (ed. Annie Becq), 19–35. Paris: Klincksieck.

Dickey, Eleanor. (2007). *Ancient Greek Scholarship*. Oxford: Oxford University Press.

Dubischar, Markus. (2010). Survival of the most condensed: Auxiliary texts, communications theory, and condensation of knowledge. In: *Condensing Texts – Condensed Texts* (ed. Marietta Horster and Christiane Reitz), 39–67. Stuttgart: Franz Steiner.

Eigler, Ulrich. (2003). *Lectiones vetustatis. Römische Literatur und Geschichte in der lateinischen Literatur der Spätantike*. Munich: Beck.

Formisano, Marco. (2012). Late antiquity, new departures. In: *Medieval Latin Literature* (ed. Ralph J. Hexter and David Townsend), 509–534. Oxford: Oxford University Press.

Formisano, Marco. (2013). Late Latin encyclopaedism. Towards a new paradigm of practical knowledge. In: *Encyclopaedism from Antiquity to the Renaissance* (ed. Jason König and Greg Woolf), 197–253. Cambridge: Cambridge University Press.

Formisano, Marco, Sogno, Cristiana. (2010). Petite poésie portable. The cento in its late antique context. In: *Condensing Texts – Condensed Texts* (ed. Marietta Horster and Christiane Reitz), 375–392. Stuttgart: Franz Steiner.

Galdi, Marco. (1922). *L'epitome nella letteratura Latina*. Napoli: Frederico & Ardia.

Gerlach, Jens. (2003). Der gedankenlose Excerptor? Anmerkungen zur Praxis byzantinischer Gnomologen und ihrer philologischen Erfassung. In: *Selecta Colligere,*

1. *Akten des Kolloquiums "Sammeln, Neuordnen, Neues Schaffen. Methoden der Überlieferung von Texten in der Spätantike und in Byzanz" (Jena, 21.–23. November 2002)* (ed. Rosa Maria Piccione and Matthias Perkams), 69–93. Alessandria: Edizioni dell'Orso.

Halporn, James W. (2004). *Cassiodorus, Institutions of Divine and Secular Learning and on the Soul* (trans. with notes J.W. Halporn; intro. Mark Vessey), Liverpool: Liverpool University Press.

Harries, Jill. (2013). Encyclopaedias and autocracy: Justinian's encyclopaedia of Roman law. In: *Encyclopaedism from Antiquity to the Renaissance* (ed. Jason König and Greg Woolf), 178–196. Cambridge: Cambridge University Press.

Henderson, John. (2007). *The Medieval World of Isidore of Seville: Truth from Words.* Cambridge: Cambridge University Press.

Herzog, Reinhart. ed. (1989). *Restauration und Erneuerung. Die lateinische Literatur von 284 bis 374 n. Chr.* Munich: Beck.

Horster, Marietta. (2016). Livius-Epitome: ein spätantiker Blick auf die (kurzgefasste) römische Republik. In: *Exzerpieren – Kompilieren – Tradieren. Transformationen des Wissens zwischen Spätantike und Frühmittelalter* (ed. Stephan Dusil, Gerald Schwedler, and Raphael Schwitter), 25–48. Berlin: De Gruyter.

Ihm, Sibylle. (2001). *Ps.-Maximus Confessor. Erste kritische Edition einer Redaktion des sacro-profanen Florilegiums "Loci communes".* Stuttgart: Franz Steiner.

Keough, Shawn W.J. (2011). Episcopal succession as a criterion of communion: The rise of rival episcopal genealogies in Alexandria according to Liberatus of Carthage. In: *Episcopal Elections in Late Antiquity* (ed. Johan Leemans, Peter Van Nuffelen, Shawn W. J. Keough et al.), 389–410. Berlin: De Gruyter.

Kitzler, Petr. (2007). *Passio Perpetuae* and *Acta Perpetuae*: Between tradition and innovation. *Listy filologické* 130: 1–19.

Konstan, David. (2011). Excerpting as a reading practice. In: *Thinking Through Excerpts: Studies on Stobaeus.* (ed. Gretchen Reydams-Schils), 9–22. Turnhout: Brepols.

König, Jason and Whitmarsh, Tim. ed. (2007). *Ordering Knowledge in the Roman Empire.* Cambridge: Cambridge University Press.

König, Jason and Woolf, Greg. (2013). Introduction. In: *Encyclopaedism from Antiquity to the Renaissance* (ed. Jason König and Greg Woolf), 1–20. Cambridge: Cambridge University Press.

Kruse, Marion. (2015). A Justinianic debate across genres on the state of the Roman Republic. In: *Shifting Genres in Late Antiquity* (ed. Geoffrey Greatrex and Hugh Elton), 233–246. Farnham: Ashgate.

Leppin, Hartmut. (2010). Das Bild der Kaiser bei Liberatus. *Zeitschrift für antikes Christentum* 14: 149–165.

McGill, Scott. (2005). *Virgil Recomposed: The Mythological and Secular Virgilian Centos in Antiquity.* Oxford: Oxford University Press.

Metzler, Karin. (2015). *Prokop von Gaza. Eclogarum in libros historicos Veteris Testamenti Epitome: Der Genesiskommentar.* Berlin: De Gruyter.

Mossman, Judith. (2010). Reading the Euripidean hypothesis. In: *Condensing Texts – Condensed Texts* (ed. Marietta Horster and Christiane Reitz), 247–268. Stuttgart: Franz Steiner.

Opelt, Ilona. (1962). Epitome. In: *Reallexikon für Antike und Christentum 5*, 944–973. Stuttgart: Hiersemann.

Overwien, Oliver. (2003). Hunayn b. Isḥāq. Ādāb al-falāsifa: Griechische Inhalte in einer arabischen Spruchsammlung. In: *Selecta Colligere, 1. "Akten des Kolloquiums Sammeln, Neuordnen, Neues Schaffen. Methoden der Überlieferung von Texten in der Spätantike und in Byzanz" (Jena, 21.–23. November 2002)* (ed. Rosa Maria Piccione and Matthias Perkams), 95–115. Alessandria: Edizioni dell'Orso.

Piccione, Rosa Maria. (2002). Encyclopédisme et *enkyklios paideia*? À propos de Jean Stobée et de l'Anthologion. In: *Philosophie antique*, 2: 169–97.

Piccione, Rosa Maria. (2003). Sammeln, Neuordnen, Neues Schaffen. Eine Perspektive der Forschung. In: *Selecta Colligere, 1. "Akten des Kolloquiums Sammeln, Neuordnen, Neues Schaffen. Methoden der Überlieferung von Texten in der Spätantike und in Byzanz" (Jena, 21.–23. November 2002)* (ed. Rosa Maria Piccione and Matthias Perkams), VII–XIV. Alessandria: Edizioni dell'Orso.

Rapp, Claudia. (2005). Literary culture under Justinian. In: *The Cambridge Companion to the Age of Justinian* (ed. Michael Maas), 376–398. Cambridge: University Press.

Reitz, Christiane. (2005). Library (CT). In: *Brill's New Pauly Encyclopaedia of the Ancient World* (ed. Hubert Cancik and Helmuth Schneider). Leiden: Brill Online. http://referenceworks.brillonline.com/entries/brill-s-new-pauly/library-ct-e1305340 (accessed 2 December 2017).

Reitz, Christiane. (2007). Verkürzen und Erweitern. Literarische Techniken für eilige Leser? Die "Ilias Latina" als poetische Epitome. *Hermes* 135: 334–351.

Roberts, Michael. (1985). *Biblical Epic and Rhetorical Paraphrase in Late Antiquity*. Liverpool: Francis Cairns.

Ronnenberg, Karsten. (2015). *Mythos bei Hieronymus. Zur christlichen Transformation paganer Erzählungen in der Spätantike*. Stuttgart: Franz Steiner.

Schamp, Jacques. (2010). Photius Abréviateur. In: *Condensing Texts – Condensed Texts* (ed. Marietta Horster and Christiane Reitz), 649–734. Stuttgart: Franz Steiner.

Schepens, Guido and Schorn, Stefan. (2010). Verkürzungen in und von Historiographie in klassischer und hellenistischer Zeit. In: *Condensing Texts – Condensed Texts* (ed. Marietta Horster and Christiane Reitz), 395–434. Stuttgart: Franz Steiner.

Schottenius Cullhed, Sigrid. (2015). *Proba the Prophet: The Christian Virgilian Cento of Faltonia Betitia Proba*. Leiden: Brill.

Searby, David M. (2011). The intertitles in Stobaeus: Condensing culture. In: *Thinking Through Excerpts: Studies on Stobaeus* (ed. Gretchen Reydams-Schils), 23–70. Turnhout: Brepols.

Sehlmeyer, Markus. (2009). *Geschichtsbilder für Pagane und Christen: Res Romanae in den spätantiken Breviaren*. Berlin: De Gruyter.

Shanzer, Danuta. (2009). Literature, history, periodization, and the pleasures of the Latin literary history of late antiquity. *History Compass* 7: 917–954.

Smith, Andrew. transl. (2004). Memnon: History of Heracleia. http://www.attalus.org/translate/memnon1.html (accessed 2 December 2017).

Van der Eijk, Philip. (2010). Principles and practices of compilation and abbreviation in the medical "encyclopaedias" of late antiquity. In: *Condensing Texts – Condensed Texts* (ed. Marietta Horster and Christiane Reitz), 519–554. Stuttgart: Franz Steiner.

Van Rossum-Steenbeek, Monique. (1997a). *Greek Readers' Digests? Studies on a Selection of Greek Sub-Literary Papyri*. Leiden: Brill.

Van Rossum-Steenbeek, Monique. (1997b). The so-called Homeric anthologies. In: *Akten des 21. Papyrologenkongresses in Berlin. 13–19.8.1995* (ed. Bärbel Kramer et al.), 991–995. Stuttgart: Teubner.

Von Möllendorff, Peter. (2010). Werbende Dichtung. Die ὑποθέσεις ἔμμετροι der Komödien des Aristophanes. In: *Condensing Texts – Condensed Texts* (ed. Marietta Horster and Christiane Reitz), 269–287. Stuttgart: Franz Steiner.

Warner, James C. (2005) *The Augustinian Epic, Petrarch to Milton*. Ann Arbor, MI: University of Michigan Press.

Ziolkowski, Jan M. (2011). *De laude scriptorum manualium* and *De laude editorium*: From script to print, from print to bytes. In: *Ars edendi Lecture Series*, vol. 1 (ed. Erika Kihlman and Denis Searby), 25–58. Stockholm: Stockholm University Press.

CHAPTER TWENTY-EIGHT

Grammar

Alessandro Garcea

28.1 A Textual Typology for Latin Grammar in Late Antiquity

According to a well-known, traditional classification best expressed in the late scholia to Dionysius Thrax's *tekhnê*, "Grammar is constituted by four parts: textual criticism, reading aloud, interpretation, and judgment; it uses four tools: glossematical, historical, metrical, and technical" (*GG* 1/3,10,8–10; cf. also 164,9–11; 170,18–20). Technical grammar, meanwhile, was divided into three subunits, which were probably isolated by Asclepiades of Myrlea (end of second century BCE), quoted by Sextus Empiricus (*M.* 1.92): "The technical part is that in which they make arrangements concerning (1) the elements and the parts of a sentence, (2) orthography, and (3) Hellenism, and what follows from these" (trans. after D. L. Blank; see Barwick 1922, pp. 223–229, with the necessary updates by Blank 2000). This chapter will show how these fields evolved in late antiquity, giving some examples for each topic that they covered. It will also emphasize that in this period the teaching of Latin gave birth not only to already familiar, elementary "cahiers d'écolier" but also to complex "livres du maître," including as many aspects of grammar as deemed necessary to represent Latin language and culture. This phenomenon is evident in the textual transmission through pre-Carolingian and Carolingian encyclopedic miscellanies (De Nonno 2000; De Paolis 2003), as well as in the conception of the *artes* themselves. They tend to become polyvalent, encyclopedic works, not necessarily written inside the schools, as proved by authors like Consentius, *uir clarissimus* from a Narbonnaise *gens*, Macrobius, *uir clarissimus et inlustris*, or Mallius Theodorus, *cos.* 399, as well as by aristocratic addressees like the *Iulianus consul ac patricius* or Q. Aurelius Memmius Symmachus *iunior*, *cos.* 485, in the case of Priscian's works (De Nonno 2009). By the presence of their names in the prefaces (Munzi 1992, pp. 110–116), they demonstrate that grammar acquired an organic and prestigious place in the cultural system of late antiquity. Thus, grammar could also become an essential feature in extensive works like the third book of Martianus Capella's *De nuptiis Philologiae et Mercurii*, providing many inflectional paradigms (*regulae nominum* and *canones uerborum*), or the first book of *Origines* written by Isidore (560–636), bishop of Seville and Toledo, who inaugurated a Christianization of this discipline.

The first subunit of the technical *ars grammatica* reveals an "ascendant," threefold structure, which, taken as a whole, represented the overall ancient conception of the language. So for example, following Varronian theories (*GRF* 237 Funaioli), Diomedes states:

> [I] the first steps of the grammar are taken from the phonic units (*elementa*), the phonic units are represented by the graphophonic units (*litterae*), the graphophonic units are associated in the syllables (*syllabae*), the lexical unit (*dictio*) is formed by the syllables, [II] the lexical units are organized in the parts of speech (*partes orationis*), the speech resumes itself to the parts of speech, [III] virtue (*uirtus*) is an ornament of the speech and it is used not to make faults (*uitia*) (*GL* 1,426,32–427,2, my translation).

Teachers and students must recognize this method of progressively "boxing up" the linguistic units of the lower levels into higher-level structures through their visual memory, which could limit itself to the internal, imaginative sight (*oculi mentis*) or be revealed by every kind of list and table, as medieval manuscripts show (Law 2000). The clearest example of this pattern is Donatus's *Ars maior* (fourth century CE), which is preceded by a basic *Ars minor*, devoted only to the parts of speech and written in the catechetic form of a *magister* interrogating his pupils. These texts became the standard manuals in medieval and modern schools. Their influence has been enormous, even for the constitution of the grammatical categories of both modern Romance and non-Romance languages (see Auroux 1994, pp. 82–85: "grammaire latine étendue").

To understand the constitution of this theoretical knowledge, it would be an error to think, as Karl Barwick (1922) did, that, except for some secondary differences that would be imputable to pedagogical practices, late grammarians passively adopted a putative Stoic model (the *tekhnê peri phônês*, for which see, e.g., Diogenes Laertius 7,44 = *FDS* 474) that supposedly circulated in Rome already in the age of Panaetius, disciple of Diogenes of Babylon and Crates of Mallos. The same pattern was allegedly followed even after the diffusion of Remmius Palaemon's Hellenizing model (first century CE), which is believed to have combined Stoic roots with the Rhodian-Alexandrian branches developed under Dionysius Thrax'a teaching (second century BCE). As a matter of fact, late Latin grammar included systematic manuals ("*Schulgrammatik*-type"), like Donatus's *Ars maior* and the *Artes grammaticae* written by Saint Augustine (extracts from an abridged version, *Ars breuiata*, of the original, lost work, in *GL* 5,494–496,14; full, new edition by Bonnet 2013), Marius Victorinus, Dositheus, Pseudo-Asper, and Pseudo-Victorinus (*GL* 6,187–205 ≃ Audax's *Excerpta*, *GL* 7,320–349). Nevertheless, there were also simple collections of basic rules and alphabetical lists for nominal and verbal analogical inflection ("*regulae*-type:" Law 1987; De Nonno 1990a, 633 n. 119), like Phocas's *Ars de nomine et uerbo* (*GL* 5,410–439,7 = Casaceli ed. 1974, fifth century CE), Priscian's *Institutio de nomine et pronomine et uerbo* (*GL* 3,443–456 = Passalacqua ed. 1999, pp. 5–41, including a section on participles), Pseudo-Augustine's *Regulae* (*GL* 5,496,15–524 = Martorelli ed. 2011), the *Frg. Bobiense de nomine et pronomine* (*GL* 5,555–566 = Passalacqua ed. 1984, 3-19) and *Regulae Palaemonis* (*GL* 5,533–547,2 = Rosellini ed. 2001). Pseudo-Probus's *instituta artium* gives not only exhaustive inflectional paradigms, but also lists of technical inquiries like *quaeritur qua de causa/quare*...(40 for the noun alone: *GL* 4,123,38–130,34). We do not know exactly if these works are the epigones of the third subunit of the technical *ars grammatica*, as Barwick strove to prove, because the *De latinitate* treatises by Pansa and Flavius Caper (second–third century CE) are lost, but, interestingly enough, this typology also contaminated grammars of the *Schulgrammatik*-type. So, for example, Sacerdos's *Artes* (third century CE) are formed of three books, which were independently redacted (De Nonno 1983): After the study of the parts of speech and the virtues and vices of the speech (book 1, the beginning is missing), come the nominal and verbal inflections according to the endings (*litterae terminales*) of each form (book 2: *GL* 6,471–495; a parallel redaction is known as *Catholica Probi* [*GL* 4,3–43]); finally, metrics occupies book 3. Similar cases are found in Consentius's *Ars de nomine et uerbo* (*GL* 5,347,8–31; 353,17–365,27), part of a systematic *ars* independently transmitted, and in the second book of a *De uerbo* written by Priscian's pupil Eutyches (*GL* 5,467,16–489,8).

Moreover, some *Artes grammaticae* elude the threefold structure. Charisius's work (*ca.* 360 CE, from Constantinople?) is formed by the juxtaposition of different sources, which mostly are declared. For example, in his chapters on adverbs, conjunctions, prepositions, and interjections (*GL* 1,180,27–242,12 = Barwick ed. 1964², pp. 233–315), Charisius first takes from Cominianus (early fourth century CE) a short, scholastic explanation; then he quotes the Alexandrian-connoisseur Palaemon; finally he adds long extracts from Julius Romanus (second half of the third century CE), probably more an amateur than a professional grammarian (Schenkeveld 2004), whose *Aphormai* (Foundations [of the study of the Latin language]) were a collection of rare and archaic words. In all likelihood, Charisius was an archivist at the imperial court (*magister scrinii*) who stated in his *praefatio* that he used his free time to write a work for his non-Latin-speaking son (Uría Varela 2006; 2009, pp. 7–11), in which he chose relevant topics that included those outside the traditional curriculum (see below, *Vices and Virtues*). Another complex *Ars grammatica*, written by Diomedes (370–380; Dammer 2001), starts with the eight parts of speech, like Donatus's *Ars minor*, but, like Charisius, it inserts before each of them specific remarks on their *accidentia* (genre, number, figure, and case) and a classification of the nouns according to their ablative; books 2 and 3 also present many peculiarities on rhetorical and literary matters (see below, *Metrics*).

One last important sign of complexity is that Donatus's acclaimed work gave birth to commentaries, in which his doctrines were explained and sometimes criticized, and on occasion his language was quoted as a linguistic model. Thus Priscian, concerning the use of *modo* with the function of *nunc* (*GL* 3,284,3–4), refers to Donatus (*mai. GL* 4,373,5–6 = Holtz ed. 1981, pp. 614,5; see also Holtz ed. 1981, pp. 240–241) in this way: *Donatus in secunda arte de nomine "sed modo nomina generaliter dicimus" pro "nunc"*. Unlike the anonymous and impersonal scholia to Dionysius Thrax, these works were written by historical individuals who could develop personal observations. Cledonius, a Roman senator and teacher at Byzantium, wrote a commentary on both Donatus's *Ars minor* and *Ars maior* (*GL* 5,9–79). Servius did the same (*GL* 4,405–448) and added a *De finalibus* (*GL* 4,449–455), conceived as a prosodic-metrical supplement. Likewise, Iulianus Toletanus's *Ars* (*GL* 5,317–324 = Maestre Yenes ed. 1973, ca. 687–690) included commentaries to both Donatus's *Artes*, supplemented by a *De finalibus syllabis* for the first part of the *Ars maior* (see the corresponding section in Pseudo-Marius Victorinus's *Commentarium*: *GL* 6,231–239 = Corazza ed. 2011, pp. 36–63, with two independent redactions), and by a *Conlatio de generibus metrorum*, derived from Mallius Theodorus's *De metris*, for its third part (excerpts from the commentary to the second part of Donatus's *Ars maior* are found in *GL* Suppl. ccxii–ccxviii, but see Munzi 1980–1981 for a new, complete edition). The African grammarian Pompeius rewrote many Servian materials on the *Ars maior* in a pleonastic and discursive form (*GL* 5,95–312): His "presentative" *ecce*, the use of the deixis, and the didactic repetitions give us the lively feeling of the work that was done in the classrooms (Kaster 1988, pp. 139–168). The first book of *explanationes in Donatum* (incompletely edited by Keil, *GL* 4,486–565; a new edition has been announced by Paolo De Paolis) testifies to the adaptation of the ancient, Peripatetic *zêtêmata* or *problêmata kai lyseis* to the scholastic practice: Some fictional, lifelike characters (*et interrogauit Filocalus...*, *et interrogauit Rusticus...*, *interrogatus...respondit*) give a lively style to the exegesis of the *magister* (De Nonno 2010, pp. 187–202).

28.2 Sublexical Level

The standard beginning of an *Ars grammatica* contains sections on graphophonemes (*de litteris*) and syllables (*de syllabis*), that is, on what we would consider to be phonological analysis of the articulated voice (Desbordes 1990; on the general *de uoce* chapter see Ax 1986). The linguistic unit called *littera* combines the written and the oral dimensions. Definitions like "*littera* is the littlest part of the articulated sound" (see *TLL* 7.2,1515,21–30) are based on articulatory parameters. Thus <X>, which corresponds to Greek <Ξ>, cannot be a *littera*, because it has a biphonematic character (velar plosive plus sibilant cluster). Other definitions distinguish the phonological and graphematic levels: "*littera* is the sign of the phonological unit and, so to speak, an image of the sound, which is susceptible to written representation" (see *TLL* 7.2,1515,38–49). So the parallel between the Latin initial aspiration and the Greek rough breathing led the grammarians to consider <H> as a graphic sign (*nota*) of a vowel's specific articulation, not a graphophoneme on its own.

The section on syllables (*de syllabis*; see Scialuga 1993) marks a profound difference from the supposed Stoic model of the Latin grammar in Barwick's reconstruction. If, pedagogically, the syllable is an essential step after having learned the alphabet and before passing to words and utterances, it has no place at all in the Stoic dialectical tripartition *phonê/lexis/logos* (cf. Diocles *ap.* D.L. 7,55–57 = *FDS* 476). Latin grammarians paid specific attention to the prosodic features of the syllables because of the importance of the metrical scansion (Leonhardt 1989, pp. 24–71): So, for instance, the *syllabae communes*, whose quantity is determined by the presence of sibilant, mute, and liquid clusters in the immediate context, are a recurrent topic.

Chapters on accents (*de accentibus*) and punctuation signs (*de distinctionibus*) refer to the suprasegmental units (see Ebbesen 1981; Müller 1964; still useful is Schoell 1876). The nature and position of the accent are studied through Greek categories, like the presence (*dasia* ⊢) or the absence (*psile* ⊣) of aspiration, and the joining (*hyphen* ‿) or separating (*diastole*ʾ) of the words of a sentence. This transfer of Greek theories causes many inconsistencies and obscurities for a modern reader (cf., e.g., Donatus *mai. GL* 4,371,31–372,13 = Holtz ed. 1981, 610,16–611,9), but, notwithstanding these difficulties, a general distinction is made between *toni breuis* (̆) and *longus* (̄), which indicate the quantity of the vowels, and *accentus acutus* (́) and *circumflexus* (^), which designate the places of a tonal heightening, respectively protracted or cursory. Almost always added by a "hand" that is different from that of the original scribe, those signs were indeed put on the Virgilian papyri and reveal the performative dimension of the literary texts, which were read aloud at school. For example, the bilingual papyrus *Nessana* II 1 (Scappaticcio 2012 no. 6: end of the fifth century–early the sixth century CE) gives *Aen.* 2,99 as follows: *Īn uulgum ambíguas et quaerere: cónscius árma* (l. 557–560), with accents that do not indicate the metrical *ictus*. Among the extant theoretical treatises, a late *De accentibus*, where one can find Priscianic materials (*GL* 3,519–528 = Giammona ed. 2012), contains interesting remarks on accents, aspiration, and instances of *sandhi*. A specific monograph on aspiration (*De aspiratione*) is jointly transmitted with Phoca's authentic work, but, in fact, it is a work of a humanist (*GL* 5,439,10–441 = Jeudy ed. 1976).

Orthography (*orthographia*) has a twofold aspect: It covers not only the correct writing but also the theoretical study of it (De Paolis 2010). Marius Victorinus's grammar (half of the fourth century CE), which is incompletely conserved, is the only comprehensive work with an extensive section on orthography (*GL* 6,7,35–26,13 = Mariotti ed. 1967, 70,18–90,11). This knowledge is justified by the scholastic *emendatio* of the books of literary authors, as shown, for example, by this remark: *non est, ut emendastis, "porca praecidanea," sed "praecidaria"* (*GL* 6,25,16 = Mariotti ed. 1967, 4,13–14). Victorinus's work also testifies to the late trend toward inclusiveness (see above, *A Textual Typology*), since traditionally autonomous fields (the second subunit of the technical *ars grammatica*: see above, *A Textual Typology*) are incorporated in that of the technical grammar. Most of the ancient monographs on orthography are lost, but two works of the age of Hadrian are preserved: Scaurus's and Velius Longus's *De orthographia* (respectively *GL* 7,11–33,13 = Biddau ed. 2008 and *GL* 7,46–81 = Di Napoli ed. 2011). Eventually, the new needs of the average readership produced a shift from the philological to a new, prescriptive approach: The written and oral competences of an increasing number of non-Latin-speaking people demanded to be emended and improved. So the well-known *Appendix Probi*, of uncertain origin and period, contains, besides miscellaneous materials, an orthographical *antibarbarus* (*GL* 4,197,19–199,17 = Asperti and Passalacqua eds. 2014, 20–27), which is immediately followed – in the MS Napoli BN lat. 1 – by a list of *differentiae* (see below, *Lexicon, lexica*), with problems of pronunciation, morphology, and semantics. The same features appear in a *De orthographia* dedicated to Eucherius (ca. 434–450), bishop of Lyon, by Agroecius, bishop of Sens (*GL* 7,113–125 = Pugliarello ed. 1978), and intended to be an integration of a homonymous compilation attributed to Caper (*GL* 7,92–107,2). These rather glossematic works had a strong influence on the high-medieval treatises by Bede and by Alcuin (redaction *a*: *GL* 7,295–312 = Bruni ed. 1997; redaction *b*: *PL* 101,902–920), henceforth alphabetically structured. Providing many extracts from ancient authors not otherwise preserved, Cassiodorus's own *De orthographia* aims at giving the classical linguistic and philological tools to a monastic community that devoted itself to the study and transcription of the Bible, so that errors in copying manuscripts could be avoided. Papiri(an)us's original work, besides a short, independent extract (*GL* 7,216,8–14), is partially preserved in Cassiodorus's excerpts (*GL* 7,158,9–166,8 = Stoppacci ed. 2010 § 4,1–109). Specific norms on <b> and <u>, which tended to overlap in their fricative pronunciation, are given in the sixth century CE by Martyrius's *De B muta et V uocali* (*GL* 7,165–199); Cassiodorus used this work too, distributing its four sections in chapters 5–8 of his treatise (Keil's edition puts Martyrius's text under Cassiodorus's, each one with its own *app. crit.* on the same page).

28.3 Morpholexical Level

Chapters on speech and its parts (*de oratione eiusque partibus*) start with the definition of *oratio* as "utterance by oral production, which is structured by words, as if it was an 'oral-ratio'." Only Priscian, who adapts Apollonius Dyscolus's model (see below, *Syntax*), takes into consideration both the grammatical consistency (*congruitas*) and the semantic autonomy (*perfectio*): "*oratio* is a coherent combination of words, which shows a complete meaning" (*GL* 2,53,28–29, my translation).

The taxonomies of the parts of speech are a recurrent topic (Garcea and Lomanto 2003). After having observed that a lexical element can replace an entire *oratio* "when it shows a full sentence (*plenam...sententiam*)" (*GL* 2,54,1–4), for example when one uses the imperative forms or answers a question by a single word, Priscian adds that there is another form of independence besides that of the monorhematic expressions. He thus refers to an Aristotelian pattern, opposing the semantically necessary and sufficient constituents of an utterance to the other parts of speech (*Ars grammatica* group 2013, pp. 11–16): "For the dialecticians, there are two parts of speech, the noun and the verb, because they are the only ones that, combined together without anything else, form a complete utterance; the other parts are called *synkategoremata*, i.e. co-significant (*consignificantia*)" (*GL* 2,54,5–7, my translation).

Chapters on morpholexical units can follow different structural orders (still useful are Schoemann 1862; Jeep 1893; new, important perspectives in Matthaios 2002). Notwithstanding Barwick's synoptic tables (1922, pp. 3–87), not only the sequence but also the definitions of the parts of speech vary significantly: Some of them are, traditionally, etymological and morphological, whereas semantic-referential definitions progressively became widespread, thanks to the diffusion of Neoplatonic terminology brought to Rome by Porphyry and assimilated by authors like Marius Victorinus and Donatus. So, for example, the stoic *definiens* "common vs. peculiar quality" of the noun (cf. Diocles *ap*. Diogenes Laertius 7,58 = *FDS* 536) recedes into the background in favor of the distinction between corporeal and incorporeal things (*corpus* as *res corporalis* vs. *res* as *res incorporalis*), be they individuals or collections. Starting from Donatus (*GL* 4,373,2–3 = Holtz ed. 1981, 614,2–3), this is considered the semantic proper feature of the noun, whose defining genus is being a part of speech and its species belonging to the case-inflection (see Luhtala 2002; 2010, pp. 224–237).

Bare inflectional paradigms are a common topic of the grammatical *regulae*-type (see above, *A Textual Typology*) and are best paralleled in the Greek tradition by Theodosius's *Basic Rules [Kanones] for Noun and Verb Inflection* (fourth-fifth century CE), commented upon by Choeroboscus and Joannes Charax (*GG* 4/1–2).

28.4 Vices and Virtues of Expression: Between Rhetoric and Grammar

According to Barwick (1922, pp. 95–101), chapters on vices and virtues of expression (*de uitiis et uirtutibus orationis*) form the "third part" of the allegedly stoic model of the Latin grammars, after the sublexical and the morpholexical sections; in fact, they are the most explicit signs of a late development in Latin grammar (Baratin and Desbordes 1986; case studies in Vainio 1999). Unlike Greek sources (cf. Diocles *ap*. Diogenes Laertius 7,59 = *FDS* 594), late Latin grammars treated multiple instances of transgressing the linguistic norm, both in a negative (*uitia*: barbarism, solecism) and in a positive (*uirtutes*: metaplasms and figures of speech) way. So, as forms of ornamentation, virtues lie beyond the grammatical correction and pertain specifically to the rhetorical field of textual analysis, already found in Cicero's ideal of the *elocutio ornata* (cf. *De orat.* 3,52–53).

The polar system "virtues vs. vices" is arranged in four categories, constituting the *quadripertita ratio* (Quintilian, *Inst.* 1,5,38: Desbordes 1983; Ax 1987): two quantitative variations, that is, addition (*additio*: A B C D) and subtraction (*detractio*: A B); a qualitative variation or mutation (*transmutatio*: A B E); and a permutation of the items (*immutatio*: A C B). Following a synchronic and normative point of view, which has no parallel in former texts (*Rhet. Her.* 4,29 on *adnominatio/paronomasia*; Varro *Ling.* 5,6; 6,2; 7,1 on etymology), late grammarians created a symmetric system, where the same type of phenomena was considered virtue or vice, depending on its presence or absence in poetry. An interesting example is given by the Gallic grammarian Consentius (fifth century CE), whose two independent sections of an autonomous reworking of Donatus's tradition are left. In his *De barbarismis et metaplasmis* (Table 28.1) he chose to take his examples of barbarism not from literary prose texts but from the lively language of his country (*GL* 5,387,29–393,3 = Niedermann ed. 1937, 3,19–13,8).

Isolated sections that are specifically devoted to rhetoric (*de rhetorica*) include an extract of Marius Victorinus's *rhetorica* placed at the end of his *Ars* (*RhLM* 238,20–239,19 = Mariotti ed. 1967, 96), the *Frg. Sangermanensis* on the synecdoche and the *hysteron proteron* (*GL* 5,328,12–20), part of a *Frg. Vaticanus* on the *chria* (*GL* 6,273,7–25), and, most notably, an entire

Table 28.1 Consentius's *De barbarismis et metaplasmis*.

uitium		*uirtus*
barbarismus		*metaplasmus*
	1) per adiectionem	
gruit ~ ruit	– prothesis	*gnatoque ~ natoque* (Virg. *Aen.* 3,12)
tottum ~ totum	– epenthesis	*Mauortis ~ Martis* (Virg. *Aen.* 8,630)
quandius ~ quandiu	– paragoge	*admittier ~ admitti* (Virg. *Aen.* 9,231)
	2) per detractionem	
onor ~ honor	– aphaeresis	*mitte ~ omitte* (Ter. *Ad.* 185)
uila ~ uilla	– syncope	*repostum ~ repositum* (Virg. *Aen.* 1,26)
magi ~ magis	– apocope	*do ~ domum* (Enn. *ann.* 576V.^{2} = 587S.)
prelum ~ plerum	3) per transmutationem	*Euandre ~ Euander* (Virg. *Aen.* 11,55)
bobis ~ uobis	4) per immutationem	*olli ~ illi*

chapter on the figures of thought in Charisius's fourth book (*GL* 1,283,15–287,16 = Barwick ed. 1964², 371,29-375,9). In fact, not only did Charisius, like Donatus, explain the Gorgian figures of speech by the same Ennian quotations that already *Rhetorica ad Herennium* (4,18) used to this purpose, but he also preserved ancient materials for all the procedures of the *ornatus*. Parallels with the exegetical field prove that grammatical commentaries to literary authors influenced Charisius's wide-ranging choice, including, among others, *dialogismos* (cf. Donatus Ter. *Eun.* 46–48), *paralipsis* (cf. Donatus Ter. *Hec.* 420,1; 473; *Phorm.* 168,1; Servius *ad Aen.* 8, 483), *ethologia – prosopopoeia* (cf. Donatus Ter. *Eun.* 15; *ad.* 308; *Hec.* 148; *Andr.* 286,1), and *epitrope* (cf. Donatus Ter. *Ad.* 132; 134; 991). This also shows that in the "third part" of the late *Artes grammaticae* "a double frontier… broke up: the frontier between grammar as system of language and grammar as text explanation; the frontier between grammar and rhetoric" (Baratin and Desbordes 1986, p. 231/2007, p. 81, my translation).

28.5 Syntax

In antiquity, the difference between morphology and syntax was not as clear-cut as it is today. Syntactic remarks could, therefore, find a place in the morpholexical sections of the grammars, like those on the *septimus casus*, on verbal constructions, on the use of some conjunctions with the accusative or the ablative, and so forth. Charisius's *De qualitatibus Latini sermonis et temporibus* (*GL* 1,262,25–264,16 = Barwick ed. 1964², 347,1–349,15) and Diomedes's *De declinatione exercitationis chriarum* and *De coniunctione temporum* (*GL* 1,310,1–29; 388,10–395,10) are particularly lengthy developments within *de uerbo* and *de nomine* chapters. An autonomous work, Arusianus Messius's *Exempla elocutionis* (*GL* 7,449–514 = Di Stefano ed. 2011, end of the fourth century CE), classified different nominal and verbal constructions with the help of many examples taken from Terence, Cicero, Sallust, and Virgil (the so-called *quadriga Messii*). In the last two books of his *Ars*, Priscian (end of the fifth–early sixth century CE; Baratin 1989, pp. 365–485) offers the most extensive treatment of syntactic, instead of rhetorical-stylistic aspects of the *oratio* (see above, *Vices and Virtues*). He here explicitly followed Apollonius Dyscolus's *Syntax*, but his work became more comprehensive (see below, *Lexicon, Lexica*) and offered a reinterpretation of the original, Stoic pattern in light of the contemporary, Neoplatonic debate on the Aristotelian categories (Luhtala 2005). This topic became widespread thanks to, among others, the commentaries on

Minucianus and Hermogenes and to the work of people involved in framing both the grammatical and philosophical discussion, like Philoponus, a sixth-century commentator of Aristotle and author of several grammatical treatises. Thus, for example, Priscian systematically used the words *substantia* and *accidens*, as only Boethius did, and rewrote his sources in order to show the reason why the noun precedes the verb in the list of the parts of speech (*Ars* 17, *GL* 3,116,25–27). In his eyes, action and passion (*agere et pati, actio et passio*) are the properties of the substance (*substantia*), whereas Apollonius (*constr.* 1,16 *GG* 2/2,18,5–9) took into consideration the dispositions of the body. The minimal utterance (*GL* 3,164,16–20) is also interpreted as the combination of a noun, that is, a *substantia* ($\simeq$ *sôma, ousia, huparxis*) and a verb, that is, an *accidens* ($\simeq$ *episumbainon*). This pattern is so extensively adopted that Priscian assigned accidental determinations not only to the substance but also to its dispositions (*GL* 3,123,13–124,3 $\simeq$ Apollonius *constr.* 1,35 *GG* 2/2,32,9–33,8): So *substantia ipsius actus* realizes the shift of the verb from its status of accident to that of a substance, whose accidents are the adverbs (*Ars grammatica* group 2010, pp. 85–105 with notes).

28.6 Lexicon, Lexica

Different semantic problems, from appropriateness (*de differentiis, de synonymis*) to valence in a bilingual perspective (*de idiomatibus*), are treated in cumulative lists, contradicting the idea of grammar as structured knowledge (Baratin 1994, pp. 153–154). Only Macrobius wrote a comprehensive essay on verbal morphology from a systematic perspective: His *De uerborum Graeci et Latini differentiis uel societatibus* (Stoppie, Swiggers, and Wouters 2007) is partially preserved in the *Excerpta Bobiensia* of the MS Napoli BN lat. 2 (*GL* 631–633), but it is also the source of the extracts taken by Johannes Scotus Eriugena in order to learn the Greek inflection (*GL* 5,599–630) and of an anonymous Latin treatise *De uerbo ad Seuerianum* from Bobbio (De Paolis ed. 1990 combines the first two and puts the third one on the opposite page). If Diomedes treats idioms especially in his section *de consensu uerborum cum casibus* (*GL* 1,310,30–320,9; see Baratin 1989, pp. 117–201), the MS Napoli BN lat. IV.A.8 adds at the end of Charisius's grammar many *idiomata, synonyma*, and *differentiae*. These sections, regarded as authentic by Barwick (1922, pp. 56–61) and accordingly edited by him (ed. 1964[2], 387-480), reveal indeed some significant parallels with the corresponding passages in Dositheus (see below) and *Ars Bobiensis* (*GL* 1,552,23–554,33 = De Nonno ed. 1982, 32,1–35,33). While this is a clear sign of a Charisian origin,

Charisius certainly did not conceive these passages in their actual form (De Nonno ed. 1982, 59 n. 7). As for Priscian, he concludes his *Ars* with a list of about 340 examples extracted from a monolingual syntactic lexicon of Attic authors (like that of *anecd. Gr.* 1,117–180 Bekker = Petrova ed. 2006) and enriched with Latin parallels (Martorelli 2014): for example, *GL* 3,281,7 = Rosellini ed. 2015, 10,3, *ausculto tibi* or *te* (with Terence *Andr.* 209 and 536) – ἀκρῶμαι σοῦ or σέ (with Aeschines 3,192). Besides the anonymous *De dubiis nominibus* (*GL* 5,571–594 = Glorie ed. 1968: 755–820; mid-seventh century CE) and Pseudo-Caper's *de uerbis dubiis* (*GL* 7,107,4–112, a list of *differentiae* including late words like *atramentarium* and *lignarium*), independent works on this topic are a typical product of the late Latin and medieval culture (Brugnoli 1955; Magallón García 1996), which could stem from different grammatical sources and from commentaries to literary authors (Stok 2008).

The bilingual *Ars grammatica* written by Dositheus (fourth century CE) is followed by a long list of Latin verbs with their Greek parallels (*GL* 7,430,1–436,4 = Tolkiehn ed. 1913, 95,7–104,10, Bonnet ed. 2005 leaves out this section). After this work, the MS Sankt Gallen StiftsB 902 also gives a collection of bilingual texts, usually referred to as *Hermeneumata Pseudodositheana* and known in nine different versions: the eight that are edited in volume 3 of the *Corpus glossariorum Latinorum* and the ninth of the MS Wien ÖNB suppl. gr. 43, containing the transcription of a lost manuscript by Conrad Celtes (1495). Parts of these texts were conceived as a tool for learning both elementary Latin and elementary Greek; others were addressed to adults who needed to learn Latin as the language of the bureaucracy in the eastern part of the Empire or Greek in provinces like Egypt. Eventually, they were used in the West by a more erudite and select Latin-speaking public, who were specifically interested in Greek. The *Hermeneumata* are formed by a multiplicity of elements: Alphabetical and thematic (*capitula*) bilingual glossaries share many resemblances with the *Appendix Probi* (see above, *Sublexical Level*); the *colloquia* provide the story of a pupil's everyday life as a bilingual conversational guide (Dickey 2012–2014); and other bilingual texts were added for reading practice.

The diffusion and mutual relationships of monolingual lexica in late antiquity are an extremely complicated issue (see the useful overview of the frequently obsolete and still incomplete editions of the Greek tradition by Dickey 2007, pp. 87–103; Dionisotti 1996 gives an excellent survey of the Latin *corpora* edited by Löwe and Goetz 1888–1923 and by Lindsay 1926–1931). Among them, Nonius Marcellus's *De compendiosa doctrina* clearly stands out as the most important Latin glossematical work of the fourth century (Barabino and Bertini 1967–1997; Bertini 2000–2005), with a vivid interest in grammatical problems, synonyms, and anomalies (books 1–12), as well as in lexical families (books 13–20). The sources are quoted following recurrent patterns, because Nonius takes extracts from 40 authors, which tend to appear in the same order (Lindsay 1901, with the noteworthy corrections by Cadoni 1987). This work was used by professional grammarians, as is shown by Priscian's use of Nonius's book 11 as a source for many of the doublets of more or less rare adverbial forms in book 15 of his *Ars* (*GL* 3,70,4–71,6 and 77,7–12). Nonius always provides the literary attestations (mostly among the *ueteres*), since they prove that these forms are acceptable, whereas Priscian is mainly interested in morphological aspects; thus he rejects *memore* (77,9–12), which is parallel to *memoriter*, even if it is used by Pomponius (*CRF*³ 109), because it does not fit into the pattern of the neutral adverbial forms ending in -*e* (*Ars grammatica* group 2013, pp. 52–54).

28.7 Metrics

Some of the *Artes* incorporate a section on metrics (*De arte metrica*: De Nonno 1990b; useful tools: Luque Moreno et al. 1987–2007; Morelli 2006). Sometimes related subjects are also developed, as in Diomedes's classification of the poetic literary forms (*De poematibus*: *GL* 1,482,13–492,14). Some commentaries also include this type of information, as shown by Evanthius's *De fabula* and the *Excerpta de comoedia* which precede Donatus's Terence. Traditionally, distinct works were written on metrics that pertained more to music (Cristante 1987, pp. 64–67; see e.g. Pseudo-Censorinus's *Epitoma disciplinarum*, *GL* 6,607–617 = Sallmann ed. 1983, 71,7–86,15) and rhetoric than to grammar. Within the grammatical field, these works were devoted more to criticism than to normative linguistic teaching (see above, *A Textual Typology*). Eventually, the inclusive character of the late Latin grammar inspired comprehensive, systematic works: Sacerdos ended up adding a third book, *De metris*, to his previous ones, whereas Diomedes planned from the very beginning a third section of his work on feet, poems, and meters, as did Charisius, although this part of his *Ars* is lost. Similar phenomena proliferate in the textual transmission: Aphthonius's monumental and erudite four books, *De metris omnibus*, were added to Victorinus's grammar without any indication, since they formed one single, unbroken text (Keil's edition still follows this incorrect presentation). Some overlaps with the rhetorical sections of the *Artes* were possible: So the treatise on prosody *De ultimis syllabis ad Caelestinum* ends with the section *de metaplasmis* (*GL* 6,262,18–264,16) and, on the other side, Consentius's *De barbarismis et metaplasmis* ends with the section *de scandendis uersibus* (*GL*

5,398,16–404,8 = Niedermann ed. 1937, 22,19–32,20). Since reading Horace (the only lyric poet who was taught at school starting from the second century) required multiple metrical competences, the commentary on *Odes* and *Epodes* of the pseudo-Acronian corpus in MS Paris BNF 7900A indicates the name of the verse as well as its interpretation and metrical scansion before the analysis of each poem. This information is also found in monographs ad hoc (De Nonno 1998). So, for example, Persius's friend Caesius Bassus first wrote a *De metris* on this topic (*GL* 6,255–272) and spread in the Roman world the "Pergamian" metrical system that obtained all metrical forms from the hexameter and the iambic trimeter through the *quadripertita ratio* (see above, *Vices and Virtues*); his work is transmitted with other metrical texts from Bobbio, especially Fortunatianus's *De metris Horatianis* (*GL* 6,278–304 = Morelli ed. 2011–2012, fourth century). Servius, who frequently quoted Horace in his commentary to Virgil and wrote two other essays on prosody (*de finalibus*) and metrics (*centimeter*: *GL* 4,456–467 = Elice ed. 2013), is also the author of a *de metris Horatii* (*GL* 4,468–472). Another example of this genre is an apocryphal *De metris Horatianis* (*GL* 6,174–184) that follows Aphthonius's work in the MSS. Priscian, who paid attention to the relationship between prosody and morphology and put a metrical *précis* at the beginning of his *Partitiones* (*GL* 3,459,3–461,14 = Passalacqua ed. 1999, 45,4–48,10; see below, *Interpretari*), participated in the debate on the ancient theater. In his *De metris fabularum Terentii et aliorum comicorum* (*GL* 3,418–429 = Passalacqua ed. 1987, 19–32), written with two other heterogeneous *opuscula*, he strove to demonstrate that Terence wrote in verse, not in prose, even if the average speaker lost a precise feeling of the vocalic quantities. To the same end, Rufinus of Antioch wrote a *Commentarium in metra Terentiana*, whose excerpts are conserved with those from his *Commentarium de compositione et de numeris oratorum* (*GL* 6,554–578 = D'Alessandro ed. 2004). Latin monographs on metrics, for their part, reveal a "boxing-up" structure similar to that of the *Artes grammaticae*: The versified treatise *De littera, de syllaba, de metris* by the former African poet Terentianus Maurus (*GL* 6,325–413 = Cignolo ed. 2002) explicitly follows this pattern.

28.8 Interpretari

Considered as one of the tools of the grammar (see above, *A Textual Typology*), the "historical" analysis of the content of a literary work gives all the relevant information on topics like mythology, law, and chronology. Specific monographs were written on this type of erudite research. Anyone who is interested in the scanty fragments of this production can find in the *Grammaticae Romanae fragmenta* (edited by Funaioli 1907 and Mazzarino 1955²) many examples of works *de dis* or περὶ θεῶν, *de iure ciuili*, *chronica*, as well as *uitae* of literary authors and works *de poetis*. This was bookish learning, conceived in relation to literary texts and extracted from them. Eventually, in late antiquity, it reappears in an atomized form, within word-to-word commentaries, which became sorts of condensed encyclopedias. Besides anonymous explanations on the margin of the manuscripts like Virgil's *scholia Veronensia* and Terence's *scholia Bembina*, vast commentaries addressed to the public of the school were written by renowned grammarians, who followed the long-standing and illustrious Greek tradition (see Dickey 2007, pp. 18–71). Donatus wrote a commentary on Terence, which is still preserved, although in an abridged form that lacks *Heautontimoroumenos*. His now lost commentary on Virgil became the basis of Servius's own, now preserved in two redactions in which the second one (*Seruius auctus* or *Seruius Danielis*) is a late expansion with different, intertwined stages and levels. At the top of this cultural work one can find philosophical, Neoplatonic-oriented commentaries, like those of Tiberius Claudius Donatus on Virgil and of Marius Victorinus on Cicero's *De inuentione*. On the other hand, a basic type of commentary, limited to a form of parsing grammar reminiscent of the Homeric *epimerismoi*, is represented by Priscian's *partitiones* (*GL* 3,459–515 = Passalacqua ed. 1999, 45–128), an analysis of the first 12 lines of Virgil's *Aeneid* in the same catechetic form as Donatus's *Ars minor* (Glück 1967). Interestingly enough, after a grammatical section containing inflectional and prosodic *regulae*, the *Frg. Bobiense de nomine* includes a glossographic section (*GL* 7,541,26–544,44 = Mariotti ed. 1984, § 14–158), with a mixture of glosses and scholia to Virgil, Horace, Lucan, Juvenal, and Sallust, the most read authors of late antiquity (generally not explicitly referred to in the text). In the case of Virgil, it is possible to demonstrate that Servius and *Seruius Danielis* are the main sources, of which the *Frg. Bobiense* sometimes transmits the original, fuller form that has been lost in the direct tradition of these commentaries (compare, e.g., *Frg. Bob. de nom. GL* 7,544,43–44 = Mariotti ed. 1984, § 158 *Epicurei definiun<t> quidquid uisu aut tactu subiacet, hoc corpus esse, unde et umbras corpora esse dicunt* with Servius *Aen.* 6,303 "*corpora cumba*": *omne quod potest uideri, corpus dicitur*; see also Mariotti ed. 1984, pp. 44–45).

Thanks to these works, reading a classical author like Virgil allowed people to obtain a form of universal knowledge, which the commentators developed and nourished (Ziolkowski and Putnam 2008). So, according to Servius, Virgil was *totus quidem...scientia plenus* (*ad Aen.* 6, prooem.), because *uariam scientiam suo inserit carmini* (*ad Aen.* 2,148). Besides conveying some linguistic models (Uhl 1998), resuscitating ancient information on institutions and *realia* of the classical world had an ideological resonance in a context of mixed Christian and pagan culture. It revealed a desire to preserve a heritage that risked being lost (Casali and Stok 2008; Bouquet, Ménial, and Ramires 2011; Stok 2013; Garcea, Lhommé, and Vallat 2016). In this period of transition, grammar ended up being the ideal medium for this preservation, both for its formal aspects and for its content. Christians were at least as interested in commenting on written texts as the imperial-era grammarians. Throughout late antiquity Christians were still trained within a classical school system in which they increasingly played important roles as professors of grammar and rhetoric, like Saint Augustine. In this way, an immense heritage, even if it resolved itself into fragments, could be the object of a "reconversion" that at the same time permitted its survival.

REFERENCES

In addition to the *Grammatici Latini* (*GL*), edited by Heinrich Keil (Leipzig: Teubner, 1855–1880), it is indispensable to use updated editions of the *artes grammaticae*, whenever available: For the references, see the *Grammatici disiecti* blog (https://gradis.hypotheses.org). A recent anthology in English translation is Copeland and Sluiter (2012). Late Latin grammars on papyrus are now edited by Scappaticcio (2015). Reliable, basic information on late Latin grammarians is found in Kaster (1988, pp. 237–440); Herzog (1989, § 521–527); Sallmann (1997, § 432–446); Stammerjohann (2009²). A first approach to the grammatical technical language must start from Lomanto and Marinone (1990) and Schad (2007).

Ars grammatica group. (2010). *Priscien. Grammaire: Livre XVII – Syntaxe*. Paris: Vrin.

Ars grammatica group. (2013). *Priscien. Grammaire: Livres XIV, XV, XVI – Les invariables*. Paris: Vrin.

Auroux, Sylvain. (1994). *La révolution technologique de la grammatisation*. Liège: Mardaga.

Ax, Wolfram. (1986). *Laut, Stimme und Sprache*. Göttingen: Vandenhoeck & Ruprecht.

Ax, Wolfram. (1987). *Quadripertita ratio*. Bemerkungen zur Geschichte eines aktuellen Kategoriensystems. In: *The History of Linguistics in the Classical Period* (ed. Daniel Taylor), 17–40. Amsterdam: Benjamins.

Barabino, Giuseppina and Ferruccio Bertini. ed. (1967–1997). *Studi Noniani*. 15 vols. Genoa: Università degli studi di Genova.

Baratin, Marc. (1989). *La naissance de la syntaxe à Rome*. Paris: Minuit.

Baratin, Marc. (1994). Sur la structure des grammaires antiques. In: *Florilegium Historiographiae Linguisticae* (ed. Jan De Clercq and Piet Desmet), 143–157. Louvain: Peeters.

Baratin, Marc and Françoise Desbordes. (1986). La "troisième partie" de l'*ars grammatica*. *Historiographia linguistica*, 13/2–3: 215–240 = Françoise Desbordes. 2007. *Idées grecques et romaines sur le langage, Travaux d'histoire et d'épistémologie*, 65–90. Lyon: Presses de l'ENS.

Barwick, Karl. (1922). *Remmius Palaemon und die römische Ars grammatica*. Leipzig: Teubner.

Bertini, Ferruccio. ed. (2000–2005). *Prolegomena Noniana*. 5 vols. Genova: Università degli studi di Genova.

Blank, David. (2000). The organization of grammar in Ancient Greek. In: *History of the Language Sciences* (ed. Sylvain Auroux, E.F.K. Koerner, Hans-Josef Niederehe, and Kees Versteegh), 407–411. Berlin: de Gruyter.

Bouquet, Monique, Méniel, Bruno, and Ramires, Giuseppe. ed. (2011). *Servius et sa réception de l'Antiquité à la Renaissance*. Rennes: Presses Universitaires.

Brugnoli, Giorgio. (1955). *Studi sulle differentiae uerborum*. Rome: Signorelli.

Cadoni, Enzo. (1987). *Studi sul De compendiosa doctrina di Nonio Marcello*. Sassari: Gallizzi.

Copeland, Rita and Sluiter, Ineke. (2012). *Medieval Grammar and Rhetoric: Language Arts and Literary Theory, AD 300 –1475*. Oxford: Oxford University Press.

Casali, Sergio and Stok, Fabio. ed. (2008). *Servio: Stratificazioni esegetiche e modelli culturali*. Brussels: Latomus.

Cristante, Lucio. (1987). *Martiani Capellae de nuptiis philologiae et Mercurii liber IX*. Padua: Antenore.

Dammer, Raphael. (2001). *Diomedes grammaticus*. Trier: Wissenschaftlicher Verlag.

De Nonno, Mario.(1983). Frammenti misconosciuti di Plozio Sacerdote. Con osservazioni sul testo dei *Catholica Probi*. *Rivista di Filologia e Istruzione Classica* 111: 385–421.

De Nonno, Mario (1990a). Le citazioni dei grammatici. In: *Lo spazio letterario di Roma antica*. Vol. 3: *La ricezione del testo* (ed. Guglielmo Cavallo, Paolo Fedeli, and Andrea Giardina), 597–646. Rome: Salerno.

De Nonno, Mario. (1990b). Ruolo e funzione della metrica nei grammatici latini. In: *Metrica classica e linguistica* (ed. Roberto M. Danese, Franco Gori, and Cesare Questa), 453–494. Urbino: Quattroventi.

De Nonno, Mario. (1998). Grammatici latini. In *Enciclopedia oraziana* (ed. Scevola Mariotti, 31–39). 3 vols. Rome: Istituto della Enciclopedia italiana.

De Nonno, Mario. (2000). I codici grammaticali latini d'età tardoantica: Osservazioni e considerazioni. In: *Manuscripts and Tradition of Grammatical Texts from Antiquity to Renaissance*. 2 vols. (ed. Mario De Nonno, Paolo De Paolis, and Louis Holtz), 1: 133–172. Cassino: Università degli studi di Cassino.

De Nonno, Mario. (2009). *Ars Prisciani Caesarensis*: Problemi di tipologia e di composizione. In: *Priscien: Transmission et refondation de la grammaire* (ed. Marc Baratin, Bernard Colombat, and Louis Holtz), 248–278. Turnhout: Brepols.

De Nonno, Mario. (2010). *Et interrogauit Filocalus*. Pratiche dell'insegnamento "in aula" del grammatico. In: *Libri di scuola e pratiche didattiche. Dall'Antichità al Rinascimento*. 2 vols. (ed. Lucio Del Corso and Oronzo Pecere), 1: 170–205. Cassino: Università degli studi di Cassino.

De Paolis, Paolo. (2003). Miscellanei grammaticali altomedievali. In *Grammatica e grammatici latini: teoria ed esegesi* (ed. Fabio Gasti), 29–74. Pavia: Ibis.

De Paolis, Paolo. (2010). L'insegnamento dell'ortografia latina fra Tardoantico e alto Medioevo: teorie e manuali. In: *Libri di scuola e pratiche didattiche. Dall'Antichità al Rinascimento*. 2 vols. (ed. Lucio Del Corso and, Oronzo Pecere), 1: 229–291. Cassino: Università degli studi di Cassino.

Desbordes, Françoise. (1983). Le schéma "addition, soustraction, mutation, métathèse" dans les textes anciens. *Histoire Épistémologie Langage*, 5.1: 23–30 = Françoise Desbordes. 2007. *Idées grecques et romaines sur le langage, Travaux d'histoire et d'épistémologie*, 55–63. Lyon: Presses de l'ENS.

Desbordes, Françoise. (1990). *Idées romaines sur l'écriture*. Presses universitaires de Lille.

Dickey, Eleanor. (2007). *Ancient Greek Scholarship*. Oxford: Oxford University Press.

Dickey, Eleanor. (2012–2014). *The Colloquia of the Hermeneumata Pseudodositheana*. 2 vols. Cambridge: Cambridge University Press.

Dionisotti, Anna Carlotta. (1996). On the nature and transmission of Latin glossaries. In: *Les manuscrits des lexiques et glossaires de l'Antiquité tardive à la fin du Moyen Âge* (ed. Jacqueline Hamesse), 205–252. Louvain: Fédération internationale des Instituts d'études médiévales.

Ebbesen, Sten. (1981). Suprasegmental phonemes in ancient and mediaeval logic. In: *English Logic and Semantics from the End of the Twelfth Century to the Time of Ockham and Burleigh: Acts of the Fourth European Symposium on Mediaeval Logic and Semantics* (ed. Henricus Antonius Giovanni Braakhuis, Corneille Henri Kneepkens, and Lambertus Marie de Rijk), 331–359. Nijmegen: Ingenium.

Garcea, Alessandro, Lhommé, Marie-Karine, and Vallat, Daniel. ed. (2016). *Fragments d'érudition: Servius et le savoir antique*. Hildesheim: Olms.

Garcea, Alessandro and Lomanto, Valeria. (2003). Varron et Priscien: Autour des verbes *adsignificare* et *consignificare*. *Histoire Épistémologie Langage* 25: 33–54.

Glück, Manfred. (1967). *Priscians Partitiones und ihre Stellung in der spätantiken Schule*. Hildesheim: Olms.

Hamesse, Jacqueline. ed. (1996). *Les manuscrits des lexiques et glossaires de l'Antiquité tardive à la fin du Moyen Âge*, Louvain: Fédération internationale des Instituts d'études médiévales.

Herzog, Reinhart. ed. (1989). *Handbuch der Lateinischen Literatur der Antike*. Vol. 5: *Restauration und Erneuerung*. Munich: Beck.

Holtz, Louis. (1981). *Donat et la tradition de l'enseignement grammatical*. Paris: CNRS.

Jeep, Ludwig. (1893). *Zur Geschichte der Lehre von den Redeteilen bei den lateinischen Grammatikern*. Leipzig: Teubner.

Kaster, Robert A. (1988). *Guardians of Language*. Berkeley: University of California Press.

Law, Vivien. (1987). Late Latin grammars in the early Middle Ages: A typological history. In: *The History of Linguistics in the Classical Period* (ed. Daniel Taylor), 191–204. Amsterdam: Benjamins.

Law, Vivien. (2000). Memory and the structure of grammars in antiquity and the Middle Ages. In: *Manuscripts and Tradition of Grammatical Texts from Antiquity to Renaissance.* 2 vols. (ed. Mario De Nonno, Paolo De Paolis, and Louis Holtz), 1: 9–58.Cassino: Università degli studi di Cassino.

Leonhardt, Jürgen. (1989). *Dimensio syllabarum: Studien zur lateinischen Prosodie- und Verslehre von der Spätantike bis zur frühen Renaissance.* Göttingen: Vandenhoeck & Ruprecht.

Lindsay, Wallace Martin. (1901). *Nonius Marcellus Dictionary of Republican Latin.* Oxford: Parker and Co.

Lomanto, Valeria and Marinone, Nino. (1990). *Index Grammaticus.* Hildesheim: Olms.

Luhtala, Anneli. (2002). On definitions in ancient grammar. In: *Grammatical Theory and Philosophy of Language in Antiquity* (ed. Pierre Swiggers and Alfons Wouters), 257–285. Louvain: Peeters.

Luhtala, Anneli. (2005). *Grammar and Philosophy in Late Antiquity.* Amsterdam: Benjamins.

Luhtala, Anneli. (2010). Latin *Schulgrammatik* and the emergence of grammatical commentaries. In: *Condensing Texts – Condensed Texts* (ed. Marietta Horster and Christiane Reitz), 209–243. Stuttgart: Steiner.

Luque Moreno, Jesús et al. ed. (1987–2007). *Scriptores Latini de re metrica. Concordantiae.* 19 vols. Granada: Departmento de filologia Latina de Granada.

Magallón García, Ana-Isabel, (1996). *La tradición gramatical de differentia y etymologia hasta Isidoro de Sevilla.* Zaragoza: Universidad de Zaragoza.

Martorelli, Luca. ed. (2014). *Greco antico nell'Occidente carolingio. Frammenti di testi attici nell'Ars di Prisciano.* Hildesheim: Olms.

Matthaios, Stephanos. (2002). Neue Perspektiven für die Historiographie der antiken Grammatik: Das Wortartensystem der Alexandriner. In: *Grammatical Theory and Philosophy of Language in Antiquity* (ed. Pierre Swiggers and Alfons Wouters), 161–220. Louvain: Peeters.

Morelli, Giuseppe. ed. (2006). *Nomenclator metricus Graecus et Latinus*, vol. 1. Hildesheim: Olms.

Müller, Rudolf Wolfgang. (1964). *Rhetorische und syntaktische Interpunktion. Untersuchungen zur Pausenbezeichnung im antiken Latein.* Tübingen: Eberhard-Karl-Universität.

Munzi, Luigi. (1980–1981). Il *de partibus orationis* di Giuliano di Toledo. *AION (Filologia)* 2–3: 153–228.

Munzi, Luigi. (1992). Il ruolo della prefazione nei testi grammaticali latini. *AION (Filologia)* 14: 103–126.

Sallmann, Klaus. ed. (1997). *Handbuch der Lateinischen Literatur der Antike.* Vol. 4: *Die Literatur des Umbruchs.* Munich: Beck.

Scappaticcio, Maria Chiara. (2012). *Papyri Vergilianae.* Liège: Presses universitaires.

Scappaticcio, Maria Chiara. (2015). *Artes Grammaticae in frammenti. I testi grammaticali latini e bilingui greco-latini su papiro*. Berlin: de Gruyter.

Schad, Samantha. (2007). *A Lexicon of Latin Grammatical Terminology*. Pisa: Giardini.

Schenkeveld, Dirk M. (2004). *A Rhetorical Grammar: C. Julius Romanus, Introduction to the Liber de Adverbio*. Leiden: Brill.

Schoell, Fritz. (1876). *De accentu linguae Latinae ueterum grammaticorum testimonia*. Leipzig: Teubner.

Schoemann, Georg Friedrich. (1862). *Die Lehre von den Redetheilen nach den Alten*. Berlin: W. Hertz.

Scialuga, Marina. (1993). La trattazione sistematica della sillaba. *Sileno* 19: 295–360.

Stammerjohann, Harro. ed. (2009²). *Lexicon grammaticorum*. Tübingen: Max Niemeyer.

Stok, Fabio. (2008). Servio fra sinonimia e *differentiae uerborum*. In: *Servio: Stratificazioni esegetiche e modelli culturali*. (ed. Sergio Casali and Fabio Stok), 132–158. Brussels: Latomus.

Stok, Fabio. ed. (2013). *Totus scientia plenus. Percorsi dell'esegesi virgiliana*. Pisa: ETS.

Stoppie, Karen, Swiggers, Pierre, and Wouters, Alfons. (2007). La terminologie grammaticale en contexte bilingue: Macrobe et l'analyse de la diathèse verbale. In: *Bilinguisme et terminologie grammaticale gréco-latine* (ed. Louis Basset, Frédérique Biville, Bernard Colombat et al.), 201–224. Louvain: Peeters.

Uhl, Anne. (1998). *Servius als Sprachlehrer*. Göttingen: Vandenhoeck & Ruprecht.

Uría Varela, Javier. (2006). Consideraciones sobre el prefacio del Arte gramática de Carisio. *STVDIVM. Revista de Humanidades* 12: 113–125.

Uría Varela, Javier. (2009). *Carisio: Arte gramática. Libro I*. Madrid: Gredos.

Vainio, Raija. (1999). *Latinitas and Barbarisms according to the Roman Grammarians*. Turku: Painosalama Oy.

Ziolkowski, Jan M. and Putnam, Michael C.J. (2008). *The Virgilian Tradition*. New Haven, CT: Yale University Press.

CHAPTER TWENTY-NINE

School Texts

Lillian I. Larsen

29.1 Introduction

In traditional reflection, the demographic and religious shifts that render late antiquity distinct have often masked the foundational pedagogical continuities of this period. Studies that frame the advent of Christianity and the emergence of monasticism as markers of "profound political and religious change" (Kaster 1988, p. ix) concomitantly define late ancient literary trajectories as registers of rupture. For example, Robert Kaster (1988, p. 12) characterizes late antique classroom models as a legacy that leads to the fragmenting of student understanding. Crystallizing a broader array of commensurate appraisal, he suggests that, at this point, an "overall view of history" was replaced with memories of "disjointed but edifying vignettes." Collections of "ethical commonplaces" supplanted the "systematic knowledge of philosophy." An "organic sense of language" was reduced to "rules and categories, divided and subdivided [into] rare lexical tidbits." Likening "the items amassed over years of schooling," to "slips filed away in a vast range of pigeonholes," he depicts accrued content as elements that might be "summoned up individually and combined to meet the needs of the moment," absent any perception of a synthetic "uniform relationship among them" (cf. Marrou 1960, pp. 1–157).

More sympathetic assessments reverse these valuations. The same catalysts faulted for the fragmenting of synthetic thought are here credited with literary production that is "complex, sophisticated and creative" (Burton-Christie 1993, p. viii). Albeit the organic work of a spiritually focused "lay movement," comprising constituencies that remain "untouched by the literary culture and refinement that formed the outlook of their bishops" (Wilken 2012, p. 105), edifying vignettes are praised for providing a particularly "clear...historical picture" of the late ancient world (Burton-Christie 1993, pp. 3–5). Ethical commonplaces are named not only "rich and varied" but also the "flowering" of unprecedented, even novel, ingenuity (pp. 3–5). Synthetically representative of a "remarkable *new* literary genre" (Ward 1986, p. xix), each is likewise deemed the "expression of an altogether *original* method of spiritual education" (Guy 1974, p. 44; emphasis mine).

The divergent character of these assessments can only give pause. Placed in conversation, they manifest the degree to which "all historical interpretive efforts and their methods and approaches illuminate some things, cast shadows over others, [and they] foreground some things, render into the background certain others" (Wimbush, 1997, p. 1). Each simultaneously displays uncanny affinity with Henri Marrou's representation of monasticism as a type of Christian school "that was wholly devoted to religion and had none of the features of the old classical school" (Marrou 1956, p. 330; cf. Larsen 2013a; 2013b). Measuring the depth of Marrou's influence lies beyond the scope of this relatively brief chapter (cf. Larsen 2013a). However, the fact that monasticism remains a kind of "absent chapter in the history of education" (Rappe 2001, p. 423) more than half a century after the publication of Marrou's epic *History*, affirms the persistent power of his premise (cf. Wilken 2012, pp. 99–108). Delimiting a primary swath of late ancient literature comprised of "text[s] without ... context" derivative of "communit[ies] with no inheritance" (Harvey 1996, p. 242), this legacy is embodied in bifurcated constituencies defined solely by categories of contest. Here, "original thinkers and radical teachers" remain "pitted against the fathers," urban intellectuals "facing off" with "desert wisdom" (Rappe 2001, p. 423).

Inadvertently bridging these binaries, George Kennedy has argued for a single system of literary reference that links pedagogical practice in space and over time. Introducing his compendium of *Greek Textbooks of Prose Composition and Rhetoric* (*Progymnasmata*), Kennedy likens the formulaically fixed and fundamentally fluid praxis that defined ancient and late antique literary habits to the "structural features of classical architecture." He suggests that not only Greco-Roman literature but also the writing produced by emergent (and established) Christian communities must be understood as uniformly rooted and shaped by "the habits of thinking and writing learned in schools" (Kennedy 2003, p. ix). This essay follows Kennedy in using classroom continuity as a lens for exploring the pedagogical landscape of late antiquity. Eschewing rhetorics of "rupture," it instead explores the stable media preserved in classroom handbooks, extant school texts, and finally, late ancient literature itself.

29.2 The "Fragments" of Late Antique Literature

The discrete elements that unite Greco-Roman literary forms with classroom pedagogical practice are well documented (cf. Marrou 1956; Bonner 1977; Cribiore 1996; 2001; Morgan 1998, 2007; Too 2001; Watts 2006; Chin 2007). By the fourth century of the Common Era, they were likewise well established. Emergent protocol, loosely referenced in the writings of Plato and Aristotle, is concretely affirmed in a lineage that finds focused articulation in the Hellenistic period and extends through late antiquity, into Byzantium and beyond (cf. Cribiore 1996; Morgan 1998). In exercises aimed at training both moral disposition and emergent intellect, students first encountered literary content in word lists, maxims, *chreiai*, and fables. In iterative progression, at every succeeding educational level, they rehearsed the same "fragmentary" material, "chewing it over...making collections... and expanding...content" until they could (at an opportune moment, or in a well-turned phrase) "aptly" incorporate lines and passages into everyday speech and writing (Cribiore 2001, p. 179). As students progressed, foundational building blocks could be variously combined in ways that linked the elementary instruction of a *grammaticus* to more advanced composition. At every stage and across generations, the goal of such instruction was not solely technical. Iterative rehearsal was understood as a conduit for simultaneously inculcating virtue and shaping character (cf. Morgan 2007).

Writing in the fourth century BCE, Plato recommends that the end purpose of "compil[ing] anthologies of the poets and mak[ing] collections of whole passages, which...must be committed to memory," is not only to enable a student to gain wide familiarity with literature but also "to make...a good and wise [individual] of him [or her]" (*Leg.* 810e–812a [Bury]). In his pedagogical treatise *Ad Demonicum*, Pseudo-Isocrates suggests that noble behavior results from a mind filled "with many noble maxims; for, as it is the nature of the body to be developed by appropriate exercises, it is the nature of the soul to be developed by moral precepts" (*Ad Demonicum* 12 [Norlin]). In the first century of the Common Era, Plutarch submits that teachers should be chosen on the basis of their ability to select and set "precepts and exhortations beside the young, in order that [children's] characters [might] grow to be upright" (*De liberis educandis* 4C [Babbitt]). Affirming commensurate practice, in his fourth-century regulatory corpus, Basil of Caesarea assigns iterative work with moral maxims, sayings, and exemplary stories to the "common children" of his fledgling monastic community (*Reg. Fus.* 15 [Clarke]; cf. Gregory Nazianzen, *Vita Macrina* 3). Like his predecessors, he notes that rehearsal of such content will not only inculcate fluid command of common compositional forms but also insure "that the soul...be lead to practise [*sic*] good immediately and from the outset, [and] while...still plastic and soft, pliable as wax, [be]...molded by the shapes pressed upon it" (Basil, *Reg. Fus.* 15 [Clarke]; cf. Morgan 2007; Larsen 2013a, 2013b).

29.3 The "Forms" of Late Antique Literary Architecture

Just as a premise of radical rupture has governed the positive and negative valence ascribed excerpted literary extracts, it has also shaped assessment of the structures used in reworking this content. Here, tradition has designated common forms of literary content as either grammatical or moral, rhetorical or spiritual (cf. Marrou 1956; Rappe 2001; Wilken 2012). However, challenging an interpretive spectrum perennially defined by fundamentally disparate media and goals, it is the case that both technical and ethical aims remain endemic to the ancient/late ancient habits of "thinking and writing" learned in school (Kennedy 2003; cf. Larsen 2001, 2008; 2013a; 2013b; 2016; 2017). These links are particularly well illustrated in the spectrum of ancient and late ancient rhetorical handbooks that remain extant. Dated from the first century of the Common Era through late antiquity (and beyond), a burgeoning record of established practice invites tracing the dissemination of both reworked moral content and structural models.

The earliest handbook that survives is the first century compendium of exercises (*gymnasmata*) attributed to Theon of Alexandria (Theon, *Gymn.* [Kennedy 2003, pp. 1–72]). Theon likens work with the included media to learning pottery on a simple pot rather than on a huge storage jar (*Gymn.* 59; Quintilian, *Inst.* 1.9.1; cf. Hock and O'Neil 1985, p. 21). Reference to commensurate practice in Quintilian's relatively contemporary commentary indicates that Theon's handbook is not the first of its kind (Hock and O'Neil 1985, p. 10). In second- and third-century sources, three other compilations are named. The handbooks of Paulus of Tyre and Minucianus of Athens are no longer extant, but a third, attributed to Hermogenes of Tarsus, survives (*Progymn.* [Kennedy 2003, pp. 73–88]).

It is late antiquity, however, that marks a "flowering of [the] genre" (Hock and O'Neil 1985, p. 11). Many handbooks are no longer extant. However, the *Suda* assigns to this period the elementary exercises (*progymnasmata*) of Epiphanius of Petra, Onasimus of Cypris, and Ulpian of Emessa. Elsewhere, a lost set of strategems is attributed to one Syrianus. The handbooks of Sirikius of Neapolis and Sopater, presumably of Apamea, have been identified in fragments. Two additional treatises, the preliminary exercises of Nicolaus of Myra (*Progymn.*

[Kennedy 2003, pp. 129–172]) and Aphthonius of Antioch (*Progymn.* [Kennedy 2003, pp. 89–127]), are preserved intact.

Of these, Aphthonius's handbook became the unrivaled standard as a source for model classroom media, "first in the Greek East and then in the Latin West" (Hock and O'Neil 1985, p. 11). In both contemporary and subsequent commentary, his singular status is often attributed to the exemplary models he includes for each exercise (cf. Hock and O'Neil 1985, pp. 211–216). An anonymous *prolegomonist* names Aphthonius's exercises "clearer than…others and more easily learned," because while "others set out the bare methods without examples [and so make] the study of the progymnasmata difficult for students at the introductory level, Aphthonius… describe[s] the methods as clearly and distinctly as possible." Through "illuminat[ing] what he says with examples, [Aphthonius] has [additionally] made his work more adapted and appropriate to the needs of the young" (*Prol.* 79 [Kennedy 2003, pp. 94–95]).

Nonetheless, even as Aphthonius's handbook became standard, its sequences might be viewed as something of a palimpsest, retaining the residual imprint of earlier models. For example, enduring influence is apparent in the late ancient resequencing of Theon's foundational models to align with Aphthonius's emergent reordered arrangement. Such reconfiguration arguably underscores Theon's continued relevance. Like the subsequent acclaim generated by Aphthonius's own models, the detailed explication included in Theon's early compendium appears implicitly foundational to late ancient classroom deployment. In fact, viewed together, the two handbooks serve as functional complements, elucidating persistent patterns that link instructional media with literary production in space and over time.

As conduits of "methodical and instrumental knowledge" (*Prol.* 79 [Kennedy 2003, p. 95]; cf. Aristotle, *Metaphysics* 6.1), both handbooks serve as repositories of uniformly iterative and variably consistent structures. Each introduces the classical forms of "literary architecture" through work with the core media of maxim, *chreia*, fable, and narrative. Albeit variable with respect to details and sequencing, the same four building blocks remain foundational to more advanced practice in refutation, confirmation, commonplace, encomion, invective, syncrisis, ethopoeia, ekphrasis, thesis, and law. Apthonius's late antique formulation reorders Theon's first-century sequencing of *chreia*, fable, and then narrative. Instead, he begins with fable (*mythos*), then moves to narrative, *chreia*, and then maxim. He likewise renders discrete Theon's elision of maxims and *chreiai* into two categories. As encountered in extant literature, however, requisite fluidity remains inherent.

29.3.1 Maxim

Both Theon and Aphthonius agree that any elaborative exercise involving the maxim should proceed in a manner that incorporates elements similar to those employed in expanding the *chreia*. In his early handbook, Theon blends the maxim (*gnômê*) and the *chreia* into a single compositional category. Simultaneously, he differentiates the two forms in multiple ways (*Gymn.* 96–97 [Kennedy 2003, p. 15]). Although Aphthonius identifies the maxim as a separate medium, he functionally defines the form relative to the *chreia* (*Progymn.* 25–26 [Kennedy 2003, pp. 99–100]). For example, echoing Theon's more particular distinctions, Aphthonius affirms that a maxim differs from a *chreia* in that a "*chreia* sometimes reports an action, whereas a maxim is always a saying." Additionally, "a *chreia* needs to indicate a person (as speaker or doer), whereas a maxim is uttered impersonally" (*Progymn.* 26 [Kennedy 2003, p. 100]; cf. Theon, *Gymn.* 96–97).

Aphthonius further delineates maxims as protreptic, apotreptic, or declarative; simple or compound; credible, true, or hyperbolic (*Progymn.* 25–26 [Kennedy 2003, pp. 99–100]). In elucidating the foundational fluidity of the form, the exemplar he selects to illustrate the "apotreptic" maxim underscores the literary character of even the simplest grammatical/*progymnasmatic* sequences: "A man who is a counselor should not sleep all the night" (*Progymn.* 25 [Kennedy 2003, 99]; cf. *Il.* 2.24). In its original narrative setting, this excerpt introduces a well-rehearsed exchange that takes place on the eve of the epic battle recounted in the *Iliad*. Here, the line is delivered by an apparition of Nestor, in a "dreamy" visit to the beleaguered Agamemnon (*Il.* 2.24–25). As redeployed in classroom settings, the same statement (or fragment) appears as one of a collection of maxims, which doubled as key components in exercises aimed at adept reformulation and elaboration.

29.3.2 Chreia

Both Theon and Aphthonius emphasize the degree to which the maxim is related in form to the *chreia*. Theon defines the *chreia* as "a brief saying or action making a point, attributed to some specified person, or something corresponding to a person." He suggests that every brief maxim attributed to a person creates a *chreia*, further distinguishing a reminiscence as an "action or a saying useful for life" (Theon, *Gymn.* 96 [Kennedy 2003, p. 15]). He gives the following example:

Alexander the Macedonian king stood over Diogenes as he slept and said:

"To sleep all night ill suits a counselor" (*Il.* 2.24)
And Diogenes responded:
"On whom folks rely, whose cares are many." (*Il.* 2.25)

Aphthonius melds these disparate aspects, more cryptically describing the *chreia* as "a brief recollection, referring to some person in a pointed way" (*Progymn.* 23 [Kennedy 2003, p. 97]).

However, the commonality that links Apthonius's exemplary maxim with Theon's model *chreia* effectively illustrates the fluid character of these intimately related forms. Adeptly rearticulated, the same *Iliadic* excerpt used to elucidate the maxim (and vice versa) readily serves as a double-*chreia*, comprised of "statements by two persons, each of which might as readily constitute a simple *chreia* by one person" (*Gymn.* 98 [Kennedy 2003, p. 17]).

Subsequent redeployment of this content is as interesting. One encounters the reattributed exchange between Alexander and Diogenes, in the philosophical discourses of Epictetus (*Diss.* 3.22.92). More striking, however, is the notation of Timaios, a third-century scribe who includes an allusion to the literary setting of the maxim in a letter to his master Heroninos (*P. Flor.* II.259; cf. Cribiore 1996, pp. 6–7; 2001, p. 179). To underscore the urgency of a certain matter needing immediate attention, Timaios pens an excerpt from the lines that preface Nestor and Agamemnon's nocturnal conversation (Homer, *Il.* 2.1–2). Preserved in the margin of a routine business document, one finds, "All the other gods and men, lords of chariots, were sleeping the whole night through, but Zeus could not have sweet sleep" (*P. Flor.* II.259; cf. *Il.* 2.1–2).

Each of the handbooks in question more broadly classifies the *chreia* as "verbal," "active," or "mixed." Theon's early treatise likewise includes additional delineation within these general categories (Theon, *Gymn.* 96–106 [Kennedy 2003, pp. 15–47]; cf. Aphthonius, *Progymn.* 23). This attaches to a graded set of exercises (*gymnasmata*), aimed at improving compositional dexterity and skill. Theon frames these as a series of discrete activities (Theon, *Gymn.* 101–106 [Kennedy 2003, pp. 19–23]; cf. Hock and O'Neil 1985, pp. 35–41, 94–107). With commensurate goals, Aphthonius outlines a single *ergasia*. This is organized according to a sequence of set "headings." As enumerated, elaboration comprises "praise, paraphrase, cause, contrary, comparison, example, testimony of the ancients, [and/or a] brief epilogue" (*Progymn.* 23–25 [Kennedy 2003, pp. 98–99]; see further discussion below).

29.3.3 Fable

Theon places the fable third in his elementary sequence of exercises. Aphthonius uses this form to introduce his sequence. Both define the fable as "a fictitious story [or statement] giving an image of truth" (Theon, *Gymn.*

72 [Kennedy 2003, p. 23]; cf. Aphthonius, *Progymn.* 21). The essence of the form is captured in practice that shifts from "imaginative falsehood" to something "sometimes false, sometimes true" (John of Sardis, *Comm.* 35–36 [Kennedy 2003, p. 194]). Theon downplays typological distinction based on whether a fable retains a human or animal protagonist. However, Aphthonius suggests that a fable can be "rational," "ethical," or "mixed," depending on whether "a human being is imagined as doing something [rational]" or whether "the [ethical] character of irrational animals" is represented (*Progymn.* 21 [Kennedy 2003, p. 96]). To illustrate, he presents an "ethical" fable about cicadas and ants:

> It was the height of summer and the cicadas were offering up their shrill song, but it occurred to the ants to toil and collect the harvest from which they would be fed in the winter. When the winter came on, the ants fed on what they had laboriously collected, but the pleasure of the cicadas ended in want. Similarly, youth that does not wish to toil fares badly in old age. (*Progymn.* 21 [Kennedy 2003, p. 96])

Emphasizing the fable's qualitative merit, both Theon and Aphthonius commend its use "for the sake of the moral" (Aphthonius, *Progymn.* 21 [Kennedy 2003, p. 96]; cf. Theon, Gymn. 73).

In ancillary commentary penned "no earlier than the late fifth century," and before the middle of the ninth (Kennedy 2003, p. 173), John of Sardis defends Aphthonius's placement of the fable at the start of the *progymnasmatic* sequence. He suggests that by virtue of offering "a glimpse of the three species of rhetoric…judicial…deliberative…[and] encomion," the fable "encompass[es] the seeds of all the art" (*Comm.* 11 [Kennedy 2003, pp. 180–181]). He additionally foregrounds the fable as a medium that "teaches students how to achieve plausibility" (*Comm.* 34 [Kennedy 2003, p. 193]), suggesting that the same skills deployed in making "speeches suitable for the supposed characters in a fable" (*Comm.* 34 [Kennedy 2003, p. 193]) remain essential to more advanced composition (*Comm.* 34 [Kennedy 2003, p. 193]).

29.3.4 Narrative

The medium of narrative (*diêgêma*) is uniformly defined as "language descriptive of things that have happened or as though they had happened" (Theon, *Gymn.* 78 [Kennedy 2003, p. 28]); cf. Aphthonius, *Progymn.* 22). In his early treatise Theon identifies six essential elements: "the person, whether that be one or many; the action done by the person; and the place where the action was done; and the time at which it was done; and the manner of the action; and sixth, the cause of these things." As enumerated, the "virtues" of narrative are "clarity, conciseness and credibility" (Theon, *Gymn.* 78 [Kennedy 2003, p. 28]).

To illustrate, Theon draws examples from familiar stories (Gymn. 80–96 [Kennedy 2003, pp. 29–42. Aphthonius, recounts "concerning the rose" (Progymn. 22 [Kennedy 2003, p. 97]). However, the features that distinguish fable from narrative are equally well illustrated in a late ancient monastic reframing of Aphthonius's exemplary fable. As reconfigured, this melding of grammatical and rhetorical, moral and spiritual is not only repackaged in an alternate medium but also repopulated with human protagonists:

> A brother visited Abba Silvanus at Mount Sinai; he saw the brothers working and said to the elder, "Labor not for the meat that perishes" [John 6:27]. "Mary has chosen the good part'" [Luke 10:42]. The elder said to Zachariah, his disciple, "Give the brother a book and put him in a cell without anything else." So when the ninth hour [time] came the visitor watched the door, expecting someone would be sent to call him to the meal. When no one called him he got up, went to find the old man and said to him, "Have the brothers not eaten today?" The old man replied that they had. Then he said, "Why did you not call me?" The old man said to him, "Because you are a spiritual man and do not need that kind of food. We, being carnal, want to eat, and that is why we work. But you have chosen the good portion and read the whole day long and you do not want to eat carnal food." When he heard these words the brother made a prostration saying, "Forgive me, abba." The old man said to him, "Mary needs Martha. It is really thanks to Martha that Mary is praised." (AP_G Silvanus 5 [Ward])

In this "rational" recounting, rather than singing cicadas and diligent ants, one meets a "spiritually" minded visitor juxtaposed with Abba Silvanus and his hard-working monks (persons). The narrative action is plausibly set at Mount Sinai (place). It is framed by the daily rhythms of monastic life (time). The manner and cause of respective protagonists' actions are "clearly," "concisely," and "credibly" woven into the details of the narrative itself.

29.4 Classroom Practice

As illustrated here, set handbook exercises could be used to transform even the most familiar content to address a new historical circumstance and/or audience. Blurring the clear compositional lines that have differentiated between the simple wisdom of rustic monks and the sophisticated rhetoric of elite authors, they affirm the scope of well-masked, shared practice. Both chronologically and geographically, such confluence argues against adhering to established dichotomies. Instead, it underscores the degree to which a text's prospective audience is refracted in the literary details that infuse the standard media being deployed. That such pedagogically informed, "habits" are mirrored in extant literary sources should not surprise. However, material examples of late ancient classroom practice also affirm broad continuity that reflects established protocol (cf. Larsen 2013a, 2016, 2017).

29.4.1 P. Bouriant *1*

Of school exercises dated to late antiquity, the content included in the notebook preserved as *P. Bouriant* 1 is particularly well researched (and well recognized). It is comprised of classroom content so quintessential that only the chrism included on each page serves to indicate Christian provenance. First published by P. Jouguet and P. Perdrizet in 1906 (cf. Carlig 2016), the notebook includes practice that begins with an extensive collection of syllabically categorized word lists. Affirming foundational use of forms elsewhere encountered in *progymnasmatic* handbooks, this is followed by a reading/pronunciation exercise comprised of five *chreiai* attributed to Diogenes. Next, one meets a full set of twenty-four, alphabetically sequenced maxims, followed by material drawn from the preface to the fables of Babrius.

In examining the relationship between classroom media and literary composition, each of these elements is of interest. The word-lists confirm that alongside Homer, Hesiod and Menander shared "a reading audience in [Christian] Egypt" (Clarysse and Wouters 1970, p. 229). The set of *chreiai* attributed to Diogenes and material related to the fables of Babrius attest continued reliance on common literary content. Given the compositional building blocks consistently encountered in extant handbooks, a subsequent list comprised of twenty-four maxims is as interesting.

The fourth maxim in this alphabetically organized sequence – predictably – begins with *delta*: "An old tree (Δένδρον παλαιὸν) is not easily replanted" (*P. Bour.* 1). Illustrating the links between classroom and literary practice, in what has been deemed the earliest collection of the "sayings" ascribed to late ancient Egyptian monks, one encounters the same maxim reframed as a simple *chreia*. Countering assessment that premises resistance to literate pursuits as "one of the most characteristic features of 'Eastern' monasticism" (Marrou 1956, p. 333), it is preserved in a collection addressed to a Latin-speaking audience: "A hermit said, 'A tree cannot bear fruit if it is often transplanted. So it is with the monk'" (AP_PJ 7.36 [Ward]).

A slightly elaborated Greek articulation remains aptly attributed to an "old man" (*gerón*): "An old man said, 'Just as a tree cannot bring forth fruit if it is always being transplanted, so the monk who is always going from one place to another is not able to bring forth virtue'" (AP_N 204/AP_GS 7.43 [Ward]). Elsewhere, the same maxim appears in a lengthier *ergasia* framed as an exhortation to young monks:

> A prolonged stay outside the cell is harmful [paraphrase]: it deprives you of grace, darkens your thinking, extinguishes your longing [cause]. Note how a jar of wine left in its place for a while to lie unmoved renders the wine clear, settled, and perfumed [contrary]. But if it is carried about here and there, it leaves the wine troubled, cloudy [comparison], and showing evidence at the same time of the unpleasantness and badness coming from the lees [example]. Compare yourself then to this example and draw benefit from the experience. Break off relationships with a multitude of people, lest your mind be distracted and disturb the way of stillness [epilogue]. (Evagrius, *Foundations* 8 [Sinkewicz])

Belying depictions of "urban intellectualism facing off with desert wisdom" (Rappe 2001, p. 423), this third expansion of late ancient fragmentary content is attributed to Evagrius, a prolific desert *abba*. Originally composed in Greek, Evagrius's deftly executed *ergasia* also survives in Syriac.

29.4.2 P. Cotsen-Princeton 1

In contrast to the century of research that attends the *P. Bouriant 1*, *P. Cotsen-Princeton 1* is among the most recently published school artifacts. Like the more familiar Bouriant notebook, this Coptic codex is comprised of a varied range of content. As provisionally catalogued by Scott Bucking (2011), its seventeen sections appear to be uniformly pedagogical in focus. Contents include an extensive syllabary and a wealth of word-lists. Largely drawn from texts in Hebrew and Christian Scripture complementary content, includes a list of *nomina sacra* and variously configured tongue twisters (*chalinoi*). The final portion of the codex is comprised of passages. Albeit less than systematically organized, the first is an excerpt drawn from Paul's letter to the Romans; the last, a series of blessings. Situated between these concluding sectors is a penultimate collection of attributed 'sayings' or *chreiai* (*P.Cotsen-Princeton* 1).

These particular *chreiai* are designated by the editor as "part of an important tradition of monastic literature known as the *Apophthegmata Patrum*." Here (as above), this genre is described as "a vehicle through which the moral and spiritual aspects of Egyptian monastic life could be taught" (Bucking 2011, p. 68). Examined within a wider literary frame, however, the pedagogical valence of such content remains implicit. Like the repurposed biblical detail that structures the codex as a whole, these texts readily serve both as technical models and as conduits for inculcating moral virtue.

Preserved at a stage more developed than the maxims encountered in *P. Bouriant* 1, the passages readily exemplify the genre's characteristic flexibility. The first, a narrative of considerable length, begins with a simple *chreia*: "Apa Basilios said that it is appropriate for the monk to live a life of poverty" ⲁϥϫⲟⲟⲥ ⲛϭⲓ ⲁⲡⲁ ⲃⲁⲥⲓⲗⲓⲟⲥ ϫⲉ ϣϣⲉ ⲉⲡⲙⲟⲛⲁⲭⲟⲥ ⲉϫⲡⲟ ⲛⲁϥ ⲛⲟⲩⲃⲓⲟⲥ ⲙⲙⲛⲧ ϩⲏⲕⲉ (*P. Cotsen-Princeton* 1, fols. 157–69; Bucking 2001, pp. 68–69). Two subsequent and relatively brief portions remain only partially legible. However, a final passage manifests classic *chreic* (and aptly monastic) form: "An old man said that ..." ⲁϥϫⲟⲟⲥ ⲛϭⲓⲟⲩϩⲁⲗⲟ ϫⲉ (*P. Cotsen-Princeton* 1, fols. 170–76 [Bucking 2011, pp. 68–69, pl. 94–100]). Examined in pedagogical context, the codex as a whole, and these passages in particular, challenge assessments that have characterized monastic literature articulated in "the language native to [a given] region" as the simple homespun wisdom of constituencies who remained "uneducated and suspicious of book learning" (Wilken 2012, p. 103). They again bely depictions that position "urban intellectualism facing off with desert wisdom" (Rappe 2001, p. 423).

29.4.3 O.Col.inv. 766

The hybrid character of a third piece of school evidence is as suggestive. Published by Raffaella Cribiore, it is inscribed on an ostracon of Theban provenance (*O.Col.inv.* 766; cf. Cribiore 1997). Penned in Greek, the preserved passage is drawn from a sermon, elsewhere attributed to Basil of Caesarea. Here, this extracted content – like the elaborated *chreia* in *P.Cotsen-Princeton* 1 – has been repurposed to serve as a copying exercise and, more explicitly, a vehicle for classroom practice with accents and lexical signs (Cribiore 1997).

Such pedagogical deployment of homiletic content adds provocative dimensionality to scholarly depictions of communities comprised of simple rustics "untouched by the literary culture and refinement that formed the outlook of their bishops" (Wilken 2012, p. 103). Further elucidating the static media and fluid content that linked ancient/late ancient classroom practice with derivative compositional habits, the sermon itself is emblematic of a textbook elaboration of the familiar maxim "Give heed to yourself:"

> "Give heed to yourself:" this admonition, like a good counselor who reminds you of human things will be useful to you when you are enjoying brilliant success and your whole life goes with the stream. And even when you are cast down by crisis it might profitably be recited again and again by your heart that

you may not fall into boastful pride because of vanity nor for desperation become ignobly disheartened. Is wealth your boast? Are you proud of your ancestors? Do you find cause for glory in your fatherland, in physical beauty, in the honors universally given to you? Give heed to yourself for you are mortal, "for dust you are and unto dust you shall return." Pass in review those persons who have enjoyed positions of eminence before you. Where are those who held the exercise of political power? Where the peerless orators? Where are they who had charge of the national assemblies – the famous breeders of horses, the generals, the governors, the sovereigns? Are not they all dust? Are not they all legend? Is it not true that a few bones are the memorial to the life of these men? (Basil, *Homilia in illud: "Attende tibi ipsi"* [*CPG* 2847]; cf. Cribiore 1997)

Like the maxims encountered in *P. Bouriant* 1 and arguably incorporated into the penultimate passages of *P. Cotsen-Princeton* 1, the core sentence – often attributed to one (or more) of the seven sages – finds echo across a broad swath of philosophical and monastic literary articulation. Rather than a "fragmenting of substantive thought" (Kaster 1988, p. 12), Basil's skillful elaboration reflects classical deployment of standard media – the reworking of malleable content to address a new historical moment and/or audience.

29.4.4 O.Cairo 44674.118

A final artifact again affirms foundational late antique links between gnomic and *chreic*, biblical and *apophthegmatic*, classroom and literary source material. Faintly visible on two faces of a small "Epiphanian" ostracon is content comprised of material most broadly defined as two Coptic maxims and a *chreia* (*O.Cairo* 44674.118; cf. Winlock and Crum 1926). Per Winlock and Crum's provisional transcription, the *verso*'s "maxims," in more familiar guise, double as Proverbs 13.7 and 13.13:

> There are those who make themselves rich, having nothing, and there are those who humble themselves, while being very [wealthy] (Prov. 13.7).

> He who despises a matter, he will be despised; the one who acts according to the commandment, [this one] is safe; nothing good will happen [(to a deceitful son)] (Prov. 13.13).

The ostracon's *recto* contains what appears to be a paraphrase of this content. It is presented as a *chreia*, again attributed to Basil. Elsewhere, it remains "unattested:"

> Apa Basilios – for who has ever been blessed because he had property, or who has been saved while in bodily rest.

Although by virtue of traditional cataloguing this artifact has long escaped categorization as school related, both adoptive form and adaptive content appear distinctive. The combination of two "moral maxims" gleaned from Proverbs and a "saying" attributed to a famous monk remain pedagogically provocative (Cf. Larsen 2013b; 2017; 2018).

29.5 Audience

In her groundbreaking work on ancient education, Cribiore has underscored the challenges inherent to identifying more advanced literary strains of classroom investment (1996). The artifacts examined here affirm these assessments. The iterative media and modes through which late ancient "literature" is disseminated, often limit the use of either descriptive delineation or material manifestation to securely distinguish whether respective articulations should be assigned school and/or literary provenance (cf. Cribiore 2001; Larsen 2009, 2018). Uniformly patent, however, is the degree to which classroom media continue to define the trajectories of composition that ultimately transferred and transformed diverse cultural, religious, and compositional threads into the literature of late antiquity. As emergent sources serve as useful measures of both confluence and re-configuration, they link disparate audiences in juxtapositions that remain implicitly hybrid.

29.5.1 *Maxim*/Chreia

As students were encouraged to report "the assigned chreia ... with the same words or in others" (Theon, *Gymn*. 101 [Kennedy 2003, p. 19]), simply mimicking the teacher may at times have been the norm. For example, in elucidating the *chreia*, Aphthonius takes as his example the rearticulation of a well-known maxim, here assigned to Isocrates: "Isocrates said: 'The root of education is bitter, but the fruits are sweet' (*Progymn*. 23 [Kennedy 2003, p. 98]; cf. *Ad Demonicum* 1.47). Ultimately, however, a student's mastery was manifested in adept elaboration. For example,

> The blessed [Praise] Syncletica said, "It is a struggle and great toil at first for those who approach God, but then it is unspeakable joy [Paraphrase]. Just as they who want to start a fire are engulfed in smoke and reduced to tears at first and in this way attain the desired object, so too [Comparison[A]] – for it says, 'Our God is a consuming fire' [Heb. 12:29] [Testimony] – must we start the divine fire within ourselves with tears and toil" [Comparison[B]] (AP_GS 3.34 [Wortley])

As elaborative elements are woven into an elegantly crafted *ergasia*, paraphrase and expansion masks the familiar form of Isocrates's simple *chreia*. Less "simple homespun wisdom" (Wilken 2012, p. 105), than sophisticated manipulation of a classic rhetorical form, the verbal tenor of this late ancient reframing preserves both the *chreia*'s technical and morally useful (*khreiôdês*) character.

29.5.2 Fable

Deft adaptation is similarly illustrated in late ancient reworking of familiar fables. For example, included among content collected by Babrius, one encounters a storyline originally excerpted from the writings of Hesiod:

> Prometheus was a god, but of the first dynasty. He it was, they say, that fashioned man from the earth, to be the master of the beasts. On man he hung, the story goes, two wallets filled with the faults of humankind; the one in front contained the faults of other men, the one behind the bearer's own, and this was the larger wallet. That's why, it seems to me, men see the failings of each other very clearly, while unaware of those which are their own (*Fabula* 66 [Perry]; Cf. Diogenes Laertius 6.27).

In late antiquity, the fable's protagonist appears in alternate guise. Simultaneously, the overall "moral" is preserved as the narrative is recast to address a new historical setting and audience:

> A brother at Scetis committed a fault. A council was called to which Abba Moses was invited, but he refused to go to it. Then the priest sent someone to say to him: "Come, for everyone is waiting for you." So he got up and went. He took a leaking jug, filled it with water and carried it with him. The others came out to meet him and said to him: "What is this, Father?" The old man said to them: "My sins run out behind me, and I do not see them, and today I am coming to judge the errors of another." When they heard that they said no more to the brother but forgave him. (AP_G Moses 1 [Ward]; Cf. AP_G Pior 3)

Underscoring the inherent malleability of requisite forms, further condensation results in the same teaching being recast as a simpler *chreia*:

> Abba John said: "We have put the light burden on one side, that is to say, self-accusation, and we have loaded ourselves with a heavy one, that is to say self-justification." (AP_John Colobos 21 [Ward]; Cf. AP_G Bessarion 7)

As each articulation renders the lines that tether classroom practice with literary production at once subtler and more patent than perhaps at any other point in history, recurrent threads weave together both continuity and change.

29.5.3 Narrative

Recognition of derivatively deployed content also lends unexpected texture to longer narration. For example, a narrative included in the pedagogical writings of Plutarch commends the importance of interspersing "rest" and "labor:"

> For, just as plants are nourished by moderate applications of water, but are drowned by many in succession, in the same fashion the mind is made to grow by properly adapted tasks, but is submerged by those which are excessive. Children must be given some breathing-space from continued tasks, for we must bear in mind that our whole life is divided between relaxation and application. For this reason there have been created not only waking hours but also sleep, not only war but also peace, not only storm but also fair weather, not only periods of vigorous activity but also holidays. In short, rest gives relish to labor. We may observe that this holds true not merely in the case of living creatures, but also in the case of inanimate things, for we unstring bows and lyres that we may be able to tighten them again. The body generally is maintained by hunger and its satisfaction, and the mind by relaxation and labor. (Plutarch, *Lib. Educ.* 9c–d [Babbitt])

Alternately, and aptly reconfigured, in late antique parlance, the same pedagogical juxtaposition supplies the structure for a familiar portrait of Antony relaxing with the brethren:

> A hunter in the desert saw Abba Anthony enjoying himself with the brethren and he was shocked. Wanting to show him that it was necessary sometimes to meet the needs of the brethren, the old man said to him: "Put an arrow in your bow and shoot it." So he did. The old man then said: "Shoot another," and he did so. Then the old man said: "Shoot yet again," and the hunter replied: "If I bend my bow so much I will break it.' Then the old man said to him: 'It is the same with the work of God. If we stretch the brethren beyond measure they will soon break. Sometimes it is necessary to come down to meet their needs." When he heard these words the hunter was pierced by compunction and, greatly edified by the old man, he went away. As for the brethren, they went home strengthened. (AP_G Antony 13 [Ward]; Cf. AP_PJ 10.2)

Here again, the subtle skein that links Plutarch's pedagogical preoccupations with Antony's investment in forming a new generation of brothers is difficult to ignore.

A final series of exemplars is characterized by eminently simple assignation. Three variations of essentially the same "active" *chreia*, are respectively preserved in both Greek and Latin:

> It was said concerning [Amma Sarah] that for sixty years she lived beside the river and never lifted her eyes to look at it. (AP_ G Sarah 3 [Ward]; Cf. AP_PJ 7.19)
>
> They said of Helladius that he lived twenty years in his cell, and did not once raise his eyes to look at the roof. (AP_PJ 4.16 [Ward])
>
> They said of Ammoi that though he was ill in a bed for several years, he never relaxed his discipline and never went to the store cupboard at the back of his cell to see what was in it. (AP_PJ 4.11 [Ward])

The appearance of parallel, but expanded, literary elements in Buddhist narrative tradition, introduces broader questions of ancient/late ancient dissemination:

> In the Great Cave of Kurandaka, it seems, there was a lovely painting of the Renunciation of the Seven Buddhas. A number of Bhikkus wandering about around the dwellings saw the painting and said, "What a lovely painting, venerable sir!" The Elder said, "For more than sixty years friends, I have lived in the cave, and I did not know whether there was any painting there or not. Now, today, I know it through those who have eyes." The Elder, it seems, though he had lived there for so long, had never raised his eyes to look up at the cave. And at the door of his cave there was a great ironwood tree. And the Elder had never looked up at that either. He knew it was in flower when he saw its petals on the ground each year." (Buddhaghosa, *The Path of Purification* 38) [Bhikku Nanamoli])

As the symbolic action assigned Christian "ammas" and "abbas" finds expression in a venerable "Elder" surrounded by visiting Bhikkus, it underscores the degree to which aptly assigned narrative detail marks the broad influence of common forms and audience in shaping emergent literary content.

29.6 Conclusion

Wedding literary media with classroom practice and contexts, the excerpts, artifacts, and exercises examined here raise as many questions as they answer. Implicit intersections elucidate not rote mechanics that render substantive thought into sound bites but, instead, a sustained trajectory of creative reframing (more transparent in broad deployment than in isolated articulation). The fact that "more [gnomic] sentences survive in schoolhands than fragments of any other literature and any other form" (Morgan 1998, p. 122) affirms the merits of viewing the "fragmentary" literature of late antiquity through a pedagogical prism. In both pedestrian and profound ways, what emerges is a kaleidoscope of literary creation and dissemination. Each hue elucidates the degree to which malleable media seem particularly suitable for addressing audiences that appear increasingly hybrid. Troubling trajectories traditionally delineated as fundamentally disparate, these literary landscapes appear to transcend chronological, geographical, religious, and linguistic divides.

Once such patterns become visible, it is difficult to ignore concomitant questions about the determinative role that perceived authorship and audience has played in shaping contemporary consideration of late ancient literature. Long-standing convention has framed Christian and, more particularly, monastic authors and educators as somehow engaged in alternate forms of praxis (Marrou 1956; Guy 1974; Rappe 2001) – or, in turn, no practice at all (Wilken 2012). However, the simple complexity encountered in melded material and literary remains raises serious questions about the adequacy of such assessment. If one is to move beyond depictions of late ancient literature as uniquely "less synthetic and sophisticated" than its Greco-Roman counterparts (Kaster 1988), it is the deployment of common classroom media that eloquently elucidates the static fluidity that characterizes established forms. Both texts and artifacts invite further exploration of the "habits of thinking and writing" (Kennedy 2003, p. ix), which persist from the classical period, through late antiquity, into Byzantium and beyond. They instead commend embracing late ancient literary models that premise reframing of core content through common media to address diverse audiences. They invite replacing simple binaries with complex configurations, manifested in multifaceted composition and disseminated along textual trajectories which link Egypt and Syria, Gaul and Central Asia, Cappadocia and Thebes.

REFERENCES

Babbitt, Frank Cole. ed. and trans. (1986). *De liberis educandis*. In: *Moralia* 1: 1–69. Cambridge, MA: Harvard University Press.

Bonner, Stanley. (1977). *Education in Ancient Rome: From the Elder Pliny to the Younger Pliny*. Berkeley: University of California Press.

Bucking, Scott. (2011). *Practice Makes Perfect: P. Cotsen-Princeton 1 and the Training of Scribes in Christian Egypt*. Los Angeles: Cotsen Occasional.

Buddhaghosa. (1999). *The Path of Purification: Visuddhimagga* (trans. Bhikku Nanamoli). Seattle, WA: BPE Pariyatti.

Burton-Christie, Douglas. (1993). *The Word in the Desert: Scripture and the Quest for Holiness in Early Christian Monasticism*. New York: Oxford University Press.

Carlig, Nathan. (2016). P. Bour. 1 (P.Sorb.inv. 826 = MP$_3$ 2643): Reconstruction Codicologique. *Zeitschrift für Papyrologie und Epigraphik*, 198: 196–201.

Chin, Catherine. (2007). *Grammar and Christianity in the Late Roman World*. Philadelphia: University of Pennsylvania Press.

Clarysse, Willy and Wouters, Alfons. (1970). A Schoolboy's Exercise in the Chester Beatty Library. *Ancient Society*, 1: 201–235.

Clark, W. K. L. trans. (1925). *The Ascetic Works of Saint Basil*. New York: Society for Promoting Christian Knowledge.

Cribiore, Raffaella. (1996). *Writing, Teachers and Students in Greco-Roman Egypt*. Atlanta, GA: Scholars Press.

Cribiore, Raffaella. (1997). An unidentified fragment of Basilius of Caesarea. In: *Akten des 21. Intenationalen Papyrologenkongresses, Berlin, 13.–19.8.1995* (ed. B. Kramer, W. Luppe, H. Maehler and G. Poethke), 187–193. Archiv für Papyrusforschung und Verwandte Gebiete Beiheft 3. Stuttgart and Leipzig.

Cribiore, Raffaella. (2001). *Gymnastics of the Mind: Greek Education in Hellenistic and Roman Egypt*. Princeton, NJ: Princeton University Press.

Gibson, Craig. (2008). *The Progymnasmata of Libanius*. Atlanta: Scholars Press.

Guy, Jean Claude. (1974). Educational innovation in the Desert Fathers. *Eastern Churches Review* 6: 44–51.

Harvey, Susan Ashbrook. (1996). Review of *The Desert Fathers on monastic community*, by Graham Gould. *Journal of Roman Studies* 86: 241–242.

Hock, Ronald and O'Neil, Edward. (1985). *The Chreia in Ancient Rhetoric: Progymnasmata*. Atlanta: Scholars Press.

Hock, Ronald and O'Neil, Edward. (2001). *The Chreia and Ancient Rhetoric: Classroom Exercises*. Atlanta: Scholars Press.

Jouguet, P. and Perdrizet, P. (1906). Le Papyrus Bouriant no. 1. Un cahier d'écolier grec d'Egypte. *Studien zur Paleographie und Papyruskunde* 6: 148–161.

Kaster, Robert A. (1988). *Guardians of Language: The Grammarian and Society in Late Antiquity*. Berkeley: University of California Press.

Kennedy, George A. trans. and ed. (2003). *Progymnasmata: Greek Textbooks of Prose Composition and Rhetoric*. Atlanta: Scholars Press.

Larsen, Lillian I. (2001). Ørkenfedrenes Apophthegmata og den klassiske Retoriske Tradisjon. *Meddelanden från Collegium Patristicum Lundense* 16: 26–37.

Larsen, Lillian I. (2008). The *Apophthegmata Patrum*: Rustic rumination or rhetorical recitation. *Meddelanden från Collegium Patristicum Lundense* 23: 21–30.

Larsen, Lillian I. (2013a). "On learning a new alphabet": The sayings of the Desert Fathers and the Monostichs of Menander. *Studia Patristica* 55: 59–77.

Larsen, Lillian I. (2013b). Re-drawing the interpretive map: Monastic education as civic formation in the *Apophthegmata Patrum*. *Coptica* 12: 1–34.

Larsen, Lillian I. (2016). Early monasticism and the rhetorical tradition: Sayings and stories as schooltexts. In *Religion and Education in Late Antiquity* (ed. Peter Gemeinhardt, Liv Van Hoef, and Peter Van Nuffelen), 13–33. Farnham: Ashgate.

Larsen, Lillian I. (2017). Monastic Paideia: Textual fluidity in the classroom. In: *Studying Snapshots: On Manuscript Culture, Textual Fluidity, and New Philology* (ed. Liv Ingeborg Lied and Hugo Lundhaug), 156–177. Berlin: De Gruyter.

Larsen, Lillian I. (2018). Excavating the excavations of monastic education in Egypt. In: *Monastic Education in Late Antiquity: The Transformation of Classical Paideia* (ed. Lillian I. Larsen and Samuel Rubenson), 101–124. Cambridge: Cambridge University Press.

Larsen, Lillian I. and Rubenson, Samuel. ed. (2018). *Monastic Education in Late Antiquity: The Transformation of Classical Paideia*. Cambridge: Cambridge University Press.

Marrou, Henri I. (1956). *History of Education in Antiquity* (trans. George Lamb). Madison: University of Wisconsin Press.

Marrou, Henri I. (1960). *Saint Augustine and His Influence through the Ages*. 2nd ed. New York: Harper.

Morgan, Teresa. (1998). *Literate Education in the Hellenistic and Roman Worlds*. Cambridge: Cambridge University Press.

Morgan, Teresa. (2007). *Popular Morality in the Early Roman Empire*. Cambridge: Cambridge University Press.

Norlin, George. ed. and trans. (1956). *Ad Demonicum*. Cambridge, MA: Harvard University Press.

O'Neil, Edward N. (1981). The chreia in Greco-Roman literature and education. In: *The Institute for Antiquity and Christianity Report: 1972–1980* (ed. M. Meyer), 18–22. Claremont, CA: Claremont Graduate School.

Rappe, Sara. (2001). The new math: How to add and subtract pagan elements in Christian education. In: *Education in Greek and Roman Antiquity* (ed. Yun Lee Too), 405–432. Leiden: Brill.

Russell, Donald A. trans. and ed. (2001). *Quintilian: The Orator's Education*. Books 1–2. Cambridge, MA: Harvard University Press.

Sinkewicz, Robert E. ed. and trans. (2003). *Evagrius Pontus: The Greek Ascetic Corpus*. New York: Oxford University Press.

Too, Yun Lee. ed. (2001). *Education in Greek and Roman Antiquity*. Leiden: Brill.

Ward, Benedicta. (1986). *The Sayings of the Desert Fathers: The Alphabetical Collection*. Kalamazoo, MI: Cistercian Publications.

Ward, Benedicta. (2003). *The Desert Fathers: Sayings of the Early Christian Monks*. London: Penguin Classics.

Watts, Edward. (2006). *City and School in Late Antique Athens and Alexandria*. Berkeley: University of California Press.

Wilken, Robert L. (2012). *The First Thousand Years: A Global History of Christianity*. New Haven, CT: Yale University Press.

Wimbush, Vincent L. (1997). Interpreting resistance, resisting interpretations. *Semeia* 79: 1–14.

Winlock, H. E. and Crum, W. E. (1926). *The Monastery of Epiphanius at Thebes*. 2 vols. New York: Metropolitan Museum of Art.

Wortley, John. trans. (2012). *The Book of the Elders: Sayings of the Desert Fathers, the Systematic Collection*. Collegeville, MN: Cistercian Publications.

Wortley, John. trans. (2013). *The Anonymous Sayings of the Desert Fathers*. Cambridge: Cambridge University Press.

Wright, Frank A. ed. and trans. (1991). *Jerome: Select Letters*. Cambridge, MA: Harvard University Press.

CHAPTER THIRTY

Literature of Knowledge

Marco Formisano

This chapter is devoted to late antique technical and scientific writing, particularly in Latin, a strand of textuality that has generally been consigned by modern scholarship to the very margins of the ancient literary and cultural system. These texts have been the object of a double condemnation; they have been perceived as marginal texts from the most marginal phase of ancient literary history. Yet the simple fact that a large number of texts on a range of disciplines – medicine, veterinary medicine, architecture, the art of war, land surveying, and others – were produced during the late Roman Empire and have been transmitted to us should be sufficient to attract the attention not only of historians and historians of science and technology but also of literary scholars.

Classicists interested in ancient literary culture can approach technical treatises from the perspective of their very marginality in the literary system; these texts have much to say about that system precisely because they tend either to reproduce or to enter into conflict with its principles. We might ask questions regarding the differences between these "technical" texts and the more traditionally "literary" texts that they cite, or regarding the argumentative strategies pursued by "technical" authors in order to present their work to a general audience that, although highly educated, was in most cases not particularly familiar with specific items of knowledge in the various fields. A related question is this: What form does the text take in order to present and maintain a certain degree of applicability and usability in extra-textual reality, something that many modern readers implicitly consider the priority of any technical text?

These questions, raised over the past decades, can *grosso modo* be classified under two general labels that well illustrate the current scholarly debate on the "literary aspects," as scholars tend to put it, of technical writings. The first label is a German word, *Wissensvermittlung*. This concept has been identified and variously articulated above all, but not exclusively, within German-language scholarship (see esp. Meißner 1999; Formisano 2001; Horster and Reitz 2003, 2005; Asper 2007; König and Whitmarsh 2007) and focuses mostly on the ways a technical text works essentially as a medium for transmitting a particular kind of knowledge by recurring to certain kinds of language, sets of arguments, logical structures, classifications of various parts and/or subfields, and responses to (sometimes highly hypothetical) readerly expectations. Particular attention has been directed at the leading principles of the systematization of the field described by a given text. In his pathbreaking *Das systematische Lehrbuch* (1960), Manfred Fuhrmann established the features of a genre – the ancient "manual" or "handbook" – by identifying its single most important characteristic as an inherent drive toward the systematization of knowledge. Connected to this key concept of *Wissensvermittlung* is that of authorial self-fashioning. Literary scholars interested in ancient technical writing often focus on the question of how authors not only introduce their field by offering an ordered classification of the subject matter but also on how they present themselves as authorities in a given discipline (for instance, Doody and Taub 2009; Fögen 2009).

Both approaches, which are often combined and presented as interconnected, emphasize significant commonalities between technical and literary texts; as a result, ancient technical treatises can be seen as part of the larger ancient literary discourse and can be read as *texts* rather than only as sources for the history of science and technology. And yet, precisely the emphasis on formal and rhetorical aspects such as argumentative and ordering strategies as well as authorial self-fashioning is based on the implicit assumption that the "literary aspects" of technical texts can be seen as detached from their technical *content*, as if their literary quality were to be considered only on the level of the linguistic surface (language, style, rhetoric), as not really connected with the subject matter. In the above-mentioned contributions to the field there is regularly discussion of "literary polish" or "literary allusions" as something that any technical writing unavoidably contains. The result of this approach is that the "literary" is conceived as something that is *added* to the technical content of these texts by various stylistic and rhetoric means, rather than as an inherent quality of the texts themselves, *qua* texts. A similar argument can be made, of course, for other genres. Epistolography in particular shares an analogous tension between a concrete extratextual goal, for instance, the transmission of certain specific information, and its intrinsic literariness.

For these and other reasons, then, instead of the label "technical writing" or the influential German term *Fachliteratur*, I prefer to use here and elsewhere (see Formisano 2012, 2017a) the term "literature of knowledge," a looser definition perhaps, but one that places emphasis on the concept of literature rather than on that of technology. Relatedly, I prefer to reverse the common trend in scholarship briefly illustrated above, by pointing to the technical core of the content of these texts, rather than just to formal aspects such as style, rhetoric, or intertextual allusions. A "technical" text, just like any other text, can certainly be read for the information it provides on a certain subject or topic. For example, we read Palladius's *Opus agri culturae* in order to obtain a view of late antique agricultural practices and political and legal measures taken in that period in order to respond to or prevent certain problems; similarly we can look for intertextual references to other authoritative texts on farming, such as those by Varro, Virgil, or Columella. Yet a text cannot be reduced to a mere instrument whose primary function is simply to transmit knowledge and instructions on how to apply it. It is equally important to remember that the text *is* that knowledge, so that even seemingly arid technical content can actually have sophisticated meaning, one that displays the highly literary quality precisely of that knowledge. Knowledge, in fact, once it takes on the form of a text, irreversibly modifies its own nature by becoming subject to the hermeneutical openness and epistemic instability that, by definition, characterize every text. Whatever content a text may have, the text is not equivalent to that content. For instance, the agriculture of Palladius's text is not *the same as* the agriculture that was actually practiced "out there;" the medicine presented by Julian's doctor Oribasius cannot be considered "medicine" itself. This perspective should not be surprising to classical scholars: Who would consider Virgil's *Georgics* to be a textbook or handbook on ancient agriculture, whatever the poem itself might claim? And yet, these same sophisticated readers of Virgil seem generally unwilling to conclude that Columella's or Palladius's texts are not mere "agricultural handbooks."

The following discussion, taking account of limitations of space, pursues three avenues simultaneously. The first two have been touched upon above: first, discussing the literature of knowledge in accordance with critical approaches valid for any other text; and second, identifying specifically late antique traits of these texts. The third large point has to do with the role played by the late antique literature of knowledge within the larger history of Western science. In a previously published article (Formisano 2013) I argue that late antiquity plays a key role in this history by advancing toward a better definition of what we might call "technical knowledge": Late antique texts display a progressive tendency toward the emancipation of technical and practical activities from the standards of traditional education, that is, from the dominion of rhetoric. This statement might appear to contradict my earlier insistence on the literariness of these texts, but in fact it is meant to complement and complicate the discussion of the rich textuality of technical knowledge. In other words, a text can, of course, be read *and used* for the content it conveys (in the terms of *Wissensvermittlung* as described above), even though the transmission of technical knowledge is not the text's primary function. I will briefly return to this point later.

In what follows, instead of producing a list of various technical texts and arranging them by discipline, I focus on a selection of passages from a variety of texts that exemplify this approach. By way of emphasizing the literariness of the texts, I organize them under three thematic headings: competition; fighting, grafting, and healing; the pursuit of practicability.

30.1 Competition

Late antique literature has been often seen as derivative: a *littérature au second degré* that derives its substance from older and thus authoritative texts. Modern readers generally have difficulties reading a late antique text that openly presents itself as reworking, rewriting, or rearranging a previous text (the most extreme example being the *centones*) without comparing the text with its model(s). This happens for a number of reasons, mostly related to the *déformation professionelle* of classicists, traditionally interested in identifying models and reconstructing genealogies. This hermeneutic principle has profoundly conditioned the reading and critical appreciation of the late antique literature of knowledge, seen as a set of vessels of information stemming from the authorities of the earlier, "classical" past.

Here I consider a text that in its very title proclaims its derivative quality: the so-called *Medicina Plini*. This text, probably composed in the fourth century, is typical of its genre in many respects, both in form and content. As is well known (Fischer 1988; Nutton 2004; Temkin 2006), late ancient medical literature progressively abandoned the highly theoretical stance that had characterized the Greek medical discourse from Hippocrates to Galen. Late medical texts instead emphasized therapeutic practices and easily obtainable natural cures and insisted on the necessity of rendering medical knowledge accessible in plain language and an intelligible style of presentation, such as the almost ubiquitous *a capite ad calcem* (from head to toe), so as to allow for easy consultation and application by these texts' "non-specialist" readers, including those suffering from illness, without the intermediary of a doctor. The *Medicina Plinii* illustrates this broader tendency, together with other texts from the same period (fourth and fifth centuries), such as Oribasius's *Epitome*, Marcellus Empiricus's *De medicamentis*, Theodorus Priscianus's *Euporista*, and Pseudo-Apuleius's *Herbarius*.

As its title suggests, most of the content of this treatise in three books directly derives from the medical section of Pliny's *Natural History* (books 20–32); interestingly enough, the manuscripts refer to the author as *Plinius Secundus Iunior*, as if he were a younger version of the elder Pliny, a point to which we will return. Already in the text's preface we find the expression of a Plinian attitude toward Greek doctors (*NH* 29.14), which in turn derives from Cato's encyclopedic *Libri ad Marcum filium*.

> Often it has happened that while traveling (*in peregrinationibus*) I have been cheated by doctors in various ways because of my own illness or that of my family: Some doctors sell very cheap remedies for huge prices, others out of greed take on cases that they do not know how to cure. I have also known certain doctors to act dishonestly in this way: They drag out the length of mild illness which could be dispelled in a few days, if not hours, and they consider it profitable for their own patients to be sick for a long time, and are more cruel than the diseases themselves. And so it seemed necessary to me to bring together aids to health from many places and collect them like in a book of extracts (*ut undique valetudinis auxilia contraherem et velut breviario colligerem*), so that I could avoid these sorts of traps wherever I happened to go. And from that time I have embarked on journeys in confidence, knowing that, if I do catch some illness, they will not make a profit out of me or assess the value of the opportunity. (trans. Doody 2009, adapted)

This passage illustrates several important and interrelated points. The frequent journeys of the author, which might appear to be a personal touch, embedded as they are in a first-person narrative, are actually a topos that recurs in other medical texts of the same period (e.g. Marcellus Empiricus and Pseudo-Apuleius). More generally, themes of travel and displacement heavily characterize late Latin textuality at large. Poems such as Ausonius's *Mosella*, Rutilius Namatianus's *De reditu suo* or Sidonius Apollinaris's *Propempticon ad libellum*, as well as Ammianus Marcellinus's *Res Gestae* among other works, are centrally based on the experiences of travel – true or fictional – of their authors (Formisano 2017b). Another topos is the bad faith of the doctors, interested in material profit rather than in the good health of their patients. Here it receives a further layer of meaning, being cited as the reason why the author decided to record in writing his collection of remedies. The idea is that, by recurring to the booklet, the author, his family members, and friends will not only stay healthy while traveling but will also be able to economize their resources.

Regarding the intricate relationship of the *Medicina Plinii* with its famous early imperial model, Aude Doody observes, "While the *Medicina Plinii* is dependent on Pliny's name and Pliny's text for some of its authority, its radical reworking of the *Natural History*'s approach to medicine could be seen as an implicit critique of Pliny's organising strategies: the book of extracts aims both to co-opt and to supplant the authority of the source-text" (Doody 2009, p. 95).

In other words, the fact that the author stays in the tradition of Pliny the Elder and shares his strong feeling against doctors does not prevent him from writing a new text. More specifically, "the *Medicina Plinii* acts on Pliny's philosophy of self-help by making his material accessible to patients in all circumstances" (Doody 2009, p. 98). Thus at the end of book 1 we find the author reporting a remedy for abscesses (*vomicae*) that he himself has successfully used on others (*aliquot a me curati sunt infra praefinitum tempus compositione ea quae infra scripta est*, 1.26. 5–6), whereas the earlier Pliny "rarely comments on his own experience of any of the cures he recommends." Thus the author of the *Medicina Plinii* "appropriates Pliny's authority at the same time as he subverts the basis on which the authority is established in the *Natural History*" (Doody 2009, pp. 99, 105).

This feature of a little-known medical treatise is extendable to many late antique texts, which tend to appropriate classical texts with the surprising effects of entering into a competition with them and then radically subverting their meaning. The best-known texts that follow this pattern are the *centones*, which programmatically use Virgil's or Homer's words in order to convey completely different meanings, some of which directly conflict with the original text. Rather as Proba in her *Cento Vergilianus* affirms that the words she uses are the very words of the revered classical poet, so Plinius Junior, playing perhaps on his own name (or pseudonym?), tells his readers that he is giving them "Pliny's medicine."

30.2 Fighting, Grafting, and Healing

One of the most distinct recurring features of the late antique literature of knowledge, as we have just seen in the case of the *Medicina Plinii*, is its epitomary nature. Almost every author conceives of his work as an epitome of previous works, which for different reasons need to be rewritten. The *Medicina Plinii*, for example, extracts cures and formulas from Pliny's *Natural History* in order to render them directly accessible. Julian's doctor, Oribasios, composes a *Synagogia iatriké*, or "medical compilation," which he later himself epitomizes with the double agenda of gathering and preserving medical texts written by previous authors (especially Galen) and selecting medical norms that are still valid and applicable. Cetius Faventinus (probably third or fourth century) epitomizes Vitruvius's architectural treatise following a similar strategy, in this case annulling the theoretical pretenses of the Augustan predecessor by emphasizing the practicability of the norms for constructing private buildings (Meißner 1999, pp. 266–268).

One of the most influential late antique technical works is without doubt the *Epitoma rei militaris* by Flavius Vegetius Renatus, who dedicated it to the emperor, probably Theodosius the Great (late fourth century), in order to propose military reform. Interestingly, although the link between the collection of past rules and norms and applicability has such a programmatic position within the treatise, Vegetius never directly quotes from or refers to specific passages of earlier authors. Vegetius's epitomatory method does not aim at a faithful if abbreviated transmission of his sources in the way we have seen in the case of *Medicina Plinii* and in other texts; and he uses the military knowledge deriving from his sources (such as Cato, Sallust, Caesar, and Frontinus) in such a way that differences between various ages are silenced, giving rise to an idealized synchronic imaginary in which recent military tactics and strategy coexist with very old institutions. The *Epitoma* has thus been described as "not a true Art of War, but a political and strategic tract" (Milner 1996, p. xxviii), although I would argue that such a synchronization of different historical phases is a characteristic feature of the textual form of military knowledge. This aspect can be seen as the main characteristic of the art of war as literary genre.

It is no accident that Vegetius's work very soon became the undisputed classic in the field: Among ancient military treatises, only the *Epitoma rei militaris* contains the characteristic features of the genre "art of war," which became highly popular in early modern Europe (Richardot 1998; Allmand 2011; Formisano 2010, 2014; Schwager 2012). Ancient military texts and their long tradition until Carl von Clausewitz at least (1780–1831) display one recurring feature in particular: Whether or not they cite specific *exempla*, the past lies at their core, for they represent as ideal the organization of the army *as it was*. For this reason historians often show impatience and dissatisfaction when using military texts in order to reconstruct the military organization of a certain period and quickly dismiss them as confused and inaccurate sources. Yet, as we have seen, precisely this particular relationship to the past is *the* mark of the ancient art of war and its tradition. Vegetius's *Epitoma* makes knowledge of the past the keystone of the art of war. Here, then, the concept of the "epitome" refers not only to the process of abridging specific texts but also, and more fundamentally, to the creation of a system of knowledge: The art of war cannot be anything else but an epitome of the past. And it is not coincidental that this development occurred precisely during late antiquity, when the confrontation with the past assumed a fundamental role in literary and cultural systems.

Some other texts that are today classified (and often dismissed) as "technical" illustrate a further fascinating aspect of this epitomatory function. They are epitomes not only in terms of content but also in terms of form: They programmatically include a poetical insertion. Palladius's *Opus agri culturae* (probably fifth century) and Marcellus Empiricus's *De medicamentis* (early fifth century), lengthy prose treatises, both end with a didactic poem (Formisano 2005). The former is an agricultural text in 15 books, the last one of which consists of a preface in epistolary form followed by 85 elegiac couplets on the topic of grafting, bearing the title *De insitione* (Martin 1976); Marcellus's pharmacological treatise of 37 books concludes with a didactic poem of 78 hexameters devoted to the preparation of remedies (*Carmen de speciebus*). In both cases, the subject matter of the poem has already been treated in the preceding prose text, so that the content of these poems does not have a structural function in terms of the transmission of knowledge. One might suppose that their function is purely "aesthetic," yet there is more to it than that: The specific subject of the two brief poems suggests a metaliterary reading. The techniques of grafting (Palladius) and of putting together or "composing" remedies (Marcellus) are transparent metaphors for their own texts.

Palladius refers to this aspect at the beginning of the poem:

> Pasiphilus, ornament of my trust, I rightly tell you whatever the shadows of my mind conceal. Twice seven books, a work on tilling fields (*opus agricolare*), my hand has written, but the feet are silent; they are not arranged in rhythms nor flowing with Apollo's river, but simple in their pure rusticity (*sed pura tantum rusticitate rudes*). You praise, value and love them, and you cherish these humble words with the affectionate concern of a friend. And so my growing confidence, which will delight (*laetificanda*) thanks to your judgment, has offered you this modest poem. (15.1–10)

The phrase *opus agricolare* (3) suggests both the subject matter and the simple, nonpoetical style of the previous 14, while *laetificanda* (10) suggests both "will delight" and "will be made fertile." A few couplets later, Palladius describes the process of grafting, using the language of marriage and copulation (13–18): *thalami, iungere, mixtus, gemina, confundere, duplicis*, and this, too, can be interpreted in a double way: The language *describes* the agricultural technique of grafting, but it also *performs* a grafting of poetry on to prose, thereby having the entire text culminate in a metaphor for the text itself taken from its own subject matter.

For his part, Marcellus Empiricus in the preface to his pharmacological treatise emphasizes the epitomatory quality of his work and then, similarly to Palladius, recurs to a poetic image which impressively fits the medical content of his book:

> I have composed this book on practical remedies with as much care and attention as I could, filling it with prescriptions for natural or man-made remedies which I gathered from many different places (*fartum undeunde collectis*). If there is anything suited to human health or healing which I have learned from others, or have successfully used myself, or have become acquainted with by reading, I took it from its scattered and hidden origins and brought it together, arranging it into a single body as Asclepius did with Virbius' scattered and wounded limbs (*id sparsum inconditumque collegi et in unum corpus quasi disiecta et lacera Asclepius Virbii membra composui*). (*pr.* 1)

The text becomes like the body of Hippolytus/Virbius reassembled by the primordial mythic doctor Asclepius (cf. Ovid, *Met.* 15, 479–551), not only because it stems from different sources but, more importantly, because the book itself *is* the remedy (compare the discussion of the *Medicinia Plinii* above).

At the end of the preface Marcellus justifies his insertion of a poem at the end of his treatise:

> We delighted with verses (*versiculis quoque lusimus*) composed so as to enumerate mixtures and drugs; not that the poetry contains anything worthwhile, but so that the poem may entice those who read and study this work, and a delightful expectation may win their favor. I have located this little text at the very end (*in infima parte*) of this manuscript, so that this work, which I have carefully (*sollertia nostra*) arranged, may come to its close in my own language (*sermone nostro*), and also so that my trifling (*nugas nostras*) play may be concealed by the superimposition of many pages. (*pr.* 7)

The poem is thus given two functions: to delight the reader after a long and tedious treatment of the medical subject matter and to close the text with the author's own words (*sermone nostro*). This very point implicitly emphasizes the fact that the text is an assemblage of parts that are in some sense *not* the author's words (for the similarity with the poetics of the cento as expressed by Ausonius, see Formisano 2007, p. 284). As with Palladius's text, *De medicamentis* is sealed with a piece of poetry that simultaneously reflects the content of the work and performs a *textualization* of the knowledge at stake.

30.3 The Pursuit of Practicability

In all texts discussed or briefly mentioned in this chapter, in addition to an emphasis on the epitome as a compositional method, another motif constantly emerges: the emphasis on practice as opposed to theory. In many cases theory is presented as being equivalent to *eloquentia*, the art of speaking well. As is well known, in the classical period, in accordance with Aristotelian and Ciceronian theorization, eloquence was thought capable of providing universal knowledge: It was the key to understanding all other disciplines or arts. To be able to talk about something well was considered equivalent to having a firm grasp and deep knowledge of it. Eloquence was not only the goal of a good education but also the means of acquiring social and political success. As Jeffrey Schnapp puts it, "Rhetoric was an *institutio* in the Latin sense: at once a method of organizing speech to achieve consensus within the city, an established body of customs and norms (linguistic, literary, and other), and a system for transmitting these customs from one generation to another" (1995, p. 101). During late antiquity, on the other hand, many factors contributed to a generally antirhetorical stance. Christianity played a fundamental role in this process, not only because of its inherent universalistic impulse to make knowledge available to everybody, including the uneducated and the barbarians, but also because it marked "the transition from a literary system anchored in the institution of rhetoric to one founded on the careful reading and exegesis of a written artifact," that is, the Bible (Schnapp 1995, p. 104). The educational and cultural system of classical *eloquentia* was thus dismantled and superseded by an equally powerful antirhetorical rhetoric. The late antique literature of knowledge acknowledges and appropriates this shift, emphasizing its own inherent conflict between practice and theory or, better, between a plain style, presented as not rhetorically adorned, and the sophistication of *eloquentia*. Whereas the strategy followed by their predecessors was one of adaptation, that is, of elevating practical knowledge to the level of theory via eloquence, technical authors now proudly declare that they are extraneous to the entire system.

In a medical text entitled *Euporista* (probably late fourth century, written first in Greek and then in Latin), Theodorus Priscianus exemplifies this tendency with great clarity, on the one hand denouncing the connection traditionally established between eloquence and medicine and on the other pleading for the return to a medicine completely based on natural remedies, instead of complex medical theories (Formisano 2004). The preface of the first book, which bears the title *Faenomenon*, touches upon a number of significant themes:

> It is fairly well known that not long ago I wrote some books on easily procurable medicine at the urging of my colleague Olympios; I wrote them in Greek

since that people has spread abroad the discipline of healing in their clear language. In the present volume, therefore, I will not aim for glory (*gloria*), and indeed in a scholarly work there is no need of eloquence, but of industry (*neque enim in logico opere eloquentia opus est sed labore*). Since the weakness of the human body demanded remedies, I decided to write them up, nature allowing me to do so with its swift cures. For not every illness permits a delay in the cure. Therefore, my dear friend, the remedies which by the agency of nature assist in the adornment of our bodies or in the obtaining or maintaining of health, I have now arranged in our language in your honor – not, I imagine, without gaining some fame (*fama*). After all, a work composed in both languages will have a greater number both of weaknesses and of judges. (*Faen.* pr. 1)

Two points are particularly interesting for our discussion. First is the rather surprising distinction between *gloria* and *fama*. While the original Greek version has already given the author a certain degree of *fama*, and he anticipates acquiring further *fama* from the new Latin version, he asserts that he is not aiming for *gloria*, a concept that he here associates with *eloquentia*. And soon thereafter, Theodorus disparagingly evokes the pursuit of *gloria* by unscrupulous doctors:

The patient lies there, tossed about in the storm of his illness. Then the flock of our profession gathers around, but instead of being motivated by pity for the dying man, instead of being mindful of the destiny imposed by our common nature, it is like an Olympic contest: One man exercising his eloquence, another engaging in argumentation, another concurring and another dissenting, they pursue an empty glory. (*inanem gloriam captant*). (*Faen.* 1.2)

Besides the contrast between *gloria* and *fama*, aligned with that between eloquence and medicine, Theodorus advocates for a type of natural medicine that directly recalls the defense of an ancient, pre-Greek and antitheoretical medicine seen above in the *Medicina Plinii*, the elder Pliny, and Cato. Theodorus introduces a powerful personification of Nature in the next paragraph of the preface of the *Faenomenon*; she speaks up in order to attack a certain type of doctor:

O race of mortals, ingrates in vain! The patient is being killed, he is not dying, and yet I am held responsible for human frailty. Diseases are dreadful, but I have given cures. Poisons lie hidden in bushes, but they contain even more healing functions. Enough of this peculiar, destructive argumentation and this vain love of verbosity (*perturbatrix disputatio atque iste loquacitatis vanus amor*). These are not the remedies I gave for the health of mortals, but rather the great potencies of seeds and fruits and herbs, and whatever else I have produced for mankind. (*Faen.* 1.2)

This call for the return to Nature – or more generally to origins – can be interpreted as a characteristically late antique cultural move, not only in the domain of the practical arts, but also in other kinds of texts such as historiography and poetry. Christian historians such as Eusebius and Orosius, for example, go back to the origins of the world in order to found a universal history. A number of anonymous antiquarian texts variously retell the origins of Rome (*Origo gentis Romanorum*, *Origo gentis Romanae*), while poets such as Claudian or Rutilius Namatianus develop the motif of the return to a natural, pre-cultural age (Formisano 2017b). Finally, both biblical and Vergilian exegesis can be seen as driven by a return to the origins, in the form of authoritative or sacred texts.

30.4 Conclusion

Within the current critical enthusiasm for late antique literature, the body of textuality called "technical literature" – which I prefer to describe as "the literature of knowledge" – has been distinctly marginalized. When they have been discussed, these texts have generally been treated as if they were fundamentally no different from technical texts written in other times and places. Scholars typically trace the historical develpoment of individual disciplinary discourses such as medicine or agriculture and discuss late antique texts in this framework, that is, interpret them from the perspective of the history of science and technology. This chapter pleads, instead, for a more carefully focused study of these texts in their specifically late antique cultural and literary context, at the same time shedding light on their inherent literariness.

NOTE

All translations are the author's unless otherwise indicated.

REFERENCES

Allmand, Christopher. (2013). *The* De Re Militari *of Vegetius. The Reception, Transmission and Legacy of a Roman Text in the Middle Ages*. Cambridge: Cambridge University Press.

Asper, Markus. (2007). *Griechische Wissenschaftstexte: Formen, Funktionen, Differenzierungsgeschichten*. Stuttgart: Franz Steiner.

Doody, Aude. (2009). Authority and authorship in the *Medicina Plinii*. In: *Authorial Voices in Greco-Roman Technical Writing* (ed. Aude Doody and Liba Chaia Taub), 93–105. Trier: WVT.

Doody, Aude and Taub, Liba Chaia. ed. (2009). *Authorial Voices in Greco-Roman Technical Writing*. Trier: WVT.

Fischer, Klaus-Dietrich. (1988). Anweisungen zur Selbstmedikation von Laien in der Spätantike. In: *XXX congrès international d'histoire de la médicine: Düsseldorf 31-VIII-5-IX-1986* (ed. Hans Schadewaldt and Karl-Heinz Leven), 315–340. Leverkusen: Vicom KG.

Fögen, Thorsten. (2009). *Wissen, Kommunikation und Selbstdarstellung. Zur Struktur und Charakteristik römischer Fachtexte der frühen Kaiserzeit*. Munich: Beck.

Formisano, Marco. (2001). *Tecnica e scrittura. Le letterature tecnico-scientifiche nello spazio letterario tardo-latino*. Rome.

Formisano, Marco. (2004). The "natural" medicine of Theodorus Priscianus. *Philologus* 148: 126–142.

Formisano, Marco. (2005). Veredelte Bäume und kultuvierte Texte. Lehrgedichte in technischen Proswerken der Spätantike. In: *Wissensvermittlung in dichterischer Gestalt* (ed. Marietta Horster and Christiane Reitz) 295–312. Stuttgart: Franz Steiner.

Formisano, Marco. (2007). Towards an aesthetic paradigm of late antiquity. *Antiquité Tardive* 15: 277–284.

Formisano, Marco. (2010). The renaissance tradition of the ancient art of war. In: *Andrea Palladio and The Architecture of Battle* (ed. Guido Beltramini), 226–239. Venice: Marsilio.

Formisano, Marco. (2012). Late antiquity, new departures. In: *The Oxford Handbook of Medieval Literature* (ed. Ralph J. Hexter and David Townsend), 509–534. Oxford: Oxford University Press.

Formisano, Marco. (2013). Late Latin encyclopaedism. Towards a new paradigm of practical knowledge. In: *Encyclopaedism from Antiquity to Renaissance* (ed. Jason König and Greg Woolf), 197–215. Cambridge: Cambridge University Press.

Formisano, Marco. (2014). Kriegskunst. In: *Renaissance-Humanismus: Lexikon zur Antikerezeption* (ed. Manfred Landfster), 490–495. Neuer Pauly Supplemente. Stuttgart: J.B. Metzler.

Formisano, Marco. (2017a). The poetics of knowledge. In: *Knowledge, Text and Practice in Ancient Technical Writing* (ed. Marco Formisano and Philip van der Eijk), 12–26. Cambridge: Cambridge University Press.

Formisano, Marco. (2017b). Displacing traditions. A new-allegorical reading of Ausonius, Claudian, and Rutilius Namatianus. In: *The Poetics of Late Latin Literature* (ed. Jas Elsner and Jesús Hernández Lobato), 207–235. Oxford: Oxford University Press.

Fuhrman, Manfred. (1960). *Das systematische Lehrbuch. Ein Beitrag zur Geschichte der Wissenschaften in der Antike*. Göttingen: Vandenhoeck & Ruprecht.

Horster, Marietta and Reitz, Christiane. ed. (2003). *Antike Fachschriftsteller. Literarischer Diskurs und sozialer Kontext*. Stuttgart: Franz Steiner.

Horster, Marietta and Reitz, Christiane. ed. (2005). *Wissensvermittlung in dichterischer Gestalt*. Stuttgart: Franz Steiner.

König, Jason and Whitmarsh, Tim. ed. (2007). *Ordering Knowledge in the Roman Empire*. Cambridge: Cambridge University Press.

Meißner, Burkhard. (1999). *Die technologische Fachliteratur der Antike: Struktur, Überlieferung und Wirkung technischen Wissens in der Antike.* Berlin: Akademie.

Martin, René. (1976). *Palladius. Traité d'agriculture.* Paris: Belles Lettres.

Milner, Nicolas P. (1996). *Vegetius: Epitome of Military Science.* Liverpool: Liverpool University Press.

Nutton, Vivian. (2004). *Ancient Medicine.* London: Routledge.

Temkin, Owsei. (2006). History of Hippocratism in late antiquity: The third century and the Latin West. In: *The Double Face of Janus and Other Essays in the History of Medicine* (ed. Owsei Temkin), 167–177. Baltimore, MD: Johns Hopkins University Press.

Richardot, Philippe. (1998). *Végèce et la culture militaire au Moyen Âge: Ve-Xve siècles.* Paris: Institut de Stratégie Comparée EPHE IV.

Schnapp, Jeffrey. (1995). Reading lessons: Augustine, Proba and the Christian détournement of antiquity. *Stanford Literature Review* 9: 99–123.

Schwager, Therese. (2012). *Militärtheorie im Späthumanismus: Kulturtransfer taktischer und strategischer Theorien in den Niederlanden und Frankreich (1590–1660).* Berlin: De Gruyter.

CHAPTER THIRTY-ONE

Inscriptions

Raymond Van Dam

Inscriptions were the most visible and public form of literature in late Roman society. Some literary texts began as oral performances in public venues, such as panegyrics or sermons, and other texts continued to be read aloud before audiences after their initial composition, such as saints' *Lives*. Some texts circulated widely between correspondents, such as letters, or among like-minded churchmen, such as theological treatises. But most literary manuscripts eventually disappeared from general public consumption to be stored in libraries or archives and read only by scribes, learned aristocrats, intellectuals, and churchmen.

By contrast, inscriptions were highly conspicuous throughout the late Roman world. In a broad definition inscriptions include almost all writings on media other than papyrus and parchment. Wood, in the form of white-washed boards, was probably the most common material, but very few wooden tablets have survived. Today the most common examples are inscriptions engraved on stones, such as marble blocks and slabs, the bases of statues and columns, the facades of buildings, and tombstones, or on bronze tablets, such as military diplomas. Inscriptions can also encompass graffiti, notations on lead seals and pipes, writing scratched on ceramics, and labels and texts set in mosaics. The most famous "inscription" from late antiquity was the caption that the emperor Constantine claimed to have seen attached to his vision of a luminous cross in the sky: "Conquer by this!" (Eusebius, *Vita Constantini* 1.28.2).

The objectives of engraving inscriptions on stones or bronze tablets were public display and permanence. Because these were goals shared with literary

---

A Companion to Late Antique Literature, First Edition.
Edited by Scott McGill and Edward J. Watts.
© 2018 John Wiley & Sons, Inc. Published 2018 by John Wiley & Sons, Inc.

works, authors and orators sometimes used inscriptions as reference points. In the mid-fourth century the priest Gregory of Nazianzus compared the treatise in which he had criticized the emperor Julian to a stone tablet, "more lofty and more prominent than the Pillars of Hercules," which would be an everlasting proclamation of infamy (*Orat.* 5.42).

Thinking about inscriptions as literature raises many issues. Even though emperors still circulated edicts and sent rescripts to their magistrates, and even though cities continued to ratify municipal ordinances, during the late antique period the quantity of legislative inscriptions in cities declined noticeably (section "Agency and Identity" below). Reading inscriptions requires familiarity with modern editorial conventions (section "Editions" below). Once edited, our first reaction is to interrogate inscriptions closely as historical "sources" in order to excavate the factual data (section "Sources" below). In contrast, evaluating inscriptions as "texts" raises the same concerns about the construction of narratives now prominent in trying to understand other literary genres (section "Texts" below). Reading inscriptions as sources or texts was not the first reaction for most people in antiquity, however. The low level of literacy transformed inscriptions into visual "images," stylized decoration accompanying monuments and statues (section "Images" below). Ancient audiences hence included many spectators and some readers, as well as censors and collectors (section "Audiences and Reception" below).

Within the regions that came to be included in the Roman Empire, most of the inscriptions were in Greek or Latin (or sometimes both languages), although other languages, such as Punic, Syriac, Hebrew, Aramaic, and Demotic, were also used. In the multitude of comprehensive modern collections, commonly known by acronyms such as *AE*, *CIL*, and *ILS* (see this chapter's abbreviations list), the dominant place of Christianity in the later Roman Empire and its successor states is apparent. Not only do most Christian inscriptions date from the period after the reign of Constantine, but the great majority of inscriptions from late antiquity were related to Christianity, either directly or indirectly (Tabbernee 2008; Cooley 2012, pp. 228–250; Salway 2014). The huge number of inscriptions, secular and Christian, is a powerful argument for more use of digital resources (Bodel 2012).

Although noting large themes and trends, the short survey in this chapter will often return to the many dimensions of one exemplary inscription from Rome. This dedication commemorated a senator whom the emperor Constantine promoted as prefect of Rome. In this case religion was not an issue. Constantine may have become the first Christian emperor, but he was still prepared to honor a pagan senator.

31.1 Agency and Identity

Emperors and their magistrates circulated many decisions. Some imperial edicts were supposed to be applicable throughout the empire. In 301 Diocletian and his fellow emperors issued an Edict on Maximum Prices: "The prices indicated in the concise list appended below are to be observed in the whole of our empire." But the reality of limited communication vanquished the rhetoric of universality. Even though fragments of inscribed copies of this edict have been discovered at more than 40 cities, its impact was restricted. No copies have been found in western provinces, and in the eastern empire it was displayed as an inscription only in three provinces. This limited dissemination suggests that individual provincial governors arranged for the engraving of the edict, or that a particular emperor, in this case, Galerius, may have been trying to strengthen his authority in western Asia Minor, Crete, and the Greek peninsula (Corcoran 1996).

Much imperial legislation took the form of responses to specific requests and petitions. Sometimes the emperors required public display. In 367 Valentinian I insisted that his new regulations about payments for pig dealers should be "engraved on a bronze tablet in the Hog Market [at Rome] as an eternal reminder" (*CTh* 14.4.4). In the later fifth century an emperor wanted a list of the tariffs imposed on ships sailing through the Hellespont "to be engraved on stone tablets next to the sea so that both collectors and payers might read the law" (Durliat and Guillou 1984). But most often the placement of inscriptions reflected local decisions. Cities might decide to honor a provincial governor or a municipal magistrate who was responsible for benefits, or local notables might want a public record of their accomplishments.

In the later empire the inscribing of imperial edicts declined. About 200 examples of imperial legislation have been found in inscriptions from the early empire; but only about 60 imperial edicts and rescripts have been discovered from the period after the Tetrarchic emperors (Feissel 2010, pp. 17–42). The inscribing of municipal laws and commemorations of civic magistrates and patrons decreased even more precipitously. At Ephesus, for instance, inscribed copies of almost 30 laws issued by the emperor and his magistrates during the fourth, fifth, and sixth centuries have been found, but no municipal laws (Feissel 2010, pp. 43–70). In cities throughout the empire the same chronological pattern appears. The engraving of inscriptions seemed almost to end toward the end of the third century but revived modestly in the early fourth century. Another decline continued to the later fifth century, but another revival lasted until the mid-sixth century. By 600, inscriptions were no longer a significant component of urban political life (Liebeschuetz 2001, pp. 11–19).

Engraving inscriptions was a deliberate choice that reflected the cultural imperatives of emperors, imperial magistrates, municipal administrators, and civic patrons. The rises and declines of the "epigraphic habit" should be correlated with larger political and social trends. In many cities the latest emperors to be commemorated were Diocletian and his colleagues or Constantine, while public inscriptions increasingly honored provincial governors rather than municipal magistrates (Robert 1948). These trends suggest that during the fourth century the very top level of imperial rule was becoming more remote among provincials even as the political institutions of cities declined in authority. Instead, local notables had the opportunity to participate in larger provincial assemblies, and provincial governors were credited for local construction projects.

By the fifth century Christianity was widespread in the empire. As more people found identities in Christian values and behavior, more inscriptions appeared in churches and cemeteries honoring churchmen and parishioners. Christian epitaphs dominated: The "epigraphic habit" survived largely as "epitaphic" practice (Galvao-Sobrinho 1995). Even imperial edicts were to be displayed in churches. In 535, when Justinian issued a new law about the behavior of provincial governors, he sent a copy to bishops, with the suggestion that they have it written on boards or engraved on stones. The bishops were to ensure that the law was available for everyone to read by displaying it "in the courtyards of the most holy church" (Justinian, *Novellae* 8, Edictum). Churches were now the preferred venues for reading official documents.

31.2 Editions

Inscriptions make stimulating but sometimes also puzzling reading. The scattering of abbreviations, the minimal use of punctuation and separation between words, the continuation of words on the next line, the grammatical and factual mistakes, and the unfamiliar scripts can turn even intact inscriptions into a challenge of deciphering. Then there are the losses due to damage. Many inscriptions are fragmentary and need reconstruction.

Modern philological editions of ancient literary works typically offer a standardized text by relegating the discrepancies among manuscripts and the grammatical uncertainties to the small font of the critical apparatus. In contrast, even though editions of inscriptions are usually derived from the actual stones, bronze plates, or other media, they are not facsimiles of the engraved or painted texts. Instead, modern editions revel in the flaws and obscurities of the engraved texts, and the omissions and reconstructions are on center stage. When properly edited, inscriptions in scholarly editions look like modernist poems, with blank spaces, asymmetrical layouts, ellipses, and inventive punctuation.

Figure 31.1 shows a typical edition of a short, but important, inscription about L. Aradius Valerius Proculus, prefect of Rome from March 337 to

Imp(erator) Caes(ar) Fl(avius) Constantinus

P(ius) F(elix) vict(or) ac triumfat(or) August(us),

pont(ifex) max(imus), Germ(anicus) max(imus) IIII, Sarm(aticus) max(imus) III,

Gothic(us) max(imus) II, Dac(icus) max(imus), trib(unicia) potest(ate) XXXIII

5 consul{i} VIII, imp(erator) XXXII, p(ater) p(atriae), p(roconsul), et

<F>l(avius) Cl(audius) Constantinus Alaman(nicus) et

Fl(avius) Iul(ius) Constantius et Fl(avius) Iul(ius)

Constans [[et Fl(avius) Iul(ius) Delmatius]]

nobb(ilissimi) Caess(ares)

vacat

10 consulibus praetoribus tribunis plebis

senatui suo salutem dicunt. Si vos liberique

vestri valetis, bene est. Nos exercitusque

nostri valemus.

vacat

Repetentibus nobis insignem nobilitate

15 prosapiam Proculi c(larissimi) v(iri), eiusdemq(ue) virtutes

privatim et publice decursis officiis cogni-

[tas] intuentibus, p(atres) c(onscripti), facilis aestima[tio est]

[Pro]culum v(irum) c(larissimum) tantundem glori[am, quam..?]

[- - -? a p]atribus acceperat e[- - -]

- - - - - -

Figure 31.1 Edition of inscription in the Forum of Trajan, Rome (modified from CIL 6.40776).

January 338, engraved on a marble block found in the Forum of Trajan at Rome, slightly modified from the edition by Geza Alföldy and Andrea Scheithauer in *CIL* 6.8.2 (1996) 4555, no. 40776.

Editions of inscriptions include all sorts of metatextual information, and understanding this inscription requires familiarity with the conventions of epigraphical markup. In particular, this edited version reveals the deployment of different types of brackets: (letters added by the editors to resolve abbreviations used in the inscription), [letters and words once inscribed but lost through damage and now restored by the editors], {letters added in error by the engraver and excised by the editors}, <letters mistakenly omitted by the engraver and added by the editors>, [[letters and words deliberately erased in antiquity]]. Underlining indicates letters that were visible to a previous editor but are now lost; *vacat* indicates an empty space on the stone; the bottom of this block was trimmed off.

In this letter Constantine was either announcing the appointment of Proculus as prefect or responding to a request from the senate to erect a statue of Proculus. The confluence of imperial titles suggest that Constantine sent the letter within a few months of his death in May 337. The protocol in the preamble included the names of his three sons and his nephew Dalmatius, whom he had promoted as his successors. After Constantine's death, however, the army murdered several peripheral relatives, including Dalmatius, to ensure the succession of only his sons. Dalmatius's name was hence chiseled off the inscription.

31.3 Sources

The historical information derived from inscriptions has contributed significantly to standard narratives of late antiquity. One field that has clearly benefited is prosopography, the study of the careers of aristocrats and noted intellectuals. Dedications to and epitaphs about senators at Rome typically listed their offices, other honors, and perhaps some comments about their families and personalities. The inscription with Constantine's letter about Proculus was engraved probably on the side of the block so that a traditional career inscription could be engraved on the front (Weisweiler 2012, pp. 310–313). In provincial cities dedications to imperial magistrates and other notables likewise typically noted their accomplishments. These offices and achievements have been collected into a vast panorama of the activities of imperial magistrates and urban elites throughout the empire. The catalogs of their careers in *The Prosopography of the Later Roman Empire* rely heavily on data from inscribed dedications and funerary monuments.

The field of late Roman law is another beneficiary. Inscribed laws are valuable for understanding aspects of the process of formulating and broadcasting laws, such as the transmission of imperial decisions from the courts to the imperial magistrates in the provinces, their reception among provincials, and the procedures for collecting and editing the constitutions in later centuries. Especially precious are inscribed versions of laws also included in the large *Codes*. In 362 the emperor Julian sent a rescript to the prefect of the East about the appointment of minor judges by provincial governors. An inscribed copy of the rescript erected at Minoa on the island of Amorgos cited the entire law but omitted the emperor's salutation to the prefect and the concluding indication of the date and place of publication. In contrast, the versions in the Theodosian Code and the Code of Justinian included the opening and closing protocols but deleted two-thirds of the actual law (*CTh* 1.16.8; *CJ* 3.3.5; Feissel 2010, pp. 205–222). In 435 the emperor Theodosius II authorized the compilers of the Theodosian Code to "excise superfluous words, add necessary words, change ambiguous words, and emend incorrect words" (*CTh* 1.1.6). But as is already apparent in the inscribed version of Julian's law, the process of revision and modification had started immediately after imperial courts issued rescripts and edicts. By deciding how much of a law to display, imperial magistrates and municipal officials became "lawmakers" themselves. Publicizing a law or an imperial letter by deciding what to have engraved in a public inscription was as much of a process of "editing" as our deciphering and correcting that inscription in a modern edition.

Even though modern historians tend to be most attracted to inscriptions about imperial laws and aristocratic careers, the survival of such elite inscriptions was quite haphazard. The two most ubiquitous categories of inscriptions were instead more humble. One was tombstones, with their epitaphs often noting the age of the deceased and the grief of their relatives. The other was milestones, which advertised the names of emperors throughout the provinces. In total, graveyards in the suburbs and roads in the countryside were tattooed with millions of inscriptions.

Tombstones and milestones seem unpromising as both historical sources and literary texts: Not only are they usually very short; they are also formulaic. In fact, though, they can become valuable for insights into Roman society. Milestones were an important technique for projecting the authority of emperors. In a society with delays in communication and slow travel, milestones allowed emperors to be everywhere at once. The names of emperors on milestones were even more pervasive than their images on coins. Milestones were how emperors "marked" their territory. As a Gallic aristocrat noted in the mid-fifth century, "The name of Caesar blossoms on very old milestones"

(Sidonius, *Carm.* 24.6–7). New milestones were being erected until at least the early fifth century in the West and at least the early sixth century in the East.

Tombstones provide important information about the demographic profile of Roman society. Many tombstones, for instance, mention the age of the deceased and the commemorators. An analysis of thousands of tombstones has concluded that spouses replaced parents as commemorators for men who died at around age 30 and women who died at around age 20. These results seem to imply that men typically married in their late twenties and women in their late teens. This conclusion about marriage customs involves the use of sampling from huge collections of epitaphs and the assumption that a shift in the commemorators can be used as proxy evidence for a change in marital status (Saller and Shaw 1984). As a result, tombstones, like milestones, can be aggregated to become a composite literary text.

Inscriptions had stories to tell: sometimes literally so. Some inscriptions addressed their readers and viewers and engaged in a virtual dialogue; sometimes the honorands on dedicatory inscriptions and the commemorated on tombstones spoke in the first person, talking from their stones. Over the centuries so many inscriptions have been lost that we cannot assume any reliable and even distribution among the surviving inscriptions. In order to overcome this "editing" through the passage of time, modern historians can resort to aggregation and sampling. Both individually and in compilations, inscriptions provide narratives, plots, characters, and motives. Inscriptions were hence literary texts twice over, both as discrete miniaturized novellas and as entries in aggregated databases.

31.4 Texts

Inscriptions preserve many texts that would be otherwise lost. In fact, inscriptions can provide many examples for most of the literary forms discussed in this *Companion*, including poetry, epistolography (such as Constantine's letter), biography and autobiography, legal texts, travel and pilgrimage literature, and translation (Trout 2009). In addition, some of the literary forms that might seem to consist of only writings in manuscripts could also incorporate texts that survive in inscriptions.

One example is panegyrics. On formal occasions panegyrists would deliver extensive orations celebrating emperors or imperial magistrates for their pedigrees and accomplishments. Inscribed dedications were likewise miniature panegyrics. At Rome the emperor was not the only source of honors for Proculus. The guild of pig dealers and butchers, the guild of bakers, and the people of the city of Puteoli all sponsored dedications and statues in honor of their "most worthy patron." These dedications were displayed in a reception room of the family's house on the Caelian Hill (Gehn 2012, pp. 16–20), and listed Proculus's many offices, including his priesthoods; his governorships and other magistracies in North Africa, Spain, and Sicily; his consulship; and his two tenures as prefect of Rome (*CIL* 6.1690 (= *ILS* 1240), 1691, 1692 (= *ILS* 1242), 1693 (= *ILS* 1241), 1694). For these dedications the marble blocks were the equivalent of an orator, broadcasting Proculus's distinctions. But in contrast to the evanescence of panegyrics, the inscribed stones kept on speaking for centuries.

Scholars of classical and theological literature have increasingly adopted interpretive approaches pioneered by literary critics. Narratology, intertextuality, speech-act theory, communication theory, memory studies, oral traditions, postcolonial theory, new historicism: Every interpretive approach applied to literary writings can also be applied to inscriptions. Proculus's dedications, for instance, were more than lists of his offices. In one dedication the inscription tried to establish a dialogue by puncturing the conventional wall between texts and readers. The "speaker" of this dedication addressed spectators directly: "Why should I remember his other accomplishments, when you are looking at Proculus [i.e. a statue], who was born for every honor?" In another dedication the honoree spoke for himself: "I am that Proculus who was born for every honor. Mention the honor that you say I do not possess." These are remarkably stylish rhetorical techniques that now require equally sophisticated literary interpretations.

One outcome of modern interpretive perspectives is to emphasize the role of authors in constructing their writings and advancing their own agendas. Even writings about past events, such as historical narratives, were dominated by present concerns. Inscriptions may seem to avoid this restriction. Not only were many anonymous, but they were also produced at the moment. Inscriptions seem to provide objective, immediate, and firsthand data uncontaminated by authorial bias or subsequent scribal adulteration. They seem to have an aura of historical authenticity, unmediated through layers of manuscript transcriptions.

In fact, no matter how close their inscribing was to the moment of the events or people they mention, inscriptions too reflected personal and social concerns. Every inscribed text was stylized and constructed, a representation of self-identity, a contribution to community solidarity, or an attempt to find solace in times of grieving.

Inscriptions were not original texts. They were not autograph documents like many papyri but rather copies like medieval manuscripts. Most inscriptions were derived from original texts that had been written on a perishable medium. The initial public display of official edicts and rescripts was often as announcements painted on whitewashed boards. Then imperial magistrates, municipal officials, patrons, or family might initiate their engraving in a permanent form on stones. In the process of transferring the words from one medium to another, the engravers, just like medieval scribes, made mistakes. Modern epigraphers are hence similar to modern palaeographers. In editing an inscription such as Constantine's letter about Proculus, scholars are trying to conjure up the original version, while restoring the derivative copy engraved on the stone and while acknowledging that a few words in that engraved copy were subsequently erased. A modern edition of an inscription is hence a palimpsest, with several layers of text hidden within the top layer that appears on the page.

Upon seeing either actual engraved inscriptions or modern edited texts, scholars read and decode them. For most people in antiquity, however, the first response was only to look at the inscriptions. Most simply could not read at all. The level of literacy was very low, perhaps as low as 10% of the population (Harris 1989, p. 22). Another handicap was the display of inscriptions in foreign languages. During the fourth century the language of imperial administration was still Latin, which could be problematic in the eastern Greek provinces (Van Dam 2007, pp. 184–216; Isaac 2009). At Aphrodisias in western Asia Minor, for instance, Diocletian's Edict on Maximum Prices was engraved in Latin on a large wall made of marble panels. The stonecutters were apparently so uneasy with both the language and the alphabet that they simply imitated the letter forms in the written copy (Reynolds 1989). From the intimidating length of the inscription viewers could perhaps deduce the authority of the emperors, but as Greek speakers, they could not read about it.

Rome too was not immune to this problem of exotic languages. In the unsanitary conditions of a big city, mortality rates were high, and only a constant inflow of migrants could sustain its enormous population. Some came willingly for the benefits given to residents of the capital, but many came unwillingly as slaves. Most of those immigrants were from the outlying provinces and frontier regions, and many were not native Latin speakers. Languages and migrations intersected without coinciding. The emperors and their magistrates exported Latin directives to the Greek provinces, while their policies encouraged the importation of non-Latin speakers to Rome. In both cases the result was the same: Most people could not read inscriptions in Latin.

31.5 Images

In late antiquity inscriptions were images first. Interpreting inscriptions hence requires an appreciation of several aspects of their visual poetics.

One aspect would highlight the appearance of inscriptions. In the inscription recording Constantine's letter to the magistrates, senate, and people of Rome, for instance, the text was engraved in majuscules. Capital letters were in fact used in most inscriptions, although in our modern context of email and texting they seem a bit strident. Font size could also denote relative ranks. In the preamble the names of the emperors and their victory titles were engraved in letters that were almost twice the height of the letters used for the content of the dispatch, and Constantine's names in the first line were slightly taller than those of his sons and nephew. The engraver further emphasized the importance of the emperors by framing their formal salutation with empty spaces before and after. This highlighting was perhaps an attempt to imitate the appearance of Constantine's actual letter, in which his secretaries had left a blank space so that he could insert the salutation in his own hand. But the outcome of this use of different font sizes and blank spaces is quite startling, because it effectively reversed the intent of the letter. Although the original letter had celebrated the honor for Proculus and the consensus between emperors and senate, the inscribed version emphasized the majesty of the emperors. Proculus seems to have been an afterthought. The appearance of the inscription trumped the words of the letter.

It is difficult to convey all of these implications in a translation into a modern language. Most translations of inscriptions render the words in lower-case letters, so that the translations look like a paragraph in a modern book. In the case of Constantine's letter, a translation could instead imitate the engraved inscription by printing upper-case letters in different sizes and by deploying the same number of lines, including empty spaces. But note too that even as a translation tries to mimic the appearance of the letters, it becomes only an evocation of the appearance of the entire inscription, resembling neither the broken stone nor the modern annotated edition. Translations tend to ignore most of the editorial brackets, excepting the double square brackets indicating erasure; and in the translation shown in Figure 31.2 parentheses enclose words added for clarification in English.

A second aspect of the visuality of inscriptions would emphasize the accompanying monuments. The surviving piece of the marble block on which Constantine's letter about Proculus had been engraved is about three feet high, and the original was taller. This block served as the base for a statue, which was probably near life-size. While the top of the inscription was set at about eye height, the statue loomed over the viewers. We prioritize the inscription, because the statue is now lost; but in antiquity the statue was the more prominent feature of the monument and overshadowed the engraved words (Smith and Ward-Perkins 2016).

EMPEROR CAESAR FLAVIUS CONSTANTINE,

PIOUS, FORTUNATE, VICTOR, AND CELEBRATOR OF TRIUMPHS, AUGUSTUS,

PONTIFEX MAXIMUS, GREATEST CONQUEROR OF THE GERMANS FOR THE FOURTH TIME,

GREATEST CONQUEROR OF THE SARMATIANS FOR THE THIRD TIME,

GREATEST CONQUEROR OF THE GOTHS FOR THE SECOND TIME, GREATEST CONQUEROR OF

THE DACIANS, HOLDER OF TRIBUNICIAN POWER FOR THE THIRTY-THIRD TIME,

5 CONSUL FOR THE EIGHTH TIME, EMPEROR FOR THE THIRTY-SECOND TIME, FATHER OF THE

FATHERLAND, PROCONSUL, AND

FLAVIUS CLAUDIUS CONSTANTINUS, CONQUEROR OF THE ALAMANS, AND

FLAVIUS JULIUS CONSTANTIUS, AND FLAVIUS JULIUS

CONSTANS, [[AND FLAVIUS JULIUS DALMATIUS,]]

MOST NOBLE CAESARS,

10 EXPRESS GREETINGS TO THE CONSULS, THE PRAETORS, THE TRIBUNES OF THE PEOPLE, (AND)

THEIR SENATE. IF YOU AND YOUR CHILDREN

ARE WELL, IT IS GOOD. WE AND OUR ARMIES

ARE WELL.

CHOSEN FATHERS, AS WE REVIEW THE FAMILY OF PROCULUS, A MOST DISTINGUISHED MAN,

15 WHICH IS FAMOUS FOR ITS NOBILITY, (AND) AS WE CONSIDER THE SAME MAN'S VIRTUES,

WHICH ARE KNOWN, PRIVATELY AND PUBLICLY, FROM THE DUTIES HE HAS COMPLETED,

IT IS AN EASY ASSESSMENT THAT

PROCULUS, A MOST DISTINGUISHED MAN, …JUST AS MUCH ACCLAIM (AS)

…HE HAS RECEIVED FROM (YOU? HIS?) FATHERS…

Figure 31.2 Translation of inscription in the Forum of Trajan, Rome.

A final aspect would emphasize the locations and topographical contexts of inscriptions. The statue of Proculus and its inscribed base was erected in the Forum of Trajan, which had been constructed over two centuries earlier to commemorate the conquest of Dacia. In the center of the enormous forecourt was a large bronze statue of Trajan mounted on a horse. Over the centuries more statues had been added, both statues of other emperors and statues of prominent senators (Chenault 2012). The statue of Proculus hence stood in good company.

Modern scholars often investigate allusions in literary writings. Not only do intertextual borrowings bring literary works into dialogue, even writings that are separated by centuries; in addition, in the process of interacting each text modifies the meaning of the other by conjuring an alternative conceptual frame. The same interpretive technique should be applied to inscriptions. In the Forum of Trajan Constantine's letter about Proculus could not be read in isolation from all the other dedications on display, and Proculus's statue could not be viewed without also looking at all the other statues. Just as the use of intertexts widened the scope and significance of literary texts, so for inscriptions (and statues), modern scholars need to evaluate the impact of inter-inscriptions.

This awareness of what we might call inter-monumentality suggests an additional implication about what should be classified as late antique inscriptions. The great modern collections contain hundreds of thousands of inscriptions from the entire period of Greek and Roman antiquity, and thousands more are being added every year. Even though only a smallish percentage of these inscriptions was actually engraved during the late antique period, many of the old inscriptions were still on display. Rome was, of course, the largest epigraphical museum in the empire, but throughout the empire cities were crowded with inscriptions, along with their accompanying statues and monuments. Through allusions and quotations, sometimes just through proximity, these old inscriptions interacted with new inscriptions. As a result, the old inscriptions from *early* antiquity that were still on display should also be counted among the inscriptions of late antiquity.

31.6 Audiences and Reception

In late antiquity literate people did read inscriptions. Emperors were readers. Constantine must have seen the names of Trajan and Hadrian on so many monuments at Rome that he called his predecessors "wall ivy" and "paintbrush" (Anonymus post Dionem (= Dio Continuatus), *Frag.* 15.2). Historians used inscriptions as sources of information. Eusebius of Caesarea cited Greek translations of imperial edicts displayed in Latin (*HE* 8.17, 9.1, 7, 9a, 10, 10.5).

In the early sixth century Cosmas Indicopleustes ("the voyager to India") quoted two ancient inscriptions still on display at Adulis in Ethiopia, one erected by king Ptolemy Euergetes in the mid-third century BCE and the other by an anonymous king of Axum (*Topographia christiana* 2.104A–107D).

The most intriguing readers were the censors, the expurgators. As in the inscribed version of Constantine's letter about Proculus, the names of discredited emperors might be chiseled off the stone. Sometimes the name of a new emperor replaced the disgraced name. Although provincial communities or senators at Rome might decide to curry favor with new emperors by updating inscriptions, emperors could order the erasure of memories. They could also permit the rehabilitation of dedications and statues. In 394 the emperor Theodosius had condemned the memory of Virius Nicomachus Flavianus as a supporter of a usurper emperor. In 431 the emperors Valentinian III and Theodosius II allowed Flavianus's grandson to erect a new statue and dedication, perhaps by reusing the original statue base. This time the imperial letter that sanctioned the restoration was inscribed in the dedication (Hedrick 2000).

This resurrected statue, with its dedication and imperial letter, was erected in the Forum of Trajan, where it would have joined the older monuments, among them the similar monument in honor of Proculus. Who might have seen Proculus's monument? One spectator was no doubt Proculus himself, who continued to hold more high offices. He was a consul in 340, when the emperor Constans was in control of Italy. He served again as prefect of Rome from 351 to 352, but this time under the usurping emperor Magnentius, who was responsible for the death of Constans. Proculus's miscalculation had made the memory of his reputation vulnerable to retaliation, and his statue and dedication might have faced removal. Yet when the emperor Constantius subsequently avenged his brother by defeating Magnentius, neither Proculus nor his dedication suffered retribution. In fact, another spectator of Proculus's statue may have been Constantius. In 357 the emperor visited Rome to celebrate his victory over Magnentius. During a tour of famous buildings Constantius studied the inscriptions: "He read the names of the gods inscribed on the pediments and inquired about the origins of temples" (Symmachus, *Relationes* 3.7). He also visited the Forum of Trajan, where he admired his predecessor's equestrian statue (Ammianus Marcellinus, *Res gestae* 16.10). Perhaps the senators who guided his entourage pointed out his father's letter to Proculus.

Fortunately for us, in the medieval period visitors continued to read inscriptions. They also started collecting them. In the later ninth century pilgrims to Rome could follow an itinerary marked by inscriptions (Walser 1987); at Tours the inscriptions engraved on the walls of the Church of St. Martin were copied into a medieval *florilegium* about the saint's cult (Van Dam 1993, pp. 308–317). These anthologies transformed inscriptions into a defined literary genre, worthy of safeguarding in manuscripts. They also preserved the texts of many inscriptions whose stones are now lost.

With the fading of memories of Roman rule the medium became more valuable than the words of the inscriptions. Over the centuries most inscribed bronze tablets (and bronze statues) were melted down (Eck 2015). Many stone blocks were reused, some for other inscriptions, others in construction projects. The statue base on which Constantine's letter about Proculus had been inscribed was essentially mutilated, probably so that it could be recycled. The block was trimmed in size, the bottom was cut off, the sides were narrowed, and three holes were drilled in the lower-right quadrant. In the medieval period used marble was often the only marble available. Bronze and stone were no guarantee of permanence after all.

Eventually, especially during the Renaissance, inscriptions were rejuvenated as witnesses to history. Towns throughout the old Roman world displayed ancient inscriptions as proof of their classical heritage, patrons collected engraved stones, and scholars published editions and commentaries (McMahon 2015). We are the heirs and beneficiaries of their antiquarian curiosity. In the great revival of late antique studies over the past 50 years the study of inscriptions has become an increasingly important discipline. The value of inscriptions as historical sources is unquestioned; their significance as literary texts and visual images should have a promising future.

ABBREVIATIONS

AE = *L'Année épigraphique*. Annually since 1888. Paris: Presses Universitaires de France.
CIL = *Corpus inscriptionum latinarum*, multiple volumes, second editions, and supplements. Ongoing since 1869. Berlin: Walter de Gruyter. http://cil.bbaw.de/cil_en/index_en.html
ILS = Dessau, Hermann. (1892–1916). *Inscriptiones latinae selectae*, 3 vols. Berlin: Weidmann.

ONLINE RESOURCES

Epigraphik-Datenbank Clauss-Slaby. http://www.manfredclauss.de/gb/index.html
Epigraphic Database Heidelberg. http://edh-www.adw.uni-heidelberg.de/home
Inscriptions of Aphrodisias. http://insaph.kcl.ac.uk/iaph2007

REFERENCES

Bodel, John. (2012). Latin epigraphy and the IT revolution. In: *Epigraphy and the Historical Sciences* (ed. John Davies and John Wilkes), 275–296. Proceedings of the British Academy 177. Oxford: Oxford University Press.

Chenault, Robert. (2012). Statues of senators in the forum of Trajan and the Roman forum in late antiquity. *Journal of Roman Studies* 102: 103–132.

Cooley, Alison E. (2012). *The Cambridge Manual of Latin Epigraphy*. Cambridge: Cambridge University Press.

Corcoran, Simon. (1996). *The Empire of the Tetrarchs: Imperial Pronouncements and Government AD 284–324*. Oxford: Oxford University Press.

Durliat, Jean and Guillou, André. (1984). Le tarif d'Abydos (vers 492). *Bulletin de correspondance hellénique* 108: 581–598.

Eck, Werner. (2015). Documents on bronze: A phenomenon of the Roman West? In: *Ancient Documents and Their Contexts: First North American Congress of Greek and Latin Epigraphy (2011)* (ed. John Bodel and Nora Dimitrova), 127–151. Leiden: Brill.

Feissel, Denis. (2010). *Documents, droit, diplomatique de l'empire romain tardif*. Paris: Centre de recherche d'histoire et civilisation de Byzance.

Galvao-Sobrinho, Carlos R. (1995). Funerary epigraphy and the spread of Christianity in the West. *Athenaeum* 83: 431–462.

Gehn, Ulrich. (2012). Ehrenstatuen in spätantiken Häusern Roms. In: *Patrons and Viewers in Late Antiquity* (ed. Stine Birk and Birte Poulsen), 15–30. Aarhus: Aarhus University Press.

Harris, William V. (1989). *Ancient Literacy*. Cambridge, MA: Harvard University Press.

Hedrick Jr., Charles W. (2000). *History and Silence: Purge and Rehabilitation of Memory in Late Antiquity*. Austin: University of Texas Press.

Isaac, Benjamin. (2009). Latin in cities of the Roman Near East. In: *From Hellenism to Islam: Cultural and Linguistic Change in the Roman Near East* (ed. Hannah M. Cotton, Robert G. Hoyland, Jonathan J. Price et al.), 43–72. Cambridge: Cambridge University Press.

Liebeschuetz, J.H.W.G. (2001). *Decline and Fall of the Roman City*. Oxford: Oxford University Press.

McMahon, Kevin. (2015). Michelangelo's marble blog: Epigraphic walls as pictures and samples of language. In: *Ancient Documents and Their Contexts: First North American Congress of Greek and Latin Epigraphy (2011)* (ed. John Bodel and Nora Dimitrova), 283–305. Leiden: Brill.

Reynolds, Joyce. (1989). The regulations of Diocletian. In: *Aphrodisias in Late Antiquity* (Charlotte Roueché, with contributions by Joyce M. Reynolds), 252–318. London: The Society for the Promotion of Roman Studies.

Robert, Louis. (1948). *Hellenica: Recueil d'épigraphie, de numismatique et d'antiquités grecques IV. Épigrammes du Bas-Empire*. Paris: Librairie d'Amérique et d'Orient, Adrien-Maisonneuve.

Saller, Richard P. and Shaw, Brent D. (1984). Tombstones and Roman family relations in the Principate: Civilians, soldiers and slaves. *Journal of Roman Studies* 74: 124–156.

Salway, Benet. (2014). Late antiquity. In: *The Oxford Handbook of Roman Epigraphy* (ed. Christer Bruun and Jonathan Edmondson), 364–393. Oxford: Oxford University Press.

Smith, R.R.R. and Ward-Perkins, Bryan. ed. (2016). *The Last Statues of Antiquity*. Oxford: Oxford University Press.

Tabbernee, William. (2008). Epigraphy. In: *The Oxford Handbook of Early Christian Studies* (ed. Susan Ashbrook Harvey and David G. Hunter), 120–139. Oxford: Oxford University Press.

Trout, Dennis E. (2009). Inscribing identity: The Latin epigraphic habit in late antiquity. In: *A Companion to Late Antiquity* (ed. Philip Rousseau with Jutta Raithel), 170–186. Oxford: Wiley Blackwell.

Van Dam, Raymond. (1993). *Saints and Their Miracles in Late Antique Gaul*. Princeton, NJ: Princeton University Press.

Van Dam, Raymond. (2007). *The Roman Revolution of Constantine*. Cambridge: Cambridge University Press.

Walser, Gerold. (1987). *Die Einsiedler Inschriftensammlung und der Pilgerführer durch Rom (Codex Einsidlensis 326)*. Stuttgart: Franz Steiner.

Weisweiler, John. (2012). Inscribing imperial power: Letters from emperors in late-antique Rome. In: *Rom in der Spätantike: Historische Erinnerung im städtischen Raum* (ed. Ralf Behrwald and Christian Witschel), 309–329. Stuttgart: Franz Steiner Verlag.

CHAPTER THIRTY-TWO

Translation

Daniel King

> If there is any offensive statement in the author, why is this to be twisted into a fault of the translator?… I did nothing more than fit the Latin words to the Greek ideas.
>
> Rufinus, *Apol ad Anastasium* 7

So, in self-defense, Rufinus of Aquileia, who had "made a Roman" of Origen, as Jerome put it in the preface to his version of *On First Principles*. Jerome's remarks raised a storm that would destroy the good names of both Rufinus and Origen – an argument over what constituted "appropriate" translation methods. Jerome contrasted his own versions of Origen with those of his opponent by pointing to a difference of *intent* rather than of *content*. Jerome aimed at unmasking the heretic lurking beneath the opaque text of *On First Principles* (so he claimed), while Rufinus wanted (at least following Jerome's reconstruction of events) to uphold him.

Both the opportunities and the dangers of translation are laid bare before us in the drawn-out conflict that ensued between the two (in)famous translators, a conflict that we can follow in their letters and *Apologies*. These documents afford us a rare insight into the liabilities of translation in late antiquity, an insight denied us in the vast majority of cases by the anonymity of these powerbrokers of culture and literature, by their lack of self-disclosure, their willingness to hide behind the cloak of the "original" text, as seemingly hidden authors who merely "fit words to ideas."

If late antiquity witnessed an explosion of activity at the boundaries of traditional cultural units, then nowhere is this truer than in the field of translation,

---

A Companion to Late Antique Literature, First Edition.
Edited by Scott McGill and Edward J. Watts.
© 2018 John Wiley & Sons, Inc. Published 2018 by John Wiley & Sons, Inc.

both literary and ephemeral. Growing bureaucracies required ever-increasing interaction across language barriers; expanding religions required proselytizing texts; and an evergreen yearning after the Greek classical canon suffused the *literati* of both the Latin West and Syriac East, while the emerging self-consciousness of once "barbarian" societies encouraged the first seeding, and also the first fruits, of indigenous literatures. Texts and ideas first conceived in Greek were reaching astonishing distances by the end of late antiquity. The cattle-herder Caedmon's first attempt to rephrase a passage from Scripture in his native Anglo-Saxon belongs to the same century (the seventh) as the establishment of Christian monasteries in Tang China, as commemorated on the eighth-century Xian Stele with its bilingual Syriac-Chinese explanation of the Christian faith. Both represent the results of impulses typical of late antiquity. Whether it be "real-time" interpretations of the Pentateuch into contemporary Aramaic, Gallic schoolmasters recasting Hellenistic epigrams into learned Latin verse, or law students in Beirut studiously transcribing Justinian's *Institutes* into Greek, late antiquity was a period of unparalleled attention to translation.

What follows will attempt to offer an overview both of the generic scope of the translational efforts of late antiquity and of the number of linguistic communities that were now beginning to partake of the traditions of classical antiquity. The term "translation" is often used in the modern literature on late antiquity in its wider sense, referring not merely to the reforming of a text in a new language but, rather, to the transference of whole ideas and genres between linguistic communities. Although this wider usage is an important conceptual category with which to analyze cultural interaction, our own overview will be concerned only with textual transfer as such. Moreover, translation was a ubiquitous activity in many walks of life, and a full study would include, inter alia, translations of legal documents such as wills and title deeds among Egyptian papyri and the Greek versions of senatorial decrees from Rome. This survey, however, will focus on texts generally deemed literary, without being unnecessarily strict in its definition.

Translation is a form of reception, and one of our prime areas of interest will be the varying reasons why certain texts and certain genres were more avidly "received" into target cultures than others. Naturally enough, the spread of the Christian churches around the Mediterranean and beyond will prove to be a major factor, and Christian texts, moreover, constitute a large proportion of all texts translated in late antiquity. Many other types of literature were also translated, however. We shall survey these genre-by-genre in order to identify key themes and motivations in the process of the late ancient reception of classical literature, asking to what extent these translations were themselves part of the formation of a new distinctive literature in late antiquity.

32.1 Philosophy, Medicine, Rhetoric, and Grammar

Prior to the fourth century very few Latin authors had made any translations of Greek philosophical works, the main exceptions being Cicero's and Apuleius's versions of some Platonic dialogues. In the days of the Republic and early Empire, Latin philosophy was barely acquainted with Aristotle, save through his lost exoteric works, and Aristotelian logic was a relative latecomer to the Latins. One early adaptation of *On Interpretation* and of *Prior Analytics* is extant, possibly from the pen of Apuleius, who also made a loose translation of Pseudo-Aristotle, *De Mundo*. But it is only in the fourth century that we witness the end of the Hellenophone grip on the discipline of logic. Marius Victorinus was the first to attempt a Latin version of the full Aristotelian curriculum as it was taught in the Neoplatonist Greek schools. Only his version of Porphyry's *Isagoge* (used as an introduction to Aristotelian logic in the schools) is extant now, though he probably also translated *Categories* and *De Interpretatione* (Cooper 2010). By introducing Aristotle as an ally to orthodox theology through his treatises on doctrine, Victorinus paved the way for the later tradition in the West of Christian Aristotelianism, which would last for more than a millennium.

Victorinus also translated portions of the Neoplatonists Plotinus and Porphyry. These had a different, albeit equally significant, impact. Picked up by the young Augustine, Victorinus's Latin Plotinus was (or so he himself claimed) fundamental to his conversion and to his later syntheses of Christian theology (*Confessions* VII,9). Augustine offers a prime example of why translation became so important in late antiquity. Like many of his contemporaries, despite being a teacher and leader of great stature, he struggled to read Greek. Yet he craved the wisdom of the Greeks in philosophy and religion and frequently worried about the reliability of the translations upon which he was so dependent (Courcelle 1969, pp. 149–223).

Victorinus's program did not have an immediate effect upon Western education, nor did the occasional interest shown in Greek philosophy by Roman worthies such as Vettius Praetextatus (d. 384) who translated Themistius's paraphrase of the *Analytics*, and a certain Chalcidius (fourth century), who translated the *Timaeus*, together with its Middle-Platonist commentary, a translation that was to become widely read in the Middle Ages (Reydams-Schils 2010). But the influence of these authors was not profound. Victorinus's true heir as translator of Greek philosophy was the renowned Roman senator Boethius, whom Cassiodorus praised for having introduced Pythagoras, Ptolemy, Nicomachus, and Euclid to Western readers

(*Variae* I,45,3). Over the first quarter of the sixth century, Boethius translated the *Isagoge* (improving Victorinus's version) together with all six books of Aristotle's logical corpus (*The Organon*), as well as commentary material on the *Prior Analytics*. Boethius's translations influenced the Western tradition in more ways than one. Over time he settled upon an approach to "scientific" translation that he deemed appropriate to teaching philosophy among those who could not read Greek, and his own translations opened up Aristotle to Western readers in a tradition that was never broken. His translations and commentaries formed the basis of logical studies in the Carolingian renaissance and in the twelfth century whetted the insatiable appetite of the European universities for new texts of the Greek philosophers.

Eastern readers were no less enthusiastic about translating Greek learning for their monolingual colleagues. Translations into Syriac of Aristotle's logic appear to have begun early in the sixth century and through the work of the polymath commentator Sergius of Reshaina continued to grow thereafter (Hugonnard-Roche 2004). The early books of the *Organon* were considered important reading for trainee priests, and the respect afforded them meant that a number of translations were made. By the eighth century knowledge of Greek was so reduced that these translations became the only means in the East of accessing Aristotle, and much of early Arabic philosophy was thus dependent on the by-then substantial and mature Syriac tradition.

Closely related was a burgeoning Armenian philosophical tradition that took off in the sixth century with a series of literal translations, originating, as had the Syriac, with the curricula of the Neoplatonist schools at Alexandria and Athens, focused on Aristotle's logical works and the late ancient commentaries on them (Terian 1982).

As was the case with philosophy, Latin and Syriac versions of Greek medical treatises were made on an ad hoc basis. This was partly the result of declining competence in Greek outside the core Hellenophone areas, while also being a function of a newly discovered self-confidence and sense of literary identity within non-Greek language communities. The full extent of cross-linguistic interaction around the Empire and beyond was considerable; the point at which borrowing begins and translation starts cannot always be isolated.

In the days of Cicero, Roman audiences still read their medical textbooks in Greek, written by Greek doctors such as Asclepiades. In the first century CE, Cornelius Celsus wrote extensively in Latin on the subject, developing the necessary lexicon of Latin terms but not yet needing to translate. Just as in philosophy, so in medicine late antiquity saw the emergence of a "canon" of texts that the student was expected to read under the tutelage of a master. The main center for the teaching of these curricula was Alexandria, but many other schools sprang up across the Empire, and hence translation of these canons became a necessity. In the West, the "school of Carthage" produced, in the fourth and fifth centuries, translations of Hippocrates (by Vindicianus) and Soranus (by Caelius Aurelianus), while another member of the school, Theodorus Priscianus, seems to have written a Greek textbook and then himself translated it into Latin for his African students. (For a full list of Latin medical translations, see Langslow 2000, pp. 70–74.)

Cassiodorus, that last great patron of Latin translations from the Greek, itemized the medical texts in his monastic library, all of which were probably Latin translations rather than Greek originals (Cassiodorus, *Institutions* I,31,2). His list includes Dioscorides, Hippocrates, and Galen. The translators of this material are unknown to us, but their existence had a significant impact on medical and other scientific knowledge in medieval western Europe.

In the East, medicine quickly became embedded in the Syriac world as a profession of great prestige. One of the most renowned doctors of late antiquity, Magnus, came from Nisibis, deep in Syriophone territory, and it is hardly surprising that so many translations were made into that language. For the Persian shahs, as for the later caliphs, the Syrians were renowned as the best purveyors of the Greek medical art. The first great Syriac translator of Galen was also a translator of Aristotelian philosophy, Sergius of Reshaina, whose medical works were standard reading in the East for 300 years, until the more advanced knowledge of Ḥunayn ibn Isḥāq was able to improve them. Ḥunayn, in turn, began the process of putting Galen into Arabic and initiated another long and glorious tradition in the reception of the Greek sciences.

Many other medical texts may have been translated initially into Middle Persian. Persian tales later told of the process by which the great learning of ancient Babylon was first plundered by Alexander and later restored by the Sassanian kings by a process of (re)translation from Greek copies. It is quite likely that some works of astrology and *Hermetica* at least were translated as early as the third century (Van Bladel 2009, pp. 23–63), and probably many more translations were made under the patronage of Chosroes I (531–579), who is said to have desired to adopt all the great philosophical knowledge of the Greeks into his language. The true extent of his success, however, is not known.

A few other branches of science may be briefly mentioned. The East, rather than the West, was the primary recipient of mathematical and astronomical-astrological works. Syriac translators rendered a number of astronomical and mathematical texts in the seventh century for their own teaching. But Theophilus of Edessa, a Syrian working at the caliph's court in Baghdad, translated a Greek compendium of astrology and thereby transmitted a broadly Ptolemaic system to the first Arabic astrologers (Pingree 2001). The sophisticated Arabic reception of mathematics and astrology, however, stands witness to a nexus of cultural interactions typical of western Asia in late antiquity; the astrological traditions of Hellenistic Egypt were translated initially into Pehlevi and Sanskrit before being reabsorbed into an Islamic milieu. Again the question of the needs of different target communities is in view. The Syriac translators of late antiquity translated only what the schools needed, while many were still able to read the originals and could, for example, still reference texts such as the *Almagest* and expect their readers to be aware of its contents. By the eighth century this was no longer the case, and even the most learned Arabs of the ninth century would need translations of these works too.

Armenia's experience paralleled that of Syria. What is known as the "Hellenizing school" of translators, in producing Armenian versions of many secular and educational texts, built upon the work of the early Armenian tradition that had been focused on bringing Greek theology to the Armenian church. A long list of works of grammar and rhetoric, logic, and astronomy were translated from the sixth century onwards (Thomson 1982, p. 144).

Much of the literature of late antiquity emanated from schools of rhetoric and grammar. Hence many of the authors of late ancient literature were brought up on translations of the Greek handbooks that had been written for the Hellenophone schools. This was true even deep within the Syriophone regions, where monasteries preserved the "rhetorical" approach to education and even translated Greek handbooks (Watt 2010). From the fourth century the Syrians also built up an increasingly sophisticated tradition of studying their own grammar. Again looking to Greek models, they made their starting point a translation of Dionysius Thrax's basic grammar. The famous work of the Arab grammarians appears to be quite independent, yet even there signs may be discerned of an unbroken intellectual tradition stretching back to the late ancient Greek grammarians (King 2012).

32.2 Law

Legal texts offer a quite different perspective on translation. The legal system of the late Empire was based on traditions of Roman law and was carried on in Latin even in the increasingly Hellenophone administration of the eastern provinces. Non-Latin-speaking students at the law schools of Beirut and Constantinople were supposed to have studied the language for a year prior to their studies, but, of course, this was never sufficient, and in the sixth century many of the professors produced translations for their classes.

This appears to be in line with a decree of the emperor Justinian, that no alternative version of his *Digest* of laws was permitted, "except if someone wants to translate these laws into Greek in just the same order and sequence in which the Latin words are found (what the Greeks call 'foot-by-foot')" (Humfress 2005, p. 168).

Such versions were simply student cribs, designed to assist those still struggling with the Latin originals. They were not designed to serve as independent texts, although some of them became just that as Latin all but disappeared from the Byzantine civil service in the following century. A comparable procedure was enacted upon the Greek of the *Novellae*, the new laws enacted under Justinian's authority. The near-incomprehensible Latin of this translation became a widely copied text in the West (Scheltema 1970).

Translations of the Acts of the major church councils should be viewed as of a type with these legal translations. Beginning with the Councils of Ephesus (in 431) and Chalcedon (in 451), translators rendered the official versions of the Acts into Latin and Syriac for wider circulation. These translations often had the desired effect of spreading among the target communities a sense of what was the orthodox doctrine espoused by their leaders. Since translators to some degree controlled access to texts and hence access to knowledge, this process could serve to underpin localized movements – witness the widespread Syriac versions of the Latrocinium Council of Ephesus (in 449) that continued to be read with sympathy by Miaphysite Syriac speakers even after Chalcedon had overturned its decisions in favor of the imperial church.

32.3 Poetry

Late ancient Latin poetry continued to plough much the same furrow as it had for centuries past, taking Greek models and imitating them in a complex variety of ways, yielding "a spectrum of textual engagement that runs from verbal echo, through allusion, to the translation of the whole" (Mulligan 2016, p. 145). In these sorts of translation quite different canons are at work from those that apply to medicine, for instance. A translator might find that metrical and phonetic equivalence gives a closer translation than semantic or functional equivalence. Ausonius and Claudian were both *par excellence* imitators/translators of Greek models, and the latter even attempted to translate his own Greek poems into Latin. The late ancient penchant for working out variations on old themes and motifs, often in long series of seemingly unimaginative combinations, was especially suited to the art of translation, which (and in this it hardly differed from the classical age) could easily become an in-group hobby for leisured intellectual elites.

Other cultures known for their translations from Greek, such as Syriac and Armenian, were less concerned with poetry. There was not there the long tradition of cultural imitation that gave Latin literature its grounding. In Syriac, an entirely native poetic tradition developed that was kept consciously apart from any Greek models, especially on account of the latter's inextricable association with religious themes distasteful to the church. So distinctive was the Syriac poetic tradition that translations tended more often in the opposite direction. Many of the hymns of the Syriac poet Ephrem were translated into Greek and then imitated in native Greek compositions that could be attributed to the Syrian. These translations varied, from being very close in word and form to being the sorts of artistic reformulations with which we are more familiar from Latin. The pioneering Byzantine poet Romanos appears to have been much influenced by the poetic genius of Ephrem and developed new genres on the basis of the Syriac tradition (Brock 1989). This "Greek Ephrem" became enormously popular throughout the late ancient world, translations being made into all the literary languages.

The Armenians also made extensive translations of Syriac poetry, not so much as a literary endeavor but, rather, because of their theological significance. Many of Ephrem's works, for instance, found Armenian translators on account of the theological authority attaching to their author. That some of these were written in, and rendered into, verse was less significant for their translators' audience than was their content.

32.4 Prose Fiction

Stories have always been among the best traveled of human inventions, and late antiquity was a productive time for the spread of stories around the Mediterranean language communities and beyond. One of the most universally known was the *Alexander Romance*, a novelistic version of the life of the great king, whose adventures became more embellished with each retelling. A Latin version was made in the fourth century, an Armenian in the sixth, and a Syriac between the fifth and seventh. From Syriac, the Alexander Romance entered both the Arabic and Ethiopic worlds. The Middle Persian version may also be from the Syriac rather than, as once thought, being an intermediary between Greek and Syriac (Ciancaglini 2001).

The ancient Jewish story of Aḥikar, known in Aramaic forms for centuries, had already been reconceived in Demotic Egyptian form in the first century BCE, and in late antiquity spread into at least Armenian, Ethiopic, Greek,

Slavonic, and Arabic. Fragments in Sogdian have now also been found of this wide-ranging and much-embellished tale of the supremacy of wisdom (Sims-Williams 2014).

Many other pieces of prose fiction were circulated around the expanding world of late antiquity, sometimes from West to East, others in the opposite direction. Such was for instance the story of Kalilah and Dimnah, and that of Sindban, both tales taken out of Middle Persian (the former originally Sanskrit) that found their way into the eastern parts of the Roman Empire. The Greek novels, too, found some fertile soil in the east even before the era of a thousand and one nights. The ancient story of Parthenope appears to have become well known in Syriac regions through live performance as much as through written material; whether or not it was performed in Syriac as well as Greek we shall never know, but within a short time its retellings had spread to Persia where a written translation was made at some time (Hägg 1986).

Closely intertwined with the cultural sharing of narrative fiction was the seemingly endless ability of saints' and martyrs' lives to be scattered, translated, and transmogrified throughout the late ancient landscape. The boundary between a saint's life and a piece of prose fiction was not always clear – many of the more elaborate parts of the Alexander Romance were taken from well-known saints' lives, while the secular Greek tale of Parthenope was transformed into a hagiography. Jerome fashioned his three saints' lives self-consciously within the genre of the Greek novel. These were the only of Jerome's works to be translated into Greek, and also thence into Syriac. For Syrian readers, Jerome was primarily an author of saints' lives rather than a theologian or polymath (King 2009).

Translation also fed the increasingly popular appetite for novelistic expansions of the biblical narrative. Tales of far-flung parts of the world were no longer read only by Greeks, and their popularity attests to a broadening of horizons and the coming-into-view of once marginalized communities. Christ had ordered his message taken to the ends of the world, and so narratives of the apostolic missions to those ends came to encapsulate Christian claims to universality. *Acta* of apostles such as (Judas) Thomas and Andrew sit somewhere between our conceptions of the genre of travel novella and New Testament pseudepigrapha. That they were translated into almost every available language of antiquity attests to their popularity as well as to the Greek language's fall from its status as sole bearer of culture.

Many of the narratives found in the Qur'ān stem from this tradition of expanding upon biblical stories. Most likely prevalent in a variety of oral modes and forms throughout the Near East, the particular genius of Arabic poetry was able to mold them into a native idiom, where they could fuel the passions of a new religion. The Suras of the Qur'ān, as much as the Arabic translations of the Gospels, were the products of a late ancient literature that was being constantly "translated" as new peoples took up the traditions of classical and of Jewish antiquity and put them to new service.

32.5 Scripture

More than any other text, it is the dissemination of the Jewish and Christian Scriptures that most clearly reflects the rise of the local vernaculars at the expense of "classical" tongues. Within late ancient Jewish communities, translations into Greek and Aramaic continued their already old traditions. The known Greek versions (Septuagint, Aquila) were still used, but there were also fresh translators who ventured versions more sensitive to the changing Greek vernaculars of their day (De Lange, Krivoruchko, and Boyd-Taylor 2009). Translation into the widely-spoken dialects of Aramaic (the *Targums*) became increasingly widespread, such that it became a major concern of the rabbinical establishment to control and authorize the versions of which they approved (Flesher 2005).

The aggressive spread of the Christian church both within and without the Empire was a particularly productive force in translation, as it was more generally in the development of vernaculars. Syriac-speaking churches took over a set of preexisting Jewish Scriptures, which they adapted to the dialect of Edessa before adding the New Testament from Greek. Congregations in North Africa started to write down their ad hoc Latin versions of Scripture from the second century, but new Latin variations continued to proliferate, of which Jerome's Vulgate was but one. In Coptic, early versions in the Sahidic dialect gave way to standardization in the Bohairic dialect, although versions in the other dialects circulated as well. Elsewhere around the borders of the Empire, versions were made in Gothic (fourth century), Ethiopic (fourth century onward), Armenian (fifth century), Middle Persian (?fifth century), Arabic (eighth century, possibly even seventh), and the Sogdian of the Turkic tribes of Central Asia (Sims-Williams 2014). Toward the end of the late antique period, the Christian Scriptures were already receiving their first Anglo-Saxon forms through Caedmon's verse, while upon the monk Alopen's arrival in Chang'an, the Tang emperor found the books he brought with him to be "mysterious, right, and well-summarized," implying that at least an oral translation of some sort must have been offered; some portions of Scripture have survived from that era that received official sanction (Tang 2004, pp. 96,104–106). Theodoret of Cyrrhus, the bishop and Christian apologist of the fifth century, claimed that the New Testament had even been translated into Scythian and Sauromatian. This may be taken as rhetorical wishful thinking, but we must continually reckon with oral versions of Christian teaching being used in missionary contexts for people whose own traditions were primarily or wholly oral.

In terms of approach and method, the Bible offers a unique case in the history of literary translation. As Jerome never tired of explaining, the words of God were not "literary" at all and ought to be treated more like a legal text than a novel, more like a senatorial decree than a wonder-working hagiography. Successive Syriac translations of the New Testament, for example, took on ever more literal styles, in imitation of the style of legal documents. A mixture of respect for the Greek philosophical heritage and an almost mathematical conception of the mode of theological discourse led to a translation style in which syntactical patterns in the original had to be mimicked in the target language, and a special form of translationese was born, one that clings to translations of religious texts even today.

These versions, however calqued upon their sources, became foundational literature for their target cultures. The early Latin versions, of which there appears to have been a myriad, and later the Vulgate, quickly became literary monuments of Latin culture; the Syriac Peshitta raised the dialect of Edessa to the heights of a standard literary dialect and ensured its dominance for centuries. The Gothic Bible, translated to quiet the barbarian peoples by civilizing their religion, remained the only monument to the literature of that tongue for generations.

Because these translations were often intentional instruments of policy, they could find themselves in conflict. In the fifth century Syrian bishops attempted to outlaw the use of the *Diatessaron*, an early Syriac version of the Gospels harmonized into a single narrative, as part of their wider efforts to bring the variegated character of Syriac Christianity under a single authority. For many, the *Diatessaron* represented local tradition over against the incursions of the government-backed episcopacy. In North Africa the new Latin version of the Hebrew Scriptures translated by Jerome was the cause of rioting in some churches – not because the congregations could understand the finer points of the arguments for this or that approach to literary translation, but simply because of the perceived threat to what were viewed as local traditions.

Similar tensions lay behind another set of Scriptural translation texts, the Aramaic Targums used in the synagogues of late antiquity, whose congregations no longer understood Hebrew. Here literature and performance once again intersect, for the written Targums are only the physical representations of public readings – the Aramaic interpreter (*meturgeman*) speaking alongside the reader of the Hebrew Bible. "He who translates a verse literally is a liar; but he who adds to it is a blasphemer," quipped one rabbi (b. Kiddushin 49a), but the efforts of the *meturgemanim* reflect the theological tendencies of rabbinic Judaism and the authorities' concern to protect their sacred text from being misinterpreted, often by the technique of (sometimes considerable) expansion. The written Targums were only guides to live performance, and we can even read in the notes to the Targums (Masora) some of the instructions given to the interpreters for this purpose (Klein 1998, p. 10).

Just as Latin and Syriac versions of the New Testament contended for prestige and authority among church groups, so Targum competed against Targum, with the wide variety of Palestinian Targums gradually being superseded by official versions from the Babylonian diaspora; Targum also competed against original as the rabbis attempted to enforce a strict and thoroughgoing distinction between them and to prevent the former from becoming an authoritative text. They were only partly successful, while for many religious communities, translations came to take on the tincture of the original's authority.

32.6 Parabiblical Texts

Alongside the core canonical books, those others must not be forgotten that lived on the boundaries. The pseudepigrapha were translated with as much gusto and frequency as those "core" books. Some, such as *4 Ezra*, underwent fascinating alterations and expansions as they passed through a variety of guises. Others, such as the novella *Joseph and Asenath*, became well-known literature throughout western Asia and beyond. The Ethiopic version of *Enoch*, translated from Hebrew or Aramaic, sometime during late antiquity, remains our principal source for this vital piece of Jewish scripture. A relatively less well-known text such as the *Testament of Adam* affords us a picture of just how easily such texts radiated – the original Syriac composition has been found in Greek, Arabic, Armenian, Georgian, and Ethiopic. Texts of this sort traveled so well and were translated and adapted so readily that it is frequently not known for sure which of a number of extant versions is the original.

The vast majority of texts of this type are located not in biblical manuscripts but in collections of monastic or other theological or popular philosophical texts. Many are narrative in style and, being open to adaptation and a cut-and-paste approach, may often be read now as political propaganda relating to the time of transmission rather than to the time of original composition. Hence their genre was in many ways closer to that of prose fiction and, in literary terms, would be better analyzed in that context.

32.7 Theology

In partly overlapping contexts are located the extensive translations made of works of a more theoretical theological nature, designed for the specialist rather than for a popular audience. We have already come across the spat between Jerome and Rufinus, which had to do with the status of translations of Origen, once their author had been condemned as a heretic. Both men published their own versions of Origen's *On First Principles*, following them up with an escalating sequence of vitriolic attacks upon one another, an exchange of views that reflects key issues facing a sociohistorical interpretation of translations (Rebenich 2002, pp. 20–24). They debated whether the translator is by default implicated in the errors of his text (is he an "author"?), and whether the translator does not have a duty rather to "correct" those errors in the interests of his audience. The translator is a powerbroker and a teacher whose bilingual talent also comes with a responsibility, just as the rabbis felt responsible for controlling the Targums. What may be defended as responsible translating by one party, to another will readily shade into deception.

In the field of translating the holy dogmas of the church and the expositions of the Church Fathers, this issue only grew in importance during late antiquity, as the Origenist controversy testifies. For many bishops in the fifth century, accurate doctrinal teaching came to focus increasingly upon the interpretation not of Scripture but of the Fathers themselves; hence, whereas for Jerome the translation of the Bible was sui generis, while all other genres could be treated otherwise, to the Syriac translators of Greek theological texts in the sixth and seventh centuries, the two genres were on a par. The techniques of extreme verbal mirroring that were brought to a peak in Thomas of Harkel's version of the New Testament (616) were also applied to the Syriac versions of Severus of Antioch, Athanasius, and Gregory Nazianzen, who were looked upon as the founders of true doctrine by the Miaphysite Syrian community (Brock 1983). Among translations of religious texts, therefore, there is good cause to treat these patristic works as generically separate from the looser and much elaborated translations of pseudepigrapha that, again in terms of the canons applied to them, belong rather with novels and popular literature.

There are some differences between the texts favored by Latin and Syriac patrons and translators at this time. Latin readers, especially from the fourth century, sought the works of the "orthodox" leaders of the Eastern church: Basil, the two Gregories, and Chrysostom, in addition to Origen, Evagrius, and the authors of hagiographies and monastic advice; the sixth-century translators Dionysius Exiguus and Rusticus were concerned to translate the *Acta* of the Eastern councils and the dogmatic works surrounding the Nestorian controversy. The Syrians were more focused on a slightly later era, on authors who constituted their "founding fathers": Theodore, Nestorius, and Theodoret for the Easterners who rejected the official theology of the Council of Ephesus; Severus and Cyril of Alexandria for the Westerners who rejected the Chalcedonian position. The explosion of Armenian translations (fifth/sixth century) included many of these same authors, while adding a particular fascination for Philo that was unparalleled in either the Latin or Syriac environments (Lombardi and Pontani 2010). In Egypt, however, much of this material lay untouched by Coptic translators (Maccoull 1984). Even the monastic works of the renowned Evagrius, which were extensively translated into Syriac and Armenian, are almost unknown in Coptic. The scribes of the Egyptian monasteries never developed that hunger for Greek learning and science that was so marked a feature of the educated Syriophone and Armenophone elites. Some theological works beyond the Scriptures and pseudepigrapha are, however, to be found in Ethiopic, which, although not numerous, serve only to render their absence in the Coptic sphere all the more marked. The spread of monasticism around the East was naturally a spur to the translation of numerous works belonging to that field of human endeavor into languages as far afield as Sogdian and Ethiopic, even before the end of late antiquity.

32.8 Conclusion

Translation offers a view of aspects of the late ancient world in microcosm. The multiple translations and retranslations of popular religious narratives embody the new ways in which religious life was being imagined: the rise of the cult of saints and martyrs, the refashioning of the classical past in the light of the Christian saeculum, the power of the book in a Judeo-Christian worldview. Competition for authority among several translations of a single text reflects in physical book form struggles between multiple elites contesting authority in the political or ecclesiastical sphere. Translations with an official imprimatur gradually push aside "provincial" competitors representing communities that had failed to "make it" at the centers of power. Conversely, the latter may be symptomatic of a democratization of literature in late antiquity. We can also learn a great deal from the canons of translation, the variety of techniques that different translators brought to their trade. Contrast the extraordinary suppleness of the Alexander legend to Justinian's strictures on the translation of his laws – the ever-negotiable canonical status of a text was a vital consideration in the translator's approach.

Late ancient translation literature was a diverse phenomenon and so reflects the characteristics of the world from which it emerged. It represents at once both centrifugal and centripetal forces: a literary force away from the traditional foci of culture, on account of the expanding self-awareness and self-confidence of non-Greek language communities – Latin and Syriac, Armenian and Coptic, even nascent Anglo-Saxon and Arabic – in their own *non*-Greekness; at the same time a force toward the center, because translation implies a longing or a need for one language community to possess the products of another, rather than to be content with introspection. In late antiquity especially, Christianity was a uniting force of empire that gave incentive to the translation of genres as diverse as martyrologies and conciliar *Acta*, into all of its constituent literary languages. If late antiquity was a world in the process both of fragmentation and of homogenization, the world of literary translation holds a mirror up to this paradox.

REFERENCES

Brock, Sebastian P. (1983). Towards a history of Syriac translation technique. In: *III Symposium Syriacum, Goslar 7–11 September 1980* (ed. René Lavenant), 1–14. Rome: Pont.Inst.Stud.Or.

Brock, Sebastian P. (1989). From Ephrem to Romanos. *Studia Patristica* 20: 139–151.

Ciancaglini, Claudia. (2001). The Syriac version of the Alexander Romance. *Le Muséon* 114: 121–140.

Cooper, Stephen A. (2010). Marius Victorinus. In: *The Cambridge History of Philosophy in Late Antiquity* (ed. Lloyd P. Gerson), 538–551. Cambridge: Cambridge University Press.

Courcelle, Pierre. (1969). *Late Latin Writers and Their Greek Sources*. Cambridge, MA: Harvard University Press.

De Lange, N.R.M., Krivoruchko, Julia G., and Boyd-Taylor, Cameron. (2009). *Jewish Reception of Greek Bible Versions: Studies in Their Use in Late Antiquity and the Middle Ages*. Tübingen: Mohr Siebeck.

Flesher, Paul V.M. (2005). Privileged versions of Scripture. In: *The Encyclopaedia of Judaism*, vol. 4 (ed. J. Neusner, Alan J. Avery-Peck, and William Scott Greem), 2414–2426. Leiden: Brill.

Garsoïan, Nina G., Matthews, Thomas F. et al. ed. (1982). *East of Byzantium: Syria and Armenia in the Formative Period*. Washington, DC: Dumbarton Oaks Center for Byzantine Studies.

Hägg, Thomas. (1986). The Oriental reception of Greek novels: A survey with some preliminary considerations. *Symbolae Osloenses* 61: 99–131.

Hugonnard-Roche, Henri. (2004). *La logique d'Aristote du grec au syriaque: Études sur la transmission des textes de l'Organon et leur interprétation philosophique*. Paris: Vrin.

Humfress, Caroline. (2005). Law and legal practice in the Age of Justinian. In: *The Cambridge Companion to the Age of Justinian* (ed. Michael Maas), 161–184. Cambridge: University Press.

King, Daniel. (2009). Vir quadrilinguis? Syriac in Jerome and Jerome in Syriac. In: *Jerome of Stridon: His Life, Writings and Legacy* (ed. Josef Lössl and Andrew Cain), 209–223. Farnham: Ashgate.

King, Daniel. (2012). Elements of the Syriac grammatical tradition as these relate to the origins of Arabic grammar. In: *The Foundations of Arabic Linguistics. Sibawayhi and the Earliest Arabic Grammatical Theory* (ed. Amal Marogy), 189–209. Leiden: Brill.

Klein, Michael L. (1998). The Aramaic Targumim: Translation and interpretation. In: *The Interpretation of the Bible: The International Symposium in Slovenia* (ed. Jóse. Krašovec), 317–331. Sheffield: SAZU & Sheffield Academic Press.

Langslow, D.R. (2000). *Medical Latin in the Roman Empire*. Oxford: Oxford University Press.

Lombardi, Sara Mancini and Pontani, Paola. ed. (2010). *Studies on the Ancient Armenian Version of Philo's Works*. Leiden: Brill.

Maccoull, Leslie S.B. (1984). Coptic sources, a problem in the sociology of knowledge. *Bulletin de la Société d'Archéologie Copte* 26: 1–7.

Mulligan, Bret. (2016). Translation and the poetics of replication in the late antique Latin epigram. In: *Classics Renewed: Reception and Innovation in the Latin Poetry of Late Antiquity* (ed. Scott McGill and Joseph Pucci), 133–169. Heidelberg: Winter.

Pingree, David. (2001). From Alexandria to Baghdad to Byzantium, The transmission of astrology. *International Journal of the Classical Tradition* 8: 3–37.

Rebenich, Stefan. (2002). *Jerome. The Early Church Fathers*. London: Routledge.

Reydams-Schils, Gretchen. (2010). Chalcidius. In: *The Cambridge History of Philosophy in Late Antiquity* (ed. Lloyd P. Gerson), 498–508. Cambridge: University Press.

Scheltema, H.J. (1970). *L'Enseignement de Droit des Antécesseurs*. Leiden: Brill.

Sims-Williams, Nicholas. (2014). *Biblical and Other Christian Sogdian Texts from the Turfan Collection*. Berliner Turfantexte 32. Turnhout: Brepols.

Tang, Li. (2004). *A Study of the History of Nestorian Christianity in China and Its Literature in Chinese*. Europäische Hochschulschriften, Ser. 27, Asiatische und afrikanische Studien 87. Frankfurt am Main: Peter Lang.

Terian, Abraham. (1982). The Hellenizing School. In: *East of Byzantium: Syria and Armenia in the Formative Period* (ed. Nina G. Garsoïan, Thomas F. Matthews et al.) 175–186. Washington, DC: Dumbarton Oaks Center for Byzantine Studies.

Thomson, Robert W. (1982). The formation of the Armenian literary tradition. In: *East of Byzantium: Syria and Armenia in the Formative Period* (ed. Nina G. Garsoïan, Thomas F. Matthews et al.) 135–150. Washington, DC: Dumbarton Oaks Center for Byzantine Studies.

Van Bladel, Kevin. (2009). *The Arabic Hermes: from Pagan Sage to Prophet of Science*. Oxford: Oxford University Press.

Watt, John W. (2010). *Rhetoric and Philosophy from Greek into Syriac*. Variorum Collected Studies. Farnham: Ashgate.

CHAPTER THIRTY-THREE

Antiquarian Literature

Christopher Kelly

Late antique Christianity was tightly bound to its past. However its Christology was to be properly formulated, all Christians recognized that the Incarnation had taken place in (fairly recent) historical time. More expansively, an informed engagement with a distant antiquity might support the claim that the comforting message of Christian salvation had run like a silken thread through human history since Abraham. But the past was not neutral territory. For all that human progress might be presented as a providential prolegomenon to Christ (and, more recently, the emperor Constantine), Christians also surveyed a past that, like some postwar landscape, was cratered with error. In Peter Brown's attractive formulation, "The question which faced Christians in the world of late antiquity was how much of the past could be put in the past, and how much could be allowed to linger in the present" (2004, p. 116). Perhaps, then, it is not surprising that so much contemporary literature was engaged with precisely this problem. A substantial number of the works discussed in this *Companion* were shaped by a set of intellectual and literary strategies that positioned them more or less explicitly in relation to canonical antecedents. In that latitudinous sense, a wide range of late antique texts might be said to be broadly "antiquarian": that is, one significant preoccupation (or anxiety) is an exploration of the possible connections – by turns tight, tense, tenuous, tendentious – between a non-Christian past and a Christian present.

Conventionally, "antiquarian" has been more narrowly deployed to denote a particular subset of interests in the classical past. (And this chapter courteously

A Companion to Late Antique Literature, First Edition.
Edited by Scott McGill and Edward J. Watts.
© 2018 John Wiley & Sons, Inc. Published 2018 by John Wiley & Sons, Inc.

resists the urge to disappoint the editors of this *Companion* by dissolving its allocated subject.) Broadly stated, the antiquarian project may be distinguished by an emphasis on some kind of systematic subject taxonomy – that is, the collection and arrangement of material thematically (as opposed, for example, to chronologically) – and by a lack of any explicit concern to interrogate the items so assembled or to explore analytically the connections between them. In Arnaldo Momigliano's tart aphorism, the antiquarian is "the type of man who is interested in historical facts without being interested in history" (1990, p. 54). But that opposition – not to be overdrawn – is perhaps better seen as pointing to a difference in approach to the past rather than to any exaggerated contrast between dull pedantry and critical sophistication. (Nor is there any need to share the disdain of the modern professionalized academy for the enthusiastic amateur, connoisseur, or gentleman scholar.) Antiquarian texts, which chiefly delight in the careful collection and display of data, with an open enjoyment of the puzzling and obscure, can profitably be set in a wider field, surveyed elsewhere in this volume, which might usefully embrace encyclopedism (with its concern as to how knowledge might be ordered, presented, and retrieved) and a range of enterprises – grammars, commentaries, paraphrases, epitomes, *breviaria*, technical treatises – that aimed to systematize, codify, and correct the past (Formisano 2012, pp. 512–520; 2013, pp. 204–15; König and Woolf 2013, especially pp. 59–63; Chin 2008, pp. 54–60; Goldlust 2010, pp. 246–261; Flamant 1977, pp. 233–252; and the magisterial survey in Inglebert 2001).

33.1 Presenting the Past

> I was persuaded to write about such things, in part, reckoning that the undertaking would secure me a lasting reputation, and, in part, that it would be both absurd and malicious to let all the hard work, as recorded by the ancients in their writings about these matters, to remain forever hidden away.
>
> John Lydus, *On Celestial Signs* 1

In these confidently self-regarding terms, John Lydus ("the Lydian": from the province of Lydia on the western coast of Asia Minor) explained to his readers his decision to assemble a sizeable body of ancient data in a treatise, *On Celestial Signs*. Two other works by Lydus survive – *On Months* and *On the Magistracies* – all three written in Greek around the middle of the sixth century in Constantinople under the emperor Justinian (527–565). Lydus, who gives a detailed account of his own career in *On the Magistracies*, retired in 552, having served as the senior-ranking administrative officer (*cornicularius*) on the judicial side of the Praetorian Prefecture, one of the largest and most important government departments in the East (*PLRE* II, 612–615; C. Kelly 2004, pp. 11–104; Caimi 1984, pp. 46–81; Maas 1992, pp. 28–37; Bjornlie 2012, pp. 113–117; Kaster 1988, pp. 306–309; Treadgold 2007, pp. 258–264; Dubuisson and Schamp 2006, I.1 pp. xvii–lii, lxxxiv–cxv).

On Months and *On Celestial Signs* were both composed in the early 540 s. Neither work survives complete or in its original form – modern editions are a jigsaw of several lengthy extracts and a scatter of smaller passages and quotations. The focus of both these antiquarian projects is firmly on amassing – rather than interpreting – data. There is a clear delight in the accumulation of technical terms (*Signs* 10a, 44, 53; *Months* 1.28, 3.22, 4.1, 4.116, frag. 12), and authorities are repeatedly name-checked (Maas 1992, pp. 119–137 offers a lengthy catalog). *On Celestial Signs* brings together information on the predictive value of solar and lunar phenomena, comets, thunder, lightning strikes, and earthquakes, as well as Greek translations of a range of Roman authors, including the first-century BCE polymath Nigidius Figulus's Latin translation of the Etruscan seer Tages's brontoscopic calendar: a list of predictions based on the daily incidence of thunder (*Signs* 27–38; see Turfa 2012 for a translation and extensive discussion). *On Months* gathers material on the Roman calendar. Book 1 (very fragmentary) deals with the reforms of the legendary king Numa; book 2, with days of the week and their numerological significance; book 3, with the number of months and their divisions – in particular, the chief festal markers (kalends, ides, nones); book 4 discusses each month in turn, offering an impressive range of information on a wide variety of subjects – (for example) laurel, the emperor Trajan, cremation, multiple births, the ibis, beans, epilepsy, volcanoes, caterpillars – and includes (for each month) detailed descriptions of traditional Roman festivals.

To be fascinated by the past, especially the distant past, was inescapably to be concerned with authors and events that were not, at least directly, biblical (see, particularly, Maas 1992, reading Lydus against the enforcement of theological and academic orthodoxy in mid-sixth-century Constantinople). Yet, as any exegesis or commentary swiftly discloses, there is a broad and ill-defined hinterland of context, connection, and allusion that can be claimed to extend outward from any key text and arguably – with varying degrees of plausibility – is necessary for its full understanding. *On Celestial Signs* opens with a clear statement of the importance of portents in the Bible, citing the plagues of Egypt and quoting the apocalyptic prophecies from Joel (2:30): "I shall give signs in the heavens above and wonders on the earth below: blood, fire, and columns of smoke" (*Signs* 1). The implicit argument of the preface – the Bible is not referenced in the rest of the (surviving) work – is that the material on ancient religious lore that follows may properly be regarded as expansively explicating subject matter that is undeniably scriptural.

On Celestial Signs thus offers its readers a capacious context in which (should they so choose) biblical portents might be more fully comprehended. It is also important to note that, for all its inconsistency (Maas 1992, pp. 105–107), Lydus's cosmology allows ample room for the beneficent operation of Divine Providence (*Signs* 8, 9, 16a).

The Christian implications of *On Months* are less immediate (perhaps, in part, because of the poorly preserved opening sections). Amid discussion of a vast array of quotations and authoritative opinions – drawn exclusively from nonbiblical texts – Lydus includes some recognizably Christian material (especially *Months* 4.47 on the Sibylline Oracles; see Kalldelis 2003, pp. 308–310). He is also clear that Greek and Roman deities are to be understood as, sometimes extended, allegories (*Months* 2.2, 2.8, 2.10, 4.2, 4.34, 4.71, 4.154, 4.159; so too, *Signs* 1, 3, 10, 45). One striking feature of the organization of book 2 is the presentation of a seven-day week beginning with Sunday (Maas 1992, pp. 57–58). The brief discussion of origins omits any archaic alternatives, passing over both the Egyptian ten-day and the Etruscan eight-day week, and ignores variations in the names of the days (and which should start the week) and their association with the planets (*Months* 2.4). Although nowhere made explicit in the text, the attentive reader might notice that the non-Christian past has been silently corrected and – along with Lydus's complicated web of numerological associations (Maas 1992, pp. 58–60) – made to run on Christian time.

Lydus also insisted on the continuing relevance of his enterprise. His researches did not signal an ivory-tower retreat from the present (Domenici 2007, pp. 30–31). One of the inspirations for *On Celestial Signs* was his eyewitness sighting of a horse-shaped comet, which he connected with the Persian sack of Antioch in 540 (*Signs* 1). He associates a solar eclipse and fire in the sky with the revolt of Vitalian against the emperor Anastasius in 513–515 (*Signs* 6, with Mass 1992, p. 109); a kite dropping an arrow from its beak while swooping over the hippodrome in Constantinople presaged the destructive Nika Riot in 532 (*Signs* 8). Conversely, the absence of an eclipse when the sun was in Leo was an affirmation of Justinian's fortunate rule (*Signs* 9). In *On Months*, Lydus records that New Year's Day in his hometown of Philadelphia was still marked by the parade of an image of a double-faced Janus, a local custom "which preserves the imprint of antiquity" (*Months* 4.2). A similar "imprint" of the non-Christian ritual of libation is preserved in the eucharistic offerings of bread and wine (*Months* 4.31). But such blurring of the past and present was not always to be welcomed. Lydus concludes his description of the Brumalia, a festival held in early December, noting that the Church rejected these ancient traditions, in part because some of the celebrations were held at night and could be associated with the Underworld (*Months* 4.158).

It is (and perhaps deliberately?) difficult to know how to take this last editorial comment on the sixth-century Brumalia. Is it a sharp protest against a too rigorist Christianity, overeager to erase traces of antiquity; or is it a more gentle indication to the reader that what is at issue is precisely how a non-Christian past should be read against a Christian present; or is it another reminder that what might seem a selection of recondite data from a safely distant past is, in fact, of immediate and pressing relevance? Of course, it is impossible here (as elsewhere) to separate with any certainty or security the aspects of Lydus's account that might reflect something of contemporary practice from those that are part of his scholarly reconstruction. (And all the more so for his explanations of these elements, their meanings, and their origin.) Even so, it is worth noting that in the sixth century the Brumalia (at least in some form) was celebrated with imperial approval (Crawford 1919, pp. 370–374), and that, despite a long Mediterranean-wide tradition of sermonizing against festivals, parades, games, and other public entertainments, the Eastern Church did not formalize its objections until the Quinisext Council held in Constantinople in 692 (Maas 1992, pp. 64–66, 69–70).

The scatter of examples briefly surveyed above should not give any misleading impression of a strongly directed text. (From that point of view, Lydus's authorial approach is the antithesis of the ideal contribution to a *Blackwell Companion*.) Reading *On Celestial Signs* or *On Months* is like wandering through a museum stripped of its labels (an experience only exaggerated by the fragmentary state of both texts). There is an overall sense of curatorial order, but is not always clear what should be made of individual items and how they might relate to each other. How far should Lydus's observations on the contemporary relevance of his researches or the continuities between the ancient and the modern be pushed? How much of this information does the author himself credit: the descriptions of ancient Roman festivals; the 360 one-line predictions in the Etruscan brontoscopic calendar; the complex cosmology or numerology? For the most part, the thick mass of data assembled in *On Celestial Signs* and *On Months* is presented in raw form. That is not much to the taste of twenty-first-century readers who may not so readily share Lydus's unstinting enthusiasm for preserving the imprint of antiquity at the expense of any sustained analytical argument. But that division should not be pressed too hard. There is more in play here than the pedantic preservation of ancient wisdom. The difficulties encountered in understanding these texts, and their deep reservoirs of arcane information, are at the core of Lydus's project. The collection and categorization of a wide variety of information and opinion resists any simple separation of the past – or knowledge of the past – into Christian and non-Christian.

33.2 Perspectives on the Past

> Nor have I haphazardly deployed these items that are worth remembering, as though in a heap. I have organized the diverse subjects, drawn from a range of authors and a mix of periods, as though in a body, so that the things I initially noted down all in a jumble, as an *aide mémoire*, might come together in a coherent, organic whole.... The work before you promises not a display of eloquence but an accumulation of things worth knowing.
>
> Macrobius, *Saturnalia*, Praef. 3–4

Sometime in the 430s (a century before John Lydus and on the other side of the Mediterranean), Macrobius Ambrosius Theodosius dedicated to his young son Eustathius a "fund of knowledge," the considered result of a lifetime's study: "All that I have toiled through – in various books of Greek or Latin, both before and since you were born" (*Praef.* 2). Macrobius (as he is conventionally known) was one of the most distinguished senators of his generation in Rome, serving as Praetorian Prefect of Italy in 430 (*PLRE* II, 1101, 1102–1103; Cameron 2011, pp. 231–239). He presented his "fund of knowledge" as a dramatic dialogue (in Latin) explicitly modeled on Plato's *Symposium* (1.1.3): the record of set-piece discussions at a gathering of 12 "leading members of the Roman nobility and other learned men" (1.1.1). The scene was set 50 years earlier – most likely in 382 or 383 – at the preceding evening and three full days of the traditional festival of Saturnalia (16–19 December) (Cameron 2011, pp. 243–247; Kaster 2011, I pp. xxiv–xxv; Consolino 2013, pp. 89–91). (Previous scholarship argued for a closer coincidence of composition and dramatic date: for example, Flamant 1977, pp. 96–126; Bloch 1945, pp. 206–208; see, too, Goldlust 2010, pp. 11–14.) The group's daytime discussions were devoted to serious subjects; the evenings, over dinner, to topics "more pleasurable and less austere" (1.1.2). In the surviving text of Macrobius's *Saturnalia* – under two-thirds of the original – the company covers (for example) the humanity of slaves; the wit of great men (including Cicero and the emperor Augustus); ancient luxury; the variety of nuts, fruits, and olives; baldness; seawater; optics; dietary regimes; the effects of moonlight; and (on the mornings of the second and third days) a lengthy discussion of Virgil (Kaster 2011, 1: pp. il–liii, with the topics conveniently catalogued at 3: pp. 428–454; Goldlust 2010, pp. 40–63). The parade of learning is impressive – as is the intimidating fiction that educated persons should have vast amounts of detailed information and a seemingly endless chain of quotations at their immediate recall (1.24.1, 5.2.3, 5.17.8, 6.6.1, but see 5.3.17).

The first full day of discussion was hosted by Praetextatus. As with other interlocutors, Macrobius's Praetextatus is modeled on a well-known historical figure: Vettius Agorius Praetextatus, a powerful senator (Urban Prefect of Rome in 367–368, Praetorian Prefect of Illyricum and Africa in 384) and prominent supporter of traditional Roman religion (holding a number of priesthoods and the highest rank in the worship of Mithras) (*PLRE* I, 722–724). Like Praetextatus, the hosts of days two and three – Flavianus and Symmachus (respectively) – are also patterned on eminent late fourth-century senators who had been appointed to high imperial offices and publicly defended traditional religion: Virius Nicomachus Flavianus (*PLRE* I, 347–349) and Quintus Aurelius Symmachus (*PLRE* I, 865–870). The opening discussions (the privilege of the host) survive only for the first day. In response to polite encouragement, Praetextatus delivers learned discourses on the meaning of his own name, on the origin of the Saturnalia, and on slaves as fully human, and he explains why the sun is worshipped under so many divine names. For some modern readers, Praetextatus – often portrayed as the poster-boy for paganism in fourth-century Rome (Kahlos 2002, pp. 12–15) – should be understood as offering a solid defense of traditional religion (see below). But his long monologue on solar deities (1.17–23) is without any significant theology or metaphysics. Rather, it is a detailed and scholarly compilation of (sometimes strained) etymology, iconography, mythology, history, and anecdote: it "sounds more like an academic dissertation than a *confessio fidei*" (Consolino 2013, p. 92; see, too, Liebeschuetz 1999, pp. 192–200; Cameron 2011, pp. 266–69; Goldlust 2010, pp. 284–287; Shanzer 1986, pp. 135–136; Van Nuffelen 2011, p. 107). Similarly, the lengthy exposition of archaic sacrificial and pontifical practice (offered on the morning of the second day) is bounded by a concern to explicate passages in Virgil (3.1–3.12, with Cameron 2011, pp. 256–257, 567–626). Praetextatus's party pieces are applauded as virtuoso displays of erudition and memory (1.24.1), constructed by Macrobius as "an unbroken stream of citations from obscure monographs many centuries old" (Cameron 2011, p. 258). Perhaps the historical Vettius Agorius Praetextatus might have spoken very differently? Certainly, Macrobius's literary Praetextatus is firmly focused on the "accumulation of things worth knowing." In approaching his allocated subjects, he is not so much an advocate of paganism as a convert to antiquarianism.

The mornings of the second and third days were entirely devoted to Virgil. The authority of the discussions is strengthened by the presence of Servius, the poet's most influential late antique critic. Although, like Praetextatus, Macrobius's Servius is not simply to be merged with the historical Servius and his surviving commentaries (Kaster 1980, especially pp. 252–260; 1988, pp. 171–175; Cameron 2011, pp. 247–252). The reader should be warned that this symposium's scholarly exchanges fall somewhat short of the expectations of modern literary criticism. What really impresses this learned gathering are long lists of example after example cited to illustrate Virgil's success (and a handful of shortcomings) in evoking emotions (book 4), in deploying conventional rhetorical styles, and in borrowing from his predecessors, notably Homer (5.2.6–5.17.4, with over 100 parallel passages quoted), Pindar, Sophocles, Ennius, and Lucretius. Most striking is the demonstration of the sheer amount of information contained in Virgil – as complex and diverse as nature itself (5.1.4, 5.1.19–20) – and correspondingly the fund of knowledge required by any serious reader to understand the text (5.18.1, 6.7.4–6.9.13). Virgil's arcane material is dissected by Servius in long discussions (for example) on the custom of combat with one foot bare (5.18.13–21), or on the use of bronze blades in collecting herbs for magical purposes (5.19.7–13), or on the precise meaning of individual words: *lituus, matura, uestibulum, bidentes* (6.8.1–6.9.7). To the evident delight of the company, Virgil is firmly established as the most academic (*studiosissimus*) of poets (6.4.1) – to be appreciated by well-read readers with (unsurprisingly) a similar antiquarian turn of mind.

The courteous camaraderie of this cultivated *table ronde* is most frequently fractured by Evangelus (also a leisured member of the Roman elite with an estate at Tibur), who unashamedly crashes the party at the beginning of the first day (1.7.1–11). Evangelus is poorly behaved: aggressive (1.7.2), argumentative (7.5.1–3), a bully (2.2.12), and a boor. In the brief discussions that bookend individual presentations, he offers the crudest challenges to Virgil's authority, claiming that a "peasant boy" from rural Mantua could not have known Greek (5.2.1) and doubting Virgil's expertise in ancient Roman religion (3.10.1–3.12.10). To think otherwise, he needles, seems "more a display of favoritism than of good judgment" (1.24.2). It may be, too, that "Evangelus" (the name is the giveaway?) should be understood as interjecting a Christian point of view, or at least as suggesting the sort of questions that might be posed by some Christians (but see the reservations of Kaster 2011, 1: pp. xxxii–xxxiv; Cameron 2011, pp. 253–254, 595–598; Gerth 2013, pp. 85–90). (And, of course, it is not exclusively a Christian critical stance to doubt the *Saturnalia*'s reverent elevation of Virgil.) Whatever its potential Christian overtones, Evangelus's conspicuous lack of convivial cooperation is certainly a reflection of his literary pedigree. The cynic at the feast plays a key role in sympotic texts: a sharp reminder to the reader not to get too caught up in the fun. After all, it is Evangelus's disruptive dialogue that prevents the *Saturnalia* from seeming (too much) like a complacent conversation among clubbable companions.

Most importantly, Evangelus's uncomfortable presence forces his fellow interlocutors to offer some justification for the steadily mounting mass of antiquarian data – "items that are worth remembering" (*Praef.* 3; and see, generally, Hedrick 2000, pp. 79–88 on patterns of memory and forgetfulness).

One significant shared concern is to anatomize Virgil's literary practice, especially his intertextual strategies. The stockpile of citations and parallel passages is key to an evaluation of Virgil's relationship with his own literary heritage. Virgil (it is suggested) is at his best when blurring the boundary between the original and his imitation in ways that transcend both quotation and plagiarism; as a result of "the good judgment he displayed in his borrowings, when we read another's material in his setting, we either prefer to think it actually his or marvel that it sounds better than it did in its original setting" (6.1.6, with McGill 2012, pp. 178–209; see, too, 5.2.13 and Virgil's failure to measure up to Pindar at 5.17.7–14, with Pelttari 2014, pp. 29–31). Virgil is most vulnerable to criticism when he departs from an identifiable model (5.17.1–4). Praiseworthy invention, then, is not a matter of brash innovation but of finding an appropriate balance between the novel and the fitting (*noue quidem sed decenter*) (6.6.1; see, too, 5.3.16; Vogt-Spira 2009; D. Kelly 1999, pp. 55–76; Goldlust 2010, pp. 278–282). For Macrobius, too, the literary past is never past; as Aaron Pelttari notes, "Macrobius endorses a theory of originality that takes full account of the importance of transmission, tradition, and repetition (in a word, the reading) of the past for any consciousness of the present" (2014, pp. 28–29; see, too, König 2012, pp. 203–214; MacCormack 1998, pp. 73–82).

Virgil's reading of his own literary antecedents thus provides an attractive model for a late antique reading of Virgil (Pucci 1998, pp. 64–69). At the core of these lengthy interventions on Virgilian reception is the implication that a critical investigation of Virgil's poetics of imitation offers a useful framework for understanding the correct relationship between past and present. The test for the reader (in the congenial company of these 12 discussants) is to extend that paradigm – with all the erudition that implies and demands – to embrace topics as difficult as "the various names for solar deities." Or perhaps better, the reader should wonder how far the paradigm can be extended. After all – aside from a not particularly witty remark by the emperor Augustus, possibly alluding to Herod's Massacre of the Innocents (2.4.11 with Cameron 2011, p. 270; Jones 2014, pp. 154–155) – this is a text without any explicit reference to Christianity. Indeed, the *Saturnalia*'s sharpest provocation may be whether such "a highly idealized and highly stylized republic of learning" (Kaster 2011, 1: p. xviii) and its antiquarian fascinations with Virgil and traditional religion must remain forever fixed in the fictive world of late fourth-century Rome, or whether, 50 years later, this past could, in its turn, yield items worth remembering – *noue quidem sed decenter* – by Macrobius's son, Eustathius, and his fifth-century Christian contemporaries.

33.3 Past and Present

Antiquarianism is (inevitably) backward-looking. Its claim (as voiced in the *Saturnalia*) is to preserve "all that the ancients developed to perfection" (1.3.1). But neither Macrobius nor Lydus was engaged in some sentimental salvage operation. Both subjected the past to scrutiny. Lydus was clear: "I have carefully reviewed the most useful theories on the subject and purged them of their fraudulent inaccuracies" (*Signs* 22). The discussion in the *Saturnalia* confronts Virgil's literary shortcomings and catalogs the moral failings of Republican Rome (3.13–17). Nor was a carefully curated past to be presented merely as a textual cabinet of curiosities (although that was certainly part of the pleasure); rather, the antiquarian project also claimed a continuing contemporary connection. One key task was the reconciliation of the divergent views of ancient authorities. "We ought to imitate bees," Macrobius reflected; "wandering about, sampling the flowers, they arrange whatever they've gathered ... and by blending in the peculiar quality of their own spirit they transform the diverse kinds of nectar into a single taste" (*Praef.* 5). It was this very process of harmonization – the active intervention of both the antiquarian and his readers – that implicated past and present. Macrobius reiterates his point to metaphorical excess. The process is fermentation, it is digestion, it is arithmetic "just as one number results from a sum of individual numbers," it is the manufacture of perfume, blending "all the aromatic essences into a single fragrant exhalation" (*Praef.* 8). Best of all, it is the process of a perfect dinner-party conversation (as the urbane company admires its own sympotic achievement on the final afternoon): "In every area of life, and especially in the jovial setting of a banquet, anything that seems out of tune should – provided the proper means are used – be reduced to a single harmony" (7.1.13; Kaster 1980, pp. 231–38; 2008, 1: pp. xliv–xlv; Goldlust 2010, 166–171; Gerth 2013, 90–103).

But, for some, the non-Christian past remained stubbornly dissonant. In his brief book report on John Lydus, the ninth-century Byzantine bishop and bibliophile Photius – no enthusiast, declaring *On Celestial Signs* mired in myth and *On Months* "replete with pointless information" – noted that it was difficult to be certain of the author's faith.

> He is a man who seems devoted to the old religion, because he honors the beliefs of the classical past and venerates them, but he also venerates ours, so that it is not possible for his readers to decide easily whether he venerates them through conviction or is just playing along. (*Bibliotheca* no. 180/125b)

Some modern scholarship has been more certain, co-opting Lydus as part of a "pagan opposition" to Justinian (Hunger 1978, 1: pp. 250–251; and, more generally, Bell 2013, pp. 217–246), or regarding any formal profession of Christianity (Maas 1992, p. 30) as the "religious dissimulation" of a Neoplatonist with a "preference for non-Christian teachers and teachings" (Kaldellis 2003, quoting 303 and 307; see, too, Bjornlie 2012, pp. 114–115). But too easy an equation between antiquarianism – inevitably fascinated with the classical past – and paganism (even in its "softest" intellectualized versions) in sixth-century Constantinople has been rightly questioned (Treadgold 2007, p. 258; Caimi 1984, p. 14; and especially the careful discussion in Maas 1992, pp. 67–82). Similarly, in his important study of the aristocratic elite in late fourth-/early fifth-century Rome, Alan Cameron (2011) has exposed the dangers of assuming any simple congruence between pagan belief and a cultivated engagement with classical culture. Even so, opinion on Macrobius remains divided. The best claim for a pagan Macrobius (at least on the basis of the *Saturnalia*) rests on a reading of Praetextatus's lengthy exposition of the names of solar deities (prominently placed on the opening morning) as a rationalizing defense of paganism offering "the clearest views of his [Macrobius's] beliefs" (Jones 2014, p. 155; see, too, Flamant 1977, pp. 652–680; Kahlos 2002, pp. 193–200; Syska 1993, helpfully summarizing a dense discussion at pp. 210–218). The case is somewhat weakened if, as suggested above, Praetextatus's monologue, with its deracinated theology, is taken as the first in a series of antiquarian interventions in a symposium whose chief interest is a critical appreciation of Virgil. Macrobius's appointment as Praetorian Prefect of Italy in 430 may also be relevant; at least after the opening decades of the fifth century it is vanishingly rare to find a non-Christian holding high office in the West (Cameron 2011, pp. 272, 187–195). Macrobius, then, was "probably a Christian" (Kaster 2011, 1: p. xxii) or perhaps – in Alan Cameron's compromise – an "uncommitted pagan" writing for an overwhelmingly Christian readership (2011, pp. 265–272, retreating from 1977, pp. 22–26; 1966, p. 36; see, too, Goldlust 2010, 15–19; Gerth 2013, 88–90).

But too great a concentration on clarifying these authors' religious confession (or level of commitment) risks impeding an appreciation of their projects. After all, some ambiguity – as Photius's assessment grudgingly concedes – was inevitable in anything less than an openly hostile engagement with a non-Christian past (and particularly with the details of archaic rituals and beliefs). John Lydus is explicit in recognizing that tension: "To be occupied with the observation of the stars does not place one beyond right religion" (*Signs* 16a, but note the text is much restored). It is implicit in the *Saturnalia*'s repeated insistence – to Eustathius, to the interlocutors, to the reader – on harmonization. (To be sure, there is no explicit mention of Christianity. But that weighty silence seems a direct challenge to fifth-century Christian readers to look beyond their religion.

To think otherwise is to elect instead to reduce the *Saturnalia* to a narrow and nostalgic exercise in literary escapism.)

Above all, late antique antiquarian texts and their authors expect their readers to work hard. Unlike encyclopedias or grammars or commentaries, which typically claim a more univocal or greater prescriptive authority over their material, antiquarian works are deliberately polyphonic. The lengthy translated extracts in Lydus and the 12 voices of "leading members of the Roman nobility and other learned men" overheard in a three-day symposium are invitations to readers to join the discussion – sometimes frustrating, sometimes uncertain, sometimes inconclusive – to determine what "items are worth remembering." From that point of view, antiquarian projects are not just about passively admiring "all that the ancients developed to perfection" or about applauding competitive academic pedantry (although both elements play a part). Most importantly, for the attentive reader, these texts hold out the active possibility of working toward a fuller understanding of an – inescapably – non-Christian past and the ways, and on what terms, it might be connected with an – undeniably – Christian present.

REFERENCES

Bell, Peter. (2013). *Social Conflict in the Age of Justinian: Its Nature, Management, and Mediation.* Oxford: Oxford University Press.

Bjornlie, Shane. (2012). *Politics and Tradition: Between Rome, Ravenna and Constantinople. A Study of Cassiodorus and the* Variae, *527–554.* Cambridge: Cambridge University Press.

Bloch, Herbert. (1945). A new document of the last pagan revival in the West, 393–394 A.D. *Harvard Theological Review* 38: 199–244.

Brown, Peter. (2004). Conversion and Christianization in late antiquity: The case of Augustine. In: *The Past before Us: The Challenge of Historiographies of Late Antiquity* (ed. Carole Straw and Richard Lim), 103–117. Turnhout: Brepols.

Caimi, James. (1984). *Burocrazia e Diritto nel* De magistratibus *di Giovanni Lido.* Milan: Giuffrè.

Cameron, Alan. (1966). The date and identity of Macrobius. *Journal of Roman Studies* 56: 25–38.

Cameron, Alan. (1977). Paganism and literature in late fourth century Rome. In: *Christianisme et formes littéraires de l'Antiquité tardive en occident* (ed. Manfred Furhmann), 1–30. Entretiens Hardt 23. Geneva: Fondation Hardt.

Cameron, Alan. (2011). *The Last Pagans of Rome.* Oxford: Oxford University Press.

Chin, Catherine. (2008). *Grammar and Christianity in the Late Roman World.* Philadelphia: University of Pennsylvania Press.

Consolino, Franca. (2013). Macrobius' *Saturnalia* and the *Carmen contra Paganos*. In: *The Strange Death of Pagan Rome: Reflections on a Historiographical Controversy* (ed. Rita Lizzi Testa), 85–107. Turnhout: Brepols.

Crawford, John. (1919). De Bruma et Brumalibus festis. *Byzantinische Zeitschrift* 23: 365–396.

Domenici, Ilaria, ed. (2007). *Giovanni Lido, Sui segni celesti* (trans. Erika Maderna). Milan: Medusa.

Dubuisson, Michel and Schamp, Jacques. (2006). *Jean le Lydien*, Des magistratures de l'état romain: *Texte établi, traduit et commenté*. 2 vols. Paris: Belles Lettres.

Flamant, Jacques. (1977). *Macrobe et le néo-platonisme latin, à la fin du IVe siècle*. Leiden: Brill.

Formisano, Marco. (2012). Late antiquity: New departures. In: *The Oxford Handbook of Medieval Latin Literature* (ed. Ralph J. Hexter and David Townsend), 509–534. Oxford: Oxford University Press.

Formisano, Marco. (2013). Late Latin encyclopaedism: Towards a new paradigm of practical knowledge. In: *Encyclopaedism from Antiquity to the Renaissance* (ed. Jason König and Greg Woolf), 197–215. Cambridge: Cambridge University Press.

Gerth, Mattias. (2013). *Bildungsvorstellungen im 5. Jahrhundert n. Chr: Macrobius, Martianus Capella und Sidonius Apollinaris*. Berlin: de Gruyter.

Goldlust, Benjamin. (2010). *Rhétorique et poétique de Macrobe dans les* Saturnales. Turnhout, Brepols.

Hedrick, Charles. (2000). *History and Silence: Purge and Rehabilitation of Memory in Late Antiquity*. Austin, TX: University of Texas Press.

Hicks, Andrew. (2012). Martianus Capella and the liberal arts. In: *The Oxford Handbook of Medieval Latin Literature* (ed. Ralph J. Hexter and David Townsend), 307–334. Oxford: Oxford University Press.

Hunger, Herbert. (1978). *Die hochsprachliche profane Literatur der Byzantiner*. 2 vols., Munich: Beck.

Inglebert, Hervé. (2001). Interpretatio Christiana. *Les mutations des savoirs (cosmographie, géographie, ethnographie, histoire) dans l'Antiquité chrétienne, 30–630 après J.-C*. Paris: Études Augustiniennes.

Jones, Christopher. (2014). *Between Pagan and Christian*. Cambridge, MA: Harvard University Press.

Kahlos, Maijastina. (2002). *Vettius Agorius Praetextatus: A Senatorial Life in Between*. Rome: Institutum Romanum Finlandiae.

Kalldelis, Anthony. (2003). The religion of Ioannes Lydus. *Phoenix* 57: 300–316.

Kaster, Robert. (1980). Macrobius and Servius: *Verecundia* and the Grammarian's Function. *Harvard Studies in Classical Philology* 84: 219–262.

Kaster, Robert. (1988). *Guardians of Language: The Grammarian and Society in Late Antiquity*. Berkeley: University of California Press.

Kaster, Robert. (2010). *Studies on the Text of Macrobius'* Saturnalia. Oxford: Oxford University Press.

Kaster, Robert. (2011). *Macrobius:* Saturnalia. 3 vols. Loeb Classical Library. Cambridge, MA: Harvard University Press.

Kelly, Christopher. (2004). *Ruling the Later Roman Empire.* Cambridge, MA: Harvard University Press.

Kelly, Douglas. (1999). *The Conspiracy of Allusion: Description, Rewriting, and Authorship from Macrobius to Medieval Romance.* Leiden/Boston/Köln: Brill.

König, Jason. (2012). *Saints and Symposiasts: The Literature of Food and the Symposium in Greco-Roman and Early Christian Culture.* Cambridge: Cambridge University Press.

König, Jason and Woolf, Greg. (2013). Encyclopaedism in the Roman Empire. In: *Encyclopaedism from Antiquity to the Renaissance* (ed. Jason König and Greg Woolf), 23–63. Cambridge: Cambridge University Press.

Liebeschuetz, Wolf. (1999). The significance of the speech of Praetextatus. In: *Pagan Monotheism in Late Antiquity* (ed. Polymnia Athanassiadi and Michael Frede), 185–205. Oxford: Oxford University Press.

Maas, Michael. (1992). *John Lydus and the Roman Past.* London: Routledge.

MacCormack, Sabine. (1998). *The Shadows of Poetry: Vergil in the Mind of Augustine.* Berkeley: University of California Press.

McGill, Scott. (2012). *Plagiarism in Latin Literature.* Cambridge: Cambridge University Press.

Momigliano, Arnaldo. (1990). *The Classical Foundations of Modern Historiography.* Berkeley: University of California Press.

Pelttari, Aaron. (2014). *The Space That Remains: Reading Latin Poetry in Late Antiquity.* Ithaca, NY: Cornell University Press.

Pucci, Joseph. (1998). *The Full-Knowing Reader: Allusion and the Power of the Reader in the Western Literary Tradition.* New Haven, CT: Yale University Press.

Shanzer, Danuta. (1986). *A Philological and Literary Commentary on Martianus Capella's* De Nuptiis Philologiae et Mercurii *Book 1.* Berkeley: University of California Press.

Stahl, William. (1971). *Martianus Capella and the Seven Liberal Arts.* 2 vols., New York: Columbia University Press.

Syska, Ekkehart. (1993). *Studien zur Theologie im ersten Buch der* Saturnalien *des Ambrosius Theodosius Macrobius.* Stuttgart: Teubner.

Treadgold, Warren. (2007). *The Early Byzantine Historians.* Basingstoke: Palgrave Macmillan.

Turfa, Jean MacIntosh. (2012). *Divining the Etruscan World: The* Brontoscopic Calendar *and Religious Practice.* Cambridge: Cambridge University Press.

Van Nuffelen, Peter. (2011). Eusebius of Caesarea and the concept of paganism. In: *The Archaeology of Late Antique "Paganism"* (ed. Luke Lavan and Michael Mulryan), 89–109. Leiden/Boston: Brill.

Vogt-Spira, Gregor. (2009). Les *Saturnales* de Macrobe: Une poétique implicte de l'Antiquité tardive. In: *Manifestes littéraires dans la Latinité tardive: Poétique et rhétorique* (ed. Perrine Galand-Hallyn and Vincent Zarini), 263–277. Paris: Institut d'Études Augustiniennes.

FURTHER READING

John Lydus's *On Months* (often known by its Latin title, *De Mensibus*) is edited by Richard Wünsch (Leipzig: Teubner, 1898); *On Celestial Signs* (*De Ostentis*) by Curt Wachsmuth (2nd ed. Leipzig: Teubner, 1897). There is a serviceable English translation of both works by Anastasius Bandy (Lewiston: Edwin Mellen Press, 2013). (It should be noted that both texts have been reordered by Bandy and no longer correspond to Wünsch and Wachsmuth, whose numbering of the fragments is followed here.) Macrobius's *Saturnalia* is edited by Robert Kaster (Oxford: Clarendon Press, 2011); the manuscript tradition is discussed in detail in Kaster 2010. The *Saturnalia* is elegantly translated in Kaster 2011 (whose translations are used here). Readers with a taste for late antique antiquarianism might also like to consult the fifth-century *De Nuptiis Philologiae et Mercurii* (*The Wedding of Philology and Mercury*) by Martianus Capella. The complete text is edited by James Willis (Leipzig: Teubner, 1983) and the standard English translation is Stahl 1971, but note that there have been several subsequent French and Italian editions and translations of individual books; see Hicks 2012 for a helpful introduction and further bibliography.

FURTHER READING

PART THREE
RECEPTION

CHAPTER THIRTY-FOUR

Late Antique Literature in Byzantium

Anthony Kaldellis

The Byzantines had no concept of "late antiquity" or "the later Roman Empire" (as they were still living in the Roman Empire), and therefore they also had no notion of late antique literature. But Constantine's conversion and foundation of Constantinople did represent a turning point in their perception of imperial history, and the Christian Roman Empire from Constantine to Herakleios was later perceived as superior to both the pagan empire that had come before and the diminished empire that came after (Magdalino 1999). So there was a sense of a Christian-Roman Golden Age, which coincided with what we call late antiquity. Byzantine emperors aspired to emulate their late antique predecessors in various ways, especially Constantine and Justinian. Their city, palace, and cathedral (Hagia Sophia) were all late antique constructions, and the Byzantine Church, its administration, and its canons were late antique institutions. That period was also distinguished by the production of foundational Christian texts in the spheres of theology, exegesis, hagiography, and liturgy. In all those fields, including that of secular law, later Byzantines wrote exclusively within the parameters set by late antiquity, just as in the area of rhetoric they followed the rules encoded in the commentaries and the instructional manuals (for example, Menander Rhetor and Aphthonios). In sum, Byzantium as a civilization took its bearings mostly from late and not from classical antiquity. Its foundational moments, in both political and religious life, had taken place in late antiquity and were commemorated in ceremonies, liturgies, texts, and art. How did this affect the Byzantine reception of late antique literature?

A Companion to Late Antique Literature, First Edition.
Edited by Scott McGill and Edward J. Watts.
© 2018 John Wiley & Sons, Inc. Published 2018 by John Wiley & Sons, Inc.

What enables us to talk of late antique literature in Byzantium as if the two were separate is the precipitous decline in literary production that occurred in the mid-seventh century during and after the Arab conquests. Though some genres never fully lapsed, most had to be revived or reconstituted, a process that began in the later eighth century and was not in full swing until the twelfth. The Byzantine experience in this regard was different from that of eastern Christian communities under Arab rule. There Greek hagiography, hymnography, other types of poetry, and philosophical theology extended late antique traditions and produced works, such as those by John of Damascus, that eventually became canonical (Johnson 2014, pp. 67–78). In Byzantium there was a greater rupture. This allows us to distinguish between "early" and "middle" Byzantium, but it is not clear that the Byzantines themselves perceived a rupture. They refer to "ancient" and "modern" literature or historical eras, but in fluid and ad hoc ways that do not correspond to modern categories (Koder 2013). Photios's reviews of hundreds of books in his *Bibliotheca* reflect no awareness of late antiquity as a distinct period or that a rupture had occurred after it. As far as the Byzantines knew, there was a continuous tradition of writing Greek, some of it older and some of it newer. The perceived unity of this tradition is exemplified in a list proposed in the thirteenth century of the four best orations: One was ancient (Demosthenes), one imperial (Aristeides), one patristic (Gregory of Nazianzos), and one recent Byzantine (Psellos) (Hörandner 2012, p. 105). The selection may have been designed to include the different periods as well as a balance between pagan and Christian authors.

The distinction between pagan and Christian was far more important for structuring Byzantine views of the past than mere chronological periods. "Ours" vs. "theirs" and "inside" vs. "outside" were fundamental polarities of thought that governed how the tradition was approached, even when it was mixed and matched in the actual manuscripts. Each side had its own greats, though little work has yet been done on how Byzantines created literary canons. Suffice it to say here that the literary canon for them consisted of the works that they copied most frequently, commented upon, invoked as authorities, and cited. In terms of the reception of late antique literature, "our authors" – that is, authors of the Christian classics – were almost all from that period, whereas the classics of "outer wisdom" came from every period between Homer and Proklos. Therefore, period, canonicity, and (perceived) religious affiliation did not entirely overlap. Nevertheless, beyond the "classics," late antiquity is overrepresented within the corpus of *all* surviving ancient literature. A work and word count in the *Thesaurus Linguae Graecae* yields, for the thousand years between Homer and 200 CE, some 4200 works for a total of 30 million words; then, for the 500 years between

200 and 700 CE, it yields 3500 texts for 47 million words, that is, almost as many works and far more words for a period half as long. While these are rough counts, they reveal a bias in favor of the survival of late antique literature over ancient literature and a tendency toward larger works in that period. Just Galen and John Chrysostom together likely account for more than all extant classical Athenian literature. This bias is confirmed by Photios's *Bibliotheca*: Five-sixths of the works reviewed there are late antique, as are most of the works that Photios seems to have preferred on grounds of style and approach (Treadgold 1984, p. 90). Photios's sample is, however, skewed, because he generally does not include ancient authors whom he could reasonably expect his readers to know already (e.g. Homer, Thucydides). At any rate, we realize again that both the ancient canon and our literary late antiquity – at least on the Greek side – are largely the product of Byzantine choices and preferences (Kaldellis 2012).

The bias favoring late antiquity makes sense. Older works had a greater chance to be lost over time, to lapse because of changing tastes, or to be absorbed by later works that subsumed or condensed their contents into comprehensive or handy compilations. Thus, we have many large collections that "digest" earlier literature in various fields, including Plutarch's *Moralia*, Diogenes Laertios, and John Stobaios (in ethics and philosophy); Dio Cassius (Roman history); Galen (medicine); Eusebios's *Chronicle*; and the corpus of Roman law (of which Greek translations were being made already in the sixth century), as well as straight-up reference works such as that of Stephanos of Byzantium (for geographical lexicography, itself quickly abridged). These "digests" had not only the competitive advantage of being later but also of reflecting the outlook of the Greek Roman Empire of late antiquity, whose natural extension Byzantium was. Moreover, the preferential survival of patristic Greek literature comes as no surprise. Finally, all works had to survive the bottleneck (and filter) of the transliteration of ancient books (i.e. being rewritten in the minuscule script), which began around 800. In sum, the Byzantines preferred late antique literature in bulk, as it spoke more directly to the concerns of their world, and so we have more of it than its antecedents. But they also kept a selection of classics, valorized in part by the prestige they had accumulated over the centuries, their entrenchment in the classroom, and their centrality to the subsequent tradition.

The question has been insufficiently asked why the Byzantines kept pagan literature from late antiquity. Their choices are understandable when it comes to rhetoric and epistolography. Libanios, Themistios, Himerios, and Julian offered templates and models to later authors, especially for writing orations in praise of emperors and others, and they were important witnesses to the key events of the fourth century and biographically connected to Church

Fathers: Libanios as the alleged teacher of John Chrysostom and correspondent of Basil the Great; Themistios as the founder of the senate of New Rome and spokesman for Christian emperors; Himerios as the teacher at Athens of Basil the Great and Gregory of Nazianzos; and Julian as a fellow student and later target of Gregory of Nazianzos. But why keep anti-Christian late antique literature, such as some of the works of Julian, the philosophical treatises of Proklos, and the history of Zosimos? Not all such works were kept, of course. Porphyry's anti-Christian treatise was burned by imperial order and survives, like that of Julian, only in fragments quoted by Christian refutations. But Byzantinists still have not addressed the question why any was kept at all, and why more was kept, in fact, than Christian heretical literature, which was entirely wiped out in the Greek tradition (anti-Chalcedonian literature survived in Syriac, translated almost as it was being produced in late antiquity). Certainly, there may have been Neoplatonist sympathizers in later times, but we also need to consider the function that this literature performed in supporting Orthodox projects. Here literary reception meets the ideology of intellectual life. Julian was the negative Evil Other necessary for understanding Gregory of Nazianzos, the most important Christian author of late antiquity, and he was also fundamental for policing the boundaries and so the very constitution of Orthodoxy. He was refuted over and over again, all the way down to Palaiologan times. Intellectual Hellenism (or paganism) never ceased to haunt the Byzantines, and its name was Julian. Proklos, by contrast, offered the philosophical expertise and conceptual sophistication that many deemed necessary for grappling with theological issues, and his thought was redeemed by Pseudo-Dionysios, who Christianized it (and who has been suspected of being a pagan Trojan horse). Finally, Zosimos seems to have been kept (in few copies, if more than one) because he made a manifestly weak case against Constantine and Christianity that could easily be refuted – and was refuted, over and over again in the margins of the single manuscript that we have (Kaldellis 2015b, pp. 46–64).

What use did the Byzantines make of other late antique texts? For the most part they read them without leaving any trace of their reaction. The rest of this chapter will survey various modalities of engagement. Some of the following categories overlap or shade into each other, yet together they offer a diverse picture of diachronic reception. What made this possible was the glacial pace of change in written Greek, especially at the higher registers of the literary spectrum. Byzantine scholars were trained to use more or less the same form of Greek as was used in late antique literature, and so they never lost touch with the tradition or had to "rediscover" it. Their intuitive sense of the continuity of the tradition was thus reinforced by linguistic stability.

34.1 Continuation

Some late antique projects called out for extension (if they were chronologically limited), supplement, or completion, and some Byzantine authors obliged. The patriarch Nikephoros (806–815) wrote a *Short History* that picks up more or less where that of Theophylaktos Simokattes, the last classical historian of late antiquity, left off. Whether or not he intended it as a continuation, the two works were transmitted together, in sequence. But other than being written in Attic Greek, the two works are different in style and format, as Nikephoros briefly covers a century and half of history as opposed to Theophylaktos's longer account of 20 years. It was, nevertheless, an attempt to pick up where a prestigious late antique tradition had left off. A more deliberate team effort to do the same in the twelfth century produced philosophical commentaries on books of Aristotle where there were gaps in the late antique commentary tradition (Barber and Jenkins 2009). This was a curious case of a multi-author corpus "completed" after a six-century hiatus. Late antique texts could be both extended and supplemented. Thus, the *Onomatologos* of Hesychios (sixth century) was an encyclopedia of pagan authors ordered alphabetically that was later extended to the ninth century and supplemented with Christian authors, while keeping Hesychios's "brand" name in the title, before it was used by Photios and in the *Souda* (Kaldellis 2005).

34.2 Absorption

Later works in a tradition could absorb earlier ones, either partially or wholly, and drive them out of circulation. An example from the other main strand of historiography is Eusebios's *Chronicle*, which survives in forms closer to the original in the Armenian and Latin translation but in Greek was absorbed into later chronicles and received indirectly – for example, through Georgios Synkellos (ca. 800). Likewise, in the sixth century Justinian's *magister officiorum* Peter the Patrician wrote up instructions for the performance of court ceremonies and protocols, but we know this "manual" only through the chapters of it that were absorbed, and possibly reworked to suit the new context, in the tenth-century *Book of Ceremonies*. This reuse, explicitly signaled in the chapter headings, was itself political, in that it linked the court of Konstantinos VII to the more powerful, authoritative, and normative empire of Justinian. The enhanced and extended *Onomatologos* of Hesychios was likewise absorbed into the tenth-century *Souda* and then lost (though smaller versions of it continued to circulate separately). Absorption did not always lead to the loss of the original, especially if it took place later in the game and the original was an already established text. In the fourteenth century, for example, Nikephoros Xanthopoulos revived the genre of ecclesiastical history, but for the period of late antiquity he relies on the same authors whom we have, fusing them into a single narrative, which is why we do not use him for that period. In fact, only now is a proper critical edition being prepared.

34.3 Rewriting

Late antique texts sometimes found Byzantine editors and were rewritten to be improved stylistically or to serve new purposes in new contexts. The classic example is the *Menologion*, a collection of 148 saints' lives arranged by calendar feast day, compiled in the late tenth century by Symeon Metaphrastes and his team. One of the goals of this collection was to provide *vitae* that met a high stylistic standard: If the original text did not, it was rewritten in a loftier and more acceptable style. Some of the lives, such as Athanasios's *Life of Antony*, were already established classics, and so Symeon included them without alteration. In some cases, for example St. Symeon the Stylite, he combined a number of sources to produce a new text (Høgel 2002). Other Byzantine practices of rewriting are harder to classify, as they defy modern conventions and even make readers uncomfortable. The military manual of the emperor Leon VI, the *Taktika* (ca. 900), lifts passages almost verbatim from the *Strategikon* of Maurikios (ca. 600), albeit without acknowledgment and acting as if nothing had changed in the practice of war and the structure of the Roman army. More troublingly, it repurposes some of the original material: For example, it transfers the chapters on the Avars to the contemporary Hungarians and Bulgarians and turns the *Strategikon*'s description of Sasanian warfare and military culture into prescriptions for contemporary Byzantine warfare. This veers closer to literary repurposing – if we must give it analytical respectability – than to lazy plagiarism.

Rewriting as appropriation could take troubling forms. The tenth-century chronicler Symeon Logothetes (likely identical to Symeon Metaphrastes) narrated the conquest of Crete (960–961) by Nikephoros Phokas under Romanos II by lifting language verbatim from Prokopios's account of Belisarios's conquest of Vandal North Africa, right down to the description of the triumph that followed (Kaldellis 2015a). The two expeditions were structurally similar, so the choice was inspired, but the result is that Symeon's account is compromised as a factual record. It can be redeemed, perhaps, as a symbolic statement: The new age of Byzantine conquests inaugurated by the Phokas family restored the empire to the dominant position it had held under Justinian. As we saw above, the reuse and reabsorption of Justinianic literature buttressed the pretensions of the Macedonian dynasty. A similar interpretation may be offered of late Byzantine encomia of cities, specifically of Constantinople by Theodoros Metochites and Trebizond by Bessarion, which extensively recycled the language, ideas, and themes of the encomia of Athens by Aristeides and of Antioch by Libanios, albeit rearranging the "raw" material to make new narratives and arguments (Saradi 2011). This textual relation both situated the Byzantine cities in the tradition of prestigious ancient cities – the very ones recommended in the rhetorical manuals as benchmarks for civic greatness – and provided ways of showcasing the Byzantine cities' superiority over them. It was this "imitation" that allowed the comparison to take place in the first place, by forming tight textual relations.

34.4 Replicating Authorial Personae

Some Byzantine authors constructed their literary personae around that of a canonical late antique writer or figure. In antiquity, Arrian had done this with Xenophon, his literary model. In Byzantium, Leon VI cast himself (among other guises) as a new Justinian, coissuing the *Basilika* (a Greek version of the *Corpus*) and then following that up with 113 *Novellae* of his own, the first of which cites Justinian as the model for the entire project. Leon was presenting himself as a new (and improved) Justinian. A more ambitious and complex refashioning of this kind was performed by the eleventh-century intellectual Psellos. In some of his political philosophical texts he presents himself as a new Themistios, offering advice in speeches to Christian emperors, while in others he channels a persona modeled on the bishop-philosopher Synesios, especially in his negotiation of rhetoric and philosophy and the public face appropriate to each. Yet more than either of them, Psellos took Gregory of Nazianzos as his main literary prototype (Papaioannou 2013). Famously, Gregory had used his speeches to engage with a range of genres, from theology and hagiography to invective and panegyric, and had also written poetry and letters. Many of these were infused with a powerful first-person presence. The diversity and ambition of Gregory's vast oeuvre was, moreover, meant to provide a canonical Christian counterpart to the prestige genres of late antiquity, claimed controversially as Hellenic (pagan) property by Julian. Psellos's own wide-ranging literary experiments replicated this project, as he covered most genres and infused most of his works with a striking albeit also deliberately vulnerable autobiographical persona. He, too, wrote funeral orations for his friends and associates, including prominent churchmen, and for his mother and other relatives, and he also produced accounts of his own life and career, including apologiae for controversies and invectives against his enemies. Gregory was the chief rhetorical inspiration for this project. Psellos also set about restructuring Byzantine theology through exegesis, infusing Neoplatonism into its methods to a degree that Gregory would have found appalling. He also wanted to overturn the traditional Byzantine monastic system of values. In fact, there are indications that Psellos sought to change the course of Byzantine thinking from the track on which Gregory and the other Church Fathers had set it, and his appropriation of Gregory's persona was an effective way to achieve this revolution from the inside (Kaldellis 2007: 158–163 and chapter 4).

34.5 Literary Criticism

Most recorded Byzantine readings, interpretations, and studies of ancient literature consist of scriptural exegesis or commentaries and scholia on classical (not late antique) literature. Notable exceptions are Photios's reviews in the *Bibliotheca*, some essays by Psellos on various Church Fathers and on Georgios of Pisidia, and a brief essay on Synesios by Theodoros Metochites, the fourteenth-century philosopher and statesman.

I will highlight here only one aspect of Photios's engagement with late antique literature, his distrust of mythography and allusions to myth, which evidently made him feel uncomfortable. We know that Christian attitudes had undergone a fundamental transformation in this regard during late antiquity. Greek mythology began as a target of apologetic ridicule and confrontation and ended up as just another cultural adornment or narrative template, to be deployed rhetorically by Christian authors in ways similar to their pagan counterparts. In Photios's time, however, Byzantine intellectual culture had reverted to its more fundamentalist mode and was not yet ready for experiments in mythological or erotic fiction (Lauxtermann 1999). In his review of the orations of Chorikios, for example, Photios felt it necessary to juxtapose the author's sincere orthodoxy with the fact that he inexcusably and inexplicably introduces Greek myths and stories, even when writing about sacred topics (cod. 160). But compare how he treats the same topic in reviewing the pagan Himerios, whose style he admired: "His writings are full of all kinds of examples from history and mythology, either for proof, or to draw parallels, or for pleasure, or to ornament what he is saying…but it is clear that he is impious when it comes to religion, and imitates those dogs that bark against us in secret" (cod. 165). Pagans are more likely to get away with using mythology in Photios's reviews than are Christian writers, perhaps because he found it less discordant in their case. Photios dislikes the "disgraceful obscenity" of mythological transformation stories and prefers Lucian, a pagan who mocks the belief in such things, over those who present them at face value, leaving Photios uncertain as to whether they believed them (cod. 129). He finds it easy to attribute a book *On Incredible Tales* to the Platonist Damaskios precisely because "such monstrosities invented in bad faith" suited an atheist who clung to idols even as the light of faith was spreading throughout the world (cod. 130).

In sum, there was no recognition in Photios's flat reading that Christian literature of late antiquity had evolved classicizing mythographical modalities. The irony was that Byzantine literature of the middle period would effectively recreate the trajectory of its late antique counterpart, moving beyond Photios's suspicious attitude to exhibit a mythographical mania of sorts, where not only emperors but bishops, too, were compared to Homeric heroes, along with erotic, pseudo-pagan, imaginative fiction (Kaldellis 2007: chapter 5). Moreover, Photios, who presented himself as a champion of images after the Iconoclast controversy, was also obsessed with finding evidence in the literature of late antiquity about the use of images in worship, thereby imposing his own cultural preoccupations on his readings of late antique texts (e.g. cod. 160 on Chorikios).

Psellos also wrote some brief treatises on the literary style of the Church Fathers, especially Gregory of Nazianzos and John Chrysostom, which attempt to uphold them as worthy equivalents on "our" side of Demosthenes, Plato, and Lysias, even if they habitually deviate from classical norms (Hörandner 1996). The parameters of his analysis are, again, provided by the rhetorical-theoretical tradition, though unfortunately Psellos does not offer close readings of specific passages to document his verdicts. At the opposite hermeneutical extreme, many of Psellos's exegetical notes (published under the title Theologica), possibly stemming from his lectures, do contain close readings of clauses or passages in Scripture and of the Fathers, especially Gregorios of Nazianzos, but these focus on technical philosophical questions, not literary style. Still, questions of grammar occasionally come up in the resolution of textual ambiguities. Psellos's guiding authorities in these notes are, more often than not, the non-Christian Neoplatonists (one cannot imagine that this would have gone over well with Gregorios). Psellos's best-known literary essay on a late antique author is his comparison of Euripides to the seventh-century theological poet Georgios of Pisidia (known today mostly for his panegyrical poems on the wars of the emperor Herakleios, but known to the Byzantines for his work the *Hexaemeron*, or *Six Days of Creation*). The essay, couched in the technical terms of rhetorical theory and metrical analysis, is unfortunately damaged in transmission, and only a page is devoted to Georgios anyway (Dyck 1986). Psellos is not interested in reading the two poets against their distinctive historical backgrounds; instead, he applies the same standards to their evaluation, as if they were contemporaries competing for the same prize. It is not clear, however, to whom he awards it. The fact that he treats them as roughly equal can disturb modern scholars, who would not think twice. But the point of the exercise is as much to showcase Psellos's own rhetorical skills, and elsewhere he advertises the fact that making a weak case seem strong was among them. Having Georgios predictably lose to Euripides would not have made for interesting reading, and, moreover, the exercise enabled Psellos to praise the literary qualities that he most prized in his own writing (Dyck 1986, p. 37).

Metochites's *Essays* have been little studied (Hult 2002), in part because his writing style is difficult and obscure. In one essay on literary criticism (17), he distinguishes between the writing styles of authors from Syria and Phoenicia, on the one hand, and Egypt, on the other. As most of his reading, too, was probably in late antique authors, the examples that he cites include Libanios and Porphyry for the first group, whose style is marked by smoothness, and then Synesios and the Egyptian Church Fathers for the second, whose style was harsh or rough. Both groups are distinct from the "Attic" writers, that is, the ancient classics. The categories of style that Metochites deploys to make these comparisons are taken from the rhetorical manuals. It is indeed difficult, if not impossible, for modern readers to reconstruct the experience of a "rough" or "smooth" style in reading Libanios or Synesios. It is likely that we have entirely lost this sense of stylistic nuance – assuming that Metochites himself could define these qualities and then actually find them in a text. Unfortunately, he does not give examples that would allow us to understand what he means.

The only late antique author to whom Metochites devotes an essay is Synesios (18), and it makes some intriguing statements. After praising him for perfectly mixing philosophy and rhetoric, Metochites says that Synesios's style did not conform to the ancient Hellenic way of writing (presumably an "Attic" standard) but was instead more "modern." Specifically, it was neither "smooth" and "simple" like the ancients nor "forceful," as so much writing was in his own time. Is it possible that Metochites was trying to articulate a late antique literary aesthetic, different from that of classical prose, but also not a standard to which Synesios himself fully adhered? Unfortunately, his frame of reference remains the conventional tradition of rhetorical theory, which is not yet amenable to modern use or appreciation. Metochites also makes a perspicacious observation about Synesios, showing that he was a superior reader to Photios. Synesios, he says, cannot be classified neatly as belonging to this or that doctrine, as he belonged to all groups, mediated among them, and chose their best elements. It is interesting that modern scholarship on Synesios has struggled with the same question, with some viewing him as a Christian and others as essentially a Platonist with only a Christian patina. Curiously, Metochites never calls Synesios a Christian at all: The question for him is which ancient philosophical school he belonged to, and his conclusion is that he was a Platonist who took in other fields and approaches as necessary.

To conclude, in terms of the history of Greek literature it is not clear that "late antiquity" ever really ended and "Byzantium" began after it at some point, such that we might postulate a clear state of reception between the two, at least not in the sense in which the term is usually understood. Byzantium was rather a living extension of late antiquity, and the Byzantines did not perceive a rupture between the two, except on the level of imperial greatness. Genres came and went, or were periodically reconstituted, but the basic modalities of Byzantine literary culture were those of late antiquity. The two were successive phases of the same culture, a continuous evolution within the same literary tradition.

REFERENCES

Barber, Charles and Jenkins, David. ed. (2009). *Medieval Greek Commentaries on the Nicomachean Ethics.* Leiden: Brill.

Dyck, Andrew R. (1986). *Michael Psellus: The Essays on Euripides and George of Pisidia and on Heliodorus and Achilles Tatius.* Vienna: Austrian Academy of Sciences.

Høgel, Christian. (2002). *Symeon Metaphrastes: Rewriting and Canonization.* Copenhagen: Museum Tusculanum.

Hörandner, Wolfram. (1996). Literary criticism in 11th-century Byzantium: Views of Michael Psellos on John Chrysostom's style. *International Journal of the Classical Tradition* 2: 336–344.

Hörandner, Wolfram. (2012). Pseudo-Gregorios Korinthios: Über die vier Teile der perfekten Rede. *Medioevo Greco* 12: 87–131.

Hult, Karin. (2002). *Theodore Metochites on Ancient Authors and Philosophy: Semeioseis gnomikai 1–26 and 71.* Gothenburg: Acta Universitatis Gothoburgensis.

Johnson, Scott Fitzgerald. (2014). Introduction: The social presence of Greek in Eastern Christianity, 200–1200 CE. In: *Languages and Cultures of Eastern Christianity: Greek* (ed. Scott Fitzgerald Johnson), 1–92. Surrey: Ashgate.

Kaldellis, Anthony. (2005). The works and days of Hesychios the Illoustrios of Miletos. *Greek, Roman, and Byzantine Studies* 45: 381–403.

Kaldellis, Anthony. (2007). *Hellenism in Byzantium: The Transformations of Greek Identity and the Reception of the Classical Tradition.* Cambridge: Cambridge University Press.

Kaldellis, Anthony. (2012). The Byzantine role in the making of the corpus of classical Greek historiography: A preliminary investigation. *Journal of Hellenic Studies* 132: 71–85.

Kaldellis, Anthony. (2015a). The Byzantine conquest of Crete (961 AD), Prokopios' Vandal War, and the continuator of the chronicle of Symeon. *Byzantine and Modern Greek Studies* 39: 302–311.

Kaldellis, Anthony. (2015b). *Byzantine Readings of Ancient Historians*. London: Routledge.

Koder, Johannes. (2013). Zur Unterscheidung von alter und neuer Zeit aus byzantinischer Sicht. In: *Polidoro: Studi offerti ad Antonio Carile* (ed. G. Vespignani), 507–521. Spoleto: Fondazione Centro italiano di studi sull'alto Medioevo.

Lauxtermann, Marc. (1999). Ninth-century classicism and the erotic muse. In: *Desire and Denial in Byzantium* (ed. Liz James), 161–170. Brookfield, VT: Ashgate.

Magdalino, Paul. (1999). The distance of the past in early medieval Byzantium (7th–10th centuries. *Settimane di studio del Centro Italiano di studi sull'alto medioevo* 46: 115–146.

Papaioannou, Stratis. (2013). *Michael Psellos: Rhetoric and Authorship in Byzantium*. Cambridge; Cambridge University Press.

Photios. (1959–1977). *Bibliothèque* (ed. and trans. René Henry). 8 vols. Paris: Belles Lettres.

Photius. (1993). *The Bibliotheca* (ed. and partial trans. N. G. Wilson). London: Duckworth.

Psellos, Michael. (1989). *Theologica*, vol. 1. (ed. Paul Gautier. Leipzig: Teubner)

Saradi, Helen. (2011). The monuments in the late Byzantine *Ekphraseis* of cities: Searching for identities. *Byzantinoslavica* 59: 179–192.

Treadgold, Warren. (1984). The Macedonian renaissance. In; *Renaissances before the Renaissance* (ed. Warren Treadgold), 75–98. Stanford: Stanford University Press.

Westerink, L. G., and J. M. Duffy. (2002). *Michael Psellus: Theologica*. Vol. 2. Leipzig: Teubner.

FURTHER READING

A different and complementary approach to the same topic:
Papaioannou, Stratis. (2009). The Byzantine late antiquity. In: *A Companion to Late Antiquity* (ed. Philip Rousseau), 17–28. Malden, MA: Blackwell.

CHAPTER THIRTY-FIVE

The Arabic Reception of Late Antique Literature

Kevin T. van Bladel

Around 940, in northern Iran, Abū Ḥātim al-Rāzī wrote in Arabic that the "best" languages were those in which God had communicated to his prophets: Hebrew, Aramaic, Persian, and Arabic. He conceded importance to Greek and Sanskrit for the sciences composed in them. But Arabic, he insisted, was the best of them all, not only because of its inherent perfection, but because, he believed, more people strove to learn Arabic than any other language at any time in history,

> to the point that they translated the scriptures, like the Torah, the Gospel, the Psalms, and the rest of the books of the prophets from Aramaic and Hebrew into Arabic; they translated the statements of the Persian sages into Arabic, and all of the books of philosophy, medicine, astral sciences, engineering, and mathematics from Greek and Sanskrit into Arabic; and every nation aspired to learn Arabic in order to translate what they had into it. Those who know the Qur'an and Arabic books have not wished to translate it into any other language, nor were any of the nations even able to render any of it into any other language. (Abū Ḥātim al-Rāzī 1994, p. 73)

By the tenth century, when Abū Ḥātim wrote, Arabic may have, indeed, seemed to be on its way to universal use. Although he grew up at the site of modern Tehran speaking an Iranian language at home, he chose Arabic as the medium for all his books, composed on subjects ranging from Arabic

---

A Companion to Late Antique Literature, First Edition.
Edited by Scott McGill and Edward J. Watts.
© 2018 John Wiley & Sons, Inc. Published 2018 by John Wiley & Sons, Inc.

lexicography to the Ismaili Shiite doctrine he professed and propagated. Because they were written in Arabic, his works could, in theory, find readers from Spain to Afghanistan, the space across which Arabic had become the preeminent language of learning and public communication, especially in cities and towns. He could feel confident that any ancient learning worth reading – be it Scripture, philosophy, science, or medicine – was, or would be, translated into Arabic and was in principle available to him. In his original writings, Abū Ḥātim shows his familiarity with a wide range of ancient sources, including not only the Qurʾān, copious early Islamic traditions, and many exemplary Arabic poems (some from before Islam) but also Arabic works attributed to Hermes Trismegistus, Proclus, and Galen; a doxography based at some removes on the *Refutatio omnium haeresium* attributed to Hippolytus of Rome (d. 230); and other late ancient material in Arabic translation. In his use of ancient sources, Abū Ḥātim is not unusual but rather typical of tenth-century Arabic authors. He was one of many who knew ancient sources in Arabic translation. Of course, he uses them only for his own purposes, but the point remains that he felt it useful to cite them.

The Arabic reception of late ancient literature followed the remarkable elevation of the status of the Arabic language after the seventh-century conquest and the stabilization of a literary standard of Arabic. In late antiquity, until the beginning of the seventh century, Arabic literature had been the product of relatively removed pastoralist and village peoples in the vast Arabian peninsula and of small client kingdoms and tribes on the arid fringes of the powerful Roman and Persian Empires. Peoples of the Persian kingdom and the Roman Empire had known speakers of Arabic primarily as brigands, mercenaries, and immigrant outsiders. Theirs was a language that very few non-Arabs ever needed, and a limited amount of its literature survives. By the year 800, however, after the far-reaching conquests of the seventh century, a standardized form of Arabic was becoming the main language of intercommunal and interregional written communication wherever Arabs had settled in Iraq, Egypt, Iran, northern Africa, and Spain. Although the conquerors had initially settled in new colonies (*amṣār*), such as Kūfa and Baṣra in southern Iraq and Fusṭāṭ in Egypt, that were intended to keep them apart and to minimize mutual acculturation while serving as bases for further conquests, the social boundaries between Arabic- and non-Arabic-speakers and between Muslim, client-convert, and non-Muslim subject were gradually eroding. Arabic became the primary language of increasingly many people, including offspring of unions of Arabic-speaking fathers and mothers who spoke other languages and even of some who had no Arabic-speakers in their ancestry. In the course of the tenth century, Arabic became the preferred medium of all learned public and intercommunal urban communication in cities almost everywhere across the Middle East and North Africa, from the Atlantic to Central Asia. By the year 1000, many members of religious communities subordinate to the Muslim, Arabic-speaking rulers – including Christians, Jews, and Zoroastrians, especially in the Muslim cities where political and military power was now based – had in many cases already shifted to the use of Arabic within their own communities and homes. Arabic would only spread further in subsequent centuries until, gradually, their traditional languages – Coptic, Greek, Aramaic, most Iranian languages, and others – would evolve into the scattered, scarcely written vernaculars of ghettos, small villages, and remote pastoralists, their old book traditions now the specialized domain of religious scholars and priests belonging to the diminishing non-Muslim religious groups.

As the use of other literary languages contracted, the role of Arabic as a medium of culture and learning was magnified through the very extensive Arabic reception, via selective translation, of the literatures surviving late antiquity, culled as needed and desired by patrons and professionals among the Arabic-speaking readership. Classical Arabic literature grew as a remarkable blend of several hitherto largely separate ingredients, creating a new, cosmopolitan culture of scholarship and letters in the process. The large-scale translation of texts from Iranian languages (especially Middle Persian), Sanskrit, Aramaic (especially the Syriac dialect), and Greek had begun already in the second half of the eighth century. Scholars and patrons of scholarship demanded old learning in the now-current medium. Old traditions from different countries were synthesized into new Arabic forms and put to new purposes. Translations from Greek, in particular, became especially numerous and prestigious in the ninth and tenth centuries.

The Arabic reception of late ancient literature is sometimes characterized as having been effected by a "translation movement." The expression was put into wide circulation by Dimitri Gutas (1998) to describe concisely the phenomenon of sustained widespread patronage of translations from earlier literary traditions, especially ancient Greek, into Arabic. While this certainly can be characterized fairly as a movement, it was not motivated by a uniform interest evenly distributed over places and times. Gutas simultaneously demonstrated generational variation in the reception. Interests changed with political and social circumstances. Translations of ancient works themselves sometimes stimulated interest in further translations. The range of topics for which translations were in demand grew. I discuss examples of these variations in what follows.

In the first 75 years of the secular and scientific translations, interest in which was centered in Baghdad (ca. 762–850), it was mostly only physicians, astrologers, and specialists in religion who used these ancient books. They needed to conduct their professions using the state of the art available in the preexisting literary traditions, as it was written in the languages of their communities of origin. Works like Aristotle's *Physics* and his logical treatises came quickly to play an important role in the interreligious and sectarian theological debates fostered by the Abbasid caliphs' courtiers and those in their orbit. Later, the audience of these translations broadened with the growth of Arabic intellectual life and the desire of intellectually inclined Muslims, especially the secretarial class (*kuttāb*), to participate in all varieties of learning. By the turn of the millennium, most educated, cosmopolitan Arabic speakers had encountered ancient learning in Arabic translations and abridgments. They could be expected to understand the basic elements of ancient Greek philosophy, medicine, science, and wisdom, even when they were not themselves professional practitioners of the ancient arts and sciences. They could name the humors of the Galenic body, describe the spherical Ptolemaic cosmos, outline the fundamental doctrines of the philosophers, and recite a fair bit of memorized gnomological lore in the name of Greek figures such as Socrates and Diogenes the Cynic or of Persians such as Buzurgmihr, legendary sage of the court of the Persian king Khusrō I (r. 531–579). They could spar with each other about first principles and God's attributes, the dualism of Zoroastrians, and the trinity of the Christians, citing late antique commentaries on Aristotelian logic while sometimes unknowingly echoing early Christian apologetic and polemic. By the mid-tenth century, such topics had become not so much a matter of the deliberate recovery of ancient thought by individuals as they were merely a part of the fabric of Arabic learned culture. In this respect, the reception had been accomplished and the material was digested. The theories, systems, and ideas translated would henceforth be elaborated and innovated upon in new ways, leading to the gradual abandonment of the direct use of ancient classics in Arabic translation in favor of recourse to the reconfigured and adapted syntheses of ancient scholarship produced from this time onward by Muslim scholars such as Ibn Sīnā (d. 1037).

The Arabic reception of late antique literature created a different canon from the literary canon of classical scholarship of modern Europe. A comparison of the two receptions is instructive. The classical Latin tradition of Europe, on which the modern discipline of classical studies is based, was fundamentally shaped by the interests of medieval Italian *humanisti*, rhetoricians who valued poetry and orations according to an ancient standard of language that they deemed excellent and that they sought to revive. The ancient masters whom they followed, such as Cicero and Ovid, were manifestly dependent on Greek rhetoric and poetry, and their interest is part of what led western European scholars to study ancient Greek directly. "Literature" in these forms became central to the European tradition of learning that would develop into classical scholarship. The reception of ancient learning in Arabic had a distinctly different character due to its different conditions. It stemmed not from the needs of Arabic rhetors, who already had adequate and socially appropriate models from ancient Arabic poetry and from Islamic scripture and sermon, models already esteemed by their patrons. In Baghdad, the Arabic reception was generated rather by the needs of other sorts of court professionals: astrologers, physicians, and experts in interreligious disputation. The Arabic reception of ancient texts in Baghdad did require some searching out and rediscovering of ancient works, but it was based at first more on the transfer of the specialized learning then current in non-Arabic languages into Arabic than on the revival of lost texts. There was no intention of pursuing that learning in the original languages, because this was not a revival of literary forms expressed idiosyncratically in those ancient and defunct tongues. It was, instead, a reception of disciplines, techniques, and methods of learning and practice. Nor was the learning particular to one language, but it was derived from any available source. It was a rather ecumenical reception, as expressed by Abū Ḥātim al-Rāzī at the beginning of this chapter. The shape of the Arabic reception of ancient literatures thus does not just throw into relief the conditioned character of western European notions of "literature." It also demonstrates that an entirely different selection process in the reception of ancient Greek literature was both possible and actual, and it entailed a mixture with materials translated from other literary languages employed to the east of the Roman Empire, not with materials from Latin. It also includes texts that do not survive in their original, but only in Arabic translation. Classical scholars have occasionally assumed that what was preserved of ancient Greek and Latin texts was simply "the best" of antiquity, destined to survive basically because of its excellence. Close historical comparison of the multiple receptions of the same body of material should help to improve this view.

There was interest in the learning of all prior nations, whenever anything of it was deemed useful. The ninth-century Arab philosopher al-Kindī wrote,

> Aristotle, the most distinguished of the Greeks in philosophy, said: "We ought to be grateful to the fathers of those who have contributed any truth, since they were the cause of their existence; let alone being grateful to the sons; for the fathers are their cause, while they are the cause of our attaining the truth." How beautiful is that which he said in this matter! We ought not to be ashamed of appreciating the truth and of acquiring it wherever it comes from, even if it comes from races distant and nations different from us. (Ivry 1974, p. 58)

The need felt by al-Kindī for the comment shows that not all of his contemporaries agreed with the notion he expressed, but it certainly describes an attitude prevalent among urbane intellectuals of the age of translations into Arabic.

When ancient works were not currently in use, they had to be sought. A substantial number of reports survive of Arabic scholars seeking copies of one ancient work or another. One way to find them was simply by hunting down ancient manuscripts surviving in nooks and crannies of old churches and monasteries, family libraries, and neglected archives (van Koningsveld 1998). Another was the commissioning of new copies of ancient scientific and mathematical works, which were now being copied anew in in Byzantium. The new copying activity has plausibly been connected to a market demand for such books in Baghdad; at least the two phenomena are fairly synchronous (Gutas 1998, pp. 175–186). These sciences had long coexisted with Christian learning and in some respects were integrated into it. For example, the Greek works of John Philoponos (fl. sixth century), a Christian philosopher of Egypt, came to be well known to Arabic philosophers in Arabic translation. His treatises addressed Greek philosophy as related to the theological needs of a monotheism of a type similar to that enjoined by Islam. For another example, one of the earliest encyclopedic cosmological works composed in Arabic, the *Sirr al-khalīqa*, or *Mystery of Creation* – written in the time of the caliph al-Maʾmūn (r. 813–833) and attributed spuriously to the ancient wonder-working sage Apollonius of Tyana – incorporates in its major recension large sections of Nemesius of Emesa's *De natura hominis*, a work of Christian anthropology written circa 390 in the ancient Greek philosophical tradition. The latter had been translated into Syriac, and from Syriac it appears to have entered Arabic in this form. The *Sirr al-khalīqa* would go on to be influential in the formation of medieval alchemy, without any explicit reference to Nemesius in it, although it incorporated some of its contents. Nemesius himself relied on Middle Platonists and Neoplatonists.

A large part of the earliest strata of translations, however, from the late eighth century, came not from Greek but from Middle Persian. The extent of Middle Persian written literature under Sasanid rule is evident more from Arabic translations than from any other source. Current scholarship sees pre-Islamic Iran as having a largely "oral" culture, at least one in which literature and scholarship were predominantly unwritten (e.g. Huyse 2008). This is misleading, as numerous Middle Persian works, lost in the original, survive only in Arabic translation, including examples of genres otherwise entirely lost. These were clearly written (not oral) compositions in their Middle Persian originals. The mistaken view exaggerating Sasanian "orality" arises because of the character of what does survive in continuous Middle Persian manuscript tradition. With the important exceptions of numerous but fragmentary Manichaean Middle Persian texts recovered from Central Asian deserts and a small number of inscriptions and other miscellaneous items, Middle Persian texts survive in Zoroastrian manuscript tradition, which preserves only such material as was of continuous interest to Zoroastrian scholars for the purposes of their religion. Zoroastrian priests praised the oral, esteeming their orally preserved liturgy above all else. These same scholars came eventually to use Arabic, New Persian, and other languages for texts with nonreligious purposes and kept Middle Persian works largely only for their religion, with a few exceptions. One has to turn to early Arabic translations of Middle Persian to get a glimpse of what else was there late in the Sasanian period (224–651) and immediately after the Arab conquest: astronomy and astrology, physiognomy, narrative history, lapidary science, agricultural lore, wisdom literature, books of manners and protocol, and more. In other words, studying Middle Persian prose literature of late antiquity today requires recourse to Arabic texts at least as much as to Middle Persian itself. This endeavor has barely begun among modern scholars. The fact of it, however, is due precisely to the large-scale adoption of ancient learning in Arabic translation between 750 and 1000, which began with Middle Persian texts.

Sanskrit texts also came into Arabic early in the period of translations, mostly during the last quarter of the eighth century. The interest in Sanskrit learning originated among men from Central Asia whose families came from beyond the former Sasanian Persian Empire, which had relatively recently fallen under Arab rule in the first half of the eighth century. These sorts of families participated in the rise of the Abbasid dynasty of caliphs. The courtiers of the Abbasid caliph al-Manṣūr and the officers and viziers of the Barmakid family, from Balkh, a city where the Bactrian language had been spoken and where Buddhist scholarship was alive into the eighth century, were the best-known patrons of translations from Sanskrit into Arabic (van Bladel 2011; 2014). When the Barmakid family was removed from power in 803, the patronage of new translations from Sanskrit effectively ceased. This clearly illustrates the connection between the background of patrons and scholars and the materials sought for translation. Sanskrit mathematical, astronomical, and medical learning of late antiquity became part of the early strata of science in Arabic. Because they were superseded by later works, many of these early translations are lost, but their traces are numerous as citations in later texts on the same genres, such as medical or astronomical compendia, whenever the competing matter from Greek did not supply much material as an alternative.

In the first half-century of Abbasid rule (750–800), while translators reworked Middle Iranian languages and Sanskrit texts into Arabic, Greek learning came into Arabic sometimes from Syriac and Middle Persian intermediaries rather than directly from Greek. With the new capital of Baghdad founded in Iraq, when the early supporters of the Abbasids, of Central Asian origin, died off, new secretaries came increasingly from a local, Aramaean background. The geographical reorientation, including regular Abbasid campaigns against Byzantium, coincided with a turning of interests toward the traditions of Hellenic learning cultivated among Syriac scholars and, soon, to increasingly numerous direct translations from Greek into Arabic where they could be had. The ninth century accordingly witnessed the birth of Arabic philosophy as such – under the name *falsafa* – with al-Kindī, whose interests followed a course that has been described as Neoplatonic, with a heavy infusion of Euclid. Several reports survive of the painstaking search for Greek manuscripts in the ancient cities of the Near East, the plunder of books from Anatolian towns on the yearly raids, and copies sought in the Byzantine Empire. Eventually hundreds of works by dozens of authors were translated, reworked, commented upon, and absorbed into the intellectual life of the new society. Translators were paid large sums in return for which they mastered ancient Greek to a high degree, as the translations themselves often bear out. As far as can be determined, everything both interesting and available to the new Muslim audience was translated over three centuries. The adoption of paper technology in the Middle East facilitated the creation of large private libraries, collections of thousands of books stocked with the works of Galen, Aristotle, and dozens of other ancients along with all the current Arabic poetry, literature, and scholarship.

This efflorescence of learning in Baghdad was one of the major bases of later medieval science, medicine, and philosophy. Both the Byzantine and Latin European learned traditions depend in part on this Arabic tradition for their form and content. Byzantinists are becoming increasingly aware that Byzantine Greek manuscripts contain numerous translations from Arabic (Mavroudi 1998, pp. 392–430), and medieval Latinists have known for many years that Western scholasticism could not have come about as it did without translations from Arabic (Burnett 2005). The different receptions of ancient learning – Byzantine Greek, European Latin, and African and Asian Arabic – are inextricably intertwined.

Scholarship in the caliphal capital of Baghdad provided a model for other courts, where increasingly independent emirs and sultans would gather scholars to serve and advise them and provide them with prestige. For example, the philosopher al-Fārābī (d. 950) spent time in the Ḥamdānid court in Aleppo. The Sāmānid emirs of Northeastern Iran and Central Asia were patrons of Arabic scholars and inaugurated the patronage of scholarship in New Persian. Ibn Sīnā (Avicenna), who came from that Central Asian region, found his last patrons in Isfahan, in western Iran, where he died. In al-Andalus (Spain), emirs sponsored astronomy, philosophy, and other sorts of learning. As sites of patronage for learning proliferated, the heritage of antiquity, synthesized as it had been in Baghdad, also spread.

Many pre-late antique texts by Greek authors were translated into Arabic, including works of Euclid, Aristotle, Plato, and Ptolemy, so long as they were deemed useful. The translators themselves had no concept corresponding to late antiquity, but if one wanted a list of just authors of scientific and philosophical works of the period 200–600, roughly our late antiquity, we can name Alexander of Tralles, Alexander of Aphrodisias, Ammonius, Cassianus Bassus Scholasticus, Galen, John Philoponus, Olympiodorus the Younger, Oribasius, Palladius the physician, Pappus of Alexandria, Plotinus, Porphyry, Proclus Diadochus, Simplicius, Themistius, Theon of Alexandria, Timothy of Gaza, Vindanius Anatolius, and Zosimus of Panopolis, with works such as the medical *Summaria Alexandrinorum* among them. This is only a portion of what became available.

In only one region did the Arab conquerors' descendants adopt another language as a regular medium for scholarship, under different demographic circumstances too complicated to be explicated here: That was the new form of Persian written in the Arabic script, in Central Asia, a language the use of which would be spread westward and eastward, beginning in the eleventh century, with the Muslim Turk warlords whose secretaries and administrators were drawn from that region. Even with its different conditions of genesis, New Persian literature began with the reception of Arabic texts and modes of expression in Persian translation, and along with it came material drawn from late antiquity through Arabic. For example, one of the earliest extant works composed in New Persian is Maysarī's medical work *Dānish-nāma*, or *Book of Knowledge* (written ca. 980), summarizing treatments corresponding with their ailments in four and a half thousand verses. It is full of material derived from ancient Greek medicine and its entire framework is Galenic. That is because Galenic medicine in Arabic translation was, in the tenth century, the norm from the Atlantic to Central Asia. Thus, even when substantial Muslim populations eventually came to use languages other than Arabic, their reception of the literatures of late antiquity came by way of Arabic. It was in Arabic that the literary products of the age we call late antiquity were interpreted for later peoples of Asia and northern Africa. Wherever Arabic learning went, the learning of late antiquity was carried along with it in continuity with the ancient past.

While this cosmopolitan and intercommunal (though largely Muslim) reception of ancient Persian, Sanskrit, and above all Greek and astronomy, medicine, philosophy, science, and mathematics was going on in Baghdad, a parallel and related reception of late antique literature was taking place among Christians. Thousands of patristic works and Christian texts in general were translated into Arabic from Greek, Syriac, and Coptic. Arabic translations of works of Christian learning were made from these languages for use by the Church of the East (Nestorians), Syrian Orthodox (Jacobites), Orthodox (Melkites), and Coptic churches. This Arabic reception of late antique Christian literature was, in a sense, still more continuous with late antiquity than was the revival of the sciences in Arabic, originating largely in Baghdad. That is because it was carried out by members of church institutions that had existed continuously since their late antique origins. It did not represent so much of a revolution in the patronage of learning as the translation movement in Baghdad did. It rather indicated the social change inherent in the shift of language in use among these Christian communities. When Christians came to speak Arabic among themselves, learning to use increasingly obsolete languages of ancient Christian learning became a special effort. Translations solved that problem by sparing the ever more numerous Arabophone Christians of the need to make that effort, while preserving their literary traditions without interruption. At the same time, Christians under Muslim rule had new problems to address. While polemic between rival churches continued unabated, the dominance of Islam meant that Christian authors had to address their socially subordinate status. For Melkite (Chalcedonian) Christians, whose churches had enjoyed Byzantine imperial support before, this was an especially big change. Christians of the various churches were, as it happened, ill-equipped to stem the tide of conversion from Christianity to Islam, lacking political, military, and economic means to retain members. The problem compelled Christian authors in each church to compose new *summae* of their faith and to harden the borders of their communities in an attempt to prevent exodus. When they wrote in Arabic, they continued to have recourse to their own Scriptures and church authorities, now also in Arabic translation. (See Noble and Treiger 2014 for an anthology of Chalcedonian Arabic texts.)

According to Alexander Treiger (2015, pp. 195–196), the earliest known translations of Christian texts were carried out in Palestine, preeminently at the monastery of Mar Saba, in the eighth, ninth, and tenth centuries. This is in parallel to the largely scientific and philosophical translations made simultaneously in Baghdad. Scholarship has not yet established what relationship, if any, linked Palestinian and Baghdadi translators, but presumably some individuals were involved in both of the two spheres of translation activity that appear to be separate both in geography and subject matter. Antioch later became a center of translations from the time of Byzantine rule (969–1084), as did other cities with Christian populations such as Damascus and Cairo. Translations of ancient Christian works into Arabic continued to be made, notably under Ottoman rule in the seventeenth and eighteenth centuries and, in general, until today. The long duration of interest in translations differentiates the Christian Arabic reception of late antique literatures from the interest in translations of works of science and philosophy. The latter waned in the eleventh century, when Arabic scholars had digested the ancient material and began to take it in new directions.

If we take just the period 200–600 CE artificially as representing late antiquity, then Greek Christian authors of that period whose works were translated into Arabic include, but are not limited to, Agathangelus, Alexander of Alexandria, Amphilochius of Iconium, Anastasius I of Antioch, Athanasius of Alexandria, Atticus of Constantinople, Basil of Caesarea, Clement of Alexandria, Cyril of Alexandria, Cyril of Jerusalem, Demetrius of Antioch, Didymus the Blind, Dionysius of Alexandria, Pseudo-Dionysius the Areopagite, Epiphanius of Cyprus, Eulogius of Alexandria, Eusebius of Caesarea, Gennadius of Constantinople, Gregory of Nazianzus, Gregory of Nyssa, Gregory Thaumaturgus, Hesychius of Jerusalem, Hippolytus of Rome, John Chrysostom, John of Jerusalem, Nectarius of Constantinople, Nemesius of Emesa, Palladius of Galatia, Paulus Alexandrinus, Peter of Alexandria, Proclus of Constantinople, Severianus of Gabala, Sophronius of Jerusalem, Theodoret of Cyrrhus, Theodotus of Ancyra, Theodore of Mopsuestia, Theophilus of Alexandria, Timothy of Alexandria, Titus of Bostra, and, of course, the books of the Bible, along with countless parabiblical and apocryphal texts. (The list is drawn from Graf 1944, vol. 1). It starts to look like a scandal that the Arabic witnesses to these authors' texts are not generally consulted in scholarship on Christian works of late antiquity.

There can be no doubt that other fields of reception remain to be elucidated in the terms described here. Scholars of Jewish Arabic, for example, may be able to represent the Jewish Arabic reception of late ancient literature (e.g. Harvey 2005). Of course, the Arabic-speaking peoples also preserved the poetry of late antique Arabia, the period they called *al-Jāhilīya*, "the age of ignorance." They are responsible for all of what still survives. The stereotyped formulae of these ancient Arabian songs were reworked in many new ways by later poets in the courts of caliphs and emirs who had no experience with the bedouin life idealized in song but appreciated the ancient types. Poets subverted the ancient categories with new subjects and topics for poems that no known ancient Arabic poem had treated. This engendered a ninth- and tenth-century debate about the relative merits of the "ancients" and the "moderns." If we use the period encompassed by this volume, classical Arabic literature included the complicated reception of late antique Arabic literature.

But Arabic scholars did not see it this way. Not only did they have no idea of late antiquity; they spent little effort on the relative chronology of ancient texts. Some of them knew, for example, that Theophrastus was Aristotle's student, and that Aristotle was Plato's student, and that Plato was Socrates's student, but, by and large, Arabic readers did not care how old a book was so much as whether its contents made sense and were true and useful. (For a rare example of an exception, see Rosenthal 1954.) They did not distinguish Themistius as a late antique author from Aristotle as an ancient author as we may, though they were well aware that Themistius commented on Aristotle long after him and they valued his works regardless of his dates of activity. Although there was scarcely any meaningful periodization of ancient works among Arabic scholars, it must be emphasized for the modern historian that everything that they received in translation was mediated by what we call late antiquity. If anything, of the numerous extended episodes of reception of ancient literature, the Arabic reception of ancient works is the most immediately derivative of late antiquity. This is partly because the advent of Arabic as a major source language defines the end of late antiquity as modern historians have construed it. As our modern late antiquity is defined, the Arabic reception is the immediate sequel. The Arabic Aristotle was, therefore, in a certain sense, a fully developed late antique Aristotle.

Relying on late antiquity as a period likewise has ramifications for how one today understands the Arabic reception of ancient texts. Usually the phenomenon has been rubricated by the languages or religious traditions from which translations were derived, not by period. Scholars of Arabic today do not normally speak of the Arabic reception of late antique literature but rather of the Arabic (or Islamic) reception of Greek thought, or Indian or Persian thought, or Jewish or Christian thought. This has much to do with our living in societies characterized by the active use of such national and religious categories. By contrast, nobody today will identify himself or herself as a late antique person. All the same, the modern historian's late antiquity is indeed the period that created the conditions for the Arabic reception of all earlier literature. This is a consequence of just how the periods are defined. Late antiquity, as usually construed, wanes with the advent of Islam, and Islam coincided with the Arabicization of many peoples. The change in major source languages (and the modern scholar's training) has meant a change of period for modern historians. Practically speaking, therefore, the texts that had physically survived in manuscript in late antiquity and so were available in the seventh century stood a good chance of being translated into Arabic, provided they were deemed useful to the interests of new readers. These observations aside, students of the widespread and prolonged Arabic reception of earlier texts in other languages must keep in mind foremost that the Arabic receptions – and their ongoing iterations in Arabic and its dependent traditions down to the present – were conditioned first of all by the highly varied and locally determined needs of the adopters. No single narrative will account for all of them. The References and Further Reading below are a selection from a vast quantity of scholarship, intended for the newcomer to this area of research.

REFERENCES

Abū Ḥātim al-Rāzī. (1994). *Kitāb al-Zīna*. ed. Ḥusayn al-Hamadānī. Sanaa: Markaz al-Dirāsāt wa-l-Buḥūth al-Yamanī.

Burnett, Charles. (2005). Arabic into Latin: The reception of Arabic philosophy into Western Europe. In: *The Cambridge Companion to Arabic Philosophy* (ed. Peter Adamson and Richard C. Taylor), 370–404. Cambridge: Cambridge University Press.

Graf, Georg. (1944–1953). *Geschichte der christlichen arabischen Literatur*. 5 vols. Studi e Testi 118, 133, 146, 147, 172, Vatican City: Biblioteca Apostolica Vaticana.

Gutas, Dimitri. (1998). *Greek Thought, Arabic Culture: The Graeco-Arabic Translation Movement in Baghdad and Early 'Abbāsid Society (2nd-4th/8th-10th Centuries)*. London: Routledge.

Harvey, Steven. (2005). Islamic Philosophy and Jewish Philosophy. In: *The Cambridge Companion to Arabic Philosophy* (ed. Peter Adamson and Richard C. Taylor), 349–369. Cambridge: Cambridge University Press.

Huyse, Philip. (2008). Late Sasanian society between orality and literacy. In: *The Sasanian Era: The Idea of Iran Volume III* (ed. Vesta Sarkhosh Curtis and Sarah Stewart), 140–155. London: I.B. Tauris.

Ivry, Alfred. (1974). *Al-Kindi's Metaphysics: A Translation of Ya'qūb ibn Isḥāq al-Kindī's Treatise "On First Philosophy."* Albany: State University of New York Press.

Mavroudi, Maria. (1998). *A Byzantine Book on Dream Interpretation: The Oneirocriticon of Achmet and Its Arabic Sources*. Leiden: Brill.

Noble, Samuel, and Alexander Treiger. (2014). *The Orthodox Church in the Arab World 700–1700: An Anthology of Sources*. DeKalb, IL: Northern Illinois University Press.

Rosenthal, Franz. (1954). Isḥāq b. Ḥunayn's Ta'rīkh al-Aṭibbā'. *Oriens*, 7: 55–80.

Rosenthal, Franz. (1975). *The Classical Heritage in Islam*. London: Routledge and Kegan Paul.

Sezgin, Fuat. (1967–). *Geschichte des arabischen Schrifttums*. 15 vols. to date plus index volume. Leiden: Brill.

Treiger, Alexander. (2015). Christian Graeco-Arabica: Prolegomena to a history of the Arabic translations of the Greek Church Fathers. *Intellectual History of the Islamicate World*, 3: 188–227.

Van Bladel, Kevin. (2011). The Bactrian background of the Barmakids. In: *Islam and Tibet: Interactions along the Musk Routes* (ed. Anna Akasoy, Charles Burnett, and Ronit Yoeli-Tlalim), 43–88. London: Ashgate.

Van Bladel, Kevin. (2014). Eighth-century Indian astronomy in the two cities of peace. In: *Islamic Cultures, Islamic Contexts: Essays in Honor of Professor Patricia Crone* (ed, Behnam Sadeghi, Asad Q. Ahmed, Adam Silverstein et al.), 257–294. Leiden: Brill.

Van Koningsveld, P.S. (1998). Greek manuscripts in the early Abbasid Empire: Fiction and facts about their origin, translation, and destruction. *Bibliotheca Orientalis* 55: 345–372.

FURTHER READING

Adamson, Peter and Taylor, Richard C. ed. (2005). *The Cambridge Companion to Arabic Philosophy*. Cambridge: Cambridge University Press.

Beeston, A.F.L., Johnstone, T.M., Serjeant, R.B., and G.R. Smith, ed. (1983). *The Cambridge History of Arabic Literature: Arabic Literature to the End of the Umayyad Period*. Cambridge: Cambridge University Press.

Endress, Gerhard. (1987–1992). Die wissenschaftliche Literatur. In *Grundriss der arabischen Philologie* (ed. Wolfdietrich Fischer), 2: 400–506 and 3: 3–152. 3 vols. Wiesbaden: Ludwig Reichert.

Gutas, Dimitri. (1999). The "Alexandria to Baghdad" complex of narratives. A contribution to the study of philosophical and medical historiography among the Arabs. *Documenti e Studi sulla Tradizione Filosofica Medievale* 10: 155–193.

Pormann, Peter E. and Savage-Smith, Emilie. (2007). *Medieval Islamic Medicine*. Edinburgh: Edinburgh University Press.

Ullmann, Manfred. (1970). *Die Medizin im Islam*. Leiden: Brill.

Ullmann, Manfred. (1972). *Die Natur- und Geheimwissenschaften im Islam*. Leiden: Brill.

van Bladel, Kevin. (2015). Graeco-Arabic Studies in classical Near Eastern Studies: An emerging field of training in its broader institutional context. *Intellectual History of the Islamicate World* 3: 316–325.

Young, M.J.L., Latham, J.D., and Serjeant, R.B. ed. (1990). *The Cambridge History of Arabic Literature: Religion, Learning and Science in the 'Abbasid Period*. Cambridge: Cambridge University Press.

CHAPTER THIRTY-SIX

Late Antique Literature in the Western Middle Ages

Joseph Pucci

Owing to the disappearance of Greek from the Western curriculum after the fourth century, late antique Greek authors never gained a foothold in the Latin Middle Ages. Pockets of Greek learning existed in the Latin West: in Ireland, in southern Italy, briefly at the court of Charlemagne, and increasingly as the Middle Ages waned. But this albeit limited engagement never touched on late antique Greek authors and, instead, focused on liturgical, pedagogical, and sacred works (Berschin 1988, pp. 3–4; Ciccolella 2008, pp. 83–85).

The reception of late antique literature in the Western Middle Ages is therefore a story of Latin authors and works and is controlled by the vagaries of manuscript transmission; pedagogical, rhetorical, and theological exigencies; and the relative attractions of individual works. A small group of writers, dominated by the church fathers, was able to resist these forces by dint of their *auctoritas* and, therefore, can be passed over with little comment. The most obvious in this regard is Augustine (d. 430), all of whose works were in wide circulation throughout the Middle Ages and whose universal presence in literate activity of all stripes is patent (Contreni 1999; Saak 1997, 1999; Backus 1997, vol. 1; Otten 1997; Kelly 1999; Wawrykow 1999).

At least in the context of Jerome's (d. 420) translations of the Old and New Testaments, the wide circulation and use of the Vulgate means that his reach was likely as wide as Augustine's, though his original writings, especially his exegetical works, were also broadly copied, read, and quoted throughout

---

A Companion to Late Antique Literature, First Edition.
Edited by Scott McGill and Edward J. Watts.
© 2018 John Wiley & Sons, Inc. Published 2018 by John Wiley & Sons, Inc.

the Middle Ages (Kelly 1975, pp. 333–334; Cain and Lössl 2009, pp. 175–252). Ambrose, too, was extensively copied and read in the Middle Ages, particularly his hymns, which gained an immediate currency upon their appearance late in the fourth century and served as models for literary and liturgical works thereafter (Fontaine 1992, pp. 11–16).

Second only to Augustine in terms of authority in the medieval commentary tradition and cited nearly as often throughout the Middle Ages (Kuzdale 2013, pp. 359–360), Gregory the Great (d. 604) perhaps reached the widest audience of any late antique author through the translations of his works into several vernaculars, including Middle Dutch, Old English, Old French (*Dialogues; Pastoral Care*), Old German (*Moralia*), and Norse-Icelandic (*Homilies on the Gospels*) (Mews and Renkin 2013, pp. 315–316). Gregory's most popular works were the *Moralia*, of which over 500 manuscripts exist, and the *Pastoral Care*, one of the few Latin texts translated into Greek for circulation in the East (Demacopoulos 2013, 223–224). The *Dialogues* were also widely read and the *Homilies on the Gospels* were influential beginning especially in the twelfth century in medieval visual art, not least in depictions of Mary Magdalene (Mews and Renkin 2013, pp. 328–29).

Boethius's (d. 524) presence in the Middle Ages is more complicated than Gregory's, because the variety of his output enabled readers to consider him, depending on the work in question, a "religious" or a "secular" writer, while the *Consolation of Philosophy* encouraged both identities in the same work (Troncarelli 2012, pp. 537–538). Given this manifold content and the "mixed" style in which it is written, which made the *Consolation* an especially appealing model for Latin, it is unsurprising that by the twelfth century the *Consolation* was absorbed into the school canon, its words fostering a rich commentary tradition represented in the interpretations of, among others, William of Conches (d. ca. 1154), William of Aragon (fl. ca. 1275), and Nicholas Trevet (d. 1334) (Moyer 2012; Love 2012).

Owing to the variety of his output and its summarizing nature, Cassiodorus (d. 585) was also widely read in the Western Middle Ages. The *Variae* were likely not known in England before the conquest but gained in popularity as the Middle Ages progressed, while the second of the two books of the *Institutiones* had a long afterlife, since it offers an introduction to the liberal arts that proved attractive in the classroom. The most popular of Cassiordorus's works was the *Exposition on the Psalms*, which appears in continental manuscript catalogs of every century and which was used extensively as early as the eighth century by Bede and Alcuin. The only commentary extant from the patristic era on the Psalms, excepting Augustine's, its wide currency is proven by the nearly two dozen authors writing between 750 and 1400 who make use of its words (O'Donnell 1979, pp. 235–264).

Likely as pervasive as Cassiodorus's reach was Isidore's (d. 636), whose *Etymologies* survives in almost 1000 manuscripts. Bede made use of the work in the early eighth century, and it was widely circulated in the Carolingian period. By the beginning of the ninth century it had been disseminated to all the cultural centers of Europe. The *Etymologies* was also important throughout the Middle Ages in the development of dictionaries and encyclopedias, which ensured its widespread use down to the Renaissance (Barney et al. 2006, pp. 24–26).

Less obvious authors emerge from the shadows of these giants, however, in the context of the classroom. Alcuin provides a first witness to these writers in the *Bishops, Kings and Saints of York* (vv. 1541–1557), where, in addition to the *auctores* just examined, grammarians, classical authors, and even some Greek authors, he reports that he also read "what Sedulius and Juvencus sang,/and what Avitus, Prudentius, Prosper, Paulinus, Arator/and Fortunatus and Lactantius wrote" (vv. 1551–1553). We might ascribe Alcuin's list to the tastes of a highly literate reader with access to an unusually excellent library, but, writing at roughly the same time, Theodulf of Orleans gathers a similar list in his accounting of "The Books I Used to Read," noting that, in addition to the *auctores*, he read "Sedulius, Paulinus, Arator, Avitus,/…Fortunatus…Juvencus/and…Prudentius" (13–16). Like Alcuin's list, Theodulf's catalog reflects presumably his training, but the similarities of the lists, given the distance separating York, where Alcuin studied, and Spain (or perhaps Italy), where Theodulf gained his formation, seem hard to chalk up to coincidence.

Instead, given their joint witness, it seems possible to see in the lists of Alcuin and of Theodulf a canon of late antique writers owed to the schools and in place by the early ninth century. Strengthening this view is the fact that many of the works of the authors mentioned by Alcuin are found in a number of composite manuscripts of the early ninth century that are themselves important witnesses to authors privileged in the schools (Godman 1982, p. lxxi;. Glauche 1970, pp. 11–12). That Theodulf represents a noninsular literary culture at a remove from Alcuin's York further ballasts the case for the existence of a canon (Godman 1985, pp. 168–169). Using Theodulf's list as a control on Alcuin's catalog thus allows us to identify a stable group of nine late antique authors mentioned by Alcuin whose works were read widely in the Western Middle Ages.

The attraction of these works is not difficult to fathom. Juvencus's *Four Books of the Evangelists* (ca. 330 CE), a poetic rendering of the four Gospels into hexameters on the model of Virgil's *Aeneid*, is a striking poem whose words explicate the history of Jesus's ministry. Attractive pedagogically, too, is the way in which Juvencus parrots biblical stories allowing his readers to follow the narrative presentation of the Gospels preserved in them. To this appeal can be added Juvencus's attention to prophetic activity, especially in the context of Christian figuration and the reading of history under the lens of Christian meaning (White 2000, p. 35).

Sedulius's *Carmen paschale* (ca. 425 CE) furthers the tradition of biblical epic on the model provided by Juvencus, and its popularity is witnessed by the 400-plus manuscripts still extant (Springer 1995). One reason for this popularity is owed to the model the poem provides for morphological and syntactical instruction and for scriptural interpretation (Wieland 1985, pp. 153–173; Green 2006, pp. 359–361; Springer 2013, pp. xix–xxi). Another reason is Sedulius's focus. Rather than cover the topics treated in the four Gospels, as Juvencus does, Sedulius concentrates on Old Testament miracles as exemplary of Christ's ministry and, then, on Christ's life, Jesus's miracles, and the events of Christ's death and resurrection. The poem was, therefore, more approachable as a source of Christian theological learning and insight, and in the Middle Ages it was more than once used to illustrate doctrinal points, especially those attending to issues of Christ's humanity (Springer 2013, p. xx). Nor did medieval readers ignore Sedulius's *Paschale opus*, which served as a model for the *opus geminatum* that became popular in Anglo-Norman Latin writing, or his two hymns, which were influential enough that he is sometimes styled one of the four chief *auctores hymnorum*, along with Ambrose, Prudentius, and Gregory (Springer, 2013, p. xxi).

The *Historia apostolica* (ca. 535) is rightly placed in the tradition of biblical epic established by Juvencus and Sedulius, but its author, Arator, stands on separate footing in his choice of materials, no doubt accounting for the work's popularity. Arator's project takes up the narrative of the Acts of the Apostles, and in this it can be understood to provide, albeit in verse, the first Latin commentary on this book of the New Testament. In addition, Arator's poem, perhaps more than Juvencus's or Sedulius's, offers material well suited to teaching, including passages devoted to typological interpretations (White 2000, p. 159).

Given his topic and the epic model he follows, Avitus (d. ca. 518) might be rightly included among the trio of biblical epicists just examined. No doubt more than a few of the qualities that attract Juvencus, Sedulius, and Arator into the canon figure also in the appeal of his *De spiritalis historiae gestis*, which treats in five books the histories of Adam, Noah, and Moses as recorded in the Pentateuch, touching on the creation of the world and original sin, the judgment of God and the expulsion from Paradise, the Flood, and the passage through the Red Sea. Although Avitus engages his biblical material typologically, so that the relationship of his themes to Christian truth is never far from obvious, his exclusive focus on the Old Testament perhaps limited his appeal. He was read widely down through the Carolingian period and even beyond, but he lost ground by the twelfth century, when his status as a canonical author seems to have waned (Curtius 1953, pp. 466–467).

A writer of some variety in both verse and prose, Prosper of Aquitaine (d. ca. 455) takes readers away from the epic and biblical spaces inhabited by Juvencus, Sedulius, Arator, and Avitus and situates them instead in the energies provided by the epigram, the basis for his inclusion in the canon. Written in elegiacs, Prosper's poems narrate moral precepts whose content and diction are often owed to the writings of Augustine. His poetry thus couples formal control with insuperable content, offering models of elegiac composition and access to some of the thought of one of the key Christian *auctores* (White 2000, p. 114).

One appeal of Prudentius's (d. ca. 405) large body of poetry was undoubtedly its metrical virtuosity, for no poet of late antiquity is more metrically accomplished. Prudentius's popularity is affirmed also by the 300-plus extant manuscripts that record all or parts of the poet's output (O'Daly 2012, p. 29). Prudentius appears in the medieval canon, however, mainly on the strength of the moralizing and allegorizing verses of the *Psychomachia* (Gnilka 1963). Adding to the appeal provided by allegory and moral exemplarism is the poet's use of personification in bringing to real and vivid life the conflicts of the abstract vices and virtues, which are pitted against one another in scenes of gore and violence that rival, as they depend on, classical Latin epic (Bastiaensen 1993; O'Sullivan 2004, pp. 3–21). Prudentius's other works were not ignored in the Western Middle Ages, to be sure, and the citations from across the poet's large output that pepper the literary output of, especially, the twelfth century prove the point.

Lactantius's (d. ca. 325) large output is dominated by prose works, including, perhaps most famously, *Divine Institutes* and the *Anger of God*. Yet he appears in the medieval canon owing to the attractions of a 170-line poem on the phoenix ascribed to him (Roberts 2017). Much like Prosper's epigrams, the phoenix poem also keys into the elegiac tradition in the telling of the story of the mythical bird that, in a cycle repeated every several hundred years, causes its own death and rebirth. The poem thus celebrates a creature whose demise and regeneration allowed it easily to be seen as a Christ-figure despite the fact that the poem is not explicitly Christian.

Paulinus of Nola (d. 431) comes into the canon as a poet writing on a variety of topics. These include poems to friends, not least his teacher Ausonius, an epithalamium, and 16 poems on St. Felix. While the pieces attending to St. Felix were perhaps most popular, owing to their Christian themes, Paulinus was not Ausonius's most famous (and, we might surmise, best liked) student for no reason. His talents as a master of Latin poetic style are clearly in evidence throughout his large output, not least his mastery of the Latin hexameter, and provide a further reason for his medieval popularity.

For much the same reason, Venantius Fortunatus (d. ca. 600) also appears in the medieval canon. Writing mostly in elegiacs, Fortunatus's large collection includes epithalamia, epitaphs, epigrams, hymns, and a life of St. Martin of Tours, the variety of which proved appealing to medieval readers. Yet Fortunatus suffered a medieval fate similar to that of Paulinus of Nola: Neither of them seems to have held onto their audiences to the end of the Middle Ages. Neither writer appears in lists of canonical writers drawn up in the twelfth century, and no manuscripts of Fortunatus survive from later than the end of the eleventh century (Roberts 2009, p. 325; Stella 2003).

Other voices from the twelfth and thirteenth centuries allow glimpses of an altered and/or expanded canon of late antique authors that developed in the High Middle Ages. Conrad of Hirsau's *Dialogus super Auctores*, written ca. 1130, offers a somewhat diminished list of writers and works that includes Sedulius, Juvencus, Prosper, Arator, and Prudentius, but omits Avitus, Venantius Fortunatus, Lactantius, and Paulinus of Nola (Curtius 1953, pp. 48–49). A century later, however, in his *Laborintus*, Eberhard the German (fl. ca. 1250) expands on Conrad's list by including Sedulius, Arator, Prudentius, and Prosper as earlier canonists had, but adding to them Boethius, Claudian, Martianus Capella, Maximianus, and Sidonius Apollinaris.

Boethius is a logical addition and the presence of the *Consolation of Philosophy* in Eberhard's list confirms the importance of a work that was read widely both in and out of the classroom (see above). Claudian's (d. ca. 405) presence, on the other hand, reveals a complex medieval reception involving two identities: Claudian *minor*, the author of the *De raptu Proserpinae*, and Claudian *maior*, the author of the other poems of his collection. Given that there are no known manuscripts of his panegyrics dating to the Carolingian period, they seem early on to have lost their medieval audience (Cameron 1970, pp. 419–420). Claudian's other poems, however, seem to have had a greater popularity. A catalog from the court library at Aix that dates to the eighth century, for example, lists the *De raptu Prosperinae* but also the *In Rufinum*, *In Eutropium*, the *De bello Gothico*, and the *De bello Gildonico*, while a manuscript from the same century contains a gathering of the *carmina minora* (Cameron 1970, p. 420). Nor should it be forgotten that Alan of Lille's *Anticlaudianus*, composed in the twelfth century, is based on and reacts to the *In Rufinum*, a century in which Claudian's words also regularly appear in *florilegia* (Cameron 1970, p. 423).

Claudian's most widely read poem in the Middle Ages was undoubtedly the *De raptu Proserpinae*, whose popularity can be measured, in addition to the copy of it at Aix, by the copies found also at Reichenau and St. Gall that date from the ninth century (Hall 1969, pp. 67–68). A resurgence of interest in the poem in the twelfth century eventually led to the writing of a commentary on it by Gaufrid of Vitry and, in the thirteenth, to its inclusion in the so-called *Disticha Catonis*, a school reader (Hall 1969, p. 71).

The popularity of Martianus Capella's (fl. 420) *Marriage of Philology and Mercury* is proven by the several hundred extant manuscripts of the work and by the commentary tradition that grew up around it beginning in the ninth century (Winterbottom 1983, p. 245). Used widely as a textbook in North Africa, Italy, Gaul, and Spain before the Carolingian period, the work received a new lease on life in the ninth century, thanks mostly to scholars including John the Scot (d. 877), Martin of Laon (d. 875), and Remigius of Auxerre (d. 908) (Stahl, Johnson, and Burge 1971, p. 63). Martianus's work comes into its own, however, in the twelfth century, owing to a newfound interest in cosmography, Platonism, and poetry that the allegorizing and mixed styles of the work naturally satisfied (Stahl, Johnson, and Burge 1971, pp. 55–71; Shanzer 1986).

Given their often prurient topics, a surprising addition to Eberhard's canon is the elegies of Maximianus (fl. sixth century). There can be no doubting the emphasis in the poet's output on obscenity, but the attraction of these poems seems to have been owed to their rhetorical flourishes and especially to the ways in which the topos of old age is carefully crafted in them (Curtius 1953, p. 50). Ironically, Maximianus's distichs were sometimes culled in order to provide aphorisms intended to promote chastity.

On the other hand, Sidonius Apollinaris's (d. 489) inclusion in Eberhard's list seems not unusual (he is also included in Alexander of Neckham's [d. 1217] gathering of preferred authors), for, along with Claudian, he was esteemed by the twelfth century as a model author. His popularity is proven by the number of manuscripts that preserve his large output (Gioanni 2014), and more than a few medieval writers praise or make use of his diction, drawing especially from the letters. John of Salisbury (d. 1180), for example, recommends Sidonius as an important author to study as does Rahewin of Freising (d. ca. 1170). Other medieval authors who recommend Sidonius and/or cite him in their works include Burchard of Worms (d. 1025), Peter Abelard (d. 1142), William of Malemesbury (d. ca. 1143), Bernard of Clairvaux (d. 1153), Peter of Cluny (d. 1156), and Gerald of Wales (d. ca. 1223) (Manitius 1911–1931, vol 3, p. 1149).

But a canon tells us only so much. What of the many late antique authors whose works seemingly were not canonical in the Western Middle Ages? Ausonius (d. ca. 395) presents an intriguing omission. That he was not read in the schools is presumably owed to some combination of the difficulty of his large output, his more than obvious nonchalance toward Christian topics, and, perhaps, to the vagaries of the manuscript tradition that continue to plague his modern editors. His reputation in late antiquity was high, as evidenced by the many authors who allude to, quote from, or otherwise mention him (Green 1991, pp xxxii–xxxiii), but that reputation seems to have diminished in subsequent centuries.

An accounting of the geographical origins of the medieval manuscripts recording Ausonius's works suggests that he was still available to those who wished to read him: France, England, Germany, and Italy are represented (Green 1991, p. xxxiv). But the poet's words appear infrequently in quotations or allusions in the works of others. The exceptions prove the rule. Reginald of Canterbury (d. ca. 1109) and Hariulf of Saint-Riquier (d. 1143), for example, wrote an imitation of the *Technopaegnion* (Manitius 1911–1931, vol 3, p. 542; Green 1991, p. xxxv), while the prayer that forms the third part of the *Ephemeris*, sometimes called the *Oratio*, is echoed by medieval writers such as Fulbert of Chartres (d. 1028), Hildebert of Lavardin (d. 1133), and Geoffrey of Vinsauf (fl. 1200), perhaps with more ease given its overt Christian content and the fact that it circulated in the Middle Ages apart from the *Ephemeris* collection. Nor are Ausonius's works found in medieval *florilegia*. A resuscitation of interest in Ausonius required a fresh set of reading eyes provided by the Renaissance.

Ennodius (d. 521) fares less well in the Middle Ages than his student, Arator, yet his omission from the canon is deceptive. Perhaps his penchant for complicated phrasing and rhetorical excesses made his inclusion difficult; yet the 100-plus manuscripts that record his work speak to an enduring presence, if not a vast acceptance (Gioanni 2004, p. 14). Ennodius earned a semblance of popularity in the twelfth century, however, with the rise of the study of the art of letter writing, the so-called *ars dictaminis*, in which his letters, for all their excesses, proved acceptable models. To the appeal of their formal qualities can be added the attractions of the letters' topics, which explains why they were extensively excerpted and quoted in moralizing and proverbial collections, not least for gatherings intended for monastic use (Gioanni 2004).

Dracontius's (d. ca. 505) large poetic output, which includes the *De laudibus Dei*, the *Satisfactio*, the *Orestes*, and a collection called the *Romulea*, was for the most part neglected in the Western Middle Ages. This is perhaps due to the classicizing topics of the *Orestes* and the *Romulea* and the personal nature of the the *Satisfactio*, in which Dracontius seeks from Gunthamund, the Vandal king, pardon for an offense. Only the *De laudibus Dei* was read widely in the Middle Ages, though not in its entirety. The poem comprises 2327 hexameters in three books, but the first book proved the most popular, owing to a recension made by Eugenius of Toledo in the seventh century that circulated separately in the Middle Ages under the title *Hexaemeron* (White 2000, p. 144).

The rich tradition of historical writing produced in late antiquity was variously received in the Western Middle Ages. Arnobius's (c. 310) *Adversus nationes* might be considered a work of history, but, perhaps owing to some of its author's questionable theological views, there remains only one extant medieval manuscript, reflecting no doubt a restricted interest in the work. Much the same textual fate befell Ammianus Marcellinus (d. ca. 400), whose history of Rome survives in fragments in two manuscripts: a ninth-century copy produced in Fulda and in fragments found in a separate codex from the same century (Reynolds 1983, p. 6). A contemporary of Ammianus, Eutropius's (fl. ca. 375) *Breviarium* was much more widely read in the Western Middle Ages, in part owing to a directness of exposition and a simple Latinity that made it a natural for the classroom. It was read beyond the schoolroom, too, and its popularity is affirmed not least by the fact that it was updated by Paul the Deacon (d. 799) in the eighth century and again by Landolf Sagax (fl. ca. 975) in the tenth. It was also translated into Greek in Eutropius's lifetime and again in the sixth century, a signal mark of its popularity and utility.

Orosius's (d. ca. 417) *Histories Against the Pagans* enjoyed an equal popularity, in part owing to its, and its author's, association with Augustine. But Orosius's Christian-centered historical perspective also had its own appeal, not least the ways in which Orosius's fresh retelling of world history concludes with the treatment of imperial history down to 417. Orosius's popularity is proven by several hundred extant manuscripts that record the *Histories*, a work that seems to have been continually read throughout the Western Middle Ages by figures as disparate as Bede in the early eighth century and Orderic Vitalis (d. 1142) and Otto of Freising (d. 1158) in the twelfth (Rohrbacher 2002, pp. 148–149). In addition to widely being quoted, the *Histories*' wide readership is also affirmed by the fact that an abridgment of the work was translated into Anglo-Saxon in the ninth century and an Arabic translation survives from the tenth.

Less popular was Victor of Vita's history of the Vandal persecution, written ca. 485, the floruit assigned also to its author. More than a few medieval manuscripts survive, which suggests a certain interest. Jordanes (fl. ca. 550), however, earned a much wider medieval readership for his *Getica*, or history of the Gothic people, though more as a historical source than as an author studied on his own merits. The Ravenna Geographer (fl. ca. 800?), for example, mined him for information, as did Paul the Deacon (d. 799), while the manuscript copies of his works prove his wide reception and preservation (Goffart 1988, pp. 110–111).

Gibbon's view that, in the *Histories of the Franks*, Gregory of Tours (d. 594) "omitted almost everything that posterity desires to learn" (Thorpe 1974, p. 55) was not shared by medieval readers. By the seventh century Gregory's *Histories* had been mined in order to flesh out the content of the so-called *Chronicle of Fredegar*, especially much of its third book (Thorpe 1974, p. 38), and by the Carolingian period nearly every historical writer cited Gregory's *Histories* or otherwise relied on it in some way, including Paul the Deacon (d. 799), Notker of Saint-Gall (d. 912), Flodoard of Rheims (d. 966), Letald of Micy (fl. ca. 1000), and Hugo of Flavigny (fl. ca. 1100) (Contreni 2002, p. 422). Excerpts from the *Histories* are found in over 80 manuscripts from the ninth through the thirteenth centuries, many of these dealing especially with saints' lives (Contreni 2002, pp. 423–424). Nor is the *Histories* the only of Gregory's works to prove popular throughout the Western Middle Ages. Because of the wide interest in hagiography, Gregory's so-called *Eight Books of Miracles* also was long-lived, demonstrated not least by some seven dozen manuscripts still extant and the many dozens of excerpts taken from the work that pepper a wide variety of collateral manuscripts (Contreni 2002, p. 425).

While grammarians and commentators such as Fulgentius (fl. ca. 500), Priscian (fl. ca. 500), and Servius (fl. ca. 400) are not likely to be considered literary authors, Servius is one of the interlocutors in Macrobius's (fl. ca. 400) *Saturnalia*, a work that perhaps more easily crosses the line separating scholarship from literature per se. Macrobius seems to have been less widely read in the early Middle Ages, but he achieved an important place especially in the twelfth century, where the *Saturnalia* and also his commentary on Cicero's *Somnium Scipionis* provided sources of scientific, philosophical, and literary knowledge (Curtius 1953, pp. 51, 443).

Some writers, such as Optatian (fl. ca. 325), wrote in forms or in styles that rendered them inaccessible to the Western Middle Ages, or, like Rutilius Namatianus (fl. ca. 415), took up topics or themes that proved less durable over the coming centuries. Other works, such as Sulpicius Severus's (fl. ca. 400) *Life of St. Martin*, offered new forms that were influential in the medieval West in their own right or as models. And, needless to say, many authors survived but were not widely read. Nor did literature provide an exclusive entry into late antique writings: In addition to the commentary and scholarly traditions that emerge in late antiquity can be added, for example, the Justinianic law code that dates from the early sixth century, monastic rules, and pieces written for liturgical and ecclesiastical purposes.

Much more might be said about the medieval reception of late antique literature than has been said here, not least because the ways in which this large body of writing was received involve more than a mere history of reading, attending also to competing pressures provided by the church, the state, the classroom, and the copying and dissemination of texts. To these pressures can be added the rise of vernacular languages and literatures and the resulting attractions of national authors and traditions and the always-fickle nature of readerly tastes. To conclude by noting these pressures, therefore, is to sketch some touchstones for a larger treatment of a much-neglected topic.

REFERENCES

Backus, Irena Dorota. ed. (1997). *The Reception of the Church Fathers in the West from the Carolingians to the Maurists.* 2 vols. Leiden: Brill.

Barney, Stephen A., Lewis, W.J., Beach, J.A., and Berghof, Oliver. trans. (2006). *The Etymologies of Isidore of Seville.* Cambridge: Cambridge University Press.

Bastiaensen, A.A.R. (1993). Prudentius in recent literary criticism. In: *Early Christian Poetry* (ed. Jan de Boeft and Anton Hilhorst), 131–134. Leiden: Brill.

Berschin, Walter. (1988). *Greek Letters and the Latin Middle Ages: From Jerome to Nicholas of Cusa* (trans. Jerold C. Frakes). Washington, DC: Catholic University of America Press.

Cain, Andrew and Lössl, Josef. ed. (2009). *Jerome of Stridon: His Life, Writings, and Legacy.* Burlington, VT: Ashgate.

Cameron, Alan. (1970). *Claudian: Poetry and Propaganda at the Court of Honorius.* Oxford: Oxford University Press.

Ciccolella, Federica. (2008). Donati Graeci: *Learning Greek in the Renaissance.* Leiden: Brill.

Contreni, John J. (1999). Early Carolingian era. In: *Augustine Through the Ages: An Encyclopedia* (ed. Alan D. Fitzgerald, John Cavadini, Marianne Djuth et al.), 124–129. Grand Rapids, MI: William B. Eerdmans.

Contreni, John J. (2002). Reading Gregory of Tours in the Middle Ages. In: *The World of Gregory of Tours* (ed. Kathleen Mitchell and Ian Wood), 419–434. Leiden: Brill.

Curtius, Ernst Robert. (1953). *European Literature and the Latin Middle Ages* (trans. Willard R. Trask). Princeton, NJ: Princeton University Press.

Demacopoulos, George E. (2013). Gregory's model of spiritual direction in the *Liber Regulae Pastoralis.* In: *A Companion to Gregory the Great* (ed. Bronwen Neil and Matthew Dal Santo), 205–224. Leiden: Brill.

Fontaine, Jacques. (1992). *Ambroise de Milan: Hymnes.* Paris: Éditions de Cerf.

Gioanni, Stéphane. (2004). *"Lumière de Rome," "Lumière de l'Église:" Édition, traduction et commentaire de la Correspondence d'Ennode de Pavie.* PhD diss., Université Lumière-Lyon II.

Gioanni, Stéphane. (2014). La Correspondance de Sidoine Apollinaire dans les Florilèges Médiévaux: L'exemple du *Florilegium Angelicum* (milieu du XIIe siècle). In: *Présence du Sidoine Apollinaire* (ed. Rémy Poignault and Annick Stoehr-Monjou). 487–500. Clermont-Ferrand: Centre de Recherches sur les Littératures et la Sociopoétique.

Glauche, Günter. (1970). *Schullektüre im Mittelalter*. Munich: Arbeo-Ges.

Gnilka, Christian. (1963). *Studien zur* Psychomachie *des Prudentius*. Wiesbaden: Otto Harrassowitz.

Godman, Peter. ed. and trans. (1982). *Alcuin: The Bishops, Kings and Saints of York*. Oxford: Oxford University Press.

Godman, Peter. ed. and trans. (1985). *Poetry of the Carolingian Renaissance*. Norman, OK: University of Oklahoma Press.

Goffart, Walter. (1988). *The Narrators of Barbarian History (A.D. 550–800): Jordanes, Gregory of Tours, Bede, and Paul the Deacon*. Princeton, NJ: Princeton University Press.

Green, Roger P.H. ed. (1991). *The Works of Ausonius*. Oxford: Oxford University Press.

Green, Roger P.H. (2006). *Latin Epics of the New Testament: Juvencus, Sedulius, Arator*. Oxford: Oxford University Press.

Hall, J.B. ed. (1969). *Claudian:* De Raptu Proserpinae. Cambridge: Cambridge University Press.

Kelly, J.N.D. (1975). *Jerome: His Life, Writings, and Controversies*. New York: Harper and Row.

Kelly, Joseph F. (1999). Late Carolingian era. In: *Augustine Through the Ages: An Encyclopedia* (ed. Alan D. Fitzgerald, John Cavadini, Marianne Djuth et al.), 129–132. Grand Rapids, MI: William B. Eerdmans.

Kuzdale, Ann. (2013). The reception of Gregory in the Renaissance and Reformation. In: *A Companion to Gregory the Great* (ed. Bronwen Neil and Matthew Dal Santo), 359–386. Leiden: Brill.

Love, Rosalind C. (2012). The Latin commentaries on Boethius' *De Consolatione Philosophiae* from the 9th to the 11th centuries. In: *A Companion to Boethius in the Middle Ages* (ed. Noel Harold Kaylor, Jr. and Philip Edward Phillips), 75–133. Leiden: Brill.

Manitius, Max. (1911–1931). *Geschichte der lateinischen Literatur des Mittelalters*. 3 vols. Munich: Beck.

Mews, Constant and Renkin, Claire. (2013). The legacy of Gregory the Great in the Latin West. In: *A Companion to Gregory the Great* (ed. Bronwen Neil and Matthew Dal Santo), 315–342. Leiden: Brill.

Moyer, Ann E. (2012). The *Quadrivium* and the decline of Boethian influence. In: *A Companion to Boethius in the Middle Ages* (ed. Noel Harold Kaylor Jr. and Philip Edward Phillips), 479–517. Leiden: Brill.

O'Daly, Gerard. (2012). *Days Linked By Song: Prudentius'* Cathemerinon. Oxford: Oxford University Press.

O'Donnell, James J. (1979). *Cassiodorus*. Berkeley: University of California Press.

O'Sullivan, Sinéad. (2004). *Early Medieval Glosses on Prudentius'* Psychomachia: *The Weitz Tradition*. Leiden: Brill.

Otten, Willemien. (1997). The role of the Church Fathers in Carolingian theology. In: *The Reception of the Church Fathers in the West from the Carolingians to the Maurists* (ed. Irena Dorota Backus), 1: 3–50. Leiden: Brill.

Reynolds, L.D. ed. (1983). *Texts and Transmission: A Survey of the Latin Classics*. Oxford: Oxford University Press.

Roberts, Michael. (2009). *The Humblest Sparrow: The Poetry of Venantius Fortunatus*. Ann Arbor, MI: University of Michigan Press.

Roberts, Michael. (2017). Lactantius's *Phoenix* and late Latin poetics. In: *The Poetics of Late Latin Literature* (ed. Jas Elsner and Jesús Hernández Lobato), 373–390. Oxford: Oxford University Press.

Rohrbacher, David. (2002). *The Historians of Late Antiquity*. Oxford: Routledge.

Saak, E.L. (1997). The reception of Augustine in the later Middle Ages. In: *The Reception of the Church Fathers in the West from the Carolingians to the Maurists* (ed. Irena Dorota Backus), 1: 367–404. Leiden: Brill.

Saak, E.L. (1999). Late scholasticism. In: *Augustine Through the Ages: An Encyclopedia* (ed. Alan D. Fitzgerald, John Cavadini, Marianne Djuth et al.), 754–759. Grand Rapids, MI: William B. Eerdmans.

Shanzer, Danuta. (1986). *A Philosophical and Literary Commentary on Martianus Capella's* De Nuptiis Philologiae et Mercurii *Book One*. Berkeley: University of California Press.

Springer, Carl. (1995). *The Manuscripts of Sedulius: A Provisional Handlist*. Philadelphia: Transactions of the American Philosophical Society.

Springer, Carl. trans. (2013). *Sedulius: The Pascal Song and Hymns*. Atlanta, GA: Society of Biblical Literature.

Stahl, William Harris, Johnson, Richard, and Burge, E.L. eds. (1971). *Martianus Capella and the Seven Liberal Arts. Vol. 1: The Quadrivium of Martianus Capella*. New York: Columbia University Press.

Stella, Francesco. (2003). Venanzio Fortunato nella poesia mediolatina. In: *Venanzio Fortunato e il suo tempo*, 269–290. Treviso: Fondazione Cassamarca.

Thorpe, Lewis. trans. (1974). *Gregory of Tours: The History of the Franks*. London: Penguin Books.

Troncarelli, Fabio. (2012). Afterword: Boethius in late antiquity and the early Middle Ages. In: *A Companion to Boethius in the Middle Ages* (ed. Noel Harold Kaylor Jr. and Philip Edward Phillips), 519–549. Leiden: Brill.

Wawrykow, Joseph. (1999). Early scholasticism. In: *Augustine Through the Ages: An Encyclopedia* (ed. Alan D. Fitzgerald, John Cavadini, Marianne Djuth et al.), 750–754. Grand Rapids, MI: William B. Eerdmans.

White, Carolinne. (2000). *Early Christian Latin Poets*. London: Routledge.

Wieland, G.R. (1985). The glossed manuscript: Classbook or library book? *Anglo-Saxon England*, 14: 153–173.

Winterbottom, Michael. (1983). Martianus Capella. In: *Texts and Transmission: A Survey of the Latin Classics*, (ed. L.D. Reynolds), 245. Oxford: Clarendon Press.

CHAPTER THIRTY-SEVEN

Early Modern Receptions of Late Ancient Literature

Diane Shane Fruchtman

37.1 Introduction

Early modern Europeans did not have a sense of a distinct, innovative, and dynamic time period akin to what we now label "late antiquity." They tended, instead, to regard the literature of the period from 284 to 600 simply as ancient, though not undifferentiated by style or quality. But within the vast epoch of classical antiquity, early modern intellectuals did, indeed, identify a separate age: the patristic age, the age of the "Church Fathers" – a time of *Christian* classical antiquity, when Christian truth encountered and engaged with classical civilization. Some early modern commentators, particularly the humanists, understood the encounter to have been one of exemplary synthesis, of the unification of piety and eloquence. They understood late ancient authors to have "charted a religious and intellectual path through Greco-Roman thought and culture," which validated their own efforts to position ancient culture as central to intellectual life; this understanding also justified further exploration of that ancient culture, as humanists sought to "understand the cultural and religious matrix that had formed the fathers themselves" (Rutherford 1997, p. 511). Other commentators, particularly scholastics, understood the encounter to have been one of antagonism, survival, and triumph, where the appropriation of pagan antiquity ("spoiling the Egyptians," in Augustine's words [Rummel 1994, p. 14]) had been achieved

---

A Companion to Late Antique Literature, First Edition.
Edited by Scott McGill and Edward J. Watts.
© 2018 John Wiley & Sons, Inc. Published 2018 by John Wiley & Sons, Inc.

to the extent that it needed to be (with the notable exception of Aristotle, whose works, translated into Latin in the twelfth century, were deeply influential to the scholastic movement); the resulting works by Church Fathers represented not the pinnacle of Christian achievement but its foundation, hallowed by antiquity but made more useful by the commentaries and interrogations of intervening generations of scholars and theologians.

The early modern era saw renewed interest in this period of Christian antiquity, as humanists, with "somewhat undifferentiated enthusiasm" and often with a tenuous grasp on issues of dating and provenance, subjected familiar texts to novel forms of analysis and sought to "locate, investigate, study, and disseminate" more obscure patristic works (Stinger 1997, pp. 506–507; for the tendency to date later texts to the apostolic age and to misattribute texts, see Rice 1962, p. 140). Fueled by their search for a "purer," simpler Christian piety and the eloquent "affective wisdom" of the generations closest to Christ, humanists elevated these texts as the antidote to the formal intellectualism of the scholastics. Scholastics, by contrast, were more circumspect about which late ancient writers should be regarded as authoritative and how they could be understood, but they, too, found themselves engaging more with the Church Fathers as they defended their readings and interpretations against humanist challenges and incorporated humanist textual findings into their assessments of the literature (or rejected them). Thus, the early modern era did not so much rediscover the works of the Church Fathers – most had been "available, read, and used" throughout the Middle Ages (Rice 1985, p. 120) – as reemphasize and rethink them.

Late ancient texts were widely read, used, and valued in the early modern period, to different degrees, to different ends, and with different emphases, such that even their detractors were forced to encounter them and address their use. And in the literary and educational culture of the time, they were ubiquitous – diffused in classrooms, in private libraries, in civic life, and at court: Elizabeth Tudor, for example, is said to have "daily turned over" Boethius's *Consolatio* and "to have translated [it] handsomely into the English tongue" (Marcus, Mueller, and Rose 2000, p. 370n). But beyond the mere fact of their use, there are few sweeping statements one can make regarding the reception of late ancient literature in the early modern era.

Thus, to provide a sense of how early modern readers received and engaged with late ancient authors, this chapter offers first an overview of some defining features of early modernity and their effect on the reception of late ancient literature: the humanist–scholastic debate, the rise of text culture, and the growth of religious diversity leading up to and during the Reformation. It then proceeds to highlight one particularly illustrative case of reception: Desiderius Erasmus's reception of Jerome.

37.2 Encountering Late Ancient Texts in the Early Modern Context

When we inquire about early modern receptions of late ancient literature, we must first define what we mean by "early modern." The term is problematically teleological (though less restrictive and ideologically infused than either "Renaissance" or "Reformation") and indicates different developments – technological, economic, intellectual, religious – depending on one's area of inquiry. "Early modern" can refer to a variety of dates ranging from the mid-fourteenth century all the way to the nineteenth (Scott 2015, p. 21; Starn 2002, pp. 298–302). To highlight developments in the reception of late ancient texts, this chapter focuses on literary, intellectual, and educational culture across central and western Europe. Thus, the most useful areas of focus for our purposes are seismic shifts in intellectual culture: the debates between humanists and scholastics that began in earnest in the fourteenth century; the proliferation of texts (both manuscript and print) in the mid-fifteenth century; and the sense of crisis attending the state of faith from the fourteenth century (with the Avignon papacy and subsequent Western Schism) through the sixteenth (as Reformations flourished).

Humanism – broadly defined as an emphasis on language skills, including philological textual critique, translation, and elegance of articulation in speech and writing – was not the invention of Francesco Petrarch (1304–1374), but his formulation of it initiated the debates about modes of intellectual inquiry that dominated the early modern period. In Petrarch's view, the humanists' primary opponents, the scholastics or "theologians" (who adhered to the centuries-honed intellectual system of Aristotelian logic and disputation that dominated the universities) were more invested in "mental gymnastics" than in a "genuine search for truth," whereas humanists sought to cultivate good morality through "wisdom and virtue" gleaned from whatever source it might be found in (Rummel 1995, pp. 30, 32–33). Petrarch further asserted that the scholastics' conflict-driven methods (dialectic, *disputatio*, *sic-et-non* reasoning) were ill-suited to studying sacred Scripture, which should be approached with more reverence and less egotism. Scholastics, like Jean Gerson (1363–1429), asserted that theology must be the foremost arbiter of academic rigor, and that theological and philosophical quandaries must be explored with precise terminology and established forms of inquiry. Thus, while in its early years the humanist–scholastic debate mainly centered on literary pursuits, we can see the seeds of the later conflict here – from its literary origins, which included intense debate about the value and danger of non-Christian classical texts, the debate expanded into the academic and institutional realms, as humanists and scholastics argued about what credentials and methodological competencies merited positions at universities. The debate then further intensified, fueling and being fueled by the religious reformations of the sixteenth century, as partisans on both sides (and in between) questioned one another's ability "to understand and interpret the Word of God" (Rummel 1995, p. 9).

Both scholastics and humanists embraced late ancient patristic authors, using the same authors and even the same texts to defend their positions. For instance, Jerome's dream of being condemned as a Ciceronian rather than as a Christian (*Ep.* 22) and Augustine's *De doctrina Christiana* were mined by both parties to defend their use or rejection of classical texts (Rummel 1995, p. 29). The fact is that many of these patristic authors held similar levels of authority for both sides; humanists and scholastics simply appreciated the texts differently, employing divergent methods of reading and analysis to glean their lessons. While humanists "were inclined to examine the source texts rather than their interpretations" and to examine biblical texts via "a philological approach, arguing on the basis of grammatical rules, etymology, and classical usage," the scholastics tended to pursue arguments that were "logical rather than philological," and to quote in support of their positions "a slate of authorities, from scriptural texts to Latin Fathers and medieval theologians" (Rummel 1995, p. 12). Patristic writings were, thus, central to all parties in the major intellectual and educational debate of the early modern period.

Also crucial to the intellectual culture of early modernity was the proliferation of texts, both in manuscript and in print. Population growth in cities, the rise of secular education, the emerging consensus that civic and political engagement required literacy, and the "unremitting enthusiasm of the bourgeoisie for edification and self-improvement" (Rice and Grafton 1994, p. 6) all contributed to an expansion of readership from aristocrats and monastics to the populace more broadly in the fourteenth and early fifteenth centuries. Humanism, indeed, played an important role in this expansion of text culture. One of its defining features was "intellectual curiosity" (Rummel 1995, p. 12), and this curiosity manifested itself not only in the exploration *of* a wide range of texts (bringing to light new things about commonly used texts by focusing on philology, translation, and an unlimited array of questions), but also in exploration *for* a wide range of texts. Humanists visited the great libraries of their day, locating and copying manuscripts of all sorts to bring home with them and share, many of them making their reputations as humanists with such ventures (Davies 1996, p. 47). Poggio Bracciolini (1380–1459), for example, found time during the Council of Constance (1414–1417), despite his role as papal secretary, to travel to Cluny, St. Gall,

Fulda, and other nearby monasteries to seek out texts, many of which he then took back to Italy (Reynolds and Wilson 1991, pp. 136–138). Most humanists did not abscond with their discoveries but, instead, copied them for their own personal use and circulation, often transcribing the text in a clear, accessible "humanist hand," which had been invented at the turn of the fifteenth century as a response to the visual difficulties presented by Gothic scripts.

The necessary components of print culture had all coalesced by 1450: affordable paper, suitable ink, movable metal type, a profusion of accessible texts to print, and, finally, a sufficient customer base – "a highly literate society with a highly organized book trade" (Davies 1996, p. 53). Over the next 50 years, printing expanded at a remarkably rapid pace, spreading across Europe and producing, by the turn of the century, roughly six million books, representing (on a conservative estimate) approximately 40 000 editions (Rice and Grafton 1994, p. 7). Though the copying of manuscripts continued to thrive and even to outpace the output of all previous centuries combined (Davies 1996, p. 58), print quickly became the dominant medium of textual transmission (Hunter 2007, p. 25). The sheer volume of texts available in print had a profound effect on intellectual culture, making a wider range of sources accessible to a wider array of people, and (for better or worse) in a generally standardized form that could be easily referenced and discussed. Demand for texts supported publishing enterprises, whose success then entrenched and increased demand for texts.

And many of the texts in high demand were late ancient. Of 53 surviving incunabula from the publishers Conrad Sweynheym and Arnold Pannartz (fl. 1465–1473), 11 are editions of the works of late ancient authors, including Lactantius (1465), Augustine (*City of God*, 1467–1470), Jerome (1468), Leo the Great (1470), Cyprian (1471), and Aelius Donatus (1472). Prior to 1502, across all publishers (and once again based on surviving incunabula, according to the British Library's Incunabula Short Title Catalogue [ISTC]), texts printed included at least 200 editions of Augustine; 166 of Jerome; 90 of Boethius; 61 of Gregory the Great; 25 of Proba; 18 of Ambrose and Prosper; 16 of Claudian; 14 of Prudentius; 8 of Juvencus, Sedulius, and Leo the Great; 7 of Cassiodorus, Orosius, and Cyprian; 6 of Ausonius and Macrobius; 4 of Sulpicius; 3 of Hilary; 2 of Sidonius, Maximianus, Tertullian, and Rufinus; and 1 of Ammianus and Symmachus. Greek works were available in print in Latin translation: The surviving incunabula include 28 editions of Basil and 4 of Athanasius. Survivals are not necessarily representative: Approximately 30,000 incunabula survive, out of millions printed, and an edition's preservation may be more likely to indicate later popularity than fifteenth-century market demands. Nonetheless, the variety and ubiquity of late ancient authors among this first generation of printed texts is striking.

These printed editions were not always of high quality. Early modern readers of any given late ancient text would likely have encountered a *textus receptus* that was largely standardized, but also typically flawed. The printing press established a level of conformity that, although not precisely intentional (more the product of expediency than anything else [Davies 1996, p. 57]), benefited scholarly communication, as all students of a work could be sure that they were reading and commenting on the same text. At the same time, these editions were based on whatever manuscripts editors had access to (many of which "had no merit except availability" [Kenney 1974, p. 5]), and they had been edited with less than exemplary care (even when care was shown, editorial theories and practices varied – see Kenney 1974, pp. 21–74). The situation was so dire, in fact, that, to combat the corruption of texts by "men of slight learning" who just happened to be in charge of publishing houses, papal curialist Niccolo Perotti proposed in 1471 that the pope appoint someone to supervise all texts printed in Rome (Davies 1996, p. 57). Nonetheless, despite the recognized shortcomings of many of the texts on offer, print editions tended to be reprinted largely without emendation: It was far easier and more cost effective to base print editions on previous print editions. Thus the process of manuscript transmission became largely monogenous – "with remarkably few exceptions the descent of any given text through the printed editions is in a single line" (Kenney 1974, p. 18). The situation improved, for some texts, with later interventions of humanist scholars, editors, and publishers. While the first generation of printers went to great effort to "rush classical texts into print…[so that] their presses should not stand idle" (Kenney 1974, p. 14), the next generation of printers, critics, and editors saw their task as improving the texts, using their erudition and intellect alongside available manuscripts and printed editions to "emend, correct, and make stainless" the texts, thus once more changing how early modern readers engaged with late ancient literature (Kenney 1974, p. 25). Nonetheless, whatever the quality of the text encountered, late ancient literature was more widely available in the early modern era than it had ever been, and it was engaged with more substantively than it had previously been.

The foregoing account of early modern text culture is only partially illuminating for late ancient texts written in Greek. Knowledge of Greek in the Latin west was relatively rare throughout the early modern period – even some humanists who recognized its importance and advocated its inclusion in the educational curriculum, like John Colet (1467–1519), did not themselves acquire the skill. Outside of Italy (where Greek instruction was regularized but still a "luxury option"), western Europeans in the fifteenth century had a difficult time finding instruction in Greek, as the experience of

Guillaume Budé, who paid exorbitantly for a mediocre Greek tutor whose instruction Budé "would soon have to unlearn," attests (Grafton 1997, p. 146). Before they became available in print, elementary Greek grammars and learning aids in manuscript form were anxiously sought, with demand vastly outweighing supply (Botley 2010, p. 115). Despite this widespread desire to learn and to read ancient Greek, printing presses were slow to supply Greek texts – both because of the difficulties of establishing an appropriate typeface and because demand was still not sufficient to make such printings profitable. Before Aldus Manutius (1449–1515) began printing and marketing Greek texts in Venice in 1495 (first a grammar, then Aristotle), only a dozen or so Greek texts had found their way into print (Reynolds and Wilson 1991, p. 155; Davies 1995, p. 9). Once this threshold was crossed, however, and it became possible for scholars to learn Greek on their own outside the classroom with an introductory grammar, the reading of Greek texts from classical and Christian antiquity flourished.

Finally, the early modern era was characterized by increased religious turmoil. The Council of Constance, which brought Poggio within hunting distance of late ancient literature ensconced in monastic libraries, had been convened in the hopes of ending the Great Western Schism, one of the significant low points in the history of the Latin Church, during which there were at one point three claimants to the chair of St. Peter. The reformers had high hopes for the Council, and its decrees, especially *Haec Sancta* (asserting the authority of church councils over the pope in matters of faith), seemed to presage change. But the very papacy the council had helped restore rejected conciliar infringement on its power, and the decrees were ignored. This only underscored the perception that the papacy and religious orders were rife with corruption, immorality, and hypocrisy, and calls for a "return" to simple piety (as exemplified by the Church Fathers) gained traction. In addition, with print facilitating the spread of ideas and humanists advocating the *ad fontes* model of scholarship – for example by reviving the study of Greek and then using it to read (and, for Erasmus, to produce a critical edition of) the Greek New Testament – diverse perspectives (both ancient and modern) on religious matters arose and were disseminated to an extent never before seen in Christian Europe. With the onset of the Reformation, which we can mark by the excommunication of Martin Luther in 1521, this diversity of opinions on matters of faith contributed to many and lasting confessional divisions.

Although Martin Luther's insistence on the principle of *sola scriptura* and his concomitant rejection of tradition as a source of authority in sacred matters precipitated a general devaluation of patristic literature among Protestant reformers, the Church Fathers, nonetheless, continued to appear as guiding lights in their thought. Lutherans, Calvinists, Anabaptists, and Anglicans all made use of patristic sources not only in establishing their own ideas but as polemical weapons in confessional debates, especially as each denomination sought to prove its continuity with Jesus and the "early church" (see, in particular, the essays collected in Backus 1997). For example, Luther excoriated the Catholic Church for abandoning Augustine's more difficult teachings about grace in favor of a "Pelagian" view of human agency in salvation; he cited Gregory the Great and other patristic sources to undercut the papacy's claims to temporal power; and he used Jerome's insights when he agreed with them but in general thought him overesteemed by Catholic thinkers (Schultze 1997, pp. 579, 599, 600). He read and engaged with patristic authors extensively but minced no words when he thought them mistaken, and he refused to allow their judgments to stand alone; everything, for Luther, boiled down to whether he thought the patristic opinion was grounded in Scripture (Schultze 1997, p. 621). Catholics, meanwhile, doubled down on the authority of the Fathers within the church – the patristic tradition, understood to be perfectly harmonious, vindicated the teaching authority of the church and could only be properly understood within that context. Thus, appealing to the Fathers to critique the church would be "inherently erroneous" (Keen 1997, p. 701).

Reception of late ancient literature in the early modern era was thus characterized by improved access to sources; altered attitudes toward reading, analyzing, and investigating them; a renewed and pointed enthusiasm among their readers; and the recognition of their utility in religious debates. A case study that illustrates all of these elements is that of Erasmus's reception of Jerome.

37.3 Erasmus and Jerome

Desiderius Erasmus (1466–1536) had a special affinity and regard for Jerome, counting him first among the doctors of the church, just as Peter had been first among the apostles (Rice 1985, p. 116; *Antibarbarians*, CWE [Collected Works of Erasmus] 23: 113). The renowned Dutch humanist encountered Jerome's works as a child studying and living with the Brethren of the Common Life, a community of education-focused pietists who followed the *devotio moderna* and who themselves held Jerome in such particular esteem that they were nicknamed *Hieronymiani* (Rice 1985, p. 116). Later, as an Augustinian canon at Steyn, Erasmus read and copied Jerome's entire correspondence (*Ep.* 22, to Cornelis Gerard 1489, CWE 1: 35), and he began to articulate his admiration for the church father in his own letters.

What appealed to Erasmus about Jerome above all else was the skill with which he navigated the demands of culture and of faith. As he wrote to his friend Antoon van Bergen in 1501, Jerome was "the only scholar in the church universal who had a perfect command of all learning both sacred and heathen, as they call it" (*Ep.* 149, CWE 2: 27). Jerome's style was, in Erasmus's view, comparable to, if not an improvement upon, Cicero's: "Look at all the classical learning, the Greek scholarship, the histories to be found in him, and all those stylistic and rhetorical accomplishments in which he not only far outstrips all Christian writers, but even seems to rival Cicero himself" (*Ep.* 141, CWE 1: 309). And Jerome's personal piety only adds to Erasmus's good opinion of him: The humanist can enjoy Jerome's style with unqualified enthusiasm, knowing that "lack of culture is not holiness, nor cleverness impiety" (*Ep.* 22, CWE 1: 35). Spiritually, Erasmus felt he was in good hands with Jerome: "with his burning energy and the divine inspiration in that amazing heart, he can at the same moment delight us with his eloquence, instruct us with his learning, and sweep us away with his religious force" (*Ep.* 335, CWE 3: 107).

It was with promulgating his own high opinion of Jerome in mind that Erasmus embarked on a critical edition of and commentary on Jerome's epistolary corpus, a project that took the better part of sixteen years, eventually grew to include various *apologia* and treatises, and was published alongside a further five volumes edited by the Amerbach brothers of Basel as the first *opera omnia* of Jerome in 1516. As he wrote to the advocate Greveradus in 1500:

> I have long had a burning desire to write a commentary on the letters of Jerome; and some god is now firing my spirit and impelling me to dare to contemplate this massive enterprise, never before attempted by anyone. What prompts me to this is the goodness of the saintly man who of all Christians was by common consent the best scholar and best writer, whose works deserve to be read and got by heart by all mankind, whereas only a very few have read them and fewer still respect them, while fewest of all understand them....I consider it most disgraceful that Jerome should be forgotten for the very reason that earned him his title to be remembered. That very excellence of style, which benefited our faith, has done harm to its creator. Many are put off by his profound learning which ought to have been the especial source of his fame; so there are few to admire an author who is comprehended by few indeed. (*Ep.* 141, CWE 1: 308)

Working primarily from previously printed editions with support from unidentified manuscripts and transcriptions of manuscripts he had at hand (Rice 1985, pp. 120–124), Erasmus used humanist principles of textual analysis to "restore" the original text, to right the wrongs that generations of poor scribes and "half-taught critics" had inflicted on the collection "through ignorance of classical antiquity and of Greek" (*Ep.* 149, CWE 2: 26). He identified passages that were stylistically divergent, anachronistic, or theologically dissonant with Jerome's broader thought and excised them as interpolations; using those same tools he identified and separated out misattributed letters (including what we now know as Pelagius's *Letter to Demetrias*); he corrected grammatical and syntactical errors; and he did all this with relative transparency, noting alterations and his reasoning for them in his commentary – though sometimes with less substantiation than modern scholars would desire, as in the case of his assessment of a spurious letter reputedly from Jerome to Pope Damasus: "Can an eye, ear, or mind be found so insensitive as to suppose that Jerome could have written such obvious rubbish?" (Rice 1985, pp. 124–129; *Ep. supp.* 47). The commentary was intended to introduce readers to the correct avenue of approach to the Church Father, that is, the humanist approach. The annotations included (in addition to textual variants and assessments of authenticity) Erasmus's rhetorical analyses of particular letters, explanations of classical figures of speech, identifications of names and places as well as literary and scriptural allusions, and, sometimes, commentary on the religious and intellectual debates of Erasmus's own era – he used his *scholia*, for instance, to weigh in against scholasticism and to note that, despite Jerome's own practice of translating Scripture into the common tongue, reading it in the vernacular would have been seen as "a sin" in the present day (Olin 1994, pp. 16–17).

For the Amerbach edition, Erasmus composed a *Life* of Jerome based upon the correspondence itself and on the accounts of Jerome's contemporaries. This was the first critical biography of Jerome (Olin 1994, p. 12; Rice 1985, p. 131). By focusing on the "mundane" aspects of the saint's life – his education, his travel to Syria and Bethlehem, his ascetic ventures, his interactions with his contemporaries, and his mastery of Latin, Greek, Syriac, and Hebrew – rather than on the miracles attributed to him, Erasmus was pointedly rejecting the type of hagiography he saw as characteristic of the medieval *Lives*, interspersed with "inventions" and unnecessary miracles that would encourage veneration and imitation (Olin 1994, p. 12). Nonetheless, the *Life* does still function as hagiography, emphasizing Jerome's sanctity by virtue of his piously applied scholarly gifts and holding him up as an exemplar to be imitated: Erasmus used his *Life* of Jerome to argue that wide-ranging scholarship, mastery of languages, and philological acumen were necessary criteria for theologians, who ought to model their explorations of Scripture and *res divinae* on the *vera theologia* of the early church, as represented by Jerome (Olin 1994, p. 13). For Erasmus, Jerome's restoration "was synonymous...with the restoration of theology itself," the chief model for how the church could accomplish a much-needed unification of eloquence and piety (Olin 1994, p. 19; see also den Boeft 1997).

Thus, Erasmus admired Jerome as a stylist, holy man, and spiritual guide, but his admiration was not distant or anodyne: It was characterized by an imperative to emulation. Like many of his humanist friends and colleagues, Erasmus believed that "you are what you read": Poetry and literature were formative (Furey 2006, p. 89), and scholarship, *ad fontes* and characterized as *askesis*, was a sacred and salvific venture (Furey 2006, pp. 44–53). That Erasmus himself sought to live out this *imitatio Hieronymi* can be seen in his own peripatetic intellectual career while he was working on his edition of the letters, which were finally published in 1516. Erasmus traveled, at Aldus Manutius's invitation, to Venice, where he spent almost all of 1508 living and working with the publisher and his community of scholars and workmen as he improved his Greek and supervised the publication of the *Adagia* (Olin 1994, pp. 46-47). Indeed, it was Jerome's knowledge of Greek that made the father indisputably superior to Augustine, in Erasmus's view, since "all philosophy and all theology in those days belonged to the Greeks" and "Augustine knew no Greek" (Olin 1994, p. 21). He later journeyed to England and spent three years (1511–1514) teaching Greek and lecturing on Jerome at Cambridge. And it was also during this time that Erasmus produced his own critical edition of the Greek New Testament (1516), sanctioned in this venture by Jerome's own editorial activity in constructing the Vulgate. It is easy to see why Eugene Rice reads Erasmus's *Life* of Jerome as an Erasmian "self-portrait" (Rice 1985, p. 132), and how Erasmus could have used his version of Jerome to assert his own scholarly credentials as the Father's consummate imitator, *Hieronymus redivivus* (Pabel 2008, p. 2; Jardine 1993, p. 164). Jerome's own promotion of himself as the foremost authority on the Hebrew Bible even served Erasmus well: He was able to reconcile "self-promotion and Christian literary labor" and thus to fashion himself "as a new Christian man of letters" (Pabel 2008, p. 11). But this imitation had limits. Erasmus saw Jerome as an authority, but not one immune to criticism or error. Erasmus noted (and excused) Jerome's lapses in orthodoxy, for instance, as relics of his passion for God or as products of his historical circumstance. Ultimately, errata were evidence of the Church Father's humanity (Rice 1985, pp. 135–136). And yet even this is imitable, for Erasmus: His Jerome is a model of discernment, weighing ideas and coming to reasoned estimations of them.

While Erasmus used the example of the Church Fathers to criticize contemporary Christianity and what he saw as the distortion and corruption of the church (most prominently in his 1511 satirical essay, *In Praise of Folly*), he sought reform of the church and the individuals who comprised it, rather than a break with the church and its traditions. Despite the persistence of the adage that "Erasmus laid the egg that Luther hatched," Erasmus did not see his forays into scriptural editing and his philological analysis of sacred texts as necessitating a break with Catholicism – he insisted instead on *pia curiositas*, "an intellectual curiosity circumscribed by considerations for the authority of the Church, and scholarship subject to the decrees of the Church" (Rummel 1995, p. 10). He was, ultimately, a firm believer in the power of the *consensus fidelium*, the shared conviction of the Christian community represented by the traditions of the church, and died a Catholic, having spent his latter decades embroiled in disputes with Luther and other Protestant luminaries. Against one attack from Ulrich von Hutten, who had expected Erasmus to support Luther and saw his failure to do so as apostasy, Erasmus responded that his aim was what it had ever been: "I am promoting literature and restoring that more pure and simple religion, and I intend to do that as long as I live" (den Boeft 1997, p. 570).

37.4 Conclusion

Erasmus's reception of Jerome is in many ways emblematic of early modern receptions of late ancient literature. His approach to the text, emphasizing Jerome's style and erudition through rhetorical and philological appreciation of his writings, highlights humanist modes of reading. The use to which he put the text – the moral aspects of what one reads and how one reads it – also reflects early modern constructions of literature's power to shape the individual. The format of the texts Erasmus encountered, first in manuscript and later in haphazard print, are typical of the early modern reading experience, as is his effort to improve the *textus receptus* by producing a critical edition. And making Jerome central to his positions in the humanist–scholastic debate as well as in the Reformation context underscores the vast importance that early modern readers placed on late ancient literature amid the most profound intellectual and religious controversies of their era. In short, engaging with and responding to late ancient literature was a crucial component of early modern culture and "self-fashioning."

REFERENCES

Backus, Irena Dorota, ed. (1997). *The Reception of the Church Fathers in the West: From the Carolingians to the Maurists*. 2 vols. Leiden: Brill.

Botley, Paul. (2010). *Learning Greek in Western Europe, 1396–1529: Grammars, Lexica, and Classroom Texts*. Transactions of the American Philosophical Society, n. s. 100, pt. 2. Philadelphia: American Philosophical Society.

British Library. (2016). Incunabula Short Title Catalogue. http://www.bl.uk/catalogues/istc (accessed 20 April 2016).

Davies, Martin. (1995). *Aldus Manutius: Printer and Publisher of Renaissance Venice*. Malibu, CA: J. Paul Getty Museum.

Davies, Martin. (1996). Humanism in script and print in the fifteenth century. In: *The Cambridge Companion to Renaissance Humanism* (ed. Jill Kraye), 47–62. Cambridge: Cambridge University Press.

den Boeft, Jan. (1997). Erasmus and the Church Fathers. In: *The Reception of the Church Fathers in the West: From the Carolingians to the Maurists* (ed. Irena Dorota Backus), 2: 537–572. Leiden: Brill.

Erasmus. (1976–). *Collected Works of Erasmus*. Toronto: University of Toronto Press.

Furey, Constance M. (2006). *Erasmus, Contarini, and the Religious Republic of Letters*. Cambridge: Cambridge University Press.

Grafton, Anthony. (1997). *Commerce with the Classics: Ancient Books and Renaissance Readers*. Ann Arbor, MI: University of Michigan Press.

Hunter, Michael. (2007). *Editing Early Modern Texts: An Introduction to Principles and Practice*. New York: Palgrave Macmillan.

Jardine, Lisa. (1993). *Erasmus, Man of Letters: The Construction of Charisma in Print*. Princeton, NJ: Princeton University Press.

Keen, Ralph. (1997). The Fathers in counter-reformation theology in the pre-Tridentine period. In: *The Reception of the Church Fathers in the West: From the Carolingians to the Maurists* (ed. Irena Dorota Backus), 2: 701–743. Leiden: Brill.

Kenney, E.J. (1974). *The Classical Text: Aspects of Editing in the Age of the Printed Book*. Berkeley: University of California Press.

Marcus, Leah S., Mueller, Janel, and Rose, Mary Beth. ed. (2000). *Elizabeth I: Collected Works*. Chicago: University of Chicago Press.

Olin, John C. (1994). *Erasmus, Utopia, and the Jesuits: Essays on the Outreach of Humanism*. New York: Fordham University Press.

Pabel, Hilmar M. (2008). *Herculean Labours: Erasmus and the Editing of St. Jerome's Letters in the Renaissance*. Leiden: Brill.

Reynolds, Leighton D. and Nigel G. Wilson. (1991). *Scribes and Scholars: A Guide to the Transmission of Greek and Latin Literature*. 3rd ed. Oxford: Clarendon.

Rice, Eugene F. (1962). The humanist idea of Christian antiquity: Lefèvre d' Étaples and his circle. *Studies in the Renaissance* 9: 126–160.

Rice, Eugene F. (1985). *Saint Jerome in the Renaissance*. Baltimore: Johns Hopkins University Press.

Rice, Eugene F. and Grafton, Anthony. (1994). *The Foundations of Early Modern Europe, 1460–1559*. 2nd ed. New York: W.W. Norton.

Rummel, Erika. (1995). *The Humanist–Scholastic Debate in the Renaissance and Reformation*. Cambridge, MA: Harvard University Press.

Rutherford, David. (1997). Gratian's *Decretum* as a source of patristic knowledge in the Italian Renaissance: The example of Timoteo Maffei's *In Sanctam Rusticitatem* (1454). In: *The Reception of the Church Fathers in the West: From the Carolingians to the Maurists* (ed. Irena Dorota Backus), 2: 511–535. Leiden: Brill.

Schultze, Manfred. (1997). Martin Luther and the Church Fathers. In: *The Reception of the Church Fathers in the West: From the Carolingians to the Maurists* (ed. Irena Dorota Backus), 2: 573–626. Leiden: Brill.

Scott, Hamish, ed. (2015). *The Oxford Handbook of Early Modern European History, 1350–1750. Vol. 1: Peoples and Place*. Oxford: Oxford University Press.

Starn, Randolph. (2002). The early modern muddle. *Journal of Early Modern History* 6: 296–307.

Stinger, Charles. (1997). Italian Renaissance learning and the Church Fathers. In: *The Reception of the Church Fathers in the West: From the Carolingians to the Maurists* (ed. Irena Dorota Backus), 2: 473–510. Leiden: Brill.

CHAPTER THIRTY-EIGHT

Edward Gibbon and Late Antique Literature

*Gavin Kelly**

Late antiquity was only called late antiquity with any frequency from the 1970s onward. Before then, one of the commonest names for the period was the "decline and fall" of the Roman Empire. Edward Gibbon's *The History of the Decline and Fall of the Roman Empire* (6 vols., 1776–1788) casts a long shadow over modern understanding of the history and literature of late antiquity. The *Decline and Fall*, of course, covers an even wider range than late antiquity "from Marcus Aurelius to Mohammed," to borrow the subtitle of the work that popularized the latter concept, Peter Brown's *The World of Late Antiquity* (1971). Gibbon's work outstrips the longest of the long late antiquities conceived in modern scholarship, taking its account down to the Ottoman sack of Constantinople and the city of Rome in the times of Petrarch and Poggio, on the brink of the Renaissance. However, the first four of the six volumes can reasonably be said to cover what is now conventionally called late antiquity, down to the Arab invasions.

In these volumes Gibbon offers a wonderful entrée into eighteenth-century reception of late antique literature, for several reasons. First, his great work had an unwieldy range, far beyond conventional political history; he based his text on a correspondingly wide range of works from many genres, Greek and Latin, prose and verse; and his acute interpretation of ancient texts, implicit in translation and paraphrase or explicit in footnotes, can be found on every page. He had also absorbed the reception of these works in

---

A Companion to Late Antique Literature, First Edition.
Edited by Scott McGill and Edward J. Watts.
© 2018 John Wiley & Sons, Inc. Published 2018 by John Wiley & Sons, Inc.

European scholarship and thought from the Renaissance to his own time. Furthermore, even if Gibbon is no longer read as a modern historian to be cited like any other – as he was until well into the twentieth century – his historical outlook and his attitude to literature has had an enduring influence and remains relevant to the reading of late antique literature to this day. To give a narrow example and a broad one: His epigrammatic characterizations of authors are still repeatedly quoted in scholarship on them – for instance, the suggestion that Ausonius's "poetic fame…condemns the taste of his age," or the dubbing of Ammianus Marcellinus as "an accurate and faithful guide" (III.xxvii.19–20n1, II.xxvi.1073). And more generally, a persistent narrative of decline is among the largest issues with which modern literary studies of late antique texts have had to struggle (see Formisano 2014).

Gibbon's massive work is multifaceted, and it has fascinated readers and scholars both as a contribution to Enlightenment thought and as a work of deep scholarly learning – and indeed it was his aim to combine "philosophical history" with the best of recent "erudite" scholarship on antiquity. Much scholarship focuses on Gibbon in the broader context of intellectual history, including the six volumes of J.G.A. Pocock (1999–2015) or, with a somewhat more philological focus, the edition and many brilliant studies by David Womersley; there is also a tradition of work on Gibbon by classical historians (e.g. Bowersock 1977; Paschoud 1977; Matthews 1996; Cartledge 2010). The focus of this chapter is on how Gibbon read ancient literature and on his work's status as a literary history – a less studied topic, but a no less essential aspect of the work. Starting from this question of how he viewed the connection between the study of literature and that of history, I shall move on to a sketch of how Gibbon read and thought of late antique literature (38.1), before making a case study of his reception of Ammianus Marcellinus, an author about whom Gibbon displayed interestingly mixed feelings (38.2). I shall close with some thoughts on the relationship between literary and historical perceptions of decline (38.3).

Gibbon's history is inescapably literary. His writing is high art and tends to narrative; he cleaves more closely to his sources and engages more allusively with them than a work of present-day historical scholarship would. Not only his explicit scholarly engagement as advertised in the footnotes but also his implicit or explicit reworking of his sources in his text can be revelatory of his interpretation and methods of reading. From his youth on he read literary texts with the eye of both the literary and historical scholar. He viewed history as arising out of the study of literary texts. A clear statement of this viewpoint can be found in his first published work, the *Essai sur l'étude de la littérature* (written 1758, published 1761). In it Gibbon gave a definition of criticism (section 23):

The art of judging writing and writers; what they have said, whether they have said it well, and whether they have said it truthfully. Under the first of these branches is included grammar, knowledge of languages and manuscripts, the identification of spurious works, and the restoration of corrupted passages. Under the second is comprehended the whole theory of poetry and eloquence. The third opens an immense field, the critical examination of facts. (Adapted from the anonymous 1837 translation, with influence from Mankin 2014, p. 13)

Historical scholarship was thus on a continuum with textual and literary criticism. Gibbon lives up to this manifesto in the *Decline and Fall*. His footnotes move constantly between these three types of problems – including not only the historical interpretation and occasional discussion of textual interpretation that one might expect but also remarks on style and judgments of literary value. Some of these have been canonized, like those on Ausonius and Ammianus quoted above, but there are many others, ranging from the harsh to the surprisingly generous:

Christodorus…composed inscriptions in verse for each of the statues [in the baths of Zeuxippus in Constantinople]. He was a Theban poet in genius as well as in birth: Bæotum in crasso jurares aere natum. (II.xviii.598n51)

In describing the triumph of Julian, Ammianus (xxii.1,2) assumes the lofty tone of an orator or poet; while Libanius…sinks to the grave simplicity of an historian. (II.xxii.849n43)

The philosophical fable which Julian composed under the name of the CÆSARS, is one of the most agreeable and instructive productions of ancient wit. (II.xxiv.909)

But literary discussion is embodied not just in passing judgments but also in longer passages, such as the biographical sketch of Libanius (II.xxiv.916–917), the praises of Claudian (III.xxx.162–164) or the characterization of Boethius (IV.xxxix.550–555). While integrated in the text, such passages, with their evaluations and conscious balance, have something of the feel of the literary and historical essays, freestanding or in his journals, that the young Gibbon had produced on his reading both ancient and modern (numerous examples can be found in the posthumous *Miscellaneous Works*). Another form of response is the close version of a passage of text. The discussion of Germany in chapter ix ostensibly owes much to Tacitus's *Germania* (though see Womersley 1988, pp. 80–88, for the more complicated truth); closer paraphrases come (to give a pair of examples) in the combined version of Ammianus's two digressions on the Romans (14.6, 28.4 ≈ II.xxxi.175-81), on which more below, or in Sidonius's description of King Theodoric (*Ep.* 1.2 = II.xxxv.364–366). Looser summaries or citations can also act as markers within the text, often standing artfully at the start or end of chapters – like the summarized version of Julian's *Caesars* that opens chapter xxiv or the story of the seven sleepers of Ephesus that closes chapter xxxiii.

38.1 Gibbon's Reading of Late Antique Literature

In turning to the question of how Gibbon read late antique literature, it is scarcely necessary to say that his reading started out from the Classics – something he has in common with the great majority both of late antique authors and of modern scholars of late antiquity. "The Classics, as low as Tacitus, the Younger Pliny, and Juvenal, were my old and familiar companions," he wrote in the *Memoirs* of his youthful reading before describing how, in order to embark on the *Decline and Fall*, he "insensibly plunged into the ocean of the Augustan History," and then in "descending series" the sources for the second to fifth centuries (Gibbon 1796, vol. 1, p. 139). As John Matthews (1996, p. 30) has remarked, the metaphorical language of lowness and descent, if not to be pressed too hard, is none the less noteworthy. It is telling that the line from Horace's epistles used in heavy-handed depreciation of Christodorus (II.xviii.598n51, quoted above) appears without identification: Gibbon's readers are expected to recognize Horace (or Virgil, or Racine, or Voltaire) without a citation. No author from late antiquity influences Gibbon's style or thought to the extent that Tacitus does, the only author, he had claimed in the *Essai*, to have fulfilled his ideal of the "historien philosophe" (Gibbon 1761, section 56), and one to whom he persistently alludes (see Womersley 1988, pp. 80–88; Cartledge 2010).

The corollary of this attitude is that Gibbon prized linguistic classicism, and that he was suspicious, in particular, of the florid Latin prose of late antiquity. This is hardly surprising: Such was the common literary consensus from the Renaissance onward (see Hernández Lobato 2014 on Sidonius), and the trend can be dated back as far as Petrarch – the central figure of Gibbon's penultimate chapter. So, for example, Sidonius's prose was "vitiated by a false and affected taste," though "much superior to his insipid verses" (III.xxxvi.393n97). Very similarly, Augustine's style, "though sometimes animated by the eloquence of passion, is usually clouded by false and affected rhetoric" – though Gibbon could admire his "strong, capacious, argumentative mind" (III.xxxiii.286; cf. the similarly ambivalent praise of the *City of*

God, III.xxviii.93n79, and, on the other hand, a catalog of praise of Christian authors at III.xxvii.59n96). A "gradation from the style of freedom and simplicity, to that of form and servitude, may be traced in the Epistles of Cicero, of Pliny, and of Symmachus" (II.xvii.603 n.73). A subsequent criticism of Symmachus's letters reinforces this sense of decline:

> In the form and disposition of his ten books of epistles, he imitated the younger Pliny, whose rich and florid style he was supposed, by his friends, to equal or excel [Gibbon cites Macrobius *Sat.* 5.1.7]. But the luxuriancy of Symmachus consists of barren leaves, without fruits, and even without flowers. Few facts, and few sentiments, can be extracted from his verbose correspondence. (III.xxviii.75n16)

With other texts, Gibbon's condemnation of their distance from classical Latin is more forceful. The Latin of the *Expositio totius mundi et gentium* was "barbarous," as was that of the second part of the *Anonymus Valesianus* (III. xxxi.183n54, IV.xxxix.534n24). Of course, such a description is for its own time entirely conventional (the modern equivalent would be "subliterary"), and in the latter case the author is conversely praised, in terms similar to Ammianus, for exhibiting "the knowledge, without the passions of a contemporary" (cf. II.xxvi.1073, quoted below).

Gibbon also prizes late antique literature on occasion due to its resemblance to earlier literature. Claudian can be mildly rebuked as a panegyrist, but surely it is no coincidence that, as the late antique poet whose style is hardest to distinguish from poets of the first century, he is the one whom Gibbon most admires – and admires in part because of that resemblance:

> In the decline of arts, and of empire, a native of Egypt, who had received the education of a Greek, assumed, in a mature age, the familiar use, and absolute command, of the Latin language; soared above the heads of his feeble contemporaries; and placed himself, after an interval of three hundred years, among the poets of ancient Rome. (III.xxx.163–164)

Gibbon thereby depreciates all other Latin poets after Juvenal, the familiar companion of his youth. Claudian's contemporaries, Ausonius and Prudentius, do indeed fare badly in his judgment (he seemingly had only indirect knowledge of Paulinus of Nola). For all that, his fondness for quoting Latin verse in his footnotes extends to Prudentius as well as to Sidonius, whom he did not in general admire. Greek quotations are markedly rarer, and indeed Gibbon's Greek was not at the level of his Latin. Overall the literary preferences of Gibbon are classicizing and secular. At the same time, he values truthfulness and informativeness—an unsurprising trait in a historian. This is apparent in a rejection of partiality that tends to affect Christian authors in particular (as we shall see in discussing Ammianus), but also in a dislike of panegyric. But Gibbon's regard for the truthful and the informative also affects stylistic judgments. Notable in the passage on Symmachus quoted above is the resentment of Symmachus's inutility as a source. We shall see that Gibbon's annoyance with Ammianus is at its strongest when his stylistic pretensions obscure his meaning.

Gibbon's approach also tends to be biographical: From Claudian's *Carmina minora* he reconstructs a story of the poet's fall from grace that few will credit (III.xxx.162–163). Likewise, he is fond of making inferences about the religious adherence of authors. The idea that Ausonius was in his heart a pagan would not convince modern readers (III.xxvii.19n1, xxxi.210n123), though the case for the cryptopaganism of Procopius and Agathias (IV.xl.561n12) has recently been reargued (Kaldellis 1999, 2004).

Many of the texts with which Gibbon was dealing had detailed commentary traditions by this stage, often variorum commentaries that could leave the text peeping out at the top of the page (cf. Gibbon 1796, vol. 2, p. 252). The means by which he had read texts is usually made clear in footnotes. So Spanheim on Julian, Sirmond on Sidonius, and hundreds of others are cited alongside the source text, praised, questioned – and sometimes quietly plagiarized. The footnotes therefore give an impression of the impressive library in Bentinck Street that Gibbon invited his adversary Davies to visit "any afternoon when I am *not* at home" (*Vindication*, in Womersley 1994, III.1154). This picture can be further clarified from the evidence of his library catalogs and of the posthumous sale of his books (see Keynes 1980). The footnotes also provide some evidence of places where he had not consulted sources directly. For ecclesiastical history in particular, Gibbon benefited from the great efflorescence of patristic scholarship of the previous century, but he notoriously used the 16 volumes of Tillemont's *Mémoires pour servir à l'histoire ecclesiastique des six premiers siècles* (1693–1712) and at times had not directly used the sources collected and analyzed there. For example, in his *Vindication* he admits having used Tillemont in place of the works of Gregory of Nyssa that he had been unable to procure (Womersley 1994, III.1147). At one point in the *Decline and Fall*, he acknowledges that the only Augustine he knows directly is the *Confessions* and the *City of God* (III.xxxiii.285n28) – and while the canonicity of those particular texts will not surprise modern specialists in late antiquity, the presence of only three direct references to the former text in the whole work might. But short cuts such as use of Tillemont also matched his inclinations. He once remarked in a footnote on Priscillianism that "Tillemont has raked together all the dirt of the Fathers: an useful scavenger"

(III.xxvii.38n51). (Gibbon was less careful in his use of Tillemont's *Histoire des empereurs* on secular history: Glen Bowersock [1977, pp. 199–201] has shown how he commits a number of errors in the history of the fourth century by relying on ancient sources directly rather than on Tillemont's analyses). The grateful use of Tillemont suggests, like much else, a less enthusiastic attitude to the explicitly Christian literature of late antiquity on Gibbon's part. And arguably, it was not until relatively recently (one thinks in particular of the scholarship of Peter Brown) that much "patristic" literature was seen as worthy of historical study or literary appreciation.

38.2 A Case Study: Ammianus Marcellinus

It is not without the most sincere regret, that I must now take leave of an accurate and faithful guide, who has composed the history of his own times, without indulging the prejudices and passions, which usually affect the mind of a contemporary. Ammianus Marcellinus, who terminates his useful work with the defeat and death of Valens, recommends the more glorious subject of the ensuing reign to the youthful vigor and eloquence of the rising generation. The rising generation was not disposed to accept his advice, or to imitate his example; and, in the study of the reign of Theodosius, we are reduced to illustrate the partial narrative of Zosimus, by the obscure hints of fragments and chronicles, by the figurative style of poetry or panegyric, and by the precarious assistance of the ecclesiastical writers, who, in the heat of religious faction, are apt to despise the profane virtues of sincerity and moderation. (II.xxvi.1073–1074)

Let us now take a closer look at Gibbon's reception of one late antique author, Ammianus Marcellinus. Ammianus, the surviving books of whose history cover the years 353–378, is a fine case study. The object of occasional references in volume 1 of the *Decline and Fall*, he is highlighted in Gibbon's *Vindication* of 1779 as one of the very few historians "since the origins of Theological Factions" who have avoided bias (Appendix III of Womersley 1994, III.1171; see also Barnes 1998, pp. 2–6), and the high praise given here foreshadows the dominant role he would play in volume 2, where he is the principal source of half the volume, chapters xix and xxii–xxvi. Near the end of chapter xxvi and the volume, after the catastrophic battle of Adrianople and the acclamation of Theodosius, Gibbon bids Ammianus the memorable farewell quoted at the head of this section. In the third volume, citations are only very occasional, with the exception of a brilliant paraphrase of the two digressions on the senate and people of Rome (14.6, 28.4 ≈ III.xxxi.175–181).

The attitude toward Ammianus is two-sided. On the one hand, he is praised in the formal farewell for accuracy, fidelity, completeness, and lack of bias. The bias of which he is free is conceived of as primarily religious, as implied by the contrast to the polemical pagan Zosimus and the equally partisan church historians on the Christian side, as well as by the reference in the *Vindication*. This praise runs deep and is often implied in discussion of detail. On the other hand, typical, albeit heavily tempered, criticism can be found in a shorter passage marking the end of Gibbon's use of Ammianus 10 pages before:

> We might censure the vices of his style, the disorder and perplexity of his narrative: but we must now take leave of this impartial historian; and reproach is silenced by our regret for such an irreparable loss. (III.xxvi.1063n91)

On many previous occasions, however, reproach had not been silenced. Occasionally criticism is historical, as with the "loose and obscure" chronology of the account of Firmus's revolt (II.xxv.1004n122, cf. 1006n123). Mostly, however, Gibbon inserts asides on matters of style: Ammianus's "inflated eloquence" (II.xix.715n74); "so eloquent, that he writes nonsense" on the death of Valentinian (II.xxv.1021n154); of the great tsunami at the end of Ammianus's 26th book, "Such is the bad taste of Ammianus... that it is not easy to distinguish his facts from his metaphors" (II.xxvi.1023n1); later in the same chapter, uncertain as to the correct interpretation of *statim ut incensi malleoli* (31.7.7), "I almost suspect, that it is only one of those turgid metaphors, those false ornaments, that perpetually disfigure the style of Ammianus" (II.xxvi.1056n81). There is absolutely no doubt that Ammianus's style is profoundly and ostentatiously metaphorical. Resistance to florid late antique *Kunstprosa* had, as remarked above, been a dominant trend since the Renaissance, though since the mid-twentieth century scholarly views have been more positive in the case of Ammianus.

This twofold approach of admiration for content and depreciation of style has arguably set the tone for modern scholarship on Ammianus, which has tended to see him as an honest reporter rather than as a partisan literary artist (for this characterization see Kelly 2008, pp. 2–4). We should not doubt the sincerity of Gibbon's reaction to Ammianus's style. And yet characterizing Ammianus as an incompetent stylist was also helpful, in that it displayed Gibbon's own judiciousness, specifically in that it could be used as a guarantee of Ammianus's veracity. In describing the Persian expedition of Julian in chapter xxiv, Gibbon provides versions of two of the emperor's speeches, one given after the sack of Pirisabora and the other on his deathbed (24.3.4–7 = II.xxvi.930–931, 25.3.15–20 = 944–945). These speeches are considered in modern scholarship as almost certainly being authorial creations typical of classical historiography, but Gibbon remarked in a note on the first, "I give this speech as original and genuine. Ammianus might hear, could transcribe, and was incapable of inventing, it" (931n63); of the second, he wonders whether Julian might even have prepared for death by composing in advance "the elaborate oration, which Ammianus heard, and has transcribed" (944n95). Ammianus's reliability is guaranteed by being a spectator (and the calumnies of Christian authors can thus be disregarded, 945n99), but also by his being incapable of inventing such speeches. Literary incompetence guarantees historical honesty.

Ammianus's impartiality (the epithet is applied to him or his testimony an extraordinary 14 times in Gibbon's work: Kelly 2009a, 355n29) is often carefully contrasted to other sources. For example, it distinguishes Ammianus from two less reliable Christian writers and confirms the bad character of Bishop George of Alexandria: "The invectives of the two saints [Gregory Nazianzen and Epiphanius] might not deserve much credit, unless they were confirmed by the testimony of the cool and impartial infidel" (II. xxiii.901n119). So, too, in discussing Julian's judicial activity (II.xxii.861n83), Gibbon places Ammianus's impartiality midway between the uncritical praise and condemnation of the pagan Libanius and the Christian Gregory. This form of triangulation helps Gibbon lay claim to (especially religious) impartiality himself.

Gibbon's use of Ammianus, I have argued elsewhere (Kelly 2009a), needs to be seen in the light of the controversy that blew up after the publication of the first volume. The two chapters on Christianity, xv and xvi, had led to an outpouring of pamphlets by defenders of the Christian faith. Although Gibbon had responded authoritatively in his *Vindication* to these "Watchmen of the Holy City," he was still careful to entrench his position (see Womersley 2002, pp. 13–42). He elevated Ammianus as an impartial historian in volume 2 (1781) as a surrogate for himself, using him in particular to preempt potential criticism of his coverage of Julian. The last pagan emperor was a hero for earlier Enlightenment thinkers such as Montesquieu and Voltaire (Womersley 1988, 156–168); Gibbon dealt with the expectation that he would heroize Julian blindly by adopting what was essentially Ammianus's approach – that is, of tempering a highly positive portrayal with serious criticism of his excessive religious zeal – and exalted Ammianus's fairness. It should be said, however, that virtually no modern scholar would consider Ammianus's treatment of Julian impartial, and that much, though not all, modern scholarship takes the view that Ammianus was very far from religiously neutral and that he was firmly but discreetly hostile to Christianity (see Rike 1987; Barnes 1998, esp. pp. 79–94; Kelly 2009a, pp. 357–360).

A nice example of how Gibbon adopted Ammianus's ostensible fairness can be found at several points in the Julian narrative. Julian, according to Ammianus, gave different Christian sects freedom of worship because he knew that lack of restraint would increase their disagreements (*dissensiones augente licentia*), and that no wild beasts are as savage to mankind as most of the Christians are to each other (22.5.4). Animal metaphors are more common in the thought of Ammianus than of Julian, and it is tempting to see this thought as primarily the historian's rather than the character's. Gibbon borrows this thought twice immediately before and during the Julianic narrative. The first time, he attributes it to Ammianus himself:

> The simple narrative of the *intestine divisions*, which distracted the peace, and dishonoured the triumph, of the church, will confirm the remark of a pagan historian.... The experience of Ammianus had convinced him, that the enmity of the Christians towards each other, surpassed the fury of wild beasts against men. (II.xxi.823–824; emphasis mine)

The second occasion comes at the proper point in the narrative:

> The impartial Ammianus has ascribed [Julian's] affected clemency to the desire of fomenting the *intestine divisions* of the church; and the insidious design of undermining the foundations of Christianity, was inseparably connected with the zeal, which Julian professed, to restore the ancient religion of the empire. (I.xxiii.877)

Quite how ideally this particular analysis appealed to Gibbon's own worldview can be seen in his apparently borrowing Ammianus's or Julian's characterization of the Christians (unacknowledged) at the end of his 16th chapter and first volume, five years before in 1776:

> We shall conclude this chapter by a melancholy truth, which obtrudes itself on the reluctant mind; that even admitting, without hesitation or enquiry, all that history has recorded, or devotion has feigned, on the subject of martyrdoms, it must still be acknowledged, that the Christians, in the course of their *intestine dissentions*, have inflicted far greater severities on each other, than they had experienced from the zeal of infidels. (I.xvi.580)

Of the three editions of Ammianus in Gibbon's library (see Keynes 1980), the working text was certainly Gronovius's edition of 1693, which contained at the foot of the page not only the notes of Gronovius himself but also the more substantial contributions of Friedrich Lindenbrog (1609), Henri de Valois (or Valesius) (1636), and the latter's brother Adrien de Valois

(1682). Their names consistently recur, with commendation or occasional disagreement, alongside citations of Ammianus. (It has also been shown that Gibbon on occasion filtered his reading of Ammianus – whether consciously or not – through the French rendering by the Abbé de la Blèterie in his *Vie de Julien* [Bowersock 1977, p. 202], just as he had done when translating Julian [201]). The scholarly benefits of his reading of Valesius and other earlier scholars affect the discussion at numerous points. For example, many of the places where Ammianus is compared favorably to other sources seem to chase up hints from the foot of Gronovius's page. From this, too, seems to come an overinterpretation of Ammianus (II.xxi.826n168), who is said to have described "eunuchs who were spoliis templorum pasti" ("gorged on plunder from temples," 22.4.3). But Ammianus nowhere calls these courtiers eunuchs: Eunuchs are mentioned in this context in other sources quoted in the footnotes of his text, and they are also specifically made the subject of the chapter in the *capitula* composed by Adrien de Valois (Kelly 2009b, p. 239). Reading through commentary also pointed Gibbon to the allusive quality of Ammianus's text: When Ammianus in a pregnant phrase (see Kelly 2008, pp. 15–18; Ross 2016, pp. 40–44) described the Gothic War battlefield of Ad Salices still white with unburied bones, *ut indicant nunc usque albentes ossibus campi* (31.7.16), Gibbon, with help from Lindenbrog's note, recognized the allusion to Virgil's *Aeneid* 12.36 ... *campique ingentes ossibus albent*, and wrote of "the wide extent of the fields (II.xxvi.1057)." But an eye for allusion and its interpretation is present in Gibbon's writing even without help from commentaries. Let me give two examples.

In paraphrasing Ammianus's famous description of Constantius's entry into Rome, Gibbon adds wider contextualization to the impressive self-control of the emperor's posture: "The severe discipline of the Persian youth had been introduced by the eunuchs into the Imperial palace; and such were the habits of patience which they had inculcated, that, during a slow and sultry march, he was never seen to move his hand towards his face, or to turn his eyes either to the right or the left" (II.xix.698; cf. Amm. 16.10.10). Aside from decorously omitting Constantius's unwillingness to spit in public, Gibbon has added the detail about Constantius's education by Persian eunuchs, found nowhere in Ammianus or any other ancient account. The grounds for this seem to be twofold: first, his knowledge that, since the capture of the Persian King Narses's harem in the year 299, eunuchs had played an important role in the Roman court; second, Gibbon's recognition and elaboration of an allusion by Ammianus to Xenophon, who describes how his fictional Cyrus trained his subjects (*Cyropaedia* 8.1.42). This allusion had not been picked up by Ammianus's early modern commentators, nor did

Gibbon note it himself. Indeed, it was not otherwise noted in scholarship until 1928 (Goodenough 1928, 79n84; cf. Classen 1988, 178, 178n6).

Another place in which Gibbon's close reading of Ammianus picked up a subtlety that other readers had missed came after Julian's death (see Kelly 2009a, p. 360). After ostensibly blaming Jovian's surrender of Nisibis on youthful inexperience (25.9.7), Ammianus moves on to a catalog of examples, which ends by pointing out how Romans under the Republic had repudiated such surrenders and handed the responsible general over to the enemy instead, as had happened to Mancinus after Numantia. The implication that this should have happened to Jovian – a position at odds with Ammianus's ostensible attitude – has not been picked up by modern scholarship. But it was clear to Gibbon (II.xxiv.954).

The closeness of Gibbon's reading of Ammianus, and his firm view that Ammianus was an unbiased and unmediated source, led him to put a particularly strong emphasis on the historian's status as eyewitness. We have already heard how he decides that Ammianus was present at Julian's deathbed and had heard his magnificent deathbed speech; but he also suggests (following La Blétarie: Pocock 1999–2015, vol. 6, p. 210) that an unnamed soldier who contributed to the debate on the appointment of a successor to Julian was, in fact, Ammianus himself (II.xxiv.946n100). Gibbon was the first scholar to infer from Ammianus's description of the bones on the battlefield of Ad Salices that the historian had himself visited the site (II.xxvi.1057). Gibbon called his splendid version of Ammianus's digression on the mores of Roman senators "an authentic state of Rome and its inhabitants, which is more peculiarly applicable to the period of the Gothic invasion" (III.xxxi.174–175), inferring the personal disappointments of the historian. Gibbon's attitude to these passages has been foundational for later scholarship. Like him, it has tended to count the two digressions, 14 books apart, as texts that can be "melted together" and read as a unity. The tendency has also been to "detect the latent prejudices, and personal resentments, which soured the temper of Ammianus himself" (III.xxxi.175): Ammianus is seen as the bourgeois interloper looked down on by the nobles. Some rather obvious points – that these biographical inferences are speculative and unlikely and the digressions themselves are remarkably timeless and closely wrapped up in the traditions of Roman satire – have been overlooked (Kelly 2008, 132-41; Ross 2015). Similarly, in a broader investigation of Ammianus's appearances or alleged appearances as a character, I found that the approach arguably founded by Gibbon was still the standard one, though a rather more artful Ammianus could be identified (Kelly 2008, pp. 31–103).

38.3 Concluding Thoughts on Decline

For Gibbon, Ammianus was "the last subject of Rome who composed a profane history in the Latin language" (II.xxvi.1074n114). One could read this as a purely factual (though actually false) statement. It is tempting, however, to see it as rather more teleological in import, akin to a remark in the character sketch of Boethius: "The last of the Romans whom Cato or Tully could have acknowledged for their countryman" – a judgment that context and choice of comparanda imply is both political and literary (IV.xxxix.550). Gibbon saw Claudian as writing "in the decline of arts, and of empire," as if these were two parallel processes. Gibbon's immensely influential attitude to the history of late antiquity was also intimately tied in to his view of the literature of the period. Modern historians of late antiquity have reacted against the description "decline and fall," and even those with a more catastrophist view of the process tend to leave out "decline" (cf. the titles of Heather [2005] and Ward-Perkins [2005]). Gibbon saw a deeper and more protracted descent. His opening three chapters on the Antonine Golden Age of the second century describe a Roman state whose population and sophistication approached those of Europe of his own time – a far more optimistic view than most modern historians of the Roman Empire would adopt – and a similar position is adopted in the "General Observations" that close the third volume of the work. The late antique world, and late antique literature, lies, as it were, in a depression between, and cannot match, the ancients or the moderns. It has been attractively argued by John Matthews (1996, p. 30) that "decline" is, for Gibbon, an attitude pervading his thinking rather than a strictly analytical approach; and moreover, that "Gibbon conceived the nature of the artistic and literary culture of a society as fundamental to an evaluation of that society in all its aspects, and saw the relationship between the two, the arts and society, as a very intimate one; if, indeed, he consciously distinguished them at all" (p. 32). In Gibbon's thought political decline and literary decline, therefore, seem to be self-reinforcing, rather than the latter being considered a product of the former. Indeed, the falling off from linguistic classicism may to some extent have seemed powerful evidence for wider decline.

Gibbon was an acute, learned, and in many ways sympathetic scholar of late antique literature, but his approach was shaped by underlying attitudes, none of them fundamentally surprising. A sense of belatedness (and decline?) in late antique literature, along with a separation of secular literature from Christian writings (not necessarily conceived of as literary), went back to late antiquity itself. A Ciceronian reaction against the ostentatious vocabulary and metaphors of much later Latin prose and the jeweled style of later Latin poetry had been conventional since the Renaissance. It makes sense that a historian would admire detailed contemporary narrative and that a man of the Enlightenment would be suspicious of Christian sectarianism. Beyond these approaches there is, of course, much subtle interpretation of many authors to be found in the *Decline and Fall*, ripe for further study. Both in the impact of these detailed interpretations – as we saw with Ammianus – and in his more general influence, Gibbon has had an enduring influence on scholarship and popular views of late antique literature.

ACKNOWLEDGMENT

My thanks to various friends who have read this piece, including Sarah Cassidy, Felicity Loughlin, and Justin Stover.

*NOTE

References to Gibbon's *Decline and Fall* give the original volume number, the chapter, and page and note references in the standard modern edition by David Womersley (1994), each of whose three volumes incorporates two volumes of the original. The original volume 1 was published in 1776, volumes 2–3 in 1781, and volumes 4-6 in 1788. Gibbon's *Vindication* (1779), a defense against critics of his treatment of Christian topics in volume 1, is cited by page numbers in volume 3 of Womersley's edition. His *Essai sur l'étude de la littérature* (1761) is cited by section number; his *Memoirs* from the first edition of 1796.

REFERENCES

Barnes, Timothy D. (1998). *Ammianus Marcellinus and the Representation of Historical Reality*. Ithaca, NY: Cornell University Press.

Bowersock, G.W. (1977). Gibbon and Julian. In: *Gibbon et Rome à la lumière de l'historiographie moderne* (ed. Pierre Ducrey, F. Burkhalter, and R. Overmeer), 191–217. Geneva: Droz.

Brown, Peter. (1971). *The World of Late Antiquity: From Marcus Aurelius to Muhammad*. London: Thames and Hudson.

Cartledge, Paul. (2010). Gibbon and Tacitus. In: *The Cambridge Companion to Tacitus* (ed. A.J. Woodman), 269–279. Cambridge University Press.

Classen, C. Joachim. (1988). *Nec spuens aut os aut nasum tergens vel fricans*. Amm. Marc. XVI 10, 10. *Rheinisches Museum* 131: 177–186.

Formisano, Marco. (2014). Reading Décadence – Reception and the subaltern late antiquity. In *Décadence. "Decline and Fall" or "Other Antiquity?"* (ed. Marco Formisano and Therese Fuhrer), 7–16. Heidelberg: Winter.

Gibbon, Edward. (1761). *Essai sur l'étude de la literature*. London: T. Becket and P.A. de Hondt.

Gibbon, Edward. (1776, 1781, 1788). *The History of the Decline and Fall of the Roman Empire*. 6 vols. London: W Strahan and T. Cadell. Cited by original volume and chapter number and page number in the edition of David Womersley (London: Penguin, 1994).

Gibbon, Edward. (1779). *A Vindication of Some Passages in the Fifteenth and Sixteenth Chapters of the History of the Decline and Fall of the Roman Empire*. London: W. Strahan and T. Cadell.

Gibbon, Edward. (1796). *The Miscellaneous Works of Edward Gibbon Esq. with Memoirs of His Life and Writings* (ed. John, Lord Sheffield). London: A. Strahan and T. Cadell.

Gibbon, Edward. (1837). *The Miscellaneous Works of Edward Gibbon Esq. with Memoirs of his Life and Writings* (ed. John, Lord Sheffield). London: B. Blake.

Goodenough, E. (1928). The political philosophy of Hellenistic kingship. *Yale Classical Studies* 1: 55–102.

Heather, Peter. (2005). *The Fall of the Roman Empire: A New History*. London: Macmillan.

Hernández Lobato, Jesús. (2014). *El humanismo che no fue. Sidonio Apolinar en el renacimento*. Bologna: Pàtron.

Kaldellis, Anthony. (1999). The historical and religious views of Agathias: A reinterpretation. *Byzantion* 69: 206–252.

Kaldellis, Anthony. (2004). *Procopius of Caesarea: Tyranny, History and Philosophy at the End of Antiquity*. Philadelphia: University of Pennsylvania Press.

Kelly, Gavin. (2008). *Ammianus Marcellinus: The Allusive Historian*. Cambridge University Press.

Kelly, Gavin. (2009a). Ammianus Marcellinus: Tacitus' heir and Gibbon's guide. In: *The Cambridge Companion to the Roman Historians* (ed. Andrew Feldherr), 438–461. Cambridge University Press.

Kelly, Gavin. (2009b). Adrien de Valois and the chapter headings in Ammianus Marcellinus. *Classical Philology* 104: 233–242.

Keynes, Geoffrey. (1980). *The Library of Edward Gibbon*. 2nd ed. Dorchester: St. Paul's.

Mankin, Robert. (2014). Gibbon's *Essay on the Study of Literature*: A new English translation. *Republics of Letters* 3.3.

Matthews, John. (1996). Gibbon and the later Roman Empire: Causes and circumstances. In: *Edward Gibbon and Empire* (ed. Rosamond McKitterick and Roland Quinault), 12–33. Cambridge: Cambridge University Press.

Paschoud, François. (1977). Gibbon et les sources historiographiques pour la période de 363 à 410. In: *Gibbon et Rome à la lumière de l'historiographie moderne* (ed. Pierre Ducrey, F. Burkhalter, and R. Overmeer), 219–245. Geneva: Droz.

Pocock, J.G.A. (1999–2015). *Barbarism and Religion*. 6 vols. Cambridge: Cambridge University Press.

Rike, R.L. (1987). Apex omnium: *Religion in the* Res Gestae *of Ammianus*. Berkeley: University of California Press.

Ross, Alan. (2015). Ammianus, traditions of satire, and the eternity of Rome. *Classical Journal* 110: 356–373.

Ross, Alan. (2016). *Ammianus' Julian: Narrative and Genre in the* Res Gestae. Oxford: Oxford University Press.

Ward-Perkins, Bryan. (2005). *The Fall of Rome and the End of Civilisation*. Oxford: Oxford University Press.

Womersley, David. (1988). *The Transformation of The Decline and Fall of the Roman Empire*. Cambridge: Cambridge University Press.

Womersley, David. ed. (1994). *E. Gibbon, The History of the Decline and Fall of the Roman Empire*. 3 vols. London: Penguin.

Womersley, David. (2002). *Gibbon and the Watchmen of the Holy City: The Historian and His Reputation 1776–1815*. Oxford: Oxford University Press.

CHAPTER THIRTY-NINE

Nineteenth- and Twentieth-Century Visions of Late Antique Literature

James Uden

Why read the authors who come at the end? Why linger at the end of an epoch, a civilization, a *Companion*? Authors of the late antique period of the Roman Empire have historically, with a few exceptions (Augustine, Boethius), occupied a marginal position within the scholarly discipline of classics. Late antique literature has been characterized by critics as uninspired and imitative and as the product of failing creative powers; or as drily exegetical, technical, or rhetorical; or as languorously decadent and dissipated. Yet for some poets, essayists, and novelists, the lateness of this literature has proven its primary attraction. Indeed, throughout the late nineteenth and twentieth centuries, the literature of Rome's final era end has enjoyed a surprisingly enduring symbolic appeal as the expression of exclusion from the canon, of romanticized or paradigmatic decline, or of the conflict between Christianity and the "pagan" Muses. In a 2009 poem, the Australian poet Peter Porter addressed the American John Ashbery: "In the end, aren't you a bit pissed/at living in the world's most powerful country?/Wouldn't you rather, like the Late Roman Poets,/coruscate in the margins of a worn-out Empire?" ("To John Ashbery," Porter 2009, 58). The *distance* of late Roman and Greek authors – their temporal distance from their models in the classical past, and frequently their geographical distance from Rome and Greece itself – makes them seductive precursors for writers who feel their own ages equally distant and late, or who perhaps feel a sort of lateness to be vital to their art.

A Companion to Late Antique Literature, First Edition.
Edited by Scott McGill and Edward J. Watts.
© 2018 John Wiley & Sons, Inc. Published 2018 by John Wiley & Sons, Inc.

This romance with lateness has found itself increasingly at cross-purposes with an academic effort to rewrite the narrative of the late Roman world. In Peter Brown's influential *The World of Late Antiquity* (1971), the later empire represents no end at all but is instead an era of "astounding new beginnings" (p. 7), of dynamic transformations in cultural, political, and religious life. The barbarian invasions that long dominated the historiographical imagination were instead "a 'gold rush' of immigrants from the underdeveloped countries of the north" (p. 122). This chapter, though, testifies to the continuing significance of narratives of decline outside the academy. It offers a brief – and necessarily selective – survey of artistic engagements with late antique literature in the late nineteenth and early twentieth centuries, in poems, novels, essays, and films. It is clear, first, that the reception of late Latin and Greek literature by these writers and artists has developed largely independently from, or in defiance of, historians' redefinitions of late antiquity. For some writers the period that encompasses Libanius, Claudian, and Procopius has seemed startlingly modern; for most, stubbornly late. Second, the critical depreciation or neglect of late antique literature within the academy has often made it attractive to those who are working outside of it; there is frequently something rebellious, countercultural, or anti-academic in a self-identification with late Greek and Roman authors. Third, in strong contrast to dismissals of late antique literature as excessively formalist or rhetorical, many of the poets and novelists surveyed in this chapter attempted to recast its works in highly personal terms. Even when it has involved no little historical invention or anachronism, nineteenth- and twentieth-century writers have tried to fill the gaps of tantalizingly unfamiliar texts with the shapes of recognizable personalities, desiring to hear for themselves the voices of late antiquity.

39.1 Decadent and Aesthetic Late Antique Literatures

One of the most famous libraries in nineteenth-century fiction is the one owned by the ailing aristocrat Des Esseintes, the central character in Joris-Karl Huysmans's influential novel *À rebours* ("Against the Grain") (1884). Des Esseintes, who became the prototypical "decadent" character for a generation of literary figures, begins the novel by retreating in disgust to his villa from the sordid banalities of urban Parisian life. Weary, impotent, and ill, he nonetheless spends his days orchestrating elaborate synaesthetic experiments of great energy and inventiveness. In one chapter, he muses upon the "sounds" of different flavors then arranges a symphony of liqueurs (2003, pp. 45–46), and in another he traces the history of perfumery in order to speak "the syntax of smells" (p. 106). Since childhood, Des Esseintes has also been an enthusiast of Latin literature (p. 4). He describes in detail the contents of his villa's blue and orange library, which is devoted entirely to Latin works that date to the period of the "Decadence," an elephantine historical category that turns out to extend from the first century CE to the tenth (pp. 27–39). Des Esseintes assaults conventional taste by denigrating "good" classical authors (Virgil, Horace, Cicero), but he praises at length several of those who have appeared in this *Companion*: Commodian, Claudian, Ausonius, and Prudentius are particular favorites (Céard 1978; McGill, 2018). These poets also become a lens through which he views nineteenth-century French literature. He compares the style of the novelists and diarists Edmond and Jules de Goncourt to that of the fifth-century poet Rutilius Namatianus – an "obvious analogy" (p. 168) – and claims that the changes wrought by Baudelaire and his successors to the French language epitomize, in less than a century, the transformations of Latin over the course of its "decline" (p. 184). Des Esseintes relishes not the content of late Latin texts but the experience their style conveys, their flavor and smell (he repeatedly likens the language he savors to meat; pp. 35, 150, 184). Des Esseintes is not fascinated by decay as such; when he returns to Paris, its "decayed nobility" holds no interest for him (p. 197). Rather, he fancies that he can trace the process of decline in the transformations of language. The "decaying" style bottles the lightning of historical change.

Scholars or readers of late antique literature who wish to find in Huysmans's character a precursor for their own enthusiasm, though, might find themselves disappointed, even deceived. Des Esseintes consumes Latin literature; he does not read it. While Huysmans demonstrated his extensive knowledge of Latin liturgy in later novels, in *À rebours*, he never actually quotes the late Latin poetry to which his character devotes elaborate praise. At one point, Des Esseintes concludes his reminiscences about taking a young boy to a brothel by taking up the poem in praise of virginity by the late antique poet Avitus of Vienne, but his perusal is interrupted by sleep (p. 69). Des Esseintes's descriptions of late Latin authors also seem markedly less accurate than his venomous characterizations of classical texts. To speak of Caesar's "pop-gun pithiness" (p. 29) is evocative; to speak of Tertullian "calmly writing" (p. 32) or of Lactantius as "obscure" (p. 33) is less so. If Des Esseintes's patchwork summaries of what we know as late antique literature reflect the limitations of Huysmans's familiarity with these works, aspects of the style of the novel do nonetheless suggest something of a late antique literary aesthetic. The novel is replete with scenes of Des Esseintes cataloging and arranging precious gems and exotic flowers, and such passages seem to symbolize the "jeweled style" of the novel, its combination of intricate artistry and encyclopedism. Oscar Wilde uses just this phrase to describe Huysmans's novel: it is written, he said, in "that curious jeweled style" of the French Symbolists (2008, p. 107). That phrase is equally familiar to classicists as the title of Michael Roberts's 1989 study of late antique literature, in which he demonstrates the tendency in late literature to offset long lists with dazzling antitheses, parallelisms, and juxtapositions within a "grid-like" structure also observable in art of the period. The static pictorialism of Huysmans' style, which manifests itself in luxuriant catalogs and vivid passages of description, seems an uncanny, even an unconscious, double of a late antique jeweled style – whether Des Esseintes would recognize it from his reading or not.

Of course, the descriptions of late antique literature in Huysmans's novel were not written for cognoscenti. They aimed to shock, provoke, and bewilder those who clung to the importance of classicizing taste. In 1834 the critic Désiré Nisard published *Études de moeurs et de critique sur les poètes latins de la décadence*, which drew disparaging connections between contemporary French Romanticism and the supposed degeneracy of early imperial Latin authors (Vance 1999, pp. 116–117). From then on, French authors advocating the cause of poetic innovation over killjoy classicism could identify themselves positively with the "degenerate" poetics Nisard rejected: an over-refined verbal subtlety, elaborate and artificial syntactic structures, an emphasis on form over plot, and a love of ekphrasis, of painting with words. Their identification with late Latin literature was a rebellion against a bland critical standard of good taste. So, Théophile Gautier, in his preface to a posthumous edition of Charles Baudelaire's *Les fleurs du mal* (1868), likened Baudelaire's style to the "language of the late Roman Empire, which was already marbled by the greenness of decomposition and over-ripe" (Travers 2001, p. 140). Baudelaire himself included in *Les Fleurs du mal* an erotic Latin poem in imitation of a hymn (*Franciscae meae laudes*), and he appended a note with polemical praise of "the language of the last Latin decadence" (Stephan 1974, p. 21). A prose poem by Stéphane Mallarmé entitled "Autumn Complaint" ("Plainte d'automne"), published in 1864 and dedicated to Baudelaire, describes how, after the narrator has lost both his sister and his cat, he can console himself only with the "authors of the Latin decadence" (Cohn 1987, p. 31). Equally wryly, Paul Verlaine declared himself to be the "Empire at the end of its Decadence" in a poem published in 1883, "Languor" (*Langueur*). With apparent allusion to France's defeat in the Franco-Prussian War, Verlaine describes "indolent acrostics" being written in the face of "barbarian" armies (1948, p. 192). Most explicitly, the English critic Arthur Symons, who did much to popularize these "Symbolist" poets in England, claimed that these French poets embody "all the qualities that mark the end of great periods, the qualities that we find in the Greek, the Latin, decadence: an intense self-consciousness, a restless curiosity in research, an oversubtilizing refinement upon refinement, a spiritual and moral perversity" (1893, pp. 858–859). This appeal to late antique literature was a rejection of the abiding power of proper classical taste, and the associations of manliness, morality, and decorum that still accompanied it.

Yet as critics of these "decadent" authors pointed out, the modish glamor of Roman decay led infrequently to the actual reading of late antique literature. Max Nordau, in his vicious denunciation of nineteenth-century aestheticism, called the French idealizing of late Latin literature a "delirium," claiming that it would be difficult to detect in any fourth- or fifth-century poet the characteristics contemporaries claim to find so charming (1895, pp. 300–301). Remy de Gourmont, himself a "decadent" poet and prose writer, observed in an 1898 essay that the popular critical comparison with late Latin authors was founded on ignorance both of late antiquity and of contemporary French literature: "Since no one – not even Des Esseintes himself, perhaps – had read the depreciated poets, it was no trick at all for any critic to compare Sidonius Apollinaris, of whom we knew nothing, with Stéphane Mallarmé, whom he did not understand" (de Gourmont 1921, p. 150). There were exceptions. In 1892, de Gourmont himself published a volume entitled *Le latin mystique*, which included translations and criticism of Commodian, Prudentius, and the biblical Latin epicists; the work exerted a particular influence on Ezra Pound. Nonetheless, late antique literature rose to the surface of literary consciousness in late nineteenth-century France, despite being little read – or, perhaps, because of it. The postclassical Latin literary world remained attractively unfamiliar, while still symbolizing an exemplary subversion of classicizing ideals.

In England, admirers and opponents of these literary trends drew parallels with the languorous style and "aesthetic" criticism of Walter Pater, the classicist and Oxford don, although Pater's vision of late antique literature is significantly different from that of his French contemporaries. For Pater, *all* literature is in some sense "late antique," haunted by the ghosts of the literatures and the layers of history that came before it. The task of Paterian criticism is not to remove this "encrustation" of prior traditions but, rather, to "celebrate syncretism, accumulation, and impurity" (Evangelista 2015, p. 649). Although Pater devoted no work of criticism exclusively to late antique Latin and Greek literature, he offers an extended appreciation of the *De raptu Proserpinae* of the fourth/fifth-century poet Claudian in his influential 1878 essay "The Myth of Demeter and Persephone," which was anthologized posthumously in *Greek Studies* (1895). Pater celebrates what he sees as the privileged position of the late poet, who, rather than being disadvantaged by coming at the end of a tradition, is blessed with a panoramic vision of preceding art and literature. Claudian has "his subject before him in the whole extent of its various development," writes Pater (1895, pp. 132–133). (Seneca had argued similarly: "He who writes last is in the best position", *Ep.* 79.6). Pater identifies the connection between verbal and visual art in the late antique poet and translates lines 1.245–274, the description of Proserpina's weaving, as a reflection of the pictorial tendencies of the whole. Claudian excels at "a kind of painting in words" (p. 133); modern scholars talk in similar terms (cf. Ware 2012, p. 36: "The poet turns artist, recreating visual scenes in words"). The poem, he says, is "pre-eminently a work in colour" (Pater 1895, p. 134). It reflects the sensibility of someone who was both artist and curator, vividly depicting – and therefore preserving – the art and ideas of the classical past.

Pater's only complete surviving novel, *Marius the Epicurean* (1885), is set in Rome under the Antonines. This is hardly "late antiquity" according to our modern definition, but Pater presents the literature of the second century as culturally late (it had "the whole world of classic art and poetry outspread before it" Pater 2008, p. 93), and his sense of chronology is fluid and forward-looking. The past, for Pater, is always a compendium of potential philosophies and literatures that will be realized in the future. Gibbon had famously imagined Antonine Rome as the apex of human happiness, but Pater's second-century Rome is on "the eve of its decline" (p. 114), with the Middle Ages "just about to dawn" (p. 75; on Gibbon, see Chapter 38 in this volume). Yet the association between late Latin literature and decadence is notable in *Marius the Epicurean* by its absence. Throughout the 1880s and 1890s, Pater resisted being associated with fashionable literary decadence, and he was silent or derogatory about the leading figures of the movement in France (Conlon 1982; Huysmans he called "a beastly man": Seiler 1987, p. 176). In his novel, he attributes a philosophical cogency to the artificiality of language that the French Symbolists were said to imitate: The mixture of archaisms and neologisms in later Latin represents not an idle ornament but an attempt to "restore the primitive power of words," Pater says, and its beauty is symptomatic of "that deeper yearning of human nature towards an ideal perfection" (2008, pp. 64–65). Pater recasts the static pictorialism and ekphrastic digressions of later Latin literature not as languorous delay but as an expanded receptivity to aesthetic experience. In place of the autumn of Mallarmé and Verlaine, he celebrates the rejuvenescent spring of the *Pervigilium Veneris*, that anonymous late antique Latin poem, in which, for Pater, the awareness of lateness is balanced by a *resistance* to time (the poem's playfulness "had still a wonderful freshness in old age" Pater 2008, p.74; Uden 2018). Not art for art's sake, then, but "life as the end of life" (Pater 2008, p. 95) is the aim of the philosophized aestheticism of Pater's novel. In *Marius the Epicurean*, the critic finds something of his famous "hard gem-like flame" in later Latin's jeweled style. In his vision, the stylistic qualities of late antique literature reflect not a degeneracy or a poverty of inspiration but, rather, an extravagant, expansive surfeit of experience.

39.2 Modernist and "Beat" Late Antique Literatures

If nineteenth-century authors romanticized the idea of civilization's slow decay, the literary aesthetics of twentieth-century Modernism were shaped by a quickened sense of crisis. The final chapter of Erich Auerbach's *Mimesis*, an analysis of Virginia Woolf's *To the Lighthouse* (1927), influentially articulated the hallmarks of the Modernist style: The use of a fragmented "multiple consciousness," in which events in a narrative are glimpsed through the subjective impressions of different characters; a disjunction between "exterior time" and characters' expansive inner monologues; and a new attention to the random, chance events of everyday life (Auerbach 1953, pp. 525–553). In the wake of accelerated technological and cultural change, and under the pall of two world wars – *Mimesis* was written in 1942–1945, while the author, a Jew, was in exile in Istanbul – Auerbach also identifies "a certain atmosphere of universal doom" clouding Modernist literature (p. 551). Auerbach's study traces the literary afterlife of the classical "levels of style," according to which the humble incidents of daily life could be admitted only to "lower" forms of literature. He sees two major periods of decisive breaking away from this doctrine: one in Modernism, and the other in late antiquity, when rhetorically educated Christian writers used their powers of eloquence to express the sublime significance of the humble life of Jesus and the writings of his followers (pp. 50–76). Despite the radical difference in the literary aesthetics of the two periods, Auerbach's book is structured in part by this unexpected parallel between Modernism and late antiquity. Of all the periods covered in Auerbach's book, these eras are presented similarly as times of remarkable ideological upheaval. Modernism and late antiquity are usually not seen as related to one another, yet important Modernist authors and critics drew surprising connections between the two periods, viewing them as times when ideological change shook the certainty of shared beliefs and the authority of the literary paradigms of the past. In this period, late antiquity itself becomes fleetingly, but significantly, modern.

No major Modernist figure is inspired exclusively or primarily by late antique literature; instead, it formed part of the "useable past" (Armstrong 2005, p. 10) from which authors drew. Parallels with late antique authors occur sporadically in criticism of the period. Edmund Wilson, in his landmark account of Modernist poetics, *Axel's Castle*, draws a suggestive if ambivalent parallel between Modernist writers and late antique literature. "In reading Eliot and Pound," he writes, "we are sometimes visited by uneasy recollections of Ausonius, in the fourth century, composing Greek-and-Latin macaronics and piecing together poetic mosaics out of verses from Virgil" (Wilson 1931, p. 111). The parallel is "uneasy" because the Ausonian cento is assumed to represent the sort of empty erudition that Eliot's critics attributed to "The Waste Land." But Wilson's image of the fourth-century poet "piecing together" fragments of classical literary culture also resonates with his earlier vision of Eliot, fashioning a psychic defense against the desolation of the postwar world out of the ruins of earlier literature (pp. 106–107; cf. Cullhed 2015, pp. 72–79 on the cento and twentieth-century literature). A very different vision of Ausonius is offered by Edmund Gosse, the Modernist biographer and essayist, in a review article on the Loeb translation by H.G. Evelyn White. Evelyn White had disparaged his own subject as a poet who lacked the "human sympathy which should pervade true poetry" (1919, p. xxvii). In response, Gosse not only constructs a vivid picture of Ausonius's life from his works (he pictures the poet as a comically breathless and over-taxed dinner party host), but he also attacks the "romantic fallacy" and anachronism of White's search for sentiment in Ausonius's verse (Gosse 1921, pp. 29–34). In Gosse's frank and funny essay, the aims of two distinct literary periods converge: the Modernist aversion to Victorian sentimentality comes to the rescue of a late antique poet whose "rhetorical" poetry was equally distant from the Romantic cult of the emotions.

In the works of Modernist writers themselves, there are moments of acutely felt identification with characters from late antique literature, whose existence in a liminal period between classical culture and Christianity captured something of these writers' own struggle to escape the inertia of Victorian ideals and realize new, modern modes of existence. Michel, the protagonist of André Gide's *L'immoraliste* (The Immoralist) (1902), is a historian of Ostrogothic Italy, who is so drawn to the "crude morality of the Goths" that he wants to leave the "fireside happiness" of his marriage. The young king Athalaric, who Procopius tells us was seduced away from the classical training of his tutors to the corrupting influence of his Gothic peers (*Wars* 5.2–4), becomes both the imagined object of Michel's lust and a symbol for his moral crisis (Gide 1996, pp. 65–66, 83, 126, 145). The Greek poet C.P. Cavafy (1992) also found in characters from late antique literature a means of expressing his homosexual desires and articulating an ambivalently modern identity. His use of late antique Greek and Latin sources is meticulous, particularly in his poems on the emperor Julian, 12 of which survive (Bowersock 2009, pp. 136–150). Writing in Alexandria in Egypt, Cavafy exposes the "barbarian" of Rome's fall as a fiction against which imperial powers define themselves: "And now, what's going to happen to us without barbarians?/They were, those people, a kind of solution" ("Waiting for the Barbarians," Cavafy 1992, p. 19). But Cavafy is also drawn to imagine small moments in the everyday life of the late antique world. His protagonists are often young, beautiful men, trapped between old and new belief systems. There is the Syrian student of the fourth century who is "in part a heathen, in part Christianized" ("Dangerous Thoughts," p. 38); the shiftless young man who wanders from the philosophy of Ammonius, to the nascent Christian church, to sensuality, and maybe back again ("From the School of the Renowned Philosopher," p. 117); and the man who grows impatient with the Greek rhetoric of the orator Libanius because, though not a Christian, he is "disturbed" and "moved" by the asceticism of Simeon the Stylite ("Simeon," p. 204). Cavafy and Gide present quintessentially modern engagements with late antiquity, since the historical figures with whom they identify do not seem "late" at all but, rather, restlessly, agonizingly, on the cusp of something new.

Late antique literature reached a far broader audience in a work of scholarship that had important connections to literary Modernism (rarely emphasized, though see Carr 2013). The ostensible theme of Helen Waddell's *The Wandering Scholars* (1927) was the goliards – rambling, rambunctious medieval scholar-poets – but she began by tracing the origins of their poetry back to late antiquity. The book was an immediate and astonishing popular success. It entered the best-seller lists within three days of publication, and went through two new editions in 1927 alone (Fitzgerald 2012, p. 121). It secured Waddell financial security – though not a permanent academic post. Like Gide and Cavafy, Waddell finds a very human voice in a literature that was still frequently dismissed as the product of stale imitation. Even in the generally sympathetic account of F.J.E. Raby, published in the same year as *The Wandering Scholars*, one could still read that the literary production of the fourth century consisted largely of "trivialities in an artificial language" (Raby 1927, p. 4). Waddell, by contrast, describes the poetry of Ausonius as "enamelled fragments of philosophy, the fading of roses, the flavour of oysters," and writes vividly of Paulinus of Nola, Prudentius, Venantius Fortunatus, and Maximianus. Her criticism of late antique literature aims, in Pound's famous phrase, to "make it new" and, indeed, *The Wandering Scholars* can itself be read as a thoroughly Modernist text. Her book "does voices" by moving in and out of lyrical poetic translations, fixes attention on the chance events of the poets' everyday lives, and draws comparisons across literary cultures in a mode beloved by Pound and others ("there is something Chinese about Ausonius," she writes). One early reviewer of the work even disparaged Waddell's mode of criticism by comparing it to the archetypal Modernist musical form, jazz, complaining that he was subjected to "saxophones for a thousand years of Latin poetry. The history of Latin song punctuated by syncopation, blues-notes, and the wistful wailing of barber-song harmonies" (Fitzgerald 2000, p. 6). But Waddell delighted readers, and the late antique Latin poets were never read so widely as they were in the translations in the opening chapters of *The Wandering Scholars* and in her next, much-reprinted work, *Mediaeval Latin Lyrics*. Waddell's picture of the scholar-poets themselves as poor but vivacious writers who lived "the life of the road" (1929, p. 197) also unwittingly prefigured an important twentieth-century literary movement that was soon to come – the Beats.

When Berkeley professor Thomas Parkinson published the first academic account of the Beat Generation, *A Casebook on the Beat*, he presented the poets of the 1950s as a vital force in experimental literature: a distinctively American literary movement centered on San Francisco, which was countercultural, collaborative, and anti-academic, and which eschewed tradition in favor of "a literature more responsive to the realities of experience" (Parkinson 1961, 289). Kenneth Rexroth, mentor to the Beats and "chief figure" (Parkinson's words) on the San Francisco literary scene, presented their poetic project in more plangent terms, as a desperate response by youthful rebels to a suffocating American postwar disaffection. In an essay anthologized in *A Casebook on the Beat*, Rexroth wrote that "against the ruin of the world, there is only one defense – the creative act" (1961, p. 181). In his own poetry, Rexroth was drawn to imitate poems and periods that seemed to him to represent the struggle of art against destruction, and thus was drawn to "Hellenistic, Byzantine, and Late Roman" poetry, because it best showed "a sense of desperation and abandon in the face of a collapsing system of cultural values" (Rexroth 1944, p. 9).

In his 1949 collection *The Signature of All Things*, alongside imitations of Ausonius and the late Greek epigrammatist Paulus Silentiarius, Rexroth wrote a version of a poem by the sixth-century Latin love elegist Maximianus (1949, pp. 43–44). Maximianus's fifth elegy describes an erotic encounter between a "Greek girl" and a central character, ostensibly the poet as an old man, while he is on an ambassadorial mission from the Roman West to the East. They are about to consummate their sexual encounter when they are foiled by the old man's impotence. This prompts an extravagant lament from the disappointed Greek woman, who claims however that she cries not for their private turmoil but for the "universal chaos" (*generale chaos*, 5.110). This extraordinary late antique text suffered its own disappointing missed opportunity in the twentieth century: It was praised by no less a critic than W.H. Auden in 1966 as a moving evocation of personal and social crisis, but the essay lay unpublished until 1995 (Bowersock 2009, p. 219). Rexroth does not include the impotence detail in his adaptation. Instead, he brings to the fore what was only a subtext in the original: Its melancholy backdrop of military failure. In Rexroth's version, the lovers' erotic encounter is interrupted when "an airplane crosses, low down/and fills the landscape with noise." He feels her "hurtling/away, abandoned on/a parachute of ruin" (1949, p. 44). Rexroth's attraction to late antique literature can be seen as part of his hostility to academic poetic criticism; like Huysmans's Des Esseintes, he is drawn to the fringes of the tradition, to the poems neglected or devalued by the academy. But he also views late antique literature through the lens of an American postwar experience, as the fragmentary records of personal life in a time of chaos. For Rexroth, the poetry of Rome's "fall," like the art of the Beat Generation, is a rebellion against the inhumanity of a nation that had lost itself at war.

Equally countercultural – though not Beat – is Gore Vidal's novel *Julian* (1964), which follows the "apostate" emperor from his childhood education to his military successes in Gaul and, then, his fateful attempt to conquer Persia. Vidal's engaging novel imagines itself as a piece of late antique Greek literature, the memoir and private diary of the emperor himself. It also describes the writing of many late Greek works (the medical texts of Oribasius, Gregory Nazienzen's invective against Julian, Julian's *Misopogon*), and it uses the orations of Libanius and the history of Ammianus Marcellinus as primary sources. Vidal's Roman emperor grows up against the backdrop of a grimly McCarthyite fourth century. "Hellenism" is blacklisted, and worship of the traditional gods has largely gone underground; "the days of toleration are over" (p. 3). Amid the "viciousness and corruption" of a newly Christianized imperial capital, "hearsay was now accepted as fact, and no one was safe" (p. 111). Julian's trenchant attacks on Christianity and Christian politics are clearly in Vidal's own satiric voice, as is his flouting of American sexual sensibilities ("among cavalry men pederasty is a tradition" p. 173). But Vidal resists merely romanticizing the apostasy of the last non-Christian emperor as a kind of Roman protoliberalism. He also gives space to Julian's own growing fanaticism, and to the contradiction between his proclamations of "universal toleration" and his ban on Christian teachers ("why if I was so tolerant of all religions did I persecute Galilean officials? For obvious reasons my answer was more sophistic than honest" p. 340). Throughout the novel, Vidal also uses the characters of the catty and eloquent Greek orator Libanius and the philosopher Priscus of Epirus to point out the absences and biases of Julian's (invented) memoir and, therefore, the holes in the historical record itself. "For better or worse, we are today very much the result of what they were then," writes Vidal in the novel's preface.

39.3 Present and Future Late Antique Literatures

In the 1980s Thomas Parkinson, the author of *A Casebook on the Beat*, would himself turn for inspiration to late antique literature. In a poem cycle entitled "Unheard of Poems by Ausonius, Certainly Forged" (Parkinson, 1987; republished and expanded, 1988, pp. 77–99), Ausonius's poetry is represented not as a dry school exercise or formal experiment; it is a poetry of melancholy, sexuality, and loss. The German slave Bissula, glimpsed tantalizingly in the extant poems, is here developed as a character. We hear for the first time Ausonius's declaration of retirement from public life, and, most poignantly, we hear his final embittered defense of the Muses against the ascetic Christian challenge of his former student Paulinus of Nola ("You say that I gave up the life of spirit/To know a world of power. Yes, to know/A world. Poets have no other business"). Parkinson envisions the relationship between Ausonius and Paulinus through a nostalgic lens of Beat camaraderie ("Abandons of poetry,/Girls, liquor, food, talk"), and he gives us one final recrimination from Ausonius to his former student ("You say I drink too much. Well, damn it, man,/I'm lonely"). In the preface to his forgeries, Parkinson toes an academic party line by introducing Ausonius only as an imitative versifier who had "no political opinions." But then Parkinson reconstructs, from fragments of Ausonius's extant texts, a vibrant inner life for the late antique poet, imagining a man who astutely critiqued the political landscape of fourth-century Rome. By juxtaposing a critical and a creative vision of the late poet's work, Parkinson implicitly draws attention to the gaps in every poetic text, gaps that the critic invariably fills according to his or her own ideological preoccupations or personal experiences. While there is nothing especially postmodern about Parkinson's desire to hear Ausonius's personal voice, a much-cited article published soon after Parkinson's poem cycle (Nugent 1990) makes such gaps in the texture of Ausonian verse a crucial aspect of the "postmodern" aesthetics of late antique Latin poetry. We are constantly being challenged, according to this argument, to transgress the boundary between poet and reader and invest the poet's text with our own meaning.

What is the future of late antique literature? Recent scholarly work has drawn valuable attention to previously neglected aspects. Queer approaches have explored homosociality and homoeroticism in late antique texts, including Christian texts; there has been more discussion of female authorship and readership in the period; and our sense of the linguistic field of the late antique period has moved beyond merely Latin and Greek. The development of new, local literary cultures in the provinces of an increasingly fragmented empire and the cultural contests over Roman identity and classical culture in Ostrogothic Italy invite postcolonial approaches. What about outside the academy? The antihero of John Kennedy Toole's Pulitzer Prize-winning *A Confederacy of Dunces* (1980) idolizes Boethius as "the very basis" of his "worldview" (1980, p. 324), and Jostein Gaarder's 1996 novel *Vita Brevis* takes the form of a letter to Augustine by the concubine he abandoned, expressing her response to the *Confessions*. Peter Porter's 2001 poetry collection *Max Is Missing* includes a poem in the persona of the sixth-century administrator and exegete Cassiodorus, on the preservation of culture in the face of impending barbarism (2001, p. 26). The Italian film *De reditu – Il ritorno* (dir. Claudio Bondi, 2003) adapts parts of Rutilius Namatianus's fifth-century travel poem, dramatizing an imagined effort to restore Rome's pagan past, and the 2009 film *Agora* (dir. Alejandro Amenábar) depicts the teaching and eventual murder of the female philosopher Hypatia in fourth-century Alexandria. But these are isolated moments of contact. Late antique literature remains a reservoir of opportunity. Traditionally devalued, it offers readers the chance for genuinely new discoveries in ancient literature. There are still great pleasures to be had for those who make it to the end.

REFERENCES

Armstrong, Tim. (2005). *Modernism: A Cultural History*. Cambridge: Polity Press.

Auerbach, Erich. (1953). *Mimesis: The Representation of Reality in Western Literature* (trans. Willard R. Trask). Princeton, NJ: Princeton University Press.

Bowersock, G.W. (2009). *From Gibbon to Auden: Essays on the Classical Tradition*. Oxford: Oxford University Press.

Brown, Peter. (1971). *The World of Late Antiquity AD 150–750*. London: Harcourt Brace Jovanovich.

Carr, Helen. (2013). Wandering poets and the spirit of romance in Helen Waddell and Ezra Pound. In: *Helen Waddell Reassessed: New Readings* (ed. Jennifer Fitzgerald), 229–251. Oxford: Peter Lang.

Cavafy, C.P. (1992). *Selected Poems* (trans. Edmund Keeley and Philip Sherrard). Princeton, NJ: Princeton University Press.

Céard, Jean. (1978). Des Esseintes et la decadence latine. *Studi Francesi* 65–66 (May–December): 297–310.

Cohn, Robert Greer. (1987). *Mallarmé's Prose Poems: A Critical Study.* Cambridge: Cambridge University Press.

Conlon, John J. (1982). *Walter Pater and the French Tradition.* Lewisburg, PA: Bucknell University Press.

Cullhed, Sigrid Schottenius. (2015). *Proba the Prophet.* Leiden: Brill.

David, Marie-France. (2001). *Antiquité latine et decadence.* Paris: Champion.

De Gourmont, Remy. (1892). *Le Latin mystique: Les poètes de l'antiphonaire et la symbolique au moyen âge.* Paris: Mercure de France.

De Gourmont, Remy. (1921). *Decadence, and Other Essays on the Culture of Ideas* (trans. William Bradley). New York: Harcourt, Brace & Co.

Evangelista, Stefano. (2015). Towards the *Fin de Siècle*: Walter Pater and John Addington Symonds. In: *The Oxford History of Classical Reception in English Literature, vol. 5 (1790–1880)* (ed. Norman Vance and Jennifer Wallace), 643–668. Oxford: Oxford University Press.

Evelyn White, Hugh G. (1919). *Ausonius.* Vol. 1. London: William Heineman.

Fitzgerald, Jennifer. (2000). "Jazzing the Middle Ages": The feminist genesis of Helen Waddell's *The Wandering Scholars. Irish Studies Review* 8: 5–22.

Fitzgerald, Jennifer. (2012). *Helen Waddell and Maude Clarke: Irishwomen, Friends, and Scholars.* Oxford: Peter Lang.

Gaarder, Jostein. (1998). *Vita Brevis: A Letter to Saint Augustine* (orig. 1996; trans. Ann Born). London: Phoenix.

Gide, André. (1996 [1902]). *The Immoralist* (trans. Richard Howard). New York: Vintage.

Gosse, Edmund. (1921). *Books on the Table.* New York: Charles Scribner's Sons.

Huysmans, Joris-Karl. (2003 [1884]). *Against Nature (A Rebours)* (trans. Robert Baldrick). London: Penguin Books.

Jenkyns, Richard. (1995–1996). Late antiquity in English novels of the nineteenth century. *Arion* 3: 141–166.

McGill, Scott. (2018). Reading against the grain: Late Latin literature in Huysmans' *À rebours.* In: *Reading Late Antiquity* (ed. Sigrid Schottenius Cullhed and Mats Malm), 85–104. Heidelberg: Universitätsverlag Winter.

Nisard, J.M.N.D. (1834). *Études de moeurs et de critique: Les poètes latins de la décadence.* 2 vols. Paris: Gosselin.

Nordau, Max S. (1895). *Degeneration.* New York: D. Appleton.

Nugent, S. Georgia. (1990). Ausonius' "late-antique" poetics and "post-modern" literary theory. *Ramus* 19: 26–50.

Parkinson, Thomas. (1961). *A Casebook on the Beat.* New York: Thomas Y. Crowell.

Parkinson, Thomas. (1987). Unheard of poems by Ausonius, Certainly forged. *New Directions in Poetry* 51: 135–144.

Parkinson, Thomas. (1988). *Poems: New and Selected.* Orono, ME: National Poetry Foundation/University of Maine.

Pater, Walter. (1895). *Greek Studies: A Series of Essays.* London: Macmillan.

Pater, Walter. (2008 [1885]). *Marius the Epicurean: His Sensations and Ideas*. Kansas City, MO: Valancourt Books.

Porter, Peter. (2001). *Max Is Missing*. London: Picador.

Porter, Peter. (2009). *Better Than God*. London: Picador.

Raby, F.J.E. (1927). *A History of Christian-Latin Poetry from the Beginnings to the Close of the Middle Ages*. Oxford: Clarendon.

Rebenich, Stefan. (2009). Late antiquity in modern eyes. In: *A Companion to Late Antiquity* (ed. Philip Rousseau), 77–92. Malden, MA: Blackwell.

Rexroth, Kenneth. (1944). *The Phoenix and the Turtle*. Norfolk, CT: New Directions.

Rexroth, Kenneth. (1949). *The Signature of All Things*. New York: New Directions.

Rexroth, Kenneth. (1961). Disengagement: the art of the Beat Generation. In: *A Casebook on the Beat* (ed. T. Parkinson). New York: Thomas Y. Crowell.

Roberts, Michael. 1989. *The Jeweled Style: Poetry and Poetics in Late Antiquity*. Ithaca, NY: Cornell University Press.

Seiler, R.M. (1987). *Walter Pater: A Life Remembered*. Calgary: University of Calgary Press.

Stephan, Philip. (1974). *Paul Verlaine and the Decadence, 1882–90*. Manchester: Manchester University Press.

Symons, Arthur. (1893). The Decadent movement in literature. *Harper's New Monthly Magazine* November, 858–869.

Toole, John Kennedy. (1980). *A Confederacy of Dunces*. New York: Grove.

Travers, Martin. (2001). *European Literature from Romanticism to Postmodernism: A Reader in Aesthetic Practice*. London: Continuum.

Uden, James. (2018). Untimely antiquity: Walter Pater and the *Vigil of Venus*. In: *Reading Late Antiquity* (ed. Sigrid Schottenius Cullhed and Mats Malm), 17–32 Heidelberg: Universitätsverlag Winter.

Vance, Norman. (1997). *The Victorians and Ancient Rome*. Oxford: Blackwell.

Vance, Norman. (1999). Decadence and the subversion of empire. In: *Roman Presences: Receptions of Rome in European Culture, 1789–1945* (ed. Catharine Edwards), 110–124. Cambridge: Cambridge University Press.

Verlaine, Paul. (1948). *Selected Poems* (trans. C.F. MacIntyre). Berkeley: University of California Press.

Vidal, Gore. (1964). *Julian*. Boston: Little, Brown.

Waddell, Helen. (1927). *The Wandering Scholars*. London: Constable.

Waddell, Helen. (1929). *Mediaeval Latin Lyrics*. London: Constable.

Ware, Catherine. (2012). *Claudian and the Roman Epic Tradition*. Cambridge: Cambridge University Press.

Wilde, Oscar. (2008 [1890]). *The Picture of Dorian Gray*. Oxford: Oxford University Press.

Wilson, Edmund. (1931). *Axel's Castle*. New York: Charles Scribner's Sons.

Wood, Ian. (2013). *The Modern Origins of the Early Middle Ages*. Oxford: Oxford University Press.

FURTHER READING

No single work examines nineteenth- and twentieth-century approaches to late antique literature, but there are fine studies on particular periods. On late antiquity in nineteenth- and early twentieth- century French literary culture, see the meticulous survey of David (2001). For Victorian England, see Jenkyns (1995–1996) and Vance (1997, pp. 195–268). On changing critical visions of late antiquity as a historical period in the twentieth century, see Rebenich (2009) and Wood (2013, pp. 268–309).

Index

À *rebours* ("Against the Grain")
  (novel by Huysmans) 628–629,
  630, 637
Abbasaid Caliphate 103, 575, 576
abbots 39, 166, 394
abbreviated texts 433, 437–439
Abelard, Peter (d. 1142) 589
Abgar of Edessa 55, 362, 410
absorption, Byzantium
  period 561–562
Abū Ḥātim al-Rāzī 569, 570
Acacius of Melitene 80, 212
accents 455, 456
Achilles Tatius 223, 244
Acts of the Apostles *see* Apostles,
  Acts of
Aeneid (Virgil) 222, 244, 436, 465,
  585, 621
Aethicus Ister 292, 407
Aetius, Flavius 229, 246
Africa 38, 87, 111, 171, 187,
  545, 577

North Africa 32, 229, 272, 419,
  513, 532, 533, 562, 571, 589
Agapetus, Pope 434
Agat'angelos 81, 82, 83, 93
Agathias (d. 582) 13, 248–249, 252
agency 507–508
Aḥikar story 530–531
Aithiopika (Heliodorus) 14
Alaha-Zekha 172
Alan of Lille 282
Alaric (Visigothic leader) 228
Albanian language 88
Alcuin 457, 585
Aldhelm (seventh-century Anglo-
  Saxon poet) 34
Alexander of Aphrodisias 56, 57
  philosophical commentary 298,
  300–305
Alexander of Neckham (d. 1217) 589
Alexander Romance, The 283, 288,
  530, 531
Alexander the Great 75, 407, 444

A Companion to Late Antique Literature, First Edition.
Edited by Scott McGill and Edward J. Watts.
© 2018 John Wiley & Sons, Inc. Published 2018 by John Wiley & Sons, Inc.

Alfoldy, Geza 510
Allegorical Content of Virgil 290
Ambrose of Milan (374–397) 30, 150, 195, 270, 329, 335, 349, 395
  biblical commentary 314, 315, 317, 319
Ambrosiaster 314, 317, 320
Ammianus Marcellinus *see* Marcellinus, Ammianus
Anastasius Sinaites 408
Anastasius the Librarian 170, 246
Anatolia 92, 98
Anaximander 297
Ancient Menippean Satire 281
Ancient North Arabian language 126, 127
Ancient South Arabian language 126, 128
andarz texts (wisdom literature) 110
anegyricus Messallae 212
Annales of Nicomachus Flavianus, lost 144, 148
Anthemius (Emperor, 467–472) 29, 229, 246
anti-Chalcedonianism 63, 70, 71, 394, 560
  see also Council of Chalcedon
Antiochus (ca. 125–68 BCE) 301, 441
antiquarian literature 539–553
  definitions/terminology 539–540
  past and present 548–550
  perspectives on the past 544–547
  presenting the past 540–543
antiquity, late *see* late antiquity
Antonine Itinerary 363–364
Aphrodite 198
Aphthonius 463, 464, 475–479, 484
apocalyptic and visionary texts 14, 108–110, 262
Apocolocyntosis (Seneca) 281, 283
Apocryphal Acts, early Christian 14
Apollinaris, Sidonius *see* Sidonius Apollinaris (d. ca.489)

Apollinarius of Laodicea 226, 260, 264, 335
Apollo 198
Apollonius King of Tyre 283, 288
apologetic chronology 183
Apologia Secunda (Athanasius) 165
Apostles, Acts of 34, 80, 231, 344, 586
apostolic preaching 345
Appendix Probi 456–457
Apuleius 284, 288, 291, 525
Aquinas, Thomas 338
Arab Conquests 16, 17, 127, 132, 558
Arab ethnogenesis 127, 128
Arabia
  "Arabization" of 125
  defining 124
  linguistic heterogeneity of 125
  maps 124
  northern Arabia inscriptions 126
Arabia Felix 125
Arabian Peninsula 124, 127
Arabian/Arabic literature 123–140
  grammatical noun endings 130
  inscriptions 126–128
  and Islam 123, 124, 127, 128, 132, 135–138
  Northern Arabian graffiti 130
  "Oral Formulaic" verse 130
  phonemic vowels 129
  poetry 129–133, 138
Arabic languages 124, 130
  Ancient North Arabian 126
  Ancient South Arabian 126, 128
  and Arabic reception of late antique literature 569, 571
  classical Arabic 127
  of everyday life 130
  Modern South Arabian 126
  Old Arabic 127, 128, 129
Arabic reception of late antique literature 569–582

Arab-Islamic conquest, seventh
    century 123
Aramaic language 13, 104, 129
Arator 34, 231, 245, 273, 586
Ardā Wirāz Nāmag (The Book of
    Righteous Wirāz) 108, 109
Ardaxšīr Romance (*Kārnāmag ī*
    Ardaxšīr ī Pābagān) 115
Argonautica (Orphic) 223
Aristides, Aelius 80, 210, 332
Aristotle/Aristotelianism 11, 12, 16,
    32, 80, 194, 213, 301, 331,
    461, 525, 561, 603
  and Arabic reception of late antique
    literature 577, 580
  Aristotelian logic 330, 338, 339,
    525, 572, 599
  Categories 57, 298, 301, 303, 525
  philosophical commentary 298–
    304, 307, 309
  Physics 303, 306, 572
  and pseudepigraphy 402, 406
Armenia/Armenian literature
    75–85, 528
  and Christianity 76, 77
  "classical" literature 76
  commencement of literature
    compared to language/oral
    culture 76, 77–78
  culture 76
  ecclesiastical/theological works, in
    prose 79–81
  historians 82–84
  and Islam 80, 84
  language of Armenia 75, 76,
    77–78, 88
  Third Council of Duin (607) 94
  written literature 77
  Zoroastrianism 79, 80, 82, 83
Arnobius (c. 310) 333, 590
Ars dictaminis (art of letter
    writing) 590
Ars maior/Ars minor (Donatus) 452,
    453, 454, 455

Arsacid regime, Parthian 75, 76, 87, 95
Artes grammaticae 453, 460
ascetics/asceticism 39, 51, 89, 226,
    247, 380, 635
  Armenian 77, 80
  and Christianity 65, 236, 247, 261,
    270, 638
    Christian poetry 261, 270
  Coptic 61, 66
  epistolography 393, 394
  female 93, 320
  monastic tales 381, 382
  Syriac 51, 52, 53
Aspasius 303, 304
astrology 115, 225, 527, 528
astronomy 115, 527
Athanasius of Alexandria 39, 62, 165,
    284, 289, 410, 434
  Christian theological literature 328,
    329, 335
  hagiography 380
  The Life of Antony of Egypt 70, 380,
    381, 562
audiences
  inscriptions 517–519
  school texts 484–487
  sermons 352–353
Auerbach, Erich 633
Augustine of Hippo (395–430) 150,
    184, 248, 270, 334, 339, 453,
    597, 600, 601
  biblical commentary 314, 317,
    318, 321
  Christian theological literature 327,
    328, 335, 336–337
  City of God 614–615
  Confessions 264, 374, 375, 376,
    525, 616, 639
  and Latin literature 27, 29, 30, 31, 34
  and letters/letter collections 390,
    395, 397
  panegyrical works 209–210, 216
  and sermons 343, 349, 353
  style 614

Aurelius Victor *see* Victor, Aurelius
Ausonius, Decimus Magnus 29, 209,
    210, 270, 443, 529, 589, 590,
    612, 613, 614, 634
  epigrams and occasional
    poetry 242–245, 249,
    254, 255
  legal texts 421–422
  Mosella 32, 495
authentication of texts 403
authorial personae,
    replicating 563–564
autobiography/autobiographical
    poems 264, 373, 374,
    375–377
  political autobiography
    375–376
Avesta 106–107, 111
Avitus (d. ca. 518) 586–587
Avitus (Emperor, 455–456) 29,
    34, 35
Avitus, Alcimus Ecdicius (bishop of
    Vienne) 232
Avitus, Flavius Eparchius 229
Avitus of Vienne 629
Ayādgār ī Zarērān (Memoir of
    Zarēr) 111

Babylonian Talmud 107
Baghdad 571, 573, 576
Balkan wars (250s–270s) 146
banquet etiquette, Iran 112
Banū Saʿd ibn Thaʿlaba, tribe
    of 133
Bar Sahde 172
"Barbarian histories" 38
Barbarus Scaligeri 180
Bardaisan of Edessa (154–222) 49,
    50, 56, 57, 329
Barhadbeshabba Arbaya/
    Barhadbeshabba
    d'Bet-'Arbaye 56, 172
Bar-Maryam, Daniel 165, 172
Bar-Tabahe, Simon 172

Barwick, Karl 452, 453, 455, 458
Basil of Caesarea 62, 77, 80, 202,
    260, 353
  biblical commentary 314, 317,
    318, 323
  Christian theological literature
    335, 336
  Hexaemeron 226, 318, 319
  and school texts 473, 482, 483
Basilikos Logis (treatise) 211
Bassae suae/Gaudentius 243
Bassius, Junius 254
Bassus, Caesius 464
Baudelaire, Charles 630
Baum, Armin D. 401, 402
Beat Generation 636–638
Bede 186, 363, 457
  ecclesiastical history 170, 173
  and Western Middle Ages 584,
    585, 591
Bentley, Richard 404
van Bergen, Antoon 605
Bernard of Clairvaux (d. 1153) 589
Bethlehem 361, 362
Bible
  see also biblical commentary;
    New Testament;
    Old Testament
  Gothic 533
  Greek as language of 11
  Hebrew 11, 65, 533, 607
  King James Version 64
  narrative 262
  paraphrase 264, 314
  poetry 34, 226, 231
    New Testament 34, 230, 231,
      232, 271
    Old Testament 34, 227, 231,
      232, 271
  Sahidic 64
  topography 363
  translation *see* translation
biblical commentary 31,
    313–325, 330

see also Bible; Christian theological literature; New Testament; Old Testament
  and literature 315–317
  origins and development 314–315
  Scriptures 314, 316, 317, 319, 321
  survey 317–322
  Syriac literature 48–49
biblical epic 230–232
Bibliotheke (Photios) 145, 558, 559
biculturalism 61
bilingualism 61, 63
biography 149, 374, 377–380
  see also hagiography
  ecclesiastical history 166
  Greek 14
  vs. hagiography 378
  historical 143
  for individual and communal self-definition 379
  as "parasitic" 378
  premodern 373
  serial 172
  Syriac 52–53
bishops 69, 273, 322, 334, 361, 432, 433, 441, 508, 565
  see also priests
  and Armenian literature 78, 82, 84
  ecclesiastical history 162, 166, 172
  and Latin literature 37, 39
  school texts 472, 482
  sermons 343, 347, 348, 350, 354
  and translation 533, 535
Blaudeau, Philippe 167
Blemmyomachy (Homerizing poem) 224
Blemyomachia 407
Bodmer papyrus 225
Boethius 283, 303, 337–338, 339, 461, 613, 623
  Consolation of Philosophy 32, 282, 284, 285–287, 289, 291, 584, 588

  pre-Boethian and post-Boethian traditions 291–292
  translation 525, 526
Book of Enoch 106, 113
Book of the Hierotheos, The (Stephen bar Sudhaili) 52
Book of the Laws of the Countries 56
Bordeaux pilgrims 364
Bracciolini, Poggio 600
breviaria (epitomes) 143, 144, 149, 170, 436, 438
  see also epitomes, historical
Breviarium ab urbe condita (Eutropius) 150, 444, 591
British Library, Incunabula Short Title Catalogue (ISTC) 601
Brown, Peter 87, 539, 611
  The World of Late Antiquity 611, 628
Budé, Guillaume 603
buildings and poetry 265
*bumberazi*s (titanic champions) 96
Bundahišn (The Book of Primal Creation) 106, 114–115
Burchard of Worms (d. 1025) 589
Buzandaran (Pseudo-Faustus of Byzantium) (Agat'angelos) 82, 83
Byzantium Empire/period 17, 64, 557–568
  absorption 561–562
  Byzantium Church 557
  continuation 561
  "early" and "middle" 558
  and Greek 16
  literary criticism 564–567
  papyri 10
  replicating authorial personae 563–564
  rewriting 562–563

Caelius Sedulius 231
Caesar Gallus 152
Caesar Julian 152

Caesarea 333
Caesares (Victor) 149–150
Caesarius of Arles (502–542) 30,
    40, 354
Caesars (Julian) 283, 284, 289,
    291, 614
Cain and Abel 226
Calcidius (scholar) 12
Calvino, Italo 391
Cameron, Alan 269, 549
Cameron, Averil 378
Candidus 155
canones (regnal lists) 183
canonical texts 404, 407, 433
Canons (Shenoute) 67, 68, 69
Capella, Martianus 27, 31,
    32, 248, 288, 292,
    437, 452
  *Marriage of Philology and
    Mercury* 283–284, 291,
    452, 589
Cappadocian formula 336
Capture of Troy (Triphiodorus) 222
Cardigni, Julieta 290, 291
Carmen contra paganos (anon)
    269, 270
Carmen Paschale (poetic version of the
    Gospels) 34, 586
Cassian, John (d. 435) 39
Cassiodorus 153, 420, 434, 437, 457,
    525, 584, 585
  and chronicles 182, 184
  and ecclesiastical history 164,
    165, 170
  *Institutions of Divine and Secular
    Learning* 28, 434
  and Latin literature 28, 29, 34,
    35, 38
Cassius Dio 145, 148
Categories (Aristotle) 57, 298, 301,
    303, 525
Catholic Church/Catholicism 38, 94,
    173, 376, 604, 608
Cato, M. Porcius 407, 495

Caucasian region 87–88, 90, 92, 94
  see also Georgia/Georgian literature
  aristocracy 95
  Caucasian Mountains 87, 88
  and Iran 91–92, 99
  Parthians 95
  social structure 91
Cavafy, C.P. 634–635
Cedrenus 147
Cellectio Avellana 420–421
Cellectio Sirmondiana 420, 421
Cento nuptialis (Ausonius) 242
Cento Probae (Proba) 267, 268
Cento Vergilianus (Proba) 496
centos 242, 264
Chalcedon, Council of *see* Council of
    Chalcedon
Chalcedonian formula 335, 336
Charisius 453–454, 460, 462, 463
chreia 476–477, 484–485
Chrestomathoi of Helladius 439–440
Christian history
  Iranic colors 97–100
  Latin 37–40
Christian literature
  see also Christian theological
    literature
  autobiographical 376
  classical/Christian binary 4–5
  Middle Persian 113–114
  pseudepigraphy 407–411
Christian poetry 225–227, 257,
    259–280
  epitaphic verse 254
  Golden Age for Christian verse
    270, 271
  Greek 260–266
  Latin 266–273
  and paganism 261, 263, 269, 270
Christian theological literature
    327–342
  see also biblical commentary
  definitions/terminology 327–331
  emergence of 331–334

end of late antiquity, consolidation and reception toward 337–338
"Long Fourth Century" 334–337
Orthodox 335
scholasticism 330
schools of 329
Christian Topography (Indicopleustes) 367–368
Christianity
  see also Christian literature; Christian poetry; Christian theological literature; Christology; church history; ecclesiastical history; hymns; Jesus Christ
  Armenia 76, 77
  and asceticism 65, 236, 247, 261, 270, 638
  Catholic Church/Catholicism 38, 94, 173, 376, 604, 608
  conversion to 48, 262
  early languages 17
  emergence as a privileged religion in Roman period 4
  legal texts 107
  literature and poetry *see* Christian literature; Christian poetry; Christian theological literature
  monotheism 125, 332, 362
  and new genres 435–437
  Nicene 50
  as official religion of Roman Empire 404
  and paganism 261, 263, 269, 270
  Protestantism 173, 603, 608
  as religion of translation 64
  and Roman Empire 4, 87, 404, 506, 508
Christodorus of Coptus 224, 247, 249
Christology 47, 48, 49, 51, 52
Chromatius of Aquileia 170
Chronici canones (Eusebius) 183
Chronici canones (Jerome) 184
Chronicle of Arbela 55
Chronicle of Edessa 55, 56

Chronicle of Fredegar (Gregory of Tours) 592
Chronicle of Joshua 56
Chronicle of Zuqnin 55, 56
chronicles 37–38, 177–192
  see also specific chronicles
  consularia 178–182
  definitions 177–178
  following sixth century 187–188
  Greek historiography 14
  and history 143
  Syriac historiography 55
  typical late antique 183–187
Chronicon Paschale 186, 188
Chronographia (Theophanes) 180, 183
Chronographia Golenischevensis 181
Chrysostom, Dio 203–204
Chrysostom, John 62, 335, 354, 410
  and Byzantium period 559, 560
  On the Priesthood 350, 353
  and sermons 343, 344, 346, 347, 349, 350–351, 352
Church Fathers 79, 336, 339, 441, 535
  and Byzantium period 559–560, 564, 565
  and early modern receptions of late antique literature 597, 598, 603–604, 606, 607
  Egyptian 566
church history 92, 153, 164, 165, 167, 169, 172
  see also ecclesiastical history
Church History (Eusebius) 328, 333
Church of St. Polyeuctus 251
Church of the Holy Sepulchre, Jerusalem 362
Church of the Nativity, Bethlehem 362
Cicero 31, 195, 212, 215, 525, 526, 592, 605
  Epistles 615
  and letters/letter collections 389, 391, 393–395, 397–398

Circus Maximus 254
City of God (Augustine) 614–615
classicizing of history/historical epitomes 143–159
classroom practice 479–484
Claudian, works of 29, 32, 195, 209, 254, 529, 632
  De raptu Proserpinae 230, 588–589
  epic poetry 223, 228–229, 230
  epigrams and occasional poetry 245, 246, 247, 254, 255
  and Gibbon 613, 615, 616
Claudius Gothicus II 214
Claudius II (r. 268–270) 145
Claudius Mamertinus 210, 216
von Clausewitz, Carl 497
Clemens, Aurelius Prudentius 233
Clement of Alexandria 162, 261, 332
Codex Gregorianus 418
Codex Hermogenianus 418
Codex of Visions 225, 262
Colet, John (1467–1519) 602
Collected Discourses (Gregory the Illuminator) 81
Collectio Avellana (collections of papal letters) 35
Colluthus 222, 224
Columba (Celtic poet) 256
Comes, Marcellinus 38
Cominianus 454
Commentaria in Aristotelem Graeca (*CAG*) 305
commentaries 6
  Avesta, on 106–107, 111
  biblical 313–325
    Syriac literature 48–49
  covering a whole work 303–305
  defining the commentator 307–309
  determining what counts as commentary 298
  and exegesis 299–300
  formal 299
  philosophical 297–312
    background 297–299
    discursive evaluation 302
    essays and short lectures 302
    forms 300–305
    isagogical issues 300
    paraphrase 302–303
    partial or selective comments 303
    summary 302–303
    techniques and strategies 305–307
  "running" 299, 300, 303–305
  scriptural 345
Commentary on Aristotle's Categories (Sergius of Reshaina) 54, 57
Commentary on Aristotle's Categories (Simplicius) 303
Commentary on Aristotle's Physics (Simplicius) 302
Commentary on Plato's Theaetetus 298
Commentary on The Dream of Scipio (Macrobius) 290
Commentary on the Gospel of St. John (Cyril of Alexandria) 264, 315
Common Era 473
Commonitorium, The (Orientius) 33, 272
competition 494–496
compilations
  see also abbreviated texts; condensed texts
  Florilegium 439–441
  forms 442–443
  transformation of texts into new and condensed forms 443–445
Complaint of Nature (Alan of Lille) 282
Concerning Iconoclasm (Vrt'anes K'ertol) 81
condensed texts 435, 437–439
  transformation of original texts into condensed forms 443–445
Conferences (Cassian) 39
Confessio of Patrick 40

Confessions (Augustine) 264, 374, 375, 376, 525, 616, 639
Conrad of Hirsau 588
Consentius 452, 453, 459
   De barbarismis et metaplasmis 459, 463–464
Consolation of Philosophy (Boethius) 32, 282, 284, 289, 291, 584, 588
   extraordinary verses 285–287
consolation of temporality 285
Constans 211
Constantina 269
Constantine Porphyrogenitus 145, 146
Constantine the Great (272–337) (Emperor, 306–337) 37, 94, 334, 343, 362, 380
   and inscriptions 506, 510
   legal texts 421, 423–426
   letter about Proculus 510, 512, 514, 515, 517, 518, 519
Constantinople 148, 170, 179, 197, 216, 261, 348, 353, 383, 432, 563
   and antiquarian literature 541, 549
   and Armenia/Armenian literature 80, 83
   Councils 183, 335, 408, 409, 411, 543
   elite 245
   and epic poetry 224, 227
   and epigrams/occasional poetry 246, 252
   and epistolography 393, 394
   foundation 557
   and Georgia/Georgian literature 94, 100
   and Greek language/literary works 13, 16
   hippodrome 542
   Justinian 153, 262
   and Latin literature 30, 34, 38
   law schools 528
   monuments 265
   Patriarch of 17, 250
   and pseudepigraphy 409, 411
Constantius 39–40, 152, 211, 216, 621
Constantius Chlorus 427
Constantius II 149, 150, 437
consularia 178–182
Consularia Caesaraugustana 182, 186
Consularia Italica 178–182, 186
Consularia Marsiburgensia 181–182
Consularia Scaligeriana 180–181
Consularia Vindobonensia 180, 181, 182
Conte, Gian Biagio 288
Contra Celsum (Origen, 248 CE) 12, 333
Contra Symmachum (Prudentius) 255, 269, 272
Conversion of K'art'li 92–95, 98
Coptic language and literary culture 61–74
   see also Shenoute (Coptic author, 347–465); White Monastery (near Panopolis)
   church history 165
   codices 64–65
   early Coptic manuscripts 64
   and Greek language/literary works 10–11, 63, 66, 71
   history 62–63
   meaning of "Coptic literature" 63
   Nag Hammadi, codices discovered at 65
   Old Coptic (traditional Egyptian religion) 63, 64
   original 66–71
   origins of Coptic literature, and translation 64–66
   problems with Coptic manuscripts 62–63
   and pseudepigraphy 411

Coptic language and literary
    culture (*cont'd*)
  replacement of Coptic with Arabic as
    language of Coptic
    Christians 62
  Scriptures 532
  syntax 68
  translation 64–66
copying of manuscripts 601
Corippus, Flavius Cresonius
    (African poet) 30, 32, 209,
    229, 245, 246
Cornelius Tacitus 144, 149
*Corpus Areopagiticum/
    Dionysiacum* 411
Corti, Maria 391
Cosmas Indicopleustes 14,
    367–368
Council of Chalcedon 47, 61, 409
  Christian theological literature
    336, 337
  Fourth Ecumenical (451)
    94, 169
  opposition to 63, 70, 71, 394, 560
Council of Constance 603
Council of Constantinople 335
Council of Ephesus 409, 529
Council of Nicaea 334, 409
Council of Trullo 409
Cox, Patricia 379
Creation, the 34, 50, 170, 256
  biblical commentary 317, 318,
    319, 321
  chronicles 182, 184
  epic poetry 231, 232
Creed, the 49
Crete, conquest of (960–961) 562
Cretensis, Dictys 444
Cribiore, Raffaella 482, 484
Croke, Brian 186
Crucifixion 268
cultural texts, Pahlavi (Middle Persian)
    literature 112–113
Cupid and Psyche (Apuleius) 291

C'urtaveli, Iakob 89
Cynic-Stoic diatribe 346, 347
Cyprian (Heptateuch Poet) 34, 40
Cyprian of Antioch, St. (Eudocia) 227,
    242, 264
Cyprian of Carthage 334
Cyprian of Gaul 314, 317, 322, 601
Cyril of Alexandria 80, 264, 336, 337
Cyrillona 50
Cyrus of Panopolis 246
Cyrus the Great 75

al-Ḍabbī of Kūfa, al-Muafaḍḍal ibn
    Muḥammad (d. 780 or
    786) 133
Dādestān ī Dēnīg 110
Daia, Maximinius 409
Damascus (ca. 458–538) 302
Damasus, Pope (ca. 305–384) 269
Damian (578–607), patriarchate
    of 63, 71
Daniel of Tur Abdin 171
Dante 108
Dares of Frigia 37, 40
Darial Gate 88
Darius the Great 75
Das systematische Lehrbuch
    (Fuhrmann) 492
Day of Judgment 262
De barbarismis et metaplasmis
    (Consentius) 459, 463–464
de Gourmont, Remy 631
De medicamentis (Empiricus) 495,
    498, 499
De principiis (Origen) 332–333,
    334, 339
De raptu Proserpinae (Claudian) 230,
    588–589
De Reditu Suo (Rutilius
    Namatianus) 32–33, 367
De Viris Illustribus (Jerome) 162, 328,
    329, 333, 377
De vita sua (Gregory of
    Nazianzus) 374, 377

decadent and aesthetic late antique
    literature 628–633
Deipnosophists (Athenaeus) 284, 289
Demosthenes 316, 558
Deñkard (Acts of Religion) 107,
    111, 114
Descriptio Consulum 178, 179, 182,
    184, 186, 188
Description of St. Sophia (Paul the
    Silentiary) 264
Description of the Ambo of St. Sophia
    (Paul the Silentiary) 265
Desiderius of Cahors (d. ca. 655) 35
Deuteronomy 69
Dexippus, Publius Herennius (of
    Athens) 145, 146, 147, 148
Dialogus super Auctores (Conrad of
    Hirsau) 588
Diatessaron of Tatian 48, 533
dictionaries 106, 113, 585
didactic poems/texts 110, 225,
    255, 263
Didascalia Apostolorum 138,
    408–409
Digest 419, 529
Dillon, John 300, 422, 423, 424
Dio, Cassius 145, 148
Diocletian (284–305) 28, 409, 418,
    508
  Edict on Maximum Prices 421,
    507, 514
Diodore (theologian of the East Syriac
    Church) 49, 50, 54, 335
Diodorus of Aphrodito 245
Diogenes the Cynic 572
Diomedes 452, 454, 460, 461, 463
Dionysiaca (Nonnos of Panopolis)
    13, 221
Dionysius of Halicarnassus 196
Dioscoros of Aphrodito 224
Dioscorus of Alexandria 70, 266
Diphilus 210
Disticha Catonis/Dicta Catonis
    255, 407

Divinarum institutionum libri vii
    (Lactantius) 333,
    334, 587
Divine Comedy (Dante) 108
Doctrine of Addai 47, 55
Donatio Constantini 411
Donatism 171
Donato, Antonio 285–286
Donatus 458, 459, 460
  Ars maior/Ars minor 452, 453,
    454, 455, 465
Donner, Fred 136
Doody, Aude 496
Dositheus 462
Dracontius (ca. 455–505) 30, 34,
    272, 273, 590
Draxt ī Asūrīg (The Assyrian
    Tree) 108
Dream of Scipio (Cicero) 31
Drepanius, Pacatus 215
Droge, Arthur J. 138
Dronke, Peter 281
Drueger, Derek 377
Dura Europos 365

early modern period
  humanism 597, 598, 599, 600
  Jerome (Saint) 604–608
  late ancient texts, encountering in
    context of 599–604
  reception of late antique literature
    in 597–610
Eberhard the German
    588, 589
ecclesiastical history 161–175
  Armenian literature 79–81
  biography 166
  conflict 38
  development 168–173
  genre 163–166
  hagiography 166
  origins 162–163
  preservation of texts 168
  and theology 166–167

Ecclesiastical History (Eusebius of
    Caesarea) 55, 70, 164,
    171, 378
*Eclogarum in libros historicos Veteris
    Testamenti epitome* (Procopius
    of Gaza) 441
Eclogues 244
Edessa 171, 362, 382
    archives 53
    dialect 532, 533
    School of the Persians in 51,
        52, 56
    and Syriac literature 47, 50–53,
        55, 56
Edict of Milan (313) 409
Edict on Maximum Prices
    (Diocletian) 421, 507, 514
editions
    inscriptions 508–510
    printed 602
Edwards, M.J. 374
Egeria 39, 362
Egypt
    see also Coptic language and literary
        culture
    10-day week 542
    Bohairic language 64
    church 70
    Church Fathers 566
    Egyptian monks 66
    Hellenistic 528
    monastic life 481
    monks of 381
    Olympiodorus of Thebes 154
    papyri 10, 524
    traditional religion (Old Coptic)
        63, 64
Ehrman, Bart D. 401, 408
Eight Books of Miracles (Gregory of
    Tours) 592
EKG (*Enmannsche Kaisergeschichte*)
    149, 150, 184, 438
ekphrastic poems 224
Elean Olympics 203

elegiacs 248, 249, 250, 255, 587, 588
Elias Of Merw 172
Eliot, T.S. 634
Elishe 82
eloquentia (speaking well) 500
Elpidius, Rusticus 250
ELQ (*Evangelium libri quattuor*)
    (Juvencus) 230
Emmel, Stephen 68
Empedocles 297
Empiricus, Marcellus 495, 498, 499
encomiastic poetry 248
encomium (praise of individuals)
    194, 205
encyclopedias 107, 145, 248, 256,
    289, 442, 465, 550, 561, 585
    abbreviated and condensed
        texts 438, 439
Endelechius 271, 272
Enipeus 199
Enmann, Alexander 149
Enmannsche Kaisergeschichte
    (EKG) 149, 150, 184, 438
Enneads (Plotinus) 12
Ennodius of Pavia (473/474–521) 27,
    29, 35, 248, 253, 254, 273,
    284, 437, 590
Ephemeris Belli Troiani (Dictys of
    Crete) 406
Ephereridos (Dictys of Crete) 37
Ephrem Syrus (d. 373) 47–50, 51, 52,
    53, 80
Epic Cycle 222
epic poetry 221–240, 321
    Christian 264–265
    Greek epic 221–227
    Latin 227–233
epic texts, Pahlavi (Middle Persian)
    literature 110–111
epideictic oratory 193–208
    defining 'epideictic,' 194–195
    epitaphios (prose eulogy) 202
    epithalamium 198–200
    festal oration 197, 202–204

geographical texturing 198–199
monody 200–201
persuasion 205
praise and blame 211
prose 193
pure display 196
rhetoric 194, 212
social aspects 196–197
sophistry 204–205
speeches as a literary genre 197
topoi 196, 201
Epigramma Paulini 272
epigrammatists 252, 253
epigrams 242, 249, 251–253, 254, 256, 376, 524
and Christian poetry 264, 269
epigraphic poems 251, 253–254
Epiphanius of Salamis 66, 80, 335
epistolary collections 245
epistolography 389–400, 492
see also *Abar Ēwēnag ī Nāmag Nibēsišnīh* (On the Manner of Book/Letter Writing)
Ars dictaminis (art of letter writing) 590
complexity 389
Constantine's letter about Proculus 510, 512, 514, 515, 517, 518, 519
forged letters 410
innovation
individual letter 396–398
late antique letter collection 394–396
late antiquity as Golden Age 390
Latin 34–36
letter collections 10, 389, 394–396
Roman letter collections in later period 390–394
macrotext 391, 395
misconduct 393
papal letters 35
senatorial 398

Syriac literature 54–55
travel/pilgrimage literature 360–362
epitaphios (prose eulogy) 202
epitaphios logos ("funeral speech") tradition 212
epithalamia 30, 198–200, 247, 248
Epitoma (Vegetius) 497
Epitoma rei militaris (Renatus) 497
Epitomē of Theophrastus' On Sense Perception (Priscian) 303
Epitomē of Theophrastus' Physics (Simplicius) 303
epitomes, historical 6, 36, 143–159, 443–445
Erasmus, Desiderius (1466–1536) 205, 604–608
Eriugena, John Scotus 12, 338
essays, philosophical commentary 302
Ethiopia, Axumite Kingdom of 14
Ethnica (Stephen of Byzantium) 144–145
Eucharist 318
Eucharisticos (Paulinus of Pella) 33, 249, 272, 376
Eucheria (Gallo-Roman aristocrat) 253
Eucherius of Lyons (d. ca. 449) 38
Euclid 525, 527, 577
Eudocia (Empress) 227, 264, 362, 369
epigrams and occasional poetry 242, 246, 251–252, 254–255
Eugenius 243
Eugenius II (Bishop of Toledo) 256
Eunapius 146–147, 148, 396
Euric (Visigothic king, 466–484) 29
Eusebius of Caesarea (ca. 260–339) 55, 76, 97, 148, 161–163, 166, 170, 172–173, 210, 246, 363
and biography 379–380
and chronicles 183, 184, 187, 188, 561

Eusebius of Caesarea (ca. 260–339) (*cont'd*)
   Church History 328, 333
   Ecclesiastical History 55, 70, 164, 171, 378
   and Greek language/literary works 13, 14
   and Latin literature 37, 38
   Laus Constantini 209, 217
   and pseudepigraphy 408, 411
Eutropius (fl. ca. 375) 37, 149, 153
   Breviarium ab urbe condita 150, 444, 591
Eutychianism 441
Evagoras (Isocrates) 200, 212
Evagrius of Pontus 52, 63, 79, 161, 164, 170
Evagrius Scholasticus 13–14, 148, 162, 169
Evangeliorum libri IV (Juvencus) 267
Evangelium libri quattuor (*ELQ*) (Juvencus) 230
Evangelus 546
Evelyn-White, H.G. 634
Excerpta Latina Barbari 180
Excerpta Sangallensia 180
exegesis 63, 81
  epic poetry 231, 233
  Homeric 222
  philosophical commentary 299–300, 305, 307
  rabbinic 314
  Syriac literature 48–49
Exempla elocutionis (Messius) 460
Exodus 34, 48, 232, 267
Expositio totius mundi et gentium 367
Expositions of the Psalms (Augustine) 347
Expositions of the Psalms (Cassiordorus) 584
Ezekiel, commentary on 31
Eznik Kolbac'i (390–455) 79–80

fables 477–478, 485–486
Facta et Dicta memorabilia (Maximus) 431
Fasti Ostienses 178
Faventinus, Cetius 497
Febronia of Nisibis, martyr text of 382–383
Felix, Flavius 243
festal oration 197, 202–204
festivals 194, 197, 203, 543
fictional writing 14
Figulus, Nigidius 541
figural poetry 242, 243, 266
Filocalus (calligrapher) 37
Firminus 396
Fisher, Greg 128, 138
Flavian of Antioch 347
Flavianus, Virius Nicomachus 144, 148, 150, 545
Florilegia 436, 437, 438, 439–441
Florilegium Marcianum 440
Florus, L. Annaeus 149
forgeries 402, 407, 410
  see also pseudepigraphy (falsely-attributed works)
  anti-Jewish 408–409
  apologetic 410
  Le Mans Forgeries 411
form, and genre 7
Fortunatus, Venantius (ca. 530–600/609) 5, 30, 33, 34, 35, 232–233, 464, 588, 635
  epigrams and occasional poetry 242–243, 250, 255
Forum of Trajan, Rome 246, 254, 509, 510, 516, 517, 518
Fotheringham, John Knight 184
Four Books of the Evangelists (Juvencus) 585
Fragmenta Vaticana 421
Frahang ī Ōīm-ēwag (Middle Persian dictionary) 113

Frahang ī Pahlawīg (Middle Persian dictionary) 113
frahangestān, "House of Culture." 112–113
French Symbolists 632
Frier, Bruce 419
Frodebert of Paris 35
Fronto 209, 212, 252
Fuhrmann, Manfred 492
Fulgentius (fl. ca. 500) 284, 288, 290, 592

Gaius 301
Galen 16, 57, 304, 405, 444, 494, 497, 527, 559, 570, 576
Gallic Chronicle (452) 185
Gallic Chronicle (511) 185
Gamaliel (Jewish patriarch) 10
Garsoian 95
Gaufrid of Vitry 589
Gaul, state of 32, 33, 36
  collapse 185, 255
  Germanic tribes in 272
  post-invasion 248
Gautier, Théophile 630
Gelasius of Caesarea (d. 395) 92, 168
Gellius, Aulus 434, 440
Genesis 34, 48, 232, 267, 323, 441
  biblical commentary 314, 317, 318, 321
Gennadius 186
genres
  ecclesiastical works 163–166
  epideictic speeches 197
  and form 7
  Greek 13, 14
  itineraries 364
  new genres and Christianity 435–437
  parahistoriographical 162
  sermons 346–347

geographical texts, Pahlavi (Middle Persian) literature 110–111
George of Alexandria 619
George/Georges of Pisidia 5, 13, 225, 226, 256, 266, 565, 566
Georgia/Georgian literature 88–102
  see also Caucasian region; K'art'li region
  acculturating Parthians 95, 96
  Christianization of eastern Georgia 93
  Church 94
  conversion stories 92–95
  earliest original 88–91
  hagiography 88–91, 92, 98, 99
  Hambavi mepʻetʻa 96, 98, 99
  historiography 95–96, 99, 100
  inscriptions 91–92
  Iranian Commonwealth 91–92
  and Islam 89, 98
  K'art'li, Christian 91–92
  K'art'velian monarchy 88, 97, 98
  and language 88, 91
  vitae 89, 90
  Zoroastrianism 87, 89, 90, 91, 94, 95, 97, 99
Georgics, books of (Virgil) 244, 271
Gibbon, Edward 151, 217, 218, 592, 611–626
  case study on Ammianus Marcellinus 617–622
  The History of the Decline and Fall of the Roman Empire 611, 613, 616, 623–624
  reading of late antique literature 614–617
Gide, André 634, 635
Gigantomachy (Claudian) 223
Gildo (African warlord) 228
Gizistag Abāliš (The Accursed Abāliš) 108
Gnostics 306
Golden Ass (Apuleius) 288
Golden Verses of Pythagoras 304

Gospels 64, 66, 230, 532
  apocryphal 163
  Christian poetry 267–268
  Christian theological literature 329
  Diatessaron of Tatian 48
  Gospel of John 13
  Juvencus's versification of 33–34
  and sermons 344
  set into Georgian 89
  synoptic 227
Gosse, Edmund 634
Grafton, Anthony 408
grammar 451–470
  accents 455, 456
  bilingual texts 462
  books 28
  grapho-phonemes 455
  Interpretari 464–466
  Latin 451–455
  lexicon/lexica 461–463
  metrics 453, 463–464
  morpholexical level 457–458
  orthography 456
  parts of speech 457–458
  punctuation signs 455
  and rhetoric 458–460
  sublexical level 455–457
  syllables 455
  syntax 460–461
  textual typology 451–455
  translation 528
  virtues vs. vices 459
grapho-phonemes 455
Gratiarum Actio (Ausonius) 29, 209
gratiarum actiones 212, 213
Graumann, Thomas 330
Great Western Schism 603
Greco-Roman historiography 163
Greek Christian poetry 260–266
  and buildings 265
  Christian epics 264–265
  liturgy 13, 261–262
  poetics, Christian 260–261
  spiritual uses 262

Greek education 403, 525
Greek epic poetry 5, 13, 221–227
  see also Greek language/literary works
  Christian 225–227
  didactic 225
  ekphrastic poems 224
  hexameters 224, 226
  iambics *see* iambics
  mythological 222–223
  panegyrical 223–225
Greek epigraphical poetry 251
Greek language
  classical vs. late antique role 10
  and Coptic language 10–11, 63, 66, 71
  dispute between Christians and Neoplatonic philosophers 12–13
  knowledge of 602
  as medium of theological exchange 11
  New Testament 11
  sociocultural role 9, 15
  translation into Syriac 12, 15, 16, 56–58, 526, 533
  value in late antiquity 9–10, 12, 15, 16, 17
Greek literature
  biography 14
  ecclesiastical history 168
  letters and letter collections 10, 390
  novels 14, 361, 531
  and Pahlavi literature 114–115
  pseudepigraphy 402
  rhetoric 68
  theological and monastic texts 15–16
Greek Middle Ages 145
Greek philosophy 11–12, 54
  see also Aristotle/Aristotelianism; Plato; Socrates

Greek Textbooks of Prose Composition and Rhetoric (*Progymnasmata*) (Kennedy) 472
Gregory of Nazianzus (late 320s–390) 47, 58, 77, 263–264, 353, 374, 506
  and Byzantium period 558, 560, 565
  Christian poetry 260, 261, 262, 376
  Christian theological literature 335, 336
  De vita sua 374, 377
  epic poetry 221, 225, 226
  epideictic oratory 202, 203
  epigrams and occasional poetry 248, 249–250, 251
  and letters/letter collections 391
Gregory of Nyssa 202, 335, 336, 361, 616
Gregory of Tours (573–594) 38, 153, 186, 592
Gregory the Great (590–604) 31, 35, 584, 604
Gregory the Illuminator 77, 78, 81, 83, 95
Grigor Arsharui (650–729) 81
Gwrobandak/Evstat'i (Iranian hero) 89–90, 91

al-Ḥārith al-Kindī, Ḥujr ibn 134
Hadjakhapatoum Djark 81
Hadrian 225
Hägg, Tomas 374
hagiography 374–375, 380–381
  see also biography
  Armenian 78
  vs. biography 378
  centrality in late antique literature 373–374
  Christian 37–40
  desert fathers 39
  ecclesiastical history 166
  epic poetry (Latin) 232–233

Georgian 88–91, 92, 98, 99
  monastic 39
  multiform nature of 380
  prologues 380
  prose 264
  scholarship 373
  Syriac 52–53
Hall, Stuart 378
Hambavi mepʿetʿa (Georgian composition) 96, 98, 99
hamīstagān (limbo or purgatory) 109
handbooks 6, 474, 475
  and *Florilegium* 439–441
Hariulf of Saint-Riquier (d. 1143) 590
Harklean/Syro-Hexaplan translations (c. 616) 15
Harpur, James 286
Harris, Joseph 281
Hazār Afsān (A Thousand Tales) 116
heaven 109
Hebraic Questions on Genesis 315
Hebrew 13, 264
  Hebrew Bible 11, 65, 533, 607
  see also Old Testament
Hebrews 352
Hector, monodies of 200
Hegesippus 162
Heliodorus 14, 406
hell 108, 109, 268
Helladius of Antinupolis 245, 256, 439–440
Hellenism/Hellenistic period 11, 148, 149, 183, 260, 285, 345
  pseudepigraphy 403, 405
Hellenization 15
Helm, Rudolf 184
Heptateuch 34
Heraclianus 245
Heraclitus 297
Heraclius 55, 93, 156, 225
hermeneutics 298, 330
Hermogenes of Tarsus 461, 474
Herod 547
Herodotus 143, 144

Heroides (Ovid) 244
hero-kings 95, 97
Herzog, Reinhart 230, 330
Hesiod 222, 227, 331, 485
Hexaemeron (Basil of Caesarea) 226, 318, 319
hexameters 224, 226, 243–245, 250, 406
   Christian poetry 266, 272, 273
   hexameter panegyrics 209
   Homeric 264
Hieracas 66
Hierocles 304
Hilary of Poitiers (315–367?) 248, 270, 335
Hill, Charles 346
Himerius 198, 199–200, 201, 203
Ḥimyar peoples 125–126
Ḥimyaritic language 125, 126
Hippocrates 304, 402
Hippolytus 55, 80, 332, 333
Historia Augusta (collection of imperial biographies) 36, 37, 149, 150, 407
Historia Nova (Zosimus) 146–147
historians 147
   Armenian 82–84
   Byzantine 148
   Latin 38
historiography
   see also historians; history
   classical 162
   Georgian 95–96, 99, 100
   Greco-Roman 163
   Greek 13–14
   Latin 36–37, 144, 149, 153, 156
   parahistoriographical genres 162
   Syriac 14, 55–56
   travel/pilgrimage literature 368
historiography/historical writing 110–111
history
   see also historians
   Christian 37–40, 97–100
   and chronicles 143
   church history 92, 153
   classicizing 143–159
   Coptic literature 62–63
   ecclesiastical *see* ecclesiastical history
   historical epitomes 6, 36, 143–159
   "real" 167
   received 95
History of the Decline and Fall of the Roman Empire, The (Gibbon) 611, 613, 616, 623–624
history writing, Latin 36–37
Holy Land 39, 361, 365
   see also Jerusalem
   monasteries in 89
   sacred sites in 361–362
Homer 37, 200, 218, 242, 331, 435, 443, 444, 480, 546, 558
   see also Iliad
   Christian poetry 260, 264, 267
   composition principles 264
   epic poetry 222, 227, 230
   hexameters 264
   philosophical commentary 297, 298, 306
   poetic language of 297
homilies 13, 63, 81, 346, 352
   Homilies (Gregory of Nazianzus) 58
   Homilies (Pseudo-Clementine) 408, 410
   Homilies on Genesis (Origen) 314, 317
   Homilies on Providence (Theodoret) 167
Honorius 228
Horace 31, 250, 251, 259, 319, 433, 614, 629
   and grammar 464, 465
Hoyland, Robert 127
Hrip'sime (martyr) 81
humanism 456, 597, 598, 599, 600
Huns 36, 50
von Hutten, Ulrich 608

Huysmans, Joris-Karl 628–629, 630, 637
Hydatius of Tuy (d. 469) 38, 185
hymnody 244, 248
hymns 48, 64, 106, 114, 226, 244, 248, 250, 256, 317, 377, 530
see also Christian poetry; Christian theological literature; Christianity; liturgy
  Armenian literature 79, 81
  and Christian poetry 261, 262, 263, 270, 271, 273
  Homeric 263
  Latin 33, 248
  liturgical 262
  Neoplatonic 248
  and Western Middle Ages 584, 586
Hypatia 393, 639

iambics 224, 250
  iambic meters 256
  iambic trimeters 250
Iamblichus (ca. 245–325 CE) 300, 304
Icarius 245–246
identity 507–508
Idylls (Theocritus) 212
Iliad 200, 222
  see also Homer
Ilias Latina (abridged version of Homer, in Latin) 37, 443
images, inscriptions 514–517
immoral poetry 261
Importunus of Tours 35
In laudem Iustini Augusti minoris 30, 229, 246
In laudibus Dei 250
incantations, Greek 13
Incunabula Short Title Catalogue (ISTC), British Library 601
Indicopleustes, Cosmas 12, 14, 367–368

inflectional paradigms, bare 458
innovation
  individual letters 396–398
  late antique letter collection 394–396
inscriptions 506–521
  agency and identity 507–508
  Arabian 126–128
  audiences and reception 517–519
  editions 508–510
  engraving 507–508
  "epigraphic habit" 508
  Georgian 91–92
  images 514–517
  milestones 511, 512
  Pahlavi 104
  sources 510–512
  texts 512–514
  tombstones 511, 512
Institutes 39, 419
Institutions of Divine and Secular Learning (Cassiodorus) 28, 434
Interpretari 464–466
interpretation techniques 317
intertextuality 6, 268
Iohannis (Corippus) 246
Iran
  banquet etiquette 112
  Christian history 97–100
  culture 76, 99
  epic tradition 96
  Iranian Commonwealth 91–92
  Iranian Plateau 103
  Iranian World 103
  Middle Iranian terminology 95
  Sasanian rule 95
Iraq 133, 570, 576
Irenaeus 63, 80
Isaac, sacrifice of 226
Isagoge (Porphyry) 81
Isagoge Saluberrima (Pseudo-Soranus) 405

isagogical issues 300
Isidore of Pelusium (bishop) 10, 390
Isidore of Seville (600–636) 5, 38,
    186, 195, 249, 368, 434,
    437, 585
  and panegyrical works 215, 216
Islam 16, 58, 172, 382, 528
  see also Arabian/Arabic literature;
    Arabic languages
  analytical theological debate 108
  and Arabian literature 123, 124,
    127, 128, 132, 135–138
  and Arabic reception of late antique
    literature 570, 573, 574,
    578, 580
  and Armenian literature 80, 84
  conversion to 107
  early Islamic period 84, 105, 106,
    108, 136, 570
  and Georgian literature 89, 98
  origins 127
  and Pahlavi literature 103–106,
    110, 111, 114–115, 116
  pre-Islamic Arabian language/
    literature 123, 127, 132,
    135–136
  Shiite doctrine 570
Isocrates 200, 212
itineraries 437
  pseudepigraphy 406–407
  travel/pilgrimage literature
    363–365
Itinerarium Alexandri 406–407
Ivry, Alfred 573
IXII Panegyrici Latini (*PanLat*)
  collection 209

Jacob of Edessa 12, 16
Jacob of Serugh (d. 521) 49, 50–51,
  52, 53
Jacob of Tsurtavi 89
Al-Jallad, Ahmad 127
Jāmāsp Nāmag 109–110
James of Edessa 188

Jerome of Stridon (d. 420) 37, 39, 67,
    150, 162, 171, 242, 254, 361,
    523, 531, 532, 535, 600, 601,
    604–608
  and biblical commentary 315,
    316, 321
  Christian theological literature
    328, 329
  and chronicles 179, 183, 184,
    185, 443
  De Viris Illustribus 162, 328, 329,
    333, 377
  and letters/letter collections 393
  and sermons 347, 350
  translations 583
Jerusalem 88, 89, 361–364, 365
Jesus Christ 55, 66, 165, 172, 227,
    333, 362, 539
  see also Christianity; Crucifixion;
    Gospels; New Testament;
    Resurrection
  and Christian poetry 266, 268
  and hagiography 380, 381
Jews of Edessa 15
Job, commentary on 31
John (biblical) 230
John bar Aphthonia 54
John of Biclar 165–166, 182, 187
John of Damascus 16–17, 558
John of Ephesus 53, 55, 165, 166,
    171, 382
John of Gaza 224, 265
John of Salisbury (d. 1180) 589
Johnson, Eleanor 282, 285
Jones, Alan 133, 134
Jordanes 38, 153, 154, 368
Joseph (biblical) 50
Joseph and Asenath 534
Juanšer Juanšeriani 97
Judaism 51, 126, 135, 334
  see also Jews of Edessa;
    Old Testament
  anti-Jewish forgeries 408–409
  legal texts 107

monotheism 125
  rabbinic 534
  and sermons 345, 346
Julian (Emperor) 36, 149, 194, 211, 217, 225, 252, 260, 328, 376, 428, 506, 620, 637
  Caesars 283, 284, 289, 291, 614
  death of 393, 622
  prosimetra 284–285, 288, 289
  Schools Edict (362 CE) 226
Juliana, Anicia 251, 264
Julius Africanus 14, 162
Julius Caesar 179
Justin II (565–574) 30, 156, 246
Justinian (Emperor, 537–565) 180, 249, 264, 367, 406, 441, 508, 524, 548
  and antiquarian literature 540, 542
  and ecclesiastical history 165–166, 171
  and Greek language/literary works 14, 17
Justinianic Code 418–419, 420, 511, 592
Juvenal 614, 615
Juvencus, Gaius Vettius Aquilinus 33–34, 230, 231, 242, 321
  and Christian poetry 267, 271, 273
  and Western Middle Ages 585, 586

Ibn al-Kalbī (d. ca 820) 128
Kārnāmag ī Ardaxšīr ī Pābagān (The Book of the Deeds of Ardaxšīr) 111
K'art'li region
  see also Caucasian region; Georgia/Georgian literature
  Christianization of 91–92, 93
  Church 93
  conversion 93
  polytheism 93

K'art' lis c'xovreba (*Kartlis Tskhovreba*) 99
K'art'velian monarchy 88, 97, 98
Kawād I 105, 110
Kennedy, George 472
Kennedy Toole, John 639
Kephalaia gnostica 52
K'ertol, Vrt'anes 81
Khalidi, Tarif 138
Khorenat'si, Movses 82
Khusro I 106
Khuzistan Chronicle 55
al-Kindī 573
knowledge
  competition 494–496
  fighting, grafting and healing 496–499
  literature of 491–504
  practicability, pursuit of 500–502
  technical 493
  textualization of 499
Kolbac'i, Eznik (390–455) 79–80, 91

Lactantius (ca. 250–320) 214–216, 242, 251, 444–445, 601
  Divinarum institutionum libri vii 333, 334, 587
languages
  see also Coptic language and literary culture; Greek language
  Albanian 88
  Arabian *see* Arabic languages
  Aramaic 13, 104, 129
  Armenian 75–78
  biblical 11
  Bohairic 64
  and Christianity 17, 64
  classical 269
  Georgia 88, 91
  Ḥimyaritic 125, 126
  imperial legislation, late antique 423–427
  Semitic 124, 128
  Syriac 171

late antiquity
  chronological limits, difficulty
      defining 5
  end of, and Christian theological
      literature 337–338
  Latin grammar, textual typology
      for 451–455
  legal texts in 418–422
  and literary history 3–4
  self-reflective correspondence 10
Latin Anthology 32
Latin Christian poetry 266–273
Latin epic poetry 227–233
  allegorical 233
  biblical 230–232
  hagiographical 232–233
  mythological 230
  panegyrical 228–229
Latin literature 27–46
  see also Latin Christian poetry; Latin
    epic poetry
  Christian history and
      hagiography 37–40
  ecclesiastical history 170
  grammar 451–455, 453
  historiography/historical
      writing 36–37, 144, 149,
      153, 156
  imperial court, removal 28
  letter writing 34–36, 390
  panegyrical and secular
      oratory 28–30
  philosophy 31–32
  religious verse 33–34
  satire 291
  secular verse 32–33
  sermons 30–31
Laudes Domini 251, 266, 267
Laus Constantini (Eusebius)
  209, 217
Laus Pisonis 212
Lausiac History (Palladius) 377
Law Book of Yišoboxt 107
Layton, Bentley 69

Lazar of Parp,' 82, 83–84
Le Mans Forgeries 411
lectionaries 78
Lector, Theodore 164, 165, 167
lectures, philosophical
    commentary 302
legal texts 417–430
  Christian and Jewish 107
  Digest 419, 529
  forms and problems 418–422
  Justinianic Code 418–419, 420,
    511, 592
  language and style, late antique
    imperial legislation 423–427
  in late antiquity 418–422
  Pahlavi (Middle Persian)
    literature 111–112
  panegyrical works 427–429
  Roman Empire 417, 418
  sources 419–420
  Theodosian Code 418, 419, 420,
    421, 422, 511
  translation 528–529
Leo Grammaticus 147
Leo the Great 601
Leon VI, Emperor 562, 563
Leonidas of Terentum 252
Leoquelle 147, 148
Lerer, Seth 286
Letter 108 (Jerome) 361
letter collections *see* epistolography
*Letter of Mara bar Serapion to His Son
    Serapion* 54–55
Letter to the Athenians (Julian) 376
letter writing *see* epistolography
Levant region 89
lexicon/lexica 461–463
Libanius (pagan orator) 10, 36, 197,
    203, 204, 245, 613
  on autobiography 375–376
  and letters/letter collections 390,
    392, 393, 396
  and panegyrical works 209, 210,
    211, 212, 213, 216, 217

Liber graduum (Book of Steps) 51, 52, 54
Liber Pontificalis (collection of papal lives) 40, 181
Liberatus of Carthage 441
Libri as Marcum filium (Cato) 495
Licinianus 254
Licinius Cyriacus 431
Life of Antony (Athanasius of Alexandria) 70, 380, 381, 562
Life of Germanus of Auxerre (Constantius) 39–40
Life of Martin (Fortunatus) 33, 39
Life of Nino 93, 94, 98
Life of St. Martin (Sulpicius Severus) 232, 592
Life of the K'art'velian Kings, The 96, 97, 98, 99, 100
Life of Vaxtang Gorgasali (ca. 800) 97, 98, 99
de Lille, Alain 397
Lim, Richard 353
Lindenbrog, Friedrich 620
literacy, Greek 10
Literal Interpretation of Genesis (Augustine of Hippo) 321
literary architecture, late antique 474–479
literary criticism, Byzantium period 564–567
literature
  see also texts; specific types
  and biblical commentary 315–317
  and Christianity 40
  commenting 313
  European concepts 573
  initial conceptualization/ systematization of 402–403
  innovation in late antique literature 3–4
  technical 502
  terminology 5–6
  wisdom 110
Lithica (Orphic) 225, 406

liturgy
  Greek Christian poetry 13, 261–262
  Greek song 248
  liturgical lectionary 81
  and sermons 345, 353
  texts 78
  translation of liturgical books 78
Lives of Pachomius 70
Lives of the Eastern Saints (John of Ephesus) 53, 382
Lives of the Sophists (Philostratus) 210
Livrea, Enrico 224
Livy 182, 433, 434
Logos, the 321, 333
Logothetes, Symeon 562
"Long Fourth Century," Christian theological literature 334–337
Lucian of Samosata 204, 216, 251, 330
  prosimetra 283, 284, 287, 288, 289, 291
Lucius Septimius 303, 406
Lucretius 251
Luke (biblical) 48, 63, 80, 230
Luther, Martin 603
Luxorius 253
Lyall, Charles J. 133
Lydus, John 549
  On Celestial Signs 540, 541, 542, 543, 548
  On the Magistracies 540
  On Months 540, 541, 542, 543, 548

McMullen, Ramsay 352, 353
Macrobius Ambrosius Theodosius 31, 461, 549
  Saturnalia 256, 290, 434, 544, 546, 548, 592
macrotext 391, 395
Madaba map, Jordan 365
Madīyān ī Hazār Dādestān (The Exposition of One Thousand Judgments) 111–112

madrasha (Syriac poetic form) 50
Maiden Song 244
Majorian (Emperor, 457–461) 29, 229
Malalas, John 14, 156
Mallarmé, Stéphane 630, 632
Mamertinus, Claudius 210, 216, 428
Mamikonian, Vardan 83, 84, 89
Mani Codex 163
Manichaean literature 113–114
   in Coptic 65
   Middle Persian 113–114
Manichaeism 47, 376
Manutius, Aldus (1449–1515) 603
maps 124, 365–366
Marcellinus, Ammianus (d. ca. 400) 36, 367, 591
   case study on 617–622
   and chronicles 184, 186
   and classicizing of history 144, 146, 147, 148, 150
   and Gibbon 612, 615
   Res Gestae 37, 151–153, 368, 495
   style 618
Marcellus, Nonius 462, 463
Marcus Aurelius 225, 304
Marenbon, John 282
Marinus 227, 254
Marius Maximus 149
Marius of Avenches (d. 596) 38, 186
Marriage of Philology and Mercury (Capella) 283–284, 291, 452, 589
Marrou, Henri 472
Martialis, Gargilius 405
Martianus Capella *see* Capella, Martianus
Martin of Tours (d. 397) 39, 232, 251, 273, 588
Martyrdom of Evstatʻi Mcʻxetʻeli, The 89–90
Martyrdom of Shushanik, The 78
Martyrdom of St. Cyprian, The (Eudocia) 264

martyrs/martyr texts 33, 285, 382–383
   martyr acts 38–39
Marx, Michael 137
Mashtots 78, 79, 80, 81
mathematics 527
Matthew (biblical) 48, 63, 267
Matthews, John 422, 623
Maurus, Terentianus 464
mawzūn (measured poetry) 130
maxim 476, 484–485
Maximianus 253, 589, 635, 636
Maximus, Magnus 209, 392
Maximus, Valerius 431
Maximus of Ephesus 225
Maximus the Confessor 338
Mayer, Wendy 352
Mazdean religion *see* Zoroastrianism
Mcʻxetʻa/Mtskheta 89
   dynastic monarchs of Kʻartʻli based at 88
medical texts 404–406
   translation 526–527
Medicina Plini 494–497, 501
medieval period 15
Medinet Madi texts 65
Mediterranean region, and Greek language 9
Mediterranean region, and Greek literary works 10
Melania the Elder 362
Memnon 442
memra (Syriac poetic form) 50, 51, 52, 53, 54
Menander Rhetor 194, 195
   treatises of 53, 211
Menander II 201, 202
Menippean satire 281, 282, 288, 290, 291
Menippean Satires (Varro) 284
Mēnog ī Xrad 110
Merčʻule, Giorgi 90
Merobaudes, Flavius 209, 229, 246, 254

Meshiha Zekha 172
Mesopotamia 381
Messius, Arusianus 460
metaliterary compositions 6, 242
Metamorphoseis 288
Metamorphoses (Ovid) 425
metaphrast 264
Metaphrates, Symeon 562
metaphysical dualism 79
metaphysics 305
Metaphysics (Aristotle) 301
Methodius of Olympus 80, 244, 262
Metochites, Theodoros 563, 566, 567
metrics 453, 463–464
Metzger, Bruce M. 401
Micah of Beth Garmai 172
Middle Ages 156, 195, 232, 299, 598
  Greek 145
  High 588
  Western 583–595
Middle Persian literature *see* Pahlavi (Middle Persian) literature
Migne, J.P. 263
Mihr-Narseh 105
milestones 511, 512
Mimesis (Auerbach) 633
Minucianus of Athens 461, 474
Miphysite church 382
miracle collections 14
miracle stories 231
miracles 586
Mirian, King (K'art'velian, r. 284–361) 91, 92, 94, 95
missionary work 345
mixed-meter satire 283–285
mnemonic techniques 297
Modern South Arabian languages 126
Modernism 633–636
Mok' c' evay k' art' lisay 98
  see also Conversion of K'art'li
Momigliano, Arnaldo 540
Mommsen, Theodor 177, 179, 180, 184

monasteries 17, 77, 89, 381, 382, 432, 441, 574, 601
  see also monastic communities; monasticism; monks
  Chinese 524
  federation of 67, 68
  and translation 524, 528, 536
  travel/pilgrimage literature 361, 363, 369
Monastery of the Archangel Michael 62
  see also Monastery of the Archangel Michael
monastic communities 39, 361, 381
  see also monks; White Monastery (near Panopolis)
  and Coptic language/literary culture 62, 65, 67, 69, 70
monastic tales 381–382
monasticism 53, 66, 94, 381, 382, 536
monks 39, 66, 84, 90, 144, 166, 255, 381, 383, 394, 433, 441
  see also bishops; monastic communities
  Coptic language and literary culture 65, 66, 67, 68, 69, 70
  Egyptian 381
  and school texts 479, 480, 481
  Syrian 381
  travel and pilgrimage literature 361, 369
monody 200–201
monotheism 125, 332, 362
moral determinism 79
Moralia (Plutarch) 559
morpholexical level, grammar 457–458
Mosaics of Time 177
Moschus, John 369
Mosella (Ausonius) 32, 495
Moses 162, 165
Mount of Olives, Jerusalem 362

Mowbedān Mowbed 106
Mroveli, Leonti (Archbishop) 96, 99
Muḥammad ibn ʿAbdallāh of Mecca (Muslim prophet) 136, 137, 138
mythological epic 222–223, 230

Nabataean Kingdom/script 128, 129
Nag Hammadi, codices discovered at 65
Namāra inscription (328) 128–129
Namatianus, Rutilius (fl. ca. 415) 495, 592, 629
Narcissus 243
narrative 40, 478–479, 486–487
  Buddhist 487
  Christian 262, 268
  narrative church histories 14
Narsē 105
Natural History (Pliny) 495
Nature, call for return to 501–502
Nazarius 215
Nazianzen 202, 204
Nemesius of Emesa 335, 574
neologisms 144
Neoplatonism 11, 224, 338
Nepotianus, Januarius 444
Nestorianism 49, 113, 169, 172, 336, 409, 441
Nestorius (theologian of the East Syriac Church) 50, 54, 335, 409, 536
Neuwirth, Angelika 137
New Persian literature 577
New Testament 64, 80, 202
  see also Jesus Christ
  compared to Old Testament 34
  Florilegia 440
  Greek 603, 607
  and poetry 34, 230, 231, 232, 271
  pseudepigraphy 531
  and sermons 344
  translation 11, 17, 49, 113, 533, 534, 535

Nicaea I (325) (ecumenical council) 11
Nicaea II (787) (ecumenical council) 11
Nicaeno-Constantinopolitan creed 335, 336
Nicander 393
Nicene Creed 330, 334, 339
Nicene faith 15, 50, 168, 333, 336, 409
Nicomachus 525, 527
Nicomedia, earthquake of 201
Nicostratus of Trebizond 146
Nikephoros (806–815) 561
nineteenth- and twentieth century writing 627–641
  Beat Generation 636–638
  decadent and aesthetic late antique literatures 628–633
  Modernism 633–636
  present and future late antique literatures 638–639
Nino (holy woman) 93, 94
Nonnos of Panopolis (fl. ca. 430) 13
  Christian poetry 264
  epic poetry 221, 223, 224, 227
  epigrams and occasional poetry 252, 256
nonsense syllables 289

O.Cairo 44674.118 483–484
occasional poetry 245–246
O.Col.inv. 766 482–483
Odes of Solomon 49, 50
Ojnecʿi, Yovhannes (650–729) 81
Old Arabic 127, 128, 129
Old Syriac (Syriac version of individual Gospels) 48
Old Testament 202
  see also Exodus; Genesis
  biblical commentary 318
  Cain and Abel 226
  commentaries 48
  compared to New Testament 34

Florilegia 440
and Greek literature 11
Isaac, sacrifice of 226
miracles 586
paraphrase 260
Peshitta translation 15, 48, 49, 533
and poetry 34, 227, 231, 232, 271
Olympiodorus of Thebes 154, 155, 224, 406, 407
Oman 126
On Celestial Signs (Lydus) 540, 541, 542, 543, 548
On God/Against the Sects (Eznik Kolbac'i) 79, 80, 91
On Human Life (George of Pisidia) 226, 256
On Months (Lydus) 540, 541, 542, 543, 548
On the Priesthood (Chrysostom) 350, 353
oracles, in verse 262
oral culture 297
"Oral Formulaic" verse 130
oral literary tradition 104
oration, festal 197, 202–204
oratory
  epideictic *see* epideictic oratory
  panegyrical and secular, in Latin works 28–30
Ordo Salutationis (legal text) 419, 420
Orestes (mythological work) 32
Organon, The (Aristotle) 526
Oribasius of Pergamum 147, 493, 495, 496
Orientius (Bishop of Auch) 255, 272, 273
Origen (ca. 186–254) 31, 63, 80, 231, 315, 318, 323, 378, 379, 408
  Contra Celsum 12, 333
  De principiis 332–333, 334, 339
  Homilies on Genesis 314, 317
  sermons 345–346

Orosius (d. post 418) 29, 153, 186, 334, 368, 591
orthography 456
Ostrogothic administration 420
Otto of Freising (d. 1158) 591
Ovid 32, 244, 251, 319, 425

P. Bouriant 1 480–481
P. Cotsen-Princeton 1 481–482
Pabst, Bernhard 281
Pacatus Drepanius 215
Pachomian federation 69, 70
Pachomius (Christian monastic founder) 10, 67, 70
paganism/pagan beliefs 79, 89, 96, 147, 251, 270, 328, 560
  antiquarian literature 545, 549
  Armenia 79, 83
  and Christianity 261, 263, 269, 270
  literary material 436
Pahlavi (Middle Persian)
  literature 103–121
  apocalyptic and visionary texts 108–110
  Avesta, commentary on 106–107, 111
  Christian and Manichaean literature 113–114
  cultural texts 112–113
  dictionaries 113
  didactic texts 110
  earliest remains 104
  geographical and epic texts 110–111
  Greek and Sanskrit literature, contact with 114–115
  inscriptions 104
  and Islam 103–106, 110, 111, 114–115, 116
  legal texts 111–112
  Manichaean literature 574–575
  philosophical and debate texts (Pahlavi) 108

Pahlavi (Middle Persian) literature (*cont'd*)
　prose fiction, translation 530, 531
　Psalms 105
　Sasanian period (224–651 CE) 103, 106, 107, 114, 115
　scientific terminology 114
　technical religious terminology 114
　Zoroastrianism 103, 105–107, 109, 112, 116
*Pahlavī Rivāyat*s 107
　Pahlavi Rivāyat of Adurfranbay 110
　Pahlavi Rivāyats Accompanying the Dādestān ī Dēnīg 110
Palaemon, Remmius 453, 454
Palatine Anthology 224, 263, 264
Palestine, 17, 88
Palladius 377, 493, 498
panegyrical (laudatory discursive) works 209–220
　consular 228
　epic poetry 228–229
　flowery style (*stylum pingue atque floridum*) 29, 30, 34
　fourth century 28
　Greek 14
　hexameter 209
　inscriptions 512
　legal texts 427–429
　mini-panegyrics 36
　oratory, Latin works 28–30
　poetry 223–225
　as propaganda 217
　prose 29
　verse 29, 30, 32
Panegyrici Latini 29, 195, 212, 215, 217
panegyricus 215
Panegyricus (Pliny) 212
Pange lingua (Fortunatus) 273
Panhellenic games 197
Pannartz, Arnold 601
Pannonius subagrestis 150
papal letters 35

papyri 298
　Arabic 136
　Bodmer papyrus 225
　consularia 178
　Egyptian 10, 524
　Greek and Coptic languages 10–11
　transition from papyrus roll to codex 144, 432
parabiblical texts 534
paradise 108
paradoxical encomium 204
paradoxography 204
parahistoriographical genres 162
paraphrase 226, 243–244
　biblical 264, 314
　Christian poetry 260, 263
　philosophical commentary 302–303
　Psalms 271
Paraphrase of the Gospel of John (Nonnus) 227, 264
Paraphrase of the Psalms 264, 411
Parentalia (Ausonius) 32
Paris, Julius 431, 444
Parkinson, Thomas 636, 638
Parmenides 297
parody 291
P'arsman (K'art'velian royalty) 91
Parthians, acculturating 95, 96
Paschale Campanum 182, 187
Paschale Carmen 231, 232
Passion of Habo (Iovane Sabanis-że') 90
Passion of Šušanik, The (hagiography) 89, 94
past, the
　perspectives on 544–547
　and the present 548–550
　presenting 540–543
Pater, Walter 631, 632, 633
Patricius 264
Patrologia Graeca (Migne) 263
Paul (biblical) 80, 329
Paul of Tamma 66
Paul the Deacon (d. 799) 591, 592

Paul the Silentiary 224, 264
Paula (aristocratic traveler) 361, 362
Paulina, Fabia Aconia 253, 254
Paulinus of Béziers 272
Paulinus of Nola (ca. 354–431) 33, 395, 635
  and Christian poetry 270, 273
  epigrams and occasional poetry 247, 249
  and Western Middle Ages 587–588
Paulinus of Pella (d. post 461) 27, 33, 249, 272, 376
Paulinus of Périgueux 232, 273
Paulus of Tyre 474
Paulus Silentarius 245, 256
Pelagia of Antioch 381
Pelagius 606
Pentadius 243, 253
Pentateuch 524, 586
Pergamene Temple of Apollonis, Cyzicus 252
Pericles, funeral oration of 202
periegeseis and *periploi* 366–368
Periochae Homeri Iliadis et Odyssiae 443
Peristephanon (verses on Christian martyrs by Prudentius) 33
Peshitta biblical translation 15, 48, 49, 533
Peter of Cluny (d. 1156) 589
Petrarch, Francesco 599
Petronius 288
Peutinger, Konrad 365
Peutinger map 365, 366
Pharr, Clyde 418
Philip II of Macedon 198, 444
Philip of Side 165
Philo of Alexandria 329
Philoponos, John 12, 574
philosophy
  see also specific Greek philosophers, such as Plato
  commentary *see* commentary

  dispute between Christians and Neoplatonic philosophers 12–13
  Greek 11–12, 54, 297
  Latin literature 31–32
  Pahlavi (Middle Persian) literature 108
  and poetry 286, 287
  and prosimetra 285–286
  Syriac literature 56–58
  systematization of 11
  translation 525–526
Philostorgius (ca. 424–438) 154, 162, 164, 168, 169
Philostratus 210
Philoxenian translations (ca. 507/508) 15
Philoxenus of Mabbug (d. 523) 48, 49, 52, 53, 55
phonemic vowels 129
Photios/Photius 146, 154, 437, 440, 442, 549, 559, 564
  Bibliotheke 145, 558, 559
Physics (Aristotle) 303, 306, 572
Piacenza pilgrim 39, 364
Piccione, Rosa 441
pilgrims 363, 364, 518
Pisentius of Koptos (569–632) 71
Plato 12, 57, 80, 284, 285, 331, 402, 473, 577, 580
  philosophical commentary 297, 299–302, 305
  Protagoras 297
  Republic 65
  Timaeus 303
Platonic Theology (Proclus) 304–305
Pliny the Elder (23–79 CE) 434, 442, 495, 496, 501
Pliny the Younger (61–112 AD) 29, 34, 212, 213, 495, 614
  and letters/letter collections 390, 391, 393–398
Plotinus (205–270 CE) 12, 299–300, 301, 302, 306, 525

Plutarch 289, 304, 440, 473, 486, 559
Pluto 230, 255
Pocock, J.G.A. 612
Poemata Arcana 263
poetry
  see also epigrams; verse
  Arabian literature 129–133, 138
  autobiographical 264
  biblical 34, 226, 231
    New Testament 34, 230, 231, 232, 271
    Old Testament 34, 227, 231, 232, 271
  Christian 225–227, 259–280
    Greek 260–266
  classical 28, 259, 377, 496
  elegiacs 248, 249, 250, 587, 588
  encomiastic 248
  epic see epic poetry
  epigraphic 251, 253–254
  female poets 133, 231
  figural 242, 243, 266
  formal 125
  Greek 5, 251
  Hebraic 264
  hexameters see hexameters
  iambics see iambics
  immoral 261
  Latin 5, 266–273
  liturgical 13, 261–262
  minor 255
  occasional 241, 245–246
  panegyrical 223–225
  and philosophy 286, 287
  poetic middle way 261
  poetics, Christian 260–261
  polemical 263
  public 29
  quasi-tragedies 376
  short-form 130, 241
  spiritual uses 262
  Syriac literature 5, 49–51
  theological 49

  translation 529–530
  "wandering poets" 245
  wedding 198
polemical poems 263
Polemon 316
Polybius 162
Polycarpus 97
polymetry 248
polytheism 93, 135, 362
Pomerius, Julianus 30
Pompeius 454–455
Pomponius 242
Pontius Pilate 410
Porphyry 12, 16, 81, 458, 525, 560
  philosophical commentary 300, 302, 304, 309
Porter, Peter 639
Possidius 39
Pound, Ezra 631, 634, 635
P.Oxy. 1786 (hymn) 261
practicability, pursuit of 500–502
Praeparatio evangelica 334
Praetextatus, Vettius Agorius 216, 253, 254, 269, 525, 545
Praetorian Prefecture 540–541
Praise of Baldness (Synesius of Cyrene) 204
Praise of Folly (Erasmus) 205
praise speeches see panegyrical (laudatory discursive) works
preaching 344, 346, 347, 349, 354
  see also sermons
  apostolic 345
  audiences 352–353
  missionary 345
  scriptural commentary 345
précis 434, 464
priests 84, 94, 144, 348, 353, 526, 571
  see also bishops
  and Pahlavi literature 106, 110
  Zoroastrian 103, 116, 575
print culture 601
Prior Analytics 525
Priscian 209, 247, 303

and grammar 453, 457, 461, 462, 463, 464
Priscianus, Theodorus 495, 500
Priscus of Panium 155
Prisoner's Philosophy, The (Relihan) 282
Pro lege Manilia (Cicero) 212
Proba, Anicia Fultonia 254
Proba, Faltonia Betitia 231, 242, 267, 268, 436, 496
Probus, Petronius 254
Probus, Titius 444
Proclus 249, 304–305
Procopius of Gaza (ca. 465–525) 13, 14, 89, 163, 368, 393, 441
  and classicizing of history/historical epitomes 144, 155–156
  epigrams and occasional poetry 247, 248
Proculus, L. Aradius Valerius 508–509, 510, 512, 513, 518
  statue of 517
Prohaeresius (rhetorician) 77
Prokopios 562
Propempticon ad libellum (Sidonius Apollinaris) 495
Propertius 425
prophecy 345
prose
  Armenian ecclesiastical and theological works in 79–81
  epideictic oratory 193
  epitaphios (prose eulogy) 202
  free psalmic 248
  hagiography 264
  and mixed-meter satire 283
  panegyrical works 29
  prose fiction, translation 530–532
  theological 80–81
  and verse *see* prosimetra
proselytizing 345
prosimetra 281–295
  Consolation 285–287
  literary shifts in the second century 287–289

  mixed-meter satire 283–285
  pre-Boethian and post-Boethian traditions 291–292
  sympotic literature 289–290
prosopography 510
Prosper, Vatican epitome 182
Prosper of Aquitaine (d. ca. 455) 33, 38, 184, 187, 244, 255, 587
Protagoras (Plato) 297
Protestantism 173, 603, 608
Proverbs 64, 66, 78
Providential History 37
Prudentius (d. ca. 405) 33, 242, 250, 255, 270–271, 273, 587, 614, 635
Psalms 64, 105, 244, 346
  and Christian epics 264
  and Greek epic poetry 226–227
  paraphrase 271
Psellos/Psellus 256, 558, 563, 566, 568
pseudepigraphy (falsely-attributed works) 401–415
  alchemical writings 405
  ascriptions deliberate or not 402
  definitions/terminology 401
  forgeries 402, 407, 408–409, 410, 411
  genuine religious 407–408
  Hellenistic era 403, 405
  historical texts 406
  imitation of canonical models, in Greek education 403
  innocent 408
  intentionality 402
  late antique pseudepigraphy 404–411
  medical, technical and similar texts 404–406
  New Testament 531
  origins in antiquity 402–404
  scholarly canons 403–404
  typology 402

Pseudo-Apuleius 495
Pseudo-Aristotle 525
Pseudo-Augustine 453
Pseudo-Callisthenes 406
Pseudo-Caper 462
Pseudo-Clementine 408, 410
Pseudo-Dionysius 16, 52, 57, 337, 338, 339, 560
Pseudo-Galen 405
Pseudo-Isidorian Decretals 411
Pseudo-Isocrates 473
Pseudo-Joshua the Stylite 167
Pseudo-Probus 453
Pseudo-Soranus 405
Pseudo-Thessalus 405
Pseudo-Zachariah 165, 171
Psychomachia (allegorical text by Prudentius) 33, 271
Ptolemy 525, 527, 528, 577
public poems 29
Pus ī Dāneš Kāmag (The Youth in Desire of Knowledge) 108
Pythagoras 525

qāfiya (rhyme of final consonants) 130
qaṣīdas (odes) 130, 133, 135
Quadratus 332
quadriga Messii 460
quadrivium (arithmetic, geometry, astronomy, and music) 27
Quaestiones medicinales 405
quasi-tragedies 376
Quenneshre, monastery of 54
Querolus (theatrical work) 33
Question 45 (Ambrosiaster) 314, 320
Quintilian 195, 215, 316, 333
Quintus 222
Quodvultdeus of Carthage 352
Qur'ān 123, 124, 136, 137–138, 531–532, 570

Raby, F.J.E. 635
Radegund 243

Rape of Helen (Colluthus) 222, 224
Rape of Proserpine (Claudian) 32
Ravenna Cosmography 407
Ražden (martyr) 90
received history 95
reception (late antique literature)
    Arabic, of late antique literature 569–582
    in early modern period 597–610
    and end of late antiquity 337–338
    inscriptions 517–519
Recognitions (Pseudo-Clementine) 410
Reformation 599, 603, 608
Refutatio (Hippolytus) 333
Reginald of Canterbury (d. ca. 1109) 590
Regulae (Pseudo-Augustine) 453
Reichl, Karl 281
religious travel 362–363
religious verse, Latin 33–34
Renaissance 391, 519, 599, 612
Renatus, Flavius Vegetius 497
Renatus, Profuturus Frigeridus 153
Republic (Plato) 65
Res Gestae (Ammianus Marcellinus) 37, 151–153, 368, 495
Resurrection 266, 268
rewriting, Byzantium period 562–563
Rexroth, Kenneth 636
Reynolds, Gabriel 137
Rhetor, Zacharias 56
rhetoric (art of discourse)
    classical 262, 347–348
    epideictic 194, 212
    and grammar 458–460
    Greek 68
    public contests 197
    schools of 213
    and sermons 30
    skill, showing off 350

Syriac literature 53–54
training 10
translation 528
Rhetorica ad Herennium 215, 460
Rice, Eugene 607
Richard of St. Victor 338
rites, books of 78
Roberts, Michael 630
Roman Empire/Roman period 37
  see also *History of the Decline and Fall of the Roman Empire, The* (Gibbon); inscriptions
  Acts of the Senate 212
  and Christianity 4, 87, 404, 506, 508
  and chronicles 185
  collapse of Empire 185
  comedy 433
  decline and fall 611
  educational system 9, 10
  epideictic oratory 214
  failure of Western Roman Empire 27
  festivals 543
  Georgian historiography 98, 100
  inscriptions 506
  law/legal texts 148, 417, 418
  letter collections in the later Roman period 390–394
  mobile society 360
  papyri 10
  praise-discourse 215
  republicanism 97, 548
  Roman identity 269
Romanos the Melode 13, 262, 377, 530
Roman–Prussian war (502–506) 56
Romanus, Julius 454
Romulea (Dracontius) 230
Rufinus 31, 92–93, 161, 164, 170, 201, 251, 252, 317, 535
Rufinus of Antioch 464
Rufinus of Aquleia 523
Rufus, John 90

Rufus of Shotep 63, 71
Rules (Pachomian) 67
Ruricius of Limoges (d. ca. 510) 34
Russell, Donald 211
Rusticus Elpidius 250
Rutilius Claudius Namatianus 32–33, 367

Sabanis-że,' Iovane 90
Sabinus of Heracleia 168
Sabinus the Arian 168
Sacerdos 453, 463
Šāhnāma (Ferdowsī') 95, 96
saints 51, 70, 363, 380, 382
  see also hagiography; martyrs/martyr texts
  Christian history and hagiography 38–39, 40
  cult of 33, 38, 536
  lives of 39, 531, 562, 592
Salvian of Marseille (ca. 440) 408
Sanskrit literature 114–115, 575
Sappho, Lesbian 198, 199
Šāpūr I 104–105, 115
Šāpūr II 105
Šāpūr Sagānšāh 105
Sasanian period (224–651 CE) 97, 98, 137, 575
  Armenia (244–651 CE) 75, 76
  inscriptions 104
  Iran, governing of 95, 103
  Pahlavi literature 103, 106, 107, 114, 115
  territorial extent of Empire 105
satire 270
  Latin 291
  Menippean 281, 282, 288, 290, 291
  mixed-meter 283–285
  Roman 283
Saturnalia (Macrobius) 256, 290, 434, 544, 546, 548, 592
Satyricon 287, 288, 289
scholasticization 345

school texts 471–490
  audience 484–487
  chreia 476–477, 484–485
  classroom practice 479–484
  fables 477–478, 485–486
  "forms" of late antique literary architecture 474–479
  "fragments" of late antique literature 473–474
  maxim 476, 484–485
  narrative 478–479, 486–487
  O.Cairo 44674.118 483–484
  O.Col.inv. 766 482–483
  P. Bouriant 1 480–481
  P. Cotsen-Princeton 1 481–482
Scriptures 4, 268, 435, 481
  biblical commentary 314, 316, 317, 319, 321
  and sermons 345, 346
  translation 78, 532–534
Scythica 146
Sebeos (historian) 84
second century, literary shifts in 287–289
Second Sophistic (ca. 100–250) 144, 145, 148, 212, 304, 329
  rhetorical style 348–349
Secretum Secretorum 406
secular verse, Latin 32–33
Sedulius, Caelius 34, 231, 232, 242, 244, 273, 586
Seeck, Otto 397
Sells, Michael A. 133
Semitic languages 124, 128
Seneca 212, 281, 283, 284, 285, 288, 425
Septuagint, the 15
Sergius of Reshaina (d. 536) 16, 54, 56–57, 527
serial biography 172
Serjeant, Robert 136
sermons 343–357
  advice about 348–351
  classical rhetoric, influence of 347–348
  Coptic literature 62
  Gallic 30–31
  as a genre 346–347
  Latin 30–31
  origins 344–346
  popularity 353
  preachers and audiences 352–353
  preservation 353–354
  and rhetoric 30
  shorthand writers 353–354
  Syriac 346
  and theology works 31
Servius (fl. ca. 400) 218, 454, 545, 546, 592
Severus, Sulpicius (fl. ca. 400) 39, 200, 301
  Life of St. Martin 232, 592
Shenoute (Coptic author, 347–465) 61, 67–69, 71
short-form poems 241
shorthand writers 344, 353–354
Sidonius Apollinaris (d. ca.489) 153, 209, 229, 259, 359, 360, 495, 589, 614, 631
  epigrams and occasional poetry 246–247, 254
  Latin literature 29, 31, 32, 34–36, 40
  and letters/letter collections 391, 395, 397
Sigibert of Gembloux 185
Signature of All Things, The (Rexroth) 636–637
Sijpesteijn, Petra 136
Silentiarius, Paulus 636
Silver Age of Statius 32
Silvestris, Bernardus 282
Simeon of Beth Ashram 55
Simeon the Stylite (d. 451) 381, 635
Simocatta, Theophylact 5
Simonides 298, 300
Simplicius (ca. 480–540 CE) 12, 301–303, 307, 308

Sinai, Nicolai 137
Sirikius of Neapolis 474
Sirmond, Jacques 421, 616
sixth century
   chronicles following 187–188
   Greek historiography 13–14
Škand ī Gūmānīg Wīzār (Doubt
     Dispelling Explanation) 108
Skuthiká 146
Slavitt, David 286
Sluiter, Ineke 309
Socrates 13, 572
   ecclesiastical history 161, 163–164,
     168, 170, 171
   philosophical commentary
     297–298, 300
Socrates Scholasticus 343, 344,
   347, 444
Somnium Scipionis (Cicero) 592
Somxit'i/Gugark' (Armeno-K'art'velian
   marchland) 88, 89, 93, 94
Sopater 474
Sophists 151, 195–198, 204, 210,
   261, 331
   see also Second Sophistic (ca.
     100–250); Third Sophistic
Soranus 405
Soterichus of Oasis 222, 227
sources, inscriptions 510–512
Sozomen 13, 161, 162, 164, 168,
   169, 170, 444
Sozomenos 154
Speyer, Wolfgang 401, 407, 408
Spiritual History 232
Stein, Peter 126
Stephanus of Alexandria 406
Stephen bar Sudhaili 52
Stewart-Sykes, Alistair 345
Stobaeus, Johannes 255, 440–441
Stobaios, John 559
Strabo, Walafrid 180
Strategios 211, 212
stylum pingue atque floridum (flowery
   style) 29, 30, 34

sublexical level, grammar 455–457
substantia ipsius actus 461
successor states 27
Suetonius 184
Sulpicius Alexander 153
Sulpicius Severus 39, 171
summary, commentaries 302–303
supra-tribal koine (language of early
   Arabic poetry) 130
Sūr ī Suxwan (Banquet Speech) 112
survey 317–322
Šušanik (daughter of Vardan
   Mamikonean) 89, 90
Swain, Simon 374
Sweynheym, Conrad 601
Symmachus, Quintus Aurelius 29, 30,
   34, 35, 209, 216, 256, 428,
   545, 616
   and letters/letter collections 390,
     391, 394, 395, 397, 398
Symons, Arthur 630
Symphosius 243
sympotic literature 289–290
synagogues 345
Synesius of Cyrene 13, 197, 204–205,
   246, 335, 360, 361, 393,
   405–406
Synkellos, Georgios 561
Synodal Discourse, Against the
   Fantasiasts (Yovhannes
   Ojec'i) 81
synoptic tables 458
syntax 460–461
Syria 77, 88, 89, 94, 124, 126, 127,
   394, 528, 566
   southeast 128
Syriac language, literature and
   culture 47–60
   biblical commentary 48–49
   biography and hagiography 52–53
   Christology 47, 48, 49, 51, 52
   division between East and West
     Syriac Churches 47
   and epideictic oratory 195

Syriac language, literature and culture (*cont'd*)
  epistolography 54–55
  historiography 14, 55–56
  and language 171
  Law Book of Yišoboxt 107
  and medicine 526
  philosophy 56–58
  poetry 5, 49–51
  and pseudepigraphy 411
  rhetoric 53–54
  sermons 346
  theology 51–52
  translation from Greek 12, 15, 16, 56–58, 78, 526, 533

Tà metà Aléxandron (Dexippus) 146
Tabula Mundi (John of Gaza) 265
Tabula Peutingeriana 365, 366
Tacitus, Cornelius 144, 149, 151, 614
Taktika (military manual) 562
Targums 533, 534
Tārīx-e Sīstān (History of Sīstān) 111
Tatianus, Flavius Eutolmius 392
Teaching of St. Gregory (Gregory the Illuminator) 81
technical texts 114 491–493
  pseudepigraphy 404–406
Temple Mount, Jerusalem 369
Tertullian (ca. 160–240) 332, 334, 408
texts
  abbreviated 433, 437–439
  apocalyptic and visionary (Pahlavi) 108–110
  authentication of 403
  canonical 404, 407, 433
  condensed 437–439
    transformation of original texts into condensed forms 443–445
  cultural 112–113
  defense of text vs. critique of tradition 291
  devotional 263
  didactic 110, 225
  epic (Pahlavi) 110–111
    see also epic poetry
  geographical 110–111
  historical, pseudepigraphy 406–407
  inscriptions 512–514
  legal *see* legal texts
  literary 491, 492
  liturgical 78
  macrotext 391, 395
  martyr 382–383
  medical 404–406
  parabiblical 534
  philosophical and debate (Pahlavi) 108
  postclassical 313
  preservation 168
  reference 313
  school *see* school texts
  secular 106
  technical 114, 404–406, 491–493
textuality 242
Themistios/Themistius 209, 211, 216, 525, 560
Theodore (theologian of the East Syriac Church) 49, 50, 54, 335, 536
Theodore of Tarsus (ca. 602–690) 14–15
Theodoret of Cyrrhus 13, 161, 164, 166, 167, 168, 381, 444, 532, 536
Theodoric (Ostrogothic king) (493–526) 29, 32, 614
Theodorus, Mallius 454
Theodosian Code 418, 419, 420, 421, 422, 511
Theodosius I (379–395) 29, 30, 246, 250, 363
Theodosius II (401–450) 169, 227, 242, 246, 409
  legal texts 418, 422

theology/theological works 11, 31, 49, 108
  Armenian literature 79–81
  Christian theological literature 327–342
  conduct of 330
  and ecclesiastical history 166–167
  prose 80–81
  Syriac literature 51–52
  translation 58, 535–536
  treatises 11, 32, 36
Theon of Alexandria 474, 475, 476, 477
Theophanes 180, 365, 367
Theophilus of Antioch 314, 317, 323
Theophilus of Edessa 171, 527–528
Theophylact Simocatta 5, 156
Third Sophistic 196
Thirteen Syrian Fathers 90, 93, 94
Thomas of Harkel 535
Thousand and One Nights 116
Thrasamund (d. 523) 247
Thrax, Dionysius 451, 453, 528
"Throne of Adulis," Ethiopia 14
Thucydides 143, 144, 162
Tigran, King of Armenia 77
Tillemont 616, 617
Timaeus (Plato) 303
To Autolycos (Theophilus of Antioch) 317
To the Lighthouse (Woolf) 633
Toletanus, Iulianus 454
tombstones 511, 512
topography, biblical 363
topoi 196, 201, 267
traditions, fusion of 97
translation 523–538
  biblical 15, 58, 78
    New Testament 11, 17, 49, 113
    Old Testament 15, 48
  Christianity as language of 64
  Coptic literature 64–66
  of Greek 12, 15, 16, 56–58, 66
  Hellenization in 15

  inscriptions 516
  law 528–529
  medicine 526–527
  parabiblical texts 534
  philosophy 525–526
  poetry 529–530
  prose fiction 530–532
  revision of earlier translations 15
  rhetoric 528
  Scriptures 78, 532–534
  Syriac literature 12, 56–58
  theological works 58, 535–536
  "translation-movement" project 16
travel/pilgrimage literature 39, 359–372
  Christianization of travel 360
  historiography 368
  itineraries 363–365
  letters 360–362
  maps 365–366
  periegeseis and *periploi* 366–368
  religious travel 362–363
  testimonies of travel and physical movement 360
  vitae 368–369
Trdat' (Armenian king) 77, 81, 83, 93, 95
Treatise on the Spiritual Life, A (Sergius of Reshaina) 57
Treiger, Alexander 578
Trilogy of Lives 382
Trinity 32, 336, 376
Troy, story of 36–37, 222, 406
Tudor, Elizabeth 598
Tur Abdin, Turkey 382

Urbano, Arthur 379

de Valois, Adrien 620–621
de Valois, Henri 620, 621
Valens (364–378) 36, 426, 434, 435, 443, 617
  and classicizing of history/historical epitomes 147, 149–152
  and panegyrical works 209, 211

Valentinian I (364–375) 29, 211, 507
　legal texts 420, 426, 428
Valentinian II (375–392) 30
Valentinian III (419–455) 246, 437
Valerius, Julius 407
Van Nuffelen, Peter 164, 350
Vandals 187
Variae 34, 420
Varro (116–127 BCE) 31, 259, 434, 439, 452, 459, 493
　prosimetra 283, 284, 290, 291
Varsk'en the *bidaxš* 94
Vaxtang Gorgasali (K'art'velian royalty) 91, 97
Venantius Fortunatus *see* Fortunatus, Venantius (ca. 530–600/609)
Venus 248
Verba Achillis in Parthenone 244
Verecundus 249
Verlaine, Paul 630, 632
verse
　see also poetry
　epistles 270
　Gospels 33–34
　homilies 13
　Latin 32–34
　occasional 241
　oracles in 262
　panegyrical 29, 30, 32
　religious 33–34
　secular 32–33
Versus ad Gratiam Domini (Pomponius) 242
Vevaina, Y.S.-D. 106
Vexilla regis (Fortunatus) 273
Victor, Aurelius 36, 37, 149–150, 438, 444
Victor of Tunnuna 165, 182, 186
Victor of Vita 38
Victorinus, Marius 248, 335, 525
　and grammar 456, 458, 459, 465
Vidal, Gore 637
Virgil 290, 319, 433, 435, 493, 614

Aeneid 222, 244, 436, 465, 585, 621
antiquarian literature 544, 545, 546, 547, 549
Christian poetry 268, 269, 272
epic poetry 222, 229, 230, 231
epigrams and occasional poetry 242, 244, 247, 251
Georgics 244, 271
and grammar 460, 464, 465
Latin literature 32, 40
Viris Illustribus (Gennadius) 186
Visigoths 32, 33
visionary literature *see* apocalyptic and visionary texts
Vita Constanini (Eusebius) 209
Vita sancti Martini (Fortunatus) 273
vitae
　see also biography; hagiography
　Georgian 89, 90
　Syriac 53
　travel/pilgrimage literature 368–369
Vitalis, Orderic (d. 1142) 591
Vitruvius 497
Vrt'anes K'ertol (550–620) 81

Waddell, Helen 635–636
Wahrām Gur (Sasanian king) 109
Wahrām I Warzāwand (The Miraculous Wahrām) 109
Wallraff, Martin 164
Wandering Scholars, The (Waddell) 635–636
Watts, Edward 396
Webb, Peter 128
wedding poems 198
Weh-andīōg-Šāpūr (city) 115
Western Middle Ages, late antique literature in 583–595
Wetherbee, Winthrop 282
White Monastery (near Panopolis) 62, 63, 68, 69
Wīdēwdād (part of the *Avesta*) 111

Wilde, Oscar 401, 630
William of Malemesbury
    (d. ca. 1143) 589
Wilson, Edmund 634
wisdom literature 110
Wissensvermittlung (technical
    writings) 492, 494
    see also technical texts; texts
Wištāsp (Kayanid king) 111
Wizārišn čatrang ud Nēw-ardaxšīr
    (Explanation of the Game of
    Chess and Backgammon) 112
Wizīdagīhā ī Zādsparam (The
    Selections of Zādsparam)
    107, 110
Woolf, Virginia 633
World of Late Antiquity, The
    (Brown) 611, 628

Xanżt'eli, Grigol 90
Xenophanes 297
Xenophon 144, 212
xrad ī harwisp āgāhīh (Wisdom of
    complete knowledge) 109

Xusrō II 90
Xwadāy-nāmag 95, 96

Yeghishe 83
Yemen 126
Yovhannes Mandakuni (575–668) 81
Yovhannes Mayravanec' (575–667) 81
Yovhannes Ojnec'i (650–729) 81

zabūr (Arabian texts) 125
Zacharias Scholasticus (492–495)
    167, 169
Zellentin, Holger Michael 138
Zeuxippus 224
Zonaras 147
Zoroastrianism 103, 383
    Armenia 79, 80, 82, 83
    dualism 105
    Georgia 87, 89, 90, 91, 94, 95,
        97, 99
    Pahlavi literature 103, 105–107,
        109, 112, 116
Zosimus 146–147, 154, 406
Zwettler, Michael 127, 130